ESSAYS PRESENTED TO
RUDOLF WITTKOWER

PHAIDON

ESSAYS PRESENTED TO

RUDOLF WITTKOWER

ON HIS SIXTY-FIFTH BIRTHDAY

═════

IN TWO PARTS

ESSAYS IN
THE HISTORY OF ARCHITECTURE
WITH TWENTY-SIX CONTRIBUTIONS

ESSAYS IN
THE HISTORY OF ART
WITH THIRTY-NINE CONTRIBUTIONS

═════

ESSAYS IN
THE HISTORY OF ART
PRESENTED TO
RUDOLF WITTKOWER

EDITED BY DOUGLAS FRASER
HOWARD HIBBARD & MILTON J·LEWINE

PHAIDON

ALL RIGHTS RESERVED BY PHAIDON PRESS LTD · 5 CROMWELL PLACE · LONDON SW7
FIRST PUBLISHED 1967
SECOND IMPRESSION 1969

PHAIDON PUBLISHERS INC · NEW YORK
DISTRIBUTORS IN THE UNITED STATES: FREDERICK A. PRAEGER · INC
III FOURTH AVENUE · NEW YORK · N.Y. 10003
LIBRARY OF CONGRESS CATALOG CARD NUMBER: 69-20281

THE FIRST PRINTING OF THIS VOLUME WAS PUBLISHED IN 1967

WITH THE GENEROUS SUPPORT OF THE INDIVIDUALS AND INSTITUTIONS

LISTED IN THE PREFACE

SBN 7148 1301 X

MADE IN GREAT BRITAIN
PRINTED BY THE PITMAN PRESS · BATH

PREFACE

THE idea of honoring Professor Rudolf Wittkower with a collection of essays on the occasion of his sixty-fifth birthday was greeted with such enthusiasm by his apparently innumerable friends that, had we not maintained a rigorous schedule of deadlines, we would have been forced to launch a periodical rather than just two volumes of essays. The warmth of the replies in response to our query was eloquent witness to the friendship and respect that Professor Wittkower has always engendered—from his university days in Munich and Berlin and his years at the Bibliotheca Hertziana in Rome (1923–1933) through what art historians might call his 'English' and 'American' periods (from 1934 to 1956 at University College, London, as Durning-Lawrence Professor of the History of Art and at the Warburg Institute, and from 1955 to the present at Columbia University, first as Visiting Professor and then as Professor and Chairman of the Department of Art History and Archaeology). During these years he accumulated impressive knowledge and developed theories of far-reaching consequence. But his thoughts have never remained sterile arcana or precious bits of private property: his titanic capacity for work is matched by characteristic generosity, and his information and ideas have always been made available to students, friends, colleagues, and the public in consultations, letters, lectures, and a staggering number of publications.

In order to reflect Professor Wittkower's own contributions to scholarship, these essays are designed to deal with subjects in each of the overlapping categories into which most of his published work falls: the migration and interpretation of symbols, problems of proportion and perspective, the iconographic interpretation of art, Italian Renaissance sculpture and architecture, Baroque art in all its manifestations, Palladio and Palladianism, and English architecture. Many of these essays expand our knowledge in these various fields; others refine ideas or explore new aspects of material Wittkower has worked on. But it is safe to say that a majority of these essays could never have been written without his pioneering work in such fields as the Italian Baroque, which opened the way to modern interest and scholarship.

The generosity and scholarly dedication of many friends made this volume possible. We owe an inestimable debt to each of the authors for their efforts to contribute essays of solid value. And we owe our warmest and sincerest thanks to those who underwrote the major costs of publication: The Edgar J. Kaufmann Charitable Foundation; The Graham Foundation for Advanced Studies in the Fine Arts; The Samuel H. Kress Foundation; an anonymous donor; Mr Philip Johnson; The J. M. Kaplan Fund, Inc., through the interest of Mrs Alice M. Kaplan; Mr Frank P. Leslie; Mr Edwin C. Vogel; Mr and Mrs John de Menil; The Luis A. Ferré Foundation, Inc., through the interest of Mr Luis A. Ferré; Mr Henry Ittleson, jr.; Mr Myron S. Falk, jr.; Mr and Mrs Henry H. Weldon; Mr Max Abramovitz; Mrs Anthony A. Bliss; Mr Armand G. Erpf; Mr Willard B. Golovin; Mrs David M. Heyman; The Four Oaks Foundation through the interest of the late Mr Donald F. Hyde; Miss Dorothy Miner; Mr Nathan Ratkin; Mr Hanns Schaeffer; and Mrs David Shiverick Smith. Additional contributions have been made by Mr Paul H. Ganz, Mr and Mrs Bernard J. Lasker, Professor James Grote Van Derpool, Mr Alfred H. Barr, jr., Mr and Mrs Robert Delson, Dr Frederick J. Dockstader, Mr René d'Harnoncourt, Mr and Mrs Howard E. Houston, Mrs Elisabeth Blair MacDougall, Mr and Mrs Leo Najda, Commander and Mrs Marsden J. Perry, Mrs Jeanne Siegel, Messrs Stephen Spector and Peter Josten, and Mrs Morton Baum.

At different stages of planning this work many friends gave helpful advice and encouragement. From the very beginning Miss Mary M. Davis, Mr H. I. Miller, and Mr Desmond Zwemmer encouraged our efforts. Professor H. W. Janson and Mr Edgar J. Kaufmann, jr., offered constant support and help throughout the entire evolution of the project in ways too numerous to mention. For the volume of studies in architectural history we owe particular thanks to the helpfulness of Mr Philip Johnson, and we are also indebted to Mr Arthur Drexler and Mr John D. Entenza. Special thanks for their aid are also due to Miss Sarah Faunce, Mrs Alice M. Kaplan, Mr Frank P. Leslie, and Mrs Henry H. Weldon. At Columbia, Miss Etta Arntzen corrected the bibliography of Professor Wittkower's published work; Mr Stanley Salmen handled the burden of all contractual obligations; and Miss Konstanze Bachmann, Mrs Russell Edgerton, Miss Helene Farrow, and Mrs Glenn Kohlmeyer cheerfully carried out the major part of the secretarial work involved. Dr I. Grafe saw the book through production, and we should like to thank the Phaidon Press for their cooperation throughout. We thank all of these ladies and gentlemen most gratefully, and finally, with particular warmth, we wish to express our heartfelt thanks to Mrs Margot Wittkower, who has helped and supported us from the beginning.

All of us join together in dedicating this book to Rudolf Wittkower with thanks, respect, and affection. May he enjoy these essays as fruits of his own labor, and may they inspire him to still more prodigious achievements.

DOUGLAS FRASER
HOWARD HIBBARD
MILTON J. LEWINE

Columbia University
22 June 1966

CONTENTS

EVELYN B. HARRISON

U and Her Neighbors in the West Pediment of the Parthenon

A subject of sufficient amplitude to do appropriate honor to Professor Wittkower is *ipso facto* too large for a *Festschrift*. So it has been necessary to substitute for the article first intended for this place, on the composition and iconography of the East Pediment of the Parthenon, a *parergon* concerning some minor problems in the West Pediment. The two themes are not unrelated, however. The general upsurge of interest in the Parthenon pediments in the last few years has been such that the literature on the subject has become very complex and it may easily happen that a scholar working in one pediment is obliged to make excursions into the other in order either to recapture a figure of his own that has been taken off to serve in the alien gable or to repatriate an unwanted stranger that has emigrated to his territory. So a student of the East Pediment reading the last article on Parthenon problems by Kristian Jeppesen[1] finds that within the three blocks 19–21 of the West Pediment one generally accepted westerner has been exiled to the east and one East Pediment piece has been tentatively inserted. It seems worthwhile, therefore, to review the evidence for the figures in these three blocks in more detail than Jeppesen has done.

The drawing made in 1674 by the artist whom we generally call Jacques Carrey (Fig. 1) does not show the cornice blocks in this part of the pediment, but the beddings on the floor (Fig. 2) indicate clearly that the kneeling youth, V,[2] second from the corner occupied the left (north) half of block 22 and overlapped some way into block 21.[3] Since this figure is still fairly well preserved, its extent can be ascertained without difficulty. In block 19 and the northern part of 20 there

are again marks that have universally been attributed to the group S-T, shown by Carrey as a woman seated on a very low couch with a boy on her knee. There has been less agreement about the *interpretation* of this group, but we shall come back to that later. Between T and V there is an empty space reckoned by Carpenter as about 1.50 m wide.[4] This agrees with Sauer's presentation of the pediment floor. Part of this gap was filled by Carpenter in the best possible way. He identified a large fragment surviving on the Acropolis (Figs. 4–6) as the figure U actually shown in the pediment by Carrey.[5] This fragment, Acropolis 1363, comprising the whole lower part of a seated female figure and all but the front edge of her rocky seat, indicates very precisely how much space was occupied by the figure U. So much is left (the base of U is 0.56 m wide) that Carpenter and most scholars following him have been convinced that there was originally another figure to the right of U in the gap which appears in Carrey's drawing. This has been dubbed U*.

Carpenter was further convinced of the existence of U* by the fact that we seem to have a copy of it in a statuette from Eleusis (Fig. 8) belonging to a group of figures (Fig. 3) that contains recognizable copies, at one-third actual size, of figures from the West Pediment. The Eleusis statuettes are themselves cut to be set on top of a cornice, not sunk into a base; that is, they too are pedimental sculpture. John Travlos has now persuasively assigned them to the pediment of a treasury of Antonine date beside the Telesterion.[6] The theme of the Eleusis pediment was different from that of the Parthenon pediment; it seems to have been the rape of Persephone. It is only some of the peripheral figures, therefore, the onlookers and not the principal actors, that can be borrowed from the Parthenon. A copy of the group of Cecrops and his daughter was recognized immediately when the statuettes were first unearthed in 1888.[7] A seated female figure with a child in her lap was thought to be copied from the frieze of the Erechtheion, and the same source was

1. 'Bild und Mythus an dem Parthenon', *Acta Archaeologica*, XXXIV, 1963, pp. 1–96.
2. The letters assigned by Michaelis to designate figures in the Parthenon pediments are still the most useful index. It does not seem worthwhile to replace these familiar appellations with the numbers proposed by Jeppesen, *op. cit.*, pp. 60–61.
3. The only complete survey of the floor-marks in the West Pediment is that made by Sauer, *Antike Denkmäler*, I, pl. 58A and accompanying text. Carpenter, *Hesperia*, I, 1932, p. 17, gives a careful re-survey of blocks 20–22 (labelled retrograde by him 5–7) and his Plate III (from which our Fig. 2 is traced) shows blocks 18–24. For a list of all studies of the pediment floor, see Brommer, *Die Skulpturen der Parthenongiebel*, Mainz, 1963 (hereafter: Brommer, *Skulpturen*), pp. 112–13.

4. *Op. cit.*, p. 20.
5. Complete publication, *Hesperia*, I, 1932, pp. 1–30.
6. *Archaiologikon Deltion*, XVI, 1960, *Chronika*, pp. 55–60.
7. *Praktika*, 1888, p. 27; *Ephemeris Archaiologike*, 1890, pp. 218–21.

conjectured for a third piece, the lower part of a seated woman.

When Carpenter found that his figure U was the one from which the third Eleusis statuette had been copied, he concluded that the woman with a child in her lap was copied also from a Parthenon figure. He therefore restored the missing U* as a woman with a child in her lap.[8] This was accepted by a number of scholars, among them Becatti[9] and Schuchhardt.[10] Then Brommer took the further step of identifying a sizable original fragment, Acropolis 888 (Figs. 16–17), as a part of the U* from which the statuette was copied.[11] The pose of the figure, the height and shape of the smooth round seat, and the general lines of the drapery conform to the Eleusis copy (Figs. 9–11). Also the finding-place, in front of the south half of the west end of the temple,[12] is specifically favorable to the attribution. There are some differences in detail, which other scholars have been quick to point out. We shall come back to them.

The most radical opposition to Carpenter's and Brommer's contributions came from Berger, who denied the identity of Acropolis 1363 with U and, recognizing rightly that there was no other spot in the pediments which this statue would fit, proposed that it, together with the prototype of the Eleusis figure with the child in her lap, formed a separate group set up somewhere near the Erechtheion.[13] Stressing the differences between Brommer's U* (Acropolis 888) and the Eleusis statuette, Berger proposed that Acropolis 888 be taken as the back (not right side) of a figure and assigned it to U. For his exclusion of Carpenter's statue from the pediment, he appealed to Langlotz' opinion that it was stylistically related to the East rather than to the West Pediment and that it appeared like a dwarf between the giants T and V.[13a] By taking 888 as the back of a figure instead of its side, Berger was able to imagine a U that spread as widely as it appears to do in Carrey. He therefore returned to the position that no other figure existed between U and V. In other words, he reverted approximately to the state of affairs before Carpenter's discoveries.

Jeppesen's solution, less cavalier and more complicated than Berger's, is no less devastating to our picture of this section of the gable. He accepts Berger's interpretation of Acropolis 888 as the back of a seated figure and even draws a picture of it,[14] but recognizing that a figure so wide as this would be too tall for U's position in the pediment, he assigns this fragment to D in the left wing of the gable. D, being one block closer to the center than Carpenter's U, would have more head-room. Carpenter's U, after detailed reconsideration, emerges as being in fact the statue shown by Carrey, but it is placed in the block south of the one where Carpenter had placed it. The reason for this shift is Jeppesen's very peculiar private vision of the group S-T.[15] Instead of seeing S as seated on the knees of a woman whose upper torso appears to the right, Jeppesen considers that the youth S has thrown his cloak over a rock and is sitting on it, while the form in Carrey's drawing that appears to be the upper part of a woman he takes to be the headless fragmentary torso of a frontally seated figure. From a study of the pediment floor and the space that would be occupied by these two figures he concludes that Carpenter's U must have occupied block 21 instead of 20, so that there would have been no room for U*.

This arrangement radically alters the iconographical as well as the esthetic picture in both West and East Pediments. If S is sitting on a rock instead of on a woman's knees, then the British Museum fragment, Smith no. 12 (Fig. 7), which comes from the right thigh of a draped, presumably female figure seated on a low seat, cannot belong here in spite of the impressive number of votes it has received for this position.[16] Jeppesen transfers it to the East Pediment and identifies it as Aphrodite, doing little service either to the goddess or to the pediment. In the space to the right of S, he places the fragment Acropolis 6713. This was first attributed to the Parthenon by Wegner, who saw in it the lower part of Athena's female charioteer, G, in the West Pediment.[17] Other scholars have accepted the piece as belonging to the Parthenon but not as a part of G, since it clearly belongs to a seated figure.[18] Berger placed it in the East Pediment, in three-quarters view facing left. Though his placement and reconstruction are unsatisfactory, it remains probable that the fragment is from the East Pediment rather than from the West. Jeppesen sets it frontally in block 20 between S and Carpenter's U, which is thereby displaced to the right into block 21. In order to do this,

8. *Op. cit.*, pp. 11–16.
9. G. Becatti, *Problemi Fidiaci*, Milan–Florence, 1951, p. 44.
10. *Festschrift Kurt Bauch*, 1957, pp. 21–28.
11. *Athenische Mitteilungen*, LXIX–LXX, 1954–5, pp. 60–62; *Skulpturen*, pp. 54–55, 60–61, 65, 169.
12. L. Ross, *Archäologische Aufsätze*, I, Leipzig, 1855, pp. 89–90.
13. E. Berger, *Parthenon Ostgiebel*, Bonn, 1959, pp. 57–59.
13a. Langlotz' own article (*Deltion*, 20, 1965, pp. 1–5) appeared while the present article was in press. His arguments remain unconvincing.

14. *Acta Archaeologica*, XXXIV, 1963, p. 73, Fig. 21.
15. First set forth in *Acta Archaeologica*, XXIV, 1953, p. 112, repeated *Acta Archaeologica*, XXXIV, 1963, pp. 67–69.
16. Michaelis, *Der Parthenon*, p. 200, lists Quatremère, Müller, Ellis, Lloyd, besides himself. Brommer, *Skulpturen*, p. 64, lists further Murray, Smith, Carpenter, Brommer and Berger.
17. *Festschrift Schweitzer*, Stuttgart, 1954, pp. 185–91.
18. Listed by Brommer, *Skulpturen*, pp. 97–98. I would no longer suggest, as in *American Journal of Archaeology*, LX, 1956, p. 303, that the piece might be classicizing. I accept it as belonging to the East Pediment.

he estimates the scale of Acropolis 6713 as much smaller than other scholars have done,[19] and takes the lowest probable restored height for U.[20] The result is a paratactic series of three frontally seated figures which Jeppesen tentatively dubs 'Eleusinian Triad'.

At this point we can safely say that things look *worse* than before Carpenter's study. It is high time to go back and look at all these pieces of evidence in more detail, in order to see whether the tangle of contradictions can be somehow unravelled and something of the familiar friendly aspect restored to the scene. Simply to review the evidence and persuade ourselves that earlier scholars were capable of drawing correct conclusions might seem a dull undertaking if there were no new evidence to be added. Fortunately, a little piece exists, and though in itself it proves nothing, it is enough to add credence to Carpenter's assessment of the relationship between his figure U and the Eleusis statuette which seems to copy it.

At the time when Carpenter wrote, this statuette consisted only of the portion below the waist (Fig. 8), so that the condition of the copy bore a striking resemblance to that of its prototype, which was broken off in just the same places. The copy gave us no information about the lost parts of the original. Now a fragment preserving the upper torso from neck to waist has been identified in the storeroom of the Eleusis Museum (Figs. 12–15).[21] This joins beautifully, though the two fragments have not been united because the lower torso is in the National Museum in Athens.[22] The photographs show the actual fragment resting, not glued, on the plaster cast of the lower part, and the break appears as a heavy line of shadow all around.

As soon as the upper torso is added, the figure becomes at once more lively and more Parthenonian than it semed before. Carpenter had remarked in the original fragment of U a strong community of style with the seated Hestia, K, of the East Pediment.[23] This becomes very noticeable also in the copy once the movement of the shoulders has been recovered. As in the Hestia the shoulders lean forward, with the right upper arm advanced and the left held back. The head, however, to judge from the slope of the neck break, turned slightly to the figure's left instead of to her right. Like the Hestia our figure wore a chiton with overfall though the overfall here was somewhat shorter, ending approximately at the line of the present break. Below this the folds model the stomach in a way that recalls the reclining Aphrodite M of the East Pediment. The neck of the chiton is not so wide as that of Hestia's, but softly rounded with a neckline somewhat resembling the neckline of the Persephone, East E. The quality of the thin, crinkly and clinging material is conveyed in this copy with almost as much fidelity to Parthenon style as in the copy of Cecrops' daughter.[24] Notice especially the deep cutting of the folds between arms and torso and the soft unsymmetrical V of complex folds that falls between the breasts. For this figure at least we can feel confident that the term 'copy' is fully valid.

The back of the figure is very summarily carved, possibly from a combination of two reasons: the back of the original was hard to get at and since the copy was itself destined for a pediment it was not necessary that the back be finished in detail. The back of the copy of Cecrops shows a comparable simplification.[25] One notices also that the proper left side is more detailed and interesting than the proper right. It may well be that in the original pediment the proper left side was less blocked from view by the adjacent figure and that this arrangement was followed in the Eleusis pediment.

The concentration of the copyist on what was to be seen from the front may account in part for the lack of depth in the upper torso, but the impression remains that the original statue also was a slender, youthful figure. The breasts, now damaged, were small, high and far apart. The elastic pose contrasts with the more solid repose of the figure with the child on her lap (Figs. 9–11).

Once we are aware of this youthful mobility in the statuette we begin also to perceive it in U. The manner

19. He gives 1.70 m, which must mean that he takes the top of the fragment to preserve the level of the top of the knee. Actually a good part of the knee is missing. The only serviceable preserved dimension is the height above the top of the plinth of the *underside* of the knee, i.e. the top of the seat. This is 0.60 m. I calculate *c.* 2.00 to 2.10 m. Wegner, *Festschrift Schweitzer*, pp. 186–7, calculated *c.* 2.25 m (without the additional plaque about 10 cm thick which he postulated between the high plinth and the floor). His height is greater than mine because he restores the semi-seated charioteer pose instead of a regular seated pose. Berger, *op. cit.*, pls. 1 and 11b places the fragment in block 16 of the East Pediment while admitting that it may seem a little small for this position.

20. Carpenter had calculated, *Hesperia*, I, 1932, p. 6, that the original height of U was 1.50–1.55 m. Jeppesen, *Acta Archaeologica*, XXIV, 1953, p. 113, complained that this was too short and called for a restored height of 1.60 m. But in the position where he later placed U (*Acta Archaeologica*, XXXIV, 1963, Figs. 22–23) the tympanon height is under 1.46 m, so that even 1.55 m would be too tall. See below, note 46. The Eleusis copy (see below) indicates that Jeppesen's first estimate of 1.60 m was more nearly correct.

21. J. Travlos, *Archaiologikon Deltion*, XVI, 1960, *Chronika*, p. 56, pl. 44a. I am grateful to Mr. Travlos for permission to publish the photographs of this fragment made under his supervision in the Eleusis Museum.

22. N.M. 201.

23. *Hesperia*, I, 1932, pp. 2–5 (Carpenter does not call K Hestia, but that is now the commonest denomination and I believe that it is right).

24. Brommer, *Skulpturen*, pl. 143, 2.

25. *Ibid.*, pl. 143, 1.

in which the front of the left lower leg has been broken off makes the lower part of the statue appear much squarer than it was in fact, but when we restore the outline of the leg and foot by comparing the folds that fan out from under the left knee to fall in loops over the left shin and ankle with those in the statuette we realize that the missing left foot must have been set as far forward in the original as in the copy. This probably means, as Berger has pointed out, that the front part of the foot would have projected beyond the front edge of the cornice,[26] but it is of course not an argument, as he would have it, for banishing Carpenter's U from the pediment. Such projections in the lower part of a figure did not break the pedimental triangle from the spectator's point of view since one always looked up at them from below. Feet that project beyond their plinths occur in more than one place in the Parthenon pediments.[27] The copy also had a projecting left foot. The sloping surface beneath it is not broken away, but roughly tooled with the point.

A comparison of the top of our statuette with Carrey's drawing of U is interesting. We seem to see the overfall and the V of folds between the breasts but the angle of the whole upper torso looks different. In the 'Nointel's Anonymous' drawings[28] the height and position of the upper torso are more like what we find in the statuette than they appear in Carrey. This is analogous to what Carpenter observed about the lower part of the figure when compared with his fragment. The artist seems to have straightened up the figure that Carrey showed tilted.

If it be agreed, then, as by now it must be, that the Eleusis statuette is truly a copy of Carpenter's U, it may be illuminating to note any significant difference, since that should be helpful in assessing the other Eleusis statuette and Acropolis 888, Brommer's candidate for U*. The most important difference shows up in the left profile (Figs. 5, 14). In the Eleusis copy of U the corner of the mantle that is drawn across the lap disappears under the back corner which falls down over it against the rocky seat. On the original fragment the front portion crosses the lap and falls straight down against the rock, while the back corner was evidently drawn up over the left arm. It is broken off at just the point where it begins to be cut free of the body, and we see the folds rising to this point. The reason for the difference between the full-scale statue and the statuette is not hard to guess. In an over-life-size figure the drapery caught up over the arm was an effective elaboration of the scheme and also a graceful form of

support for the heavy arm held free of the body. In the small statuette the difficulty of undercutting such a thin wall of drapery would have outweighed its advantages. The small forearm could be, and probably was, cut separately and dowelled on. The other statuette, N.M. 202, preserves the remains of an iron dowel in the stump of the right arm (Fig. 9).

In the fragment Acropolis 888 something very similar happens. This piece belongs to the proper right side of a draped figure sitting on a smooth seat. The himation appears to be wrapped around the back of the figure and the folds rise as they come forward. Just as in Carpenter's U the drapery is broken away at the point where it begins to be cut free of the body. Here it seems to have been more deeply undercut, however, for the ends of the big drill-holes remain visible (Fig. 17). Once again we must assume that the end of the cloak was caught up over the arm, this time the right arm, and once again we must expect that the statuette will show a significant difference at this point. It is just here, in the statuette, that the legs of the child cut across the mother's lap, and the folds of the himation disappear under them. On Acropolis 888 the child, if there was one, must have been somewhat differently placed, for no trace of its attachment is to be seen at this point and if it had been very close the drill could not have reached in to undercut the mantle as it does. It would appear, then, that the Eleusis statuette N.M. 202 differs more strongly from its prototype than N.M. 201. In fact the style of the statuette itself is the strongest argument that this is so. Though the drapery of the lower part exhibits a normal fifth-century aspect, the scheme and style of the upper part would not be possible before the middle of the fourth century. With its sleeved chiton beneath the peplos and with the high girding generating stiff vertical folds between the heavy breasts, the figure from the waist up resembles nothing so much as the routine votive images of the Mother of the Gods.

It seems clear that this statuette was not simply copied at one-third the scale from a Parthenon figure but is a kind of pastiche, following the prototype more closely in the lower than in the upper part. Such mixtures are not surprising once we realize the purpose the figures served. The Eleusis pediment was not a miniature reproduction of the Parthenon pediment; it was a classicizing composition full of recognizable quotations in a new context. Therefore any degree of imitation from outright copying of a whole figure or group to almost wholly new inventions might be possible. One can see from comparing almost any two of the figures assigned to the Eleusis pediment that it contained a wide range of styles of carving and degrees of imitation. The torso of the Athena, for example, closely

26. *Op. cit.*, pp. 57–58.
27. East E-F.
28. Carpenter, *Hesperia*, I, 1932, pp. 8–10, Fig. 5. Omont, *Athènes au XVIIe Siècle*, Paris, 1898, pl. 25.

resembles the Athena of the West Pediment of the Parthenon, but the scale of one-third is not maintained (Athena is not a central figure and so has to be smaller), and the execution of the folds is coarse and monotonous.[29] The head, if it belongs, is of a different type.

We therefore have to ask whether the basic idea of a mother and child group was present in the original as well as whether Acropolis 888 belongs next to U in the pediment. Actually, the presence of the child cannot be proven. The markedly youthful look of U as we now see her in the supplemented Eleusis copy adds weight to Becatti's suggestion that she is the daughter of the figure next to her, and Becatti had suggested that the child served principally to identify the mother as such.[30] We have shown a child in Fig. 2, but there is no evidence for its type or pose. It is indeed conceivable that U* was characterized as the mother simply by her dress. The undergarment, though indistinct, seems to be a peplos rather than a chiton, and the himation caught up over the *right* arm suggests the symmetrically worn cloak of Demeter. It is possible, too, that the form of the seat, though hard for us to interpret, had some significance in this connection.

When we come to discuss the position of Acropolis 888 in the pediment, the first thing that needs to be established is that the fragment is from the side, not the back of the figure. Michaelis described it as 'nur ein Stück der ziemlich flachgehaltenen Rückseite (oder der r. Seite?)'.[31] In attributing the piece to the back of the figure he was perhaps influenced by Ross' opinion that the workmanship was casual because this side had been turned away from the spectator: 'aus diesem Grunde weil diese Seite von dem Beschauer abgewandt war, ist die Arbeit von keiner grossen Vollendung'.[32] Ross, however, believed that the fragment came from the right side of the figure. Actually the unfinished look comes partly from the fact that the peplos is preserved only in the awkward space between the body and the raised right arm with its undercut himation. What we see of it would not have been visible to the spectator. The tubular folds of the himation that fall down against the seat are very carefully carved and finished. Below these folds we see (Fig. 17) the beginning of the projecting plinth on which the feet rested. There is no doubt that the right edge of the fragment represents the front corner of the seat. The undercut broken edge of the upper part of the

himation is even surer proof that we are not dealing with the back of a figure. Jeppesen's reconstruction[33] with the himation draped over the right shoulder makes nonsense of the undercutting besides characterizing the lady as an eccentric who drapes her himation on the wrong shoulder.

The next important question is that of scale. Here we cannot help noticing that though the seat is lower than that of U[34] one has the impression that we are looking at a bigger woman. But we need to consider the evidence for the pose before deciding that Acropolis 888 would be too tall for the position of U*. The seat is lower at the back and slopes up to the front, implying that the thighs, as in T, sloped upward to the knees. The folds of the peplos slant forward, suggesting that the body is in a slumped rather than an upright position. Both these things make the height of the figure less in proportion to its scale than if it were in an upright posture such as Jeppesen has drawn. The Persephone, E, of the East Pediment, who occupies a precisely analogous position in the inward half of the fifth block from the corner, provides an excellent illustration of how far a slumped pose can reduce the height of a figure. The side view of E presents many analogies with our fragment.

Such a reconstruction of U* as a large figure compactly seated on a low seat does something toward answering Langlotz' objection that U and U* look like dwarfs between the giants T and V. That U should be smaller in scale than U* is acceptable, since she is a young person. When we come to the reconstruction of T we shall see that though large she is not so gigantic as Carpenter's artist drew her.

So long as Acropolis 888 is not too tall for the position of U*, there is no persuasive reason to assign the fragment to the seated figure D in the other side of the pediment. Both the finding-place and the type of Acropolis 888 are against this identification. The marble was excavated by Ross in front of the south half of the west front of the temple. Pieces that fell from the north half of the pediment are not likely to have become buried in front of the south, and Ross did not himself consider the possibility of its belonging to D. As for the type, the drawing by William Pars of the left corner of the gable[35] shows the right arm of D still preserved, and there is no himation draped over it.

29. *Ephemeris Archaiologike*, 1893, pl. 14, 3. Mayer, *ibid.*, p. 199, calculates the height of the Eleusis Athena around 0.86 m. Three times that would be 2.58 m. The Parthenon Athena must have measured around 3 m.

30. *Problemi Fidiaci*, p. 45.

31. *Der Parthenon*, p. 195.

32. *Archäologische Aufsätze*, I, p. 90.

33. *Acta Archaeologica*, XXXIV, 1963, p. 73, Fig. 21.

34. The height from the floor to the lower edge of the drapery at the back (left edge of fragment) is 0.40 m. At the front it is 0.47 m. The average height is therefore approximately the same as on the British Museum fragment of T. The front edge of the seat of Acropolis 888 measured on top of the mass of drapery that falls down over it is 0.52 m high. The plinth below this drapery is 0.07 m high.

35. Brommer, *Skulpturen*, pl. 80.

The front of the figure is shown by Pars as entirely split away. We may reasonably conclude that this was caused by the fall of the cornice block above the statue. The fact that the knees were split off may well account for Dalton's odd representation of this figure.[36] He may have misread accidental breaks as modelled surface. If Acropolis 888 is, as we have seen it must be, from the side of the figure, D as shown in Pars' drawing does not preserve enough depth to accommodate it. In any case, the seat of Acropolis 888 is so deep that it does not seem that the figure could have fitted into D's space. In the position of U*, on the other hand, in block 21 the diagonally placed setting-table suggests that the statue also was set at an angle, which would allow some extra room. Since the front part of block 21 is lost, we cannot say exactly how far the statue extended, whereas in the case of D we can see that the frontally seated figure left a strip of cornice bare in front of the right foot.[37]

We can say, then, that the identification of Acropolis 888 as U* is not open to any insuperable objections on the grounds of scale and pose and we are therefore free to accept the strong excavational evidence in its favor.

So far, in considering the space available for U and U*, I have accepted Carpenter's placement of U in the right-hand half of block 20, not overlapping the joint between 20 and 21. This too, however, now needs to be defended in detail, for Jeppesen makes U straddle the joint,[38] while Brommer's drawings show two different positions. Jeppesen pushes U so far over the line that there is positively no room for U*. Brommer's drawing of surviving fragments[39] keeps Carpenter's placement, but the drawing which combines the evidence of the fragments with that of Carrey[40] pushes U to the south, still leaving space for a U* restored directly from the Eleusis statuette but not for one in which Acropolis 888 is realistically incorporated. The reason is that Carrey's drawing of the group S-T shows it taking up so much room that no other solution would be possible. This is a problem which Carpenter did not fully discuss. He admitted in his text that the group was drawn too large in the reconstruction made for him by Fomine[41] but he did not speak of the fact that it was thus made to encroach

on the space known to have been occupied by P-Q-R. When Q with her twins is put back into her proper place something has to give, and Brommer and Jeppesen decided that it should be U. But this seems rash before one has considered all the evidence for T.

Carpenter mentions that a fragment 'presumably from T' in the British Museum was not taken into account in Fomine's drawing. 'The figure should probably be smaller in scale and be raised upon a fairly high couch (which Carrey's acute angle of vision foreshortened or left invisible).' Michaelis gives a perfectly accurate description of the British Museum fragment (Fig. 7): 'Auf einem Felsblock, über den ein Gewand gebreitet ist, war eine reichbekleidete Frau hingestreckt, so dass sie mit dem Schoss tiefer lag als mit den Knieen. Das vorhandene Stück, dessen gute Erhaltung zusammen mit der schmucklosen Glätte des Felsblockes dafür spricht, dass es die innere Seite der Figur war, ist ein rechter Schenkel.'[42] He says the question-mark should be removed from the attribution, but since his time the identification has again been disputed by Jeppesen, who banishes the fragment to the East Pediment,[43] and Brommer has reverted to the pre-Michaelian mistake of taking the piece for a left thigh instead of a right.[44]

Jeppesen's objection, apart from the fact that he believes S is sitting on a rock rather than on a human lap, is that the diameter of the thigh on the British Museum piece calls for a figure twice life size. He calculates its height as about 2.00 m and remarks that in the space available for T the cornice height is only 1.70 m. He is measuring the thigh together with all its heavy drapery, and he is putting T farther to the right than Carpenter placed her. These arguments are therefore both open to question. At the point where Carpenter places T the tympanon height is about 1.68 m, and there is a possibility of 6 to 8 cm extra under the soffit of the raking cornice.[45] The available floor space between the group P-Q-R and U Jeppesen reckons at barely a meter, whereas his twice-life-size figure would need at least 1.50 m. The fact that the foot of T is clearly seen in Carrey to extend in front of part of the plinth of Q does not concern him, since he remains somehow unable to see this foot.

The outline which extends to the very front edge of the cornice near the middle of block 19 is logically to be taken as marking the plinth under the right foot of the seated boy S (Fig. 2). The plinth of T, unless we

36. *A Series of Engravings Representing Views of Places, Buildings, etc., in Sicily, Greece, etc.*, London, 1751–2, pl. 3. Brommer, *Skulpturen*, pl. 65, 2, reproduces the whole engraving; Jeppesen, *Acta Archaeologica*, XXXIV, 1963, p. 68, Fig. 19a, gives a detail. Brommer, *Skulpturen*, p. 34, rightly rejects the idea that Dalton is showing F instead of D.
37. *Antike Denkmäler*, I, pl. 58A.
38. *Acta Archaeologica*, XXXIV, 1963, Figs. 22a, 23b.
39. *Skulpturen*, pl. 152, 2.
40. *Ibid.*, pl. 152, 3.
41. *Hesperia*, I, 1932, p. 21, n. 1.

42. *Der Parthenon*, p. 200, no. 20.
43. Above, note 15.
44. Cf. *American Journal of Archaeology*, LXIX, 1965, p. 185.
45. Jeppesen comments (*Acta Archaeologica*, XXIV, 1953, p. 113) that the space is maximally 9 cm higher than the top line of the tympanon. But except for the horses no head was so close to the tympanon as to use this maximal space.

are to disbelieve Carrey completely, must then have extended some distance to the left of this. Jeppesen calls the hole in the left half of block 19 a pry-hole and makes this a boundary between plinths. Sauer, however, draws it as a dowel-hole and calls it one in his text.[46] That would mean that a plinth covered it. Brommer's location of the right foot of S and the left foot of T seems to correspond both to Carrey's drawing and to the pediment floor. It must be correct.

The difficulty is not with the north but with the south boundary of the group S-T. If one takes Carrey literally it has to come as Brommer has shown it, with the back of T projecting beyond the middle of block 20 so that there is not enough room left in the block to accommodate U. But can one take Carrey literally? One can, but only if we assume that part of the figure T was no longer in its original place when he drew it. When we look closely at the head, neck and torso of T we are struck by the complete absence of plastic form and surface detail. Compared with S and the lap on which he sits, the upper part of T is a faceless ghost. The whole outer portion appears to have been split off. Now a blow which would have been heavy enough to split the head and torso in this fashion might also have separated the upper torso from the legs. Another look at Carrey is enough to persuade us that this is just what happened. The shoulders come much too close to the level of the thighs to be reconcilable with any normal human posture, and the length from the knees to the back of the figure is too great in proportion to the lower legs. Also the torso appears to be leaning against the side of U, and U itself is shown tilted toward the right. Carpenter took the position of T to be original and believed that the proper right side of the rock on which U sits had been worked away to make room for the neighboring figure when the statues were being set in the pediment.[47] But there are no tool marks in this supposedly worked strip. What we have is simply a micaceous streak in the marble along which part of the rocky seat has been split away.[48] A very similar surface is to be seen on the split face of the British Museum fragment of T.

Now Carpenter has mentioned good reasons for believing that some of the raking cornice in this section of the gable had already fallen before Carrey's time. We cannot prove it, because Carrey did not draw either the raking or the horizontal cornice in the right wing, but the break in the left knee of U is already shown by Carrey and could most easily have been

caused by a falling cornice block.[49] Carpenter suggests that a falling block, either the same one or its neighbor, also knocked U* out of the pediment, taking with it the front of the horizontal block on which she sat.

From what we have observed about T it would appear that the block above her head also fell and that the upper torso of T falling over against U pushed it a little way to the south into the gap vacated by U* so that it tilted as Carrey shows it. Carpenter dismisses the idea that U is tilted over the edge of the broken cornice block because he assumes that U is still in its original position: 'The front of mutule-block 6 was broken away when U* fell, but U itself could not have been affected or have tipped over the edge of the break, because U rested wholly on the next block, 7, which is virtually unbroken.'[50] But since U was never dowelled to the floor, a lateral displacement would be perfectly possible. It offers the best explanation for all the oddities that have plagued this section of the pediment: the seemingly overlarge scale of T, the disjointed look which inspired Jeppesen's schism, the tilt of U, and the inadequate space left for U*. Since we can probably never reconstruct the precise order and position of the falling blocks it may never be possible to explain just exactly how all this happened, but I think we have to assume that it did.

We may then sketch the original aspect of this section of the pediment as follows (Fig. 2): T was a female figure seated in profile with her legs much as Carrey has shown them but with her upper torso in a more erect position. The British Museum fragment, Smith no. 12, preserves part of her right thigh which was toward the tympanon. This gives us the height of the low seat, around 0.42 m. The boy S perched on her left knee. The drill-holes on the top of the surviving fragment of T near the broken front edge suggest the proximity of his body and some of the folds adjacent to these drill-holes may belong to his drapery. This again conforms to Carrey. The left foot of T extended a little to the north of the dowel-hole in block 19. The south end of her plinth was close to the middle of block 20. The total length of the figure may have been something like 1.30 m, the height not more than 1.70 m.

U, now the best-documented of all these figures, sits frontally, as Carpenter has placed her, in the south half of block 20. Acropolis 1363 is indeed the lower part of this statue. The figure seems to have been accurately copied in the Eleusis statuette N.M. 201 except that the motif of the mantle caught up over the left arm is omitted as impractical for the small scale

46. *Antike Denkmäler*, I, pl. 58A, p. 50.
47. *Hesperia*, I, 1932, p. 5.
48. Cf. Brommer, *Skulpturen*, p. 54, 'eher eine Verwitterung auf Grund der Glimmerstelle'.

49. Carpenter, *Hesperia*, I, 1932, p. 6.
50. *Ibid.*, pp. 7–8.

of the statuette. U was represented as a slender young woman wearing a chiton with buttoned sleeves and an overfall of moderate length. Her head seems to have turned a little to her left. The height of the figure as calculated on the basis of the Eleusis statuette, which lacks only the head, should be about 1.60 m. This is what Jeppesen calculated before he had the idea of moving the figure into block 21, which obliged him to reduce the height somewhat. It helps to confirm the placement in block 20.[51]

U* occupied all but the southern end of block 21. Acropolis 888 can be assigned to this figure by elimination. Its finding-place makes it certainly a West Pediment piece, and probably from the south half. All other figures are known to some extent from drawings and no other corresponds to the fragment. The general motif of a mother holding a child is suggested by the Eleusis statuette N.M. 202, but this is seen by the fourth-century scheme of its upper part to be an adaptation rather than a copy. Acropolis 888 seems to represent a fairly large woman sitting slumped on a low seat with a smooth rounded profile. The Eleusis statuette shows a very similar form if we allow as in U for the mantle being carved flat against the body instead of lifted free over the raised arm. Though the height of the seat of the Eleusis statuette bears to that of the seat of Acropolis 888 the expected ratio of 1:3, the depth seems to be proportionately less in the statuette than in the actual fragment. It would appear that the actual scale has been somewhat reduced. The conversion from a slumped to an erect posture was made easy in the statuette by giving the figure a high girdle.

It seems established that U represents a young woman and that U* is her mother. The types of the two figures show something in common with types of Demeter and Kore, but it remains uncertain whether this is because the Parthenon artist was influenced by existing statues or whether the Parthenon types were subsequently borrowed to represent the divine mother and daughter. Two statuettes from the Athenian Agora which appear to be votive rather than pedimental and which are unrelated to one another in scale and style help to illustrate, though they do not solve, this problem.

Slender proportions and a generally youthful aspect characterize a figure which is so close to U and the Eleusis copy of U that it must derive from the same type (Fig. 18).[52] She sits on a throne with footstool rather than on a rock, but her pose is the same and she wears the same chiton with an overfall which comes only to the waist in front. The himation, drawn across the lap with one end falling down on the proper left side, is closer to the arrangement of the original U than to the Eleusis copy, but the Agora figure does not show the himation rising on the left side to be draped over the left arm. Rather it appears to have been pulled up over the left shoulder in back, leaving the left side of the chiton visible. This may again be a variation aimed at avoiding the undercutting needed to show the himation draped over the arm. Here, however, it is possible that the left arm was cut in one piece with the statuette, for there is an awkwardly cut area on top of the left knee which recalls the traces of some kind of interference on the left knee of Acropolis 1363. Though the proportions are made slenderer than in the Parthenon figure and the lower folds of the chiton around the feet are made longer and more agitated, direct inspiration from the pedimental figure seems possible. The Agora figure looks ill-suited to the square throne on which she has been placed, especially on the proper right side, where the drapery collides most ungracefully with the chair-leg. The drapery itself is carved in a hard, stiff style with strong shadows and broad, smooth surfaces. It should belong to the Roman Period, quite possibly to the second century after Christ. We have no direct clue to the meaning of the Agora statuette. If it was not pedimental but votive it should represent a goddess, as the throne also suggests. For the youthful type Persephone is the most likely candidate.

---

51. The height without the head is 0.475 m, from which we may subtract 0.045 m for the height of the plinth, and perhaps 0.005 m for a slight projection of the preserved back of the neck above the height of the chin. If we say that the head of a normal seated figure of this period goes about $5\frac{1}{2}$ times into its height, we get 0.52 m for the restored height of the statuette minus its plinth. Multiplying by 3 and adding 0.05 m for the plinth of U, we get 0.161 m. Calculations such as this are open to various uncertainties, but Fig. 3 shows that N.M. 201 is definitely taller in proportion to N.M. 202 than Carpenter restored the prototypes. The height of the tympanon joint just to the left of the head of U is 1.567 m according to measurements kindly furnished by W. B. Dinsmoor. Carpenter's drawing agrees. Where the head of U would come the tympanon height is about 1.54 m. If the figure was actually 1.60 m tall she will have been using up a good part of the head-room under the cornice (see above, note 45). This seems perfectly possible. It does not seem possible, on the other hand, to restore the figure with a low enough height to fit into block 21. The noticeable gap which Jeppesen leaves between U and V may stem from this difficulty.

52. Inv. S 289. Catalogued February 1933 from marbles found in the southwest corner of the Agora (this suggests a late, probably modern context). Broken off at waist, upper part missing. Back legs of throne missing. Edges battered, chipped and worn. Pentelic marble. Pres. H. 0.365 m. Brommer, *Skulpturen*, p. 106, no. 2, pl. 145. Mentioned by Schuchhardt, *Festschrift Kurt Bauch*, p. 28, n. 21. Also by E. Harrison, *American Journal of Archaeology*, LXIX, 1965, p. 186. I am grateful to Homer Thompson, Field Director of the Agora Excavations, for permission to publish this and the other Agora statuette mentioned below.

The second Agora piece (Fig. 19) recalls a known Eleusinian motif, that of Demeter holding Kore in her lap. A votive group from Eleusis shows the daughter full grown, so that she towers over her mother.[53] The statuette from the Agora probably again represents Demeter and Kore.[54] The girl is here half-grown, small but with already clearly defined breasts. She is held on the lap in the same position as the child in the Eleusis pedimental statuette N.M. 202, and the whole scheme of the figures and the drapery is so close that the two groups appear to be based on the same type. The Agora statuette again has a smooth rounded seat but it is somewhat higher in proportion to the figure than in the other versions. It seems to have been a separate votive group rather than a pedimental piece, for the structure as a whole has been made more schematic, symmetrical, rectangular, than in the Eleusis statuette. The whole scale is a little smaller. There is no clear indication of the date of the Agora group. It might be as early as the fourth century or it might be much later. In any case it should be earlier than the Eleusis pediment, for the fine shallow carving of the drapery is not likely to be so late as the Antonine Period.

One thing which the Agora group seems to share with the Eleusis statuette and with U* is the diagonal point of view from which it was meant to be seen. Both the back and the proper left are so little worked out that it seems obvious that no one was meant to look at those views.

If the Agora statuette represents an Eleusinian type and conforms to the Eleusis pedimental figure in most respects but has an older child on her lap, it seems quite likely that the Eleusis group itself has modified the Parthenon original in the direction of this same Eleusinian type. The child is larger than any that Acropolis 888 can have held. The drapery again implies that the child is female, since the folds of a chiton appear below the himation. She cannot, of course, represent Kore, for Kore appears in the middle of the pediment being carried off by Hades. These onlookers in the Eleusis pediment are even harder to name than those in the Parthenon.

If U* held a child it may have been male or even an infant whose sex was not clearly indicated to the spectator. Thus, though the identity of Acropolis 888

with U* seems established, and though it is clear that the Eleusis statuette N.M. 202 is related to N.M. 201 in the Eleusis pediment as U* was related to U in the Parthenon, it remains unclear how far we can use N.M. 202 as evidence for the interpretation of U*.

It is scarcely possible to solve the iconographical puzzles of one corner of the West Pediment without taking the whole story into account, and for this the time seems not quite ripe.[55] But it may count as some gain if the existing material evidence is set firmly enough into place in any one section to keep it from being shaken or dislodged by the waves of new interpretations washing over it. This, we can at least hope, our newly enhanced knowledge of the Eleusis statuettes has enabled us to do for U and her neighbors.

53. G. Mylonas, *Eleusis and the Eleusinian Mysteries*, Princeton, 1961, Fig. 73. Jeppesen, *Acta Archaeologica*, XXXIV, 1963, p. 67, Fig. 18.

54. Inv. S 1429. Found October, 1949, in the scarp east of Shop 9 of the Stoa of Attalos, in late fill about two meters below the modern surface. Both heads missing. Upper part weathered and battered. Pentelic marble. Pres. H. 0.30 m. Brommer, *Skulpturen*, p. 106, no. 3, pl. 147, 1. Mentioned by Schuchhardt and Harrison, *loc. cit.*, above, note 52.

55. The following speculations should therefore be regarded as extremely tentative. If we accept Becatti's suggestion that U* is Praxithea and U her daughter, the persistent suggestion of some Eleusinian connection tempts us to see in the youth V and the reclining woman W Eumolpos and his mother Chione, who bore him to Poseidon and hid him in the depths of the sea. Eumolpos belongs to the family of Erechtheus as well as to the offspring of Poseidon, for Chione was the daughter of Boreas and Oreithyia. His kneeling, emergent posture (the right leg is cut away below as in A and like A he seems to have had drapery falling down his back as if he were shedding it) could be symbolic of his rise from the sea, and the quiet reclining pose of Chione would fit her name, which means 'snow'. (It would scarcely be fair to invoke the 'melting' quality of her drapery, since this is largely due to weathering.) Eumolpos would fill the requirement that all the human participants of the scene should be significant ancestors. It seems altogether probable that the Periklean Parthenon would include Eleusis in symbolic recognition of the unity of Attica and the importance of the mysteries. The ancient war between Eleusis and Athens might be seen as a human parallel to the struggle between Athena and Poseidon. Cf. Isokrates, XII (*Panathenaicus*), 193. Eumolpos would be the youngest in generation of those present in the pediment and would thus be in place at the right end of the pediment, especially if, as I believe, the first figure, A, was Aktaios. Since Jeppesen (*Acta Archaeologica*, XXXIV, 1963, p. 64) has correctly identified the rock-torso as an autochthon supporting the horses of Athena, I would no longer call it Kranaos, but I still believe that A and A* represented Aktaios and Kranaos. It would appear that no male figures belonging to a generation later than that of Kekrops are shown full-grown. The women are so simply because they are present in the role of mothers. The assembled company is then rather a panorama of the future than a contemporary family gathering. This may explain the seeming anomaly that Erechtheus appears, if at all, as a boy in the family of Kekrops, whereas his daughters and perhaps even his granddaughter are shown as grown women.

A very tentative roster might then read as follows:

A	Aktaios	M	Poseidon
A*	Kranaos	N	Iris
B	Kekrops	O	Amphitrite
C	Pandrosos	P-Q-R	Oreithyia, Zetes and
D	Aglauros		Kalais
E	Erichthonios (= Erechtheus)	S-T	Ion and Kreousa
F	Herse	U	Daughter of Erechtheus
G	Nike	U*	Praxithea
H	Hermes	V	Eumolpos
L	Athena	W	Chione

MARION LAWRENCE

The *Birth of Venus* in Roman Art

When the birth of Venus is mentioned one of two visual images inevitably comes to mind, either the Ludovisi Throne or Botticelli's painting. Both are favorites with museum visitors and both still present many unsolved problems in spite of the attention they have attracted over the years among scholars. This paper is written in the hope that an examination of the Roman forms, which have never been studied systematically, will throw light on the origin of Botticelli's iconography.

For the Greek versions we have some important literary references. Pausanias lists Eros receiving Aphrodite as she rises from the waves as among the scenes on the base of Pheidias' statue of Zeus at Olympia.[1] Of Apelles' famous painting at Cos, which was later taken to Rome by Augustus, we are told by Pliny that Aphrodite is emerging from the sea but that the lower part was damaged and no one could be found to restore it. He also says that it is known as the *Anadyomene*. Ovid and the *Aetna* as well as epigrams in the Greek Anthology describe how the goddess wrung the foam out of her wet hair; one of these, Democritus, says she showed only her breasts, another, Leonidas, describes her breasts 'firm as quinces'. Cicero, Propertius and Strabo also eulogize the painting, the latter speaking of the many cures of women recorded on votive offerings at the shrine. None of them, however, mention the shell.[2] Many statues and statuettes have come down to us of Venus with both arms raised wringing water from her hair, the so-called *Anadyomene* type.[3] The legend that Venus was born from the genitals of Uranos, thrown into the sea by

Cronos which gathering the foam produced the goddess, is recounted by Hesiod but Plautus, Tibullus and Pompeius Festus speak of Venus as born of a shell.[4] The latter belief must have been widespread for a number of Greek vases and many small terracottas show Aphrodite, usually kneeling, in a large shell and often between its two open valves.[5] The problem of the origin and symbolism of this shell and of Venus as the pearl within it is, however, beyond the scope of this paper as are the variants of the Greek types.

In Roman art since the birth of Venus is a popular subject and Apelles' painting, as we know, was in Rome one would expect to find copies, or at least echoes, of it. But in spite of the efforts of many scholars no surviving work has been discovered that conforms at all to the ancient descriptions.[6]

1. v, 11, 8. The beautiful silver medallion in the Louvre found in 1877 at Galaxidi (Locrida) may have been copied from this as de Witte suggested since Aphrodite is being pulled out of the waves by an adolescent Eros who stands on a rock at the left. 'La naissance d'Aphrodite', *Gaz. arch.*, 5 (1879), 171-4, pl. 19, no. 2. E. Simon, *Die Geburt der Aphrodite* (Berlin, 1959), 42, pl. 26.
2. Pliny, *Nat. Hist.*, xxxv, 91 f.; Ovid, *Ars Amat.*, xiv, 81, *Trist.*, ii, 529, *Amores*, i, 14, 35, *Ex Pont.*, iv, 1, 29; *App. Verg.*, *Aetna*, line 592; *Greek Anth.*, xvi, no. 178-82; Cicero, *De Nat. Deor.*, i, 27, 75, to *Attic.*, ii, 21, *De Divin.*, i, xiii, 23; Propertius, iii, 9, 11; Strabo, xiv, 2, 19. A second painting of Venus by Apelles, which was left unfinished at his death, is mentioned by Pliny, *op. cit.*, and Cicero, *Ep. ad famil.*, i, ix, 15, and *De off.*, iii, 2, 10, but only the head and shoulders were completed.
3. J. J. Bernoulli, *Aphrodite* (Leipzig, 1873), 284-95; S. Reinach, *Répertoire de la statuaire grecque et romaine*, ii, pt. 1 (Paris, 1897), 341-4; M. Bieber, *The Sculpture of the Hellenistic Age* (New York, 1955), 20 f., 82 f.

4. Hesiod, *Theog.*, 188 f.; Plautus, *Rud.*, iii, 3, 43; Tibullus, iii, iii, 34; Festus, iii, 23.
5. L. Stephani, 'Erklärung einiger im südlichen Russland gefundener Kunstwerke', *Compte rendu de la com. imp. arch.* (St. Pétersbourg, 1874), 5-290. He gives pictures of five examples in the Hermitage of Venus kneeling in front of a bivalved shell. Since the Berlin Museum has three terracottas of this type it must have been quite common. G. Perrot, 'Une statuette de la Cyrénaïque et l'Aphrodite Anadyomène d'Apelle', *Mon. Piot.*, 13 (1906), 117 f., pl. 10; W. Deonna, 'Aphrodite à la coquille', *Rev. arch.* (1917, 2), 392-416; M. Brickoff (later M. Bratschkova), 'Afrodite nella conchiglia', *Boll. d'Arte*, 9 (1929-30), 563-9; *idem*, 'Die Muschel in der antiken Kunst', *Bull. Inst. arch. bulg.*, 12 (1938), 1-128. This repeats the four illustrations of the first article but adds to them. She attempts the almost impossible task of listing all examples of the shell including not only the symbol but its use as a vessel, ornament or architectural element as well. In spite of a catalogue of 988 examples her list is far from complete. Aphrodite appears here and there but many of my examples are omitted and the author states that the standing type of Venus on the shell is unknown before Botticelli, an error quoted by several scholars. Nor is M. Bratschkova interested in iconographic types. Her article, however, is extremely useful for its great mass of material and no list, no matter how long, is ever complete, especially as new examples are excavated. See A. A. Barb, 'Diva Matrix', *Jour. Warburg Courtauld*, 16 (1953), 204 ff.; E. R. Goodenough, *Jewish Symbols in the Greco-Roman Period*, 8 (New York, 1958), 95 ff., for discussion of the shell and its symbolism.
6. Curiously enough several manuscripts of the late fourteenth or early fifteenth century show Venus in the water up to her waist, accompanied by birds, Cupid and other figures. She is nude but on three examples wears a crown or wreath of flowers. These are three Ovids Moralisés, E. Panofsky, 'Renaissance and Renascences in Western Art', *Figura*, 10 (1960), Figs. 56-58, and an Albricus, *Libellus de deorum imaginibus*, A. Warburg, *Gesammelte Schriften*, 2 (Leipzig-Berlin, 1932), 471, Fig. 112. There may well be other medieval representations of this form which in the half-figure of Venus in the water is the closest parallel that I know to Apelles' conception.

A lost fresco from a house on the Celian in Rome, known only from a seventeenth-century engraving (Fig. 1), showed Venus swimming, her body covered by water to the waist and with both arms outspread.[7] It thus could not have been modelled on Apelles' version since she is neither emerging from the waves nor wringing water from her hair. Venus is accompanied by cupids, two of whom are swimming below her while two more fly high in the sky overhead holding a veil or mantle. Another one jumps into the water and a sixth stands on a rock. On the shore in the foreground flowers are blooming and figures are dancing a *thiasos*. Curiously enough this version of Venus' birth which, as far as I can discover, is unique in Roman art, appears in two Byzantine manuscripts, commentaries by Pseudo Nonnus on the homilies of Gregory of Nazianzus. One of these is in Rome, the other in Paris and both are of the eleventh century.[8] There Venus is fully clothed as she swims and the genitals of Uranos appear falling from the sky, a feature, as far as I know, never shown in ancient art.

The usual rendering of the birth of Venus in Roman times was, however, quite different. It illustrates the description by Lucian since Venus, seated or reclining, in a large shell is guided ashore by two tritons although the flowers that he says were sprinkled over her are omitted.[9] A mosaic, found in 1961, in the small Baths at Sétif in Algeria (Fig. 2) is the liveliest example of a group of ten or more Roman pavements with this theme.[10] More than half of them are in North Africa and all are late in date ranging from the third century at the earliest to the late fourth or early fifth century. Here Venus already wearing necklace, armlets,

bracelets and what seems to be a diadem, is arranging her hair with both hands.[11] She is thus the *Anadyomene* type. Her long legs dangle over the shell which is held by an older and bearded triton at the left, the rear view of his body in antithesis to the front view of the young, beardless triton who holds it at the right, a contrapposto not found on the other examples. Two cupids with fluttering drapery fly above, the one at our left carries a mirror, a detail that appears frequently. Below, cupids play in the water. The one at the right stands on the side of a floating vase using a scarf as a sail, in the center two dolphins, whose tails are intertwined, support a cupid who is offering the goddess a golden diadem, while at the left another cupid is kneeling on a board pulled by a pair of dolphins, a strange form of water-skiing. Cupids often gambol with dolphins, riding them or standing on their backs, on Roman pavements and on sarcophagi but I know of no exact parallels for these three. Finally above Venus, nicely focusing attention on her head, is a triangular fluted object which does not look like another shell, although one appears in this position on a mosaic from Halicarnassus.[12] Can this be a parasol such as we see in the painting of the personification of Alexandria from the House of Meleager in Pompeii?[13]

Another interesting example of this iconography is at Ostia in the House of the Dioscuri (Fig. 3).[14] Venus, in a pose similar to hers on the first mosaic but with her direction reversed, sits in a shell held by two tritons, both of whom face us and who are beardless. The goddess is without jewelry but wears a mantle draped over her left shoulder and thigh. Both arms are raised as she wrings out the water from her long golden hair. There are no cupids but two large dolphins face each other below the shell and nereids riding various sea creatures, sea-horses, sea-tigers, sea-bulls, etc., and led by another triton encircle the central group. Thus it is a fine sea *thiasos*.

Venus sits in a similar pose in her shell on six other examples that I know of the scene: mosaics at Bulla Regia (Fig. 4),[15] Carthage (now in the Musée Alaoui

7. Found in 1639 in the garden of the monks of S. Gregorio and engraved along with its companion painting by P. S. Bartoli, J. P. Bellori, *Picturae antiquae cryptarum romanarum et sepulcri Nasonum* (Rome, 1750), 89, pl. 7; O. Benndorf, 'Bermerkungen zur griechischen Kunstgeschichte', *Ath. Mith.*, 1 (1876), 50 ff., pl. 2; A. M. Colini, 'Storia e Topografie del Celio nell'Antichità', *Mem., P. Accad. Rom. Arch.*, 7 (1944), 208–12, Fig. 169a. Colini dates the fresco as mid-third century from the coiffure of a female portrait adjacent to it.

8. *Vat. gr.*, 1947, fol. 147 v, and *Bib. Nat. Coislin*, 239, fol. 121 v. K. Weitzmann, *Greek Mythology in Byzantine Art* (Princeton, 1951), 52–53, Figs. 63, 64. He compares these to the Roman fresco, Fig. 65, which he labelled 'Domus Aureus', apparently following the caption in S. Reinach, *Répertoire de peintures grecques et romaines* (Paris, 1922), 59, no. 6. We know from Pliny, *Nat. Hist.*, xxxv, 91 f., that Nero had substituted another painting by Dorotheus of the birth of Venus for Apelles' original which had 'suffered from age and rot'. Perhaps this accounts for Reinach's error.

9. *Dial.*, 15, 330.

10. This is the ancient Sitifis. *Fasti Arch.*, 16 for 1961 (1964), nos. 4858, 7299, mention its discovery during excavations by M. Gaspary and date it from a rare decorative motif in the border as of the end of the fourth century or early fifth. I wish to thank M. P. A. Fevrier for sending me the photograph.

11. Hesiod, *Hom. Hymn.*, vi, describes the Horae at the birth of Aphrodite as putting 'a fine, well-wrought crown of gold on her head', hanging earrings in her ears and 'adorning her with golden necklaces over her soft neck and snow-white breasts'.

12. R. P. Hinks, *Catalogue of the Greek, Etruscan and Roman Paintings and Mosaics in the British Museum* (London, 1933), 131–2, no. 52a, Fig. 150. This was found in 1856.

13. Now in the Museo Nazionale in Naples. G. E. Rizzo, *La pittura ellenistico-romana* (Milan, 1929), pl. 83.

14. *Scavi di Ostia, Mosaici e pavimenti marmorei*, iv, ed. G. Becatti (Rome, c. 1962), 119–22, pls. 149–53, 214–16. They date it in the second half of the fourth century.

15. G. C. Picard, 'Mosaïques africaines du IIIᵉ siècle apres J.C.', *Rev. arch.* (1960, pt. 2), 46, Fig. 5.

in Tunis) (Fig. 5),[16] Djemila,[17] Henchir-Thina (Mus. at Sfax),[18] Susa,[18a] and Halicarnassus (British Museum).[19] She usually wears jewelry and holds her hair or at least raises her arms. Once, at Bulla Regia, she is nimbed. Cupid holds a mirror on two examples, at Bulla Regia and at Djemila, and Venus holds it herself at Carthage and at Halicarnassus. In the latter and at Djemila her image appears in the mirror. Thus the scene is sometimes called the toilet of Venus. As a rule tritons support the shell but at Henchir-Thina and on a mosaic at Sainte-Colombe,[20] near Lyons, cupids hold it. The last named differs also from the others in showing Venus reclining in the shell with a mantle behind her body. On none of them do we find the playful cupids of the Sétif mosaic, although at Bulla Regia they ride dolphins.

The reclining Venus seems to have been especially popular in Pompeii where two frescoes and two mosaic fountains show this type. The first painting has been known for many years and is today in the Museum in Naples.[21] Here she is almost in a swimming pose but with her arms raised to hold an air-inflated mantle overhead. A small cupid at the right seems to be pushing the shell while dolphins swim below. Venus wears bracelets and anklets and holds what seems to be a palm-leaf fan. The second example (Fig. 6) is a very large painting found in the new excavations along the Via dell'Abbondanza.[22] Venus' pose is almost identical and the flying mantle very similar. She now has in addition a gold diadem, earrings and necklace. A cupid, as before, propels the shell but another one, with a banner or small sail and riding a dolphin, leads the way. The sky is blue and limpid, the water wet and green as befits the goddess of love.

A modification of this form appears on a mosaic fountain in the Casa dell'Orso in Pompeii.[23] Here the cockle shell with its hinge at the bottom as on all our

examples so far, fills the semi-dome of the niche so that Venus is without companions. She lies in the semi-recumbent position often seen on sarcophagi with her right knee bent behind the straight left leg. Both arms are extended, the right one holding her yellow mantle which billows overhead but also, unlike the complete nudity of the last two examples, covers her body from the waist down. A second fountain, discovered in 1881 in the Regia IX, Isola 8, has a more interesting and much fuller scene (Fig. 7).[24] The shell now is a small craft on a large blue sea. Venus from a reclining position reaches out to put her hand on the head of a small cupid at the right who is guiding the shell as he swims in the water as in the two frescoes, a curious object, a stick with a cloth filled with air like a sail, in her right hand. Two other cupids helped by a half-submerged triton push or guide the shell. Farther away another cupid plays with a dolphin, a nereid holds her mantle overhead, Cupid and Psyche embrace and a dove has alighted on a large rock. Finally on the shore at the left are two women who must be Horae, the one in the foreground seated, while, at the right, a third stands with a mantle over her arm as she waits ready to clothe the goddess. Still another woman squats on the ground in the center but what she takes from her open box or what the other seated one holds, is hard to determine. Thus we have a full and graphic illustration of Hesiod's lines in his Homeric *Hymn to Aphrodite*, 'There the moist breath of the western wind wafted her over the waves of the loud-moaning sea in soft foam, there the gold-filleted Horae welcomed her joyously. They clothed her with heavenly garments, on her head they put a fine, well-wrought crown of gold', etc., etc.[25]

The sarcophagi present a somewhat different form. On a few examples of the many renderings of a marine *thiasos*, Venus appears in the center in her shell which is held by the usual tritons who are flanked by nereids riding them or other sea animals. Usually, as on the fine sarcophagus in the Palazzo Borghese (Fig. 8), the figure of the goddess is small in relation to the shell which completely encloses it.[26] One or more cupids are also within the shell. Venus, here accompanied by a cupid with a lighted torch, the Eros *Psychopompos*, is crouching on one bent knee, holding a billowing mantle in her right hand and covering herself with her hand, a pose repeated but with its direction reversed

---

16. *Inventaire des mosaïques de la Gaule et de l'Afrique*, II, P. Gauckler (Paris, 1909), pl. 671; *Catalogue des Musées et collections archeologiques de l'Algérie et de la Tunisie*, xv, suppl. (1910), pl. 2.
17. *Inventaire des mosaïques*, III, F. G. de Pachtere (1911), pl. 293.
18. *Ibid.*, II, pl. 18; *Catalogue des Musées*, xvII (1912), pl. 2.
18a. *Inventaire des mosaïques, Atlas Archéologique*, feuille 57, L. Foucher (1960), 72–73, pl. 35b, c.
19. *Supra*, note 12.
20. *Inventaire des mosaïques*, I, G. Lafaye (1909), pl. 217. Found in 1894.
21. P. Herrmann, *Denkmäler der Malerei des Altertums*, I (Munich, 1904), 256, pl. 189; Goodenough, *op. cit.* (*supra*, note 5), Fig. 62.
22. Regia II, isola 6, no. 3, A. Maiuri, *Roman Painting* (Geneva, 1953), 7 (color plate). Found in 1952.
23. R. Gusman, *La décoration murale a Pompei* (Paris, 1924), pl. 25 (color).

24. *Notizie Scavi* (1881), 23; Herrmann, *op. cit.* (*supra*, note 21), text 258 ff., Figs. 77, 78. I have followed Herrmann's identification of the various figures.
25. *Supra*, note 11.
26. A. Rumpf, *Die Meerwesen auf den antiken Sarkophagreliefs, Die antiken Sarkophagreliefs*, v, pt. 1 (Berlin, 1939), pl. 36, no. 92. He dates it as early third century by comparing the coiffure of Venus with that of Julia Domna.

on a cruder sarcophagus now in the Louvre (Fig. 9), which was, however, originally also in the Villa Borghese.[27] A third sarcophagus now in the Lateran collection (Fig. 10) shows Venus even smaller but seated, her leg covered by a mantle while she fixes her hair.[28] Two cupids accompany her; the one at the right probably, as Rumpf suggested, held a mirror. Below in the waves on all three examples cupids either swim or ride on sea creatures, among them the ketos. The tempo is rapid as is usual on these 'meerwesen' sarcophagi. They show a veritable riot of nereids, cupids and animals, making a fine rhythmic but clearly balanced pattern. The theme of 'laughter-loving Venus' is obviously appropriate for a mosaic pavement, particularly in a bath or for the walls of a private house, but why should it appear on sarcophagi? Is it a sepulchral subject? Clearly the cockle shell which so frequently enclosed the portrait of the deceased on the sarcophagi had the meaning of birth or rebirth into a new life.[29] Perhaps that is the explanation for Venus here. In any case it is a rare subject on sarcophagi and I know of only one example where the birth of Venus appears on a grave altar, one in the Museo dei Conservatori.[30] This shows a variant of the type that we have seen on the sarcophagi for here Venus kneels, a pose derived from the statue by Doidalsas of the goddess bathing. Two cupids are also in the shell, one holding a vase, the other a shell as a mirror. Two young tritons clasp the shell.

Closer to the type of the mosaics are a few scattered examples of the theme in metal. One of the scenes on the bronze *tensa* in the Conservatori Museum shows Venus seated nude except for some drapery over her legs and arranging her hair while three cupids fly above her.[31] The shell is held by the usual tritons, one young, one old, and Venus' feet dangle over into the water in which dolphins swim. The famous Projecta casket from the Esquiline Treasure, today in the British Museum (Fig. 11), has a similar and rather elegant rendering in spite of its fourth-century date.[32] Venus seated with a foot on the water, holds a lock of her hair in one hand while the young triton on the right balances a large mirror. Cupids with gifts stand on the tritons' fish tails. Also from the same treasure and of silver is the patera now in the Palais des Beaux-Arts in Paris (Fig. 12).[33] This simplifies the scene as the shell fills the interior of the bowl completely. We thus have no tritons but Venus alone seated in an up-right position with her mantle as before over her right thigh. She wrings out her wet hair with both hands while cupids offer her a flower and a mirror. We have thus seen Venus seated, reclining, crouching or kneeling in her shell. There is still another type in Roman art. Sometimes she stands in the birth scene. A mosaic found at El-Djem, ancient Thysdrus in North Africa and today in the Museum in Susa (Fig. 13) shows Venus completely nude except for a necklace and bracelets standing at the edge of the water while she wrings the foam from her long golden hair.[34] A cupid on either side holds garlands, the one at the left a veil and mirror as well. It is clearly the edge of the sea with a rocky mound under each cupid and the shore onto which the goddess is stepping is indicated in the center. On one side water plants appear across the waves. There is no shell of any sort. But this appears in our next example, a mosaic in the British Museum which was found at Hemsworth in Dorset (Fig. 14).[35] It, alas, is fragmentary and Venus' whole body from

27. *Ibid.*, pl. 37, no. 93. For a discussion of the Eros *Psychopompos* see my article, 'The Velletri Sarcophagus', *A.J.A.*, 69 (1965), 213.

28. *Ibid.*, pl. 36, no. 91.

29. Barb, *op. cit.*, 204; Goodenough, *op. cit.*, 95 ff. (*supra*, note 5).

30. Venus alone appears on a few sarcophagi as well as in a group, usually of Mars and Venus, a use that I think is accounted for by the Roman habit of representing individuals, from the emperor down, in the guise of gods or goddesses. See my discussion of this 'Season Sarcophagi of Architectural Type', *A.J.A.*, 62 (1958), 279–82. Two other possible examples should perhaps be mentioned, a small fragment published by P. Sticotti, *Arch. Epig. Mith.*, 16 (1893), 37, Fig. 1, as in a private collection in Ossero. It consists of a nude woman (head, shoulders and legs broken) in a semi-recumbent position in a cockle shell which is held by two enormous hands. Whatever was originally underneath the shell is broken away. It is described as of limestone, which, if accurate, does not point to a sarcophagus. The other is a curious relief pictured by R. Venuti, *Vetera Monumenta Matthaeiorum* (Rome, 1779), III, pl. 2, Fig. 1. Venus, holding her long hair spread out like a tent, sits in a fluted bowl held high by two tritons, her feet dangling in mid-air. Cupids stand on the tritons' fish tails, one with a mirror. This is very odd in many ways. Is the lower half a restoration? Since Rumpf omits it completely from his corpus he obviously did not believe it to be part of a sarcophagus. For the marble altar see D. Mustilli, *Il museo Mussolini* (Rome, 1939), 29, pl. 23, no. 79, inv. 2101. He dates it in the middle of the first century A.D. Compare the pose of Venus with Bieber, *op. cit.* (*supra*, note 3), Fig. 292.

31. H. S. Jones, *The Sculptures of the Palazzo dei Conservatori* (Oxford, 1926), 183, pls. 68–72. He dates the reliefs in the mid-third century, identifies the objects in the cupids' hands as a mirror with the reflection of Venus' face, an arm-band and a wreath. Both of the latter, however, look like garlands and the young triton, that he calls female, is clearly male.

32. O. M. Dalton, *Catalogue of the Early Christian Antiquities in the British Museum* (London, 1901), 61, 177, pls. 13–18. Found on the Esquiline in 1793.

33. P. Gusman, *L'art décoratif de Rome* (Paris, 1908), I, pl. 26.

34. *Inventaire des Mosaïques*, II, 2 (*supra*, note 16), 14–15, pl. 71 f. Found in 1911–12. Our scene is flanked by busts of the four Seasons in squares to right and left. *Tunisia, Ancient Mosaics*, Unesco (Paris, 1962), pl. 24 (color). Gauckler gives no date but this is undoubtedly fourth century. It looks earlier than the Sétif mosaic.

35. Hinks, *op. cit.* (*supra*, note 12), 99–100, pl. 30. The catalogue gives no date and there is little to work with except for the border patterns which look like fourth-century ones.

the waist up is gone but she is clearly standing in the shell, nude with her red mantle falling in many folds behind her. Two ivy leaves appear on the sides. She could have had her arms raised and, if so, was probably without cupids since there would hardly have been room for them. Dolphins and other fish swim in the semi-circular border of the mosaic which is slightly horseshoe in shape.

Venus stands triumphant on the handle of a silver platter found at Bourdonneau, now in the Louvre (Fig. 15).[36] Below her in the water is a small shell, behind her a large one with its two valves open forming a figure eight. This is held by two young tritons while cupids stand on dolphins, neatly filling the space beyond the central group. Venus, completely nude, holds her hair with one hand, the shell behind her with the other. This curious form with the double valves seems to be a revival of the Hellenistic type although I have found no exact parallel for the upright figure eight. It is without doubt like the earlier examples a reference to the theory of the birth of Aphrodite from a shell.[37]

For the type of Venus standing alone in a shell which completely encloses her a carved gem in Berlin (Fig. 16), probably of the Augustan period, can be cited.[38] This shows an Aphrodite *pudica* of the Medici form and is closely paralleled on a lamp, possibly of the same date, found in Cyprus (Fig. 17), iconography which also appears, as we shall see, in Coptic art.[39]

Among the many survivals of classical themes in Egypt the birth of Venus appears quite frequently. There are three examples in the sculpture from Ahnâs of the late fourth or early fifth century, today in the Coptic Museum in Cairo.[40] One (Fig. 18) in which the shell fills the major part of the semi-dome of a small niche

shows the goddess crouching, holding her mantle which billows behind her. She is nude except for a necklace and an armlet. In a second relief (Fig. 19), also of limestone, she stands in a shell which encloses her, stepping over her mantle, as it were, as it falls between her legs, but which is draped over both arms. A curious demon at the left, the Coptic version of a triton, holds the shell; the one on the other side is broken. Here Venus has long curly locks and wears huge earrings as well as a necklace with a big circular pendant. In the third relief she stands in a tall, oblong shell, holding her hair. She wears pendent earrings, several necklaces and a mantle draped over her body from the waist down. Also of the same period and probably of the fourth century is a fragment of a limestone relief from Egypt in the Museum in Berlin.[41] Venus crouches in her shell holding her long hair with both hands; a small cupid, who seems to be sleeping, lies at the right, his head projecting from the shell. A bone carving from Alexandria, also in Berlin, shows the fuller rendering of the scene, for here are the two swimming tritons and Aphrodite in her shell with her hands to her hair.[42] She seems to have been seated but the lower part of the relief is broken. In both of these examples, unlike the sculpture from Ahnâs, the goddess is shown completely nude and without jewelry.

In metal a tiny bronze plaque, which originally was part of the decorative sheathing of a wooden chest, shows a seated Venus in a bivalved shell, making an upright figure eight as on the silver handle in the Louvre (Fig. 15). This is in the Museum in Cairo.[43] Minute tritons are just visible below. Venus' arms are held outstretched and her left foot dangles in the water. The style is very crude indeed and it is hardly more than a pictograph.

On my last two examples Venus stands completely enveloped by her shell. The first is an ivory diptych, probably of the mid-fifth century, today in Sens (Fig. 20), which shows a triumph of Dionysus on one wing, of Selene on the other.[44] On the latter in the upper left-hand corner, a Venus of the *Anadyomene* type appears but holding her mantle behind her. The reference here would seem to be to Venus as a planet. Also Coptic but somewhat later in date is the beautiful lapis and gold pendant in the Dumbarton Oaks Collection in Washington (Fig. 21) where Venus stands, her

36. Gusman, *op. cit.* (*supra*, note 33), II, pl. 61. Of excellent style this may easily be work of the early empire.
37. See *supra*, note 4.
38. A. Furtwängler, *Beschreibung der geschnittenen Steine* (Berlin, 1896), 112, pl. 22, no. 2385.
39. Cyprus Museum, inv. no. 2578. Goodenough, *op. cit.* (*supra*, note 5), 98, Fig. 68. Bratschkova, *op. cit.* (*supra*, note 5), in her catalogue, no. 862, lists a lamp in the Antiquarium in Rome, no. 96, which was fragmentary but showed Venus standing naked in a shell. She gives no reference and I have not been able to find an illustration of it. She did not know the Cyprus lamp.
40. Inv. no. 44068, 46727, 44072. U. Monneret de Villard, *La scultura ad Ahnâs* (Milan, 1923), Figs. 18–19, 16, 17; G. Duthuit, *La Sculpture Copte* (Paris, 1931), pls. 27b, 28a, b, 29b. Also probably from Ahnâs are two limestone reliefs which were unpublished until they were exhibited in the Exposition, *L'Art Copte*, Petit Palais, Paris, in 1964. The first is in the Louvre and shows Venus rising from a shell held by two tritons (no. 47, p. 81). The second, today in the museum at Recklinghausen, is the capital of a pilaster where cupids hold the shell in which Venus squats (no. 71, p. 97).

41. O. Wulff, *Altchristliche und mittelalterliche Bildwerke, Konigliche Museen zu Berlin*, III, 1 (Berlin, 1909), pl. 5, no. 57.
42. *Ibid.*, pl. 18, no. 384.
43. J. Strzygowski, *Koptische Kunst*, Cairo, Musée des antiquités égyptiennes, II (1904), 255, pl. 25a. It is 0.163 cm long, 0.075 cm high. He dated it 'third to fifth century'.
44. R. Delbrueck, *Die Consulardiptychen* (Berlin–Leipzig, 1929), 232, pl. 61.

mantle covering one leg, the other long and svelte.[45] Her arms are raised as she wrings out her wet coils of hair. She wears a necklace with a pendant which falls between her 'quince-like' breasts. Her face is small with a pointed chin but with enormous eyes. The chiasmic position sways slightly to the right and almost suggests that she is about to dance. The one unusual feature here is that the hinge of the shell is at the top undoubtedly because, were it the other way which affords a better support for the figure, it would be an awkward form for a pendant. On the sea this type would be impossible since Venus' boat would take in water.

Thus in the late survivals of the theme in Coptic art we find a variety of types, the goddess crouching or seated but with at least some examples of her standing. More often than not she is partly covered by her mantle and frequently wears jewelry but there is no characteristically Coptic form.

*   *   *

With these many Roman illustrations in mind perhaps one can look at Botticelli's *Birth of Venus* with fresh insight. Could he have seen one of these Roman monuments or something like them and how much was he inspired by them? Clearly he has altered the form of Venus. His is the Medici type, the *pudica*, not the Venus *Anadyomene* although he has kept the latter's long hair.[46] The two symmetrical tritons are now male and female winds, placed on one side, closely interlocked as they fly on huge wings, blowing the goddess ashore, a unique and original conception. One Hora stands on the land holding a billowing mantle ready to clothe Venus. Here, as generations of scholars have recognized, Botticelli seems to be following Poliziano's poem, the *Stanze*, written for Giuliano de' Medici's *Giostra*, which in describing the birth of Venus draws heavily in its turn on Hesiod.[47] Both poets, however,

speak of the Horae in the plural, Poliziano listing three; both have them ready to clothe the goddess, Hesiod says 'with heavenly garments', Poliziano 'a starred mantle'. Both describe the jewelry with which they adorn her. Botticelli eliminates all but one Hora, Spring, paints the garment as sprinkled with daisies and omits the jewelry. Hesiod speaks of the western wind, Poliziano makes this plural and adds the shell. He describes Venus with her right hand on her hair, her left 'the sweet apple hiding'. Botticelli reverses this, raising Venus' right hand to cover her breast; with the other she holds her hair over her *mons Veneris*, a departure both from the poem and from antique models. Botticelli also adds the wind-blown flowers in the air, mentioned by Lucian, and blossoming trees. Thus the correspondence with the poem is not too close. In fact reading Poliziano's description of the doors of the Palace of Venus where the bas-relief is found, the visual image that comes to mind is of the Gates of Paradise; its borders of leaves, flowers and birds, the verisimilitude of heaven, sea and shell, which he praises, the lightning glance of the goddess' eyes and his description of a second and then a third incident in the story when Venus is received by the gods, all make us think of Ghiberti's work. There also one sees a woman, beautiful as an ancient Venus, rising from the sleeping Adam, wafted up, as it were, by little angels.

Botticelli or Poliziano might have seen a Roman mosaic, now lost, like the Pompeian fountain (Fig. 7) with its extensive sea and the Hora standing on the shore at the right or one in which, as on the pavement from Hemsworth (Fig. 14), Venus stood on a relatively small shell, or the model might have been a silver object such as the handle in the Louvre (Fig. 15). Finally Botticelli himself might have modified the standing but shell-enclosed type which, as we have

45. *The Dumbarton Oaks Collection, Handbook* (Washington, 1955), no. 184, plate; H. Peirce and R. Tyler, *L'art byzantin* (Paris, 1934), II, pl. 154b.

46. Although the famous Medici Venus was not yet in Florence and apparently still unknown, there are many copies of this type. G. A. Mansuelli, *Galleria degli Uffizi, La scultura*, I (Rome, 1958), 70 ff. One copy at least must have been known' in Tuscany in the early fourteenth century because the form appears used for Prudence on the base of Giovanni Pisano's pulpit in Pisa Cathedral. A. Venturi, *Giovanni Pisano, sein Leben und sein Werk*, II (Munich, 1927), pl. 102; J. Pope-Hennessy, *Italian Gothic Sculpture* (New York, 1955), pl. 19.

47. A. Warburg's basic study, his doctoral dissertation, *Sandro Botticelli's Geburt der Venus und Frühling* (Hamburg–Leipzig, 1893), reprinted with addenda in *Gesammelte Schriften* (*supra*, note 6), 1, 6 ff., 308 ff., prints Poliziano's *Stanze*, v. 99–103, as does H. Horne, *Sandro Botticelli* (London, 1908), 148 ff. For an English translation see J. A. Symonds, *Sketches and Studies in Italy and Greece*, 2 (London, 1914), 338. Later discussions:

J. Seznec, *The Survival of the Pagan Gods* (New York, 1961), 112 f., French ed. 1940; E. Gombrich, 'Botticelli's Mythologies', *Jour. Warburg Courtauld*, 8 (1945), 53 ff.; A. B. Ferruolo, 'Botticelli's Mythologies, Ficino's *De Amore*, Poliziano's *Stanze*', etc., etc., *Art Bull.*, 37 (1955), 17–25; W. S. Heckscher, 'The *Anadyomene* in the Mediaeval Tradition, Pelagia, Cleopatra Aphrodite. A Prelude to Botticelli's Birth of Venus', *Nederl. Kunsth. Jaarb.*, 7 (1956), 1–38; Panofsky, *op. cit.* (*supra*, note 6), 86 f. These are all concerned with the interpretation of the allegorical meaning or layers of meaning of Botticelli's painting in the extraordinarily gifted and humanistic circle of the Medici court. Roman iconographical parallels, if they are mentioned at all, are usually relegated to a footnote. Although Heckscher illustrates two examples, he omits any discussion. Warburg's attempt, *Gesammelte Schriften*, 311, to explain Botticelli's use of the shell by the early fifteenth-century MS. (Vat. Pal. lat. 1066) of Fulgentius Metaforalis, H. Liebeschutz, *Studien Bibl. Warburg*, 4 (1926), pl. 8, Fig. 10, is rightly challenged by Panofsky, 192, n. 4, as too remote visually to seem a likely source.

seen, was not uncommon and which he might have known from a gem in the Medici collection.[48] In any case his Venus is unadorned, coming to us in her new-

48. The gem in Berlin shows Venus *pudica* as does the lamp in Cyprus (*supra*, notes 38, 39) but this type is rare with Venus on or in the shell.

born purity and loveliness, without cupids or distracting companions. Like any great artist, Botticelli has changed and interpreted his material, expressing new ideas and not hesitating to disregard Poliziano or other literary sources but selecting from earlier models whatever pleased his fancy.

Addendum

La Mosaïque Gréco-Romaine, Colloques internationaux du Centre national de la Recherche scientifique (Paris, 1965) appeared after this paper was submitted. It has two important articles on my subject although neither author is concerned with the Birth of Venus as a theme. The first by D. Joly, 'Quelques aspects de la mosaïque pariétale au Ier siècle de notre ère d'après trois documents Pompéiens', 57–76, illustrates both the fountain of the Casa dell'Orso, Figs. 1 and M (color) and of the Casa, Regia IX, 7–8, Figs. 2, 27, 28, 32 and N (color). These latter photographs which Mlle Joly took herself are very welcome and her careful descriptions of both the semi-dome and its borders. The second article by J. Lassus, 'Vénus Marine', 175–90, gives a detailed description of the Sétif mosaic, Figs. 3 and D (color) which he also dates *c.* 400. His plates confirm both Venus' diadem and her parasol. Then comes a mosaic of slightly later date which had just been excavated at Cherchel, Fig. 4, pp. 178 f. It

shows Venus sitting in her shell which is held by two centaurs with tritons' horns. Nereids riding sea-creatures, a griffin and lion, are below surrounded by dolphins and other fish with a cupid whose legs end in fishtails riding a dolphin in the center. Venus with a red mantle falling across her legs holds a heavy gold necklace as if to fasten it around her neck. In a footnote on p. 181 M. Lassus refers to another unpublished mosaic in the Museum of Guelma, found at Khamissa, where two centaurs carry a shell with Venus above their heads, the goddess holding an air-inflated veil over her head. The mosaic at Djemila is Fig. 9 and this he places along with the one at Cherchel in the early fifth century. Consequently two more mosaic pavements in North Africa, both of which run true to type, must be added to my list on pp. 11–12. The subject obviously is a popular one there and we may expect more examples.

MEYER SCHAPIRO

An Irish-Latin Text on the Angel with the Ram in Abraham's Sacrifice

In a paper in *Ars Islamica* (X, 1943, 134–47) I investigated a variant of the medieval representation of the Sacrifice of Isaac, in which an angel is shown bringing the ram.[1] This variant not only ignores the text of Genesis 22:13 that tells of the ram appearing miraculously, 'caught in a thicket by his horns'; it also excludes by implication the familiar symbolism of that miracle, the analogy with Christ on the Cross which is often brought out by commentators and illustrated in art.[2] I showed that this variant, exceptional in Christian art but typical in Moslem images of the Sacrifice, comes from early Jewish tradition.[3] The Jewish legend of the angel bringing the ram entered Latin question-books on Genesis through Alcuin who in speaking of the ram at the Sacrifice posed a problem that had engaged the thought of Jewish commentators: was the ram created then and there for the Sacrifice or was it an existing sheep brought by the angel?[4] In the first case one must suppose that God continued to create after the six days; in the second, the intervention of God is in accord with an already established order of nature. In the Hebrew *Sayings of the Fathers* (*Pirkē Aboth*) the ram was included in a series of beings created by God on the evening of the sixth day in prevision of their future use;[5] and in the Midrash an angel was said to have brought this ram, browsing in Paradise since the sixth day, to the place of Sacrifice.[6]

Another version identified the ram as the bell-wether of Abraham's flock.[7]

In accounting for the acceptance of the variant by Romanesque sculptors, I pointed to a tendency in their art to introduce into Biblical scenes some explanatory details and episodes that made the action more intelligible. These details referred to the efficient and material cause, to what preceded and prepared the action, as distinct from the final religious sense which, for the schooled believer, was implicit in the form of the story and was sometimes indicated by a symbolic device or a parallel typological image.[8]

This explanation would hardly fit the primitive character of the Irish stone sculptures of the tenth century at Arboe and Durrow which are the oldest known images of the angel carrying the ram.[9] I had first supposed that the motif in Ireland was based on Alcuin's book; but I have since found an Irish-Latin text of the seventh century that anticipates Alcuin. We can assume now that the variant in question could appear in Ireland as an illustration of the idea presented in that native text.

It is a passage in the book *De Mirabilibus Sacrae Scripturae* written in 655 by an Irish author who calls himself Augustinus.[10] Reflecting on the nature of miracles in the Old Testament, he asks how the ram got to the place of Abraham's Sacrifice. He answers that according to some writers the earth brought forth the ram at that very hour in the same way that it originally begot sheep. But he knows a second and better explanation: since it cannot be said that God continued to create from the earth after the sixth day, he believes that an angel brought the ram from another place, just as an angel transported Philip from

1. 'The Angel with the Ram in Abraham's Sacrifice: A parallel in Western and Islamic Art' (cited hereafter as S.).
2. For some medieval texts see S., p. 143, n. 57; for the early Christian texts, see Isabel Speyart van Woerden, 'The Iconography of the Sacrifice of Abraham', *Vigiliae Christianae*, xv, 1961, pp. 216 ff. and 239.
3. S., p. 139. The oldest text is by Alexander Polyhistor ('Concerning the Jews'), a writer of the first century B.C. who perhaps excerpted the story from a work of the chronographer Demetrius. The text is preserved in Eusebius' *Preparation for the Gospel*, IX, 9, 421 b.
4. *Interrogationes et Responsiones in Genesin, Pat. lat.*, C, col. 545, Inter. 206.
5. *Pirkē Aboth* 5:9—R. H. Charles, *Apocrypha and Pseudepigrapha of the Old Testament*, Oxford, 1913, II, p. 708. This passage was quoted in the eleventh century by Rashi of Troyes in commenting on Genesis 22:13, and through Rashi in the Christian *Extractiones de Talmud* (1248–55)—see M. Hailperin, *Rashi and the Christian Scholars*, Pittsburgh, 1963, p. 278, n. 63.
6. See S., p. 139, n. 34.

7. *Ibid.*, p. 140, n. 40.
8. *Ibid.*, pp. 142–7.
9. *Ibid.*, Figs. 1, 2.
10. *Pat. lat.*, XXXV, cols. 2149 ff. In the prologue the author addresses the book to the clergy of 'Carthage'—perhaps a copyist's error for an unfamiliar Irish place-name. On Augustinus, see M. Esposito, 'On the Pseudo-Augustinian Treatise, *De Mirabilibus Sanctae Scripturae*, written in Ireland in the year 655', *Proceedings of the Royal Irish Academy*, XXXV, 1919, C, pp. 189–207. See also P. Duhem, *Le Système du Monde*, Paris, 1915, III, pp. 12 ff., 15, 16.

[17]

the eunuch to Azotus (Acts 8:39) and as an angel is said to have brought Habakuk to Daniel in the lions' den in Babylon (Daniel 14:35).[11]

The language of this Irish writer recalls in several phrases the text of Alcuin. The latter asks: 'was the ram suddenly created there out of the earth, or was he brought from another place by the angel? The learned suppose that an angel brought him from some other place rather than that God created him then and there from the earth, after the work of the six days.'[12]

Since, as I have shown, Alcuin's question and answer are new in the type of question-book upon which he drew—for we do not find them in the question-books on Genesis by Jerome, Augustine, Isidore and Bede, utilized by Alcuin[13]—the close resemblance to the Irish writer's text makes it probable that this was indeed, directly or indirectly, Alcuin's source. A scholar who has catalogued the surviving manuscripts of the Irish Augustine has already inferred Alcuin's acquaintance with this work from another passage in Alcuin's question-book that reproduces the text of the Irish author.[14] We do not have to assume then, as I had done, a direct acquaintance of Alcuin with Jewish oral or written tradition for this detail, although it is ultimately of Jewish origin. The Irish text enables us to establish more fully, though not completely, the line of transmission of an attempted rationalistic account of the ram at the Sacrifice from its older Jewish sources to the Romanesque period. Alcuin, who went to school at York of which he praised the exceptionally rich library, appreciated the learning of the Irish scholars in his native Hiberno-Saxon world.[15]

If the Irish sculptors who represented the angel bringing the ram on the stone crosses of Durrow and Arboe repeated an idea that had become part of native religious lore, it was for the writer of the seventh century a significant example of a theological principle which he illustrated by other scriptural incidents. His book is devoted to the explanation of the miracles in the Old and New Testaments. His aim, he says, is to show that whenever in the Bible something happens contrary to the everyday conduct of things, there God is not creating nature anew ('non novam ibi Deum facere naturam'), but is governing nature as He had established it in the beginning.[16] The miracles He performs are in accord with His laws and utilize existing means. So, in commenting on Joshua's miracle he remarks that the movement of the moon as well as the sun had to be arrested in order not to disturb chronology.[17] The change of Lot's wife into a pillar of salt, he explains, was effected by the spread of the small quantity of salt, normally in the organism, throughout the whole body ('totum corpus infecit').[18] However fantastic the explanations of the miracles in this book—for they depend on the acceptance of supernatural forces—they show also a rationalistic temper which is indebted to classical thought and anticipates tendencies of the later middle ages.[19] The Irish Augustine is interested particularly in calendrical computation and in explaining rainfall and the tides. One cannot help noting that although he wrote in the seventh century and was known to Alcuin, the many surviving manuscripts of his book belong to the period of the twelfth to the fifteenth century.[20] It seems to have attracted attention again in the Romanesque period, a time when the interest in natural phenomena and rational explanation began to revive.

* * *

11. *Op. cit.*, I, 14, col. 2162. 'Hunc in illa hora terra protulit, quomodo et in principio pecora gignit. An etiam, ne illud opus post diem sextam condidisse de terra Deus dicatur, istum aerietem detulisse angelum aliunde credimus, quomodo et Philippum angelus ab eunucho transtulit in Azotum, et ad Danielem in Babylonem Habacuc transtulisse ad lacum leonum fertur angelus.'

12. *Pat. lat.*, C, col. 545, Inter. 206: 'Unde aries iste, qui pro Isaac immolatus est, venerit, solet quaeri: an (de)terra ibi subito creatus esset, vel aliunde ab angelo allatus?—*Resp.* Aries iste non putativus, sed vero credendus est. Ideo magis a doctoribus aestimatur, aliunde eum angelo atulisse, quam ibi de terra, post sex dierum opera, Dominum procreasse.'

13. S., p. 141.

14. Esposito, *op. cit.*, p. 201.

15. For Alcuin on the Irish scholars, see the texts assembled by J. F. Kenney, *The Sources for the Early History of Ireland*, New York, 1929, I, pp. 534, 535.

16. *Op. cit.*, col. 2151.

17. *Ibid.*, col. 2175. Interesting for early medieval rationalism in this context is the question of Gunzo, an Italian writer of about 970, who asked whether, when the sun and moon stood still at Joshua's command, the other planets also stopped moving and the music of the spheres was changed. See M. Manitius, *Geschichte der lateinischen Literatur des Mittelalters*, I, Munich, 1911, p. 534.

18. *Op. cit.*, cols. 2161–2. The rationalistic tendency of the Irish writer will be evident from a comparison with an example of folklore reasoning about the same episode. The anonymous fourth- or fifth-century author of the poem *De Sodoma*, following Jewish writers (Wisdom 10:7, Josephus, *Antiqu. Jud.*, I, 11, 4), describes the pillar of salt as still standing in the Palestinian plain, undissolved by rains or destroyed by winds; and to confirm the belief, he adds that the pillar, formed as an image of Lot's wife, menstruates (*Pat. lat.*, II, cols. 1161–2). This legend reached the artist who painted the scene of the burning Sodom and Lot's wife in a thirteenth-century French manuscript of World History (British Museum, Add. MS. 19669, fol. 20); a red cross is drawn over the place of the vulva in the whitened figure. The text says nothing of this detail, though it recalls the preceding verses of the ancient poem: '... devint une pierre salee ausi com se ce fust une ymaige com eut par grant diligence samblent ali tailliee et contrefaite' (fol. 22).

19. The author refers in several places to the ancients and to learned literature: 'duabus autem causis, ut sapientes aiunt' (I, 35); 'ut multi magistri putant' (II, 15); 'physiologi aiunt' (III, 2); 'ut antiqui ferunt' (III, 8). All these are cited by Esposito, *op. cit.*, p. 206.

20. Forty-two manuscripts are listed by Esposito, *op. cit.*, pp. 189 ff.

I take this opportunity to add several works to the previous list of examples of the angel carrying the ram in art.

In the Schocken Library in Jerusalem I have seen in a Haggada manuscript of the late fourteenth or early fifteenth century, written in Northern Italy, a miniature of the Sacrifice with an angel bringing the ram. Although he does not carry the ram in his arms, as in the clearest examples, he stands behind it with one hand on the ram's shoulder. Since the ram is not near the tree, we may interpret this version as one that replaces the traditional literal type, in which the ram appears miraculously in the bush or beside it, by the physically more plausible variant. I do not know another example among the numerous Jewish representations. Like some other Biblical pictures in Jewish manuscripts it was probably based on a Christian model. In the same book there is a calendar with miniatures of the labors of the months, which include even the slaughtering of the pig.

Other examples are:

Nîmes, Musée Archéologique, Romanesque capital from the apse of the church of Les Saintes-Maries-de-la-Mer. The angel holds the ram by the horn. See V. Lasalle, 'Fragment roman d'un Sacrifice d'Abraham au Musée Archéologique de Nîmes', *La Revue du Louvre et des Musées de France*, XV, 1965, p. 176.

Parma, Duomo, capital. See H. Decker, *Romanesque Art in Italy*, New York, 1959, pl. 236.

London, Victoria and Albert Museum, French Romanesque capital.

Paris, Bibliothèque Nationale, MS. fr. 20125. See H. Buchthal, *Miniature Painting in the Latin Kingdom of Jerusalem*, Oxford, 1957, pl. 150b—thirteenth century.

Bordeaux, St. Michel, tympanum of north transept portal, *c*. 1500. On a second tympanum of the same doorway is the scene of Isaac with faggots and the ram on the altar.

Pietro Testa (1611?–1650), etching. One angel stays Abraham's arm; a second, flying, carries the ram. This work was kindly called to my attention by Dr. Konrad Hoffmann of Tübingen University.

Abraham's sacrifice with an angel bringing the ram. Miniature in a Haggada manuscript of the late fourteenth or early fifteenth century, written in Northern Italy. Reproduced by courtesy of the Schocken Library, Jerusalem.

ERWIN PANOFSKY

Hercules Agricola: A Further Complication in the Problem of the Illustrated Hrabanus Manuscripts

'Ea memorare volo, explicare nequeo.'
(W. M. Lindsay)

Magnentius Hrabanus Maurus, born in 780, received his education at Tours under Alcuin but spent the greater part of his adult life in the Monastery at Fulda which he directed as Abbot from 822 to 842. After five years (842–847) of withdrawal to the nearby Monastery on the Petersberg—his own foundation—he was elected Archbishop of Mayence, where he died in 856.[1]

In his retreat he composed—or, rather, compiled—a big encyclopedia entitled *De naturis rerum* (but mostly cited as *De universo*) which he dedicated to his old friend, Bishop Hemmo of Halberstadt, and a copy of which he offered to King Louis the Germanic. Concerned with 'omnibus rebus et quibusdam aliis', this work is largely copied from the *Etymologiae* (occasionally quoted as *Origines*) by Isidore of Seville (*c.* 560–636); but it differs from its model in several respects. The vast material is presented in a different order (there are twenty-two books instead of twenty, and the discussion starts, as Hrabanus thought proper, with God, the Trinity and the angels instead of with the liberal arts); some of Isidore's entries are omitted; and most of them are lengthily 'moralized' by the application of an *interpretatio Christiana* still foreign to Isidore.[2]

1. Cf. M. Manitius, *Geschichte der lateinischen Literatur des Mittelalters*, Munich, 1911–31, I, pp. 288 ff.; III, p. 1062.
2. So far as I know there is no critical edition of Hrabanus' *De universo* based on a comparative study of the manuscripts which tend to differ not only in individual readings but also in the numbering of the chapters and, as will be seen, in the presence or absence of single sentences or even whole sections. For the time being the text is normally quoted from vol. CXI of Migne's *Patrologia Latina* (hereafter referred to as *P.L.*), cols. 9–614, which is a straight reprint of G. Colvenerius (George Colvener or Colveneer), ed., *Magnenti Hrabani Mauri opera omnia*, Cologne, 1626–7 (not 1617, as stated in *P.L.*). This in turn largely agrees with the *editio princeps*: *Rabanus, opus de universo seu de sermonum proprietate et mystica rerum significatione*, Strasbourg, probably Adolf Rusch, shortly before 1467 (Hain-Copinger, *13669); photostats of this *incunabulum* were kindly placed at my disposal by Dr. Curt F. Bühler of the Morgan Library. In referring to the text I keep to the order of chapters adopted in *P.L.* Isidore's *Etymologiae* is accessible in *Patrologia Latina*, LXXXII, cols. 74–1054, and in the critical edition by W. M. Lindsay, Oxford, 1911. Cf. J. Engels, 'La Portée de l'Etymologie Isidorienne', *Studi medievali*, Spoleto, Series III, 1, 1962, pp. 1 ff.

I

Since the end of the nineteenth century, Hrabanus' *De universo* has aroused the interest not only of palaeographers and students of medieval literature but also of art historians. Of the *c.* thirty manuscripts which have come down to us, ranging from the tenth to the fifteenth century, no less than five are illustrated, though only two provide us with a nearly complete set of miniatures. And these illustrations bear witness to a constant representational tradition still rooted in the art of classical antiquity.

The two completely illustrated and completely preserved manuscripts, separated by about four centuries, are, first, the 'Codex Casinensis 132' (hereafter referred to as '*Cas.*'), which has never left the Monastery of Montecassino where it was both written and illuminated in 1022–1023;[3] and, second, a manuscript in the Vatican Library, Cod. Pal. lat. 291 (hereafter referred to as '*Pal.*'), which was written in South or Central Germany in 1425 (the *explicit* even states the precise date: November 8) and is no less fully—as a matter of fact, a little more fully—illustrated in a charmingly provincial version of what is now generally called the 'International Style of around 1400'.[4]

3. Many—unfortunately not all—of its three hundred and sixty-one illustrations are reproduced in P. A. Amelli, *Miniature sacre e profane dell'anno 1023*, Montecassino, 1896, but only in chromolithographs which, being hand-made, obscure the style of the miniatures and isolate them from the script. Photographic reproductions exist only of some thirty pictures or pages selected according to the requirements of a given context. See, e.g., E. A. Lowe, *Scriptura Beneventana*, Oxford, 1929, I, p. 344, and II, pl. 59; R. Wittkower, 'The Marvels of the East', *Journal of the Warburg and Courtauld Institutes*, V, 1942, pp. 159 ff., pl. 42b; E. Panofsky, *Il Significato nelle arti visive*, Turin, 1962, p. 52, Fig. 13; and, above all, F. Saxl, 'Illustrated Medieval Encyclopaedias', *Lectures*, London, 1957, I, pp. 228 ff., and II, pls. 155 a ('p. 107' should read 'p. 106'), c, e ('p. 290' should read 'p. 291'); 156 b–d; 157 a, c; 158 a, c, e; 159 a, c; 160 a, c ('p. 474' should read 'p. 472'), e; 161 a, c, e; 162 a, c; 163 a, c; 164 a, e; 165 a, c; 167 c; H. Giess, 'The Sculpture of the Cloisters of Santa Sofia in Benevento', *Art Bulletin*, XLI, 1959, pp. 249 ff., Fig. 26. For the general problem of illustrated medieval encyclopedias, see Saxl, *loc. cit.*, and 'Die Bibliothek Warburg und ihr Ziel', *Vorträge der Bibliothek Warburg*, I, 1921–2, pp. 1 ff.; further, A. Goldschmidt, 'Frühmittelalterliche illustrierte Enzyklopädien', *ibid.*, III, 1923–4, pp. 215 ff.
4. *Pal.* was discovered and excellently described as well as analyzed by P. Lehmann, 'Illustrierte Hrabanus Codices; Fuldaer Studien, II', *Sitzungsberichte der philosophisch-his-*

Of the three other illustrated manuscripts two are mere fragments: two isolated vellum leaves, probably written and illuminated in West Germany about 1200, which belong to Book IV, Chapters 2–5 (*De martyribus, De Ecclesia et Synagoga, De religione et fide, De clericis*), in Paris, Bibliothèque Nationale, MS. lat. 17177;[5] and the *disiecta membra* (more than one hundred pages or clippings from pages) of a manuscript ascribed to a Catalonian hand of the late fourteenth century, fairly good in quality with respect to script as well as illustrations but barbarously cut apart. Most, though not all, of its surviving fragments were acquired and assembled by the Preussische Staatsbibliothek in Berlin (Cod. fol. lat. 930) and are at present on deposit in the University Library at Tübingen.[6] The fifth manuscript (Vatican Library, Cod. Reg. lat. 391, hereafter referred to as '*Reg.*') dates from the early fifteenth century and was most probably produced in Italy (it was in fact owned by an Italian humanist as early as *c.* 1450). The text is complete, except that it abruptly ends in the middle of the antepenultimate chapter (XXII, 14); but the rather rustic illustrator either died, was dismissed or lost heart after having produced seven pen drawings and one lapis sketch at the beginning.[7] Late, scantily illustrated, indifferently written, and careless in the rendering of the text, this manuscript would not be of

great value were it not for the fact that blank spaces are left for all the pictures planned but not executed— which enables us to compare its organization with that of *Cas.* and *Pal.*

II

That these five illustrated manuscripts are interrelated cannot, I think, be doubted.[8] There arise, however, two questions. First, do all the manuscripts postdating *Cas.* depend on it, or do some derive from a common archetype now lost? Second, if we do have to postulate such a parent manuscript, how do we have to imagine the genesis of this *chef d'œuvre inconnu*?

The first of these questions has been conclusively answered by Paul Lehmann. He demonstrated that *Pal.* and *Reg.* constitute a family related to but different from *Cas.*, and that, therefore, these two manuscripts derive from a model antedating *Cas.* And, since *Pal.* was written and illuminated in Germany, this model was presumably produced at Fulda, perhaps within the orbit of Hrabanus Maurus himself.[9] This Lehmann proved by pointing out that no less than four pictures present in *Pal.* and planned for *Reg.*—witness the

torischen Klasse der Bayrischen Akademie der Wissenschaften zu München, 1927, pp. 13 ff. The only trivial objection which may be raised is that the chapter references do not consistently refer to either the order adopted in *P.L.* or to the occasionally deviant numeration in *Pal.* itself. Cf. also E. Panofsky and F. Saxl, 'Classical Mythology in Medieval Art', *Metropolitan Museum Studies*, IV, 2, 1933, pp. 228 ff., particularly p. 258, and Figs. 37, 41; E. Panofsky, *Renaissance and Renascences*, Stockholm, 1960, p. 207, Fig. 157. My grateful memory belongs to the late Dom Guy Ferrari, O.S.B., who kindly provided me with a complete set of photographs.

5. P. Lehmann, 'Mitteilungen aus Handschriften', *Sitzungsberichte der philosophisch-historischen Abtlg. der Bayrischen Akademie der Wissenschaften zu München*, 1930, pp. 45 ff.; cf. H. Swarzenski, 'Recent Literature, Chiefly Periodical, on Mediaeval Minor Arts', *Art Bulletin*, XXIV, 1942, pp. 287 ff., particularly p. 293.

6. P. Lehmann, 'Reste einer Bilderhandschrift des Hrabanus in Berlin', *Zentralblatt für Bibliothekswesen*, LV, 1938, pp. 173 ff.; cf. also Swarzenski, *loc. cit.* Some of the fragments, then thought to belong to a manuscript of Isidore's *Etymologiae*, were offered in E. van Scherling's *Rotulus, A Quarterly Bulletin for Manuscript Collectors*, Leiden, III, 1933, pp. 3 and 8 ff. In spite of the erroneous attribution, this publication is still important in that it includes a number of miniatures which the Berlin Library was unable to secure and at least one of which (the Decapitation Scene referred to in notes 8 and 17 and illustrated in our Fig. 3) is known to have been destroyed by fire (kind communication of Professor Bernhard Bischoff).

7. P. Lehmann, 'Fuldaer Studien, II', pp. 41 ff. The illustrations begin with I, 1 (*De Deo*) and end with III, 1 (*De aliis quibusdam viris sive feminis, quorum nomina in Veteri Testamento scripta leguntur*). In this case, too, I have to thank the late Dom Guy Ferrari for photographs.

8. This also applies to the Berlin fragments which, according to Swarzenski, *loc. cit.*, 'seem to deviate from the other known illustrated copies of this work'. It is true that Paul Lehmann, 'Reste einer Bilderhandschrift', cannot see a 'direct connection between the Berlin fragments and one of the other manuscripts'; but he admits that 'not infrequently an affinity is evident' between them and *Cas.* In my opinion this affinity is so close that even a direct descent of the Berlin fragments from *Cas.* might be considered. The destroyed miniature, showing a Decapitation Scene and formerly illustrating the chapter *De theatro* (XX, 36, illustrated in *Rotulus*, no. 1583, and our Fig. 3), agreed with *Cas.*, p. 489 (Amelli, pl. CXXX), in that it showed four spectators, two victims already beheaded and the henchman putting back his sword into the scabbard; whereas *Pal.*, fol. 248 v (here XX, 35), shows only three spectators, one victim still alive and the henchman raising his sword for action (our Figs. 4 and 5). Cf. also below, note 17. Pan (XV, 6) bears a staff, as he should, in the Berlin manuscript, Cod. fol. lat. 930, fol. 73, as well as in *Cas.*, p. 389 (Amelli, pl. CXII), but a snake in *Pal.*, fol. 191 v; and the Theseus shown at the entrance of the Labyrinth (XIV, 12; Berlin, Cod. fol. lat. 930, fol. 65) is, if not a sword-bearing warrior as in *Cas.*, p. 348 (Amelli, pl. LXXXVII), at least not a monk as in *Pal.*, fol. 170 v (where, incidentally, the chapter is numbered 13 rather than 12). If the personification of Terra (XII, 1) apparently lost but reproduced in *Rotulus*, no. 1582) makes an orant gesture as she does in *Pal.*, fol. 142, but not in *Cas.*, p. 294 (Amelli, pl. LXXI), it should be noted that this orant gesture occurs in the very similar personification of the *Rubrum Mare* in *Cas.*, p. 276 (Amelli, pl. LXII). Be that as it may, on no account can the Berlin fragments be said to represent a tradition different from that which is reflected in the four other illustrated manuscripts.

9. Of the Paris manuscript Bibl. Nat., MS. lat. 17177, too little is preserved to establish a filiation; but the very fact that it was written and illuminated in West Germany at a comparatively early date suggests that it, like *Pal.*, depends not on *Cas.* but, directly or indirectly, on the Fulda archetype. For the Berlin fragments, apparently more closely akin to *Cas.* than to the *Pal.-Reg.* family, see the preceding note.

spaces left for them in the text—are without parallels in *Cas.*: *Pal.*, fol. 117 v (IX, 24 [not 'X, 24']), *A Heap of Ashes*; *Pal.*, fol. 126 v (X, 10), *The Occupations of the Months*; *Pal.*, fol. 241 (XX, 4), *Four Men with Horns and Trumpets*; *Pal.*, fol. 272 (XXII, 12), *Sleighs and Their Runners in a Wintry Landscape*. And it may be added that *Pal.*, in spite of its late date, occasionally avoids iconographical inaccuracies committed by the illuminator of *Cas.*, whereas the opposite is true in other cases.

In the left-hand column of fol. 190 (XV, 6), for example, the illuminator of *Pal.* correctly equips Mercury with footwings (our Fig. 2) whereas the illuminator of *Cas.* (p. 386, Amelli, Pl. CIX, our Fig. 1) misunderstood these footwings as a complete bird flying between the legs of the god.[10] In *Pal.*, fol. 187 (XV, 4), the subject, taken from Exodus 7:20 (*Moses Changing the Waters into Blood*), is much more clearly indicated than in *Cas.*, p. 379 (Amelli, Pl. CIV), even though the illuminator of *Pal.* forgot to provide Moses with a halo. The Saturn in *Pal.*, fol. 190, left-hand column, has retained the classical sickle; whereas in *Cas.*, p. 386 (Amelli, Pl. CVIII), he carries the more modern scythe. And in the initial miniature of the chapter *De diis gentium* (XV, 6) the demoniacal nature of the winged figure on the right is correctly emphasized by horns in *Pal.*, fol. 188 v; whereas he looks like an angel in *Cas.*, p. 383 (Amelli, Pl. CVI).

Conversely, the counterpart of this figure (Silvanus?) is omitted in *Pal.*, and there are other miniatures which, from an iconographical point of view, are less nearly correct in *Pal.* than in *Cas.* Where the illustration of XVIII, 5 in *Cas.*, p. 448 (Amelli, Pl. CXXIV), correctly shows the nimbed Apollo instructing his son, Aesculapius (also nimbed), in the art of medicine, the corresponding picture in *Pal.*, fol. 222 v, transforms Aesculapius into a patient walking on crutches. And that the staff of Pan in *Cas.*, p. 389 (Amelli, Pl. CXII), has become a snake in *Pal.*, fol. 191 v, has already been mentioned.[11] In certain cases it may thus be possible to 'reconstruct' the archetype by synthesizing, as it were, the renderings in *Cas.* with those in *Pal.*[12]

With regard to the second question—the genesis of what may be called the 'Hrabanus Cycle'—it is now generally conceded that the illustrations of the—presumably Carolingian—archetype are firmly rooted in the classical tradition and that the models they reflect were produced in what Ernst Kitzinger felicitously called the 'sub-antique' period of the sixth or seventh century. The wealth of comparative material brought together by Fritz Saxl[13] leaves little doubt about these points. What is in doubt, however, is whether the 'Hrabanus Cycle' was assembled *de novo* or—like the illustrations of the *Aratea* manuscripts, the *Psychomachia*, the *Notitia dignitatum*, the *Comedies of Terence*, etc.—is based upon a cycle already established several centuries before; in other words, whether the original illustrator of Hrabanus' *De universo* collected his more than three hundred and sixty pictures from a great number of separate sources or merely appropriated, revised and rearranged a basically identical set of compositions originally intended to illustrate the parent work of Hrabanus' encyclopedia, the *Etymologiae* of Isidore of Seville.

The first of these alternatives would be at variance with the known habits of Carolingian and Ottonian book illuminators, who normally did not invent, or assemble from many heterogeneous sources, a whole

individual figures, *Cas.* and *Pal.* differ as follows. *Cas.* shows fifteen species of monsters arranged in four rows (the Pygmies are represented by two specimens). *Pal.* shows, in the left-hand column of fol. 75 v, twelve species in three rows of four figures each, and in the right-hand column of the same page—a miniature not mentioned by either Lehmann or Wittkower—two further species in one row: a Hippocentauress and the Chimaera. Ten species are common to both *Cas.* and *Pal.* *Cas.* lacks four species present in *Pal.*: the people blessed with a lower lip large enough to cover the entire face so as to protect it from the sun ('labeo subteriore adeo prominente, ut in solis ardoribus totam ex eo faciem contegant dormientes'); the people whose mouths are so small that they can 'suck up nourishment only by means of straws' ('aliis concreta ora esse modico tantum foramine, calamis avenarum haurientes pastus'); the Hydra; and the Chimaera, the two last-named *portenta* mentioned in *P.L.*, col. 198 B. *Cas.*, on the other hand, has five species not present in *Pal.*: the Androgyni (or Hermaphrodites); the Antipodes; the Hippopodes; the Minocentaurs; and the Onocentaurs. We may thus assume, with all due reservations, that the archetype exhibited nineteen species (10 plus 4 plus 5), distributed, I think, over two miniatures as in *Pal.* One of these would have shown twelve species in four rows (again as in *Pal.*), beginning with the Androgyni and ending with the Antipodes. The other, considerably smaller, would have shown seven species in one row of four (showing the Hippopodes, the Pygmies, the Hydra, and the Chimaera) and one row of three (containing the more space-consuming representatives of the Centaur family, viz., the Minocentaurs, the Hippocentaurs and the Onocentaurs).

10. This discrepancy was already pointed out by Panofsky and Saxl, 'Classical Mythology in the Middle Ages'; for the cynocephalous aspect of Mercury, see below, note 37. In the same miniature, however, Bacchus wears his rightful wreath of vine or ivy leaves in *Cas.*; whereas he appears bareheaded in *Pal.*

11. See note 8.

12. This may apply not only to the miniatures showing Hercules, Mars and Apollo, which form the main subject of this article (see below, pp. 23 ff.), but also to the illustration of the 'monsters' described in the chapter *De portentis* (VII, 7): *Cas.*, p. 166 (Wittkower, *op. cit.*, p. 173, pl. 42b, our Fig. 6, reproduced from a photograph kindly supplied by the Warburg Institute in London); and *Pal.*, fol. 75 v (Wittkower, p. 174, pl. 42c, our Fig. 7). Apart from minor discrepancies in the sequence of the

13. *Lectures*, cited in note 3. Cf. also E. Panofsky and F. Saxl, *Dürers Kupferstich 'Melencolia. I'* (Studien der Bibliothek Warburg, II), Leipzig and Berlin, 1923, pp. 125 ff., now superseded by R. Klibansky, E. Panofsky and F. Saxl, *Saturn and Melancholy; Studies in the History of Natural Philosophy, Religion and Art*, London and New York, 1964 (here p. 309, n. 89, and *passim*).

series of compositions for the sole purpose of illustrating a contemporary or nearly contemporary text. We should find it hard, moreover, to imagine how an artist probably active at Fulda between, say, 850 and 950 should have gained access to so many different pictures, all dating from the sixth or seventh century (that is to say, precisely from the lifetime of Isidore of Seville), which could serve as models for the Trinity as well as for the pagan gods; for the celestial bodies and such meteorological phenomena as clouds, hail and thunderstorms as well as for an infinite variety of serpents, worms, insects, plants, and minerals; for all kinds of public and domestic buildings (most of them late-'classical' in character) as well as for technological devices from glass ovens to carts and sleighs. Whereas a scriptorium active in the very humanistic, 'subantique' environment of Isidore of Seville—whose *Etymologiae*, we recall, begins with the liberal arts—would have had no difficulty in producing all the illustrations required by the text on the basis of a tradition still very much alive in the Iberian Peninsula.

Against the second alternative, however, there militates the ineluctable fact that we do not have a single manuscript of Isidore's *Etymologiae* (and their number is legion) which contains illustrations even remotely comparable to those encountered in the manuscripts of Hrabanus Maurus' *De universo*.

In view of this negative evidence such eminent scholars as Paul Lehmann[14] and Adolph Goldschmidt[15] are understandably reluctant to postulate an illustrated Isidore manuscript as the prototype of the 'Hrabanus Cycle'. But there are those, particularly Fritz Saxl, for whom the improbability of a 'Hrabanus Cycle' freely assembled from many different yet stylistically homogeneous sources, all of them antedating the middle of the ninth century by more than two hundred years, outweighs the difficulty presented by the absence of illustrated Isidore manuscripts. It is quite possible, Saxl thinks, that there existed an illustrated *édition de luxe* of the *Etymologiae*, unique and now lost (just as the models of the *Aratea* manuscripts, the *Psychomachia*, the *Notitia dignitatum*, the *Comedies of Terence*, etc., are lost), which was accessible to the originator of the 'Hrabanus Cycle'.[16]

Inclined to accept what may be called the 'Isidore hypothesis',[17] this writer attempted to look for tangible evidence in its favor by examining the text as well as the pictures. But in doing so he soon found himself confronted with a problem which, instead of clarifying the situation, complicates it even further. He wishes, for this very reason, to submit the whole question to the judgment *di color che sanno*.

III

In Hrabanus' chapter *De diis gentium* (XV, 6) the pagan gods and demi-gods (beginning with Bel, Beelphegor and Beelzebub and ending with the 'Pilosi' and Faunus Ficarius) are enumerated in exactly the same order, and described in largely identical terms, as in the corresponding chapter of Isidore's *Etymologiae* (VIII, 11). There is, however, one notable exception: the section on Hercules. From Isidore's extensive list Hercules is conspicuously absent.[18] With Hrabanus, the situation is quite different and very complex.

As printed in *P.L.*, col. 430 C, as well as, with minor differences in spelling and punctuation, in the *editio princeps* of *c.* 1465, fol. o 1 v f., the text contains an elaborate though somewhat loosely constructed description, inserted between those of Mars and Apollo (the emendations in brackets are supported by the manuscripts): 'Herculem [*ed. pr.*: *Hercolem*] credebant deum virtutis: dicitur autem Hercoles [should read: *Heracles*] Graece, quasi heris cleos, id est, litis gloriosus, ab heris, id est, lis, et cleos, gloria; vel quasi herocleos [should read: *Heroncleos* or *Heron Cleos*, viz., ἡρώων κλέος], quod Latine virorum fortium famam dicimus. Fuit autem (ut scribit Sextus Pompeius) agricola: ideoque Anchei [should read: *Augei*,

14. 'Fuldaer Studien, II', p. 46.
15. 'Frühmittelalterliche illustrierte Enzyklopädien', p. 219.
16. *Lectures*, I, pp. 233–9. Saxl's opinion is shared, for example, by Hanns Swarzenski (personal communication) and E. Schenk zu Schweinsberg, 'Des Hrabanus Maurus Kapitel vom Glase', *Glastechnische Berichte*, XXXVII, 1964, pp. 129 f.
17. One small point in favor of the Isidore hypothesis may perhaps be found in the fact that Hrabanus' chapter *De theatro* (XX, 36) is illustrated by the Decapitation Scene reproduced in our Figs. 3–5 and referred to in note 8. There is nothing in the text of this chapter (literally taken over from Isidore, *Etymologiae*, XVIII, 42) to suggest so sanguinary a subject. Its presence might, however, be accounted for by the assumption that the composition now serving to illustrate Hrabanus' chapter *De theatro* was originally intended to illustrate the related and nearly adjacent chapter *De tragoedia* in Isidore's *Etymologiae*, XVIII, 45, where the tragedians are defined as those who 'antiqua gesta atque *facinora sceleratorum regum* luctuoso carmine, *spectante populo*, concinebant' (italics mine). This chapter, like the intervening chapters *De scena* and *De orchestra* (*Etymologiae*, XVIII, 43 and 44), expatiates on the chapter *De theatro* but was omitted by Hrabanus Maurus. In other words, we seem to be confronted with a picture purporting to illustrate a text in Hrabanus' *De universo* while actually illustrating a text found only in Isidore's *Etymologiae*.
18. In Isidore's *Etymologiae* Hercules is mentioned only in other contexts and only in passing. First, he occurs in the chapter *De discretione temporum* (V, 39, 11, not in Hrabanus), where he is said to have died in the 'third age of the world'; and, second, in the two nearly-identical passages concerned with the Hydra: in *De portentis*, Isidore, XI, 3, 34 (hence Hrabanus, VII, 7; *P.L.*, col. 198 B), and in *De serpentibus*, Isidore, XII, 4, 23 (hence Hrabanus, VIII, 3; *P.L.*, col. 233 A). In both these passages the Hydra is defined as a 'locus evomens aquas' and both contain the sentence: 'quod Hercules videns, loca ipsa exussit, et sic aquae clausit meatus.'

a by-form of *Augeae* which already occurs in Seneca, *Hercules furens*, line 248] regis stabulum stercoribus purgasse refertur, quia proprie agricolarum est stercorare agros.' This reads in English: 'Hercules was held to be the god of virtue. In Greek, however, he is called "Heracles", *heris cleos*, as it were, which means "famed by strife", from *heris*, viz., strife [*heris*, needless to say, is a faulty transliteration of ἔρις], and *cleos*, fame; or else "Heroncleos", which we would call in Latin "the fame of brave men". But according to Sextus Pompeius, he was a husbandman; and for this reason he is said to have cleaned King Augeas' stables of dung, because it behooves the husbandman to fertilize the fields with manure.'

I am unable to name the manuscript or manuscripts from which this 'printed version' is derived and must leave its or their identification to the experts. The manuscripts which have come to my very limited knowledge fall into two classes.

In the first class—beginning with what may be the earliest extant manuscript but also including a manuscript as late as the fourteenth century—no mention is made of Hercules at all; the sequence of divinities is, precisely as in Isidore: 'Mercury, Mars, Apollo'. This class is represented, for example, by a tenth-century manuscript in the Badische Landesbibliothek at Karlsruhe (Cod. Aug. perg. 68, p. 113);[19] a twelfth-century manuscript in Paris (Bibliothèque Nationale, MS. lat. 16879, fol. 190 v);[20] a very beautifully written manuscript of the same century in the British Museum (MS. Royal 12 G. XIV, fol. 196);[20a] and a fourteenth-century manuscript, probably of Italian origin, in the University Library at Leiden (Cod. Voss. lat. F 5, fol. 121).[21]

Of the manuscripts of the second class with which I am familiar, ranging from 1022–1023 to the fifteenth century, all but one (Stuttgart, Würtembergische Landesbibliothek, M.S. theol. 2° 45, fol. 202) happen to be illustrated: *Cas.*, p. 387 (Amelli, Pl. CX, our Fig. 8); *Pal.*, fol. 190 v–191 (our Fig. 9); and *Reg.*,

fol. 111 (our Fig. 10).[22] These manuscripts do include a textual description of Hercules, accompanied by a miniature in *Cas.* and *Pal.* and intended to be accompanied by a miniature in *Reg.* But this description differs from the 'printed version' in three respects. Firstly, Hercules is discussed not between Mars and Apollo but between Mercury and Mars so that the sequence is not, as in the 'printed version', 'Mercury, Mars, Hercules, Apollo' but 'Mercury, Hercules, Mars, Apollo'; and it is this order which is observed in the illustrations. Secondly, there are some differences in spelling, one of them crucial; to this we shall shortly revert. Thirdly, and most importantly, the derivation of the name 'Hercules' from *heris* (strife) is absent so that the text in *Cas.*, *Pal.* and *Reg.* is limited to what follows (abbreviations expanded and proper names capitalized): 'Herculem [*Cas.*, *Reg.* and Stuttgart: *Erculem*] credebant deum virtutis. Dicitur autem Hercules [*Cas.* and *Reg.*: Ercules] grece [Stuttgart: *grate*] Eracles quasi eron cleos [*Pal.*: *heroncleos*; *Reg.*: *croncles*], quod latine uirorum fortium faman dicimus. Fuit autem, ut scribit Festus [*Pal.* and Stuttgart: *Sestus*] Pompeius, agricola ideoque Augei [*sic* in *Cas.*, *Pal.*, *Reg.* and Stuttgart] regis stabulum stercoribus purgasse refertur, quia proprie agricolarum est stercorare agros [the clause beginning with *ideoque* inadvertently omitted in *Reg.*].'

IV

In Hrabanus' chapter *De diis gentium*, then, we have to distinguish, as far as the treatment of Hercules is concerned, between three strata. In 'Stratum A', represented by the manuscripts in Karlsruhe, Paris (Bibl. Nat., MS. lat. 16879), London, and Leiden, there is, as in Isidore's *Etymologiae*, no reference to Hercules at all. In 'Stratum B', represented by *Cas.*, *Pal.*, *Reg.* and Stuttgart, a section devoted to Hercules is inserted between those devoted to Mercury and Mars but is confined to the following statements: (1) 'Hercules was the god of virtue'; (2) his name derives from *heron cleos* [ἡρώων κλέος], 'the fame of heroes': (3) according to 'Festus' or 'Sestus' Pompeius, the cleaning of the Augean stables identifies him as a husbandman (*agricola*) who fertilizes his fields by manuring them. In 'Stratum C', finally (known to me only from the printed editions), the section on Hercules is inserted not between Mercury and Mars but be-

19. The Karlsruhe manuscript is divided into two parts, the first (containing Books I–XII) bearing, somewhat paradoxically, the signature 'Cod. Aug. perg. 96'. For this information (Manitius, *Geschichte der lateinischen Literatur* . . . , I, p. 300, cites only Cod. Aug. perg. 96) as well as for a photostat of the pertinent page I have to thank Dr. Jan Lauts, Director of the Staatliche Kunsthalle at Karlsruhe.

20. A photostat of this page was kindly presented to me by Dr. Robert Klein, to whom I am also indebted in other respects (see note 32).

20a. This manuscript (G. F. Warner and J. P. Gilson, *British Museum, Catalogue of Western Manuscripts in the Old Royal and King's Collections*, London, 1921, II, pp. 73 f.) was brought to my attention by Miss Carla Greenhaus (now Mrs. Lord) to whom I wish to express my gratitude.

21. A photostat of this page was kindly presented to me by Professor H. van de Waal of Leiden University.

22. For the photograph reproduced in Fig. 9 I am indebted to the Warburg Institute at London. The fragments in Berlin (Cod. fol. lat. 930) and Paris (Bibl. Nat. MS. lat. 17177) do not contain the pertinent folios. The unillustrated manuscript in Stuttgart (fifteenth century) was brought to my attention by Dr. Florentine Mütherich who also provided me with a microfilm; I am most grateful to her on both counts.

tween Mars and Apollo; 'Festus' or 'Sestus' Pompeius has become 'Sextus' Pompeius; and the text is augmented by another derivation of the hero's name: 'Hercules' means *heris cleos*, 'famed by strife'.

'Stratum A' presents no difficulties. Omitting Hercules altogether, and thus refraining from any alteration of the Isidore text, it may be held to represent the primary redaction or 'Urfassung' of Hrabanus' chapter *De diis gentium*.

'Stratum B' does not, however, seem to be much later. Since it is exemplified by *Cas.* (dated 1022–1023) as well as *Pal.*, *Reg.* and Stuttgart, this shorter form of the Hercules section must have been present in the 'Carolingian archetype' from which the extant illustrated manuscripts derive. Nothing militates against the assumption that the insertion was made by Hrabanus himself;[23] and this assumption would agree with the fact that all the sources of this shorter text are classical or late-antique.

That Hercules was held to be the 'god of virtue' was a commonplace ever since Xenophon had popularized Prodicus' story of Hercules at the Crossroads, wherein the young hero prefers Virtue to Pleasure. The derivation of his name from the Greek equivalent of *virorum fortium fama*, 'the fame of brave men', is found in Fulgentius' *Mythologiae*, II, 2: 'Hercules enim Eracles [should probably be followed by something like 'id est, *eron cleos*'] Grece dicitur, quod nos Latine virorum fortium famam dicimus';[24] and hence it passed not only into Hrabanus' *De universo* but also into the mainstream of the mythographical tradition. It is paraphrased, for example, by the 'Mythographus III', who (whether he be identical with Alexander Neckham, with a 'Magister Albericus Lundoniensis' or with a great Anonym) was active in the latter part of the twelfth century and may be considered the most authoritative mythographer of the High Middle Ages: 'Hercules igitur quasi ἡρώων κλέος, virorum fortium gloria, interpretatur.'[25] And this paraphrase is repeated in the *Libellus de imaginibus deorum* of *c.* 1400: 'Hercules enim quasi Hercleos, quod est virorum gloria fortium.'[26] Boccaccio in his *Genealogia deorum* (XIII, 1), how-

ever, directly appropriated it from Hrabanus.[27] But who is the author credited with the interpretation of Hercules as a husbandman and the inventor of manuring?[28]

Even if the reading 'Sextus Pompeius', adopted in the 'printed version' of Hrabanus' *De universo* as well as in Boccaccio's *Genealogia deorum*,[29] were correct, the author referred to could only be Sextus Pompeius Festus, the well-known Roman lexicographer flourishing near the close of the second century A.D. His *De verborum significatu* is accessible to us only in one incomplete and sadly damaged manuscript, the so-called 'Farnesianus' (Naples, Bibl. Naz., Cod. IV A 3). It had already been deprived of its first seven quaternions (which included the 'Hercules' entry) when it was discovered in 1476 and later lost three further quaternions which are, however, preserved in Renaissance transcriptions; for the portion already missing in 1476 we depend on scattered quotations and on a much abbreviated digest (*Epitome*) composed by Paulus Diaconus of Montecassino in or shortly after 782 and dedicated to Charlemagne. But the whole work was available to the Middle Ages from pre-Carolingian times to at least the thirteenth century; what was preserved of it enjoyed a genuine revival in the Renaissance, and its author is indiscriminately referred to as 'Sextus Pompeius', 'Festus Pompeius', 'Festus', or even 'Pompeius' *tout court*.[30]

23. For the reappearance of this shorter form of Hrabanus' Hercules section in another text, the *Scholia in Isidorum Vallicelliana*, see below, pp. 26 f.

24. *Fabii Planciadis Fulgentii V.C. opera*, R. Helm, ed., Leipzig, 1898, p. 41 (apparently overlooked by Lindsay and Whatmough, cited in notes 30 and 31).

25. G. H. Bode, ed., *Scriptores rerum mythicarum latini tres*, Celle, 1834, p. 246 (XIII, 1).

26. Cod. Vat. Reg. lat. 1290, fol. 5a. The text is transliterated in H. Liebeschütz, *Fulgentius metaforalis; Ein Beitrag zur Geschichte der antiken Mythologie im Mittelalter* (Studien der Bibliothek Warburg, IV), Leipzig and Berlin, p. 124 (with *Hercleos*, obviously a depraved form of *Heroncleos*, misprinted into *Hereleos*) and reproduced in pl. XXVI, Fig. 45.

27. Boccaccio, *Genealogia deorum*, V. Romano, ed., Bari, 1951, p. 638: 'Rabanus autem in libro de origine rerum dicit, quod cum crederent Herculem deum virtutis, eum dici quasi Heruncleos, quod Latine virorum fortium famam dicimus.' Boccaccio quotes Hrabanus' *De universo* no less than twenty-six times.

28. In a somewhat different form the connection between the Augeas incident and the invention of manuring is also implied by Pliny when he writes (*Nat. hist.*, XVI, 50): 'Augeas rex in Graecia excogitasse traditur [*scil.*, the idea of fertilizing the soil by means of dung], divulgasse vero Hercules in Italia, quae regi suo Stercuto, Fauni filio, ob hoc inventum immortalitatem tribuit.'

29. Boccaccio's text, quoted in note 27, continues with another specific reference to Hrabanus: 'Et scribit ipse Rabanus a Sexto Pompeio Herculem fuisse agricolam...' I had no opportunity to check the manuscripts used in Romano's edition; but 'Sextus' invariably appears in the early printed editions of the *Genealogia deorum*: Venice, 1481, fol. x, 1 v; Venice, 1494, fol. 96; Venice, 1511, fol. 96.

30. For Festus' *De verborum significatu* and its transmission, see the admirable edition by W. M. Lindsay, *Sexti Pompei Festi de verborum significatu quae supersunt cum Pauli Epitome*, Leipzig, 1913, revised and augmented by the same scholar in *Glossaria latina iussu Academiae Britannicae edita*, IV, Paris, 1930, pp. 73–467, where many fragments absent from the edition of 1913 are included and where a good case is made for the availability of a pre-Carolingian manuscript in North Italy (p. 74). For two Festus manuscripts described in high-medieval library catalogues, the 'Great Catalogue' of Cluny, written there between 1158 and 1161, and the Catalogue of Glastonbury, written there in 1247, see M. Manitius, 'Zu Pompeius Festus', *Hermes*, XXVII, 1892, pp. 318 ff. In the Cluny Catalogue, Festus' work is described as *Liber Festi Pompeii ad Arcorium Rufum*, and in the Glastonbury Catalogue as *Liber Pompei de signifi-*

There is, moreover, evidence that the Hrabanus manuscripts originally had 'Festus' rather than 'Sextus'. This is the way in which he is referred to, we recall, in *Cas.* and *Reg.* (see our Fig. 10, here with 'Fes. Pomp.' added *in margine* by a humanistic hand). And 'Festus' is also what we read in the marginal glosses, known as *Scholia Vallicelliana*, which are found in an eleventh-century manuscript of Isidore's *Etymologiae*; in these scholia Hrabanus' Hercules section, as it appears in 'Stratum B' (from *Herculem credebant* ... to *stercorare agros*), is taken over—lock, stock and barrel—by a glossator possibly identical with a certain Grauso or Grausus, supposedly Bishop of Ceneda (not far from Belluno) in 998. We are thus faced with the curious fact—apparently unnoticed by the Latinists—that one of the precious Festus fragments found neither in the 'Codex Farnesianus' nor in its Renaissance transcripts nor in Paulus Diaconus' *Epitome* (where Hercules is mentioned only as an astrologer), was preserved for posterity by Hrabanus Maurus.[31]

cacione verborum. But Paulus Diaconus in his dedicatory letter to Charlemagne (quoted, e.g., in Manitius, *Geschichte der lateinischen Literatur des Mittelalters*, I, p. 264) refers to the author as 'Sextus Pompeius' (as in the 'printed version' of Hrabanus' Hercules section and in Boccaccio's *Genealogia deorum*), and so does Pietro Vettori (Victorius) in *Variae lectiones*, xvii, 2 (Florence, 1553), as quoted in Lindsay's edition of 1913, pp. xii f. By the middle of the sixteenth century the work of Festus was familiar enough to be quoted in Vincenzo Cartari's popular handbook of classical mythology, *Imagini dei Dei de gli antichi* (first published in 1556), with reference to the belief that the chariot of the moon goddess was drawn by a mule (Festus, p. 135, line 11, in Lindsay's edition of 1913; Cartari, p. 106, in the edition of 1571); and, after him, by Annibale Caro in his program for the bedchamber of Alessandro Cardinal Farnese, composed in November 1562. But what Jean Seznec, to whom credit is due for having observed Caro's extensive use of Cartari (*The Survival of the Pagan Gods*, New York, 1953, pp. 291 ff.), fails to mention is that Cartari, as so often, merely transcribes L. G. Giraldi's *Syntagmata*, first published (under a different title), in 1548: L. G. Gyraldus, *Opera omnia*, Leiden, 1696, I, col. 358.

31. For Paulus Diaconus' reference to Hercules as an astrologer, see Lindsay's edition of 1913, p. 89, lines 22 f. As far as the *Scholia Vallicelliana* are concerned, those which are or seem to be based on Festus were incorporated in Lindsay's revised edition in *Glossaria latina*, *loc. cit.*; the Hercules passage, pp. 221 f. They were published *in toto* by J. Whatmough, 'Scholia in Isidori Etymologias Vallicelliana', *Bulletin du Cange*, II, 1926, pp. 57–75, 134–69 (the scholium containing the Festus quotation added *in margine* to Isidore, *Etymologiae*, viii, 11, 50–55). A problem is posed by the personality of Grauso (called 'Guasone' in P. Gams, *Series episcoporum*, Ratisbon, 1873, p. 783) as well as by the continuation of the text after *stercorare agros*: 'Quod mala ab Hesperidibus petisse fertur, pecorum per hoc cura signatur, quae graece *mila* (μῆλα) dicuntur. Item armenta, cum Geryonis boues abegisse narratur. Per aprum autem quod supinum portasse fingitur, sues mansuetos fecisse demonstratur. Per canem tricipitem uenandi studium gessisse ostenditur.' Lindsay accepts the statements referring to the apples of the Hesperides and to the oxen of Geryones as coming from Festus; but then the reference to the Erymanthean boar, which also attempts to support the interpretation of Hercules as a husbandman, should not be excluded. I suspect that every-

V

While there is every reason to believe that the shorter form of the Hercules section ('Stratum B') goes back to the ninth century—possibly to Hrabanus Maurus himself—the 'printed version' ('Stratum C') must be of considerably later origin.

As will be remembered, 'Stratum C' differs from 'Stratum B' not only in that Hercules appears between Mars and Apollo rather than between Mercury and Mars, but also, and more significantly, in that it includes, in addition to the derivation of his name from *cleos* (fame) and *heron* (of heroes), the stranger and, as is evident from the awkward repetition of *autem*, interpolated derivation from *cleos* (fame) and *heris* (strife). So far as I know, this second derivation cannot be traced back beyond the twelfth century where we find it in two nearly contemporaneous and probably interdependent texts: William of Conches' *Glosses on Boethius* and Bernardus Silvestris' *Commentary on Six Books of Virgil's Aeneid*. 'Hercules vero', says William of Conches, 'ponitur pro sapiente. Qui bene Hercules dicitur, id est lite gloriosus,—"her" [*sic*] enim lis, "cleos" gloria, quia sapiens lite et pugna contra sapientes gloriosus apparet' ('Hercules, however, signifies the wise man, and he is aptly called "Hercules", that is to say, a man glorious by strife—

thing which follows *stercorare agros* represents an elaboration on Festus' agricultural interpretation of Hercules rather than a direct quotation. Be that as it may, certain it is that the first half of the scholium (from *Herculem credebant* ... to ... *stercorare agros*) is literally identical with the Hrabanus Maurus text and that the interpretation of Hercules as 'virorum fortium fama' comes from Fulgentius. But this identity confronts us with another problem.

That the Isidore scholiast and 'Hrabanus Maurus' should independently have produced two absolutely identical texts, both ushered in by a statement to the effect that Hercules was the 'god of virtue' and both composed of the same excerpts from Fulgentius and Festus, is, of course, unthinkable. We have therefore to consider three possibilities: (1) the Hrabanus text depends on the Isidore scholium; (2) the Isidore scholium depends on the Hrabanus text; (3) both depend on a common source, presumably an Isidore manuscript already containing the shorter form of the Hercules section. Possibility number three is not too probable because, even assuming that such an Isidore manuscript existed (which may or may not have been the case; cf. below, p. 28), it would have been unique and could hardly have wandered from Fulda to an obscure little diocese in North Italy. Possibility number one is even less credible because the shorter form of the Hercules section, occurring as it does in *Cas.* as well as in *Pal.*, *Reg.* and Stuttgart, must have been present in the 'Carolingian archetype' and therefore antedates the Isidore scholium—quite apart from the fact that the Vallicellian manuscript does not seem to have been exploited or even noticed until the twentieth century. We are thus left with possibility number two, that is to say, with the hypothesis that the Vallicellian scholiast owes his acquaintance with Festus' interpretation of Hercules as a husbandman to Hrabanus Maurus' *De universo* and not, as Lindsay and Whatmough seem to assume, to Festus' *De significatu verborum* itself. This hypothesis is concordant with the fact that Hrabanus' work was easily accessible and widely read in Italy at all times, including the eleventh century.

L. D. ETTLINGER

Muses and Liberal Arts

Two Miniatures from Herrad of Landsberg's *Hortus Deliciarum*

Herrad of Landsberg's celebrated *Hortus Deliciarum* contained apart from the text no less than 636 miniatures on some 650 folio pages. Yet we should not assume that this twelfth-century encyclopaedia was so lavishly illustrated simply because the abbess of Hohenburg was as fond of fine pictures as she was learned. The miniatures are in fact an integral part of her book, setting out the argument by way of visual demonstration.[1] Herrad's didactic purpose is particularly striking where she links two miniatures in a kind of 'typological' demonstration, for example when comparing the principal tenets of the Old Covenant with those of the New. In this case the first of her pictures illustrates the blood sacrifice of the Old Testament as prescribed in the law of Moses while the second shows Christ, King and High Priest, holding a chalice above His Church.[2] This juxtaposition expresses theological views which can be traced back to the early Fathers and even the Gospels, and imagery of this kind was common enough in medieval art. But Herrad applies the same method also to secular topics and one such case merits our special attention because of its unusual features: the conjunction of Muses and Liberal Arts on neighbouring pages. The most widely known of Herrad's delightful drawings shows *Philosophia* enthroned and surrounded by personifications of the seven Liberal Arts, with Socrates and Plato sitting at her feet (Fig. 1).[3] This miniature in isolation has often been regarded as a graphic account of medieval learning and its branches. It is not always realized, however, that in the (lost) original manuscript it was preceded by a clearly related image showing the Nine Muses (Fig. 2).[4] Nine busts, each in a round frame, are arranged in three rows which form a large square. Herrad, well read in ancient and medieval literature, was surely aware of some subtle connection between the classical Muses and the medieval *Artes*,

and in the text which accompanies these two miniatures she explicitly links them on account of their tutelage over humane studies, so that the Arts seem to duplicate the function of the Muses.[5] We may ask, therefore, how and why these blue-stockinged personifications came to replace the more comely Greek deities. Medieval writers and artists paid scant attention to the nine sisters but the seven Liberal Arts were ubiquitous, and Ernst Robert Curtius has appropriately said of them that they were, at least until the twelfth century, the *Fundamentalordnung des menschlichen Geistes*,[6] a phrase which seems to echo the sentiments of Vincent of Beauvais, who had referred to them as the foundation of all the knowledge which the philosopher has to master.[7] Wherever this system of learning is pictorially represented in medieval art—in the great sculpture cycles of the cathedrals, on stained glass, or in manuscripts—the personified *Artes* make their appearance, so that Emile Mâle has rightly called them together with Philosophy 'the eight Muses of the middle ages'.[8] The following attempt to trace the ancestry of Herrad's two miniatures may throw some light on the curious transformation by which nine Muses changed into seven Liberal Arts.

A well-known sarcophagus in the Louvre (among many examples) preserves the pictorial types of the Muses most widely current in classical antiquity.[9] The nine goddesses are assembled on the front and raise no serious iconographic problems (Fig. 3). The reliefs on the two sides, however, are more problematic. Each shows a seated man in the company of a standing

1. This was recognized by Fritz Saxl: 'Herrad's texts are an accompaniment to the pictures. It is the pictures that are the main feature; the texts do no more than give explanations of particular points. The language of the picture has to be read first, and then the words.' 'Illustrated Medieval Encyclopaedias', *Lectures*, London, 1957, p. 253.
2. Saxl, *op. cit.*, p. 250 and pls. 170b/c.
3. Herrade de Landsberg, *Hortus Deliciarum*, ed. A. Straub and G. Keller, Strassbourg, 1899, pl. XI bis. See also Saxl, *op. cit.*, pp. 248 f.
4. Straub and Keller, *op. cit.*, pl. XI.

5. *Musae novem quaerendae scientiae modos designant . . . In monte habitant, quia in sublimibus habitat sapientia . . . His autem sigillatim liberalia distribuuntur studia.* Herrad's text is preserved in a nineteenth-century copy, Paris, Bibliothèque Nationale, MS. nouv. acq. franç. 6083–4 and 6044–6. In Herrad's original this passage occurred on fol. 31.
6. E. R. Curtius, *Europäische Literatur und lateinisches Mittelalter*, Bern, 1954, p. 52.
7. *Primum operam esse dandam artibus maxime septem liberalibus, quae sunt fundamentum omnis doctrinae et ita sibi cohaerent, alteriusque vicissim rationibus indigent, ut sibi vel una defuerit ceterae philosophum facere non possunt. Speculum Doctrinale*, II, 31.
8. E. Mâle, *L'art religieux du XIIIe siècle en France*, Paris, 1925, p. 75.
9. On the iconography of the Muses in classical antiquity see Pauly-Wissowa, s.v. *Musai*.

female figure and the men are clearly differentiated by their appearance. The one on the left relief represents the common type of a bearded philosopher and because of his very marked features must be Socrates (Fig. 4). The man on the right conforms to a type usually reserved for poets; perhaps he is Homer (Fig. 5). The two female companions cannot be Muses since—other reasons apart—all nine appear already on the front of the sarcophagus. But if the identification of the men as poet and philosopher is accepted, they could represent Poiesis with the former and Sophia with the latter.[10] Thus the nine Muses and two personifications would appear to be united on the same monument, and such a combination would demonstrate pictorially a fact well known from ancient literature: the daughters of Zeus and Mnemosyne often led a rather shadowy existence in an ill-defined territory between the Olympic Gods and less substantial figures.[11] Yet for this very reason they were also eminently adaptable, and when Christianity vanquished the pagan gods, the Muses could transfer their office to the less tainted Liberal Arts.

Moreover the function of the Muses helped such a transformation. They had acquired their specialized protectorates over the various arts, such as comedy, dance, song and so forth, only gradually, and the process became complete only in Roman times. But to the end they remained associated with the sciences and with education in general. Cicero, expanding Pythagorean and Platonic concepts, used a significant phrase like *cum Musis, id est cum humanitate et cum doctrina*,[12] while Virgil asked the Muse to teach him the laws of the cosmos.[13] The term εὔμουσος described not an artistic but a well-educated man, and 'Good Education' was even personified, as is proved by a marble statue of the familiar seated Muse variety inscribed EUMOUSIA.[14] The Museion in Alexandria was not an academy of dance and drama, but an institute of advanced study.

Two Roman sarcophagi illustrate vividly the wider educational role of the Muses.[15] One of them (Villa Torlonia) shows in the centre the couple for which it was destined (Fig. 6). The man is seated, holding a

scroll, and his wife is standing before him. They are flanked by six bearded men, clearly characterized as philosophers, and by eight female figures. Obviously, the deceased is meant to be the equal of the six bearded scholars and we must call the ensemble the Seven Sages. By the same token his wife becomes the ninth Muse.

Another sarcophagus (Lateran Museum) again has for its central figure a philosopher (for no good reason sometimes identified with Plotinus) who is this time flanked by two female figures (Fig. 7). He is turning to the one on his right, who like himself is holding a scroll and should therefore be identified with Sophia. While neither sarcophagus shows seven female personifications, it can nevertheless be said that by the third century A.D. a scholar could be represented with allegorical figures, modelled on the Muses and symbolizing his spiritual guides.

In spite of the difference in date, these two sarcophagi help to establish the context in which we should set the fifth-century text which is generally held to have furnished both Middle Ages and Renaissance with standard descriptions of the seven Liberal Arts, Martianus Capella's *De Nuptiis Mercurii et Philologiae*.[16] It is an odd allegory of the pursuit of learning in which Philologia is wooed and won by Mercury, and in her highly intellectual love-making the bride is assisted by the seven Liberal Arts. But the Muses also put in an appearance and have to play an important part.

Martianus' first two books are a kind of romance, taken up with an account of the preparations for the wedding. Apollo chooses the bride, and after the other gods have accepted her, the Muses invite her into heaven. Before the journey begins Athanasia touches Philologia's heart, who on being touched spits out many books which are eagerly gathered by the Liberal Arts. While for Martianus and his readers this abstruse incident allegorizes the origin of all knowledge, it is in our present context more important to observe that a fifth-century author still speaks of the Muses, but brings the personified Arts to the same ceremony.

In the second book Martianus describes the heavenly journey of the learned bride and her introduction into the circle of the immortals. Finally Apollo presents

10. This plausible identification was suggested by F. Cumont, *Recherches sur le symbolisme funéraire des Romains*, Paris, 1942, pp. 311 ff.

11. P. Boyancé, *Le culte des Muses chez les philosophes Grecs*, Paris, 1938.

12. *Tusc.*, v, 23, 66.

13. *Georg.*, ii, 475.

14. A. H. Smith, *A Catalogue of Sculpture in the Department of Greek and Roman Antiquities, British Museum*, London, 1904, iii, no. 1687.

15. G. Rodenwaldt, 'Zur Kunstgeschichte der Jahre 220–270', *Jahrbuch des deutschen archäologischen Instituts*, li, 1936, pp. 101 ff.

16. Martianus Capella, *De Nuptiis Mercurii et Philologiae*, ed. A. Dick, Leipzig, 1925. E. R. Curtius, *op. cit.*, pp. 47 ff. About the representation of the Liberal Arts see F. Rademacher, 'Eine romanische Kleinbronze der "Grammatik"', *Bonner Jahrbücher*, clix, 1959, pp. 260 ff., and particularly p. 261, n. 5, where an extensive bibliography is given. For illuminated Martianus texts see L. H. Heydenreich, 'Eine illustrierte Martianus Capella Handschrift des Mittelalters und ihre Kopien im Zeitalter des Frühhumanismus', *Kunstgeschichtliche Studien für Hans Kauffmann*, Berlin, 1956, pp. 59 ff., and the same author in *Atti del V Convegno Internazionale di Studi sul Rinascimento*, 1958, pp. 265 ff.

Philologia's ladies-in-waiting, the Liberal Arts, and the book concludes with the words

> Nunc ergo mythus terminatus, infiunt
> Artes libelli qui sequentes asserent.

In fact, the remaining seven books of the *Nuptiae* are dedicated in turn to each of the liberal arts. The physical appearance of Grammatica, Logica, Rhetorica and so forth is described in some considerable detail, and the famous practitioners accompanying each Art are enumerated before the functions of each branch of learning are discussed. In this manner Martianus' books III to X become a synopsis of academic studies and an extension of the second book of Cassiodorus' *Institutiones*.

Early illustrated texts of the first two books of the *Nuptiae* apparently have not survived, but there is some literary evidence of the visual appeal of Martianus' weird imagination, albeit from a later period. Countess Hadwig of Swabia gave to the Monastery of St. Gall a cope embroidered with figures taken from his book, and Baudri de Bourgueil has described scenes taken from Martianus which allegedly decorated the bedchamber of William the Conqueror's daughter.[17] But we still have fragments of the famous Quedlinburg tapestry, dating from the early twelfth century, which preserve a picture of the crowning scene of the feast: Mercury and Philologia are joining hands in a ceremony which in this very form occurs also on Roman reliefs illustrating the wedding ritual (Fig. 8).[18] There are other details suggesting that the designer of this tapestry may have used a model ultimately derived from a late classical prototype, perhaps even illustrations to Martianus dating back to the time of his writing. Unfortunately no part of the Quedlinburg tapestry is extant which can show how close in type Muses and Arts had been in the imagination of the original illustrator.

Martianus designated the Muses as Philologia's companions on her celestial journey and in the intellectual setting of his allegory this choice may not seem surprising. However, it gains added significance once we remember that the ascent can only begin after Athanasia has touched the bride, and we may assume that eschatological beliefs played a part in it. For the Muses were a favourite motif on Roman sarcophagi, and Franz Cumont has offered an interpretation of their presence there which may also be relevant to their role in the *Nuptiae*. He argued that the nine sister goddesses govern the harmony of the spheres and awaken through music in the human heart a deep nostalgia for heaven and its divine melodies. At the same time, since they are the daughters of Memory, they cause reason to remember the truth which it had known in a previous life. 'They impart to wisdom a pledge of immortality . . . and after death the divine virgins summon to themselves into the starry spheres the soul which has sanctified itself in their service, allowing it to share the life of the immortals.'[19]

If this is the context in which Martianus' Muses fulfil their role, we can understand why Christian writers had to reject them. The Liberal Arts, on the other hand, were mere personifications originally without cosmological or eschatological significance, and could act as protectresses of learning without usurping a power which belongs to God alone. They could be absorbed into the Christian system by becoming handmaidens of Theology and Philosophy. The opening of Boethius' *Consolationes* is a magnificent poetic allegory indicating this change, for we witness the lament of the Muses and the appearance of a christianized Philosophia.

When a medieval poet invented an allegory describing a journey to heaven the Muses could no longer play an active part in it. The *Anticlaudianus* of Alanus de Insulis may be called a Christian transcription of Martianus' *Nuptiae*. But when Phronesis accompanied by Ratio and Prudentia gets ready to set out upward through the spheres in order to seek the advice of Theologia her carriage is built by the seven Liberal Arts. Arithmetic, Geometry, Music, and Astronomy are the wheelwrights, Dialectics makes the axle, Grammar the shaft and Rhetorica guilds the vehicle.[20] This insistence on the function of the Arts and the exclusion of the Muses is all the more noteworthy, since in other instances Alanus did not exclude non-Christian elements from his poem.[21]

Alanus' concepts and his imagery are complex because they form part of a larger poetic structure. In the later Middle Ages the role of Arts could be depicted in a more straightforward manner. Even so, the connection with Theology was strictly maintained. A late fifteenth-century woodcut probably coming from the Wolgemut workshop, for example, shows Theologia being carried to heaven in a chariot which is pulled by the Trivium while the ladies of the Quadrivium assist by turning the wheels. Petrus Lombardus is acting the part of the

17. Baudri de Bourgueil, ed. P. Abrahams, 1926, pp. 221–8. P. d'Ancona, 'Le rappresentazione allegoriche delle Arti Liberali', *L'Arte*, v, 1902, p. 215.
18. B. Kurth, *Die deutschen Bildteppiche des Mittelalters*, Vienna, 1926, I, pp. 53 ff. and pls. 12–21.

19. Cumont, *op. cit.*, p. 350.
20. For illuminated manuscripts of Alanus' poem see F. Mütherich, 'Ein Illustrationszyklus zum Anticlaudianus', *Münchner Jahrbuch der bildenden Kunst*, III, 1951, pp. 73 ff.
21. E. R. Curtius, *op. cit.*, p. 131.

coachman (Fig. 9).²² But whether the Arts build the chariot, as Alanus describes it, or whether they propel Theologia to heaven, they do *mutatis mutandis* what the Muses had done for Philologia in Martianus' story. Yet there is one important difference. The classical Muses had promised immortality. The Christian Arts, of course, cannot do this, but they can help the soul toward the revelation of Divine Wisdom, a concept of their function already outlined by Cassiodorus and St. Augustine.

It was precisely this function of the liberal arts within the scheme of human salvation and divine revelation which occupied the medieval authors of *Summae* and *Specula*. Their works were not books of reference like classical or modern encyclopaedias, but carefully arranged schematic guides designed with the theological end in mind, and the illustrations had to match this purpose.²³ Herrad's *Hortus Deliciarum* is visually the most splendid of these 'encyclopaedias', even if her text is little more than a learned florilegium.

The Muses and Liberal Arts appear in a chapter entitled *De philosophia et de septem artibus liberalibus*. When discussing the function of the nine Muses Herrad drew naturally on classical sources, and she took most of her text verbatim from Fulgentius' *Mythologiae*, where the relevant section significantly begins with the words: *Nos vero novem Musas doctrinae et scientiae dicimus modos*.²⁴ The picture which belongs to Herrad's text (Fig. 2) is also directly derived from a classical source. Representations of the Muses are in any case extremely rare in medieval art, but the very form of this particular example betrays its classical origin. The same arrangement of nine busts is found frequently on Roman mosaics in many provinces of the Empire (Fig. 10). It makes little difference that in classical art the Muses were usually distinguished by their attributes, which Herrad (or her immediate source) has omitted, though on her original drawing the names had been inscribed on tituli.²⁵

But the typological counterpart to this miniature demonstrates a medieval concept and its classical derivation is not immediately obvious (Fig. 1). The subject is Philosophy, or more precisely Divine Wisdom. Philosophia is enthroned in the centre and the seven Liberal Arts are standing under arcades surrounding her. Inscriptions explain the image, emphasizing that all wisdom comes from God and that Philosophy is the ruler of the seven liberal arts.²⁶ Seven fountains flow from Philosophy, three to the right and four to the left, and this formula likens by an obvious symbol the seven liberal arts to the seven gifts of the Holy Spirit. The same equation occurs also in Lambert's *Liber Floridus*²⁷ and on a miniature of the Salzburg School, dating from the twelfth century.²⁸ In the last-named instance Philosophy is crowned, she holds book and sceptre and the seven rivers from her body flow to the Liberal Arts below.

F. Saxl has pointed out the significance of one particular pictorial device employed by Herrad in the Philosophy miniature. Only those enclosed within Philosophia's circle, even if they were not Christians, partake of divine inspiration, but in the writers sitting outside the circle black birds evoke unholy thoughts. Herrad's inscription refers to these two men as *poetae vel magi*, and in her text she speaks of those who after the deluge, instead of studying philosophy proper, engaged in poetry and magic because their reason was blinded.²⁹ Herrad, therefore, argues through picture and word both the good and the evil results of studies, but at the same time she stresses the positive function of the liberal arts within the structure of a truly Christian philosophy.

In composing an image to fit this complex concept Herrad used two different pictorial formulae and combined them. The *magi* with their black birds are modelled on traditional representations of the Evangelists. The nature of Philosophia, however, is demonstrated with the help of a diagrammatic device which —with many variations—Herrad employed frequently in the *Hortus Deliciarum*. Nevertheless, in this particular case she seems to have adapted a classical prototype which could be transformed into a diagram with-

22. For a manuscript with a related representation (Salzburg, Studienbibliothek) see H. Tietze, *Beschreibendes Verzeichnis der illustrierten Handschriften Österreichs*, Vienna, 1908, II, p. 58.
23. Hence Martianus Capella's *Nuptiae* were of little use when a visual demonstration of the function of the Liberal Arts was required. While the first two books contain an involved cosmological allegory, the others are little more than a dry textbook. The elaborate descriptions of the seven personifications with their trains of followers are difficult to visualize. Above all, there is nothing in Martianus suggesting an interrelated system of the arts.
24. Fulgentius, *Opera*, ed. R. Halm, Leipzig, 1898, p. 28.
25. R. Parlasca, *Die römischen Mosaiken in Deutschland*, Bonn, 1959, pp. 141 ff. The Muses appear in medallions—even if differently arranged—on the famous 'AER' miniature, Bibliothèque Municipale, Reims, MS. 672, fol. 1. See H. Swarzenski, *Monuments of Romanesque Art*, London, 1954, pl. 210, Fig. 492. C. de Tolnay, 'The Music of the Universe', *Journal of the Waters Art Gallery*, VI, 1943, pp. 83 ff. H. von Einem, *Der*

Mainzer Kopf mit der Binde (Arbeitsgemeinschaft für Forschung des Landes Nordrhein-Westfalen, Geisteswissenschaften, 37), Cologne, 1955, p. 26.
26. The inscription to the left of Philosophia reads: *Omnis sapientia a Domino est.* (Eccl. 1.) On the ring between Philosophia and Liberal Arts appear the words: *Arte regens omnia quae sunt/ego Philosophia/subjectas artes in septem divido partes.*
27. Saxl, *op. cit.*, p. 249.
28. G. Swarzenski, *Die Salzburger Malerei von den ersten Anfängen bis zur Blütezeit des romanischen Stils*, Leipzig, 1913, p. 94, and Rademacher, *op. cit.*, p. 265, n. 20.
29. Saxl, *op. cit.*, p. 248.

out losing all its characteristics. She may have known such a prototype only indirectly through some post-classical derivation, for her image is not unique in medieval art and two comparable examples must be mentioned.

One is a curious wooden dish in the cathedral treasure of Halberstadt, usually described as an alms-dish, though it must have been made for some secular purpose since the inside is decorated with the painted portraits of fourteen classical authors set in roundels. In the centre are Virgil, Ovid, Juvenal and Plato; among others, arranged along the rim, are Aristotle, Cicero and Diogenes. The dish dates from the early fourteenth century, but the subject matter as well as the arrangement suggest some classical model, most likely a Roman floor mosaic.[30] There is no resemblance to Herrad's miniature, but the concentric arrangement and the reference to classical learning allow us to set the two side by side.

Closer to Herrad's Philosophia miniature comes the engraving on a twelfth-century bronze bowl, both in form and in subject matter. In the centre we find Philosophia seated on a throne. Like Herrad's similar figure she is wearing a triple crown which is inscribed ETHICA/PHYSICA/LOGICA. Socrates and Plato are standing at the side of Philosophia and this group of three figures is framed by a circular band inscribed: SEPTEM PER STUDIA DOCET ARTES PHILOSOPHIA/ HAEC ELEMENTORUM SCRUTATUR ET ABDITA RERUM. Six of the Liberal Arts do in fact appear in a circle outside this band. They are small female figures, each with a scroll on which her name is inscribed. They are accompanied by six bearded men. As on Herrad's picture Grammatica is placed directly above Philosophy, and Rhetorica, Dialectica and so on follow clockwise. Astronomia has been omitted.[31]

This bronze bowl obviously shares many significant features with Herrad's illustration, but the differences are also telling. From a didactic point of view Herrad's diagram is clearer and its Christian content is more accentuated through reference to the Holy Ghost.

Moreover, Herrad has given companions only to Philosophy, but the Artes are alone. Nevertheless the same kind of model must stand behind both images. It is here suggested that it was in the last resort again a classical prototype, that is to say a representation of 'Education' in the manner of the Monnus mosaic from Trier (Fig. 11), which dates from the third century A.D.[32]

In spite of the poor state of preservation it is still possible to reconstruct the composition of the Monnus mosaic. In a central octagon were placed Homer with Calliope and the personification of *Ingenium*, and around this central panel were arranged eight further octagons, each containing the picture of an author and a Muse. Between central and outer octagons were eight small squares with portraits of classical authors. Around this realm of arts and literature were grouped the portraits of actors, masks, the signs of the zodiac, the Seasons and the Months. Though the whole scheme is fairly comprehensive, the accent is clearly on the Muses and their disciples, who have been given the most prominent position. Yet as far as we can judge from the surviving fragments not all the companions of the Muses were poets. Moreover, the presence of *Ingenium* right in the middle of the mosaic may be regarded as a pagan counterpart to Herrad's Holy Ghost as the source of inspiration. Finally it should be remembered that the Monnus mosaic is only a particularly splendid specimen of a widespread type of Roman floor decoration.[33]

There is yet another significant similarity between the Monnus mosaic and Herrad's illustration: the combination of a personification or deity—Philosophia taking the place of a Muse—with an author, or in Herrad's case two authors. We know these juxtapositions not only from mosaics, but also from Hellenistic and Roman reliefs.[34] The conventional label used for such representations *Poet and Muse* is, however, somewhat misleading. We can rarely be sure about

30. W. Vöge, *Jörg Syrlin der Ältere und seine Bildwerke*, Berlin, 1950, II, p. 183 and Fig. 85.
31. J. Weitzmann-Fiedler, 'Romanische Bronzeschalen mit mythologischen Darstellungen. Ihre Beziehungen zur mittelalterlichen Schulliteratur und ihre Zweckbestimmung', *Zeitschrift für Kunstwissenschaft*, XI, 1957, pp. 21 f. and particularly pp. 30 ff. The same circular arrangement can still be found on the Heiningen Tapestry (dated 1516), London Victoria and Albert Museum. Philosophia, accompanied by Teoretica, Practica, Logica, Mecanica, and Physica, is in the centre. The Liberal Arts appear in an outer ring, alternating with the Virtues. In the four corners Ovid, Boethius, Aristotle and Horace are shown. For a detailed description and a transcription of the inscribed texts see, *Victoria and Albert Museum. Department of Textiles, Guide to the Collection of Carpets*, London, 1931, pp. 51 ff., no. 399.
32. Parlasca, *op. cit.*, pp. 41 ff. K. Scheffold, *Die Bildnisse der antiken Dichter, Redner und Denker*, Basel, 1943, pp. 168 f.
33. 'Fundamental' schemes of moral and scientific knowledge were often used to decorate the floors of medieval churches. In this case too the Arts would appear together with the Virtues, the zodiac, the Seasons, and so on. See A. Katzenellenbogen, *The Sculptural Program of Chartres Cathedral*, New York, 1959, p. 15. A purely schematic unfigured circular pattern of Muses and poets is found in Oxford, Bodleian Library, MS. Rawl. B. 214, fol. 202, see F. Saxl and H. Meier, *Verzeichnis astrologischer und mythologischer illustrierter Handschriften des lateinischen Mittelalters*, London, 1953, III, edited by H. Bober, p. 398. The same subject, but in a severely abbreviated form, occurs in the decoration of the early thirteenth-century Trivulzio Candelabrum, O. Homburger, *Der Trivulzio Kandelaber*, Zürich, 1949.
34. R. Hinks, *Myth and Allegory in Ancient Art* (Studies of the Warburg Institute, VI), London, 1939, pp. 98 ff.

the occupation and identity of the so-called poet, and his companion may be either a Muse or a personification. As was pointed out when referring to the Torlonia and Lateran sarcophagi, the female figures are in the end simply indications of 'inspiration'. It follows that the character of this imagery, for the most part, is neutral as far as religious implications are concerned, since there is nothing specifically pagan in it. Therefore it became possible to use the *Poet and Muse* formula both in heathen and in Christian contexts without any fundamental alterations.

On the late-antique Monza ivory diptych we see a 'poet'—sometimes identified with Claudianus—and a 'Muse'. But strictly speaking neither figure can be identified, and the architectural setting can hardly mean that the hallowed subject of divine inspiration has now been transformed into a simple genre scene in which we are witnesses of a poetry lesson. It should be noted that 'poet' and 'Muse' do not look at each other. Only we, the spectators, are aware of her unseen presence in the room, and we are reminded that, though invisible to him, inspiration speaks to us through an author's works.[35]

In this form the image was taken over into Christian art, whether we think of the famous miniature in the Paris Psalter, where Melody stands behind David, again unseen by him, or of the picture of St. Mark with his instructress in the Codex Rossanensis.[36]

When the motive occurred in Carolingian art (where we know of examples only through descriptions or surviving tituli[37]) the Liberal Arts have definitely taken over the role of the Muses, and as far as the visual arts are concerned this pattern remained in force well into the Renaissance. But, as Wilhelm Vöge argued in a memorable passage, where the Liberal Arts occur in medieval sculptural cycles, they are usually alone, and the depiction of their classical representatives—Cicero, Aristotle, Euclid, and so forth—is rather an exception, as at Chartres and Laon. Vöge suggested that there must have been some influence from the philosophical tenets of the School of Chartres and its hardly veiled admiration for the sages of classical antiquity.[38]

This convincing argument may be adduced here in support of the evidence already given to explain the sources of Herrad's diagram. The explicit inclusion of Socrates and Plato, instead of two nameless scholars, adds an important element which bridges the gulf separating the twelfth century from the days when the Monnus mosaic and similar monuments were made. Yet this classical flavour notwithstanding, Herrad's picture of Philosophia inspired by the Holy Ghost, and in her turn inspiring the Liberal Arts, remains in all essentials a Christian image. For as on the Royal portal at Chartres the Liberal Arts occupy literally a peripheral position and their placing implies the dependence of human learning on divine inspiration.[39]

The Christian character of Herrad's drawing becomes even more palpable if we now read it in an entirely different manner. For, apart from thinking of it as a didactic diagram, we may also regard it as a flattened-out or planimetric representation of a circular temple with Philosophia and her companions sitting in the centre, and the Liberal Arts standing under the surrounding arcade. The text illustrated in such an image can be found in Proverbs (9:1): *Sapientia sibi aedificavit domum, excidit columnas septem* and in Alcuin's gloss on this passage: *quae sententia licet ac divinam pertinet sapientiam tamen sapientia liberalibus literarum septem columnis confirmatur.*[40] A miniature in a late eleventh-century French manuscript illustrates the same concept. Sapientia is enthroned between Dialectica and Grammatica, the other arts stand under a colonnade below together with the author of a poem on the same page.[41] But unlike Herrad's picture of divinely inspired learning this miniature does not seem to stem from a pictorial tradition going back to classical antiquity. The reason for this may well be found in the difference of date and all its implications.

In the *Hortus Deliciarum* the Muses made one of their rare and not altogether appropriate appearances during the Middle Ages, but the learned Herrad was well aware that these heathens belonged into the realm of *fabula*. Two hundred years later Boccaccio praised Dante for having roused 'those half-asleep sisters' and he gave credit to Petrarch for having given them once more their erstwhile beauty.[42] Yet this was hardly more than a brilliant metaphor, for when Dante had des-

---

35. I should like to thank my friend Professor Philip Fehl for discussing with me the problem of the 'unseen figure', on which he is working.

36. Hinks, *op. cit.* For the Paris Psalter see H. Buchthal, *The Miniatures of the Paris Psalter* (Studies of the Warburg Institute, II), London, 1938, pp. 13 ff. and pl. 1.

37. J. v. Schlosser, *Schriftquellen zur Geschichte der karolingischen Kunst*, Vienna, 1892, pp. 373 ff.

38. Vöge, *op. cit.*, pp. 175 ff. See also the detailed argument in Katzenellenbogen, *op. cit.*, pp. 15 ff.

39. On Giovanni Pisano's pulpit in Pisa Cathedral the subservient role of the Liberal Arts is demonstrated in another fashion. They support the platform from which the word of God is proclaimed. See H. von Einem, *Das Stützengeschoss der Pisaner Domkanzel* (Arbeitsgemeinschaft für Forschung des Landes Nordrhein-Westfalen, Geisteswissenschaften, 106), Cologne, 1962, p. 28.

40. Alcuin, *De grammatica*, P.L., CI, 853.

41. Paris, Bibliothèque Nationale, MS. lat. 3110, f. 60 r. See M.-Th. d'Alverny, 'La sagesse et ses sept filles', *Mélanges Félix Grat*, Paris, 1946, pp. 245 ff. and pl. III.

42. Letter of 1372 to Jacopo Pizzinga. Giovanni Boccaccio, *Opere*, Paris, 1928, IX, p. 195.

cribed in the *Convito* the order of the spheres he linked to them the Liberals Arts, but not the Muses.[43] When, however, in the middle of the fifteenth century that 'improving and educational game',[44] the *Tarocchi*, was designed, Apollo and the nine Muses took their place between a set of cards depicting the 'Conditions of Man' and another showing the seven Liberal Arts, Astrology, Philosophy and Theology. Herrad could

43. *Convito*, II, 13–15.
44. J. Seznec, *The Survival of the Pagan Gods*, New York, 1953, p. 138.

hardly have disapproved of this catholicity of choice. But would she equally have appreciated the subtleties of Raphael's Stanza della Segnatura? Theology and Philosophy are no longer served by the seven Liberal Arts, for Apollo and his Muses have returned to Parnassus. Still, this is no pagan revival. Dante, the most Christian of poets, appears among the devout and faithful of the *Disputá*, and he is also present on Parnassus in the company of Homer and Virgil. Only now have the daughters of Zeus and Memory been made harmless.

HUGO BUCHTHAL

Notes on a Sicilian Manuscript of the Early Fourteenth Century

In a recent paper I published two single miniatures of the late thirteenth century representing New Testament subjects, and showed that they were direct copies of mosaics in the aisles of the Cathedral at Monreale.[1] Unfortunately, the Gospel manuscript from which they were cut out, which must have been produced at Palermo, and which probably contained a whole cycle of miniatures based on the Monreale mosaics, seems to be lost. It might have taught us a great deal about Sicilian illumination of the period, which is still practically unknown and unexplored, as well as about the original state of the mosaics before they were progressively disfigured by successive campaigns of restoration. But the two fragments allow us to attribute several other manuscripts illuminated in the same easily recognizable style to the same scriptorium working in the Sicilian capital during the late thirteenth and early fourteenth centuries.

One of these is in the National Library of Turin.[2] It was only slightly damaged in the fire of 1904, and contains the lives and passions of about sixty saints. The choice of saints, some of them Greek, but the majority Latin, is significant. Most enjoyed special veneration in Sicily, and many had been represented among the mosaics of Monreale. Every saint's life is illustrated with a more or less comprehensive cycle of miniatures ranging in number from two or three to almost thirty; it goes without saying that their iconographical interest is considerable, if not unique. There are well over three hundred miniatures in all, mostly in the margins, without frames or backgrounds; more often than not, two or three of these small scenes are arranged on the same page, on top of each other. The system of illustration is that found in a number of Byzantine manuscripts of the eleventh and twelfth centuries. Occasionally, a scene occupies part of the lower margin of a page and extends laterally into the zone of the script, thus framing the last few lines of the text,

exactly as the two cut-out Gospel fragments must have done when they were still in their places.[3] Moreover, each saint's life starts with an illuminated initial, which sometimes includes a figure or scene on a gold ground.

Two miniatures should be singled out, and treated separately from the others. The *Passio apostolorum Petri et Pauli* is illustrated with two scenes referring to the apostles' activities in Rome: their Disputation with Simon Magus in the presence of the emperor Nero (Fig. 1), and the Fall of Simon (Fig. 2). These, the only outline drawings in the manuscript, were perhaps intended to be finished in colour like the others, but were left uncompleted. One suspects a particular reason for the difference in technique; the model may have been different from those of the other miniatures, perhaps a monumental work, as in the case of the two Gospel fragments, which were copied from mosaics. A comparison with the mosaic cycle from the lives of the two apostles at Monreale (Fig. 3), to which one naturally turns first, will indeed reveal many similarities. In both panels the composition and arrangement of the figures, and also most of their gestures and details of costume, are to all intents and purposes identical. But there are also some significant differences which argue against the theory of direct copying. In the first miniature Peter stands in front of Paul, not behind, and turns round towards him; Nero sits with his legs crossed, and does not hold a sceptre, but raises his right hand in a gesture of allocution; and Simon wears a garment with long sleeves, and with broad *segmenta* decorating the chest and both wrists. The second drawing shows Peter standing more upright than in the mosaic, the lower part of his body all but hidden by Paul who kneels at his side. The Magus falling to the ground is shown in a more natural position, more spread out in space, with his arms bent at right angles, and his feet wide apart; and the scaffold from which he falls to his death has only horizontal and no diagonal bars.

Still, in spite of these divergencies, there must be some connection between the two drawings and the Sicilian mosaic tradition. In addition to the similarities which

1. H. Buchthal, 'Some Sicilian Miniatures of the Thirteenth Century', *Miscellanea pro arte, Festschrift für Hermann Schnitzler*, Düsseldorf, 1965, pp. 185–90.
2. MS. I.II.17, cf. F. Pasini, *Codices manuscripti bibl. Reg. Taurinensis*, 1749, no. DLXI (k.VI.19); Carta-Cipolla-Frati, *Atlante paleografico-artistico*, Turin, 1899, tab. LXIII; A. Poncelet, *Catalogus codicum hagiographicorum latinorum Bibl. Nat. Taurinensis*, Brussels, 1909, pp. 445–8.
3. Buchthal, *op. cit.*, p. 185.

have been mentioned, there is one iconographical detail which may be considered decisive. In practically all surviving representations of the second incident—the Fall of Simon—the emperor Nero is again present; indeed his presence is indispensable for a true understanding of the event.[4] There is only one exception to this rule: the mosaic in the Cappella Palatina in Palermo, where this episode, the concluding scene of the cycle, had to be squeezed into a particularly narrow space. The cogent reason for the absence of Nero in Monreale is that this scene, together with most others in the Peter-and-Paul cycle, was copied from the Palatina mosaics direct.[5] Thus the drawing in the Turin manuscript, where Nero is also left out, ranges itself quite clearly with the two Sicilian works; and as the comparison with Monreale is not conclusive, one is led to consider the relation of the two miniatures to the corresponding mosaics at Palermo.

Unfortunately, the cycle of the story of SS. Peter and Paul in the Cappella Palatina is even more extensively restored than that at Monreale. But a confrontation of the relevant panels (Figs. 4, 5) with the drawings in the Turin manuscript will immediately show how closely the two belong together. Just as in the miniature, Peter stands in front of Paul, and turns round to him; Nero sits with his legs crossed and his right arm raised, and wears a crown of the *camelaukion* type and a cloak fastened with a clasp and hanging down over his shoulders; and Simon has the same long-sleeved garment with broad embroidered *segmenta*. The second drawing, too, shares with the Palatina mosaic a number of features which are different at Monreale: the position of the falling Magus, the shape of the scaffold which has no diagonal bars, and, especially, the attitudes of the two apostles; every single fold of St. Peter's garment is identically reproduced. The inevitable conclusion is that the two miniatures were copied from the mosaics in the Cappella Palatina. The copies are indeed so faithful that one is tempted to use them for a reconstruction of the original appearance of the mosaics before their various restorations. Thus, in the first Turin drawing Simon Magus is shown with his left arm and hand pointing downwards; but in the Cappella Palatina as well as in Monreale he holds his left hand in front of his body. As it is known that the figure of the Magus in the Palatina is entirely renewed from the waist down,[6] one would like to assume that the miniature shows the original gesture, and that the restorer completed the missing part of the mosaic by introducing a motif which he borrowed from the cor-

responding figure at Monreale. The left-hand devil in the second scene of the Palatina cycle, with his scaly body and bat-like wings, seems to be another total restoration, since both at Monreale and in the Turin drawing the devils appear as winged putti, and this is what they must originally have looked like in the Palatina mosaic too. Whether the devil also faced the same way as in Monreale or was turned round as in the drawing is a matter which cannot be so easily settled. But it is obvious that the two drawings have a certain documentary value as early and reliable copies of the Palatina mosaics.

The procedure of copying mosaics in this way is, of course, not unique as such. Thus, it appears that the cycle of mosaics of New Testament scenes which adorned the church of the Holy Apostles at Constantinople served as a model for some of the representations of the great feasts in Byzantine lectionary manuscripts.[7] The illuminators of Palermo followed a Byzantine precedent. But they did so for very different reasons. The Byzantine miniaturists turned to mosaic models because those large-scale hieratic compositions were eminently suitable to be converted into full-page feast pictures. The Byzantine or Byzantine-inspired mosaic decorations of Norman Sicily, on the other hand, stood as a symbol and a reminder of the island's artistic heritage. During the troubled years of the unpopular Angevin occupation, artistic activities in Palermo must have come practically to a standstill. The Turin manuscript and its relatives, which were produced soon after the Sicilian Vespers, i.e., after the liberation from the hated foreign oppression, presented, as it were, a new departure. The Norman mosaics were copied in a conscious attempt to revive the local tradition on essentially retrospective lines, in order to claim some kind of continuity with the past. The link was particularly appropriate in the case of the story of SS. Peter and Paul: they had been the patron saints of the Norman Kingdom. They had been represented flanking the mosaic of the enthroned Pantocrator above the royal throne on the west wall of the Cappella Palatina, one of the last mosaics set by a member of the Hauteville dynasty.[8] After the Vespers, the new king, Peter of Aragon, and his consort, Constance, daughter of King Manfred, commemorated their accession by a fresco in the 'Cappella dell'Incoronazione' in the Cathedral of Palermo, which showed again the Pantocrator enthroned and flanked by the standing figures of SS. Peter and Paul, but this time in the act of crowning the royal couple kneeling

4. E. Kitzinger, *The Mosaics of Monreale*, Palermo, 1960, p. 43.
5. *Ibid.*, pp. 42 f.
6. O. Demus, *The Mosaics of Norman Sicily*, London, 1949, p. 31.

7. K. Weitzmann, 'The Narrative and Liturgical Gospel Illustrations', in *New Testament Manuscript Studies*, edd. Parvis and Wikgren, Chicago, 1950, pp. 164 ff.
8. Demus, *op. cit.*, p. 57, pl. 39.

at His feet[9]—an unmistakable demonstration that dynastic continuity had been re-established. The illuminator of the Turin manuscript gave, in his own modest way, expression to the public feeling when he based his version of the legend of the two apostles on 'authentic' Norman models.

Why the two scenes were copied from the mosaics in the Cappella Palatina rather than from those at Monreale, which were of more recent date and had served as models for the two Gospel fragments, one can only guess. The reasons may have been mainly practical. In Monreale, the cycle from the life of St. Peter is in the chapel which precedes the southern side apse, i.e., in a place which was not so easily accessible, and where the mosaics did not offer themselves for copying with the same facility as in the Cappella Palatina where they are in the aisles, in a location where they could be more readily studied and copied. It is also possible that they were chosen as models in preference to Monreale because the Cappella Palatina was dedicated to St. Peter. However this may be, there can be little doubt that the copying of the twelfth-century mosaics, the Peter-and-Paul scenes as well as those from the Gospels, was a piece of pro-Norman propaganda. As the manuscript in which the two Gospel fragments were once contained is lost, the full extent of this revival movement is difficult to assess. But one would like to think that the many reminiscences of Comnenian style which are found throughout the illustrations of the manuscript in Turin are at least in part due to the impact of the Norman mosaics.

*　　　　*　　　　*

On balance, those remnants of Comnenian style are not, however, the dominating element. It is only to be expected that a 'polycyclic' manuscript of this kind, based on a variety of models and executed by several different masters, in a scriptorium without an established stylistic tradition of its own, should be illuminated in a composite and very individual style made up of a number of distinct and even contradictory features. To some extent the various stylistic sources can still be determined from a study of the hagiographical affiliations of the single cycles: the copying of a number of heterogeneous models also left its mark on the style.

A general survey of the illumination of this fascinating manuscript cannot be attempted here. Only one saint's life will be briefly discussed in the present context: that of St. Benedict. This is by far the largest

cycle in the manuscript, probably because the scriptorium in which it was produced was attached to a Benedictine monastery, and had access to an 'authoritative' illustration of its patron saint's life. Thus it will hardly come as a surprise that the cycle can be compared almost scene by scene with the even more comprehensive set of pictures in the well-known eleventh-century lectionary in the Vatican Library[10] which was written at Monte Cassino itself, the home of the Benedictine order. Of the twenty-nine Benedict scenes in Turin, twenty are so close to their counterparts in the Vatican manuscript that they may be said to represent the same pictorial tradition; in other words, the model which was used by the illuminators of Palermo must have been a near relative of the Vatican manuscript.

A detailed iconographical comparison of the two cycles would be outside the scope of these notes. Only a few examples will be singled out to illustrate the similarities and the differences between the two manuscripts. One is the story of the monk Exhilaratus, who was sent by his superior to St. Benedict with a present of two flagons of wine. The monk, however, hid one in a bush, in order to collect it on his way home and to keep it for himself. The saint gratefully accepted the gift, but when Exhilaratus took his leave he warned him not to drink from the flagon he had hidden, but first to turn it upside down. The monk, confounded by Benedict's omniscience, followed his advice, whereupon it turned out that the flagon contained a poisonous snake.[11]

In the Cassino manuscript (Fig. 6) two consecutive scenes are combined in a single picture: Exhilaratus handing one flagon to the saint, and emptying the other one from which the snake escapes. In Turin (Fig. 7) the two incidents are represented separately; in the first the figures are transposed, and in the second the bush in which the flagon had been hidden is included, but otherwise they are iconographically identical. Moreover, there is one additional scene, at the beginning of the cycle, showing the monk carefully concealing the flagon in the bush. In other words, the illustration of the later manuscript is more complete, and the inference is that it follows a common archetype more faithfully than the surviving version from Cassino itself.

This is by no means the only instance of its kind. In the Benedict miniatures in Turin quite a number of details are rendered correctly which are misunderstood or even entirely suppressed in the Cassino

9. P. Gramignani, 'La Cappella dell'Incoronazione di Palermo', *Archivio storico siciliano*, 54, 1934, pp. 227 ff.

10. Vat. lat. 1202, cf. M. Inguanez and M. Avery, *Miniature Cassinesi del secolo XI*, 1, Montecassino, 1934.
11. Gregorii Magni *Dialogi libri IV*, Rome, 1924 (Fonti per la Storia d'Italia, 57), cap. XVIII, pp. 108 f.

lectionary. One of the most striking examples is the illustration of the last meeting of St. Benedict and his sister, St. Scholastica, whose prayer for rain caused a downpour from a previously cloudless sky so that the saint was forced to stay indoors.[12] In the Cassino manuscript (Fig. 8) both St. Benedict and his companion acknowledge the miracle with their glances and gestures, but the miracle itself is not shown. In Turin (Fig. 9), on the other hand, the cloudburst, the answer to St. Scholastica's prayer, is included in the picture, and we may take it that its presence was equally prominent in the archetype. No doubt the lectionary, which may be said to contain the finest illuminations ever produced at Monte Cassino and has a dedication picture showing Abbot Desiderius offering the manuscript to St. Benedict,[13] was the result of a special effort, an epitome of the unique achievements of the Abbey during the period of its greatest splendour. But our comparisons show that, comprehensive as it is, it was not itself the original recension, but reflects an even more complete archetype, from which the cycle in Turin, too, is an excerpt. Still, the model that was actually used by the illuminators of Palermo must have been close enough to the lectionary, not only in iconography but also in style. The Benedict cycle in Turin, and more especially the depictions of the protagonist himself, preserve many stylistic features which are characteristic of the Cassinese school of illumination during the later part of the eleventh century. Outstanding are the triangular or near-circular divisions of the garments patterned with parallel angular lines in local colours and a technique reminiscent of *cloisonné* work, a heritage from Byzantine illumination as found in manuscripts such as the Paris Gospels, gr. 74.[14] There is every reason to assume that the Sicilian masters took them over from their model, and that the model, though not identical with the Vatican lectionary from every point of view, was stylistically related to it, and also a product of the Cassino scriptorium during the most active period of its history.

It is perhaps possible to be more precise on this point. One of the more obvious differences between the two cycles concerns the figural type of St. Benedict himself. In the Turin manuscript he is always very distinct, and easily recognizable: a sturdy, oldish man with a broad face and a short, grey, semi-circular beard, bare-headed, and with a large tonsure. In the Cassino lectionary, on the other hand, his facial features are not so pronounced; he is younger, and appears more slender, and he always has his hood on his head. There is however one exception. In the miniature where he meets Totila, the Ostrogoth king (Fig. 10), whose approaching end he predicts,[15] he is represented as a big man, broad-faced and bare-headed; and though he still looks somewhat younger and his tonsure is not so prominent, it is clear that he is much closer to his various counterparts in Turin than to any of those in the lectionary. A comparison with the preceding scene in the lectionary[16] will at first glance show the difference. If, on the other hand, the figure is confronted with that in the miniature in Turin illustrating the mysterious fire in the monastery kitchen (Fig. 11), it will at once be obvious how closely the two belong together. Iconographically as well as stylistically one might almost be a direct copy of the other. This is the figural type of the saint which must have been predominant in the cycle of the sister manuscript of the lectionary, which served as a model for the Benedict miniatures in Turin.

The questions here discussed are only a tiny fraction of those raised by the Turin illustrations. Unfortunately, only few other cycles of saints' lives can be compared in any detail with those surviving in other manuscripts. Of very special interest are the lives and passions of some Greek saints, which were certainly copied from Greek models direct, and which will add considerably to our knowledge of Byzantine illumination once they are published. In the meantime, it is hoped that these notes will give sufficient proof of the extraordinary importance of this neglected manuscript.[17]

---

12. *Ibid.*, cap. xxxiii, pp. 125 f.
13. Inguanez and Avery, *op. cit.*, pl. i.
14. Cf. M. Schapiro, *The Parma Ildefonsus*, 1964 (Monographs on Archaeology and Fine Arts, xi), pp. 41 ff.

15. Gregorii Magni Dialogi, *op. cit.*, cap. xv, pp. 102 ff.
16. I.e., the scene to the left in our Fig. 10.
17. A more detailed account by this writer of the Turin manuscript and its sister manuscript in the Vatican Library will be found in the *Dumbarton Oaks Papers*, 20, 1966.

CARLO BERTELLI

The *Image of Pity* in Santa Croce in Gerusalemme

Few iconographic themes have been studied so thoroughly and still remain so highly controversial as that of the *Man of Sorrows* and its twin subject, the *Mass of St. Gregory*. In particular, the role played in the making of the Gregorian legend by a small mosaic icon preserved in Rome, in the church of Santa Croce in Gerusalemme, has been eagerly discussed since the publication of the image some thirty years ago[1] (Fig. 1). According to the inscription on a well-known engraving by Israhel van Meckenem,[2] the mosaic should be the faithful reproduction of a vision that appeared to Pope Gregory the Great while he was celebrating mass. To some authors this story seems entirely unconvincing, and they tend to place the origin of the legend in St. Peter's; others are inclined to accept Sta. Croce but do not credit the mosaic, favouring the hypothesis that there was a much older prototype, from the eighth or even late sixth to early seventh century.[3] Where they all meet, however, is in attributing

the mosaic not to a Byzantine school, but to some thirteenth-century Italian master, an opinion which would make of it a possibly unique case of this Byzantine technique in Italian art.[4]

I hope it might prove a sort of tribute to Wittkower's taste for a factual approach, to which we owe so much, to try and disentangle this small work of art from the various theories that have grown around it, and to try and look at it as it is. A new scrutiny seems now all the more necessary because it was restored some years ago,[5] and the confused array of little cubes (Fig. 3) that A. Thomas, who first studied it, saw in the 1930's[6] has now regained a correct unity, with its many fragments duly put in their proper places.

The mosaic, on a small wooden panel measuring 23 × 28 cm (with the frame; 13 × 19 cm without it), is encased in a large wooden reliquary having the shape of a triptych. This consists of a central panel, surmounted by a curved pediment, bronze-coloured, and of two lateral wings. It has a wooden, brass-covered pedestal, where some holes still indicate the position of ornamental stones, which have now disappeared. There

1. A. Thomas, 'Das Urbild der Gregoriusmesse', in *Rivista di Archeologia Cristiana*, x, 1933, pp. 51 ff. A comprehensive survey of the literature on the subject has been recently offered by R. Bauerreiss, O.S.B., 'Ο ΒΑΣΙΛΕΥΣ ΤΗΣ ΔΟΞΗΣ, Ein frühes eucharistisches Bild und seine Auswirkung', in *Pro mundi vita, Festschrift zum Eucharistischen Weltkongress, 1960*, Munich, 1960, pp. 49 ff. See now also: E. M. Vetter, 'Iconografia del "Varon de dolores", Su significado y origen', in *Archivo Español de Arte*, xxxvi, 1963, 143, pp. 199 ff.; cf. the entries 'Gregoriusmesse', by Thomas, in *Lexikon für Theologie und Kirche*, iv, 1960, cols. 1217–18; and 'Ablass-Bild', by Otto Schmitt, in *Reallexikon zur Deutschen Kunstgeschichte*, i, cols. 81 f. All the literature on the subject draws on a pioneering article by J. A. Endres, 'Die Darstellung der Gregoriusmesse im Mittelalter', in *Zeitschrift für christliche Kunst*, xxx, 1917, p. 152 (preceded by X. Barbier de Montault, 'La Messe de Saint Grégoire', in *Œuvres complètes*, vi, Paris, 1892, pp. 235 ff.; and *Revue de l'art chrétien*, Oct. 1887, pp. 498 f.) and seems to have taken great advantage of the thesis discussed in Berlin by H. Löffler ('Ikonographie des Schmerzensmannes', 1922) which was never published. I have not seen M. Lorenz's thesis, 1956, referred to by Thomas in his article of 1960.
I here thank Father Bauerreiss and Doctor Vetter, who kindly sent me offprints of their work. I am particularly indebted to Professor Francis Wormald, London, and to Professor Otto Pächt, Vienna, for their invaluable assistance and for many suggestions.
2. Bartsch, 135. A good reproduction in W. Mersmann, *Der Schmerzensmann*, Düsseldorf, 1952, pl. 1.
3. A. Thomas, *op. cit.*, p. 55, attributes the icon to a western workshop; H. Schrade, 'Beiträge zur Erklärung des Schmerzensmannbildes', in *Deutschkundliches, Friedrich Panzer zum 60. Geburtstag, Beiträge zur neueren Literaturgeschichte*, xvi, Heidelberg, 1930, p. 166, supposes some connections between the mosaic and the 'umbella' attributed to John VII, a Byzantine epitaphion which was kept in the chapel of the Veronica in

St. Peter's; P. Ortmayr, 'Papst Gregor der Grosse und das Schmerzensmannbild in S. Croce zu Rom', in *Rivista di Archeologia Cristiana*, xviii, 1941, pp. 97 ff., tried to relate this iconography to the teaching of St. Gregory himself and supposed that the mosaic derived from a large composition going back to the time of Gregory; W. Mersmann, *op. cit.*, p. vii, takes also the Roman *Image of Pity* as the former 'Mittelpunkt einer vielfigurigen Komposition'; R. Bauerreiss, in his last contribution to the subject (see note 1) rules out the Roman mosaic entirely from the development of the Gregorian legend but still supposes the existence of a much older 'Prothesisbild' in Sta. Croce.
4. The only miniature mosaic which, to my knowledge, has been rumoured as being of Italian origin, the Crucifixion in the Staatlichen Museen in Berlin, has been rightly referred to a metropolitan workshop by J. Beckwith, *The Art of Constantinople*, London, 1961, pp. 134 ff. See also note 18.
5. In Rome, at the Istituto Centrale del Restauro, in 1960. The restorers were Signor Paolo and Signora Laura Mora. I wish to thank here Professor Cesare Brandi, then director of the Institute, who so enthusiastically supported my project of restoring the mosaic, for his advice and for his assistance. The mornings we spent together trying to combine the many minute fragments seem now the last mark of a whole period in the life of the Institute. A report on the restorations undertaken should appear in the *Bollettino dell'Istituto Centrale del Restauro*. Small gaps were filled with coloured wax and are clearly visible in the black and white photographs. A full photographic documentation is kept in the archive of the Istituto Centrale del Restauro, and other photographs, made after restoration, in the Gabinetto Fotografico Nazionale.
6. *Op. cit.*, Fig. 1.

are handles to carry it in processions, and some other clumsy decorations. When the reliquary is shut (Fig. 5), the outside surface of the two wings shows a gold-tooled leather cover similar to a bookbinding; when open, it reveals a number of small cases, glass-faced and framed by metallic strips (copper? brass?), held together by small nails with rosette-shaped heads. Each case is carved into the thickness of the wooden panel and contains a relic wrapped in green silk[7] (Fig. 4).

The whole thing, with closed wings (under the pediment a gilt inscription reads: *Fuit S. Gregorii Magni Papae*), looks like any plain eighteenth-century aedicula. There are, however, a few elements pointing to an earlier date. A triptych shape would be at least unusual for a reliquary after the Renaissance, while it would be fairly common in the thirteenth and fourteenth centuries.[8] When the reliquary is open, if we avoid looking at the pediment and at the ornaments of the pedestal, the irregular grid-iron pattern of the intersecting metallic strips has a distinct medieval accent, enhanced by the simple presentation of the single relics. If we look at it more closely and try to read the labels on the single relics, we discover that a number of them are written in 'gotica rotunda' while

only a few are in a later hand. Even the scale of gold and red, the colours of the metal and that of the wood —wherever it is visible—is a common device in many Italian 'fondi oro'.[9] Signor Riccardo Ventura, a restorer in the Soprintendenze, was kind enough to detach the leather lining of the reliquary for me, so making it possible to examine the original outer surface of the two wings (Fig. 6). This is painted with a very simple decoration: a roundel of veneered 'verde antico', delimited by a thin white line; a similar white line goes around the edges of the panel.[10] A pattern like this may be attributed to any period between the fourteenth and the sixteenth centuries. There is enough to conclude that, as it is, the reliquary must have undergone several alterations and embellishments but that it is certainly earlier than it looks at first glance today. A dating to the end of the fourteenth century, if supported by other elements, would not seem unlikely.

The handling of the reliquary has been uncommonly discreet—due perhaps to the superstitious belief that the mosaic itself had been composed by Pope Gregory with his own hands, using fragments of bones of the martyrs (a tale which I myself heard related by a sacristan of our own days). This discretion has allowed the bits and pieces of the mosaic to be kept together, though oddly arranged, even when the image was damaged, having fallen down or received a severe blow at an unknown date. That it was not touched was a happy circumstance, which enabled us to restore the figure almost in its entirety.

The Sta. Croce mosaic, after restoration, is obviously to be compared with another portable mosaic of the same subject from the monastery of the Birth of the Virgin in Tatarna (now Tripotamon) near Evrytania, in Aetolia, that is attributed to a Byzantine workshop of the early fourteenth century[11] (Fig. 7).

There is, however, a remarkable difference in the iconography. The Sta. Croce mosaic shows the Lord's body down to the waist, the bleeding wound and the crossed hands well in sight. In the Tatarna mosaic the Saviour is represented only as far as the chest, and His hands are not depicted at all. Both types are well known from a large series of monuments,[12] but while

---

7. We were not allowed to open the small bags in order to inspect their contents. This reliquary seems to be the same which was described by Onofrio Panvinio (*De praecipuis urbis ...basilicis*, Rome, 1570, p. 221); Francesco del Sodo (*Compendio delle chiese con le loro Fondationi, Consecrationi, et Titoli* [after 1575], cod. Vat. lat. 11911, particularly fol. 32 r); and Abbot F. Besozzi (*Storia della basilica di S. Croce*, Rome, 1750, p. 149). Panvinio states that there were 220 'sorti di reliquie' collected in '137 cassette'; Besozzi, echoed by the *Nota delle Reliquie* affixed in the church (Fig. 23), also counts '137 cassette'; Del Sodo speaks of 220 relics. I count 197 and suspect that Besozzi depends on Panvinio in his counting; they both state, in fact, that the labels with the names of the martyrs cannot be read 'per vecchiezza' or 'per l'antichità'. A cross which was kept in the vertical cell right over the mosaic, with the label *Fuit Scti Petri*, has been stolen, and the present Abbot, Monsignor Moscatelli, has substituted for it a bronze cross found inside the altar of St. Helen.

Rosette-headed nails are documented as early as the thirteenth century (e.g., a casket of St. Ebbo, at Serrancoulin, Hautes-Pyrénées—a Limousin work: see the catalogue of the exhibition, *Les trésors des églises de France*, Paris, 1965, n. 473, pl. 56). I must add here that not all the nails are decorated with rosettes and that there is a certain pattern in the distribution of the nails. As for the plain strips of brass, cf. another French example: the bookbinding of the Pontifical in the Bibliothèque Municipale of Châlons-sur-Marne, MS. 45, of the second half of the thirteenth century (see *Notre-Dame de Paris, 1163–1963, Exposition du huitième centenaire*, Paris, 1963, no. 49, pls. VIII and IX).

8. Some illustrious examples: the 'reliquiario del libretto' in the Museo dell'Opera del Duomo in Florence (E. Steingräber, in *Mitteilungen des Kunsthistorischen Instituts in Florenz*, XX, 1960, p. x); the triptych of Conques (*Les Trésors ...*, Paris, 1965, no. 548, pl. 126); the triptych of Sainghin-en-Mélantois, Nord (*ibid.*, no. 20, pl. 127; with a statuette of St. Nicholas in the central panel).

9. For instance, Giotto's Stefaneschi triptych is tinted red in its exposed wooden parts, as it also appears in the scene of the cardinal's presenting the very same triptych to St. Peter.

10. It is rather curious, as we shall see, that this simple pattern appears on the frames of some frescoes of the late fourteenth–early fifteenth century in the church of SS. Niccolò e Cataldo in Lecce, in the territory of Raimondello Orsini.

11. *Byzantine Art, Ninth Exhibition of the Council of Europe*, Athens, 1964, no. 167. I am obliged to Professor M. Chatzidakis, director of the Byzantine Museum in Athens, who kindly supplied me with a photograph of the icon.

12. See note 1. On the Byzantine iconography in particular:

the Tatarna type is usually referred to as of Greek origin, the Sta. Croce one is said to be distinctly Western.[13] This view might be reconsidered if only we could produce some examples of the Sta. Croce type of certain Eastern origin. Besides those published by Millet, I should now like to point out at least one more instance of just that kind; an icon in the monastery of Mount Sinai, probably of the fifteenth century. Here the Sta. Croce type is provided with a convenient sarcophagus, which, according to current theory, would represent only a later stage in the western development of the iconography. An earlier representation of the same subject (twelfth century?), on an enamel plaque in the former Botkin collection in St. Petersburg, was quoted by Schrade.[14]

Not less striking are the differences in style. The Tatarna mosaic does not aim at the eurhythmy of proportioned horizontal zones which is such a prominent feature of the Sta. Croce mosaic. It is marked, instead, by a sort of casualness in the way Christ's body is represented, fallen, as it were, down to the bottom of the panel; even the horizontal bar of the Cross is missing. But in its own way the Tatarna image is no less impressive. The heavy body of Christ has a powerful muscular structure still reminiscent of the athletic figures in Roman mosaics; His face, contracted by suffering, has the struggling quality which was the attribute of virile endurance in Pergamene sculpture. Moreover, while in the Tatarna mosaic the figure is interpreted as a whole form, in which the leonine head is firmly attached to the strongly-built torso, in the Sta. Croce icon breast and waist constitute a sort of strigilated support to the beautiful head. This is displayed like a relic, as detached from the rest of the

figure as the severed head of a Martyr put on a vessel. In contrast with the tender and beautiful head, the anatomy of the body is coldly descriptive: it follows a symmetrical arrangement of ribs and muscles, and it delimits the perfect ogee arch of the belly and the round masses of the breast, distributing here and there tiny highlights and composing linear rows of shadows. Bauerreiss and Thomas,[15] who saw the mosaic before restoration, attributed it to an Italo-Byzantine artist of the thirteenth century; Vetter, who saw it afterwards and published a photograph of it in its present state,[16] also regards it as a replica by an Italian Dugento artist. To add weight to this attribution, Vetter points out the 'grafía incorrecta' of the inscription on the titulus of the Cross, which 'hace suponer que no es obra bizantina'. But my limited knowledge of Greek does not allow me to discover there any gross mistakes.[17]

Considering the many differences between the two mosaics, of Tatarna and of Rome, one would indeed be tempted to deduce the possibility of a western origin for the latter. But on a closer scrutiny the mosaic in Sta. Croce reveals some significant analogies with other, certainly Byzantine, works of the same class. The minute highlights, resembling tiny pieces of straw scattered all over the surface, are even more marked in the mosaic icon of St. John Chrysostom in the Dumbarton Oaks collections.[18] The technique of inscribing the lettering with bitumen on a golden background (a detail at hand in Sta. Croce but not in Tatarna), is also to be found on the same icon.[19] The body of Christ is heavily built in a way that can be easily compared to what we see in another icon mosaic in Dumbarton Oaks, the one with the 'Forty Martyrs', which, on a reduced scale, presents several variations on the same theme.[20] The soft and delicate handling of the faces, although a certain firmness in the Sta. Croce mosaic may indicate a slightly earlier date, makes them even closer to each other.

*   *   *

During restoration, the Sta. Croce mosaic revealed one more secret. When it was removed from the encasing reliquary, on the back of the panel a standing figure of *St. Catherine*, painted on a golden background, came to light (Fig. 9). This is a very intriguing

G. Millet, *Recherches sur l'iconographie de l'évangile aux XIVᵉ, XVᵉ et XVIᵉ siècles*, Paris, 1916, pp. 483 ff.; R. Dölling, *Aus der byzantinischen Arbeit der Deutschen Demokratischen Republik*, Berlin, 1957, pp. 170 ff., with further literature.
13. Cf. E. M. Vetter, *op. cit.*, pp. 204–5.
14. The Sinai icon is reproduced in A. Champdor, *Le Mont Sinaï et le Monastère de Sainte Catherine*, Paris, 1963, p. 71 (photo Allan). The Botkin enamel was first published in the catalogue of the collection (*Sobranie M. P. Botkin*, St. Petersburg, 1911, II, pl. 85) and then by H. Schrade, *op. cit.*, p. 165, Fig. 1. According to Vetter, the half-figure should have succeeded the bust after the conquest of Constantinople brought to the West the Holy Shroud; the Byzantine examples referred to by Millet, *op. cit.*, p. 484, would be regarded by this author as works under the influence of the Italian Trecento. The influence of the Shroud on western iconography has been discussed by H. Wentzel (*Miscellanea*. I. Das Turiner Leichentuch Christi und das Kreuzigungs-Bild des Landsgrafenpsalters Schwabens, in *Beiträge J. Baum*, Stuttgart, 1952). Nevertheless, for what concerns the Italian Trecento, I find it remarkable that the Shroud was never heard of after the sack of 1204 until it was recorded in the possession of Geoffroy I de Charny in 1353; in 1452 Marguerite de Charny gave it to the Duke of Savoy, who kept it in Chambéry until 1578 when it was brought to Turin. See N. Chevalier, *Étude critique sur l'origine du Saint Suaire de Lirey-Chambéry-Turin*, Paris, 1900.

15. See note 1.
16. E. M. Vetter, *op. cit.*, pp. 198 and 205.
17. A possible mistake, the use of *I* for *H* in the word *THC*—which, eventually, would confirm that the mosaicist spoke the language he wrote—is corrected by the English drawing of Fig. 15.
18. O. Demus, 'Two Paleologan Mosaic Icons in the Dumbarton Oaks Collection', in *Dumbarton Oaks Papers*, 14, 1960, pp. 89 ff., Figs. 22 and 23.
19. It was Professor Ernst Kitzinger who drew my attention to this detail.
20. See O. Demus, *op. cit.*, Figs. 2, 3.

Tracing of the title of the Cross on the mosaic icon in Sta. Croce piece of painting. The frontal pose, the huge nimbus, the *loros* and the rest of the garment, the small basilical building in the background, the *sgraffito* inscription above (✛ 'Η ΑΓΙΑ ✛ ΚΑΤΕΡΙΝΗ), which is now only scarcely visible, are all elements pointing to an Eastern origin. But certainly not Eastern is the lily crown worn by the saint, nor the diapered background, or the fragmentary Latin (?) inscription at the lower edge. One can note that the way the saintly princess wears the *loros* is inappropriate, and the suspicion that a Western artist is here playing with an alien model becomes more insistent.

The back of the panel therefore seems to put forward as many questions as it answers. I think it wiser to leave them aside for the moment and to turn to the last element we have not yet examined, the silver-gilt frame of the mosaic (Fig. 1). It consists of a flat band with beaded borders, on which an acanthus scroll is embossed, enclosing in its rinceaux more or less heraldic fauna—three leopards, an ape, a dragon, several fowls—and ten barbed lozenges. Each lozenge originally contained an enamel plaque; three of them have been missing for a long time, and the gaps are filled with a bluish paste. The oblique section of the frame, all along the icon, bears a decoration of very rough four-petalled flowers.

The technique is that of repoussé, with a great use of the punch to flatten the background; some minor details are incised. On the whole, it is a rough and clumsy piece of work, miles away from the elegance of the stamped frames from Venice and Istria.

Of the seven enamels that are still in place, three represent scenes from the Passion of Christ (namely, from left to right: the Flagellation, Christ bearing the Cross, and the Crucifixion), while the four at the corners are decorated with coats-of-arms. Italian translucid enamels are seldom of such bad quality; those showing coats-of-arms, however, are sufficiently clear to allow their identifications. Thomas[21] rightly recognized the shield of the Holy Sepulchre in the one at the upper right corner, that of Anjou on the left, and, below, the coat-of-arms of the Orsini-Montfort family on the left corner, while the one on the right he identified as del Balzo. The association of Anjou with the Holy Sepulchre is a royal connotation: the Angevins claimed in fact to be both kings of Hungary (as is indicated by the white and red fesses surrounding the shield with the lilies) and of Jerusalem. Besides, it seems that Louis of Hungary was particularly fond of small devotional images of the sort of the Sta. Croce one. We know he presented to the shrine of Charlemagne in Aachen a Byzantine icon, which had an enamelled frame adorned with the Angevin lilies (a gift clearly intended to underline his political claims), and, short of Byzantine objects, he gave a Sienese (?) panel, with an enamelled cover in the Oriental manner, also displaying his heraldic lilies, to the sanctuary of Maria Zell.[22] But if our mosaic were a royal present, it would not bear the coat-of-arms of two subject families. Thomas supposed that the frame was a gift from Nicola Orsini, Count of Nola, the husband of Maria, the only daughter of Raimondo del Balzo, and that it was presented shortly after the foundation of a charterhouse in Sta. Croce, in 1371. Nicola, with his brother Napoleone, had been in fact the patron of the new Carthusian establishment.[23] But even if Nicola Orsini, as an Italian husband of the Trecento, may have been more respectful than the average of the prerogatives of his wife, I still doubt that so many years after his marriage,[23b] in the presenting of such a modest gift to his beloved church, he would have felt bound to display the coat-of-arms of his wife's family next to his own. The more so since his brother's will had left him a considerable amount of money to be spent on the charterhouse,[23c] a circumstance which put the balance even more on the side of the Orsinis.

It must be remembered that there was still someone else who liked to go around showing the arms of the Orsini and those of the del Balzo families joined together. This was Nicola's second son, Raimondello (Fig. 11).

As a second-born, he was deprived of the family rights,

---

21. *Op. cit.*, pp. 52 ff.

22. To the Hungarian chapel in Aachen, founded in 1367, Louis gave two panel paintings with the *Coronation of the Virgin* and an icon with the Virgin and Child (see the catalogue of the exhibition, *Unsere Liebe Frau*, Aachen, 1958). After 1365–6 he offered to Maria Zell an 'icon', attributed to Andrea Vanni but too extensively overpainted to allow any attribution, which, according to a legend, had granted him a victory over the Turks (O. Wonisch, *Mariazell*, Munich, 1957, pp. 4, 39, 42). Professor Pächt drew my attention to the 'Ikonenstiftung' of the king.

23. Thomas, *op. cit.*, p. 54. On this branch of the Orsini family see: F. Sansovino, *Historia di Casa Orsina*, Venezia, 1565; P. Litta, *Le famiglie celebri italiane*, fasc. LXII, disp. 114, 'Orsini di Roma', tab. XI and XII, Milan, 1847; cf. V. Spreti, *Enciclopedia storico-nobiliare italiana*, I, Milan, 1931, p. 493. On the role of Napoleone and Nicola in the foundation of the charterhouse in Rome: Tromby, *Storia del patriarca S. Brunone e dell'Ordine Certosino*, VI, Naples, 1777, pp. 300 ff., 311–12; VII, Naples, 1777, pp. 1–3, 67 (and cf. VI, Appendix II, with the bull of Urban V on the establishment of the Carthusian house, addressed to the two Orsini brothers); see also M. Armellini, *Le chiese di Roma*, Rome, 1887, p. 205, with further documentation.

23b. In 1357 Nicola's first wife, Gorizia di Guglielmo di Sabrano, dictated her will (Litta, *op. cit.*, tab. XI). Soon afterwards Nicola must have married Maria di Raimondello del Balzo, since in 1387 her son Raimondello was of an age to command a host against the bandits in the Neapolitan territory (*ibid.*, XII).

23c. On Napoleone's will see Armellini, *op. cit.*

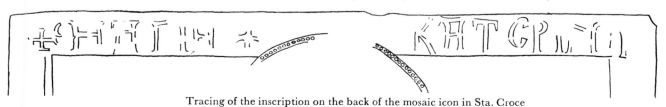

Tracing of the inscription on the back of the mosaic icon in Sta. Croce

which passed to his elder brother; he had therefore to fight his claims in order to acquire an independent status of his own.[24] In his youth he may have been impressed by his father's love for learning and interests in the mystical,[25] but he very soon found himself opposed to his father, and received support from his mother, whose coat-of-arms he eventually adopted. In the early eighties he took possession of the county of Soleto and of the principality of Taranto, which his mother had inherited from her brother; in 1386 he became Count of Lecce. As the ruler of a rather large territory—actually one of the widest feudal states in the kingdom of Naples—he acted as an ambitious patron of the arts, only restrained by the peripheral situation of his county with respect to the main currents of western art in that period.[26]

Hostility between the Durazzo and the Anjou made life uneasy in the circle of minor southern nobility to which Raimondello belonged; and necessity, ambition, and the fierce struggle to assert his authority or just to survive had taught him very early in life the risky game of keeping a foot in both camps, or of quickly switching from one patron to the other. These circumstances make the period when he might have been eager to show his coat-of-arms associated with that of the Anjou quite special and restricted.

Looking at Raimondello's biography, we can find only a brief space of time when this adventurous knight can be presumed to have presented the Carthusian church in Rome with a gift marked with the symbols of the Angevin party.

On September 21, 1384, Louis of Anjou died and Raimondello Orsini del Balzo became chief of the army of the Angevin pretender to the throne.[27] He was already on the march against Carlo di Durazzo when an appeal reached him from Pope Urban VI. The pope had been previously allied to the Durazzos against the Angevins, but he had now started a quarrel with his ally on the question of the partition of Capua and Amalfi, which he wanted to give to his nephew Buttillo Prignano. Carlo di Durazzo had therefore turned against the pope, and at that very time Durazzo's army was besieging him in the fortified town of Nocera de' Pagani.[28] Raimondello succeeded in liberating the pope (July 7, 1385), receiving a wound during the exploit.[29] Some months later Durazzo was killed in Hungary (February 17, 1386). Urban VI aligned himself again with the Durazzos and, in order to protect Ladislao, the pretender, who was but a child of ten, he committed him to Raimondello. By that time the short union between the latter and the Angevins had come to an end. The Orsinis were well known to Urban VI; in 1378 Nicola had sided with him against Giovanna of Anjou, and this had in fact been the pretext for Raimondello to leave the family.[30] So we may think that there was ground enough for a family reunion and for offers to be made to the family church, the flourishing Carthusian establishment of Sta. Croce—after the fight, the wound and a long exile.

Urban VI was generous with his rescuer. Among the honours he granted, there is one which is perhaps of little significance to the general historian but which may be of some interest to the art historian.

In two bulls[31] Urban VI conceded special blessings

24. On Raimondello's career see also: H. Krass, *Storia di Lecce*, Bari, 1936, pp. 205 ff.; A. Cutolo, *Maria d'Enghien*, Naples, 1929.

25. Nicola was a friend of Boccaccio's (see *Decameron*, ed. V. Branca, Florence, 1952, p. 40, n. 2, p. 100) and it was he who presented to Boniface IX the cause for the canonization of Bridget of Sweden (Litta, *ibid.*). A souvenir of Nicola's patronage in Sta. Croce has come down to us. It is the MS. Sessorianus 1467/20 in the Biblioteca Nazionale, Rome, which he gave to the church on September 5, 1390 (see fol. 20). It contains the *officium invencionis sanctae crucis* and bears the coat-of-arms of Gregory XI, the pope who introduced the use of reading nine lessons, instead of three, in the office for the Invention of the Holy Cross. It is an attractive, but very simple manuscript.

Besides the mosaic, there was another important 'orientalizing' item in Sta. Croce, namely the part preserved in the Vatican Library of a fully illustrated *Vitae Patrum*, which is being studied by Professor Hugo Buchthal (cf. P. Toesca, *Il Medioevo*, III, Turin, 1927, p. 1143, n. 14; *id.*, *Il Trecento*, Turin, 1951, p. 842).

26. For a survey of Raimondello's patronage see: R. Pagenstecher, *Apulia*, Leipzig, 1914, pp. 170 ff.; Krass, *op. cit.*, pp. 225 ff. See also: A. Putignani, O.F.M., *Il tempio di S. Caterina a Galatina*, Galatina, 1947. For the chronology of Raimondello's career cf. B. Papadia, *Memorie storiche della città di Galatina, nella Japigia*, Naples, 1792, p. 47; cf. Putignani, *ibid.*, p. 17.

27. Krass, *op. cit.*, p. 220; Litta, tab. XII.

28. Litta, tab. XII. Cf. A. Valente, *Margherita di Durazzo vicaria di Carlo III*, Naples, 1919.

29. According to Litta, tab. XII, he was wounded in the foot. Sansovino, *op. cit.*, p. 7, has a more adventurous story to tell: in the Holy Land 'Raimondello fece prodezze maravigliose, essendosi in un fatto d'arme portato animosamente, intanto ch'egli solo haueua attorno, quasi come a sembianza di un muro, i corpi morti de gli infedeli, usò poi in segno di quella notabile et memorabile fattione, di portare una calza bianca fin quasi presso à talloni, & da indi in giù tutta rossa, dalla qual si trasse non l'arme, ma l'impresa ò liurea che si dica. Et il pontefice con singolar fauore gli fece un presente della Rosa ch'egli suol donare à Prencipi honorati & di cuore che si trouan à tempi suoi.' Sansovino certainly shows some confusion with the action of Nocera.

30. H. Krass, *op. cit.*, p. 210; cf. Litta, *op. cit.*, tab. XII.

31. The bull 'Piis votis fidelium' and the bull 'Sacrae vestrae religionis sinceritas'; they are both printed by B. Papadia, *op. cit.*, pp. 29, 97 and 98, who seems to have read them as reported in the chronicle by Silvio Arcudi, a MS. which was the property of a notary, Mattia Luceri, in Galatina. There seems to be a certain discord between the dates attributed to the bulls— March 25, 1384, and April 8, 1385—and the ascertained dates of the events in Nocera. Maybe Urban granted his benefices before his rescue. Nevertheless the bull of April 8 is dated 'pontificatus anno septimo', and Urban was elected on April 8,

and a number of indulgences to the church and the hospital that Raimondello was building in Galatina, his residence in the Salento. The church and the annexed hospital, dedicated to St. Catherine, were the major achievement of Raimondello as a patron of the arts, and they had, in his view, a very high religious and political meaning.[32] The church was intended as the shrine of an exceptional relic, which he made into the palladium of his state and the talisman of his good luck. It sheltered the relic of that finger of St. Catherine which, according to the legend, Christ Himself had encircled with His ring during the mystical wedding. The relic was brought to Galatina by Raimondello himself, who, according to some sources,[33] stole it from the shrine on Mount Sinai, tearing it from the body of the Saint by his own teeth. (It may be remembered that, in the end, his successors were to add St. Catherine's wheel to their coat-of-arms.[34]) But the extremely poor quality of the reliquary of St. Catherine (G.F.N. Phot. R. 1467) proves the serious limitations of these provincial ambitions.[35]

The presence of an image of St. Catherine on the back of the mosaic icon seems thus not without significance. Raimondello, in fact, was a collector not only of relics but also of rare art objects, in the class of small portable mosaics. The treasury of the church of Sta. Caterina in Galatina, we need only remember, possesses another such mosaic icon (Fig. 12).[36] I wonder if the rather unusual representation of the *Man of Sorrows* on the pediment over the main door of the church in Galatina (Fig. 13) is not a memory of the temporary stay there of the mosaic which is now in Sta. Croce.[37]

If the representation of St. Catherine on the back of the mosaic may be taken as an indication of its former owner, it can also point to its provenance. Painting in Apulia in the fourteenth century is still a little-known field, and the few surviving monuments seem to yield highly contradictory evidence. In our case, it is to be lamented that the frescoes which Raimondello had painted in his church of Galatina are no longer visible, as they were later covered with new frescoes ordered by his wife.[38] Nevertheless it is difficult to believe that the St. Catherine of Sta. Croce was executed just before the mosaic was sent on to Rome. If it were, there would have been no reason to have inscribed it with the Greek words 'H AΓIA KATEPINH; and if the mosaic had to be encased in the reliquary—which is likely to be contemporary with the silver frame—the painting would have been concealed, as indeed was the case until its restoration. It is possible that Raimondello had the St. Catherine painted when he brought the mosaic to Galatina; but it is also to be remarked that the other mosaic icon in Galatina has a plain back. I am rather inclined to think that the painting on the back was meant to be more a dedication to St. Catherine than a mark of origin or of ownership. Considering that in 1380–1381 Raimondello climbed Mount Sinai and that he came back carrying the relic of St. Catherine, we may think it not unlikely that he also might have taken along from the sanctuary the mosaic icon itself. In this case, the painting ought not to be attributed to the man who took the icon away, but to the one who first gave it to the monastery.

Presenting the monastery of St. Catherine with icons was by no means unusual, as we know from the studies by Sotiriou and by Weitzmann.[39] About the same years with which we are concerned, in this case 1387, a citizen of Barcelona, Bernardo Manresa, at that time the Catalonian consul in Damascus, sent to the monastery a similar icon with an image of St. Catherine, painted by a Catalonian artist.[40]

1378. Another bull in favour of Galatina, also reproduced by Papadia, p. 100, is dated Genoa, June 15, 1386.
32. See Putignani, *op. cit.* For a critical appreciation of the architecture see: H. W. Schulz, *Denkmäler der Kunst des Mittelalters in Unteritalien*, Dresden, 1860, I, pp. 247 f., and *Atlas*, pl. 46; W. Krönig, in *Römisches Jahrbuch für Kunstgeschichte*, II, 1938, p. 58; P. Toesca, *Il Trecento*, pp. 60, 73.
33. Bonaventura da Lama, *Cronica de' Minori Osservanti Riformati della provincia di S. Nicolò*, Lecce, 1724, p. 101.
34. See the tomb of Giannantonio di Raimondello, in the same church in Galatina, reproduced by Litta, *op. cit.*, tab. XII.
35. Richer, but hopelessly crude, is the chalice attributed to Raimondello or to Maria d'Enghien in the same church. See M. D'Elia, *Mostra dell'Arte in Puglia*, Bari, 1964, no. 86, pl. 91.
36. It was published by G. Castelfranco, 'Opere d'arte in Puglia', in *Bollettino d'Arte*, 1927, pp. 289 ff. See now M. D'Elia, *op. cit.*, no. 9, with further literature. Following a local tradition reported by D'Elia, the mosaic should be the gift of the Galatina friars to Raimondello after his return from the Holy Land. But Raimondello's return from his pilgrimage falls several years before he summoned the Franciscan friars to Galatina for his newly-founded church.
37. G. van der Osten, *Schmerzensmann, Typengeschichte eines deutschen Andachtsbildwerkes von 1300–1600*, Berlin, 1933, p. 29, n. 23, seems to believe that the representation of the *Man of Sorrows* on church portals was much rarer than what it actually is. Cf. E. M. Vetter, *op. cit.*, p. 226. It is displayed also on many chapels represented in Italian Trecento paintings, not to mention Fermo cathedral.

38. A detailed description of the frescoes in Putignani, *op. cit.*, pp. 37 ff. For a critical appreciation see M. Salmi, 'Appunti per la storia della pittura in Puglia', in *L'Arte*, 1919, pp. 149 ff., pp. 153 ff. (with the surprising statement that 'agli inizi del Quattrocento, a Venezia si dipingeva poco meglio che in Terra d'Otranto, sotto l'influsso del bizantinismo'); and P. Toesca, *Il Trecento*, p. 692. One of the painters of Galatina painted the Annunciation in S. Stefano in Soleto; one of the Galatina stonemasons carved the fount in the parish church of Soleto, an attractive version of his repertory of Byzantine, Gothic and Romanesque motives.
39. G. and M. Sotiriou, *Ikones tis Monis Sina*, Athens, 1958; K. Weitzmann, 'Thirteenth Century Crusader Icons on Mount Sinai', in *The Art Bulletin*, XLV, 1963, 3, pp. 179 ff. G. and M. Sotiriou point out the connections of some icons with wall painting in Apulia.
40. J. de Contrera, *Historia del Arte Hispànico*, Barcelona, 1934, p. 344, pl. xxiv, with further literature. I owe this reference to Professor Pächt.

The peculiar blend of Eastern and Western elements in the painting now in Sta. Croce makes one think of Latin outposts in the Near East, or, better, of some Eastern settlement on the western coasts. There are certainly no connections with the group of manuscripts and icons studied by Buchthal[41] and Weitzmann,[42] which are of a much earlier date; nor can I point, as far as I know, to any affinity with the icons produced in Cyprus during the fourteenth century.[43] On the other side, it seems too hazardous to compare our small icon with the mosaics in the Baptistry and in the chapel of St. Isidore in San Marco, although these are apt to provide us with an excellent reference position with respect to the *Zeitstil* of the Sta. Croce painting. No more conclusive are comparisons with the frescoes in Apulian crypts.[44] Thus I am afraid one has to leave the painting aside, among the 'quadri senza casa'. To sum up, I feel rather inclined to believe that the Sta. Croce mosaic is a Byzantine work of the late thirteenth or early fourteenth century; that it was very likely brought to Mount Sinai before 1380–1381, when it came to Italy; and that it was finally given to the church of Sta. Croce in Gerusalemme as late as 1385–1386.

If these data are correct, they may modify the current views on the origins of the Mass of St. Gregory. For one thing, we no longer have to look for a supposed sixth–seventh century prototype in Rome, of which the mosaic icon would be a copy. When the mosaic was imported to Rome, the iconography of the great *Basileus tes doxes*, the Western *Man of Sorrows*, was so widespread and so popular throughout Europe that the mosaic cannot be claimed to be the first image to have introduced these features into the West.[44b] As it is, before going farther, we have first to ascertain whether it is really to this mosaic and to this church that references are made in the early versions of the legend.

* * *

The earliest references to the Mass of St. Gregory, collected by Endres in his pioneer article published in 1917,[45] are to be found in some indulgence charts. They describe where the miracle took place, because their purpose is to assure the pious onlooker that a few prayers recited in front of the image provided an easy substitute for a pilgrimage to the holy place itself.

The oldest text, inscribed on a relief in Regensburg,[46] from the beginning of the fifteenth century, is rather laconic: 'Wer dies figur ert mit einem Pater Noster und ave maria, der hat uon der erscheinung dy s. gregorius erschien in ainer kirchen haist porta cruc. denselben aplas derselben kirchen.' Other texts give more information: 'Unser herr ihesus'—declares a relief of 1428 in Münnerstadt[47]—'erscheint sant greiorio v rom i der burg, di man nent porta crucis uf dem altar iherusalem.' In 1448 a relief in Karlstadt am Main[48] uses more words: the miracle, it says, happened 'in der borg die man da nennet auria vor dem Altar Jehrusalem'. According to a Latin manuscript of 1475, which Abbot Besozzi—the author of a monograph published in 1750 on Sta. Croce in Gerusalemme—had acquired for the convent's library, 'Reperitur in caeremoniis Romanorum, quod D.N.J.Ch. . . . semel apparuit in specie pastoris[49] sub effigie pietatis beato Gregorio celebranti super altare Jerusalem in ecclesia s. Crucis.'[50] Finally, the engraving by Israhel van Meckenem, already referred to, reproduces precisely the Sta. Croce mosaic, with the legend: 'Hec imago contrefacta est ad instar et similitudinem illius primae imaginis pietatis custoditae in ecclesia sanctae crucis in urbe Romana, quam fecerat pingi ss. Gregorius pontifex . . . propter habitam ac sibi ostensam desuper visionem.'[51]

All the authors who tried to make sense out of these distant sources concluded that they all referred to a common place, namely the church of Sta. Croce, although under a variety of denominations. But lately R. Bauerreis,[52] the learned Benedictine from Munich, submitted all these sources to systematic criticism. The engraving of 1495 excepted, none of them, he says, can be taken as a certain reference to Sta. Croce;

41. H. Buchthal, *Miniature Painting in the Latin Kingdom of Jerusalem*, Oxford, 1957.
42. K. Weitzmann, *op. cit.*
43. D. Talbot Rice, *The Icons of Cyprus*, London, 1937.
44. A. Medea, *Gli affreschi delle cripte eremitiche pugliesi*, Rome, 1939.
44b. The memorable exhibition *Europäische Kunst um 1400*, Vienna, 1962, counted no less than seventeen items which were more or less related to the representation of the Man of Sorrows. Significant is the frequent appearance of the *Image of Pity* in the representations of altars in the Coronation Book of Charles V, dated A.D. 1365 (British Museum, Cotton MS. Tib. B. VIII, fol. 46, 47 v, 48, 50 v, 51, 54 v, 56, 57, 59, 64). E. Panofsky, 'Imago Pietatis', in *Festschrift für M. J. Friedländer zum 60. Geburtstage*, Leipzig, 1927, pp. 261 ff., has acutely interpreted the relevance of the *Imago Pietatis* to the *Andachtsbild* practice and theory.

45. See note 1.
46. J. R. Scheergraf, *Geschichte des Doms von Regensburg*, Regensburg, 1849, II, pl. IX; Endres, *op. cit.*, p. 148.
47. *Kunstdenkmäler Bayerns*, X, 166.
48. *Ibid.*, VI, 97.
49. A German fifteenth-century engraving, formerly in the Kupferstichkabinett in Berlin (Schreiber, *Manuel*, III, nos. 2645 and 2646), is inscribed 'in specie ignis'. Bauerreiss, *op. cit.*, 1960, p. 63, correctly assumes that both the engraving and the lost manuscript derive from the same source. See also note 65.
50. R. Besozzi, *La storia della basilica di S. Croce in Gerusalemme*, Rome, 1750, p. 149.
51. See note 2.
52. *Op. cit.*, 1960 (see note 1).

moreover, he continues, apart from the confused inscriptions from Bavaria, or in a lost manuscript of 1475, no-one ever heard of the Sta. Croce miracle before 1495. Accurate descriptions of Rome in the fifteenth century simply ignore it.

One of the most curious of these travel-books, written by a Nuremberg patrician, Nikolaus Muffel, after a journey in 1452,[53] not only ignores the miracle of Sta. Croce but, as Bauerreis points out, seems to play with the same words of the German indulgence charts when he refers to some precious relics in St. Peter's.[54] There Muffel saw the 'gulden pfort, dadurch Christus das heylig creutz getragen hat', which Bauerreiss identifies with the 'Porta Crucis' and the '(Porta) Auria' of the inscriptions quoted above. Then, Muffel continues, as one goes into the church ('als man in das münster geet'), besides several wonderful things, one sees in front of the door ('vor dem thor') two silver crosses: one is on the tomb of Saints Peter and Paul and gives seventeen years of indulgence to everyone who kisses it; over the other 'stet da heylig sacrament, das sich verwandelt in fleisch, do sant Gregorius mass hielt'. That, Bauerreiss concludes, ought to be a Mass of St. Gregory.[55]

There are, however, other pieces of evidence which have escaped notice up to now; they seem to indicate that, at the time of Muffel's visit and in spite of his silence, the legend was already connected with Sta. Croce.

In the year 1454 the monks of the charterhouse of Villeneuve-lès-Avignon put Enguerrand Charonton's celebrated painting of the *Crowning of the Virgin* on the altar of the 'sainte cité' in their church.[56] The theological program of this masterpiece is to connect the celestial event with the salvation and the damnation of mankind. The souls of the damned and of those who still suffer in Purgatory are shown under the rocky crust of the earth, while Christ crowns His Mother in Heaven; above, at the two sides of the Crucifix, in front of which a Carthusian monk is kneeling, the two towns of Rome and Jerusalem are depicted. The view of Rome is no less imaginative than that of Jerusalem: St. Peter's is just a gothic cathedral, Castel Sant'Angelo a circular *donjon*. The most prominent feature of the townscape is a huge church near the walls. The building is represented so as to show a view of both the interior and the exterior. Inside one sees a number of Carthusian monks attending a service celebrated by a saintly pope, in front of whom is Christ, His hands crossed in the familiar pose of the *Man of Sorrows*. There can be no doubt that the church depicted here is the Carthusian church in Rome, namely Sta. Croce in Gerusalemme[56b] (Fig. 21). There are more references to the Man of Sorrows, from the fifteenth century, that can be connected with the Carthusians—a connection which did not escape Campbell Dodgson.[57]

---

53. W. Vogt, *Nikolaus Muffels Beschreibung der Stadt Rom*, Stuttgart, 1886.

54. Bauerreiss, *op. cit.*, 1960, pp. 61 ff.; Vogt, *ibid.*, pp. 17 ff.

55. Bauerreiss, *op. cit.*, p. 62: 'Man wird sich "das heylig Sacrament, das ob demselben creutz stet" kaum anders vorstellen können als eben eine "Gregoriusmesse".' I wonder whether we really have to imagine a *Mass of St. Gregory*. What Muffel was shown was possibly a miraculous host, possibly exhibited in a monstrance, and not a figure of the *Man of Sorrows*; in any case not a *Mass of St. Gregory*. The Monk of Whitby, followed by Paulus Diaconus and by Johannes Diaconus (F. A. Gasquet, *A Life of Pope St. Gregory the Great, written by a Monk of the Monastery of Whitby*, Westminster, 1904; cf. *Acta Sanctorum*, Mens. Martii, 12, Anon. Auctor, IV, 19) relates the miracle of a host which changed into a bleeding phalanx during a mass of St. Gregory's. Two hosts with the imprint of the cross have been preserved in Andechs, Bavaria, since at least 1182 and are known as the 'sacramentum Gregorii'. (They are preserved together with a third host, bearing the imprint of a bleeding phalanx, which is supposed to be the imprint of a miracle that occurred in Bamberg in 1051.) After having been missed for a considerable time, the three hosts were miraculously found again in 1388, and in 1392 they were exhibited in Munich in the ducal chapel of the Alt Hof. Duke Albrecht III returned them to Andechs in a Gothic monstrance, the same one in which they are still kept today. The three hosts are believed to have been found in a case which is painted on the inside with the figures of the Lamb and of the *Man of Sorrows*. These images may have been painted after the recovery of the case and, however, I would not call them a *Missa Gregorii*. A painting attributed to Michael Wolgemut, also in Andechs, represents the miraculous mass of a pope (Gregory? or Leo IX in 1051?) but does not introduce the *Man of Sorrows*. For an accurate description of Andechs, see R. Bauerreiss, *Andechs, den Besuchern des 'Heiligen Berges' gewidmet*, Andechs, 1925; cf. H. Schnell, *Wallfahrtkirche Andechs*, Kunstführer no. 394, 1939, 5th ed., Munich, 1960. On the three hosts and their relationship with the *Man of*

Sorrows see the fundamental studies by Father Bauerreiss: 'Der "gregorianische Schmerzensmann" und das "Sacramentum s. Gregorii" in Andechs', *Studien und Mitteilungen zur Geschichte des Benediktinerordens*, XLIV, 1926, pp. 57 ff.; *Pie Jesu. Das Schmerzensmannbild und sein Einfluss auf die mittelalterliche Frömmigkeit*, Munich, 1931. On eucharistic miracles in general see: P. Browe, S.J., 'Die eucharistischen Wunder des Mittelalters', *Breslauer Studien zur historischen Theologie*, N.F., IV, 1938.

56. Ch. Sterling, *Chefs-d'œuvre des Primitifs Français: Le Couronnement de la Vierge par E. Quarton*, Paris, 1939, with further literature. The painting was ordered from Charonton by Jean de Montagnac on April 23, 1453, and was finished before September 1454. See also G. Ring, *La peinture française du quinzième siècle*, London, 1949, pp. 209–10, cat. no. 116.

56b. The contract for the painting, reproduced by Sterling, *op. cit.*, p. 25, n. 4, indicates the church *apertis verbis*: 'l'église Sainte-Croix de Jerusalem où saint Grégoire celebra et lui apparut Notre Seigneur en forme de pitié en la quelle sera peinte l'istoire selon l'ordonnement dudit maistre Enguerrant, en la quelle ystoire sera sainct Hugue chartreux assistant audit saint Grégoire avec autres prélatz'.

57. Campbell Dodgson, 'English Devotional Woodcuts of the Late Fifteenth Century, with Special Reference to Those in the Bodleian Library', *Walpole Society*, XVII, pp. 94 ff.; cf. also *id., Woodcuts of the XV Century in the Department of Prints and*

A woodcut by Caxton, which he discovered pasted into a miscellaneous volume in the University Library, Cambridge (Inc.5.F.6.3), shows the *Image of Pity* surrounded by a frame displaying the *Arma Christi* and a Carthusian monk devoutly kneeling in front of it. The print is stuck to the last, blank leaf of a printed Antwerp edition of 1487 (M. van der Goes) of the *Colloquium Peccatoris et Crucifixi Jhesu Christi*. The print is dated by Dodgson, on several grounds, to 1492, i.e., to the same year in which is dated another, manu-script, text bound in the same volume, a text which was transcribed in the London Charterhouse.[58] Another woodcut in a primer printed by Caxton about the year 1487, now in the Print Room of the British Museum, does not introduce the figure of a Carthusian monk, but besides the usual list of indulgences,[59] it does show an inscription on the cross, Ó : BĀCíΛEVS hōrá:3á, that is an attempt at transcribing the original Greek in a form very close to that of the engraving by Israhel van Meckenem. With other details, it points to the same source, the mosaic in Sta. Croce[60] (Fig. 8).

Finally, thanks to the great kindness of Francis Wor-mald, I can here add one more piece of evidence which seems to stamp the final seal on these English connec-tions. A British Museum MS., Add. 37049, is a MS. in Middle-English of the fifteenth century. Its content is a very peculiar miscellany of symbols of pity and devotion, a curious cross-section of popular and religious practices otherwise seldom documented, in-cluding, among other things, the exact reproduction of Christ's wounds according to their size (fol. 20) and a Chart of Human Redemption (fol. 23). On fol. 22 we read a poem on the Carthusian Order, and Carthusian monks are found in large numbers in the many boldly coloured illustrations. Beyond any doubt, this is a Carthusian manuscript, and it is with good reasons that its origin has been sought in the south of England, with most probability in Sheene.[61]

The first two sheets of the MS., consisting now of two different pages of parchment, are deliberately intended to form a diptych, constituting a sort of solemn and devout introduction to the book (Figs. 14 and 15). They both reproduce a well-known devotional painting (*Andachtsbild*), a circumstance which makes them all the more significant in the peculiar context into which they are inserted. The bust of the Virgin on fol. 1 v, wrapped in a mantle and surrounded by red flames, goes back to an Eastern prototype, recently detected by O. Pächt,[62] a replica of which had been presented to a pope, identified as Clement VI or, more likely, Urban V, in Avignon. It is here to be noted that the Avignon gift was also a diptych, in which the image of the Virgin was confronted by the Holy Face.[63] In the Carthusian MS. we find, in place of the Holy Face, an *Image of Pity* (fol. 2 r) which is unmistakably a close copy of the Sta. Croce mosaic, and an extremely accur-ate one even in some elusive details, such as the inner design of the nimbus and the Greek inscription on the titulus of the cross.[64]

Even if the English MS. fails to give any account of

Drawings in the British Museum, London, 1934, I, no. 42, pl. LXXI; cf. Bradshaw, 'On the Earliest English Engravings of the Indulgence Known as the Image of Pity', 1867, reprinted in *Collected Papers*, Cambridge, 1889, pp. 84–100. I owe to Pro-fessor Wormald these precious references.
58. Bradshaw, *op. cit.*, p. 95.
59. Campbell Dodgson, *British Museum*, pl. XXXI c. The text reads: 'Seynt gregor' with oÞir'. popes.—& bysshoppes yn feer'. —Hauge graū——ted' of pardon xxvj daeys: 8 xxvj. Mill'—yeer. To Þeym Þat befor' Þis iy-—gur' on Þeir knees. —Deuoutly say I.v. pater noster. &. v. Auees.'
According to Campbell Dodgson, another woodcut is slightly older, one that is stuck in MS. C 939 of the Bodleian Library, Oxford, with a very similar figure into a frame displaying the *Arma Christi* and the inscription: 'To them that before this Yma-ge of pyte deuoutly say — .V. Pr — noster, v. Aueyes & a credo py- — tously beholdyng these armes of — xps passyon ar graunted xxxij — M,vij C. & Iv, yeres of pardon.' Of another woodcut with the *Image of Pity*, inserted at the beginning of a copy of *Directorium Sacerdotum* by Clement Maydeston (British Museum, Dept. of Printed Books, C.10.b.16; see Gordon Duff, *Fifteenth-Century English Books*, p. 81, no. 290; Campbell Dodgson, *op. cit.*), only the numeral *vij* remains from a probably similar text. W. Y. Ottley, *Inquiry Concerning the Invention of Printing*, London, 1863, p. 198, remarked that the first engrav-ing mentioned in this note had been previously seen in two other books, 'besides which, it appears from the back of the print, that in the first instance it had been folded, and that for a length of time it had been carried about by the devout possessor of it in a small pocket book'.
60. See the position of the cross, the letters ĪC̄ and X̄C̄ on the background.

61. This MS. has a wide reputation among students of Middle-English literature and language. It was first made known by Herrig, in *Archiv f. d. Studium d. neueren Sprachen und Literatur*, CXXVI, 1911, pp. 58, 360; CXXVII, 1912, p. 388; recently part of its contents has been published by J. W. Ross, 'Five Fifteenth-Century "Emblem" Verses from British Museum Add. MS. 37049', in *Speculum*, XXXII, 1957, pp. 247 ff. Of some interest for the art historian is the story about the monk whose enthusiasm for the Virgin cooled down when he saw an image of Her which he disliked, and, on fol. 21, the text entitled 'of ye fayrnes of saynt mary gods moder our lady', illustrated with a figure vaguely resembling a 'schöne Madonna'. The Charter of the Human Redemption was published by M. C. Spalding, *The Middle English Charter of Christ*, Bryn Mawr Coll. of Mono-graphs, XVI, 1914, p. 80.
62. O. Pächt, 'The "Avignon Diptych" and its Eastern Ances-try', in *De artibus opuscula in Honor of E. Panofsky*, New York, 1961, pp. 402 ff. It seems that the association of the Virgin and Her Son—possibly as the Man of Sorrows—was a favoured theme of diptychs: see K. A. Wirth's *Diptychon* article in Schmidt's *Reallexikon zur Deutschen Kunstgeschichte*, IV, Stutt-gart, 1958, cols. 61 ff. The 'Passion diptych' (*Passio Christi* and *Compassio Mariae*) is rightly connected by Wirth with the tendencies of the *devotio moderna*.
Also the presence of St. Catherine, the *sponsa Christi* and the patron saint of pilgrims to the Holy Land, could mean more than a tribute to a local saint.
63. O. Pächt, *op. cit.*, Fig. 1.
64. As noted before (note 17) the drawing helps restore the original inscription.

the Mass of St. Gregory, it certainly provides a precious clue about who was busy spreading the cult of this particular image and how they were doing so.

We can now confidently attribute to the same Carthusian network the woodcut in Caxton's primer with its faulty transcription of the titulus of the cross, very likely deriving from an English drawing similar to the one in Add. MS. 37049 and mentioning 'Seynt gregor' with oþir'. popes. & bysshoppes' in the list of indulgences which goes with it.[65] Two English statues from the early fifteenth century, now on the altar dedicated to St. Gregory in Sta. Croce, are perhaps a relic of exchanges between the English and the Roman charterhouses.

An indicative trace of the busy activity of the Carthusian Order around the 'Gregorian' mosaic remains at its very centre of origin. In a Carthusian Missal from Sta. Croce, now in the Casanatense Library in Rome (MS. 1394),[66] the Image of Pity on f. 191 (Fig. 16) certainly does not belong to the thirteenth century, as Bauerreiss inferred from the supposed dating of the codex,[67] but, as Vetter rightly suggested, to the middle

of the fifteenth century.[68] Its interest lies just in its not being part of the codex. In fact it is a three-fold sheet of parchment, as it were a miniature triptych, which was bound with the codex only when it was already considerably worn by use. It is inscribed with parts of the Credo and passages from the Gospels, with reference to the Eucharist. Though the type of the Man of Sorrows here represented is—not surprisingly—purely Quattrocento without any direct reference to the mosaic, all the same the 'holy picture' included in the Carthusian Missal seems to be only a late specimen of a sort which must have had a rather wide circulation.[69] So great was the impact of the Image of Pity in Carthusian circles that even visions of the Crucifix were interpreted as apparitions of the Man of Sorrows. Reporting a vision which, according to Dorlandus, had appeared to a Carthusian monk in the year 1367, of Christ 'in eo schemate quo . . . olim in crucis ligno pependerat, clavis affixus', Bohic is ready to inform us that there are 'nonnulli ex nostris' who affirm that 'in ea forma conspectum esse, sicut eum sanctissimus papa Gregorius inter Missarum suarum solemnia vidit'.[70]

In spite of such active Carthusian propaganda, in some distant provinces the name of the church where the miracle took place was chosen at random from among the most illustrious or the most legendary buildings of Rome. About the same years of Charonton's painting for the Avignon charterhouse, a painter, probably from Picardy, stated under his representation of the Mass of St. Gregory, in the cathedral of Burgos, that the event had occurred 'a rome e leglise nomee pantheo'.[71] But with the support of the evidence produced in favour of Sta. Croce, the confused topographical information of the German indulgence tables does seem to indicate a reference to that same

65. On the 'Gregorian' indulgences in general see N. Paulus, *Geschichte des Ablasses im Mittelalter*, III, Paderborn, 1923, pp. 247 ff., 293 ff. They would be worthy of a critical edition, as they have much more in common than is immediately apparent. From the German charts, according to Hind, *Early Italian Engraving, A Critical Catalogue*, I, London, 1938, p. 43, engraving A.I.44, derives a Florentine woodcut of about 1460–70, the obscurities in the text being explained by comparison. Oddly enough, the Italian charts are rare, and so it may be useful to mention here one that, in Sicilian dialect, is inscribed on a Quattrocento fresco in the church of S. Andrea del Priorato in Piazza Armerina (see: R. Delogu, *Mostra degli affreschi restaurati del Gran Priorato di S. Andrea di Piazza Armerina*, Palermo, 1963, pp. 3–5, with further bibliography). It begins: 'Summanu tuti lip[ecca]ti in—dulgentis concesi . . .' There are two more English references to the Mass of St. Gregory. One is a stone relief in Kirkham Chantry, Paignton, Devonshire (1490–1500), which seems to be connected with the German engravings (see G. McN. Rushforth, 'The Kirkham Monument in Paignton Church', in *Exeter Diocesan Architectural and Archaeological Society Transactions*, XV, 1927–9, quoted by L. Stone, *Sculpture in Britain: The Middle Ages*, Harmondsworth, 1955, pp. 223, 268, pl. 181). The other instance is in a fifteenth-century manuscript in Dublin (Trinity College, MS. D. 4, 3, p. 207: see P. Grosjean, 'Catalogus Hagiographicorum Latinorum Bibliothecarum Dubliniensium', in *Analecta Bollandiana*, XLVI, 1928, p. 94). It states that Christ appeared to St. Gregory, while he was celebrating the Mass, *in tali effigie sicut hic videtur depicta*, but in spite of these words, there is no illustration, nor, as Mr. W. O'Sullivan, the Keeper of MSS. in Trinity College, kindly informe me, is there any space left blank for any miniature. Therefore we have to take this passage as a copy of a lost, illustrated, text. There is also the usual list of indulgences, with the supplement of some days which *a domino Clemente papa quinto conceduntur*.
66. Formerly B.II.9. See: Ebner, *Das Missale Romanum im Mittelalter*, Freiburg i. Br., 1896, p. 158; R. Bauerreiss, *Pie Jesu*, p. 3, n. 5; Thomas, *op. cit.*, p. 67 (with illustration).
67. R. Bauerreiss, *op. cit.*, attributed the drawing to the end of the thirteenth century and supposed that it was earlier than the

initial in Clm 23094, which, according to Löffler, would be the first western representation of the Man of Sorrows. The thirteenth-century dating of the whole codex was already suggested by the eighteenth-century compiler of the entry on its first folio. The palaeographic elements, the initials, and the rough illumination depicting a Crucifixion in this same manuscript make a date in the late fourteenth century quite convincing.
68. Vetter, *op. cit.*, p. 199.
69. A systematic research in other Carthusian archives is still wanted. Particularly rewarding might prove the archives in the former charterhouse in Trisulti, which has not been explored for many years and which possesses many charts belonging to Sta. Croce. I have not found anything related to our subject in the charts from S. Maria degli Angeli (where the Carthusians from Sta. Croce moved in the sixteenth century), now in the Archivio di Stato, Rome.
70. Cl. Bohic, *Chronica Ordinis Carthusiensis*, Parkmonasterii, 1922, p. 244, 'ad annum 1367'. In the Casanatense MS. the crude miniature of the Crucifixion (see note 67) curiously reminds one of the prestige enjoyed by the Sta. Croce mosaic.
71. J. Lavalleye, *Les Primitifs Flamands—Collections d'Espagne* —2, Antwerp, 1958, no. 89.

church when they mention a 'porta crucis' and an 'altar Jehrusalem'.

The claim of Sta. Croce was, however, challenged in Rome itself. In S. Gregorio al Celio, the most obvious place for the Gregorian legends,[72] Muffel was shown 'der sal . . . so ist die capellen do im (Gregory) Christus erschienen ist mit der Zeichen und waffen des leyden Christi, da man nennet Gregorius-erscheinung'.[73] It would seem that the type of image referred to as the Gregorian one, very probably a *Man of Sorrows* surrounded by the *Arma Christi*, was known to Muffel and to his guide but that it was not kept in S. Gregorio al Celio, or, if it was, that it was very different from the type of the *Basileus tes doxes* in Sta. Croce. This can be deduced from the marble relief which Luigi Capponi carved in 1470[74] and is still to be seen on the Gregorian altar in the church on the Celio. Although the inscription on it refers to 'Gregorio I.PM. celebranti.Iesus Christus.patiens.heic.visus.est', the scene there represented shows an image of Christ pressing His wound, from which His blood is pouring into the chalice of the Mass. After considering so many proofs concerning the great reputation which the mosaic in Sta. Croce enjoyed in the early fifteenth century, and knowing its history, one would expect that at least this church had some historical or legendary connection with St. Gregory.[75] But it had neither. The only link with St. Gregory that I have so far been able to trace— admittedly a very loose one—is in the proper liturgy of the church. The feast of the consecration of Sta. Croce was on March 13, and was followed, a week later, by the feast of the consecration of the 'capella nostra Jerusalem', a major event in the daily life of Sta. Croce when the chapel was open to the public, although women were admitted only on the 21st of the same month, the only day in the whole year when they were so permitted.[76] Thus the feast of St. Gregory,

which was especially celebrated in the basilica,[77] immediately preceded the most momentous octave of the church. One cannot of course make too much out of this piece of liturgical information.

The 'chapel Jerusalem', or of St. Helen, where the reliquary with the *Image of Pity* was kept, was certainly a very impressive place. To reach it the pilgrims had to descend through a dark, narrow and bending corridor,[78] and when they entered the badly lit, subterranean chapel, they knew that the pavement on which they stood covered earth brought there from Golgotha.[79] The place was so much like Jerusalem, one was told, that a pope had died there because he had been not aware of this close connection. A great number of relics had been assembled in the chapel, described by a huge inscription ('da findet man den schatz der gnaden', commented the German Rombüchlein[80]); most of them were gathered in a single large reliquary, making a curious collection which was almost a materialization of the dominical insignia that were depicted on the glittering mosaics of the vault.[81] Topographical views of the Holy Land, like that from the seventeenth century which is now kept in the sacristy, probably aimed at underlining the sacred character of the place and endorsing the many indulgences with which the pilgrims were rewarded.[82] Even

72. F. Wüscher-Becchi, *Le memorie di S. Gregorio Magno nella sua casa del Monte Celio*, Roma, 1902. Cf. Thomas, *op. cit.*, pp. 58–59.

73. Muffel, *op. cit.*, p. 58.

74. A. Venturi, *Storia dell'arte italiana*, VII, Roma, 1901, Figs. 656–8.

75. Besozzi, *op. cit.*, p. 38, also sought some historical connections with St. Gregory. He found that the placing of Sta. Croce among the cardinal's tituli, instead of St. Nicomedes, was attributed to him. But there is nothing to support this attribution.

76. A short interdiction of women during the liturgy in Sta. Croce was already practiced at the end of the eighth century: see the 'Appendix liturgica in codice Einsiedlensi', fol. 87 v, published by G. B. De Rossi, *Inscriptiones Christianae Urbis Romae septimo saeculo antiquiores*, II, I, Roma, 1888, p. 34. See the 'Nota delle indulgenze' (Fig. 22), a parchment-covered tablet still preserved in the new relics chapel in Sta. Croce, probably copied from the original one in Besozzi's time (cf. Besozzi, *Storia . . .*, p. 149). See also the German *Rombüchlein*, quoted by J. E. Weiss-Libersdorf, *Das Jubeljahr 1500 in der Augsburger*

Kunst, Munich, 1901, pp. 188 ff. Cf. R. Krautheimer, *Corpus Basilicarum Christianarum Romae*, I, Vatican City, 1937, p. 178, n. 2.

77. I know of two calendars of Sta. Croce: one is in the Casanatense MS. 1394, already referred to, the other is in the *Liber Sacerdotis Hebdomadarii*, also from Sta. Croce, now in the library at Trisulti, MS. 2693, of the beginning of the fifteenth century. There are some slight differences between the two calendars; I hope to be able to publish a collation of both of them in the near future.

78. On this corridor, which at that time was not yet adorned with the majolica tiles we see today, see the article by Ilaria Toesca in this same volume. See also R. Krautheimer, *op. cit.*, p. 189. The original plan of this corridor is preserved in a drawing by Antonio da Sangallo il Giovane (Uffizi, Disegni architettonici 898; repr. in Bartoli, *I monumenti antichi di Roma nei disegni degli Uffizi*, III, Rome, 1922, CCXCIX, Fig. 489).

79. This is stated in another parchment, also exhibited in the chapel of the relics, which Besozzi assures us he ordered copied (Fig. 23; Besozzi, *op. cit.*, p. 146), and in a marble inscription on the floor of the chapel of St. Helen (the old 'chapel Jerusalem').

80. See Weiss-Liebersdorf, *op. cit.*, note 76, *ibid*. Incidentally, Burgkmair's painting puts a strong accent on the wide reputation of Sta. Croce as a 'treasury of graces'. An account of the relics preserved there, is to be read in Cod. Vat. lat. 4265, published as an Appendix to the *Mirabilia* by Parthey (see *Mirabilia*, ed. I. Ferrante Corti, Rome, 1930, p. 61).

81. J. Wilpert, *Die römischen Mosaiken und Malereien in der kirchlichen Bauten vom IV. bis XIII. Jahrhundert* (2nd ed.), III, Freiburg i. Br., 1917, p. 341. Cf. also Krautheimer, *op. cit.*, p. 168, n. 3.

82. The large canvas hanging in the sacristy has been recently restored by the Soprintendenza alle Gallerie. The numbers painted beneath the various scenes or buildings may have

the 'Gregorian' mosaic, as a replica of a well-known icon in the church of the Holy Sepulchre in Jerusalem and a memory of an illustrious pilgrim, enhanced the ideal connections of the 'chapel Jerusalem' with the Holy City.[83] In fact, it might have been presented precisely to this shrine just because of its connections with the *Sepulchrum Domini*. Finally, only the pope, we are informed, was allowed to celebrate Mass in the chapel.[84]

It would seem that all this would provide the right setting in which to stage the legend. In many fifteenth-century representations of the miracle of St. Gregory the Mass is being celebrated in a church filled with the symbols of the Passion, as indeed the 'chapel Jerusalem' actually was. But it will suffice to remember that the representation of the *Image of Pity* among the *Arma Christi* was already an established iconographic scheme long before our small mosaic was brought to Sta. Croce (Fig. 17).[85] To put things the other way round, the mosaic in fact went only in order to complete the rich collection gathered in the chapel. It fit perfectly, because it had already resulted from the same line of thought found in the complex array of relics and symbols there assembled.[86]

It has been assumed that the cult of the Roman *Image of Pity* and the related indulgences were connected with the celebration of the Holy Year. The pope Clement mentioned in many charters of indulgences has therefore been identified with Clement VI, to whom two bulls are attributed: the first, an authentic one ('Unigenitus Dei Filius'), confirms all the indulgences which his predecessors had conceded to the churches of Rome; the second, apocryphal, proceeds on the same lines[87] but, for the first time, mentions Sta. Croce as the first of the non-patriarchal basilicas which the pilgrims ought to visit for their benefit. As we have seen, at the time of the Jubilee celebrated by Clement VI (1350), the mosaic icon was not yet in Sta. Croce; but to anyone who wanted to attach to it an 'authentic' list of indulgences the name of Clement was bound to appear as the most suitable. And it actually was added, if indeed the manipulations took place before the Jubilee of 1400, indicted by Boniface IX, and after 1350.

There is one more interesting feature in the same apocryphal bull of Clement VI. This is the first bull to guarantee indulgences to pilgrims who would look with devotion at some of the venerated images in Rome.[88] The images mentioned are the *Veronica* in St. Peter's and that miraculous bust of the Redeemer which had appeared on the apse of St. John Lateran when Pope Sylvester consecrated the basilica.[89] To

referred to an inscription now lost. The picture is to be dated in the late sixteenth century (photo: Rome, G.F.N. E56441).

83. On the Jerusalem icon see the catalogue of the exhibition, *Byzantine Art*, Athens, 1964, n. 475, p. 406 (with further literature). At the exhibition, the enamel frame was shown, thus leaving the icon itself covered. The original icon has in fact disappeared (though there are still hopes that a thorough research may lead to the discovery of some remains of it), and the panel, as it appears from Kondakov's reproductions (*Archeologiceskoe pytemecttbie po Sirie i Palestini*, St. Petersburg, 1904, pl. LXV) and Mersmann (*op. cit.*, pl. 2), has been substituted for by an upright bust of Christ. But the inclination of the crossed nimbus leaves no doubt that the original painting was in every respect a faithful *Basileus tes doxes*.

84. See the 'Nota delle reliquie', quoted above. The original *Nota* was written after 1492, as it mentions the titulus of the Holy Cross, a relic discovered in that year (and the fame of which was bound to obscure that of all the other relics in the church). The same list makes a distinction between the two chapels: the chapel of the relics, above, and that of St. Helen, below. According to Besozzi, p. 31, over the door which gave access to the corridor leading to the chapel of St. Helen there was a balcony on which the relics were displayed on certain given occasions. The church underwent several restorations from 1470 on (see Bohic, *op. cit.*, III, pp. 231, 232; IV, p. 443).

85. On the *Arma Christi* see: W. Scheffer, 'Das Wappen Christi', in *Der Herold für Wappen- und Siegelkunde*, 3–4, 1943, pp. 89 ff.; M. Mackeprang, 'Christi Lidelseredskaber, Christi Vaaben, En arkaeologisk-heraldisk Skitse', in *Aabøger for Nordisk Oldkyndighed og Historie*, Copenhagen, 1951; Ch. Carter, *The 'Arma Christi' in Scotland*, Edinburgh, 1959. I was not able to consult F. Wimmer, 'Die Waffen und Wappen Christi', in *Organ f. christl. Kunst*, 1868, pp. 159 ff.

86. Interesting analogies with the 'chapel Jerusalem' in Sta. Croce are offered by the chapel of the Holy Cross in the castle of Karlstein in Bohemia (J. Neuwirth, *Mittelalterliche Wandgemälde und Tafelbilder der Burg Karlstein in Böhmen*, Prague, 1896; A. Stange, *Deutsche Malerei der Gotik*, II, Berlin, 1936, pp. 19 ff.; A. Matějček and J. Pešina, *La peinture*

gothique tchèque, Prague, 1950, pp. 49 ff.). Even more than the chapel in Sta. Croce, this was a precious and secluded oratory, covered with golden vaults, the walls incrustated with shining marbles, and it guarded some rare relics of the Passion. Over the altar, over the locker which contained the relics, with Tommaso da Modena's triptych below and a representation of the Crucifixion by Master Theoderich above, there was hung a painting, by the same Master Theoderich, representing the Man of Sorrows in the sepulchre. It is surrounded by two angels and by three holy women, as it were a fragment of a 'Non est hic' scene, but the character of the devotional picture (*Andachtsbild*) is unmistakable, and it is stressed by the relationship with the relics. In fact it is as though the eternal image of the suffering Man had interrupted the narrative which followed after the Crucifixion. As the date of the paintings in Karlstein is 1357–1367, or 1365–7, and the mosaic with the Man of Sorrows arrived in Rome in the 1380's, in this case it is not Rome which influences the art of the North. The close connections linking Rome, Avignon and Prague in this period are a well-known fact.

87. Endres, *op. cit.*, p. 152; cf. N. Paulus, *op. cit.*, p. 241; the text of the bull was printed by Ae. Amort, *De origine ... indulgentiarum*, Vienna, 1735, pp. 81 ff. Vetter remarks that the Trinity College MS. D 4 mentions Clement V as the pope who granted the indulgences. Otherwise, a German engraving (Schreiber, *Manuel*, I, no. 918) calls him 'Clemens der sechst', and so do other sources.

88. Paulus, *ibid.*

89. Endres was wrong when he interpreted the words of the bull as referring to the Acheropita in the Sancta Sanctorum. On the bust of Christ in the Lateran mosaic see now O. Pächt, *op. cit.*, p. 407. For the aspect of the *Veronica* in the fourteenth century a first-hand document is the miniature Fig. 4 in the *Regula Sancti Spiritus* in the Archivio di Stato, Rome.

anyone who was zealous for the new charterhouse and concerned about its status as a place of pilgrimage, the thought may have occurred of producing another 'authentic' portrait of Christ, thus opening the way for it to be provided with a number of indulgences. After all, the tale introduced in Sta. Croce was no less credible than many others which were offered in several places of the town to the reader of the *Mirabilia* or were told in other churches to pilgrims like Muffel. As we know from Delehaye's research, this was a period which saw many a serious change in the way indulgences were distributed,[89b] transformations which must have been a blessing for the faked charters of Sta. Croce. These so bluntly break the limits established by the Fourth Lateran Council that we have to suppose that they must have run through side-channels, possibly an underground network, without coming to the surface until the legend was well established. The erratic propaganda for the Holy Year and the scattered outposts of the Carthusian Order joined to make the tale more vigorous and widespread. But even if the peculiar situation at Sta. Croce at the end of the fourteenth century allowed a powerful backing of the legend, there are many questions still open about the very origin of the story and its immediate appeal.

Endres[90] rightly pointed out that the main difficulty in dealing with the origin of the Mass of St. Gregory lies in the fact that it is not connected with any historical event or any dogmatic belief but is rooted in the unpredictable vagaries of folk-lore. Certainly, we cannot follow all the more or less individual acts of worship, the rumours and the pious tales which made the legend grow: still, there are a few tracks that can be followed in order to discover what we can about these obscure beginnings.

The legend of the prodigious Mass of St. Gregory, to which the mosaic icon is referred, has been considered to be the result of a number of other eucharistic legends related to this saint.[91] But when this group of legends materialized into that particular image of Christ, a significant, and probably new, element was introduced. While the other legendary Masses of St. Gregory are concerned with the power of the Mass in

healing souls in the Purgatory, or with the mystery of Eucharist itself,[92] here the emphasis is mainly put on the vision of Christ. The mosaic in Sta. Croce, we read in Israhel van Meckenem's engraving, was ordered by St. Gregory 'propter habitam visionem'. This was obviously the only way to focus attention on it: thus it might be taken as an exact counterpart to the venerated 'acheiropoietai' of Rome. It was not, however, an image made by no human hand, but, on the contrary, a man-made, carefully executed and historically documented reproduction of a vision of Christ which a saintly pope had experienced during his own life. So, though not losing its connections with the subject of the redemption of souls—a prerogative of the pope who rescued even the soul of the emperor Trajan[93]—the legend hinted at it in a subtle and new way, venturing on a difficult path. Could a man have a vision of God during his lifetime? The problem had been long debated throughout the whole history of Christendom and was a passionately debated one in a century during which even the possibility that the beatific vision could be enjoyed by the souls of the righteous before the Last Judgement had been put into question.[94] The 'locus communis' of all the speculations was the vision of Moses in the burning bush. Did Moses see God 'face to face'—as the souls of the righteous are believed to do[95]—or did he only see a semblance of Him? According to some authors, only 'a vision of a much lower order' was granted to the prophet,[96] for the vision of God can be experienced in this life only through a mirror or a fog, seeing, as it were, the sun through a cloud.[97] This theory, which was the basic idea of the fourteenth-century English mystical trea-

---

89b. H. Delehaye, 'Les lettres d'indulgence collectives, IVe, Les lettres collectives du XIVe siècle', in *Analecta Bollandiana*, XLV, 1927, pp. 323 ff.; *ibid.*, XLVI, 1928, pp. 149 ff. 'Les lettres collectives au XVe et au XVIe siècle.' The Great Schism must have carried great weight in this development. On the Avignon issue of this sort of letter see now O. Homburger and Chr. von Steiger, 'Zwei illustrierte Ablassbriefe in Bern', in *Zeitschrift für Schweizerische Archäologie und Kunstgeschichte*, XVII, 1957.

90. *Op. cit.*, p. 147. Endres speaks of 'bild- und bildsame Stoff des Volkglaubens und einer volkstümlicher Andachtveranschaulichung'.

91. Endres, *ibid.*, and Bauerreiss, *Der gregorianische Schmerzensmann*, quoted at note 55.

92. See note 55.

93. *Acta Sanctorum 12 Martii: Anonimus Auctor* (Monk of Whitby), v, 25; Joh. Diaconus, II, 44; Paulus Diaconus, c. 27. Cf. Dante, *Purgatorio*, x; Vincent de Beauvais, *Speculum historiale*, XXII, c. 22. The 'miracle' of Trajan was the subject of many theological speculations, from Aquinas to Bellarmine. Another miraculous redemption of a soul is quoted by Johannes Diaconus (I, 2) and Paulus Diaconus (VI, 45).

94. As is well known, the controversy was started by John XXII on All Saints' Day, 1331. Among the pope's most active opponents was Cardinal Napoleone Orsini (*not* Nicola's brother). On the theological issues, see: X. Le Blanchet, in *Dictionnaire de théologie catholique*, II, Paris, 1905, cols. 657–9; and N. Valois, in *Histoire littéraire de France*, XXXIV, Paris, 1915, pp. 551–627.

95. The expression 'face to face' appears in John's XXII recantation.

96. The problem of the vision of God in the doctrine of the Latin mystics is acutely investigated by Dom Cuthbert Butler, *Western Mysticism*, London, 1922. St. Bernard (*Canticles*, XXXIV, 1; see Butler, *op. cit.*, p. 176) was almost rigorous towards Moses, for the latter's daring presumption to aim at a 'certain great vision'; he says that the Prophet only obtained a 'vision of a much lower order'.

97. This theory was introduced particularly by St. Gregory. See Butler, *ibid.*, p. 127.

tise 'The Cloud of Unknowing', was brought forth by St. Gregory of Nyssa[98] in the East and by St. Gregory the Great in the West.[99] Oddly enough, the latter, who was apparently unaware of the conclusions of his Greek namesake, admits, in his comment on the vision of Moses and against his own usual doctrine, that the prophet saw the 'eternal brightness of God' by piercing contemplation.[100] It seems that this exceptional passage of St. Gregory's did not remain unnoticed by the person who gave instructions to Charonton for his painting in the Avignon charterhouse. Side by side one can see there God the Father appearing to Moses in the burning bush—actually calling out to him, 'Moyses, Moyses'—and God the Son appearing on the altar to St. Gregory (Fig. 21).[101]

The compiler of *Omne Bonum*, the English fourteenth-century encyclopedia to which we have already referred (B.M., Royal MS. 6 E VI), also contains a passage from St. Gregory which is worthwhile quoting here. It is the well-known account of the vision which occurred to St. Benedict who, according to Gregory's narrative, suddenly saw at dead of night a light shed from above and then the whole world, gathered as it were under one sun-ray, brought before his eyes while the soul of Germanus, bishop of Capua, was carried to Heaven by angels in a fiery ball.[102] *Omne Bonum* associates this vision with St. Paul's rapture to the third heaven, another *locus classicus* of the philosophical speculations on the mystical experience of the vision of God. In the MS. in the British Museum, the page opposite that with the two accounts of St. Paul's and St. Benedict's visions (f. 16 r) is adorned with a highly elaborate composition (Fig. 18), also known from another English MS. now in Glasgow,[103] inspired

by the two visions. On the back of this full-page miniature (f. 16 v, Figs. 19 and 20) is diffusely reported Benedict XII's sanction, of January 1336, of the beatific vision, i.e. the vision of God enjoyed by the blessed. This theological couplet is preceded (f. 15 r) by the display of the *Arma Christi* we have already considered (Fig. 17). Thus three different degrees of approach to the vision of God are shown: the first one reserved to the souls of the righteous; the second which can be attained through piercing contemplation by a few; and in the third place the more accessible *Arma Christi*, which occupy the lowest, and initial, order.

Under the illustrations of the *Arma Christi*, *Omne Bonum* reproduces the prayer composed by Innocent III for the *Holy Face*, granting a certain number of indulgences to those devoutly reciting it. But we have to remember that quite often the *Arma Christi*—as well as the *Veronica*—were reproduced with the caution that one had to look at them intently and devoutly in order to take advantage of the indulgences. It was just their contemplation that blessed one's soul,[104] as if their sight provided a sort of mystical experience free to everybody. Thus it was believed that the Saviour would appear on Doomsday surrounded by the *Arma Christi*, carried by His angels, with the outward appearance of the *Man of Sorrows*. Therefore the *Arma Christi*, along with the *Image of Pity*, were to be considered as the preview of the day to come, the expectation of the full Brightness of God which the repentant sinner could hope to see after the Last Judgement.[105]

98. In his *Life of Moses* (critical edition by W. Jaeger and G. Pasquali, 1921). It provided the ground for Gregory's allegorical interpretation. See H. Freiherr von Campenhausen, *Die griechischen Kirchenväter*, Stuttgart, 1956, pp. 114–24, with further literature. On the *Cloud of Unknowing*, see Butler, *ibid.*, p. 127.
99. Butler, *ibid.*
100. Butler, *op. cit.*, pp. 129 f. *Moralia in Job*, XVIII, 88, 89. Butler points out that in this passage 'St. Augustine makes his influence felt'.
101. The contract simply requested: 'et la aparut audit Moyses Notre Seigneur en forme de feu' (Sterling, *op. cit.*, p. 25, n. 4); but where other painters generally followed various schemes (in Froment's *Buisson ardent* the Virgin and Child are holding a mirror, meaning that Moses saw the 'Eternal Brightness' only 'in speculo', not in its reality), here above the flaming bush the figure of God (the Father?) is distinctly represented. The ambiguities (*in specie pastoris, ignis, panis*) of the family of charts of indulgences to which the MS. of 1475 quoted by Besozzi belongs (see Bauerreiss, *Pie Jesus*), betrays a theological preoccupation.
102. Gregorius, *Dialog.*, II, 35. On the significance of this passage, which is the only one where the pope relates the actual process of a mystic vision, see Butler, *op. cit.*, pp. 123 ff.
103. O. Pächt pointed out this MS. to me (Glasgow, Hunterian

Library, MS. W.3.4). According to Richard Hunt, it is possible to identify the Roger, who is seen kneeling on the Glasgow miniatures and to whom the general iconographic outlay is probably due.
104. See the frequent caption (also in Royal MS. 6EVI, fol. 15): 'quicumque arma superius descripta sive insignia domini nostri Ihesu Christi devote inspexerit a summis pontificibus subscriptam indulgenciam consequetur, etc.' Useful reading is provided by A. Rosenberg, *Die christliche Bildmeditation*, Planegg b. München, 1955.
105. See E. Panofsky, *op. cit.*, p. 299.
The Nuremberg engraving, referred to in note 87, reports a prayer attributed to Clement VI which begs Christ to appear to the repentant sinner as He appeared to Peter, to the Magdalen, etc.: 'O herr Jhesus Christus. Siehs an mich armen sünder mit zeugen deiner erbärmde. mit denen du angesehen hast Petrum im vorhoff . . . und mit dem gerechtem schacher in dem hymlisch baradeyse ewiglich dich sehen möge .amen.' Cf. Thomas, *op. cit.*, p. 69.
Finally I wish to mention a much more ambitious work of art also dealing with the *Man of Sorrows* and the *Arma Christi*. It is the grandly tragic 'retable de Boulbon' now in the Louvre. It comes from St. Marcellin de Boulbon, a church which in 1457 was annexed to the Chapter of the collegiate church of St. Agricole in Avignon, a foundation of John XXII. There the problems which stirred the mind of the founder of the collegiate church (whose coat-of-arms adorns the panel) seem to be acutely stressed. The donor, who is introduced by his patron Saint Agricola, kneels in front of a dramatic vision. Over an

This interpretation is clearly stressed by the representation of the Mass of St. Gregory on tombs; there the promise of sharing the same vision which the saintly pope had had during his mass becomes openly transparent.[106]

Up to now we have tried to follow through a certain process which seems to link together different elements from the cult of St. Gregory: his miraculous masses; his accounts of visions;[107] and his concern with the souls in the Purgatory. But in spite of all these elements I would not take them as firm evidence and would not claim that it was the concourse of these three ingredients together that accounts for the origin of the legend; nor does this process allow an attribution to St. Gregory.

In the vernacular literature of the Middle Ages the name of St. Gregory was in fact likely to be used as an overall denomination of a pope's—a legendary pope's—personality, just as, for example, Constantine's was a misused name for any sort of emperor. The complicated story of Gregory auf Stein, or the Italian *Leggenda di Vergogna*, is a conspicuous instance of a dramatic development for which St. Gregory was by no means responsible.[108] But what we can take for certain is that, even if at an indetermined moment a legend about a miraculous vision was circulating under the name of Gregory, the circumstances which we have tried to describe are likely to have corroborated the tale, putting it on a higher, mystical level.

As a Greek icon, the mosaic played a quite unexpected role.[109] Most likely, it had been placed in the 'chapel Jerusalem' because of its Eastern provenance and as a reminder of the Holy Sepulchre. But its origin was soon forgotten, and the long-established connections of the image it shows with the Eucharist, a theme which had struck western onlookers as early as 1054,[110] became almost unnoticed. In the late fourteenth or early fifteenth century its iconography was so naturalized in the context of Western, and particularly Italian, art that it could not cause any liturgical or theological question. But its unusual technique, its remote beauty, its intimately Eastern character, together with its location among an array of highly reputed relics in a 'Constantinian' church, were apt to stimulate imagination. The result was an exegesis, which went very far from the teaching of the Greek fathers, on the relationship between the painted image and its prototype.

---

open sarcophagus, surrounded by the emblems of His Passion, Christ stands in the likeness of the *Man of Sorrows*; at His right the Dove is flying, while God the Father's majestic face appears through a window. 'Salvator mundi, miserere mei' invokes the donor, while the Saint solemnly states, 'Hec est fides nostra', thus repeating the words of John XXII's recantation. This is certainly the most impressive illustration of the beatific vision and one of the most powerful elaborations of the subject of the Man of Sorrows in western art. (See G. Ring, *op. cit.*, n. 205, pl. 107, ill. p. 224.)

106. Many examples are gathered by G. van der Osten, *op. cit.* The subject of the redemption of souls connected with the *Missa Gregorii* is exemplified in Charonton's *Coronation of the Virgin*.

107. Not of *his* visions, however. See the spiritual portrait of Gregory traced by Butler.

108. L. Olschki, *Die romanischen Literaturen des Mittelalters*, Potsdam, 1928, pp. 20 f.; H. de Boor, *Geschichte der deutschen Literatur*, II, Munich, 1953, pp. 74–77. On the Italian legends see: G. Ciccone, 'Un poemetto abruzzese del sec. XV sulla leggenda di S. Gregorio papa', in *Bullettino della Società di Storia Patria degli Abruzzi*, 2 s., xx, 1911, pp. 93 ff.; A. D'Ancona, *Saggi di letteratura popolare*, Leghorn, 1913, pp. 47 ff.; F. Lanzoni, *Genesi, svolgimento e trame delle leggende storiche*, Rome, 1925, p. 63; P. Toschi, *La poesia popolare religiosa in Italia*, Firenze, 1935, p. 240; and G. Tomasetti, 'San Gregorio e la leggenda', in *Rivista di Archeologia Cristiana*, xiv, 1937. My friend Tilmann Buddensieg informs me that during the Renaissance St. Gregory was the subject of fierce attacks by the humanists, partly based on his own teaching—on image worship and on pagan cult places—and partly influenced by the strange

legends which were following his name. An echo of the Gregorian controversies is still found in the seventeenth century: Io. H. Gradonici (Gradenigo) *S. Gregorius Magnus Pontifex Romanus a criminationibus Casimiri Oudini vindicatus*, Rome, 1753 (against C. Oudinus [Oudin], *De scriptoribus ecclesiasticis a Bellarmino et aliis omissis*, Paris, 1686).

Fantastic legends about St. Gregory flourished in Ireland. See J. Vendryes, 'Betha Grighora', in *Revue Celtique*, xii, 1925, pp. 119 ff. Cf. P. Grosjean's review in *Analecta Bollandiana*, xlv, 1927, p. 167.

109. The Greek attitude to icons has been admirably investigated by A. Grabar, *L'iconoclasme byzantin*, Paris, 1957; E. Kitzinger, 'The Cult of Images in the Age Before Iconoclasm', in *Dumbarton Oaks Papers*, viii, 1954, pp. 85 ff.; and G. Ladner, 'The Concept of Image in the Greek Fathers', *ibid.*, pp. 1 ff.

110. Vetter, *op. cit.*, p. 215, points out that the origins of the *Image of Pity* in Byzantine art are to be sought in the same school of thought in which originated the representation of the dead Christ in the Crucifixion, a subject that scandalized Cardinal Humbert de Silva Candida and was one of the causes of the schism. The title *Basileus tes doxes*, which marked the Byzantine *Image of Pity*, was originally applied to the Crucifix, as is documented by the famous ivory triptych in the Cabinet des Médailles (A. Goldschmidt and K. Weitzmann, *Die Byzant. Elfenbeinskulpturen*, Berlin, 1934, no. xx). See L. H. Grondijs, *L'iconographie byzantine du Crucifié mort sur la croix*, Leyden, 1941; and P. Thoby, *Le Crucifix des origines au Concile de Trente*, Nantes, 1959 (and the review by E. Lucchesi-Palli, in *Zeitschr. f. kathol. Theologie*, 84, 1962, 3, pp. 359 ff.). In Western eyes this devotional image had a two-way effect. It provided material for the raptures of mystics like Elizabeth of Schönau (see Vetter, *op. cit.*, p. 224), and it was used by painters as an iconographic scheme of the mystical experience of the vision of God. In a Passionary of 1293–1300 (Florence, Laurenziana, Plut. xxv, 3, fol. 183 v; see Vetter, Fig. 4), the image is somehow associated with a bust of St. Bernard. In a German Life of St. Augustine, from the second half of the fifteenth century (Boston, Public Library, MS. 1483: P. Courcelle and J. Courcelle-Ladmirant, *Vita Sancti Augustini imaginibus adornata*, Paris, 1964), the vision is attributed to St. Augustine. In a Hungarian MS. of the fourteenth century in the Pierpont Morgan Library (part of the same book is in the Vatican Library, Vat. Lat. 8541) the vision is connected with the story of a Dominican Saint (M. Harrsen, *The Nekcsei-Lipócz Bible*, Washington, D.C., 1949).

I do not know of any Greek icon believed to be the reproduction of a historical vision. The Greek fathers thought that an icon should mirror an unaffected, unchangeable, eternal prototype. Legends told of icons painted by hands not human or made by direct imprint on the material. Icons belonged more in the realm of intellect than of nature; and, if they acted as real beings, performing miracles on their own, talking, moving and so forth, this happened because they were nothing but an extension of their prototype's power. But in the story of the Sta. Croce mosaic the prevailing accent is a sort of realistic preoccupation with affirming that it was deliberately executed according to a vision.[111] This is a truly Western approach, marked by the same realism applied to mystical experience that made the Meditations of the Pseudo-Bonaventura or St. Bridget's Revelations such a rich source for iconographers. No wonder that one of the earliest representations of the *Missa Gregorii* may claim to go back to the founders of the new way of painting in the Northern countries.[112]

111. From this point of view the Gregorian legend was widely different from other stories related to man-made images. In the legend of the *Volto Santo*, for instance, Nicodemus is said to have carved his sculpture according to a vision he had had in a dream. In the Gregorian legend there is nothing comparable to the interior inspiration attributed to Nicodemus: the name of the artist remains unknown and what matters are the instructions he receives from the pope. Such an emphasis on the patron would have looked outrageous by Byzantine standards because the relationship between the artist and his work was thought of in a quite different way.

112. H. Beenken, *Rogier van der Weyden*, Munich, 1951; H. Th. Musper, 'Die Brüsseler Gregormesse, Ein Original', in *Bulletin des Musées Royaux des Beaux-Arts*, 1952, 3, pp. 89 ff. In the case of the Virgin in René d'Anjou's prayer-book (Paris, Bibliothèque Nationale, MS. lat. 17332, fol. 15 v), O. Pächt (*op. cit.*, p. 417), has shown that an Eastern model was chosen not 'to simulate a hieratic style', but to 'present a historically accurate likeness'. Byzantine art in the West was coming to the end of a path which began at least from the days of the golden Evangeliary of Henry III in the Escorial, where the cultivated Western artist had left to his Byzantine colleague the task of painting the flesh and the 'real' parts of the figures of Christ and of the Virgin (see Ph. Schweinfurth, 'Das goldene Evangelienbuch Heinrichs III. und Byzanz', in *Zeitschrift f. Kunstgeschichte*, 10, 1941–2, 1–3, pp. 40 ff.).

POST-SCRIPTUM.—This paper was already at the printer's, when I received from Professor Weitzmann the photograph, here reproduced as Fig. 10, of an icon from the Sinai monastery. It represents Saint Theodore and is attributed, by Professor Weitzmann, to the late fourteenth or the early fifteenth century. It should be compared with the painting on the back of the Sta. Croce mosaic-icon, points of reference being the punched background, the stiffness of the whole figure, the dry folds of the habit and even certain features of the face on both paintings. As it is, this new addition seems to provide some more support to the 'Sinai theory' and also some clues about the possible localization of this particular school of painting in an Eastern center closely connected with the Latin world.

MILLARD MEISS

The First Fully Illustrated *Decameron*

In the course of the fourteenth and fifteenth centuries the characteristic medieval enthusiasm for illustrated writings encompassed an ever-increasing number of texts not connected with the cult and with prayer. In Italy the great religious poem of Dante was multiplied from the 'thirties on in numerous illuminated manuscripts, a few containing a picture for each of the hundred cantos. Petrarch's writing enjoyed no comparable vogue, the one exception being a mural cycle in the Salone in Padua based on his *De viris illustribus* and an imitation of this cycle on the pages of a manuscript.[1] Boccaccio's *De mulieribus claris* and *De casibus virorum illustrium* not infrequently bore frontispieces, and at the end of the century one manuscript of the *Decameron* was even given an illustration for each of the ten parts of the text.

In France Dante was not well known, Petrarch was admired by scholars, but Boccaccio found an enthusiastic audience, which included the princes who could and did commission splendid illustrated manuscripts. Interest in three of Boccaccio's works led to a series of translations or paraphrases. The *Cleres et nobles femmes* was completed in 1401 by an anonymous writer. The indefatigable Laurent de Premierfait, who had written a French version of *De casibus* in 1400, continued to produce the *Cas des nobles hommes et femmes* in 1409, and finally the *Décaméron* on June 15, 1414.[2] Of the first two texts several beautifully illustrated copies survive and are well known from numerous publications. With regard to the *Décaméron* the miniatures in the manuscript in the Bibliothèque de l'Arsenal of around 1440 have frequently been studied and reproduced (Figs. 5, 10) but those in the earliest copy of the translation remain virtually unknown. Only one of the hundred miniatures in this manuscript—Vatican, Pal. lat. 1989—has to my knowledge ever been reproduced, and that one more than fifty years ago by the excellent Paul Durrieu, who identified the manuscript and announced his discovery in two short papers.[3] He claimed that the cycle served as a model for the manuscript in the Arsenal, and then left the matter at that point. Even this observation, essentially correct but requiring important qualifications, has been ignored in subsequent accounts of the much-discussed copy in Paris.[4] The present brief note aims to enquire a little further into the nature of the relationship of the two cycles and to locate the one in the Vatican on the pictorial map of the time. Some of the miniatures will be reproduced also, and in color, in the interesting volume that Professor Vittore Branca is now preparing on the illustrations of the *Decameron*.[5]

Durrieu proved beyond any possible doubt that the Vatican codex, though it now bears no arms, belonged to Jean sans Peur.[6] It appeared in the inventory compiled after the Duke's assassination in 1419. The manuscript in the Arsenal, on the other hand, though lacking in that inventory, is identifiable with an item in the inventory of 1467 of the books of Philippe le Bon, for whom it was presumably made.[7] Durrieu's belief that Laurent de Premierfait had himself written Pal. lat. 1989 was challenged by Henry Martin,[8] but regardless of the authorship of the script the manuscript is, philologists agree, the earliest extant copy of

1. T. E. Mommsen, 'Petrarch and the Decoration of the Sala Virorum Illustrium in Padua', *Art Bulletin*, XXXIV, 1952, pp. 95 ff.
2. In the *Cas* Laurent said the *Roman de la rose* served Dante (during a visit to Paris) as a model for the *Commedia*.
3. 'Le plus ancien manuscrit de la traduction française du Décaméron', Paris, *Académie des inscriptions et belles-lettres, comptes rendus*, 1909, pp. 342–50, and 'Découverte de deux

importants manuscrits de la "Librairie" des ducs de Bourgogne', *Bibliothèque de l'École des Chartes*, LXXI, 1910, pp. 58–71; K. Christ, *Die altfranzösischen Handschriften der Palatina*, Leipzig, 1916, p. 20, adds nothing to Durrieu's discussion. The manuscript is mentioned also by V. Branca, *Boccaccio medievale*, Florence (1956), pp. 223, 229.
4. For example, F. Winkler, *Die Flämische Buchmalerei*, Leipzig, 1925, pp. 29, 194, who otherwise gives the best account hitherto published of the Arsenal manuscript. Earlier Winkler mentioned Durrieu's observation ('Studien zur Geschichte der niederländischen Miniaturmalerei des XV. und XVI. Jahrhunderts', *Jahrbuch der Kunsthistorischen Sammlungen des A. H. Kaiserhauses*, XXXII, 1915, p. 320, n. 5).
5. To be published by Sansoni in Florence.
6. The first two words on the second folio and the last words of the text given by the inventory are identical with those in the manuscript. See G. Doutrepont, *Inventaire de la 'librairie' de Philippe le Bon (1420)*, Brussels, 1906, p. 160, no. 238. The manuscript measures 29.8 × 22.5 cm. A note on the verso of the first four added folios states that the old binding was signed by 'Stuvaert Lieum' (a famous binder) at Bruges.
7. J. B. J. Barrois, *Bibliothèque protypographique, ou librairies des fils du roi Jean, Charles V, Jean de Berri, Philippe de Bourgogne et les siens*, Paris, 1830, p. 185, no. 1262. The Vatican manuscript passed from Jean sans Peur to his successor, Philippe, and appears as item 1259 of this inventory (*ibid.*).
8. H. Martin, *Le Boccace de Jean sans Peur*, Brussels, 1911, pp. 10 ff.

the *Cent nouvelles.*[9] This view is, as we shall see, confirmed by comparative study of the pictorial cycles.[10] Apart from the delightful small portrait busts drawn, probably by Boccaccio himself, in the margins of a holograph,[11] the earliest surviving illustrations of the *Decameron* are the drawings in a manuscript written by Giovanni d'Agnolo Capponi, who died in 1392.[12] These charming illustrations, drawn in brown ink and shaded in the same color by one good draughtsman and his assistants, extend across the two columns of the text at the beginning of each of the Ten Days. The events they represent are drawn either from the first story of the day or, as in the instance of the Fourth Day, from the introduction by Boccaccio (Fig. 1). The scene at the left shows Filippo Balducci, who holds the hand of his two-year-old son, lamenting the death of his wife. Though the text speaks of Filippo's sorrow only, without reference to any other persons, the illustrator has taken the opportunity to introduce into the foreground a group that in arrangement and pantomime resembles one very familiar to him, the Lamentation over the dead Christ. The grief-stricken Filippo retires from the world with his son, and to the right they appear a few years later in the hut they occupied on Monte Asinaio. When the boy reached eighteen without ever having left the wilderness he persuaded his father to take him to Florence. The draughtsman shows the couple entering the city, their holiness signified by monastic habits. In the background rise the Baptistery, the Palazzo Vecchio, what seems to be the Campanile (though with a fanciful crown), and to the left of it the façade of the Cathedral, surmounted by a series of statues. It is not these structures that attract the youth but six wholly novel creatures who stand at the right. Informed by his father that they are called 'ducklings', the boy asks whether he might take one back to the mountain.

The miniatures in Pal. lat. 1989 were not made much later than these drawings, for Laurent completed his

translation, as he tells us, June 15, 1414, and Jean sans Peur, who owned the manuscript, died in 1419. The cycle of illustrations is much larger than in the Florentine manuscript: one for every story rather than for every day, and thus one hundred in all. Pal. lat. 1989 is the first manuscript illustrated on this scale. As in most large cycles the miniatures were executed by several painters, here however, as we shall see, associates in one atelier.

The painter who was asked to design the first illustrations of the *Decameron* had of course no representative tradition to guide him. The lack of pictorial models was as true of the French illuminator as of the Italian, because there seems to be no link between the drawings in ital. 482 and the miniatures in Pal. lat. 1989 (or, for that matter, Arsenal 5070). The designer of the illustrations in the Vatican manuscript, a master active in Paris, apparently read his text; that at least seems the most likely explanation in the light of at least one miniature, rather naïve theologically though effective pictorially (Fig. 2). In the fifty-sixth *nouvelle* Michel Fallace (*recte* Scalzo) tells his companions a tall tale about the antiquity of the Baronci family and their ugliness. 'Les baroncionnois comencerent estre au monde des que dieu comenca a prendre art de painture ... [ils] ont les visages bien [*sic!*—an error for *mal*] proportionnes ainsi telz comme ont acoustume de faire les enfans quand de nouvel apprennent art de painture. ...'[13] The illuminator transformed the comparison of God learning to paint with children at the same stage of development into a representation of the youthful Lord producing (with effort) the malformed Baronci on his panel while the adult Lord displays a specimen of the well-proportioned human kind that he has learned to design.

The less specific the instructions given to the illustrator the more he tended to tell the new stories with groups of figures from his repertory that seemed to suit. Rudolf Wittkower has shown us the consequences of this process in the illustration of the *Merveilles du monde*, painted by the Boucicaut Master and his associates shortly before 1413, where the fantastic creatures are often those familiar to the illuminator rather than what the text described.[14] We have mentioned the application of the Lamentation or *Pietà* to the story of Filippo Balducci in ital. 482 (Fig. 1), and we may observe the same resolution of the novel into

9. See for example G. S. Purkis, 'Laurent de Premierfait, First French Translator of the *Decameron*', *Italian Studies*, IV, 1949, pp. 22 ff. Laurent was unable to read Italian, so that he had the *Decameron* translated into Latin by Antonio d'Arezzo, and the Latin he then translated into French.

10. H. Martin, *Les peintres de manuscrits et la miniature en France*, 2nd ed., Paris, 1927, p. 93, for reasons not stated dates Arsenal 5070 between 1414 and 1420, though it was not in the inventory of 1420.

11. The manuscript has been published by V. Branca, *Un autografo del Decameron*, Padua, 1962; for reproductions of the drawings see Meiss (with P. Brieger and C. S. Singleton), *The Illuminated Manuscripts of the Divine Comedy*, Bollingen Series, New York (in press).

12. Paris, Bibliothèque nationale, ital. 482. See Branca, *Boccaccio medievale*, cit., p. 220. Reproductions of several of these drawings—which Branca is inclined to date a little after 1392—may be found in the first 72 pages of his book.

13. See the printed edition: *Le liure Cameron autrement surnomme Le prince Galliot ... Translate de latin en francoys par Laurens du Premierfaict*, Paris, Michel Le Noir, 1521, p. 69. All subsequent extracts are from this edition. I am much indebted to Mr. Lessing Rosenwald for having made accessible to me the copy in his rich library of this very rare text.

14. 'Marco Polo and the Pictorial Tradition of the Marvels of the East', *Oriente Poliano*, 1957, pp. 155-72.

the familiar, of the imperfectly understood into the habitual, in the early French illustrations of the *Decameron*.

The *nouvelle* numbered thirty-six by Laurent, the sixth story on the fourth day, tells of the tragic end of the love of Androlla (*recte* Andreuola) and Gabriel (*recte* Gabriotto). On one of the many occasions when they were secretly enjoying each other's company in her father's garden Gabriel fell to the grass gravely ill. Androlla drew him into her lap and there he died.[15] The image suggested by these lines is realized in a drawing in the first fully-illustrated Florentine *Decameron*, dated 1427 (Fig. 3). The painter of the Vatican miniature has given to this sad farewell the much more formal composition, widely diffused in the North, of the *Vesperbild* (Fig. 4). The illustrator of the Arsenal manuscript copied this composition (Fig. 5). Identical too is the subsequent episode of the intervention of the police as Androlla and a servant carry off the body.

Nouvelle number 26, the sixth story on the third day, is devoted to a highly successful though improbable ruse (Fig. 7). A Neapolitan nobleman, Richard Minutile (*recte* Minutolo), who has fallen in love with Catelle, the wife of another nobleman, has finally contrived to have a few words alone with her by joining a gay group that has foregathered at the seashore on a hot day. He persuades her to go to a certain bath,[16] where she will discover that her husband has been meeting another woman. Richard of course goes there first, rents from the bath-woman an absolutely dark room and, pretending to be Catelle's husband, shortly receives her there. The illuminator managed to show both important episodes in the story by placing the house at the seashore. To describe the setting of the second meeting as clearly as possible he has put the bath, which Boccaccio locates simply in the house, in the dark room itself.

The corresponding miniatures in the Arsenal codex, by a different illuminator than the author of the story of Androlla, are clearly related in general but very different in detail (Fig. 10). The sea and the strand described in both the Italian and French texts have been replaced by a meadow and a river. The view of the town has been shrunk to the room itself, still dark and with a tub, but now very much reduced in size. A woman bearing two containers of water, presumably for the bath, enters the room; all very practical but

destructive of the privacy of the lovers. Wrong, too, is the evident connection of the room with the street. Whereas the master who painted the miniature of Androlla in the Arsenal manuscript followed the Vatican composition exactly the illuminator of the Neapolitan story—the Master of Guillebert de Mets[17] —produced something different. This relative independence is puzzling. By good luck we can come closer in this instance to what actually happened.

The visual evidence is rather startling. For the tryst in the *étuve* the Master of Guillebert de Mets borrowed from another manuscript nothing other than the scene of the Birth of the Virgin, making of course the minor modifications that were needed (Fig. 8). These included the moderate enlargement of the infant's tub. There is no doubt whatever that the Master of Guillebert de Mets knew the miniature of the Birth of the Virgin. First of all, it is in the beautiful Breviary illuminated for Jean sans Peur and his wife Margaret of Bavaria, so that it formed part of the Burgundian library.[18] The *Birth of the Virgin* is one of several miniatures in the Breviary that were painted either by the Egerton Master or an assistant, under the influence of the *chef d'atelier* whom I have named, after this manuscript, the Master of the Breviary of Jean sans Peur.[19] The Master of Guillebert de Mets knew the manuscript very well because he himself early in his career added many miniatures in it. Thus the line of communication is completely re-established. It does not, however, tell us unequivocally *why* the choice was made. The new interior no doubt looked more modern, but the narrative was, we must admit, not improved.

We have already observed that the setting of the episode at the left failed to conform with the text. It does however follow exactly a note in Flemish in the lower margin of the folio that by chance escaped the usual erasure: '.j. mann enn .j. wijf, .j. man enn .j. wijf, staende neven .j. riviere' (a man and a woman, a man and a woman, standing near a river).[20] Now this description differs in two respects from both Boccaccio's Italian and Laurent's French. Boccaccio wrote that 'molte brigate di donne e di cavalieri . . .

15. 'Et [Gabriel] sans plus dire mot cheut tout plat a terre. Lors Androlla ce voyant bien esbahye se print en son giron et disoit Las mon cher amy quelle maladie avez vous Gabriel . . . ' (*op. cit.*, p. 49).

16. 'Bagno' in Boccaccio's text, 'estuves' according to Laurent (*op. cit.*, p. 36).

17. A well-known Flemish illuminator named after this manuscript, which was written by Guillebert de Mets at Grammont in eastern Flanders, according to the colophon.

18. E. G. Millar, *Souvenir de l'exposition de manuscrits français à peintures organisée à la Grenville Library (British Museum) en janvier-mars, 1932*, Paris, 1933, pp. 29 ff.

19. See Meiss, 'The Exhibition of French Manuscripts of the XIII–XVI Centuries at the Bibliothèque Nationale', *Art Bulletin*, XXXVIII, 1956, pp. 194 f.

20. Published without comment by S. Berger and P. Durrieu, 'Les notes pour l'enlumineur dans les manuscrits du moyen âge', *Mémoires de la Société Nationale des Antiquaires de France*, LIII, 1893, p. 28, n. 1.

andassero a diportarsi a' liti del mare. . . .'[21] By way of the Latin this became in Laurent '. . . sur le rivage de la mer Catelle estoit en deduyt avecques plusieurs aultres femmes. . . .'[22] The note omits Laurent's decisive 'de la mer' and substitutes for *rivage*, which could refer to the shore of a sea as well as of a river, the word *rivière*, which refers to the bank of a river only.[23] Laurent's text had already been written of course on the folios of the Arsenal manuscript before the note was added in the margin, so that the substitution was either inadvertent or the consequence of a misunderstanding of the corresponding miniature in the Vatican manuscript.

Who was responsible for the content of the note? Clearly the bilingual adviser of an illuminator who knew only Flemish. It is certain that this adviser was familiar with the Vatican manuscript, because his instruction 'two men and two women' follows the miniature in that manuscript and not the words of Laurent, who speaks only of 'Catelle . . . avecques plusieurs aultres *femmes*.' Perhaps then he mistook the sea or bay of Naples in the Vatican miniature for a river.

Below the scene in the bath-house there is a legible inscription also. '.j. man en .j. wyf deen neven dand in een bedde neven .j. badecupe' (a man and a woman, the one near the other in a bed near a tub of water). This is indeed what the illuminator represented, adding however the woman carrying water, who was not mentioned by the text either. Again he apparently did not see, or at least did not follow, the miniature in the Vatican manuscript, and, as we have observed, he omitted the town visible in that work.

Similar inscriptions are still preserved on three other folios, though I have not been able to study them.[24] It has not been noticed that all of them appear on folios painted by the Master of Guillebert de Mets or an assistant. Now the style of this illuminator is Flemish, he worked in Flanders, and he undoubtedly was a Fleming.[25] The miniatures by him that I have

been able to compare with corresponding illustrations in the Vatican manuscript are closely copied from the latter.[26] Either, then, he followed the pictorial model or the instructions of the adviser. He did not read the French text.

The performance of his chief collaborator in the manuscript, the so-called Master of the Mansel, was quite different.[27] The style of this illuminator derives from the French tradition, and particularly from the Bedford Master. Several miniatures by him, while following even in small details the designs of the corresponding scenes in the Vatican manuscript, introduce one or two differences, and in every instance these changes make his miniatures more effective—and sometimes even more correct—illustrations of the text.[28] Unlike his associate he probably could read French, and himself undertook to correct or enlarge upon his pictorial model.

Though the adviser was responsible for the error mentioned above, we have seen that he was familiar with the Vatican miniatures, and he also knew Laurent's text well. He felt capable of improving upon both. In the scene of the initial courtship of Catelle he instructed the illuminator (who, we remember, could not read the text) to paint on Richard's sleeve a motto and a badge expressive of his state of mind. MON ESPOIRE is written large on the sleeve, and between the two words there is a heart.

Neither the original text of Boccaccio nor Laurent's translation suggests such a visualization; it derives no doubt from late medieval chivalric and feudal practices. Mottoes were frequently woven into mantles, and a record of payment of 1414 informs us that the sleeves of a robe of Charles d'Orléans were embroidered with:

21. *Decameron*, ed. V. Branca, Florence, 1951, I, p. 369.
22. *Op. cit.*, p. 36.
23. See E. Verwijs and J. Verdam, *Middelnederlandsch Woordenboek*, and Godefroy, *Dictionnaire de l'ancienne langue française*, s.v. *rivage* and *rivière*. See also Du Cange, s.v. *rivera* and *riveria*. The connotation of river in the Latin *ripa* is retained by most of these derivatives, though there was some ambiguity in *ripa* itself from the time of Augustus on. In medieval Latin *costerium* was used specifically for the seashore.
24. The other three are on fols. 120, 128, 132 v. See H. Martin and P. Lauer, *Les principaux manuscrits à peintures de la Bibliothèque de l'Arsenal*, Paris, 1929, p. 42. None of these has been published by Martin here nor in his *Catalogue des manuscrits de la Bibliothèque de l'Arsenal*, Paris, v, 1889, p. 37.
25. See Winkler, *Flämische Buchmalerei*, *cit.*, with list of miniatures by him. Also P. Durrieu, *La miniature flamande*, Brussels, 1921, pp. 15 f., and Brussels, Palais des Beaux-Arts, *La minia-*

ture flamande. Le mécenat de Philippe le Bon, ed. L. M. J. Delaissé, Brussels, 1959, pp. 17, 21 f. Delaissé was the first to propose a specific date for the Arsenal manuscript: between 1434 and *c.* 1450.
26. Miniatures for *nouvelles* 4 (I, 4), 12 (II, 2), 24 (III, 4), 46 (V, 6), 49 (V, 9). The left half of I, 1 corresponds also but the right half is different, and less close to the text.
27. For this master see Winkler, *op. cit.*, p. 36, and Delaissé, *op. cit.*, pp. 22, 65.
28. *Nouvelle* 14 (II, 4): Landolfo clings far more effectively to the chest and he is correctly lifted from the water by his hair. *Nouvelle* 15 (II, 5): the latrine, lacking in the Vatican manuscript, is represented and Andreuccio rightly retains some clothing. *Nouvelle* 77 (VIII, 7): the courtyard is properly closed, not partly open as in the Vatican manuscript (Durrieu, *op. cit.*, 1910, p. 68, overlooks this difference and overstates generally the dependence of the Arsenal manuscript on Pal. lat. 1989). *Nouvelle* 81 (IX, 1): the guard with a lantern, important to the story, is represented. *Nouvelle* 86 (IX, 6): five persons are represented, not six. It is true that in the miniature for *Nouvelle* 69 (VIII, 9) the miniature in the Arsenal manuscript adds a hedge that is not mentioned by the text, probably to clarify the reclining figures in the Vatican manuscript. Furthermore *Nouvelles* 69 and 86, both illustrated by him, follow the Vatican MS. rather closely.

MADAME JE SUIS PLUS JOYEULX.[29] Occasionally in art the sleeve of a figure bears an inscription or an emblem, such as the wolf on the *houppelande* of Charles VI.[30] Perhaps in actuality or in plays figures sometimes wore emblems appropriate to a particular situation or brief inscriptions resembling the spoken words that earlier were written on scrolls.

The emblem in the Arsenal manuscript is especially interesting to an English-speaking audience because of the established metaphor 'to wear one's heart upon one's sleeve'. The image, extremely rare in German, French or Italian, was given currency by Shakespeare. In *Othello*, Act I, scene I, Iago says:

> For when my outward action doth demonstrate
> The native act and figure of my heart
> In compliment extern, 'tis not long after
> But I will wear my heart upon my sleeve
> For daws to peck at. . . .

The heart upon Richard's sleeve is only one instance of the much broader 'compliment extern'—the exhibition of the inner self—signified by Shakespeare's image, but there may be a literary link as yet undiscovered between it and the convention implied by the Arsenal miniature.[31]

At first sight the remarkable conjunction of subject and scene in the miniature of the *étuve* might look like the relatively innocent handiwork of an illuminator given scanty instructions and lacking, for whatever reason, his usual model (Fig. 10). He knew quite well, however, that he was illustrating a racy secular text, with which an episode in the life of the Virgin was not compatible. Could a half-hidden sacrilegious joke have been intended? The mode is not different from parts of the *Decameron*, and Boccaccio himself would probably have been amused.

II

Though illuminators of the Arsenal codex were identified, or rather reintegrated, years ago nothing whatever has hitherto been said—beyond 'French'—about the main master of Pal. lat. 1989. He seems to me clearly

the *chef* of one of the largest ateliers in Paris in the first two decades of the fifteenth century. In 1956 I listed around two dozen manuscripts that this workshop produced in whole or in part, calling the *chef* the Master of Christine de Pisan[32]—a name that is better changed to the Cité des Dames Master to distinguish his style from that of another important illuminator who worked for this author, and who may be called the Master of the Epître d'Othéa (Bibliothèque nationale, fr. 606). The Cité des Dames Master tended to specialize in the illustration of secular texts, especially of Boccaccio and Christine, but he occasionally contributed to religious books, and his earliest extant dated miniatures, derived directly from Jacquemart's style in the phase of the *Brussels Hours*, are in a Book of Hours of 1401 in the Biblioteca Central, Barcelona (Fig. 9).[33] In that manuscript he worked with the Master of Luçon, and this association—at least of certain hands in the ateliers—continued in later manuscripts such as the complex *Térence des Ducs* (probably around 1408) and the famous so-called *Boccace de Jean sans Peur*, actually a *Cas des nobles hommes et femmes*, probably illuminated in 1409–1410. The workshop collaborated with all the leading masters in Paris, the Egerton Master, the Bedford Master, and above all the Boucicaut Master.

Our illuminator learned from the Boucicaut Master the kind of landscape composition he employed in the *Décaméron* for the famous story of the encounter in a rainstorm of the jurist 'Sire Frosin' and 'le meilleur paintre de la ville de Florence nommé Iosse' (Fig. 6).[34] This is the earliest surviving representation of Giotto. He is an engaging figure as he moves along in the foreground in his borrowed, mud-splattered hat and coat. The illuminator probably knew who he was because he probably had visited Italy. The composition resembles closely several by the Boucicaut Master in the *Merveilles du monde*, illuminated shortly before 1413.[35]

'avoir le cœur sur la main' is normal), it may occasionally be used, as Dora Panofsky has kindly pointed out to me (A. Camus, *La chute*, Paris, 1956, p. 24).

32. *Art Bulletin*, 1956, p. 193, including three copies of Christine's *Cité des Dames*. I ascribe additional manuscripts to the workshop in *French Painting in the Time of Jean de Berry, The Late Fourteenth Century and the Patronage of the Duke*, now in the press.

33. The inscription, 'L'an de grace mil quatre cens et un furent faites ces heures par Colin le besc', was written on fol. 25 v, in the central part of the manuscript illuminated, I believe, by the Master of Luçon. The Cité des Dames Master illuminated (probably at the same time) a double folio (1 v and 2) at the beginning, and the last six miniatures beginning on fol. 183. I have discussed this important manuscript in the book cited in the preceding note.

34. *Nouvelle* 55 (VI, 5).

35. Bibliothèque nationale, *Livre des merveilles*, ed. H. Omont, Paris, 1907, pls. 20, 98.

---

29. L. Laborde, *Les ducs de bourgogne*, III, Paris, 1852, p. 267.
30. In a miniature by the Cité des Dames workshop in Bibliothèque nationale, fr. 23279 (1409), the King's mantle bears his motto 'James', and the wolf on his sleeve (see J. Evans, *Dress in Medieval France*, Oxford, 1952, Fig. 26).
31. Shakespeare scholars connect this passage with lines in Lyly's *Euphues*: '. . . if Thou pretende such love to Euphues, carrye thy heart on the backe of thy hand . . .' (*A New Variorum Edition*, 11th ed. H. H. Furness, Philadelphia, 1886, VI, p. 16, n. 71). See also the Arden Shakespeare, 7th ed. M. R. Ridley, London, 1959, XXVII, p. 8. What is common to the two images is pecking or plucking, not the sleeve. The heart on the sleeve did not appear in *The Proverbs, Epigrams, and Miscellanies of John Heywood* (1562), ed. J. S. Farmer, London, 1906. Though the metaphor is not established in French (the form

The Cité des Dames Master shared with the Boucicaut Master an interest in city-scapes as well as landscapes. We have seen a view of Naples and of another town in the *Décaméron* (Figs. 4, 7),[36] and there are similar representations—bold in their general conception though uncertain in linear perspective—in another manuscript for Jean sans Peur for which the workshop was largely responsible (Fig. 11). This is the well-known copy of Laurent's preceding translation—or rather version—of Boccaccio, the *Cas des nobles hommes et femmes*. The manuscript was probably illuminated during 1409–1410, as we have said, at the same time as the Duke of Berry's copy now in Geneva.[37] Thus the work was done about six years before the *Décaméron*.

The Cité des Dames Master was interested in the appearance of nature seen from nearby as well as from afar. He was attentive to phenomena such as the mantle of snow depicted in *nouvelle* 77 (Fig. 12). The footprints, the flakes glistening on the bare branches of the trees and clinging to all possible surfaces of the wall and house, are all attractively rendered. To this master must be accorded, furthermore, the honor of designing the first real snowstorm in the history of painting (Fig. 14). Like the snow in the *Décaméron* the representation here was required by the text. The scene, illustrating a passage in the *Miroir historiale* of Vincent of Beauvais,[38] shows Emperor Henry III witnessing an unusual sight from his palace window: at night a nun carries a cleric across the square through the snow. The illuminator has regarded the requirement as an opportunity, and depicted the snowfall lustily.

The five miniatures that we have reproduced from the Vatican *Décaméron* were not all executed by the same illuminator. The painter of Giotto and his companion (Fig. 6) was clearly superior to the painter of God as beginner and master (Fig. 2)—probably the result of an accidental allotment, but droll nevertheless. These two miniatures are on successive folios. In the first part of the book the best illuminator normally did at least the first miniature in each gathering.[39] Despite the variations within the manuscript the miniatures have common qualities that differentiate them from the earlier products of the workshop.

The miniatures in Pal. lat. 1989 are conspicuous for their pale colors and open brushwork (Fig. 6). 'Iosse' and 'Sire Frosin' are painted in gray and buff against a more strongly colored landscape. Often the relationships are reversed, and the figures bear the saturated colors. The roofs in the miniature of 'Androlla' compose a charming pattern of pastel blue, pink and green alongside the deeper greens of the hedge and arbor at the left (Fig. 4).[40] In the snow scene the walls are violet, the man wears purple and the lady green (Fig. 12).

This technique of pale wash was frequently employed in the last phase of the workshop, around 1415, the probable date of the Vatican manuscript. In a *Chronique de Normandie* in Vienna, probably painted a few years later, the orange-brown terrain and light green trees of the *Décaméron* reappear (Fig. 13).[41] The other forms are rendered in washes of pale gray, blue, or brown, brought up in small patches here and there to bright red or pink.[42]

Several scenes in the Vatican *Décaméron* show two interiors set side by side as two rooms of one building. A composition of this kind has notable narrative advantages, and it was indeed first popularized around 1408 by the *Térence des Ducs*, on which the Cité des Dames workshop collaborated.[43] The *Décaméron* also seems to take account of contemporary Flemish painting in its costumes (especially hats) and figure-types. Perhaps the illuminators looked at the very early work of the Master of Guillebert de Mets,[44] who later modeled his miniatures in the Arsenal *Décaméron* on the Vatican manuscript. The complexity of history is the handiwork of the 'players' no less than of the historians.

---

36. The most remarkable in his miniatures in Bibliothèque nationale, fr. 23279 of 1409. See fols. 5, 19, 54, 59 v, 65, 81, 119.

37. Bibliothèque publique et universitaire, fr. 190. The Duke received the copy at New Year, 1411.

38. Book 26, chapter 18.

39. Fols. 11, 34 v, 105 v. Fol. 65, the work of a less advanced hand, is an exception.

40. The strange folds in the dress of the woman at the extreme right reappear in the miniature on fol. 163 v.

41. For Vienna 2569 see H. J. Hermann, *Französische und iberische Handschriften der ersten Hälfte des XV. Jahrhunderts* (Vienna, Nationalbibliothek, *Beschreibendes Verzeichnis der illuminierten Handschriften in Österreich*, VIII, VII, pt. 3), 1938, pp. 41–43.

42. Another fully illustrated *Décaméron*, Vienna 2561, illuminated probably in North France in the third decade of the fifteenth century, reflects to a degree the cycle in the Vatican manuscript. Except for the first scene on fol. 18 the miniatures are by poor masters, and many were repainted later. See Hermann, *op. cit.*, pp. 64–86.

43. The *Heautontimorumenos*. See the ed. H. Martin, Paris, 1908, pls. XIV ff.

44. He painted for Jean sans Peur the Book of Hours, Paris, Bibliothèque nationale, Nouv. acq. lat. 3055 (see V. Leroquais, *Un livre d'heures de Jean sans Peur*, Paris, 1939).

OTTO J. BRENDEL

A Kneeling Persian: Migrations of a Motif

The migrations, transformations and re-uses of an identical motif found in different regions, in different contexts, and at different times constitute a special problem of art. This problem is of a broader scope—and implies something more—than the simpler and more direct relation between a copy and its original. 'Transformation' differs from 'copy' and, in comparison, is the looser term. Yet whenever among various manifestations of art we find reason to posit a migration, the members of the chain so described ought to be related in a manner more definite—more concretely traceable—than when we speak of mere influences. In comparison to 'influence', 'transformation' is the stricter term. Migrations of motif are mostly carried on by means of transformations, not straight copies. An instance of migration, then, in the sense indicated, is what I wish to add to the materials collected in this volume. The example chosen involves a wide sweep of art, ancient, Byzantine, Renaissance, and beyond; it also covers a vast range of territories. Nor is the case which I have in mind one of recent discovery. On the contrary, it has been under discussion for a considerable time. As the discussion progressed, however, it revealed complexities hardly foreseen at the start, or even foreseeable. This attending circumstance seems to me quite as interesting as the underlying problem itself.

Before turning to the case in question, we should also briefly consider the second term included in the above title, namely 'motif'. By this term shall here be understood the posture of a human figure, represented in a way sufficiently impressive to be remembered and re-used. by its inventor or by others. Such re-use, of course, has happened countless times, in many arts. There is no need to pursue the matter further as a general problem of art. But one aspect of this situation touches the present inquiry closely enough to require some attention. This is the problem of meaning. In the continued propagation of an established motif of art a question of meaning is also involved. It is true that, if the motif consists of a figure of an animal or of a human figure in action, as it does in the case before us, the prototype can, in the process of prolonged re-use, become regarded as little more than a patterned image or a ready-made formula. In that event, interest concentrates on the formal effectiveness of the proto-type, without regard or even awareness of its original significance. It would be erroneous, however, to presume that this prevailing formal interpretation of an image excludes the factor of meaning by necessity and altogether. Like other visual shapes, the images of human action may suggest multiple meanings.[1] As far as they represent specific characters—mythical, political, religious, or whatever—the primary purpose of such images is to show individuals: identifiable and nameable persons in a certain situation of their known lives. Not all representations of art are so specific, however. In other instances the same kind of images may render, not individuals but impersonal beings defined as members of ethnic or social groups, and identifiable by actions and situations habitually associated with their groups. Thus for example we recognize Greeks and Amazons in battle, even though we need not attribute personal names to them. Either way the images are apt to partake of still other categories of meaning, no less definite than their primary denotations but of different specifications. For instance human figures shown in action, quite aside from their personal histories or group characteristics, are likely by the same token to demonstrate human reactions to a given situation or manifestations of will and intent. The more impressively a certain image performs the latter functions the more it invites interpretations that dwell on these emotive qualities. What matters then is no longer the person represented as an individual in its own right, nor the tribe to which it may belong, nor even the history with which it may be involved. Instead the image, as it stands before us, becomes first of all evaluated as an archetype—a consummate visualization—of a certain human sentiment, passion, or emotion. We may assert that whenever this comes to pass the affective interpretation of an image of art has prevailed over the personal or historical associations that may also be connected with it. The affective —rather than personal—interpretation of given image-types must be recognized as a potent incentive for the creation of new art. A tendency to view works of art in this rather detached manner lies at the roots of the 'Pathos-Formeln' of the Italian Renaissance, to

1. R. E. Kantor, 'Art, Ambiguity and Schizophrenia', *Art Journal*, xxiv, 1965, pp. 234 ff. Ambiguity in visual forms: pp. 237 ff., with bibliography.

name one outstanding example.[2] But the same tendency can be detected in many other series of 'motifs', of the kind here contemplated, and in arts other than the Renaissance. Apparently in all such cases, the motif which the members have in common was evaluated chiefly as an iconic formula or archetype, expressive of a human situation. Thus freed from the specifics of time and circumstances, including the specific meaning of the original, the image as an established formula became available for re-use and a novel interpretation whenever and by whomever it so pleased.

Having stated these preliminaries, we now proceed with the particular case to be presented. Its rather unusual history in modern scholarship began in 1885, when F. von Duhn first noticed the similarity between the statue of a kneeling Persian, now in the Musée des Beaux-Arts of Aix-en-Provence (Fig. 1), and the kneeling figure of Adam in an illuminated page of the 'Très Riches Heures du Duc de Berry', folio 25 r (Fig. 3).[3] The formal agreement between the two figures is indeed striking, the differences of period, material and content notwithstanding. It is close enough to exclude all thoughts of mere chance. In addition it implies the interesting assumption that in posing his Adam as he did, Pol De Limbourg restored the left arm which the Persian now lacks, apparently on his own judgement yet, as we shall soon see, in keeping with other similar ancient monuments. Von Duhn's suggestion was in due time confirmed by J. von Schlosser[4] and, most recently, by J. Adhémar.[5] Thus the case was opened and, one may add, at once revealed the typical range of problems that arises from almost all such comparisons of art across the ages.

Of these problems one concerns meaning, as was already mentioned. The ancient statue represents a kneeling Persian. It is a Roman copy, the original of which probably formed part of a series of groups of battle commissioned by King Attalos of Pergamon and exhibited near the south wall of the Athenian Acropolis.[6] The group in which the Persian may have found

his place represented the battle of Marathon. The Attalos who commissioned it was more probably the second king of this name than the first, and the date of the entire donation may be set accordingly in the decade before 150 B.C.[7] The 'Hours' of the Duc de Berry gave the identical pose to a picture of Adam in Paradise. In this respect the contrast of meaning is a glaring one; the two themes, 'Persian' and 'Adam', are totally unrelated and incommensurate. Moreover, this discrepancy caused important changes. The Persian is fully clothed, Adam entirely nude. The former has a bearded face, savage, and distorted. The face of Adam is young and handsome. On the other hand the psychological significance of the posture, in either figure, is very much the same. It expresses defense, in a moment of danger. With the Persian we must assume that the threat against which he shelters himself, perhaps hopelessly, stems from a situation of combat. Adam defends himself against the temptation offered by Eve. In brief, the affective meaning of the motif was preserved in spite of the differences of illustrative content and in fact was interpreted in remarkably similar fashion by both artists. The proper recognition of the motif by the painter of the 'Hours' and its application to a story so different, meant a truly creative act—a flash of insight.

The other problem which the formal correspondence between these two figures involves is of a different order. An iconographic motif can only be transmitted through prototypes known by, and accessible to, those who transmit it. It is a demand of historical method that the accessibility of an assumed prototype must be capable of proof, or at least be made plausible. If one is not satisfied with regarding the similarity between the Pergamene statue and the work of Pol De Limbourg as fortuitous, he must ask what actual connection between them can be plausibly construed. This, however, constitutes a vexing question. The likely date of the 'Très Riches Heures' lies between 1413 and 1416. Of the three brothers mentioned as collaborators in this project, at least Pol, the master of the workshop, seems to have traveled in Italy, and especially to have visited Florence, shortly before those years.[8] On the other hand, the various statuary copies preserved, attributable to the Pergamene ex-voto, appear to have been found a century later in Rome, in 1514.[9] They have

2. A. Warburg, *Gesammelte Schriften*, Leipzig-Berlin, 1932, II, pp. 447 ff. Cf. E. Kitzinger, *Hellenistic Heritage in Byzantine Art*, Dumbarton Oaks Papers, VII, 1963, pp. 114 ff. For the methodical distinction between 'copying' and 'borrowing' see R. Wittkower, 'Imitation, Eclecticism, and Genius', in E. R. Wasserman (ed.), *Aspects of the Eighteenth Century*, Baltimore, 1965, pp. 143 f.
3. *Gesammelte Studien Zur Kunstgeschichte (Festgabe für A. Springer)*, Leipzig, 1885, pp. 1 ff. About the artist, possibly Pol de Limbourg, see below, note 8.
4. J. von Schlosser, 'Die ältesten Medaillen und die Antike', *Jahrbuch der Kunsthistorischen Sammlungen des Allerh. Kaiserhauses*, XVIII, 1897, pp. 94 ff.
5. J. Adhémar, *Influences antiques dans l'art du moyen âge français*, London, 1937, pp. 301 f.; Figs. 125, 126.
6. M. Bieber, *The Sculpture of the Hellenistic Age*, New York, 1955, pp. 109 f., Fig. 437.

7. Bibliography in T. Dohrn, 'Pergamenisches in Etrurien', *Mitteilungen des Deutschen Archaeol. Instituts, Röm. Abteilg.*, LXVIII, 1961, pp. 5 f.
8. U. Thieme and F. Becker, *Allgem. Lexikon d. bildenden Künstler*, vol. 23, Leipzig, 1929, s.v. 'Limburg', p. 228 (F. Winkler).
9. A. Michaelis, 'Der Schöpfer der Attalischen Kampfgruppen', *Jahrbuch d. Kaiserl-Deutschen Archäologischen Instituts VIII*, 1894, pp. 119 ff. Cf. Ph. Pray Bober, *Drawings after the Antique by A. Aspertini*, London, 1957, p. 82 and Fig. 117.

meanwhile become dispersed in sundry collections, chiefly in Italy. The statue now in Aix was acquired between 1725 and 1732 by the then French Ambassador to the Curia, Cardinal de Polignac.[10] It was at that time still in Rome. Thus the known facts, at least at present, leave unanswered the question as to how the motif came to be repeated in the 'Hours' of the Duc de Berry.

The case rested at this stage until 1954. In that year L. Curtius, without knowledge of the kneeling Adam in the 'Très Riches Heures', pointed out that two northern Renaissance paintings, one by a follower of Dierick Bouts and the other by the Master of the Lyversberg Passion, contain each one figure that bears a surprising resemblance to a different kneeling Persian; this statue is now in the Vatican (Fig. 2).[11] Both paintings represent the Betrayal of Christ; the ancient warrior was cast into the role of Malchus, protecting himself from the sword of angry Peter (Fig. 4). That Curtius was right in stating a significant similarity between the Vatican statue and the two figures of Malchus in the two Flemish paintings is evident at a glance; but equally clear is the typical relation of all three representations to the motif of Adam in the 'Hours' of the Duc de Berry. To that extent all these observations, though made independently of each other, corroborate each other. Yet, while they put the investigation on a broader basis, they do not make the case less puzzling. In the first place, we are now faced with two possible prototypes instead of one. Secondly, the chronological dilemma has by no means disappeared. The older of the two Flemish paintings, by Dierick Bouts or a close follower, which once formed part of an altar, must be dated no later than 1460. The ancient statue is a Roman copy, probably after an original forming part of the same Pergamene ex-voto as the Persian at Aix. Like the latter it may have belonged to the find of 1514, but the documentary evidence reaches no further than 1771. In that year the statue was restored by the sculptor Cavaceppi, who sold it to the Vatican together with other sculptures from the erstwhile Giustiniani collection.[12]

From these initial findings a definite iconographic type can now be established, based on the following characteristics. A male figure is represented kneeling in a tense and even contorted fashion. One knee touches the ground. The other knee is raised and the foot rests on the ground; in some instances this leg stretches forward. The upper part of the figure leans forward rather strenuously, while at the same time one arm reaches down for support. The other arm is held high above or across the head, which usually looks up and always turns toward the side of the raised arm and the raised knee. The result of this combination of opposites is a strong as well as a complicated contrapposto, contained in a distinctive silhouette which opposes a closed side (lowered arm) to an open one (raised arm). One senses in it the Hellenistic taste for contrasting directions and sharply set accents; the two ancient examples so far listed are actually traceable to Hellenistic, Pergamene art. There can be little doubt that we are faced with a chain of interdependent members, each one representing a more or less free re-creation of the common motif, rather than a sequel of faithful copies. Aside from the obvious changes of costume and context, one may notice especially that both knees are not in every instance shown equally clearly (Fig. 4); nor do the various representations always render the same view of the figure. Yet however it is varied, the motif retains the marks of its Hellenistic origin. Like many another ancient image-formula which the art of the Renaissance accepted and cultivated this one, also, had originally been invented for a representation of battle.

It is now well known that the various statues of the so-called 'small' Pergamene Dedication enjoyed considerable popularity among Renaissance artists. Signs of interest in these statues begin to appear in Renaissance art around 1540.[13] After this date a reference to any of them poses no problem of chronology. But when one believes that he has encountered echoes of the same statues in works of the Quattrocento, or indeed at any time before 1514, he deals with a more difficult situation. L. Curtius faced this dilemma most decidedly; it led him to the conclusion that the Persian, now in the collection of the Vatican, must in fact have been discovered some time before 1500. The suggestion does not seem altogether impossible since, after all, nothing is really known and anything may be surmised about this statue prior to its sale from the

10. M. Collignon, *Histoire de la Sculpture Grecque*, II, Paris, 1897, p. 508, n. 3.
11. Kneeling Persian: Galleria dei Candelabri, VI, 32. W. Helbig and W. Amelung, *Führer durch die öffentl. Sammlungen Klass. Altertümer in Rom*[4] (ed. H. Speier), vol. I, Tübingen, 1963, pp. 450 f., no. 574. Paintings by the Master of the Lyversberg Passion, Cologne, Wallraf-Richartz Museum, and by a follower of D. Bouts, Munich, Alte Pinakothek: L. Curtius, 'Wirkung in die Ferne', *Neue Beiträge zur Klass. Altertumswissenschaft* (Festschr. B. Schweitzer), Stuttgart, 1954, pp. 378 ff., pl. 86.
12. G. Lippold, *D. Skulpturen d. Vatikanischen Museums*, vol. III, 2, Berlin, 1956, pp. 436 ff., no. 32; Cf. C. Pietrangeli, *ibid.*, *Anhang*, p. 556.

13. A. Michaelis, *l.c.*, pp. 121 f.; drawing by Heemskerck, Fig. 1. For other statues from the same Pergamene dedication, now in Venice (first Grimani collection), see this author, 'Borrowings from Ancient Art in Titian', *The Art Bulletin*, XXXVII, 1955, pp. 121 ff.

Giustiniani collection.[14] But in the absence of any other evidence supporting the earlier date the reasons for ascribing the Vatican Persian to the find of 1514 still appear stronger; they are not yet invalidated. Nor is it the only possible answer to the problem, to pre-date the discovery of the Vatican statue. Another answer has already been forthcoming. According to T. Dohrn, neither the Persian in the Vatican nor the one in Aix can be regarded as a likely model for paintings from the circle of Dierick Bouts that date around 1450–1460.[15] Nor, we may add, do the known circumstances make it seem probable that either statue was accessible to the Limbourg brothers in the second decade of that century.

If their histories cause the two Pergamene Persians to be eliminated from this search, at least for the time being, alternatives nevertheless exist. Similar if not strictly identical attitudes occur not rarely among the reliefs decorating Etruscan cinerary urns of the Hellenistic period, as Dohrn has demonstrated (Fig. 6).[16] This new observation opens up interesting aspects. In the first place, the contribution of Etruscan art to Renaissance classicism has hardly as yet been assessed. When attention focuses more than it has so far on the Etruscan sources of Renaissance art, examples of their impact will probably increase.[17] Secondly, since much of this material was mass-produced in antiquity, it was probably available in some quantity also at later times. There exists therefore a statistical probability that the more frequent Etruscan urns instead of certain famous statues transmitted the Pergamene motif of the kneeling combatant to the Quattrocento artists of the north, and perhaps to those of Italy as well. On the other hand, if such was the case, our chances of finding the actual model—as distinguished from the general motif—of the Malchus in the northern paintings or the Adam in the 'Hours' of the Duc de Berry have probably diminished. Objects considered minor for their size or value, or both, disappear more easily than big marble, figures. One must assume that the Etruscan urns, owing to their relative frequency in central Italy and their often rather cursory workmanship, belonged to a group of antiquities which changed hands lightly, were sometimes admired and sometimes neglected, and were always in danger of being lost.[18] Yet, while

their reliefs often resemble each other they are rarely quite alike unless they were actually imprints of the same mold.[19] When their decorations were molded or carved by hand, variations rather than replicas resulted. In the latter cases hardly any specimen can fully replace another.

Here it may be in order to reflect briefly on the aesthetic character of the ancient objects themselves, that seem to carry so much weight in this investigation. It is not difficult to show that the Pergamene statues and the reliefs on the Etruscan urns have more in common than a mere similarity of posture.[20] The very attitude that their artists took towards the postured figure as a patterned image appears to be the same. Nothing shows this attitude more clearly than the obvious fact that the two kneeling Persians in Aix and in the Vatican constitute antithetical representations that repeat each other's actions in opposite directions. With respect to posture the statues in the Vatican and in Aix are twins. But each repeats that posture in an inverted sense. The ultimate reason for this arrangement escapes us, since nothing is known about the original order of these battling groups.[21] At any rate, both Persians must be judged as parts of one plan. The method of their duplication confirms this. It involves a calculated reversal of left and right just as one might expect in figures designed in relation to one another. With the Persian in Aix the left is the 'open', his right the 'closed' side; while the left is the 'closed' side of the statue in the Vatican. Thus when they were seen together the two were apt to enter into formal correspondence with one another. They also established a common connection with the human world outside them: both are simultaneously 'open' to the observer. The outcome of this rather complicated inversion was not simply a pair of replicas but two statuary variations of a common theme, with sides exchanged. A procedure of this kind presupposes a special concept of an image, in whatever art it may happen. Antithetical duplication attaches to the images a formal, decorative evaluation over and above their representational meanings. In Greek art the classical style shied away

14. C. Pietrangeli, l.c., note 12. The fact that Cavaceppi restored and sold this statue in 1771 does not of course exclude an earlier date of discovery.

15. Dohrn, l.c., pp. 7 f.

16. L.c., pl. 1, Figs. 1–2.

17. Etruscan revival in the Italian Renaissance: A. Chastel, Art et Humanisme à Florence au temps de L. le Magnifique, Paris, 1959, pp. 63 ff. See also below, note 18.

18. Etruscan cinerary urns: C. Laviosa, Scultura tardo-Etrusca di Volterra, Florence, 1964; bibliography, pp. 19 f. The most

striking, early borrowing from an Etruscan urn occurs on N. Pisano's fountain in Perugia: Pisano's 'Goliath' is a close imitation of the dying warrior to the right of the antithetical group found on many Etruscan urns, representing Eteocles and Polyneices. Cf. the urn in Chiusi, L. Banti, Il Mondo degli Etruschi, Rome, 1960, pl. 106; the identification was made by P. Jacobsthal, Early Celtic Art, Oxford, 1944, 1, p. 52.

Illustration of the 'Goliath' relief: G. Swarzenski, Nicolo Pisano, Frankfurt/Main, 1926, pl. 82.

19. Terracotta urns with molded decorations: C. Laviosa, l.c., p. 40, no. 4.

20. See also Dohrn., l.c., pp. 4 ff.

21. See bibliography in Helbig and Amelung, l.c., p. 451; also above, note 11.

from such configurations. Perhaps the underlying reason was the classical tendency to dissolve traditional, archaic, statuary types, and the ensuing emphasis on the quality of uniqueness, in images freely invented. The more it must seem a matter of importance that in the Hellenistic period the antithetical use of human figures did become an accepted device of Greek art.[22] This change of attitude probably came in the wake of an evolution, then already of long duration. A new trend towards standardization can be observed in much Greek art around and after 400 B.C., chiefly in the representations of struggle and combat.[23] The case of the kneeling Persian illuminates the eventual consequences of this renewed traditionalism. The image, a coined form, has definitely assumed the value of a motif in the sense stipulated above. It is now ready for re-use and variation. Within its own historical context, which is the series to which it belongs, each new instance of a motif so regarded by the subsequent generations of artists may fulfill a dual function, as a receptacle of past experience and a potential exemplar for the future.

Under the circumstances it is not necessary to assume that the statues in Aix and in the Vatican, or rather their lost originals, really mark the beginning of the series. It seems more likely that they, in turn, had forerunners in the High-Hellenistic, probably Pergamene, art of the advanced third century B.C. But it is a curious fact that the inclination to turn out variants with reversed sides comes to the fore, time and again, in the post-Pergamene history of this motif. The Etruscan terracotta urn at Perugia (Fig. 6) inherited this device, together with the kneeling posture itself,

from the Pergamenes. Surrounding the infernal monster that rises from what appears to be a well-head, two terrified onlookers fallen on their knees are rendered as reciprocal figures.[24] Their postures were clearly derived from the kneeling Persians, but the aspect in which each is shown differs significantly. The figure to the left retains the broad, relief-like aspect of the Pergamene statues while the one to the right transposes the motif into a more compact and statuesque form, seen frontally. I should add that, even more surprisingly, the ancient device of repeating this kneeling figure inversely recurs in the workshop of Dierick Bouts. The kneeling guard in the Munich 'Resurrection' (Fig. 5) is the exact counterpart of Malchus in the Judas episode from the same altar (Fig. 4), but with sides exchanged.[25] The compact, frontal position, which the several repetitions of this type from the circle of Dierick Bouts have in common, greatly strengthens the probability that an Etruscan monument similar to the urn at Perugia, or a drawing of such a monument, provided their immediate model. Moreover, the derivation from an Etruscan relief rather than from a single Hellenistic statue explains plausibly the variable renditions of left and right throughout the Renaissance tradition of this motif. The same theory offers a more comprehensible account than the comparison with the Persian of Aix alone, for the representation of Adam in the 'Hours' of the Duc de Berry (Fig. 3). This last figure shows the 'left-handed' version of the motif, to call it so. But there can be no doubt that it belongs to the same series of kneeling figures. In fact, the Adam of the Limbourg brothers gives us the earliest example so far identified in Renaissance art. He also represents the most naturalistic interpretation of the motif on our list up to now. It will have to be shown later that antecedents and companions of this remarkable image existed nevertheless, reaching back as far as the art of Giotto (see note 42).

In the main, the above observations may be deemed sufficient to present the case. But there still is room for an epilogue, even though this one may be of somewhat disproportionate length. In a study which deals with the diffusion of a certain motif of art, and does not attempt to name a particular model for every single instance, the constituent characteristics of the motif must not be lost from sight as the search advances. This ought to be the first condition whenever

---

22. 'Amazonomachia' on the Sarcophagus from Ephesus, and related monuments: this author, *American Journal of Archaeology*, LXV, 1961, p. 213. A comparable antithetical use of identical postures occurs among the Niobid groups in the Uffizi. Cf. the two statues, G. Mansuelli, *Galleria degli Uffizi, le sculture*, Florence, 1958, vol. 1, pp. 118 f., nos. 79, 80; young son of Niobe fleeing up a rock. This figure was duplicated in much the same way as the two Persians of the Pergamene dedication, moving toward a common center; except that if shown together, one of the Niobids must be seen from the back, the other from the front. I should date the original of the Niobid group to the same stylistic level as the small Pergamene ex-voto, about the middle of the second century B.C.; though a different school probably produced it. Recent suggestions of a date in the first century B.C. are too late, in my opinion: F. Weber, *Jahrbuch des Instituts*, LXXV, 1960, pp. 112 ff.; cf. Helbig and Amelung, pp. 104 f., no. 139. The group in the temple of Apollo Sosianus (founded 38 B.C.) may have been plundered art, or a copy. See also L. Hamburger, 'Symmetrie und Umkehrung in der römischen Kunst', Dissertation, Halle, 1916; I thank M. Bieber for this reference. Greek archaic art where antithetical representations of identical, or nearly identical, motives are not unusual requires a separate discussion.

23. G. Rodenwaldt, 'Das Problem der Renaissancen', *Archäologischer Anzeiger*, 1931, p. 320; cf. also this author, *American Journal of Archaeology*, LIII, 1949, p. 87.

24. Dohrn, *l.c.*, p. 8.

25. E. Buchner, *Alte Pinakothek in München*, Munich, 1957, Fig. 101 and p. 16; from the same altar as the 'Betrayal', above, Fig. 4, by a follower of D. Bouts. Further bibliography in E. Panofsky, *Early Netherlandish Paintings*, Cambridge, Massachusetts, 1953, p. 491, note 4 to p. 315.

we weigh a new suggestion to increase the list of examples. Two such suggestions that have already been made require re-examination. I now feel doubtful whether, as Adhémar proposed, the figure of Isaac in the famous bronze relief by Brunelleschi meets our criteria.[26] To be sure, the boy kneels with one knee raised. But since his hands are tied, the characteristic counterpoise between the raised head and the raised shoulder must needs be missing. Yet, the action of the raised arm must be held essential to the motif of the 'Fencing Kneeler', which is the object of our query. I find the discrepancy sufficient reason to drop Brunelleschi's figure from our list. To have the boy, Isaac, kneel on the altar with one knee raised was, after all, established custom in Christian iconography.[27] Beyond this obvious adherence to tradition, there is hardly a need to look for the model in someone else's art for Brunelleschi's highly personal and atypical invention. The second suggestion by Adhémar poses an entirely different problem. It regards an executioner dressed as a Roman soldier in a scene from the martyrdom of Saints Cosmas and Damianus, painted by a close if not overly talented follower of Fra Angelico, probably in the 1440's.[28] The man has fallen to his knees, struck with terror by the flames about to engulf him, while he props himself on his right arm. The left arm, held high, shelters his face from the searing heat. The up-turned head looks back across the raised arm to the miraculously saved saints (Fig. 7). This description alone will make it apparent that essential traits of our kneeling motif are also present in this composition. The trouble is that side by side with the features that agree one notices others, no less important, that do not agree. In spite of its light forward tilt, this figure appears more relief-like, more adapted to a plane surface, than any other so far discussed. Its posture seems even more emphatically open to the observer than can be said of the Pergamene statues. The principal cause of the last-named peculiarities lies in the simple fact that, different from all the others, the executioner in the Florentine painting is shown with both knees on the ground. In the foregoing examples the raised knee was apt to become a source of formal tension or even a barrier from behind which the figure acts; in the present case both knees move much more smoothly, parallel to each other and in the same direction. No doubt the soldier in the Florentine painting also represents a 'Fencing Kneeler', even with Hellenistic overtones reminiscent of the representations with

which we began. But as a formal device it must be separated from their series. It constitutes a type in its own right, however closely related to the first type it may be in certain respects. I propose to call it our Type Two.

Fortunately the history of this new type, which emerges from a critical examination of the first group, can be traced in a number of examples which agree very well amongst themselves. Again an Etruscan urn furnishes the probable point of departure (Fig. 8).[29] A close imitation—almost a copy—of the central figure of this urn occurs in the foreground of the large drawing attributable to Antonio Pollaiuolo, now at Windsor Castle (Fig. 9).[30] One notices at once how readily the Etruscan relief lent itself to pictorial reproduction. The reliance on silhouette and the suppression of the third dimension, so conspicuous in the ancient prototype, could easily invite rendition by an outline drawing. Actually, the drawing makes a palpable effort to restore a degree of roundness to the figure. As a result a slight difficulty arose in the representation of the right leg; this the Renaissance artist was forced to restore by his own lights because his model suppressed it completely. This predicament remained with the motif throughout its later vicissitudes; it was inherent in its origin. The painting in the Accademia at Florence also shows the problem quite clearly (Fig. 7). But there are other instances as well. It is regrettable that Leonardo's preserved drawings for the Trivulzio monument do not tell us explicitly enough how he wished to deal with this detail when he considered the motif for the fallen warrior beneath a rearing horse.[31] Even prior to Leonardo, one may list the engraving, probably from a drawing by Mantegna, on which Albrecht Dürer based his famous 'Orpheus' of 1494 (Fig. 10).[32] The same kneeling image left other traces in Dürer's work. It is clearly recognizable in the woodcut of Christ succumbing under the cross, from the 'Large Passion' of 1498–1499 (Fig. 11).[33] A belated

26. Adhémar, l.c., p. 302.

27. As in the mosaic in S. Vitale: S. Muratori, *I Mosaici Ravennati della chiesa di S.V.*, Bergamo, 1945, pl. 8.

28. Adhémar, l.c., p. 302; F. Schottmüller, *Fra Angelico di Fiesole*, Stuttgart and Leipzig, 1911, pl. 215.

29. Florence, Museo Archeologico; from Chiusi. G. Q. Giglioli, *L'arte Etrusca*, Milan, 1935, pl. 397, 2.

30. A. E. Popham and J. Wilde, *The Italian Drawings of the XV and XVI Centuries (The Ital. Drawings at Windsor Castle)*, London, 1949, catal. no. 27, Fig. 6: 'Battle of Naked Men'. Cf. A. Mongan and P. J. Sachs, *Drawings in the Fogg Museum*, Cambridge, Massachusetts, 1940, vol. I, p. 33.

31. L. Heydenreich, *Leonardo da Vinci*, London and Basel, 1954, pp. 69 ff. Sketches which include the fallen warrior vary greatly. Those closest to the type here discussed show the forward leg nearer the observer and partly overlapping the other leg—a naturalistic correction of the flattened-out, highly formalized prototype.

32. Dürer, 'Orpheus': drawing, Hamburg, Kunsthalle. A. Warburg, *Gesammelte Schriften*, Leipzig and Berlin, 1932, pp. 445 ff. and pl. 55; E. Panofsky, *Albrecht Dürer*, Princeton, 1943, vol. II, p. 95, no. 928 and illustration, Fig. 49. Cf. also above, note 30.

33. Panofsky, l.c., p. 32, no. 230; illustration, Fig. 89.

echo of the same invention appears in the grisaille 'Bearing of the Cross' of 1527, now known only through workshop copies.[34] Returning to Italy, I find the Mantegnesque interpretation of the motif as Orpheus once more revived by Giulio Romano.[35] I conclude this preliminary catalogue with an etching by Picasso, 'Fight in the Arena', dated 1937, in which the young and evidently imperiled opponent of the bull-headed monster assumes this same pose of the kneeling fighter that here concerns us (Fig. 12).[36]

At least temporarily the search can be halted here. There is now substantial evidence that since the Quattrocento, at the latest, the motif of the 'Fencing Kneeler' has split into two concurrent types, related by pattern and affective content but distinct from one another by important formal qualities. Both types have separate, if parallel, histories; and each can be related to a different Etrusco-Hellenistic prototype as its source or starting point. But this description applies only to Renaissance examples. It leaves the question open as to what happened to the same motif in the art between the end of antiquity and the year 1400. One factor which demonstrably had a share in these developments has not thus far been mentioned: the Byzantine tradition. Yet postures obviously related to the two types of kneeling figures discussed above are indeed found in Byzantine monuments long before the Renaissance. This material cannot be collected here. It requires a special study, a task which I must leave to others more competent to carry it out. I shall limit myself to one example only, in order to illustrate the point at issue. The mosaics of the Cathedral at Monreale include a most elegant version of our 'Fencing Kneeler', in a courtly Byzantine style of the late twelfth century (Fig. 13).[37] The figure represents Abel assailed by Cain. Again the motif appears as part of a fighting group. It also introduces to this study a new subject: the murder of Abel. There are other interesting circumstances about this representation. Its wide open contour would seem to compare well with the examples of our second type; so does the posture,

leaning vehemently sidewise, with arms extended from the torso almost at a right angle. But what about the principal criterion, the manner of kneeling? Strangely enough, the artfully planar design of the mosaic makes it difficult to decide at a glance whether both knees touch the ground, as they should if one were to count this figure among the examples of type two; actually the representation seems ambivalent in this respect. The version in Monreale may be read several ways, either as raising one knee or resting both knees on the ground.

An answer to the question can perhaps be deduced from a supporting document. A representation of the same scene is included with the Barberini Codex in the Vatican (cod. Barb. lat. 4406, folio 32), which renders the lost cycle of Genesis illustrations commissioned by Pope Leo the Great for the Basilica of S. Paolo fuori le mura, about the middle of the fifth century. If the artist of the seventeenth century who drew the illustrations in the Barberini Codex copied his original correctly, the left knee of Abel was raised, the right knee touched the ground. On the whole, the mosaic in Monreale followed the same iconography. But the kneeling motif was interpreted differently and rather more vaguely.[38] It seems that the separation between our types one and two was not heeded in Byzantine art shortly before the Renaissance, or at least it did not have the same significance that it assumed later. Instead, the representation in the Monreale mosaic, of Abel falling to the ground, is best understood as a spontaneous if relatively late reshaping of a common ancient image signifying a fallen adversary, which had become standard in Greek art around 400 B.C. The Attic tombstone of Dexileos, who died in battle in 394 B.C., may serve as an early example (Fig. 15).[39] The Byzantine version in Monreale, descending from an iconographic ancestry which harks back to the transition from Classical to Medieval art, must be evaluated accordingly. It represents the product of a continuous tradition, a true case of survival. By contrast, the two similar types of kneeling figures in

34. Panofsky, l.c., p. 7, no. 13. Cf. H. Tietze and E. Tietze-Conrat, *Kritisches Verzeichnis der Werke A. Dürers*, Basel and Leipzig, 1938, Catal., vol. II, pp. 70 f., no. W129 and illustration, Fig. 212.
35. F. Hartt, *Giulio Romano*, New Haven, 1958, vol. I, p. 252; illustration, vol. II, Fig. 515. An interesting interpretation of the same motive, close to the Windsor drawing (Fig. 9) but in Fontainebleau style, can be recognized in the fallen soldier to the right of the 'Risen Christ' by A. Caron, at Beauvais: *Art News*, LXIV, 1965, p. 23.
36. J. Bourbet, *Picasso, dessins*, Paris, 1950, pl. 78; not included in C. Zervos, *Pablo Picasso*, vols. VIII–IX, Paris, 1957–8 (works from 1932 to 1939).
37. O. Demus, *The Mosaics of Norman Sicily*, London, 1950, pp. 250 ff. Cf. E. Kitzinger, *The Mosaics of Monreale*, Palermo, 1960, pls. 19–20 and pp. 70 f.

38. Old Testament cycle in S. Paolo fuori le mura: St. Waetzold, *Die Kopien des 17. Jahrhunderts nach Mosaiken und Wandmalereien in Rom*, Vienna and Munich, 1964, pp. 56 f., no. 599; illustration, Fig. 337. Relations between Monreale and the lost frescoes of S. Paolo: Demus, l.c., pp. 250 ff.; also H. von Einem, 'Zur Hildesheimer Bronzetür', *Jahrbuch d. Preussischen Kunstsammlungen*, LIX, 1938, pp. 16 f. with Figs. 7 and 9. A somewhat different variant, more similar to the Barberini drawing, was used for the figure of Abel in the mosaics of the Capella Palatina, Palermo; for restorations see Demus, l.c., p. 67, no. 167. The motive persists among representations of Abel slain by Cain, into the Renaissance; e.g. in the painting by Bacchiacca, 'The Death of Abel', Bergamo, Galleria dell'Accademia Carrara, no. 564.
39. K. Friis Johansen, *The Attic Grave-Reliefs*, Copenhagen, 1951, pp. 48 f.

Renaissance art were revivals which came into being by means of a conscious return to two distinct, ancient sources. Both these sources were Hellenistic-Etruscan, but only one favored the statuesque and compact rendition which characterizes the northern tradition of the motif. Among the northern artists Dürer alone, who almost certainly derived the motif from Italy, followed the second, Italianate type. In either case one may assume that the preceding Byzantine tradition helped to sharpen the sensibility of the moderns to the artistic possibilities inherent in the inherited image-formula. Subsequently the Renaissance revitalized the ancient motif, much as grapevines may be revitalized by grafts from the original stock.

Precisely how the motive became domesticated in the art of the north is still difficult to say. Evidently its career in northern painting started early. It may even be possible to propose an intermediary example, between the Byzantine tradition and the use of the revised motif by the northern schools. In the so-called 'Neville-Hours', datable perhaps to the year 1407, folio 32 v illustrates the betrayal of Christ (Fig. 14).[40] Just as in the painting related to Dierick Bouts (Fig. 4),[41] Malchus was placed into the nearest foreground, in the lower left corner. Peter brandishes his sword above him. One recognizes that Malchus kneels with the right knee raised, but one hardly arrives at this answer without some scrutiny. His posture retains much of the uncertainty in this respect that might be expected in a Byzantine model. At the same time his left arm, the one closest to the observer, reaches forward and down, overlapping the chest; the head turns upward and back, counter to the governing direction. The latter movements anticipate essential elements of the statuesque contrapposto that the later Flemish paintings elaborated so obviously. Thus, in its entirety, the figure seems to combine a degree of early Renaissance modernism with Byzantine reminiscences. It may be a fusion of both, antedating by only a few years the much more refined work of the Limbourg brothers.[42]

We are nearing the end. The last item on our list is also a Byzantine work, but its general character and its problem differ from the monuments just discussed. It is an icon in the Ikonen-Museum at Recklinghausen, Italo-Byzantine of origin and datable approximately near the year 1600; its theme, the 'Transfiguration of Christ' (Fig. 16).[43] The three disciples, Peter, John, and James—eyewitnesses of the event—are assembled in the foreground near the lower border, in accordance with the customary Byzantine iconography of this scene. John has fallen headlong at the feet of Christ. Peter to the left makes an effort to speak. James kneels, the left knee slightly raised, and supports himself on the left arm while raising the right hand to his forehead, to shelter his eyes from the blinding light. This is the figure which interests us. The same action of protecting his eyes has traditionally been ascribed to James on this occasion.[44] What sets aside his portrayal in the Recklinghausen icon from other, analogous representations is not the action—the content—which agrees with tradition but the manner in which that action is shown—the form of the image. There can be no doubt that this form repeats the motif which by now we know so well: the 'Fencing Kneeler'. Dürer's Orpheus (Fig. 10) would be immediately recognized as an almost exact parallel if it were not for the differences of costume and context.

I regard the image of James the apostle in the Recklinghausen icon as a member of our second Renaissance group, the 'Italianate type'. Only in the position of the knees does the Byzantine tradition linger on resulting, here also, in a slight ambivalence of meaning. The figure half sits, half kneels on the ground; one cannot be certain which alternative was really intended. Nevertheless, while traditional habits of representation persist, the customary posture was thoroughly redrawn in a Renaissance fashion. A point was reached where a Renaissance 'revival' could occasionally replace continuous 'survival' in the Byzantine tradition itself. Yet

40. C. L. Kuhn, 'Herman Scheerre and English Illumination of the Early Fifteenth Century', *The Art Bulletin*, XXII, 1940, p. 148 and Fig. 10.

41. Above, note 25. The diffusion of Italianate motives in northern painting poses many kindred, methodological problems; see, e.g., M. Meurer, 'Zwei antike Figuren bei Rogier van der Weyden', *Schülerfestgabe für H. von Einem*, Bonn, 1965, pp. 172 ff. It may also be noted here that the kneeling 'elect' in the second panel from the left of Roger's 'Last Judgement' at Beaune looks remarkably like a variation of the kneeling Adam in the 'Trés Riches Heures'. E. Panofsky, *Early Netherlandish Painting*, vol. I, pp. 268 ff. and illustration, vol. II, pl. 188.

42. The connection suggested above, p. 66, between the art of the Limburg brothers and the Etruscan urns can probably be confirmed by another illustration in the 'Trés Riches Heures'. E. Panofsky, *Early Netherlandish Painting*, vol. I, p. 63, already

observed that the '*contrapposto* attitude' of the St. John on Patmos in the 'Hours' (Fig. 18) represents 'almost a mirror image' of Giotto's 'St. Francis Receiving the Stigmata', in the painting of Santa Croce in Florence (Fig. 17): *ibid.*, vol. II, Figs. 83 and 86. Actually both figures appear to be variants of the kneeling onlooker to the right of the miracle-story on the terracotta urn at Perugia, here illustrated in Fig. 6. As the work of Giotto represents the earliest instance known at present of the re-use of this particular model in modern times, it bears out R. Wittkower's remarks on the leading role of Giotto in the development of the Renaissance practice of 'imitatio': 'Individualism in Art and Artists: a Renaissance Problem', *Journal of the History of Ideas*, XXII, 1961, pp. 300 f.

43. Recklinghausen, Ikonen-Museum, Inv. no. 343. For this information and the photograph reproduced in our Fig. 16, I thank the Museum and its acting director, Dr. A. Schröder.

44. G. Millet, *L'iconographie de l'Evangile*, vol. I, Paris, 1916, pp. 222 f.

whatever steps now unknown to us led to this particular result, they hardly included a fresh study of the Antique by the anonymous painter of the icon. Clearly we are looking at another instance of a migration of motif. One recognizes the stable elements of the motif alongside the formal changes that go with adaptation. But the actual circumstances which linked the painter with the origin of his chosen motif remain uncertain. This state of the matter is hardly an isolated experience; on the contrary, it appears to be symptomatic of the condition under which motifs migrate. The reason is not difficult to understand. Most series of motifs come into being through internal borrowing from one member of the chain to another rather than through direct contact with the original from which the series took its start. Perhaps we should say that in the psychology of art, 'motif' and 'prototype' are not of the same order. They fulfill different functions. A 'prototype' becomes selected because of its singularity; a 'motif' serves as a generalization which can be reduced to particulars. Any given form—any model, that is—may of course be viewed either way. The difference lies not in what form is used as a model but in how that form is applied to the creation of new art.

ERNST H. GOMBRICH

From the Revival of Letters to the Reform of the Arts

Niccolò Niccoli and Filippo Brunelleschi*

Cultural history is passing through a crisis, the crisis engendered by the slow demise of Hegelian 'historicism'. Its repercussions have been felt with particular force in Renaissance studies because it is here that the link between developments in art and in other fields has proved to modern research to be so much more complex and problematic than it appeared to the philosopher of progress. It was Hegel even more than Burckhardt who had first projected a unifying vision of the Renaissance as a forward surge of the spirit, a phase that expressed itself with equal authenticity in the revival of learning, the flourishing of the arts and the geographical discoveries, three facts representing for him the 'dawn that precedes the sunrise of the Reformation'.[1]

However little Hegel's optimistic metaphysics may have appealed to individual historians, the need for a unifying principle made it hard to forgo this conception of a new age without being left with unrelated fragments of an unintelligible past.

Rudolf Wittkower is one of the students of the period who has shown that this dilemma is unreal. Boldly challenging the traditional view that the Renaissance predilection for centralized church buildings is the expression of a new paganizing aestheticism he has also refused to withdraw into a positivist collection of dates and groundplans.[2] He could thus show that in one particular area a bridge exists between ideas and forms without falling back on generalizations about the new age and the new man.

It is the purpose of this study to follow up this success by facing Hegel's questions once more, to look for an answer not in the metaphysics of history but in the social psychology of fashions and movements. Maybe the solution it tries to offer is premature. It is certainly one-sided. But it will have served its end if it shows once more that if we follow Wittkower in concentrat-

ing our attention on living people in concrete situations we are more likely even to find texts and cues that explain the interaction of changes in various fields than if we are satisfied with the pseudo-explanation of a 'spirit'.

The Renaissance is the work of the humanists. But to us this term no longer denotes the heralds of a new 'discovery of man' but rather the *umanisti*, scholars, that is, who are neither theologians nor physicians but rather concentrate on the 'humanities', principally the *trivium* of grammar, dialectic and rhetoric.[3] How was it, we must ask, that these preoccupations could lead to a revolution not only in classical studies but also in art and ultimately even in science? What started the landslide that transformed Europe?

Any movement that thus conquers society must have something to offer that establishes its superiority in the eyes of potential converts. Where what is offered is a useful invention the historian need hardly puzzle his head why it was accepted. We know only too well why gunpowder was quickly taken up in Europe which it had reached from the East, and we are not surprised that spectacles were a success when they were first invented about 1300 in Pisa.[4] What 'movements' offer their new adherents, however, is generally something a little less tangible but psychologically more important. They offer them a feeling of superiority over others, a new kind of prestige, a new weapon in that most important fight for self-assertion which the English humorist Stephen Potter has so aptly described as the game of 'one-up-manship'. The early humanists evidently had both to offer, real inventions or at least discoveries which established their superiority in some respects over more old-fashioned scholars, but also a new emphasis on that superiority, a new glamour and self-confidence that carried everything before it, even though it was based at first on precariously narrow foundations. The humanists, as Ruskin once put it, 'discovered suddenly that the world for ten centuries had been living in a ungrammatical

* This paper is based on a lecture originally given at the New York Institute of Fine Art in December 1962.

1. *Vorlesungen über die Philosophie der Geschichte* (ed. E. Gans), Berlin, 1840, pp. 493–6. I have referred to this problem in my inaugural lecture on 'Art and Scholarship' (1957) now reprinted in *Mediations on a Hobby Horse*, London, 1963, pp. 106–19.
2. *Architectural Principles in the Age of Humanism*, 2nd ed., London, 1952.

3. Augusto Campana, 'The Origin of the Word "Humanist"', *Journal of the Warburg and Courtauld Institutes*, IX, 1946, pp. 60–73; P. O. Kristeller, *Studies in Renaissance Thought and Letters*, Rome, 1956, esp. p. 574.
4. Charles Singer, E. J. Holmford *et al.*, *A History of Technology*, II, Oxford, 1956; III, Oxford, 1957.

manner, and they made it forthwith the end of human existence, to be grammatical. . . .'[5]

To be sure this interpretation has been increasingly challenged in recent years. Many students of the period have come to emphasize the importance of 'civic humanism'[6] in the outlook of such great humanists as Coluccio Salutati and Leonardo Bruni Aretino who had certainly cared for many things besides grammar. The question is only whether it was these virtues which secured humanism its ascendancy and ultimate triumph. The time may have come to focus attention once more on those representatives of the movement who are nowadays sometimes censured for their exclusive concentration on classical studies. Of these, by common consent, the most outstanding and the most extreme example is Niccolò Niccoli, 1365–1437, a Florentine merchant of a well-to-do family.[7]

Every student of the period knows the charming portrait of the aged Niccoli that Burckhardt quoted from Vespasiano da Bisticci's biography: 'always dressed in the most beautiful red cloth which reached to the ground . . . he was the neatest of men . . . at table he ate from the finest of antique dishes . . . his drinking cup was of crystal . . . to see him at the table like this, looking like a figure from the ancient world, was a noble sight indeed.'[8]

Every line of Vespasiano's beautiful biography breathes his veneration for a man he is proud still to have known, and whom he described as a central figure in that great circle of enthusiasts who experienced the exhilarating tide of new texts and new information. We can confirm from the correspondence of Poggio Bracciolini, Ambrogio Traversari, Bruni, Aurispa and others that in this respect Vespasiano had not exaggerated. Niccolò Niccoli was the man to whom discoveries were reported from abroad and who passed on information and codices. His library that went to San Marco testifies to his industry and devotion to the cause of classical studies.

Many decades after his death, when Vespasiano looked back, Niccolò Niccoli's role as one of the originators of the humanist movement was no longer a point of contention. 'It may be said that he was the reviver of Greek and Latin letters in Florence . . . although Petrarch, Dante and Boccaccio had done something to rehabilitate them, they had not reached

the height which they attained through Niccolò.'[9] In all its deceptive simplicity the sentence still sums up the theme of Niccoli's life, his ambivalence towards the three great luminaries of Florentine literature who had to be surpassed if the recovery of Greek and Latin standards was to be attempted in earnest. It was his respect for these standards, we learn from Vespasiano, that accounts for the fact that Niccolò himself never published anything. His taste was so fastidious that he never satisfied himself.

Even in this idealized portrait it is possible to discern the type of pioneer to which Niccolò Niccoli belongs. They may be called the catalysts, men who effect a change through their mere presence, through conversation and argument, but who would be unknown to posterity if others had not left records of their encounters. Socrates is the most exalted example (save for religious leaders). Like Socrates, Niccoli is known to us mainly in the dual reflection of hostile satire and pious evocation. He was singled out for scurrilous diatribes and as an interlocutor in many a humanist dialogue that tried to evoke the atmosphere of discussions in Florence during its most creative period.[10]

The most telling of these dialogues was composed at a time when Niccolì was in his middle thirties; it is the first of Leonardo Bruni's famous *Dialogi ad Petrum Histrum*[11] which is often quoted for Niccoli's unbridled attack on Dante, Petrarch and Boccaccio in which it culminates.

> What are these Dantes, these Petrarchs, these Boccaccios you remind me of? Do you expect me to judge by the opinion of the vulgar and to approve and disapprove of the same as does the crowd? . . . I have always suspected the crowd, and not without reason.

Quite apart from Dante's anachronisms and mistakes he was devoid of Latinity. Niccoli had recently read some of Dante's letters

> by Jove, nobody is so uneducated that he would not feel ashamed to have written so badly. . . . I would exclude that poet of yours from the company of literate men and leave him to the woolworkers. . . . [12]

5. *The Works of John Ruskin*, ed. E. T. Cook and A. Wedderburn, London, 1904, XI, p. 69 (*Stones of Venice*, III, ch. 1).
6. Hans Baron, *The Crisis of the Early Italian Renaissance*, Princeton, N.J., 1955, and bibliography on p. 444.
7. Giuseppe Zippel, *Niccolò Niccoli*, Florence, 1890. For a sympathetic appraisal of Niccolì's position, see E. Müntz, *Les précurseurs de la Renaissance*, Paris, 1882.
8. Vespasiano da Bisticci, *Vite di Uomini Illustri*, ed. P. d'Ancona and E. Aeschlimann, Milan, 1951, pp. 442–3.

9. *Ed. cit.*, p. 440.
10. For Bruni's dialogues see below. Niccoli is also introduced in the dialogues by Poggio Bracciolini, *An Seni uxor sit ducenda*, *De Nobilitate* and *De infilicitate principum*, in Lorenzo Valla, *De voluptate* and in Giovanni Aretino Medico, *De nobilitate legum aut Medicinae* (first published by E. Garin, Florence, 1947).
11. The most accessible edition (and Italian translation) is in E. Garin, *Prosatori Latini del Quattrocento*, Milan, 1952, pp. 44–99.
12. *Ed. cit.*, pp. 68–70.

After similar tirades against Petrarch and Boccaccio Niccoli exclaims that he rates 'a single letter by Cicero and a single poem by Vergil far higher than all the scribblings of these men taken together'.[13]

It is hard to understand, let alone forgive, this sensational blasphemy unless one reads it in the context of the dialogue. For Bruni is careful both in the setting and in the argument to prepare the reader for this denunciation of Florence's proudest tradition. In the opening section Coluccio Salutati, the chancellor, a sage as well as a scholar, is found politely reproaching the young men, Bruni, Roberto Rossi and Niccolò Niccoli because they neglected discussion or disputations of philosophical matters. Niccolò agrees that such exercises would be beneficial but it is not his fault but the fault of the times in which they live that they are not worth pursuing.

> I cannot see how one can pursue the mastery of disputations in such wretched times and with such a shortage of books. For what worthy skill, what knowledge can be found in these times that is not either dislocated or totally degraded? ... How do you think we can learn philosophy these days when large parts of the books have perished and those that survive are so corrupt that they are as good as lost? True enough, there are plenty of teachers of philosophy who promise to teach it. How splendid these philosophers of our age must be if they teach what they do not know themselves.[14]

They refer to Aristotle's authority, but those harsh, hard and dissonant words they quote as Aristotle cannot be by the same of whom Cicero writes that he wrote with incredible sweetness. And as with philosophy so it is with all the Liberal Arts. It is not that there are no talents nowadays, or no wish to learn, but without knowledge, without teachers, without books it cannot be done. 'Where are Varro's writings, where Livy's histories, where Salust's or Pliny's? A whole day would not suffice to enumerate all the lost works.'[15]

It is here that Salutati interposes and asks his opponent not to exaggerate. They have works by Cicero and Seneca, for instance, and he reminds him of the three great Florentines, thus provoking the final outburst.

In the second dialogue this attack is withdrawn. Niccoli maintains that he had only said these outrageous things to provoke Salutati into a eulogy of the Florentine 'triumvirate'. Since it was not forthcoming it is he who shows that he can argue the other side and give due praise to the Great Three.

The contrast between these two speeches is so startling that Hans Baron has concluded that they cannot date from the same period and must be indicative of a change of heart, at least on the part of Bruni.[16] But quite apart from the fact that the marshalling of effective arguments on both sides is part of the rhetorical tradition, Niccoli's conversion is perhaps not as complete as it looks on the surface. Bruni slipped in a malicious joke that turns out to be a very backhanded retraction of the original remark about Vergil and Cicero:

'As to those who assert that they rate one poem of Vergil and one letter by Cicero more highly than all the works of Petrarch', Niccoli is now made to say, 'I frequently turn this round, and say that I prefer one speech by Petrarch to all Vergil's letters and that I rate Petrarch's poems much more highly than all Cicero's poems.'[17]

Cicero's poems, of course, were notoriously wretched, and Petrarch's speeches exist as little as do Vergil's letters. The retraction, therefore, is quite in character.

There is no doubt that it was this sensational irreverence that attracted most attention among Niccoli's contemporaries, and that in revolutions of this kind to have gained attention is half the battle. The baiting of authority, the cry 'burn the museums' belong to that ritual of 'father killing' that we associate with new movements. But the first dialogue shows us also that this attack was launched from a secure base. The humanists had probed the enemies' defences and found out their weakest spot. They were right in their complaint about the lack of good texts, right in their suspicion of the Aristotelian doctrine as it was taught in the universities, right in their demand that in such a situation first things must come first and that the greatest need was to find out what the ancients had in fact written and taught. Without these preliminaries there can be no valid disputations within a framework that relies on authorities. It is a temper that is not unfamiliar to those of us who have witnessed similar if less spectacular reactions in present-day scholarship against the grand generalizations of philosophical historians. The proper edition of texts and charters acquires an almost moral significance for those rebels who submit to a self-denying ordinance in order to atone for the vapid rhetoric of their elders.

It is against this background that both the hostility aroused by Niccoli's group and its ultimate European triumph become more intelligible. Documents of this hostility there are plenty. No less than five formal

13. *Ed. cit.*, p. 74.
14. *Ed. cit.*, pp. 52–56.
15. *Ed. cit.*, p. 60.

16. H. Baron, *op. cit.*, pp. 200–17.
17. *Ed. cit.*, p. 94.

'invectives' against Niccoli and his circle are known,[18] among them vicious attacks by the greatest of fellow humanists such as Guarino and Bruni himself. The burden of their complaint is always the same: irreverence towards the great Florentine poets, excessive arrogance backed by no creative achievement, a foolish pedantry concerned with finicky externals of manuscripts and of spelling instead of an interest in their meaning.

Thus Cino Rinuccini pretends in his invective written around 1400 that his 'sacred wrath' drove him from Florence to seek refuge and peace from the

> empty and stupid discussions of a gang of prattlers. To appear very erudite in the eyes of the vulgar they shout in the piazza how many diphthongs the ancients had and why today only two are in use . . . and how many feet the ancients used in their verses and why today only the anapaest is used . . . and with such extravagances they spend all their time . . . but the meaning, the distinction, the significance of words . . . they make no effort to learn. They say of logic that it is a sophistic science and not much use. . . .

And so through the whole gamut of the Liberal Arts each of which the arrogant *brigata* is accused of dismissing and which the writer feels called upon to defend against these 'vagabonds'.[19]

Rinuccini does not mention the offending party. Guarino's invective dated 1413 is much more personal; though he does not name his victim he must have been easy to identify.

The letter exists in two versions.[20] Both of them contain the gravamen of the charge that Niccoli forgets that 'it is not the eagle but the spider who catches flies'.[21] One of them expands on this point at some length with heavy sarcasm describing Niccoli as a student of 'geometry'.

> Neglecting the other aspects of books as quite superfluous he expends his interest and acumen on the *points* (or dots) in the manuscript. As to the *lines*, how accurately, how copiously, how elegantly he discusses them. . . . You would think you hear Diodorus or Ptolemi when he discusses with such precision that they should be drawn rather with an iron stylus than with a leaden one. . . . As to the

paper, that is the *surface*, his expertise is not to be dismissed and he displays his eloquence in praising or disapproving of it. What a vacuous way to spend so many years if the final fruit is a discussion of the shape of letters, the colour of paper and the varieties of ink. . . . [22]

Guarino had recently seen a little work by Niccoli, an Orthography compiled for the education of small boys.

> It shows that it is the author who is a small boy who is not ashamed, against all rules, to spell syllables which are contracted by nature with diphthongs. . . . This white-haired man does not blush to adduce the testimony of bronze and silver coins, of marbles and of Greek manuscripts in cases where the word offers no problems. . . . Let this Solon tell us, if he can, which living author of his age he does not find fault with.[23]

Leonardo Bruni picked up these and other motifs when it was his turn to quarrel with Niccoli around 1424.[24] He offers a vivid caricature of Niccoli strutting through the streets looking left and right expecting to be hailed as a philosopher and a poet, as if he said:

> Look at me and know how profoundly wise I am. I am the pillar of letters, I am the shrine of knowledge, I am the standard of doctrine and wisdom. If those about him should fail to notice he will complain about the ignorance of the age. . . . [25]

It is Bruni now who confirms that Niccoli does not stop at abusing Dante, Petrarch and Boccaccio, that he despises St. Thomas Aquinas and anyone else who lived during the last thousand years.[26] Yet what has he done himself? He cannot put two Latin words together, he is sixty now and all he knows is about books and the book trade, he knows neither mathematics nor rhetoric, nor law. Allegedly he is interested in grammar, a subject fit for boys. He ponders about diphthongs. . . .[27]

Making allowance for the obvious distortions of these caricatures they still supplement the picture of Niccoli in an important respect. If Bruni's Dialogue has shown us the rebel who wants to break with the immediate past in order to restore the higher standards of antiquity, the caricatures emphasize the weapon he was using in this fight. The old men should go back to school, they could not even properly spell or write.

18. For four of them, see below, for the fifth, by Lorenzo di Marco de' Benvenuti, see Hans Baron, *op. cit.*, pp. 409–16. In addition there are Francesco Filelfo's many attacks.
19. *Invettiva contro a cierti caluniatori die Dante, etc.*, in Giovanni da Prato, *Il Paradiso degli Alberti*, ed. A. Wesselofsky, vol. I, pt. 2, Bologna, 1867, pp. 303–16.
20. Guarino Veronese, *Epistolario*, ed. R. Sabbadini, Venice, 1915, I, pp. 33–46.
21. *Ed. cit.*, p. 36.
22. *Ed. cit.*, p. 37.
23. *Ed. cit.*, p. 38.
24. *Leonardo Bruni Oratio in Nebulonem Maledicum* in G. Zippel, *Niccolò Niccoli*, Florence, 1890, pp. 75–91.
25. *Ed. cit.*, p. 77.
26. *Ed. cit.*, p. 78.
27. *Ed. cit.*, pp. 84–85.

It was easy to ridicule this concern as tiresome pedantry, but the very resentment it caused betrays anxiety. For clearly Niccoli was often right. The spelling of Latin had been corrupted in the Middle Ages. In itself this was no new discovery. Salutati was also interested in orthography.[28] But for him this was certainly not the most important issue. He could freely cultivate the heritage of Petrarch and pursue the study of the classics without being totally diverted to such concentration on minutiae. He could never contemplate a breach with tradition. As Ullman has brought out so well in his recent book on Salutati's humanism, medievalizing and modern elements do not clash in the mental universe of the Florentine chancellor.[29] To the young rebel this must have looked like compromising with the devil. Their programme 'first things first' now started with spelling and writing.

At first sight such a programme does not look like a promising start for a fashion and movement that was to embrace the whole of the Western world. It is understandable therefore that in Hans Baron's book this pedantic classicism is mainly used as a foil to bring out the 'civic humanism' of Bruni.[30] The pedants stand condemned as men lacking in patriotism and glorying in their isolation. Not all of the few facts we know about Niccoli fit this image. Niccoli quite frequently held public office and some of the posts he occupied were not without importance.[31] But even if the picture of Niccoli's detachment were entirely correct this need not prove that he might not have influenced the course of events. It is rash to assume that a concern with spelling and similar issues cannot have more far-reaching consequences than the best-intentioned participation in local politics. We have seen in our own days that spelling reforms can become an issue of no less explosive a kind than the design of flags. It only depends what context such questions are raised in.

There are indications that the concern with these famous diphthongs was aroused in this circle by an outsider. Manuel Chrysoloras, the admired sage from Constantinople whom Salutati had called to Florence to teach the young scholars Greek, was interested in this question of orthography[32] which probably impinged on the correct transliteration of Greek names. It must have been startling to be told by a Greek that

Latin had been corrupted in the Western world and to find confirmation of this in inscriptions on coins and tombstones. The spelling *etas* was clearly wrong, it should be *aetas*, and so with many similar forms. No wonder that these matters could become a symbol of the new emphasis on accuracy, a banner to be raised in the fight against the corruption of language.

Even now, as it happens, the question of diphthongs can make hackles rise. We need only watch the reaction of a proud English scholar who has to accept American spelling of such words as color or labor, though in this case etymology favours the transatlantic usage. But the dropping of that old-fashioned 'u' becomes identified in the mind of the conservative with 'false quantities' or even with that proverbial dropping of aitches which marks the uneducated Cockney on the stage and in real life. No wonder tempers could be frayed over matters of spelling. Salutati still clung to the medieval usage of *michi* and *nichil* and wanted to enforce this barbaric tradition against the 'stiff-necked' opposition of Poggio Bracciolini who called the spelling of *nichil* a 'crime and a blasphemy'.[33] He may have been joking but he surely felt strongly about the need to revert to the purity of ancient orthography.

It would be interesting to study in a wider context the importance which language has played in the formation of social groups. Bernard Shaw's Professor Higgins knew that language and accent are the passport to society. But language is more, it can create a new allegiance. The purist who claims special insight into language and castigates current abuses will always attract attention and arouse both hostility and passionate allegiance among users of language. Karl Kraus in Austria was a case in point, a satirist to whom little else was sacrosanct beside the rules of correct German which he saw threatened and corrupted by journalistic jargon. Healthy as was his campaign in many respects, the feeling of superiority he gave to those who had learned to spot certain common mistakes was a noteworthy by-product of his pamphleteering. It appears that it even spread to England through his admirer Ludwig Wittgenstein who, in his turn, wanted to reform the language of the tribe and succeeded mainly in raising the self-confidence of those who had learned to spot linguistic muddles in others.

We need not overwork this possible parallel to realize that the movement which Niccolò Niccoli represents may have owed some of its dynamism to what Potter calls 'one-up-manship'. The humanists were reformers of style and language and in this field they could show their demonstrable superiority over the old men who

28. B. L. Ullman, *The Humanism of Coluccio Salutati*, Padua, 1963, pp. 108–12.

29. *Op. cit.*, pt. III.

30. *Op. cit.*, esp. pp. 289–90; 2nd ed., Princeton, 1966, pp. 322–323.

31. Lauro Martines, *The Social World of the Florentine Humanists, 1390–1460*, London, 1963, pp. 161–3.

32. B. L. Ullman, *The Origin and Development of Humanistic Script*, Rome, 1960, pp. 70–71, where more passages on diphthongs are quoted.

33. Ullman, *Humanistic Script*, pp. 25 and 53.

still betrayed their ignorance by spelling *nichil* instead of *nihil* or *autor* instead of *auctor*. It may well be true that this passion sometimes crowded out all other interests. Niccoli, at any rate, was not a rebellious spirit in metaphysical matters. There is no reason to doubt Vespasiano's words that he was *cristianissimo*[34] and that 'those who harboured doubts concerning the truth of the Christian faith incurred his strongest hatred'.[35]

In a sense that concentration on form rather than on content that so much aroused the wrath of Niccoli's enemies in his own time and in ours, facilitates this conservatism in religious and philosophical matters. Neither for him nor, a century later, for Erasmus was there any contradiction between this regard for philological accuracy and a respect for the Gospel.

Far from being a weakness therefore, this emphasis on form was an added asset for the success of the humanist movement. It established the superiority of those who adhered to it, but it did not cut at the root of their beliefs. From this point of view it is not surprising that it was in this circle and at that moment of time that the direct transfer occurred from a literary concern and attitude to a change in a visual style. We have heard from Guarino how much Niccoli worried about 'points, lines, and surface' in books. Another satire[36] is even more explicit on this point. It complains once more about a group of irreverent men who fail to respect the three great Florentine poets but have never created anything of themselves. It is true,

> one of them may claim to know very much about books. But I should reply, yes, perhaps, whether they are well bound, and that might make a good beadle or stationer. For this turns out to be the height of genius of that professional fault-finder, to want to see a beautiful ancient script, which he will not consider beautiful or good, if it is not of the ancient shape and well spelt with diphthongs, and no book, however good it may be pleases him, nor would he deign to read it if it is not written in ancient characters [*lettera antica*].[37]

Here we know that what struck contemporaries as a fad and an affectation in one man was to affect the whole of the Western world. For it was this *lettera antica* that replaced the Gothic script first in Italy, whence it spread in the wake of humanism wherever the Latin alphabet is now used, including the printers of this volume.

The story of this first tangible innovation which we owe to the Florentine circle of humanists is exceptionally well documented. An art historian may well envy the palaeographer the precision with which he can here follow a stylistic change. It has been treated with masterly clarity and acumen by L. Ullman in his book on the *Origins and Developments of Humanistic Script*.[38] Thanks to Ullman we can see this development in terms of particular people expressing preferences and making a choice rather than in terms of those anonymous collective forces and trends which are the bane of history. Not unexpectedly the story begins with Petrarch who still wrote a Gothic script but who had strong opinions about the quality of lettering he preferred. What he wants, he writes to a friend, are not fine luxuriating letters which delight the eye from afar but fatigue it in reading. In 1395 Petrarch's heir and disciple Salutati tries to procure a book from France and writes: 'If you could get one in antique lettering I would prefer it, since no letters are more welcome to my eye.'[39]

There is little doubt that what Salutati meant by antique lettering was the type of lettering used before the arrival of Gothic script, the type we now call Carolingian Minuscule which is indeed much more lucid and easier to read. Very likely Salutati whose eyesight was deteriorating preferred it for that reason; but he must also have noticed that the earlier manuscripts offer on the whole a better text. His expression 'antique lettering' even suggests that he may have wrongly believed the oldest codices of this kind to go back to the classical age. Ullman has shown that there exists at least one manuscript by Salutati himself, a Codex of letters by Pliny, which the aged humanist and chancellor copied out for himself, and in which he experimented with an imitation of this earlier form of lettering, though he did not sustain the attempt. The first dated manuscript known to Ullman written in the new script is a codex written by Salutati's pupil and subsequent successor in the chancellery Poggio Bracciolini dating from 1402 to 1403[40] (Fig. 1). It still shows traces of Gothic form but is written with the discipline and care of the professional scribe—for that is what Poggio apparently was in his youth.

It is interesting to follow Ullman here into an analysis of the spelling which reflects the very discussions in this circle which had attracted so much hostility and ridicule.[41] In the first part of the manuscript Poggio still writes *etas* but later *aetas*. On the whole Poggio is careful to employ the sacred diphthong, occasionally

34. *Ed. cit.*, p. 435.
35. *Ed. cit.*, p. 438.
36. This anonymous attack was published by Wesselofsky together with *Il Paradiso degli Alberti, ed. cit.*, vol. I, pt. II, pp. 321–30, but does not form part of it.
37. *Ed. cit.*, p. 327.

38. Rome, 1960.
39. *Op. cit.*, pp. 13–14.
40. *Op. cit.*, p. 18 and Fig. 8.
41. *Op. cit.*, pp. 24–25.

even too careful. As Ullman noticed he had some diffi-culty in not introducing it where it does not belong. Thus he once wrongly writes *fixae* for the adverb *fixe* and twice *accoeptus* for *acceptus*.

Poggio himself was not to become an extremist in matters of diphthongs. But what is important here is not so much the individual spelling as the emphasis on a standardized orthography and a standardized script. We can trace the efforts by which Poggio spread the new form of lettering for we know from his letters that he had set himself the task of teaching it to the scribes who served the circle of the Florentine human-ists.[42]

In a letter of June 1425 to Niccolò Niccoli he men-tions a scribe who can write fast and 'in that script that savours of antiquity' (*litteris quae sapiunt anti-quitatem*). By then he also had a French scribe at his disposal whom he had taught to write *litteris antiquis*. In 1427 Poggio complains that for four months he had done nothing but to teach a blockhead of a scribe to write 'but the ass was too stupid'. Maybe he would learn in two years. By that time, of course, the manu-scripts tell their own story; we can see the spread of the *littera antiqua* in manuscript after manuscript.

As far as we can tell the amateur Niccolò Niccoli him-self did not write in the same perfect hand—as little indeed as he wrote in a perfect Latin style. According to Ullman he had developed instead a more cursive utility version of the *littera antiqua* which must have served him well in his labours of copying ancient texts and which developed later into the type we know as italic.

And yet, if the picture painted by the satirists is any guide, the single-minded passion of this man must have had a share in that reform of letters that still affects us today. It was a reform in the true sense of the word. A turning back from a corrupt style and lettering to an earlier phase. Otto Paecht has shown how closely fifteenth-century manuscripts in Italy came to be modelled on twelfth-century exemplars both in their scripts and their initials.[43] He drew atten-tion to the similarity between the Oxford Lactantius of 1454[44] (Fig. 4) and a Gregory manuscript of the twelfth century[45] (Fig. 3).

It is obvious therefore that there is a striking parallelism between this spread of the *littera antiqua* thát was really a twelfth-century form and the momentous change in the style of architecture which we connect with the name of Filippo Brunelleschi. Brunelleschi too rejected the Gothic mode of building that was current in Europe in his day in favour of a new style that became known as *all'antica*. His reforms, as that of the humanist scribes, spread from Florence through-out the world and remained valid for at least five hundred years wherever the Renaissance style was adopted or modified. And like the humanists, Brunel-leschi derived his alternative to the Gothic style less from a study of Roman ruins than from pre-Gothic exemplars in Florence which we now know to be in a form of Romanesque but which he probably invested with greater antiquity and more authority.[46]

The order and magnitude of Brunelleschi's achieve-ment is of course on a different level from that slight adjustment in letter-forms carried out by Salutati and his disciples. And yet that comparison would perhaps have sounded less extravagant to the fifteenth century than it sounds today. Lorenzo Ghiberti, who, what-ever his relations were with Brunelleschi, was after all in constant touch with him for many years, makes the explicit comparison in his *Commentarii*. Discussing proportion as a key to beauty he switches from the example of the human body to that of writing: 'In writing too script would not be beautiful except when the letters are proportionate in shape, size, position and order and in all other visible aspects in which the various parts can harmonize.'[47]

Now it is this discovery of an underlying harmony that is stressed by Brunelleschi's first biographer as the true revelation that was granted to Brunelleschi in his con-templation of ancient statues and buildings where 'he seemed to recognize quite clearly a certain order in their members and bones . . . whence he wanted to re-discover . . . their musical proportions . . .'[48]

This is not the place to revive the discussion that has centred round the problem of Brunelleschi's Roman journey.[49] The story which Vasari took over from that

42. Ullman, *Script*, pp. 86–87.

43. *Italian Illuminated Manuscripts from 1400–1550*, Catalogue of an Exhibition held in the Bodleian Library, Oxford, 1948.

44. MS. Can. Pat. Lat. 138.

45. MS. Can. Pat. Lat. 105.

46. Hans Tietze, 'Romanische Kunst und Renaissance', *Vorträge der Bibliothek Warburg 1926–27*, Berlin, 1930. The point is also discussed *inter alia* by E. Panofsky, *Renaissance and Renais-sances in Western Art*, Stockholm, 1960, p. 40, and recently by Eugenio Luporini, *Brunelleschi*, Milan, 1964, esp. notes 31 and 33.

47. 'Similmente la scrittura non sarebbe bella se non quando le lettere sue proportionali in figura et in quantità et in sito et in ordine et in tutti i modi de' visibili colle quali si congregano con esse tutti le parti diverse . . .' *Lorenzo Ghiberti's Denkwürdig-keiten* (I Commentarii), ed. J. v. Schlosser, Berlin, 1912, MS. fol. 25 v. I am indebted for this reference to Mrs. K. Baxandall.

48. Antonio Manetti (attrib), *Vita di Ser Brunellesco*, ed. E. Toesca, Florence, 1927. 'E nel guardare le sculture, come quello che aveva buono occhio ancora mentale, et avveduto in tutte le cose, vide el modo del murare degli antichi et le loro simmetrie, e parvegli conoscere un certo ordine di membri e d'ossa molto evidentemente. . . . Fece pensiero di ritrovare el modo de' murari eccellenti e di grand'artificio degli antichi, e le loro proporzioni musicali . . .'

49. See above, especially E. Luporini, note *cit*.

same biography according to which Brunelleschi left Florence for Rome because he was not awarded the commission of the Baptistry doors, so obviously bears the stamp of a pragmatic reconstruction that it need not be taken seriously. Of course this would not exclude any number of trips by Brunelleschi to Rome during which he may have studied ancient methods of vaulting and ancient forms of capitals.

But seen in the light of the palaeographic parallel such studies of detail may well have come after the main reform. Humanistic script also came to embody features, especially in majuscules, that were directly taken from Roman monuments, but the basic structure of the *bella lettera antica* was not Roman but Romanesque. Like the reform of script the reform of architecture was certainly due to the new and exclusive enthusiasm for antiquity, but its inspiration came mainly from monuments of the Florentine past that were venerated as Roman relics. In this respect there is evidence, not yet considered by art historians, that strongly suggests a link between these two reform movements, for once more the clues point to Niccolò Niccoli and to Coluccio Salutati.

Vespasiano actually tells us that Niccolò 'especially favoured Pippo di Ser Brunelleso, Luca della Robbia and Lorenzo Ghiberti and was on intimate terms with them'.[50] But this testimonial is rather vague and late in date. More precious and more startling evidence is buried in Guarino's invective of 1413 against Niccolò Niccoli, a date that is a few years earlier than any of Brunelleschi's first efforts in the new style. This is what Guarino writes about Niccolò Niccoli:

> Who could help bursting with laughter when this man, in order to appear also to expound the laws of architecture, bares his arm and probes ancient buildings, surveys the walls, diligently explains the ruins and half-collapsed vaults of destroyed cities, how many steps there were in the ruined theatre, how many columns either lie dispersed in the square or still stand erect, how many feet the basis is wide, how high the point of the obelisque rises. In truth mortals are smitten with blindness. He thinks he will please the people while they everywhere make fun of him. . . . [51]

Here is a precious document therefore which shows

Niccolò Niccoli as interested in the externals of ancient buildings as he was in ancient lettering and spelling. We can even infer what spurred this interest in Florence at this particular moment. The clue is found in a famous pamphlet by Salutati which strangely enough has also escaped the attention of architectural historians. Once more we are in the context of polemics. Salutati, the Florentine chancellor, was out to defend and exalt the dignity of Florence against the attacks of the Milanese Loschi.[52] The background of this polemic has been illuminated in Hans Baron's book on *The Crisis of Humanism*.[53] Baron has emphasized how the civic pride of Florence was aroused by the moment of mortal danger from the north when the Visconti of Milan made ready to snuff out the last of the independent city states. It was in this patriotic propaganda that the legendary links between Florence and the Roman Empire loomed large and Salutati was out to prove that this claim is well founded. He proved it by art historical arguments:

> The fact that our city was founded by Romans can be inferred from the most compelling conjectures. There is a very old tradition obscured by the passage of years, that Florence was built by the Romans, there is in this city a Capitol and a Forum close by, . . . there is the former temple of Mars whom the aristocracy believed to be the father of the Roman nation, a temple built neither in the Greek nor in the Etruscan manner, but plainly in the Roman one. Let me add another thing, though a matter of the past; there was another sign of our origin that existed up to the first third of the fourteenth century, . . . that is an equestrian statue of Mars on the Ponte Vecchio, which had been preserved by the populace in memory of the Romans. . . . We also still have the traces of the arches of the aqueduct built according to the custom of our ancestors . . . and there still exist the round towers, the fortifications of the gates now joined with the Bishop's Palace, which anyone who had seen Rome would not only see but swear to be Roman, not only because of their material and brickwork, but because of their shape.[54]

50. *Ed. cit.*, p. 441.
51. *Ed. cit.*, pp. 39–40. 'Quis sibi quominus risu dirumpatur abstineat, cum ille ut etiam de achitectura rationes explicare credatur, lacertos exerens, antiqua probat aedificia, moenia recenset, iacentium ruinas urbium et "semirutos" fornices, diligenter edisserit quot disiecta gradibus theatra, quot per areas columnae aut stratae iaceant aut stantes exurgant, quot pedibus basis pateat quot (obeliscorum) vertex emineat. Quantis mortalium pectora tenebris obducuntur.'

52. For an (abbreviated) edition and translation into Italian see E. Garin, *Prosatori Latini del Quattrocento*, pp. 8–36.
53. *Op. cit.*, esp. pp. 81–85; for the question of date B. Ullman, *Salutati*, p. 33, and Baron, 2nd ed., pp. 484–7.
54. 'Quod autem haec urbs romanos habuerit auctores, urgentissimis colligitur coniecturis, stante siquidem fama, quae fit obscurior annis, urbem florentinam opus fuisse romanum: sunt in hac civitate Capitolium, et iuxta Capitolium Forum; est Parlasium sive Circus, est et locus qui Thermae dicitur, est et regio Parionis, est et locus quem Capaciam vocant, est et templum olim Martis insigne quem gentikitas romani generis volebat auctorem; et templum non graeco non tusco more factum, sed plane romano.

There is more literary evidence for this interest in the architectural style of the monuments we now assign to the Florentine 'proto-Renaissance'. Giovanni da Prato's *Paradiso degli Alberti* which Baron dates around 1425, the very years of Brunelleschi's reform, contains another discussion of the Roman origin of Florence which is probably dependent on Salutati but gives more details. Its description of the Baptistry as an ancient temple of Mars scarcely has a parallel in pre-Renaissance literature:

> This temple can be seen to be of singular beauty and in the most ancient form of building according to the custom and method of the Romans. On close inspection and reflection it will be judged by everyone not only in Italy but in all Christianity the most notable and singular work. Look at the columns in the interior which are all uniform carrying architraves of finest marble supporting with the greatest skill and ingenuity that great weight of the vault that can be seen from below and makes the pavement appear more spacious and more graceful. Look at the piers with the walls supporting the vault above, with the galleries excellently fashioned between one vault and the other. Look at the interior and the exterior carefully and you will find it as architecture useful, delightful, lasting, solved and perfect in every glorious and happy century.[55]

While these lines were being written Brunelleschi was probably already at work to revive this form of building. We do not know for certain to which building should go the honour of having been the first in which Brunelleschi ventured this deliberate break with current usage to become the *risucitatore delle muraglie antiche alla romanescha* as he is called by Giovanni Rucellai.[56]

Brunelleschi's ascendancy in the Cathedral *Opera* coincides with the work on three important projects, the Ospedale degli Innocenti, the San Lorenzo Sacristy, and, if we can believe his early biographer, the Palazzo della Parte Guelfa.[57] That there was some give and take between two of these projects at least is indicated by the fact that a certain Antonio de Domenico '*capomaestro della parte Guelfa*' was detailed in March 1421 to do some work on the building of the Innocenti.[58] If it could ever be shown that the Parte Guelfa was the first project in which the new reformed style was used, a certain link could perhaps be established between the interest of the 'civic humanists' in the Roman monuments of Florence and the revival of the style. For though the *Parte Guelfa* appears to have lost much of its power in the course of the fourteenth century it may still have been true, to use Gene A. Brucker's formulation, 'that it remained a visible symbol of the Guelf tradition. Most Florentines had come to accept the Parte's contention that it was the city's most vital link with her past and also the guardian of her destiny.'[59] Among their ceremonial rights and duties was the precedence given to the captains of the *Parte* to lead the annual procession to the Baptistry at the Feast of San Giovanni, the patron saint of Florence.[60] Would it not have been fitting to build their palace in the admired style of that ancient shrine? A new statute of the *Parte Guelfa* was approved in March 1420. It had been prepared by a commission whose members 'in this preparation could rely on the work and aid of Leonardo Bruni'.[61] It would certainly be tempting to connect the new building with this attempt at reviving the institution. According to Manetti Brunelleschi was only called in when the building had already been begun. In the absence of further evidence we cannot tell whether this may have

'Unum adiungam, licet nunc non extet, aliud originis nostrae signum, quod usque ad tertiam partem quarti decimi saeculi post incarnationem mediatoris Dei et hominum Jesu Christi apud Pontem qui Vetus dicitur, erat equestris statua Martis, quam in memoriam Romani generis iste populus reservabat, quam una cum pontibus tribus rapuit vis aquarum, annis iam completis pridie Nonas Novembrias septuaginta; quam quidem vivunt adhuc plurimi qui viderunt. Restant adhuc arcus aquaeductusque vestigia, more parentum nostrorum, qui talis fabricae machinamentis dulces aquas ad usum omnium deducebant. Quae cum omnia romanae sint res, romana nomina romanique moris imitatio, quis audeat dicere, tam celebris famae stante praesidio, rerum talium auctores alios fuisse quam Romanos? Extant adhuc rotundae turres et portarum monimenta, quae nunc Episcopatui connexa sunt, quae qui Romam viderit non videbit solum, sed iurabit esse romana, non solum qualia sunt Romae moenia, latericia coctilique materia, sed et forma' (*ed. cit.*, pp. 18–20).

55. 'Vedesi questo tempio di singulare belleza e in forma di fabrica antichissima al costume e al modo romano; il quale tritamente raguardato e pensato, si giudicherà per ciascuno non che in Italia ma in tutta cristianità essere opera più notabilissima e singulare. Raguardisi le colonne che dentro vi sono tutte uniforme, colli architravi di finissimi marmi sostenenti con grandissima arte e ingegno tanta graveza quanto è la volta, che di sotto aparisce rendendo il pavimento più ampio e legiadro. Raguardisi i pilastri colle pareti sostenenti la volta di sopra, colli anditi egregiamente fabricati infra l'una volta e l'altra. Raguardisi il dentro e di fuori tritamente, e giudicherassi architettura utile, dilettevole e perpetua e soluta e perfetta in ogni glorioso e felicissimo secolo' (*ed. cit.*, vol. III, pp. 232–3).

56. *Giovanni Rucellai ed il suo Zibaldone*, ed. A. Perosa, London, 1960, p. 61.
57. For a calendar of dates and documents see Cornelius von Fabriczy, *Filippo Brunelleschi*, Stuttgart, 1892, pp. 609–17, and the same author's 'Il palazzo nuovo della Parte Guelfa', *Bulletino dell'Associazione per la difesa di Firenze antica*, IV, June 1904, pp. 39–49.
58. Fabriczy, *Brunelleschi*, p. 559.
59. Gene A. Brucker, *Florentine Politics and Society, 1343–1378*, Princeton, N.J., 1962, pp. 99–100.
60. Fabriczy, *Brunelleschi*, p. 292.
61. H. Baron, *op. cit.*, p. 612, n. 18.

happened as early as 1418 as some have conjectured[62] or whether the Innocenti project which was started in 1419 has the priority. One thing is likely—Brunelleschi's departure from the traditional Gothic methods was at first confined to certain commissions.[63] In all probability he continued to use the earlier idiom for some of the private *palazzi* which he apparently built in the twenties.

In any case it is clear that Brunelleschi's reform parallels the humanist reforms also in that respect that it is more concerned with the weeding out of corrupt practices than with an entirely fresh beginning. What strikes us, in the vocabulary of Quattrocento architecture, is less its classical character than its link with the medieval past. The typical form of the palace window as we see it on Michelozzo's Medici palace is a case in point (Fig. 7). There is nothing here that matches Roman forms, but much that goes back directly to medieval practice as exemplified by the Gothic window of the Bargello (Fig. 8). All the Renaissance architect did was to remove the solecism of the pointed arch and so to make the general shape conform to the rules abstracted from Vitruvius and Roman buildings. The relation can be taken as typical. It is this type of continuity behind diversity which we so often find when we analyse the manifestations of the Renaissance. No wonder opinions differ so widely as to the degree of novelty we should attribute to the period. Would it not be correct to say that the novelty lies frequently in the avoidance of mistakes that would infringe the classical norm?[64] This avoidance in its turn springs from the new freedom to criticize the tradition and to reject anything that seems 'a crime and a sacrilege' in the eyes of ancient authority.

It is this after all that distinguishes the humanists from the more conformist scholastics. It is this that made Niccolò and his friends so unpopular and so startling. He arrogated to himself the right to feel superior over the greatest figures of the Florentine past because he knew certain things better—diphthongs for instance. Is it not possible that it was this same critical attitude

that connects the humanist movement also with the second of Brunelleschi's momentous reforms, the introduction of scientific perspective into the vocabulary and the practice of painting?

The first great work of art, of course, in which Brunelleschi's style *all'antica* is combined with his achievement of mathematical perspective is the presentation of the Christian mystery of the Trinity in Masaccio's fresco in Santa Maria Novella, painted about 1425.

Much, perhaps too much, has been written about perspective and the claim has been made in various forms that this new style reflects the new philosophy, the new *Weltanschauung*, centred on man and on a new rational conception of space. But cannot Occam's Razor be applied to these entities? Can it not be argued that perspective is precisely what it claims to be, a method of representing a building or any scene as it would be seen from a certain vantage point? If it does, Brunelleschi's perspective represents an objectively valid invention, no less valid than the invention of spectacles a century earlier. Nobody has as yet claimed that to look at the world through lenses to correct one's bad eyesight is due to a new *Weltanschauung*, though we may claim that it is due to inventiveness.

Maybe the invention of scientific perspective can be seen as a reform that originated from the same critical scrutiny of tradition as did the introduction of diphthongs. The Trecento tradition that had its origin in Giotto was as vulnerable from that point of view as was the poetry of Dante, Petrarch and Boccaccio. Boccaccio could claim of Giotto that he was able to deceive the sense of sight,[65] but looked upon with cool detachment and with the legendary fame of ancient painters in mind this claim could hardly be upheld. There are inconsistencies in the spatial construction of Trecento paintings which must have jarred increasingly on critical minds the more the narrative style demanded a convincing setting.[66] It fits well with this interpretation that in Bruni's first Dialogue of 1401 there is also a critical reference to painting put into the mouth of Niccolò Niccoli. The passage which has also escaped the attention of art historians occurs in the context of Niccoli's attack on Petrarch and the advance publicity he was accused of giving to his *Africa*.

What would you say of a painter, who would claim to have such knowledge of his art that when he started to paint a scene people would believe that another Apelles or Zeuxis was born in their age, but when his paintings were revealed it would prove to

62. A. Chastel, *L'Art Italien*, Paris, 1956, I, p. 191. It appears, however, that this date which is sometimes found in the literature is based only on the negative evidence mentioned by Fabriczy in the article quoted under note 57: in the *protocolli notarili delle provvisioni dei Capitani e Consuli della Parte* of 1418–26 there is a reference under 17th September 1422 to the construction of the palace and to the *Operai* previously appointed to supervise this venture. Since this appointment is not recorded in the volume concerned Fabriczy concluded that it must have been referred to in an earlier (and lost) volume. So far, therefore, we have no means of knowing when the new palace was begun nor can we tell when Brunelleschi was called in.

63. G. Marchini, 'Il Palazzo Datini a Prato', *Bolletino d'Arte*, XLVI, July to September 1961, pp. 216–18.

64. E. H. Gombrich, 'Norma e Forma', *Filosofia*, XIV, July 1963. Now published in English in *Norm and Form*, London, 1966.

65. *Decamerone, Giornata VI, Novella 5*.

66. E. H. Gombrich, 'Visual Discovery through Art', *Arts Magazine*, XL, 1, November 1965.

be laughably painted with distorted outlines? Would he not deserve universal mockery?[67]

Whether or not Niccoli's darts are here directed against any particular artist, one thing is sure, at the time when they were published there was really nothing painters could do to rectify this strange impression of distorted outlines—indeed the closer they came to a naturalistic narrative, the more noticeable were such inconsistencies. Help had to come from outside, and looking at the matter *post factum* it is not at all surprising that it came from an architect.

The story of Brunelleschi's invention has been discussed and analysed by Panofsky, Krautheimer and John White.[68] According to Manetti the first perspective painting was a view of the Baptistry (Fig. 5) as seen through the door of the Cathedral. Looking at the painting, or rather its mirror reflection through a peephole, and looking at the real scene, the startled beholder could see that the two images were identical. It may be no accident that Brunelleschi took the Baptistry for his demonstration piece. For this famous landmark of Florence which Dante calls '*il mio bel San Giovanni*' had figured on many traditional views of the city. We can discern it well, both on the Biadaiuolo Codex on grain distribution, of the Trecento (Fig. 10), and again on the fresco in the Bigallo of 1352 (Fig. 9). The examples show one of the difficulties in rendering this beautiful building without distorted lines; the representation must be consistently constructed if the patterns of the incrustation are not to get you into trouble. Even on that later Cassone (Fig. 11) which may well have been influenced by Brunelleschi's panel, this inconsistency is disturbing, once attention has been drawn to it.

How was it that it fell to an architect to find the remedy for this awkward distortion of lines? Maybe, because an architect is used to asking a different question from the painter. The painter is apt to ask 'What do things really look like?' while the architect is more often confronted with the more precise question of what can be seen from a given point. It is the answer to this simple question which must have given Brunelleschi the means to solve the painter's puzzle. For obviously, if Brunelleschi was asked, for example, during the work on the cupola of the Cathedral whether the lantern would be visible from the door of the Baptistry he would have replied that this could

easily be found out by drawing a straight line from the one point to the other. If the line hits no obstacle the points must be visible. Even today, whenever the problem is raised whether a new building is likely to obscure or spoil a famous view the architect will be called upon to show exactly how much of his projected building will be visible from a given point and how its silhouette will relate to the city's skyline. Needless to say this is a question that allows of an exact answer. None of the arguments that have been customarily adduced to stress the conventional character of perspective materially affect its accuracy—neither the fact that we see with two eyes nor the fact that the retina is curved or that there is a conflict between the projection onto a plane and onto a sphere. The same objective laws secure of course an uncontrovertible answer to the question as to what part of a room can be seen from a given spot through a window. It all follows from the fact that visual lines are straight and that Euclidean geometry works, at least here on earth.

It also did in 1420. What Brunelleschi had to demonstrate to his painter friends was precisely a view through an opening that corresponds to a window or frame. He chose the door for the Florentine Cathedral. What such a door offers is of course a frame of reference at a given distance against which the view out there can be plotted. If it has a gate in form of a grille, or if a net is placed in front, so much the better. With the help of this simple demonstration it can be shown that a perspective picture can be projected onto a plane. The geometrical problems of projection may not yet be solved by this simple answer, but at least they can thus be correctly posed.

Why is it, then, that this simple solution did not occur to anyone? Why is it even asserted today by the most eminent students of the problem that there is a flaw in this argument? It is because it may be claimed in fact that we always *see* the world *liniamentis distortis*. For we must not confuse this simple question of *what* we see from a given point with the similar-sounding question of how things appear to us from that point. Strictly speaking that second question allows of no objective answer. It will depend on many circumstances, a building will look small when 'dwarfed' by a neighbour, a room may look larger with one wallpaper than with another. Most of all, our knowledge and expectation will invariably transform the appearance of familiar objects or identical shapes receding in depth through what are technically known as the constancies, the stabilizing mechanism of perception that counteracts the objective fluctuations of the stimuli impinging on our retinas.

The paradox is only that this transformation does not justify the criticism that has been made of the validity

67. 'Quid igitur, si pictor quispiam, cum magnam se habere eius artis scientiam profiteretur, theatrum aliquod pingendum conduceret, deinde magna expectatione hominum facta, qui alterum Apellen aut Zeuxin temporibus suis natum esse crederent, picturae eius aperirentur, liniamentis distortis atque ridicule admodum pictae, nonne is dignus esset quem omnes deriderent?' *Ed. cit.*, p. 72.
68. For a full bibliography see Luporini, *Brunelleschi*, n. 63.

of Brunelleschi's invention. For where perspective is applied convincingly it enables and even compels us to read a projection on a flat panel as a report of a three-dimensional configuration.[69] It can be shown and has been shown that in this reading the constancies come into their own and we again transform the appearance of the objects represented much as we would transform it in reality. This transformation must not be confused with the total illusion we call *trompe l'œil*. It even applies to schematic images of three-dimensional views. A few moments spent on architectural photographs with a pair of dividers will demonstrate the degree to which we underrate the objective diminution of distant windows or houses as compared to the corresponding features in the foreground.

These discussions may seem to lead far off the problem of this paper. But we are unlikely to get a clear picture of any movement in history before we try to assess the advantages it offered its adherents. These advantages, we have seen, may be utilitarian, psychological, or both. They can spring from the feeling of superiority that follows even from a slight improvement that makes earlier methods look first old-fashioned and soon ridiculous. Even the early humanist reform of Latin orthography had this effect of superior knowledge backed up by genuine philological and archaeological training. The reform of lettering had the added advantage of greater clarity and beauty. Both were in fact a symptom, but not a symptom of a new philosophy so much as of an increasingly critical attitude towards tradition, a wish to eradicate mistakes that had crept in, of getting back to better texts and an unclouded

view of the wisdom of the ancients. Brunelleschi's reforms went further, but in the same direction. We may call the success of his architectural innovations a mere fashion though for him the eradication of such solecisms as the Gothic arch unsanctioned by Vitruvius was certainly a genuine improvement, a return to the correct manner of building. In his reform of painting methods he could feel the assurance that he had really discovered, or re-discovered, the tool that had enabled the famous ancient masters Apelles or Zeuxis to deceive the sense of sight. Here was tangible progress and this progress, in its turn, reacted back on the self-confidence of his generation and those who followed.[70] From the preoccupation of a small *brigata* of arrogant young men the Renaissance had become a European movement, irresistible in its appeal. But perhaps it is no mere paradox to assert that this movement had its origin not so much in the discovery of man as in the discovery of diphthongs.[71]

---

69. E. H. Gombrich, *Art and Illusion*, New York and London, chaps. VIII and IX.

70. E. H. Gombrich, 'The Renaissance Concept of Artistic Progress and its Consequences', *Actes du XVII Congrès International d'histoire de l'art*, now reprinted in *Norm and Form*, London, 1966.

71. After completion of this manuscript I received, through the courtesy of the author, Professor Frederick Hartt's paper on 'Art and Freedom in Quattrocento Florence', *Essays in Memory of Karl Lehmann* (ed. L. Freeman Sandler), New York, 1964, pp. 114–31, in which he does me the honour of referring to my views on Hegelian art history and bases his fresh interpretation largely on Hans Baron's book to which I am also indebted. It would be both premature and presumptuous of me at this stage to enter into a critical discussion of his rival hypothesis beyond stating that a transition from letters to art seems to me more natural than a direct reflection of political events in the themes and expressions of individual works of art. This general remark, of course, is not meant to detract from the interest of Professor Hartt's attempt to break through the vicious circle of Hegelian *Geistesgeschichte*.

H. W. JANSON

Ground Plan and Elevation in Masaccio's
Trinity Fresco

A little more than half a century ago, G. F. Kern published a detailed study of the perspective construction of Masaccio's *Trinity*.[1] His findings—though not his art historical conclusions—have been so widely accepted that it has remained the only scholarly paper on the subject. These findings may be summarized as follows: the projection of the architectural interior is mathematically correct, permitting us to derive from it an unambiguous ground plan (Fig. 1) whose central feature is a square covered by a barrel vault. The figures inside this chapel, on the other hand, fail to show the same mastery of the new scientific perspective; they are not seen *di sotto in su*, as they ought to be, and the position of God the Father in space is irrational, since His feet rest on a platform attached to the rear wall of the chapel while His hands support the arms of the cross, which is in the same plane as Mary and John, near the entrance.

That the perspective of the architecture is accurate enough to yield an unambiguous ground plan is certainly true, but in every other respect Kern's analysis leaves ample room for doubt. It contains, in fact, one gross factual error, which should have alerted Masaccio scholars not to take Kern's reliability for granted. The author states that he took all important measurements from the fresco itself,[2] yet the only figure he cites—the depth and width of the area covered by the barrel vault—is far off the mark: 320 cm, more than the maximum width of the entire fresco.[3] While the depth of the area in question (VTZG, Fig. 1) is conjectural, its width can be measured directly; it corresponds to the distance between the pilasters, which is 204 cm. Nor can Kern's figure be a printer's error. It agrees with the scale included in his perspective diagram,[4] according to which the width of the mural is 490 cm, the width of the aisle of S. Maria Novella 685 cm,

and the distance between the central and the lateral vanishing points (i.e., the distance of the beholder from the picture as set by the artist) 775 cm. Only one of these figures is correct: the width of the aisle, measured from the wall to the center of the piers. If we change the scale in Kern's diagram to accord with the actual size of the mural, the distance of the beholder as determined by Kern becomes 520 cm, only three-quarters the width of the aisle and suspiciously short. Kern was quite unaware of the confusion, since in his text he claims to have corroborated Schmarsow's observation that the distance of the beholder approximately equals the width of the aisle.[5] An error of 35 per cent in these basic measurements makes one wonder about the trustworthiness of Kern's conclusions regarding the shape of the area covered by the barrel vault.

The vault, as Kern correctly observed, consists of seven bands of eight coffers each, the nearest band hidden from the beholder by the arch over the entrance to the chapel. In order to fit this vault over a square, Kern is forced to assume that the coffers are not uniform squares but rectangles of varying sizes, the two rows at the top of the vault being the most nearly square, those at the bottom the most elongated. Is it likely that Masaccio—or Brunelleschi, if we grant him the role of consultant—planned such irregular coffers? To maintain this is about as plausible, it seems to me, as to claim that the columns in the *Trinity* were intended to have oval instead of circular cross-sections. While oblong coffers and oval columns are not entirely unknown in later times, neither belong to the architectural vocabulary of classical antiquity and would be inconceivable in any design based on the style of Brunelleschi. If in the fresco the two bottom rows of coffers, half concealed behind the columns of the entrance, appear elongated in relation to the rest (as in fact they do), we must regard this as a slip—or perhaps an intentional departure from accuracy to mitigate the extreme distortion of these coffers—in the process of executing the mural, rather than as part of the plan of the architectural structure. That Masaccio had a ground plan of the chapel, and that this ground

1. 'Das Dreifaltigkeitsfresko von Santa Maria Novella, eine perspektivisch-architekturgeschichtliche Studie', *Jahrbuch der königlich preussischen Kunstsammlungen*, XXXIV, 1913, pp. 36–58.
2. *Op. cit.*, p. 39, footnote.
3. This width, including the protrusions beyond the vertical edges, is 317 cm; see Eve Borsook, *The Mural Painters of Tuscany*, London, 1960, p. 143. Without the protrusions, the width of the fresco is just under 300 cm.
4. *Op. cit.*, p. 38; this is the only one of Kern's drawings to show a scale.
5. *Op. cit.*, p. 43.

plan must have reflected the thinking of Brunelleschi, can hardly be doubted; how else could he have worked out a perspective view so intricate and precise? We must also postulate that the plan of the chapel was a square; a less regular form would be inconsistent with the solemnity of the subject.[6] But the plan of the chapel is not coextensive with the barrel-vaulted area. The interior depicted by Masaccio includes, in addition, four space compartments: two on the flanks (containing the four columns on which the barrel vault rests), the entrance area, and its counterpart in the rear of the structure. In Kern's plan (Fig. 1), these four compartments have identical dimensions, so that, together with the square of the vaulted area, they form a Greek cross. Here, however, Kern disregards a bit of visual evidence which he explicitly acknowledges elsewhere in his paper.[7] The columns at the entrance—and their counterparts in the rear—are set so closely against the wall that about one-quarter of the (originally square) abacus has been cut off. These abacuses, then, are rectangles of the ratio 4:3, with the shorter side toward the beholder. Their longer side defines the depth of the entrance area and its equivalent in the rear, while the shorter side corresponds to the width of the lateral compartments.[8] Thus the lateral compartments are narrower than those at the front and rear, and the complete symmetry of Kern's ground plan becomes illusory. Another argument against the assumption that the barrel vault covers a square is purely aesthetic: if it did, the interior of the chapel would give the impression of being wider than it is deep, since in the perspective view the lateral space compartments are partly visible while those in the front and rear do not enhance the depth aspect of the interior (note that the arch over the entrance obscures the first band of coffers). In order to balance the *apparent* width and depth of the chapel, Masaccio had to make the vaulted area oblong rather than square; and the barrel vault in the fresco does, in fact, look deeper than it is wide.

How did Masaccio manage to design a square ground plan for his chapel despite the oblong shape of the vaulted area? I suggest that he did so by making a square of the vaulted area *plus* the lateral compartments; the front and rear compartments he treated as 'entrances' that do not form part of the chapel proper (Fig. 2). In order to retrace the steps by which he arrived at this solution, we shall find it helpful to measure the component parts of the structure, not in centimeters but in the unit employed in Florence at the time, i.e., the braccio (58.36 cm). For our purposes, the half-braccio, or palmo (29.18 cm), is even more convenient; the scales in Figs. 2 and 3 are calibrated in palmi. It turns out that the distance between the pilasters in the fresco, and thus the diameter of the barrel vault, equals seven palmi (204 cm); the width of the abacus over the columns at the entrance, which as we have seen equals the width of the lateral space compartments, is one palmo. The total width of the chapel interior, therefore, is nine palmi, and its depth —i.e., the length of the barrel vault—must also be nine palmi (leaving aside the 'entrance areas'). The true size of the coffers cannot be measured directly, since the nearest visible band of them is more than two palmi behind the picture plane, but it is clear that they are three times as wide as the intervening ridges (excepting the anomalously elongated first and last sets of coffers). Masaccio's choice of seven palmi as the diameter of the vault (by trial-and-error or calculation) must be regarded as a singularly fortunate one, since it made the circumference of the vault another integer, eleven palmi ($r\pi = 3.5 \times 3.1416 = 10.996$).[9] By making each coffer one palmo square, and the width of the ridges a third of a palmo, he achieved an even distribution of eight coffers and nine ridges over the full length of the circumference by the simplest of arithmetic ($8 + \frac{9}{3} = 11$; cf. the lower part of Fig. 3). Had he wanted this vault to cover a square area, he could have done so easily enough; for five bands of coffers, plus six ridges, would have made the depth of the vault seven palmi—the same as its diameter. Instead, he chose to make the vault nine palmi deep, and in order to do so he added an extra band of coffers in the front and rear but omitted the accompanying ridges, so that the farthest band of coffers abuts directly against the arch of the 'rear entrance', as clearly visible in the fresco.

We might pause at this point to inquire how Kern arrived at the—in my view mistaken—conclusion that the vaulted area is a square. The analytical drawings he provides are entirely consistent within themselves,

6. On the pervading importance of the square as a 'perfect figure' in Renaissance religious architecture, see Rudolf Wittkower, *Architectural Principles in the Age of Humanism*, London, 1952, *passim*.
7. *Op. cit.*, pp. 38 (diagram) and 39.
8. By analogy, we must assume that the columns in the lateral compartments are as close to the wall as those at the entrance.

9. Seven is the only simple integer which, when taken as the diameter of a semicircle, yields a circumference closely approximating another integer. Did Masaccio learn this from Brunelleschi, or did he consult a mathematician such as Paolo Toscanelli or Fra Ubertino Strozzi? The latter, a Dominican, was living in the monastery of S. Maria Novella in the early fifteenth century, according to P. Vincenzo Marchese, O.P., *Memorie dei più insigni pittori ... domenicani*, Florence, 1845, I, p. 275, who cites Borghiniani's chronicle of S. Maria Novella (II, p. 217, *ad ann.* 1413). The chronicle has recently been published in its entirety by Stefano Orlandi, O.P., in his *Necrologia di S. Maria Novella*, Florence, 1955. 22/7 as the ratio of the circumference of a circle to its diameter had been known to mathematicians ever since Archimedes.

despite the confusion of scales mentioned earlier, and yield the result he claims; the source of the trouble is the diagrammatic representation of the painted architecture, which does not simply record the principal lines of the fresco but simplifies and 'idealizes' them. Thus, in the diagram, all the orthogonals meet perfectly in a single vanishing point just below what was then the bottom line of the picture, i.e., the platform with the kneeling donors. In reality, the level of the vanishing point cannot be fixed with precision. All the available orthogonals are comparatively short, far above the vanishing point, and close together; they converge at rather sharp angles, so that the exact point of intersection is difficult to establish. Some of them are blurred by the damaged condition of the surface, and must have been even harder to make out before the recent cleaning and restoration. A few do indeed appear to meet at the spot indicated by Kern, but others meet at a lower level. Kern simply selected the highest among several possible vanishing points, under the impression that it corresponded to the average beholder's eye level.[10] That Masaccio placed the vanishing point at what he considered normal eye level does indeed seem highly plausible. But Kern, of course, did not know at what height above the church floor the fresco had been before its transfer to the façade wall. Now that, thanks to Ugo Procacci, the mural has been returned to its original location and reunited with its lower portion, the skeleton in the niche (Fig. 5), it is apparent that Kern's vanishing point, 175 cm from the floor, is too high. It demands a beholder some 184 cm tall, a good deal above average in present-day Italy and even more so in the Quattrocento, when people were shorter than they are now (as indicated by any collection of suits of armor).[11] What Masaccio regarded as the normal height of human beings is evident from the skeleton in the fresco, which is 'life-size', being exactly in the picture plane; it measures five and a half palmi (160 cm).[12] For Masaccio, normal eye level must thus have been about five and a quarter palmi from the floor, or 153 cm, some 20 cm lower than Kern's vanishing point. Considering the dimensions of the whole mural, this difference may seem unimportant, yet it has considerable significance, as will be seen below.

The lateral vanishing point, or distance point (since it indicates the beholder's distance from the picture as set

by the artist), is even more precarious in Kern's diagram than the level of the central vanishing point (i.e., the horizon). Kern locates it by 'restoring' the oblong abacus of one of the columns at the entrance to its original square shape, by drawing a diagonal through this foreshortened square and continuing it to its intersection with the horizon. Theoretically, the method is unexceptionable; in practice, it cannot be carried out with any precision. The smallest error in reconstructing the square of the abacus—and such errors are impossible to avoid under the circumstances—will cause a minute change in the angle of the diagonal, which will produce a sizeable shift of the distance point, and a consequent shift of all the points in Kern's diagram that depend on the location of that point. Moreover, since the two lines whose intersection defines the distance point meet at a rather sharp angle, a lowering of the horizon by as little as 20 cm will displace the distance point some 40 to 60 cm. It would be futile to argue the matter in greater detail. Suffice it to say that the beholder's distance from the picture as determined by Kern—520 cm, as pointed out before—is clearly too short; it ought to be about seven meters, roughly equal to the width of the aisle. We might add, however, that it was not at all necessary for Masaccio to assume a fixed distance of the beholder from the picture. He could—and probably did—achieve a correctly foreshortened image without reference to this distance.[13]

---

10. Cf. op. cit., p. 43.

11. The present placement of the *Trinity* corresponds exactly to its original one, since a portion of the architrave was found *in situ*, as reported orally by Procacci and noted in Ursula Schlegel, 'Observations on Masaccio's Trinity Fresco . . .', *The Art Bulletin*, XLV, 1963, p. 21, n. 12. See also Fig. 7.

12. From the head of the (restored) cranium to the heel. The donors, though kneeling, are of the same size; see below, p. 87.

13. See H. Wieleitner, 'Zur Erfindung der verschiedenen Distanzkonstruktionen in der malerischen Perspektive', *Repertorium für Kunstwissenschaft*, XLIII, 1920, p. 254. The distance point in the fresco can be verified—and the degree of Masaccio's accuracy measured—by a simple method, which Kern surely knew but failed to utilize, based on the difference between the apparent height of the vault and columns in the rear of the chapel and their real height (i.e., the height of the vault and columns at the entrance), as shown in Fig. 2. In this longitudinal section, the length of the vault is assumed to be nine palmi, and the horizon is placed five and a quarter palmi above the church floor. The visual ray descending from the top of the vault in the rear passes through the surface of the picture at *a* (four and a third palmi lower than the real height of the vault) and intersects the horizon at A, 24½ palmi (7.15 m) from the wall. The ray descending from the abacus of the columns in the rear ought to intersect the horizon at the same point, but does so at B, somewhat closer to the wall (23 palmi, or 6.71 m). The two rays meet at C, 28½ palmi (8.30 m) from the wall and three palmi (88 cm) above the floor of the church. In a fully consistent perspective projection these three points would coincide. C obviously is not the true distance point, being more than two palmi below the horizon as determined by the convergence of the orthogonals. Who is at fault here, we wonder—we or Masaccio? If the fault were ours, it should be possible to make the two rays meet at the horizon line by changing the variables in our diagram, i.e., the level of the horizon and the length of the vault. But this proves to be impossible: if we raise the horizon to the level postulated by Kern (it obviously cannot be lowered), we increase the distance between A and B; and if we shorten the vault to seven palmi in accordance with Kern's ground plan, we move A and B closer to the wall but the

Once we realize the importance of seven palmi as the key measure for the design of the vault, we may hope to discover the same unit elsewhere in the fresco. Such is indeed the case, as evidenced by Fig. 4, which shows a grid, calibrated in palmi, superimposed on a photograph of the mural in its present state.[14] The most striking recurrence of seven palmi is the distance from the floor of the church to that of Masaccio's chapel. Seven palmi above the chapel floor we reach the bottom line of the arms of the cross. The apex of the vault (i.e., the bottom line of the entablature) is exactly twenty palmi from the floor of the church. The abacuses of the columns at the entrance are three and a half palmi below the entablature, as we would expect; but it is something of a surprise to find that the abacuses of the columns in the rear are three and a half palmi below those in front. Thus the perspective projection of the vault is inscribed within a square of seven palmi on the picture plane, in what seems to be an attempt to harmonize surface design and depth. The harmony is somewhat forced, however, as shown by the two distance points in Fig. 2. In order to make distant point A coincide with B, Masaccio should either have made the rear columns a bit taller, or the rear arch somewhat smaller.

By perusing Fig. 4, the reader will readily find other important distances measured in whole palmi, such as that from the church floor to the rear edge of the skeleton's sarcophagus (three palmi) and that from the church floor to the top of the donors' heads (ten palmi, half-way from the church floor to the entablature). At present, the height of the kneeling donors is somewhat less than four palmi. However, as Ursula Schlegel has pointed out, the true edge of the platform on which they kneel is lost, and the present edge the work of restorers (cf. Fig. 7). She suggests that the donors originally knelt at a slightly lower level (see Fig. 6). In the grid of Fig. 4, this would be exactly the six-palmi line above the church floor, and the donors' height would then become exactly four palmi—an interesting confirmation of Miss Schlegel's conjecture. Our grid also lends support to another aspect of Miss Schlegel's

reconstruction: the area covered by the fresco, she believes, must have been slightly wider and taller than it is today, to accommodate a painted frame. By extending the present edges of the mural at the top and sides to the nearest whole palmo, we gain the additional margin needed for such a frame. The original height and width of the mural were in all likelihood twenty-three and eleven palmi, respectively.

What could have been the purpose—or, better, purposes—of the numerical relationships pervading the *Trinity*? They bring to mind, of course, the Pythagorean tradition of harmonious numbers, whose significance for Renaissance architecture has been pointed out by Rudolf Wittkower.[15] They also serve to correlate ground plan and elevation, surface and depth. Finally—and this is by no means their least important function—they made it possible for Masaccio to transfer his complex and exacting architectural design intact from the small scale of the preparatory drawings to the 'lifesize' scale of the fresco. No earlier artist had had to face this task, hence no established procedure was available. The architecture in Gothic painting, whether conceived as background or (in the case of interiors) as a 'cage' for the figures, invariably lacks the structural solidity, the consistent scale of real buildings, even when it portrays existing structures such as Florence Cathedral. The third dimension may be effectively suggested but is never measurable. Masaccio, in contrast, wanted the chapel of the *Trinity* to be as measurable in every respect as an actual piece of Brunelleschian architecture. Thus the Trecento technique of large-scale preparatory drawings (sinopie) on the first coat of plaster (arriccio), which were covered up area by area as the second coat (intonaco) was applied for each day's work of painting (giornata), would obviously not have been precise enough for his purpose; and there is no indication that he ever made a sinopia on the arriccio of the *Trinity*.[16] The time it took Masaccio to paint the mural could not have been

distance between them remains unchanged (A would be 18 palmi, or 5.25 m, from the wall, B 16½ palmi, or 4.81 m). The fault, then, is Masaccio's: there is an error of slightly more than six per cent in his perspective projection—not a very serious one, since it can be detected only by measurement rather than by direct inspection, but an indication that he very probably did not take a fixed distance of the beholder from the wall as his starting point.
14. The photo, Soprintendenza neg. no. 104648, has been taken with such care that it shows no significant linear distortion horizontally or vertically. I have verified this by checking a number of measurements based on the photo against the same measurements in the original and the tracing of the fresco, made by Leonetto Tintori, in the Uffizi.

15. *Op. cit.*
16. When the main portion of the fresco was transferred about 1860, only the intonaco was detached from the wall; the arriccio was destroyed. There is no record of what if anything appeared on its surface. (If it had held drawings comparable to the sinopie underneath the *Triumph of Death* in the Camposanto in Pisa, one might expect someone to have noted the fact.) After the return of the upper part of the mural to its original location in 1952, the bottom part, which had always remained *in situ*, was stripped from the wall (and then reattached), to see if the arriccio held a sinopia; there was none. I am indebted for the above information to Leonetto Tintori, who was in charge of the entire project. In Piero Sanpaolesi's monograph on Brunelleschi (Milan, 1962) there are two illustrations (Figs. 24, 25) described in the captions as tracings after the sinopia of the *Trinity*; they actually reproduce the tracing of the mural itself referred to in note 14 above.

much more than a month;[17] the work is done almost wholly in true fresco technique, with a minimum of additions 'a secco'. Nor did he use the cartoon method, which made its appearance only in the 1440's.[18] How, then, did he proceed? Did he superimpose a uniform grid of squares on his final drawing and transfer the entire design to a corresponding grid on the wall? There are remains of grid lines on the surface of the fresco, but these, as Oertel has pointed out, cover only limited areas (the figure of Mary and the capitals) and the several 'islands' of grid lines are unrelated to each other; they did not form part of an over-all system but served only for the transfer of certain particularly difficult details. For the composition as a whole, Masaccio must have relied on a different method that has left no visible trace: a grid not mechanically superimposed but one whose lines represented the main horizontal and vertical divisions of the design. He could, for instance, have marked the vertical divisions by plumb lines hanging from a board attached to the wall above the mural, and the horizontals by strings weighted at both ends and passed over hooks driven into the wall on either side of the working area. Such an arrangement would have permitted him to move the strings out of the way and put them back in place as needed. But in order for the system to be workable, the intervals had to be defined as simply as possible—in whole palmi or half-palmi.[19]

The standardization of measurements we have seen in the architecture of the *Trinity* may also be observed in the figures. The skeleton, we recall, is lifesize, five and a half palmi. The donors must have been intended to have the same scale. Kneeling, they are four palmi tall, if we accept the slight lowering of their platform advocated by Miss Schlegel; were they shown standing, they would very probably be five and a half (i.e.,

the tops of their heads would be on a level with those of Mary and John).[20] We may conclude from this that donors and skeleton are at the same distance from the beholder. The Sarcophagus is directly beneath the donors' platform, and the depth of both is identical—if the skeleton were placed three palmi higher, it would rest on the donors' platform but would retain its present size. The four figures inside the chapel occupy a spatial zone that is about two palmi farther from the beholder, and their height, therefore, is less: five palmi, with slight variations. Christ, measured from the heel to the top of the head, is exactly five palmi, God the Father a bit more (about 5.2 palmi), perhaps in order to leave enough space for the dove, while John is four and a half and Mary four and two-thirds. The feet of the latter two figures, however, are hidden from the beholder; if we allow for this by adding half a palmo to John, and a third of a palmo to Mary (who seems somewhat closer to the entrance), they too become five palmi tall.

The lesser height of the figures inside the chapel, as against those outside it, takes account only of their greater distance from the beholder measured along a line perpendicular to the wall; that we see them from below (so that, e.g., the feet of Christ are a good deal closer to the beholder's eye than His head) is disregarded as a factor in reducing their apparent height. The same is true, of course, of the architecture—the apparent width of pilasters and columns remains constant throughout their length; if the pilasters had horizontal instead of vertical flutes, these too would have the same size at the bottom as at the top. Parallel lines running at right angles to the plane of the horizon are not permitted to converge in Early Renaissance perspective, regardless of their length. In extreme cases, such as the upper part of the triumphal arch in Mantegna's *St. James Led to His Execution* in the Eremitani or in the Ionic capitals of the *Trinity*, this rule produces oddly distended shapes. Had Masaccio applied the rule to the figures of Christ and God the Father as rigidly as he did to the capitals (he attempted it in the face of Mary), the results would have been frightening. His lack of consistency here is thus entirely understandable, even though Kern censures him for it.

More consequential is Kern's complaint that God the Father arches illogically through the space of the chapel, His feet resting on a platform attached to the rear wall while His hands support the arms of the

17. Leonetto Tintori was kind enough to tell me that he has discerned 24 giornate and thinks that there may have been a few more.

18. See Robert Oertel, 'Wandmalerei und Zeichnung in Italien', *Mitteilungen des kunsthistorischen Instituts in Florenz*, v, 1940, pp. 309 ff. Oertel, however, postulates the existence of a sinopia, an assumption which, in the light of Tintori's findings, is almost surely mistaken, since it is hard to believe that Masaccio made a sinopia for the upper part of the fresco but not for the lower part.

19. Common fractions are awkward to calculate with, and decimal fractions were unknown until the seventeenth century. A detailed study of the partial grids must await publication of the full report of the restoration of the mural by Procacci and Tintori. For the capitals the horizontal intervals of the grid, according to Oertel, are 14.8 cm each, closely approximating half of a palmo (14.6 cm), while over the figure of Mary, oddly enough, the grid intervals vary from 12.5 to 13.9 cm but are always less than half a palmo (in the area of the head, the squares of the grid are subdivided into sixteen smaller squares). Could this be an experiment in proportional diminution so as to render the figure more accurately *di sotto in su*?

20. There is, of course, no absolutely fixed relationship between the height of a given figure kneeling and standing, but experiments I have made with normally proportioned adults five and a half palmi tall have yielded a close approximation of four palmi for their height when kneeling in the manner of Masaccio's donors.

cross close to the entrance. Until very recently, this view seems to have been shared by every scholar who commented on the fresco, including Krautheimer,[21] Tolnay,[22] and Schlegel.[23] Kern had defined the platform—the area $\alpha\beta\gamma\delta$ in his ground plan (Fig. 1)—as 'offenbar für die Aufnahme eines Sarkophags bestimmt'; he meant, I take it, not that the platform was originally intended to hold a sarcophagus in the fresco but that it resembles the platforms on scroll brackets supporting sarcophagi in such Quattrocento tombs as that of Baldassare Coscia. According to Tolnay, the rectangular area visible above the platform and behind God the Father actually *is* a sarcophagus—the sarcophagus of Christ—rather than the upper portion of a wall or screen closing the rear of the chapel, as assumed by Kern and Schlegel. His interpretation, however, is clearly in error, for the length of the putative sarcophagus cannot be more than five palmi (i.e., the distance between the abacuses of the columns to either side of it), too short for a body of normal size; the sarcophagus of the skeleton is six palmi long, and that of Christ would have to be at least equal to it, unless we wish to tax Masaccio with an error in perspective far graver than any we have found so far in the architecture of the fresco. We must continue, then, to regard the area in question as part of the rear closure of the chapel. But can we be certain that the platform is attached to the rear wall? Or to put the question another way, is the vertical surface above the platform continuous with that below the platform? The only scholar so far to suggest that they are not has been Sanpaolesi; in his Brunelleschi monograph[24] he published a plan and longitudinal section of Masaccio's chapel (unfortunately, without analytical comment) that show God the Father's platform attached to a box-like structure protruding from the rear wall, so that the front edge of the platform is equidistant from the front and rear of the chapel. In principle this is, I believe, the right solution.[25] Once we accept it as a working hypothesis, we begin to realize that Masaccio has carefully differentiated the two surfaces. The area above the platform is framed by a carved molding,

while the one below is divided into vertical panels by means of inlaid strips of dark marble (Fig. 8). The latter surface, moreover, shows a clearly defined shadow cast by John;[26] it must be located immediately behind that figure and thus cannot be the rear wall. The vertical plane to which God the Father's platform is attached would then be about three palmi from the entrance to the chapel; its height (including the shelf) would be equal to that of Mary and John, i.e., five and a half palmi in a longitudinal section of the chapel. Since God the Father, too, is five and a half palmi tall, the top of His head would be eleven palmi above the chapel floor, or two palmi below the apex of the vault. If the above reading of the visual evidence is correct, Kern's claim that the position of God the Father is spatially ambiguous must be abandoned. But we are now faced with a new problem: how to interpret the nature and significance of the object that supports God the Father's platform. Its height, as we saw, must be five and a half palmi; its width can be inferred, approximately, from the length of the platform, whose right-hand corner is visible just below John's chin (Fig. 8). The object in question, then, appears to be about four palmi wide. Of its depth we have no indication; if it extends all the way to the rear of the chapel, it could be six or seven palmi. Is the object, as Sanpaolesi's drawing suggests, a kind of architectural promontory thrust forward from the rear wall for the sole purpose of bringing God the Father's platform close to the plane of the cross? I prefer to think of it as a tall box rising from the chapel floor, a piece of church furniture rather than part of the architecture of the chapel. Masaccio gives us a strong hint as to what kind of church furniture the box might be: the three panels on its front, outlined by inlaid strips of dark marble, strikingly resemble the three panels, again defined by inlaid strips, on the front of the skeleton's sarcophagus. Unless we are willing to dismiss this relationship as fortuitous, it indicates that God the Father's box, too, is a tomb, although a far more monumental one than that of the Everyman skeleton below. This could only be the sepulchre of Christ, its long axis placed at right angles to that of the skeleton's sarcophagus. Tolnay, then, was right in claiming that the sarcophagus of Christ is shown in the picture, even though he located it in the wrong spot. The presence of Christ's sepulchre, strange as it is, does not necessarily upset Miss Schlegel's interpretation of the symbolic meaning of the chapel itself. It may, however, lead her to modify some of her conclusions.

21. Richard Krautheimer and Trude Krautheimer-Hess, *Lorenzo Ghiberti*, Princeton University Press, 1956, pp. 201, 243.
22. Charles de Tolnay, 'Renaissance d'une fresque', *L'Œil*, January, 1958, pp. 17 ff.
23. *Op. cit.*, p. 26.
24. *Op. cit.*
25. In other respects, Sanpaolesi's drawings show many of the same faults as Kern's, including discrepancies of scale (in one of them, the horizon is 182 cm above the floor of the church, in another only 140 cm). Sanpaolesi also shares Kern's opinion that the area covered by the barrel vault is a square. Since the drawings are unaccompanied by verbal explanations, one wonders to what extent they represent the views of the draughtsman, rather than the author's.
26. I am grateful to John Coolidge for drawing my attention to this feature. Leonetto Tintori assures me that the shadow, which was invisible before the recent cleaning of the fresco, is entirely authentic.

XAVIER DE SALAS

The *St. John* of Niccolò dell'Arca

This note claims only to introduce a work of Niccolò dell'Arca which remains unknown although it is important and kept in a much visited place. This seems impossible, but it is so. The *St. John the Baptist* published here is to be found in one of the show-cases in the so-called 'Hall of Treasure', next to the Chapter Room at the Escorial.

Even if its appearance were not sufficient to confirm its authorship, it is clearly signed in capital letters NICOLAUS. In spite of this, everyone writing on Italian Renaissance sculpture has ignored it, perhaps because it has never been published nor described in the guide books of the Monastery and the guides continue to state that it is a work of Niccolaus Vergara,[1] a Spanish sculptor of the mid-sixteenth century.

The mistake seems all the more difficult to explain when we find that the sculpture is not only signed but also mentioned in the old literature on the sculptor. It is referred to by all the first writers on Niccolò dell'Arca and one of them even records that it was acquired by the King of Spain. This was done by Girolano Borselli, Fileno della Tuata and Cherubino Ghirardaci[2] in texts brought together by Gnudi who, in the

light of these, included the statue in the list of lost works.[3] But it has always been in the Escorial: given by King Philip II in 1586, it appears listed in the third relation of the objects that were sent to the Escorial on July 31, 1586.[4] And the photographs published here bring out its exceptional beauty and morbid character (Figs. 1–3).

Following the traditional iconography, Niccolò showed the Baptist standing on some rocks. His athletic body is partially covered by a ragged camel-skin chiselled with great virtuosity; it falls stiffly, and one of the camel's hooves hangs from his waist. The edges of the dry skin are twisted outwards, and the garment is held together in several places by ligatures. The sculptor has contrasted the tufts of hair and the stiffness of the skin with the tense muscularity of the body.

The rocks on which the figure of St. John is poised are of strange forms; I can find a parallel for them only in some oriental carvings. I have no words with which to describe them, except that they are of complex shapes, rounded and polished. Whether derived from oriental forms or not they seem to be of arbitrary shape and have a decorative intention. The rocks correspond to the attire of the Saint, rugged and harsh, and are linked in appearance with it and with the twisted stem of the ivy climbing up the tree-stump by the figure.

The face is framed by his long hair, falling in twisting strands. This great mass of hair, with its restless lines, and the beard, falling apart into two long curls, reinforce the anguished but restrained expression of the Saint. One of his hands holds up the mystical lamb, with its halo and flag forming a strange jewel, to which

1. There were two Nicolás de Vergara, sculptors. Nicolás de Vergara, el Viejo, the father, was appointed sculptor by the Cathedral of Toledo in 1542, and he did several works of importance, among them the silver urn containing the body of St. Eugene. He died before 1576, and the iron work of the railings of the sepulchre of Cardinal Cisneros (in Alcalá) and the bronze lectern for the Cathedral of Toledo were finished by his son, Nicolás de Vergara, el Mozo. He did several works with his father, finishing the above-mentioned ones. In 1580 he also completed the stained-glass windows for the Cathedral of Toledo. Both were highly praised by Ceán Bermudez in his *Dictionary* (v, p. 206). This is why their names have been kept in memory, so that the signature on the *St. John* suggested the attribution of this work to one of them. But it is hardly necessary to compare it with the works of either of the Vergaras although this is so easily done today. (For the sculpture of Niccolò dell'Arca, see the studies of Gnudi, Bottari and Pope-Hennessy, where various photographs appear. For the relief of the lectern at Toledo by Vergara, see Manuel Gomez Moreno, *La gran época de la escultura española*, Barcelona [1964]; for the urn of St. Eugene at Toledo, see J.-F. Rivera Recio, *S. Eugenio de Toledo y su culto*, Toledo, 1963.)

2. Girolano Borselli, *Cronica gestorum ac factorum memorabilium civitatis Bononiae* (1494): 'Uxore habuit de Boateriis cum uno filio et una filia, figuram ex marmore Sancti Johannis Babtiste a se factam reliquit vendendam ducatis auri quingentis...' Fileno della Tuata, *Cronaca*, MS.: '1494 a di 2 de marzo mori maestro Nicolò Schiavo... Havea fatto molte degne cose fra le quali avea fatto un San Zoane Baptista de marmore fino lungo sette palmi che se vendé duccati settecento e fu

portato in Spagna...' Cherubino Ghirardaci, *Historia di Bologna*, pt. III, pp. 284–5. 'Hebbe per moglie una donna de Boateri, di cui nebbe un figliolo maschio et una femina a cui lascio per dote una figura di san Giovanni Battista di marmo alta due piedi di valori di 500 scudi, ch'egli fatta haveva.' (Texts quoted from Cesare Gnudi, *Niccolò dell'Arca*, Turin, 1942, pp. 67 and 71.)

3. *Ibid.*, p. 77.

4. 'Nº 1604 Una figura de bulto de Sanct Juan Baptista en el desierto, vestida de una piel de carnero [debe decir de camello] con el cordero puesto dentro de un çerco redondo en la mano yzquierda, señalandole con el dedo de la mano derecha, puesta la figura sobre una peaña quadrada hecha de follaxe abierto con sabandijas, que entran y salen por los follaxes; todo de alabastro; tiene de alto una vara escassa.' Eª. 5ª. 1586, IIIª, 31 de Julio. Published by Julian Zarco Cuevas, 'Inventario de las alhajas, relicarios, estatuas, pinturas, tapices y otros objetos de valor y curiosidad donados por el Rey don Felipe II al Monasterio de El Escorial, años de 1571 a 1598', *B.R.A.H.*, 1930.

[89]

one finger of the other hand is pointing. Everything contributes to bring out an extreme tension and nervousness and to emphasize the virtuosity of the chiselling and finishing.

That to Niccolò dell'Arca, an exceptional artist of so few works, may be attributed one more masterpiece of quality and beauty forces us to consider his life and the chronology of his works if we are to place the *St. John* within such a small series.

The old texts, when writing of this *St. John*, do not say at what moment it was done. They only state that it was sold after the sculptor's death and that it was left as a dowry for his daughter, as Ghirardaci wrote. This might incline us to think that it was one of his final works. But that the sculptor, according to Borselli, 'Fantasticus erat et barbarus moribus; adeo agrestis ut omnes a se objeceret'[5] opens up the possibility that it was an earlier work and that its fantastic character made him keep it for himself, as 'caput durum habens consilium amicorum non acquiesebat'. In any case it was a work much valued by its author and one which the chroniclers record as exceptional, among other reasons because of the price at which it was sold to Spain.

But although such dates as we know do not place it in time, we can attempt to date it on the basis of its intrinsic character. First, however, we shall examine the chronological problem of Niccolò dell'Arca's works. We know four documented and unquestioned works: his part in the *Arca di San Domenico*, the *Madonna di Piazza*, the *Holy Burial* in the church of Santa Maria della Vita and the *Eagle* of San Giovanni in Monte.

Until Gnudi, following intuitions of Venturi, discussed the chronology, the works in the *Arca di San Domenico* and the *Holy Burial* were considered to be the first ones done in Bologna. The records tell us that he signed a contract with the Community of the Dominicans for the decoration of the Arca del Santo in 1469, and this was still not completed in 1473 when on July 16 he put the decoration of the upper part in place. On the basis of certain compiled records, the *Holy Burial* was considered to be one of his very early works, to be dated 1463. Gnudi, basing his arguments on stylistic grounds, considered that this chronology should be altered. After the works of the *Arca di San Domenico* (1469–1473), he placed the *Madonna di Piazza* (1478), the *Eagle* (1481), and, as the final one, the group of the *Holy Burial*, sculpted when Niccolò was under the influence of Ferrarese painters. The date might be around 1485–1490, for the sculptor died in 1494.

5. *Cronica gestorum . . . Bononiae* (1494), in Gnudi, *op. cit.*, p. 67.

I do not think this theory can be maintained; I give my reasons in a note.[6] I think we should return to the

6. Without wishing to start a polemic, we must analyse the bases from which Gnudi started to reach his conclusions and give the reasons which make us think that the traditional chronology is the true one.

Gnudi, following Venturi, supposes that Niccolò dell'Arca (probably a Dalmatian) formed his style in Naples, where the atmosphere was composed of varied artistic currents. There he learnt the artistic idiom of the Italian sculptors working on the triumphal arch of King Alfonso. After that Gnudi supposes that the sculptor went to France, where he acquired a direct knowledge of Burgundian art (Sluter and his followers), and after settling in Bologna, where he did several works which show his non-Italian personality and his not quite Tuscan art, his instincts revived and he remembered what he had learnt abroad from the examples of the Ferrarese painters (Ercole da Roberti, Cossa). Their example caused him to express himself with that extreme passion we see in the *Holy Burial*.

I think that to accept these conclusions it is necessary in the first place to force the meaning of the records that we have. (Gnudi's arguments on the value of the records can be read in *op. cit.*, chap. I, p. 19, n. I.) He considers that the chronology of the *Holy Burial* is based on a mistake on the part of the author of the 'Narratione delli veni stabili dell'Hospitale [di Madonna S. Maria della Vita]' who, in making an inventory of the hospital, describes: 'Della banda sinistra di detto altare . . . vi [è] un sepolcro cioè un Cristo morto disteso con la Madonna et altre figure in piedi a torno a detto Cristo, in forma grande, di pietra cotta, fatto per mano di Maestro Nicolò da Puglia, del quale l'hospitale le ebbe nell'anno MCCCCLXIII, come appare al libro nominato Campione . . . alla partita di maestro Antonio Zanolino lanarolo, in suo credito, sotto li VIII aprile del medesim'anno in una partita di L. 24, 7, 6, il qual sepolcro prima fu posto . . .' The book called *Campione* has been lost, but there exists a Papal bull signed in 1464 by Pope Paul II in which he pointed out to the faithful the need to support the hospital, recalling: 'quod ibidem constructa est commemoratio sepulchri Dominici cum figuris et imaginibus pulcherrimis ad cuius manutentionem ipsius hospitalis non suppetant, facultates sed christifidelium suffragia quam plurimum sint opportuna . . .' Gnudi supposes that the compiler was confused since, after describing the *Holy Burial* of Niccolò dell'Arca, he gives the date 1463 because this was the date of a payment of Lit. 24-odd from the money given by Maestro Antonio Zanolino, the wool dealer. This amount Gnudi considers insufficient for the payment for the sculptures, but he does not take into account the fact that, because of the medieval system of accounting, the entry quoted would indicate only that the credit of the wool dealer had been applied to the payment of the *Holy Burial*, not that its price was Lit. 24-odd.

But Gnudi considers that the entry of Lit. 24-odd refers to some ceremonies or theatrical performances on the subject of the Holy Burial, which he considers to be of the kind performed in 1780. In them there were used several sculptures and, as some of them were of wood, that is to say fragile, he supposes that the above-quoted bull refers to them and recommends alms-giving for their maintenance.

Without taking into account the coincidence of date (the 1463 payment to Niccolò and the Papal bull given in 1464)—a coincidence that I cannot overlook and which makes me think that the bull was given a year after the *Holy Burial* was finished and placed—we could still suggest that the 'manutentionem' refers to Niccolò's work, the maintenance of which could incur such expenses as candles for illumination. Nor need we exclude the possibility that Niccolò's figures took part in some kind of representation, as happens today in Spain, where the works of our greatest carvers take part in the Holy Week and other processions.

But in any case the phrase 'constructa est commemoratio

traditionally accepted chronology. To understand the work of dell'Arca we must start from two points that Gnudi has not taken into account. The first is that he did most of his work in marble but that the *Holy Burial* is in terracotta and thus, for technical reasons, this

sepulchri Dominici' cannot, I think, be applied to an ephemeral work for theatrical festivities. I do not think that such could be called 'constructa'. In a word, I do not think that Gnudi is right in his suppositions.

The style of the *Holy Burial* should also be analysed. This is the crux of the problem. When Gnudi published his study on Niccolò dell'Arca in 1942, that issue of the *Art Bulletin* of 1939 in which Wethey's study of Sagrera was published most probably had not yet reached Italy. This is perhaps why Gnudi forgot the existence of this sculptor, as he did when quoting Spanish sculptors influenced by Sluter (*op. cit.*, p. 17, n. 13). Yet every day the personality of Guillermo Sagrera comes out as greater and greater. He was an architect and sculptor who worked in Naples and Mallorca, his birthplace. And after all that is now known there can be no doubt that Niccolò formed his style on that of Sagrera. The comparisons made by Stefano Bottari (*L'Arca di S. Domenico in Bologna*, 1964, p. 66) confirm this. In the examples of Sagrera, Niccolò dell'Arca could find ways which he was to use later to express his fantastic sensibilities and innermost reactions.

Lastly we must discuss the relationship of gestures and expressions that exists between some painters of the Ferrarese School and the Marys of the *Holy Burial*, especially the unforgettable Mary Salome, at first sight a convincing approach. Ercole de' Roberti, in the predella of the Griffoni altar, represents a woman with outstretched arms and garments blown backwards in heavy folds (Gnudi, *op. cit.*, pl. 60). Another woman appears in the Crucifixion housed in the sacristy of San Petronio in Bologna (a copy of Roberti, Gnudi, pl. 61). The arms are rigid with the fingers parted, the mouth is opened in a deep cry and the garment is twisted. The St. Joan in this Crucifixion is also crying with a wide-open mouth.

But this way of expressing grief in an open cry is not exclusive to the Ferrarese School. We could find many examples in the schools of the north, and the gestures so similar between the Mary Salome of the *Holy Burial* and the woman of the predella of the Griffoni altar are not original. Roberti was neither the only one nor the first to show grief with such an expression. Contemporary with Roberti's work is the small panel by Domenido Veneziano in the Fitzwilliam Museum at Cambridge (*Miracle of S. Zenobius*) in which there is a female figure throwing herself forward with arms stretched behind her back and her lips opened in a terrifying expression of grief. It does not seem that Domenico Veneziano had anything to do with Niccolò or ever came across him.

It is not necessary to suppose that Niccolò knew or needed any of these paintings to find examples for the gestures. In a superficial search of Roman sarcophagi representing the death of Adonis we could find similar gestures. We shall give only two examples: the sarcophagus in the Louvre, on which one of the women coming to tend the wounded Adonis is also throwing herself forward with arms stretched behind her and crying with wide-open mouth, and a sarcophagus in the cathedral of Bieda, in Italy, where another woman is represented with similar gestures. This makes us suppose that Niccolò dell'Arca could well have found inspiration for his striking expression of grief in some Roman sarcophagus representing the death of Adonis.

We must also add that the great book of Longhi, *Officina ferrarese* (Florence, 1956), publishes most of the works of this school: the plates show clearly its fantasy and inventiveness and in the case of Roberti, his great possibilities of pathos. But I think that Cossa has little to do with what is characteristic of Niccolò dell'Arca if we exclude certain similarities in the folding of the robes.

group is treated in a different way from the rest of his work. Niccolò dell'Arca, like other sculptors, worked differently according to his medium. When working in marble, he tried to achieve monumentality and to make the volume dense with a clear-cut silhouette, even where his taste for the picturesque appears, as in some figures of the Arca. But when he worked in clay, as in the *Holy Burial*, he brought out his figures violently with expansive gestures and sharp angles. He tried to make expression the first quality, and the exalted expressions were brought out by the polychromy.

The second and even more important point of departure is that of his formation. Pope-Hennessy, when alluding to the Mallorcan sculptor Guillen Sagrera, seems to me to have made the right suggestion.[7] It is not necessary to suppose that dell'Arca went to France or to Mallorca, as Gnudi does, since he came from Naples where Sagrera, the great architect and sculptor, was working for King Alfonso. In his atelier Niccolò could have learnt what the style of the Burgundian Sluter was, without travelling to the north. This influence seems at times to overcome that of the Italian sculptors working in Naples, as is first shown in his sculptures of the Arca.

If all this is accepted, where shall we place the *St. John*?

It is a work showing all the characteristics of a mature style. From the complexity of the design it seems to be the most perfect of all that have come from his chisel. In spite of its 'Gothicism', the intensity of the expression of faith is differently conveyed from the drama which moves the figures of the *Holy Burial*. This figure of St. John is essentially different from those of the *Burial*. There the pain is manifested not only in the profound agitation of the bodies, the distorted faces and the hands clutching at the garments, but in the wide gestures of the Marys, whose robes are thrown backwards or pressed on their bodies. On the contrary, in the *St. John* of the Escorial we see the Baptist in profound spiritual agitation, but revealing his passion only in a restrained tension. He stands like a shuddering flame. Niccolò dell'Arca managed to contain in a restrained silhouette a tremendous spiritual passion. All this, and the texts reassembled by Gnudi, incline us to consider this sculpture as one of the artist's last works. In his maturity, Niccolò dell'Arca did not need to represent a cry of grief to express a passion.

Dell'Arca managed to fuse in this work the dissimilar elements of his formation. He interpreted them in a personal, exquisite manner, showing the subtleties of a

7. John Pope-Hennessy, *Italian Renaissance Sculpture*, London, 1958, p. 343.

great sculptor, a profound virtuosity and his strange originality.

We must add that Niccolò was not alone in this ambiguous position. A Gothic strain moved the sure poise of many artists of the Renaissance. In this connection Ferrarese painters are an important group, full of fantasy and grace, but we do not need to refer to them in order to understand the art of dell'Arca.

On the other hand, the *St. John* belongs to a type that appealed to Philip II. He bought works by painters of the Venetian Renaissance, Titian in the first place, but at the same time he was buying devotional Flemish paintings. In the great building of the Escorial—for some historians a *capolavoro* of mannerist architecture—he assembled, besides many masterpieces of the Flemish Gothic painters, Venetian Renaissance paintings, works of Northern and Italian mannerist painters and many works of the fantastic Hieronimus Bosch.

The *St. John* of Niccolò dell'Arca manifests a blend of Renaissance and medieval and, as well, his taste for the fantastic and the extreme. Thus, in coming to the Escorial, it reached its right setting.

JAMES HOLDERBAUM

The Birth Date and a Destroyed Early Work
of Baccio Bandinelli

With an Archival Contribution by Edward Sanchez

Sixteen years ago, the writer presented himself at the door of the Wittkowers in London—an unannounced stranger avowing interest in the sculpture of sixteenth-century Italy in general and of Giovanni Bologna in particular. The warm generosity with which he was received has remained one of the most gratifying and sustaining memories of his life.

Professor Wittkower's scholarly hospitality was fully as generous. The literature available in those days was not very helpful to the student seeking a general view of Cinquecento sculpture. The bewildering riches of Venturi's three indispensable volumes offered something more like a census (with some beautiful and even apposite commentary, it is true) than a real historical dissertation; while an attractive pamphlet by Dottoressa Becherucci[1] was full of insight but severely limited by its slight proportions. As Professor Wittkower's published writings contained many illuminating remarks on sixteenth-century sculpture and clearly demonstrated his command of the whole field,[2] it can be imagined with what keen anticipation this student heard the professor's modest confession that he had himself undertaken a history of Cinquecento sculpture

many years earlier and that his files contained a copy of the highly developed manuscript. As though it were in no way an unusual favour, permission to read it was given without hesitation.

It even exceeded expectations. The way the author surveyed his multifarious material was a prophecy of those astonishing powers of synthesis and exposition which much more recently have distinguished his *Art and Architecture in Italy, 1600–1750* of 1958. In the eventful decades since the manuscript was put aside, knowledge of *cinquecento* sculpture has grown apace; yet the present writer's view of its history as a whole remains firmly based on this early reading of Professor Wittkower's survey.

The pages on Baccio Bandinelli come to mind as an especially useful model of objective stylistic analysis and historical interpretation. A series of then more or less recent publications had provided the young Wittkower with some stimulating reassessments especially of the painters who came after Michelangelo and Raphael. Unfortunately, the sculpture of these generations was still neglected. Although Bandinelli's reputation had reached one of its later apogees around 1800, the critics of Romanticism had turned him into a scapegoat, and for several generations he had been the butt of almost totally indiscriminate contempt. But Rudolf Wittkower had returned to the monuments themselves and subjected them to long and thoughtful scrutiny. The resulting passages on works like Bandinelli's Hercules, or his Adam and Eve for the Florentine Cathedral Choir, came to this reader as a revelation. They showed how changing and sometimes profoundly different impulses had deflected Bandinelli and his contemporaries from the principles that had guided the classical art of the first dozen years of the sixteenth century, and had led them to learn new lessons from a variety of models which their predecessors would have avoided—the radically altered art of the end of antiquity, with its strange and awesome imagery and its many devices of style whereby earlier formulas had been transformed; the art of Northern Europe; the art of early Italian eras before Leonardo. At the time the young Wittkower began

This paper, in a slightly different form, was read before the College Art Association in Philadelphia, in January, 1964. Recently, some of the auxiliary material serving here to support main arguments has inevitably been mentioned in Dr. Detlef Heikamp's exemplary edition of Vasari's life of Bandinelli (Club del Libro, Milan, 1964, vol. VI, pp. 9–84). However, the two principal topics indicated by the title of this article both revise and augment Dr. Heikamp's authoritative commentary. The article incorporates results from several campaigns of research made possible by a Sheldon Fellowship from Harvard University and by Fulbright and Guggenheim Fellowships.

Since this book went to press, another of Dr. Heikamp's admirable Bandinelli articles has appeared (*Paragone*, 191, 1966, pp. 51–62) and made mention in passing of what were meant to be two scholarly novelties in my essay. However, as his purpose was the publication of mature works known only to specialists, he did not have the opportunity to discuss the implications of this new information about Bandinelli's early life and style, and my short article will therefore perhaps serve as a preface to his more extensive contribution.

1. Luisa Becherucci, *La scultura italiana del cinquecento*, Florence, 1934.
2. E.g. the illuminating remarks on the principles of Giovanni Bologna's sculptural composition as contrasted with Bernini's, in 'Le Bernin et le baroque romain', *Gazette des Beaux-Arts*, sixième période, vol. XI, 1934, 1er semestre, pp. 329–31.

work on his study, the discoveries of such pioneering scholars as Poggi, Middeldorf and Kriegbaum were not yet available, while the photographic material and the libraries equipped for this research were later to be vastly augmented and improved. But in spite of this subsequent multiplication of new data, Professor Wittkower's succinct summary of Bandinelli's accomplishment remains unrivalled.

Here is an instance of the kind of scholarly treatment which until recently has been the lot of most sixteenth-century sculptors, but especially of Bandinelli. No one seems to have cared that he is given two quite different birth dates in modern literature: 1488 and 1493. Those who have turned to German sources, especially to the Thieme-Becker lexicon, have adopted 1493; while those who have consulted Milanesi's edition of Vasari have followed him in pushing it back to 1488. As Mr. Edward Sanchez has devoted years of painstaking research in the Florentine archives to correct just such discrepancies, the writer went to him for help in settling the matter, and this he was able to do at once.

The Florentine baptismal records (*Libri dei Battezzati*), preserved in the Opera del Duomo, clear up the mystery. Under November, 1493, on Wednesday the thirteenth, the following entry occurs: 'Bartholomeo e giovanni di michelan'glo di viviano' of the parish of S. Pier Maggiore, who had been born late on the previous day, November 12. This Bartolommeo is Baccio (a common nickname for Bartolommeo) Bandinelli, whose later claim to that distinguished old Sienese patrician name is dubious, to say the least, but who is well known to have been the son of the respected goldsmith, Michelangiolo di Viviano, named in the document. This same archival source, under October 1488, on Wednesday, October 7, records the birth of one 'Bartolomeo donnino diviviano di ba'tolomeo' of the parish of S. Lucia di Ognissanti. As the latter entry contains the two names Bartolommeo and Viviano, it is not surprising that it was mistakenly identified with Bandinelli; but since the father's name is clearly given as Viviano di Bartolommeo, and not Michelangiolo di Viviano, the baby recorded cannot be the future sculptor. It is therefore certain that Baccio Bandinelli was born on November 12, 1493.

We are grateful to Mr. Sanchez for an art-historical datum of larger consequence than may at first be obvious. For even though it may seem that a difference of a little more than five years in a birth date should not matter very much, the fact is that it does indeed matter for an artist coming into his own during those crucial years of artistic transition, the second decade of the sixteenth century. If Bandinelli's birth had occurred as early as 1488, he would have been the contemporary of Jacopo Sansovino and Andrea del Sarto, both of

whom were born in 1486. But as in fact it took place more than five years later, at the end of 1493, he is rather the contemporary of a very different group of artists, of men like Pontormo (born soon after in 1494) and of Rosso Fiorentino (born early in 1495). When Bandinelli's first sculptural experiments from about 1515 to 1520, and when especially the extraordinary pictorial designs which he produced in this period to be engraved by Agostino Veneziano, are considered in the context of the work of Pontormo and Rosso from these same years, it will be seen how significantly they increase the precise evidence for the induction of critical trends in Florentine art at this juncture.

Furthermore, the certainty that Bandinelli's birth date is as late as the end of 1493 now permits a better understanding of his position during the new Medicean ascendancy and the papacy of Leo X. For example, in 1515, the first year from which a considerable quantity of certainly identifiable and datable work by Bandinelli survives, he was not twenty-seven, but rather a promising young man only twenty-one years old.

This is not the occasion for a discussion of the engravings after Bandinelli's designs dating from the decade beginning in 1515, but they conspicuously demonstrate how Bandinelli's drawings in particular, and graphic material in general, have been seriously slighted in the voluminous modern literature on the development of pictorial art in these crucial years. 1515 is also the year in which Bandinelli's statue of St. Peter for the cathedral was commissioned and undertaken—and here, in the search for alternatives to the art of Michelangelo, the Sansovinos, and antiquity, the young sculptor turned to Donatello (the St. Mark, Orsanmichele), and restored to currency one of the most valuable resources of the Florentine artistic patrimony. In this same decisive year of 1515, the prolific young artist was also assigned a surprisingly large part in the elaborate decorations for the ceremonies celebrating the entrance into Florence of its pope, Leo X de' Medici,[3] and produced, in addition to a major share of the decoration for the Sala del Papa at S. Maria Novella, four ambitious independent compositions: a triumphal arch at the junction of Via Tornabuoni and Via Panzani; another rich decoration in Via della Scala; a great column where the Mercato Nuovo was later erected; and, most important of all, a colossal Hercules for the Loggia de' Lanzi.

Bandinelli's colossus of 1515, which was much larger

3. See P. Minucci, *Archivio storico italiano*, ser. IV, vol. III, 1879, p. 482; and Luca Landucci, *Diario fiorentino dal 1450 al 1516*, ed. Jodoco del Badia, Florence, 1883, pp. 353–9. Miss Eve Borsook has kindly informed the writer that many now unknown details of the 1515 celebrations are disclosed by ample unpublished documentation in the archives.

than Michelangelo's nearby David,[4] occupied the position where Cellini's bronze Perseus was placed some forty years later. But although, like nearly all of the thousands of these *ornamenti* made by most of the masters of the Renaissance and the baroque, it was executed in the impermanent material of stucco, unlike so many of the others it fortunately has not vanished without a trace. Vasari's fresco cycle of the life of Leo X in the Sala di Papa Leone of the Palazzo Vecchio in Florence includes a large and minutely detailed representation of the climax of the 1515 festivities, with the triumphal entry of the pope into the Piazza Signoria; and a prominent feature of the accurately reconstructed background is Bandinelli's Hercules (Plate XIII, Fig. 1). While the identity of this detail has not wholly escaped attention,[5] it has been ignored by students of Bandinelli, perhaps on the assumption that it would have been more or less a figment of Vasari's imagination, since it was painted forty-six years later, in 1561.[6]

There is, however, considerable evidence that Vasari's image is a good record of the actual appearance of Bandinelli's statue. In the first place, it was painted during that phase of Vasari's career which culminated soon afterwards in the vastly augmented second edition of his *Vite*, and it is therefore reasonable to assume that this is one of the uncommon instances where the art historian is actually justified in imputing art-historical methods and thinking to a practicing artist. Indeed, the elaborate program of research which preceded Vasari's history paintings in the Palazzo Vecchio was scarcely very different in nature from that which produced the enlarged *Vite*. Furthermore, although Bandinelli had died early in 1560, when Vasari's research for the Sala Leone could have been barely under way at best, the sculptor left an enormous legacy of papers, drawings and models of all sorts and sizes, and this material may very well have preserved a visual record of what had been Bandinelli's first major work to be unveiled to the public. To this material Vasari would of course have had access. A detail of Vasari's account proves that his knowledge of the original was very exact. Had it not been, he would have given its height in a round figure, say eight or ten

braccia. The fact that he could specify down to the fraction of a braccio—9½ braccia, hardly a figure one would improvise as an approximation—is another indication of his familiarity with the precise actualities of the colossus.

The hypothesis that Vasari's representation is a faithful record, strengthened by a variety of such evidence, is virtually proved by two extant statues of exactly the same nature which Bandinelli turned out shortly afterwards, probably about 1520 or not long thereafter. All writers on Bandinelli have been unaware of the survival of two very similar stucco colossi by Bandinelli in the garden of the Villa Madama just outside Rome (Plate XIII, Fig. 2) which shows them before the drastic restorations of the 1930's—an oversight hard to explain, since they have been included in several topographical publications.[7] Unfortunately, the distinguished eighteenth-century scholar, Giovanni Bottari, wrote that they were destroyed[8]—one of his rare errors, but one that has been perpetuated by a long list of later writers. Although they are weathered and mutilated to a point where some of Bandinelli's intentions can only be surmised, they nevertheless present a complete series of correspondences to Vasari's painted image— resemblances which cannot be duplicated in any other works of art from the period, and which therefore leave little doubt that Vasari's fresco is based on fact and is indeed a pretty faithful reproduction, a visual documentation, of the appearance of Bandinelli's original. In addition to the many morphologically distinctive details which they share and which could hardly be coincidental, the conclusive similarity lies in the truly extraordinary proportions of the figures as a whole. These are entirely unlike the characteristic proportions of rather long torso and shortish legs which are the only invariable feature of the otherwise exceedingly various Florentine sculpture of the entire sixteenth and early seventeenth centuries, including most other works by Bandinelli himself. These three statues are unique in their exceptional proportions of relatively much longer legs to much shorter torso; the tibia is especially elongated. The many correspondences are all the more convincing since they are qualified by some striking differences both in general composition and in specific detail, particularly in the heads, where there is a change in shape, in features and in their distribution. It was to be expected that the maturing master of 1520, in returning to exactly the same problem which had occupied him in the youthful Florentine experiment of 1515, would subject it to just such

4. The David is 4.10 meters high. Vasari reports the height of Bandinelli's Hercules as 9½ *braccia*, or *c.* 5.21 meters—well over 17 feet and thus almost 30 per cent taller than the David. See G. Vasari, *Le Vite*, ed. G. Milanesi, vol. VI, Florence, 1881, p. 141.

5. See E. Schaeffer, *Monatshefte für Kunstwissenschaft*, vol. III, 1910, p. 112.

6. As the Sala del Papa Leone was undertaken at the very beginning of January, 1561, presumably the preparatory research and drawing would have started at least some months earlier in 1560. See Alessandro del Vita, *Il Libro delle Ricordanze di Giorgio Vasari*, Arezzo, 1927, p. 83.

7. See Hermann Egger, *Codex Escurialensis*, Vienna, 1906, p. 137, Fig. 57; and Theobald Hofman, *Raffael als Architect*, vol. I, *Villa Madama zu Rom*, Leipzig, 1908, pl. 43.

8. See G. Vasari, *Le Vite*, ed. G. Bottari, Rome, 1759, vol. II, p. 582, n. 1.

revisions. In short, there can be little doubt that Vasari's fresco is based on fact and is indeed a reasonable facsimile of Bandinelli's lost original.

What inferences, then, can be made about the nature of the Florentine Hercules as a work of art? Obviously any colossus of 1515 presupposes the art of Michelangelo, but Bandinelli would have been astonished at the judgment of later nineteenth- and twentieth-century criticism, which indiscriminately found almost all of Michelangelo's successors, but especially Bandinelli, guilty of 'misunderstood Michelangelism' (a phrase fondly remembered from the lectures of Professor Chandler R. Post). Nothing could have been further from Bandinelli's intentions that an overt act of artistic homage to Michelangelo. Obviously, like Jacopo Sansovino just before him, the young Bandinelli was searching rather for alternatives to Michelangelo's art, and a main point of all the early sculptures of Bandinelli (both this and the two Roman colossi, the St. Peter in the Florentine Cathedral, the Orpheus in the Palazzo Medici, etc.) is that they achieve their non-Michelangelesque purposes by virtue of their very divergence from the art of Michelangelo. It has already been observed that the images are morphologically most distinctive: from their short bull necks and compact, powerful shoulders, down through their broad, barrel-like torsos and their bulky hips, to their long legs with massive thighs and swelling calves, they compose an anatomical canon wholly unMichelangelesque. Both intentions and results are like nothing in the sculpture of Michelangelo up to 1515. As usual, the initial impulse came from the antique; but not classical antiquities—rather, what might be called anticlassical antiquities. A wide variety of ancient representations—of Hercules, gladiators and the like, especially in grotesque painting and mosaic—has been so thoroughly assimilated that specific prototypes cannot readily be adduced. Above all, Bandinelli has turned to models which would have been avoided by most of the previous generation. The drawings by Bandinelli's contemporaries document their sympathies with works like the colossal bronzes of the Campidoglio and Barletta; and Bandinelli's three huge stuccoes unmistakably evoke the more brutal of antique colossi, works overpowering by sheer bulk and through their strange and slightly monstrous imagery—not just superhuman, but stupendously antihuman. Not Michelangelo, but rather Bandinelli, makes stunning immensity an end in art.

Vasari's painting indicates that the disquieting effect of Bandinelli's ogreish image of 1515 was clinched at its apex in a curious head, underproportioned by Bandinelli's later or indeed most other standards, with its little eyes and other mean features cramped curiously low in a smallish face crowned by a towering brow. While it would be excessive to argue photographic scrupulousness on Vasari's part in all these details—which differ from Bandinelli's later types but also, and radically, from Vasari's own—the probability that the head presented a grotesque extreme is confirmed by its affinities with the bust of the St. Peter statue, begun the same year. Details have been changed and these affinities are generic rather than specific; but the shocking realism especially at the throat of St. Peter, with its hideously riled tendons, together with the malevolent glare of his eyes, demonstrates how rashly the young Bandinelli capped the climax in the heads of his first statues.

That the Hercules of 1515 was found perplexing one can easily understand. Within a dozen congested years the Florentines had seen a bewildering succession of sculptural innovations. They had experienced the definitive realization of a truly classical art in the sculpture of Andrea Sansovino, exalting humanity in harmony with God. Then they had been stunned by the sublimities of Michelangelo. Then there had been the triple group of the *Preaching Baptist* by Giovanni Francesco Rustici for the Baptistry (1507–1511), reflecting the restive Faustian spirit of the aging Leonardo, who was constantly at Rustici's side during its creation—a group whose images have something of that curiously indefinable intensity, that quality of the magnetic, the fabulous, which radiates like a mysterious glamour from Leonardo's humanity. Then the interesting early works of Jacopo Sansovino, those suave expositions of statuary form, imagery and technique, had proffered a rich intellectual and esthetic feast. But an informative diary entry by Luca Landucci (d. 1516), made soon after the exhibition of Bandinelli's statue, indicates that a substantial number of Florentines could not assent to the new extreme hazarded by Bandinelli in this strange giant of 1515[9]—and thus began Bandinelli's long feud with the sceptics in the Florentine audience, which continued until his death liberated the reputation of the artist from that of the personally odious man. The mixed reception of the 1515 colossus brings to mind the objections to Rosso's equally bold and disquieting altarpiece for Santa Maria Nuova three years later—and indeed when one considers Bandinelli's statue in relation to the sequence of works by Rosso, Pontormo, Alonso Berruguete, and Francesco da Sangallo, and to a few later works by Bandinelli himself, one sees the significance of the Hercules of 1515 as an historical symptom.

Bandinelli himself, in his next works, did not pursue the implications of *antigrazioso* made in the colossus of 1515 and in the extraordinary flesh passages of the St.

9. See Landucci, *loc. cit.*

Peter undertaken in the same year—even though, in this aspect of his early style, he discovered a fertile vein of Florentine *cinquecento* sculpture; one which eventually yielded a great part of the strange work of Baccio's contemporary, Francesco da Sangallo, and years later, some of the most interesting sculpture of Bandinelli's follower, Vincenzo de' Rossi. It was, however, only after a decade that Bandinelli himself returned to the artistic potentialities and indeed the very theme of the 1515 colossus, and produced, in that stunning little masterpiece of brutal violence and cruelty, the Hercules and Cacus *bozzetto* in Berlin, a quintessential realization of the Florentine artistic spirit during the 1520's. But in most of his intervening works Bandinelli cultivated a more widely palatable if still highly personal antiquarianism, seen precociously in the relief of the *Birth of the Virgin* in Loreto (mainly 1517–1519)—which, in its evocation of an exotic and rarefied fantasy-antiquity, anticipates, in both style and spirit, not only the pictorial arts of the future *Maniera*, but also, centuries later, a major phase of Neoclassicism; indeed, Bandinelli exerted powerful influence upon a large group of late eighteenth- and early nineteenth-century artists. Then follow the far from literal copy of the Laocoön in the Uffizi and the almost Canovan Orpheus in the Palazzo Medici, which eulogizes the Apollo Belvedere.

The probability that Vasari's representation of the 1515 Hercules is faithful is thus reinforced by the early development just summarized, which would lead us to expect what is in fact the case: the grotesque extreme of the head in the earlier colossus is mitigated in the more characteristically Bandinellian face well enough preserved in the left of the Villa Madama stuccoes.

Furthermore, the terribility of the earlier and considerably larger colossus, which must have seemed all the more immense since it loomed more than a meter above Michelangelo's David, has been domesticated in the Villa Madama statues. They are made pendants and become therefore wholly decorative objects, garden ornaments subordinant to the architectural ensemble. *Disegno* prevails over expression. The unbridled violence of the later Berlin *bozzetto* is thus a somewhat aberrant singularity in Bandinelli's maturing art of the 1520's. But the extraordinarily enhanced mastery of figure composition which the *bozzetto* demonstrates is not. For however unorthodox the imagery and morphology of the 1515 Hercules, Vasari indicates that the body was disposed according to the most conventional *contrapposto* formula. The postures of the later Villa Madama giants, on the other hand, are subtly enlivened by suggestions of gyral movement in the trunks and by a somewhat wider spacing of the legs—small revisions, to be sure, but evidence that the more developed artist found the earlier composition insipid and pedantic.

It is precisely in this concentration on strictly esthetic considerations that Bandinelli's works around and just after 1520 are most prophetic of mid-sixteenth-century art. In most of them, beginning with the Loreto relief —and it is significant that this work was done largely outside Florence, close either to Andrea Sansovino or the Raphael school—Bandinelli seems wholly impervious to the exciting atmosphere in which Rosso and Pontormo produced their contemporary paintings. The content of these sculptures, as cool as the marble in which they are carved, is their esoteric imagery, their form, design, style. Their content is *maniera*.

JAMES H. BECK

A *Sibyl* by Tribolo for the 'Porta Maggiore' of San Petronio

In the second edition of his *Lives* Vasari devotes considerable attention to the biography of Niccolò Tribolo and describes how, in 1525, the Florentine sculptor was called to Bologna:

> Mentre che queste opere dal Tribolo si facevano in Firenze, essendoci venuto per sue bisogne messer Bartolomeo Barbazzi gentiluomo bolognese, si ricordò che per Bologna si cercava d'un giovane che lavorasse bene, per metterlo a far figure e storie di marmo nella facciata di San Petronio, chiesa principale di quella città. Perchè ragionato col Tribolo, e veduto delle sue opere gli piacquero, e parimente i costumi e l'altre qualità del giovane, lo condusse a Bologna; dove egli con molta diligenza e con molta sua lode fece in poco tempo le due Sibille di marmo, che poi furono poste nell'ornamento della porta di San Petronio che va allo spedale della Morte.[1]

The two *Sibyls* of marble referred to by Vasari are the subject of this paper.

Over the years Vasari's notice has been interpreted as referring to two of the twenty Sibyls that are on the jambs of the side portals of the basilica of San Petronio that flank Jacopo della Quercia's central portal. The portal specifically designated by Vasari, the one that lies towards the 'spedale della Morte', is located on the left side of the façade, the side toward the Pavaglione. Both side portals were made and decorated with sculpture during the 1520's by a group of sculptors and architects that included Arduino Arriguzzi, Girolamo da Treviso, Alfonso Lombardi, Properzia dei Rossi, Amico Aspertini, Francesco da Milano, Ercole Seccadenari, Zaccaria da Volterra and others with some additions made nearly fifty years later by Silla de' Longhi and masters Teodosio and Lazzaro [Casario].[2]

It is my contention that Vasari erred; the two *Sibyls* he mentioned must have been made for the central portal. In fact, two centuries after Vasari's notice (1767), Marcello Oretti wrote that in addition to other works carried out by Tribolo for the side portals of San Petronio, he executed some ('alcune') *Sibyls* for the central portal.[3] Shortly after Oretti's description, the seventh edition of Malvasia (which contains additions by Oretti himself as well as by Longhi and Giusti) reported a similar notice:

> La Porta maggiore fu commessa nel 1429 a Giacomo di M. Piero dalla Fonte, che prevenuto dalla morte nel 1442 (e non nel 1418 come dicesi nelle note al Vasari) non potè compire, avendovi però fatte nelle due Pilastrate laterali, e nell'architrave sopra di esse in bassi rilievi di marmo 15 storie dalla Creazione del Mondo fino al Diluvio, ma nel sott'arco le statue della B.V. col Figliuolo, S. Ambrogio, e S. Petronio sono di Domenico Aimo detto il Varignana; *le Sibille poi annesse alle dette Pilastrate sono di Niccolò Tribolo* [my italics] delle cui mani sembrano le tanto più belle Storie, e Profeti annessi, che ornare le Porte piccole di un tal gusto, che a giudixio degl'intendenti non invidiano l'eleganza, e la correzione di Rafaello.[4]

These *Sibyls* are mentioned as pertaining to the central portal in the Guide of 1803 by Gatti,[5] and in the 1820 and 1826 editions of Bianconi's Guide, but in the 1844

3. 'Le pitture nelle chiese della città di Bologna', MS. marked B30, Biblioteca Comunale dell'Archiginnasio, Bologna, p. 210.
4. *Pitture, scolture e architetture a Bologna e suoi sobborghi*, 7th ed., Bologna, 1782, p. 229. Precisely the same text is used in the edition of 1792 (p. 250). I have included the full text because of the complicated grammar of the sentence. For an extremely useful article on Bolognese guide-books see G. Zucchini, 'Catalogo critico delle guide di Bologna', *L'Archiginnasio*, XLVI–XLVII, 1951–2, pp. 135–68. See also L. Frati, *Opere della bibliografia bolognese*, Bologna, 1888, I, pp. 1031–5.
The references to the central portal in the citation above are manifestly incorrect. For a summary of Jacopo della Quercia's work on the portal see J. H. Beck, 'Jacopo della Quercia's Design for the "Porta Maggiore" of San Petronio', *Journal of the Society of Architectural Historians*, 1965, pp. 115–26, and O. Morosani, *Tutte le sculture di Jacopo della Quercia*, Milan, 1962.
5. G. Gatti, *Descrizione delle più rare cose di Bologna e suoi subborghi*, Bologna, 1803, p. 119.

1. Ed. G. Milanesi, VI, Florence, IV, 1881, p. 59. For recent discussion of the artist see J. Pope-Hennessy, *Italian Renaissance and Baroque Sculpture*, London, 1963, catalogue, pp. 58–60; M. G. Ciardi Duprè, 'Presentazione di alcuni problemmi relativi al Tribolo scultore', *Arte antica e moderna*, 13–16, 1961, pp. 244–7; J. Holderbaum, 'Notes on Tribolo', pts. I and II, *Burlington Magazine*, XCIX, 1957, pp. 336–43, 369–72.
2. See I. B. Supino, *Le sculture delle porte di San Petronio in Bologna*, Florence, 1914, pp. 37 f. See also G. Zucchini, *Guida della Basilica di San Petronio*, nuova edizione illustrata, Bologna, 1953, pp. 20–24.

edition of the same guide-book there is no longer any reference to them.[6]

The first monograph on the sculpture of the portals of San Petronio published in 1834 also fails to allude to these figures.[7] It must be assumed, therefore, that sometime between 1826 and 1834 they were removed from the central portal.

In 1929 the Bolognese scholar Francesco Filippini published a relief figure that had been brought up from the *cantina* of San Petronio upon his suggestion (Fig. 1).[8] He described the figure as a 'Virgin Annunciate' and attributed the work to Niccolò Tribolo on the basis of a stylistic analysis. From an examination of the relief—now located on the right wall of the left aisle of the basilica of San Petronio directly opposite the entrance to the Museo dell'Opera —it can be ascertained that the head had been severed from the body and restored, that the chin and mouth were also repaired, as was a break at the mid-section. It is equally apparent that an effort was made at some point to clean the relief; the cleaning, begun at the base, was abandoned at the level of the waist—due, doubtless, to a fear of further injuring the relief. Filippini sought to include this figure within the project that Tribolo and his Florentine assistant Antonio Solosmeo began at the behest of Bartolomeo Barbazzi for his father's tomb during the years 1525 and 1526— during precisely the same period that Tribolo's name appears among those artists working on the decoration of the side portals of San Petronio, and during the period when Barbazzi was Operaio of the Fabbrica of San Petronio.[9] Barbazzi died while the work on the tomb was under way (1527) resulting in the suspension of the project. Filippini quite rightly dismissed the possibility that the 'Virgin Annunciate' had been planned as part of the Barbazzi monument on the

grounds that the quality of stone is diverse. Marble from Carrara had been stipulated for the Barbazzi monument; the relief under examination, on the other hand, is of Istrian stone.[10]

Filippini did conclude that the relief was part of a monument that had been located at a considerable height above the eye level, probably, he supposed, for one attached to a wall inside the church. The relief, however, on the part that is uncleaned, reveals incrustations that could only have been accumulated out of doors. At the same time the vigorous turn of the figure's head, the manner in which she supports the small book, the gesture of her left arm and large robust hand, held close to the breast, all make it quite unlikely that she represents a 'Virgin Annunciate' at all. More likely she represents a Sibyl, and must have had a companion of similar design facing her. The gesture of the arm across the body may be found in Sibyls as well as in figures of the Annunciate and in this case is quite similar to a *Sibyl* by Giovanni Pisano on the pulpit in Sant'Andrea, Pistoia (Fig. 2).[11]

The evidence leads to the inescapable conclusion that the relief was one of a pair set out of doors, that it was made to be seen from below, that it was executed by Niccolò Tribolo, and finally that it was formerly part of the decoration of the central portal of San Petronio. Like the other sculptural elements of Jacopo della Quercia's portal, it is of Istrian stone and its height (155 cm) is consistent with the height of the figures in the lunette of the portal (the *San Petronio* measures 180 cm). The *Sibyl* and a companion must have been placed on the same zone of the portal as the lunette

6. Bianconi, *Guida del forestiere per la città di Bologna*, Bologna, 1820, p. 232, and ed. of 1826, p. 107.

7. V. Davia, *Le sculture delle porte della basilica di San Petronio in Bologna*, Bologna, 1843.

8. F. Filippini, 'Opere del Tribolo in S. Petronio', *Il comune di Bologna*, March, 1929, pp. 15–19.

9. V. Davia (*op. cit.*, p. 17) found payments to Tribolo from July, 1525 to December, 1526. In reviewing the account books of the archives for these years, it can now be reported that Tribolo's name appears as late as August 9, 1527 (Giornale XIX della Fabbrica, fol. CXC). It should also be noted that the first clearly defined payment to the sculptor was made on July 15, 1525 (Libro Mastro XIX della Fabbrica, fol. CCCXII, and Giornale XIX della Fabbrica, fol. CXXXVIII) and payments to him continued with extreme regularity until August more than two years later. Unfortunately in these payments no mention is made of the specific works upon which he was engaged at any given moment but merely mention a sum (usually, but not always, £7 soldi 6 per week) credited to his account. The payments made to him were almost inevitably within the entries for all of the other sculptors who were engaged on the decoration of the 'porte picchioli'. See also A. Gatti, *La fabbrica di S. Petronio*, Bologna, 1889, docs. 218–27.

10. Filippini, *op. cit.*, p. 15. Michelangelo, it will be remembered, supplied a design for the tomb and two letters addressed to him, one from Barbazzi and the other from Tribolo, are published in Supino, *Le sculture . . .*, *op. cit.*, doc. 79.

11. The motif of the small book Tribolo's *Sibyl* carries and the way she holds it are analogous to several Sibyls by Agostino di Duccio in the Tempio Malestestiana. For Sibyls in Italian art see A. Rossi, 'Le sibilli nelle arte figurative italiane', *L'Arte*, XVIII, 1915, pp. 205–21, 272–85, 427–58, and L. Freund, *Studien zur Bildgeschichte der Sibillen in der Neuer Kunst* (dissertation), Hamburg, 1936. Freund points out (p. 10) that the Sibyls in Pistoia developed from the motif of the Virgin Annunciate.

The internal portal of the right side of the façade (Notai) contains a *Virgin Annunciate* that crowns the left-hand pilaster that is of very similar design to our Sibyl. It has been attributed to Properzia dei Rossi by Venturi (*Storia dell'arte italiana*, XI, Milan, 1935, p. 604 and Fig. 476) who correctly singles out the influence of Tribolo. Zucchini (C. Ricci and G. Zucchini, *Guida di Bologna*, Bologna, 1950, p. 19) considers the Virgin to be by Francesco da Milano as does Supino (*L'Arte nelle chiese di Bologna*, II, 1938, p. 61). I hope to discuss some of the problems connected with the sculpture of the internal portals of San Petronio at some future time, but from external evidence it appears that the Virgin Annunciate derives from our Sibyl. In this way the type derived in the first instance from a Virgin Annunciate was adapted for a Sibyl, and re-adapted for the Virgin Annunciate.

figures, directly above the two main historiated pilasters ('Le dette pilastrate'). The areas of the portal directly above these main pilasters (the presumed location of the Sibyls) do not have the marble facing that covers the rest of the façade at this level, a fact that helps to reinforce the conclusion already reached (Fig. 3).

The quality of the relief is somewhat misleading. The carving appears to be somewhat forced and even heavy-handed in places but the conception of the figure is impressive. The short block placed under the right leg allows for a forceful contrapposto; this relaxed leg is rendered with swelling masses that project beyond the relief plane. On the same side of the figure, the right arm hangs loosely as it balances the small book; heavy folds of drapery fall freely about it. The left side of the figure, on the contrary, is more rigid: beginning with the severe profile of the head and the decisive gesture of the arm, the vertical silhouette of drapery parallels the weight-bearing function of the left leg. The carving is noteworthy too because it combines the more common procedure of bas-relief with a stiacciato-like execution of the front plane, allowing thereby an impression of a relatively high projection when in point of fact the overall relief is quite shallow except for the head. There are several borrowings from Quercia's panels on the lintel and pilaster immediately below the original location of the Sibyl. The massive, flat, rectangular hand that lies on the breast of the Sibyl is a parallel to Joseph's hand in the Nativity relief on the lintel (Fig. 6). The sharp, almost ferocious turn of the head displayed by the Sibyl has its equivalent in Antique reliefs (Fig. 4), but is also a motif in Quercia's figure of Adam in the *Temptation and Fall of Adam and Eve*.[12] The net effect of such a pose is uncommonly rich, for it affords highly characteristic views of the body, in full front, and the head, in profile, simultaneously.

Once its high conceptual level has been recognized, we may now return to the question of the rather modest quality of the *Sibyl*'s execution, especially the somewhat forced modelling.[13] The relief has been caked with incrustation that tends to reduce the subtleties of the carving. But more important is the quality of the stone and its limitations. The Florentine sculptor Niccolò Tribolo was accustomed to work with Carrara marble, which affords the representation of even the most delicate nuances; Istrian stone, on the other hand, must have been something of an obstacle for him. Vasari's comment on Tribolo's relief of the *Assumption of the Virgin* (1537), also executed in Bologna and now in San Petronio, might explain the nature of the difficulties. In this case Tribolo was not altogether pleased with the results 'perchè essendo il marmo che lavorava di quelli di Milano, saligno, smeriglioso e cattivo, gli [Tribolo] pareva gettar via il tempo senze una dilettazione al mondo'.[14] The stylistic arguments presented by Filippini in favor of an attribution to Tribolo are sound and to them may be added the similarity of the head of the Sibyl to the head of the figure in the background of the relief *Lot Fleeing from Sodom* (of Carrara marble, incidentally) on the left pilaster from the portal on the right side of the façade (towards the Palazzo dei Notai), a work generally attributed to Tribolo and datable between the years 1525 and 1527 (Fig. 5).[15]

By substituting the central portal for the portal 'che va allo spedale della Morte', Vasari's notice takes on new meaning. He must have been referring to the *Sibyls* that once made up part of the decoration of the 'Porta Maggiore'. It is consistent with the iconographic program of the central portal to have Sibyls as part of the decoration since, along with the prophets of the jambs and the archivolt, they serve to link Old and New Testament representations. The *Sibyl* can be dated with the other works by Tribolo executed for the Fabbrica, whose records contain payments to him from July 1525 to August 1527.[16]

We have already seen that this relief statue by Tribolo has a strong Quercesque air, as do the prophets in the archivolts and the figure of Sant'Ambrogio in the lunette, executed in 1510. The stylistic relationships to Jacopo della Quercia's sculpture on the portal is, in fact, further evidence that the *Sibyl* was designed for the portal. Especially in his handling of the drapery and in the manner by which the immense left hand of the Sibyl lies flatly on her breast Tribolo reveals a dependence upon the quattrocento master (Fig. 6). It is clear that Tribolo sought a degree of conformity with the existing sculpture on the central portal of San Petronio, as the sculptors of the 1510 campaign,

12. The best example from Antique reliefs I have been able to find is from a muses sarcophagus in the Villa Medici, Rome. It is datable to the first half of the second century and may have its derivation in Hellenistic painting, rather than sculpture. For this sarcophagus see M. Cagiano de Azevedo, *Le antichità di Villa Medici*, Rome, 1951, cat. no. 57 (p. 71) and pl. XXIX.
13. C. de Tolnay, s.v. 'Michelangelo', *Encyclopedia of World Art*, IX, 1964, col. 870. It had been suggested to De Tolnay that this figure may have been by Michelangelo, but he considers the 'Virgin of the Annunciation' as probably by a pupil of Michelangelo, dating from about 1545. Although De Tolnay holds that the invention is elevated, he considers the execution 'rough' and 'clumsy'.

14. Vasari, Milanesi, VI, p. 70.
15. Venturi, *op. cit.*, p. 201; Supino, *Le sculture . . .*, *op. cit.*, p. 164. Also to be recorded is the stylistic correspondence between the *Sibyl* and the figure of the Virgin in the lunette of the same (right) portal, also by Tribolo (see Venturi, *op. cit.*, Fig. 162).
16. See note 9.

Antonio del Minella, Antonio da Ostiglia, Amico Aspertini and Domenico da Varignana had done earlier when they were completing Quercia's portal decoration in the zone at the level of the lunette.[17] Tribolo ingeniously accommodated his style to the existing statuary but maintained at the same time a high degree of invention.

17. J. H. Beck, 'A Document Regarding Domenico da Varignana', *Mitteilungen des Kunsthistorischen Institutes in Florenz*, Band XI, Heft II–III, November 1964, pp. 193–4.

ILARIA TOESCA

A Majolica Inscription in Santa Croce
in Gerusalemme

So little is generally known about Roman majolica during the fifteenth and sixteenth centuries that one is inclined to assume that higher-quality wares—either decorated pottery or floor-tiles—were usually imported. Among the few extant examples the most notable are certainly the Spanish tiles found in Castel Sant'Angelo and those still in place in the Della Rovere chapels in S. Maria del Popolo, ascribed to Deruta. In 1494 Pope Alexander VI is also known to have ordered tiles from Valencia for his new Vatican apartments.

Even if we limit investigation to the restricted field of floor-tiles—a type of decoration which does not seem ever to have been too popular in Rome—, we see that the few scattered items said to be locally made are more often in fact of alien origin. And indeed no dated ceramic marked Rome is as yet known before the year 1600. Thus the picture remains a rather blurred one, chiefly for lack of sufficient material.[1]

Still, surprisingly enough, a major monument of majolica-craft has been so far totally overlooked by specialists, a very curious fact because it is located in an extremely conspicuous place, one of Rome's 'seven churches', S. Croce in Gerusalemme. In addition, it is not used for a pavement, but, what makes it highly noteworthy as an exception in Italian practice, it is related to the architectural setting in a quite unusual way, being applied as wall decoration.[2]

The subterranean chapel of St. Helen had been for centuries the most holy place in the basilica when the titular Cardinal, Bernaldín Lopez de Carvajal (Plasencia, Estremadura, 1459–Rome 1523) decided to renew the access to it after extensive restoration— or, rather, radical rebuilding—had been carried out, and another underground chapel, dedicated to St. Gregory, had been added. The work, which may have started just after 1495, was finished by 1520, in the pontificate of Leo X, as is stated in a long inscription, giving both an historical account of the place and of its ultimate remodelling.[3] It is precisely to this inscription, now only partly preserved but still imposing enough, that I should like to call attention. It has the peculiarity of being on majolica tiles.

The two corridors descending from both sides of the apse of S. Croce to the twin chapels of St. Gregory and of St. Helen are still, in their present structure, as the Cardinal left them (Fig. 1).[4] Plunged in almost total

1. See A. Lane, *A Guide to the Collection of Tiles* (Victoria and Albert Museum), London, 1960, for a number of examples and for the relevant bibliography. The tiles found during excavations in Castel Sant'Angelo were first published by R. Papini ('Gli antichi pavimenti di Castel Sant'Angelo', in *Faenza*, II, 1914, pp. 69–71). See also: B. Rackham, *Catalogue of Italian Maiolica* (Victoria and Albert Museum), London, 1940. J. Chompret's *Repertoire de la majolique italienne*, Paris, 1949, as well as G. Ballardini's *Corpus*..., Rome, 1933–8, are of no help in this case. There are no new elements in the recent book by A. Berendsen, M. B. Keezer, S. Schoubye, J. M. dos Santos Simões, and J. Tichelaar, *Fliesen*, Munich, 1964.
The extremely fine set of majolica tiles existing in the church of S. Silvestro al Quirinale (Fra Mariano's chapel) may be mentioned here. It has been said to have come from the original pavement of Raphael's Logge and was thus attributed, on Vasari's authority, to Luca della Robbia the Younger (G. Tesorone, *L'antico pavimento delle Logge di Raffaello in Vaticano*, Naples, 1891; and D. Gnoli, 'La cappella di fra Mariano del Piombo in Roma', in *Arch. Stor. dell'Arte*, IV, 1891, p. 124). But this is pure inference because there is no proof that the three fragments really come from the Vatican. The splendid border decoration, with the Medici ring, is not enough to affirm so. What puzzles me is the fact that although the tiles are obviously loosely rearranged, the ones simulating a 'punta di diamante' show such differences in perspective that they cannot have been planned as a floor decoration but rather for a wall. Their date seems to be early sixteenth century, while the manufactory which produced them may well have been Tuscan. A dated Roman majolica pavement is the one in the apse of S. Maria della Consolazione. The square tiles, painted with a simple pattern of a yellow rose, are fairly preserved only along the walls, where they have not been so much walked upon. The name of the donor and the date are given in an

inscription now transferred to the pavement of the nave ('Gundisalvus de Salazar Hyspanus prot. scrip̃. ap̃. huius ecclesiae guardianus ornamentum et pavimentum istius maioris altaris impẽsis suis fieri fecit anno dñi MDXXI').
It may also be noted here that during recent restorations more tiles were found in S. Maria del Popolo.
2. For a discussion of the buildings and full bibliography see R. Krautheimer, *Corpus Basilicarum Christianarum Romae*, I, pp. 165 ff. (especially pp. 193–4).
3. The inscription in itself has been, of course, duly considered (Krautheimer, p. 168, n. 3; p. 194, n. 1), but the peculiarity of its material does not seem to have been noticed by anybody concerned with this special subject.
4. Their plan at the beginning of the sixteenth century is known through a drawing by Antonio da Sangallo il Giovane (Florence, Uffizi, Disegni architett. 898, reproduced by A. Bartoli, *Monumenti*..., III, CCXCIX, Fig. 489), showing the north corridor already rebuilt as it is while the southern one still has its earlier semicircular shape. Krautheimer suggests that they might have had two storeys. There is no other record of their aspect before the sixteenth century.

darkness and rather awe-inspiring—a feeling well-suited to the mood of pilgrims about to see a venerated receptacle of treasured relics—, they lead down to the sanctuary by a slow ramp. The first impression one gets when entering them from the church is that their walls have an irregular shape. This is not so in reality, but the impression is due to the fact that in the first section they are curved inwards. The architect seems to have felt it necessary to counterbalance the external curve of the apse, which limits them on one side and, for some reason, had to be left visible. The two funnel-shaped passages get broader as they approach their end, towards the entrance to the chapels, a rather subtle device that gives some illusion of greater depth and space. This was certainly increased by the extensive decoration in wall-tiles, tiles that would glitter in the darkness to the passing torchlights.

It is quite difficult for us today to recapture the original effect of the ambiance. On the ceiling of the north corridor—the one through which visitors entered the chapels—Cardinal Carvajal's coat-of-arms is still to be seen, but no trace is left of the majolica facing except for one single row of tiles above the arched entrance to the chapel of St. Gregory, with the inscription: 'Ave crux spes unica vite mortalis tem [. . .] reis indulge veniam piis auge iusticiam.' The loss of the first part of the entire inscription, which originally adorned both lateral walls of this ambulatory, was due to the over-scrupulous ecclesiastical supervisors of the eighteenth-century restorations: since what it contained did not quite agree with historical truth, the section of tiling on the left wall was destroyed. For symmetry's sake its continuation on the right wall was also deleted although it gave only the most factual statements about the sixteenth-century rebuilding and the date of its completion (1520).[5] Thus an appreciation of the whole setting is now possible only on the basis of the second half, which was allowed to remain in place in the south corridor—the one through which pilgrims went back to the church. Even there, however, present conditions are far from excellent since only the tiling is left: but nothing else exists any more of the other original decoration. The walls are at present entirely bare and shabbily whitewashed; and there are no elements that may help to suggest how they were connected to the majolica surface. Even so, although totally deprived of any architectural or decorative framework and apparently floating on a shapeless

background, the extant fragment is still impressive enough by itself.

It consists of a number of rows (eight on the left wall and nine on the right) of square painted tiles,[6] forming a continuous frieze, respectively about 8 and 6.50 m long, and about 1.10 m high. This uncommonly large surface displays, on as many lines as are rows of tiles, beautiful lettering in Roman capitals, designed in dark blue against a white ground. The single lines are separated from each other by a strip that shows a continuous interlacing pattern in blue, yellow and green (Figs. 2, 3, 4). The end wall of the corridor, over the entrance to the chapel of St. Helen, bears a shorter, independent inscription, on three lines of tiles of a slightly different design (Fig. 4), similar to those on the entrance to the St. Gregory chapel.

The text relates at length how the *titulus* of the Holy Cross was happily found in the church of S. Croce on the same day of the year 1492 when the news of Granada's capitulation to the hands of the Catholic monarchs, Ferdinand and Isabella, first reached Rome.[7] The coincidence was then interpreted as a meaningful event, if not a wonderful one—the more so since the discovery of so precious a relic had been caused by the works of restoration being carried on at that moment by order of the Spanish titular Cardinal of the time, Pedro Gonzalez de Mendoza, primate of Toledo. For his successor, Carvajal, another Spaniard, it was only too proper to record these facts, even twenty-eight years later, and to put a strong emphasis on the names of Mendoza, Ferdinand and Isabella, these three having been his steady patrons from the beginnings of his interesting career at the Roman curia.[8]

---

5. These facts are related by the contemporary Besozzi (whose monograph, *Storia della basilica di S. Croce*, Rome, 1750, is our principal source of information), who for the same reasons omits quoting the incriminated part of the inscription. Fortunately this was printed by L. Schrader (*Monumentorum Italiae quae hoc nostro saeculo & a Christianis posita sunt libri quatuor*, Helmstedt, 1592, p. 128: see Appendix).

6. Measuring 12.5 cm per side (see tracing, below).
7. See Appendix.
8. Carvajal's fascinating personality need not be discussed here. Incidentally, it may be remembered that in 1493 (June 19) he, by that time acting as Spanish ambassador and as the King's and Queen's own speaker to the Holy See, delivered the solemn 'obedience speech' on their behalf to the newly elected Alexander VI: a speech in which he insisted, with proud nationalism, on the subject of the defeat of the last Moorish kingdom. This happened just before he became a Cardinal (August 20, in the same creation with Cesare Borgia, whose gaoler he was later to be), with the title of SS. Pietro e Marcellino. At Mendoza's death (1495) he took over his patron's titular church of S. Croce in Gerusalemme. Carvajal had always been one of the chief fighters for a Catholic Reformation, and later he became the leader of the schismatic Council of Pisa (1511). After this he was excommunicated, to be readmitted into the Church and reinstated with his former titulus of S. Croce by Leo X (1513). He then appears to have taken special pride in embellishing his church, promoting restorations which included, among other things, the rebuilding of all the side-altars, which he dedicated to various sanctified Cardinals. A man of letters and erudition, whose best friends were Pietro Martire d'Anghiera and whose secretary was, for many years, Fedra Inghirami, he remained throughout his life first of all a Spanish priest, although more inclined, in his later years, to

Tracing of a tile,
right wall, South Corridor

Cardinal Carvajal himself may easily be credited with the text of our inscription.[9] The highly elaborate Latin phrasing echoes the Ciceronian touch he was aiming at in his oratory, not so much distinguished by elegance as 'docte concocta', as Pietro Martire d'Anghiera defined it. But what appears chiefly to be due to his personal taste (or at least to what we may guess his personal taste was) is the very idea of making use of wall-tiling in order to display an inscription, the monumental quality of which—stressed by the solemn Roman lettering—should obviously demand, by Italian Renaissance standards, the use of stone or marble.

In fact, the whole scheme does not fit in with the personality of any architect or decorator that we can think of who worked in Rome about 1520, and it appears entirely alien to Italian taste, if not frankly awkward, because of its looseness of general outline and lack of a distinct articulation. Even so, I have not been able to trace any other instance of a similar device even in Spain, where the common 'azulejos' decoration, or the type of tile-picture inaugurated by Francisco Niculoso Pisano, has a quite different character.[10]

As has been pointed out, nothing is unfortunately visible now of the decoration of the lower portions of the walls, and any guess at reconstructing what it

might have looked like thus appears gratuitous.[11] In any event, if we consider the monument just as it has been allowed to come down to us, what still strikes one most is the fact that the inscription is practically unreadable. People coming to pray to the holy 'Jerusalem', as the St. Helen chapel was called, went down through the north corridor and back up through the southern one after they had halted to pray in the sanctuary. Presumably the words inscribed all along their way were intended as an adequate accompaniment. But this could hardly have been the case: in order to read such a lengthy text (each line about 8 m long) one has to pace up and down the whole place a great number of times, something that would have been even more inconvenient to do in a crowd waiting for admission than it is now, to say nothing of the scarcity of light. So the value of Carvajal's inscription appears to be mainly psychological. Words are not used here so much to be carefully read as to impart a feeling of authoritative authentication to the place, to its history and to what were its treasured possessions. Perhaps one can go so far as to suppose that, in Carvajal's view, those shining lines might have constituted a sort of Christian counterpart to the Moslem religious-decorative tile-inscriptions of his own country.

Whether the actual tiles are the product of a Spanish or a Roman (or Italian) manufacture remains, to me, an open question.[12] They were executed to meet a very special order from a rather special man. In that respect they remain, I should think, unique, at least in Rome.

---

purely political speculations. For Carvajal, see H. Rossbach, *Das Leben und die politisch-kirchliche Wirksamkeit des B. Lopez de Carvajal, Kardinal von S. Croce*, Breslau, 1892. Rossbach's work does not include Carvajal's last years, nor any section on the Cardinal as a humanist and a patron of the arts. This part of his study was announced, but, as far as I know, was never published.

9. As suggested by Besozzi, who adds that this is what Severano says. Severano, however, only affirms that the inscription was commissioned by the Cardinal (p. 623).

10. See J. Ainaud de Lasarte, *Ceramica y Vidrio (Ars Hispaniae*, x), Madrid, 1952.

11. Unless tests are made, by removing the plaster-coating of the walls, nothing can be seen of what may still be left underneath.

12. An answer may come from examination of the back of the tiles, which might somehow be marked. But removing them without breaking them is quite difficult, given the present circumstances.

APPENDIX

Text of Carvajal's inscription in S. Croce in Gerusalemme.

Part I (from *Monumentorum Italiae quae hoc nostro saeculo & a Christianis posita sunt libri quatuor, editi a Laurentis Schradero*, Helmstedt, 1592, p. 128).

(Ad dextram ingredientibus capellam)
Anno Domini MIII tempore Otthonis III Sylvester Papa II qui fuerat antea eiusdem Otthonis Praeceptor, non satis rite forsan Pontificatum adeptus, a Spiritu praemonitus, qua die Hierusalem accederet, se fore moriturum, nesciens forte hoc sacellum esse Hierusalem secundum, sui Pontificatus anno quinto, statuta die, rem hic divinam faciens, ipsa die moritur. Eo tamen

divina gratia ante communionem, cumse iam tunc moriturum intellexisset propter dignam poenitudinem et lacrymas ac loci sanctitatem ad statum verisimilem salutis reducto:reseratis enim post divina populo criminibus suis et ordinatione praemissa, ut in criminum ultionem exanime corpus suum ab indomitis equis per urbem quaqua versum discurrentibus traheretur, et inhumatum dimitteretur, nisi Deus sua pietate aliud disponeret, equisq., post longiorem cursum intra Lateranam aedem moratis, isthic ab Otthone tumulatur. Sergiusque III successor mausoleum deinde expolitius reddidit. Sunt qui dicunt historico referente Vincentio Asylum Romae quod primum inter duos lucos Tarpeium et Palatinum impunitati virorum et foeminarum Romulus dicaverat, aucta Urbe ex Caeliomonte per Tullum Hostilium III. Roman. Regem ad finem ipsius montis intra Urbis pomerium translatum, fuisse ex ipso ferme loco ubi nunc Basilicam Hierusalem constructam cernimus, ut ubi olim fuerat flagitiis impunitas, ibi sub Christo accedentibus omnium peccatorum venia tribuatur.

(Ibidem ex alio latere)

Ad gloriam Dominicae Crucis et spem recuperationis sacri gloriosi sepulcri Hierosolymae sub S. in Christo Patre et D. N. Leone X Hetrusca gente familia Medices clarissimo, ac serenissimo D. Carolo V Hispaniarum et utriusque Siciliae ac Hierusalem universaeque Insulae Athlanticae seu terrae Sanctae Crucis et Hispaniensis, ac aliarum insularum Africae et Indiae Rege Catholico, Archiduce Austriae &c in Rom. Imp. electo, Reverend. in Christo Pater D. Bernard. Cardinal Vaial [sic!] Episc. Sabinensis et Card.S.Crucis Patriarcha Hierosolymitanus ante capellam hanc ulteriori sacrae capellae S.Crucis in Hierusalem adiungendam curavit Anno Salutis Christ. MDXX.

Text of the extant inscription (the missing letters in brackets).[1]

Sacra ulterior capella. dicta Hierusalem q. Beata Helena magni Constantini mater Hierosolima rediens anno domini CCCXXII:Dominici trophei insigniis repertis:in proprio eam cubiculo erexerit:terraque sancti montis Calvariae navi inde advecta supra quam/ Christi sanguis effusus fuit redemptionis humanae praecium:ad primum usque inferiorem fornicem repleverit ex quo sacellum ipsum et tota basilica ac universa urbs:secunda Hierusalem meruit appellari: apud/qam [sic] et Dominus ad illius robur fidei:in Petro iterum crucifigi voluit ubique unius dei veneratio ac fides indeficiens et Domini praecibus et Petri favore:ad ultimum usque Domini iudicantis adventum in urbe sublimi et valente ac inde veriore Hierusalem: creditur permansura (hunc ergo locum Regina ip)sa multis Christi et Sanctorum reliquiis ornavit et a beato Sylvestro XIII k(al)l.aprilis cum multiplici peccatorum venia visitantibus indulta consecrari obtinuit.Inde centum ferme labentibus annis:Valentinianus.II.imperator filius/(Constantii Caesaris Arcadii) Honorii imperatorum nepos ex sorore Galla Placidia filia magni Theodosii hispani:in solutionem voti sui ac matris Placidiae et Honoriae sororis:opere vermiculato eam exornavit.Inde quasi MC an(n)is evolutis:(titulus verae Crucis ab Helena Romam dela)tus qui supra ar(cu)m maiorem istius basilicae in parva fenestra (plumbea t)heca muro lateritio clausus tandiu latuerat: musivis tame(n) litteris ab extra id referentibus quod

illic titulus staret quae iam litterae prae vetustate vix legi (poterant, sedente Innocentio) V(III p)ientiss(imo Pontifice anno Domini) MCCCCXCII.Pontificatus sui an(no VIII cum bonae memoriae) R.mus D.Petrus Gundisalvi d(e Mendo)za nobiliss. Cardinal.S.Crucis in Hierusalem Toletan. primas . tectum basilicae istius et musivas illas litteras fenestrae/(reparari faceret fabris bitumen) quo literae fi(n)g (ebantur in)discrete diruentibus ape(rto) fen(estrae foramine con)tra eorum et Cardinalis beneplacitum:gloriosus titulus verae crucis post tot annos ab Helena Romae visibilis apparuit eaque die magna Granata olim dicta[2] Hiliberia a filia Hispani regis condita et appellata deinde sub Christo sincera mente Deum reverens tum post cladem Hispaniae a Mahumetanis aphricanis sub Roderico Rege illatam multo tem/pore Mahumetis militiae serviens tandem Ferdinando & Elisabeth sacris coniugibus Hispaniarum rege et regina catholicis valida illam tum obsidione cingentibus dedita illis Romae nuntiatur/ut apparente signo filii Dei in urbe quae universum orbem refert simul contra Mahumetem praecipuum Christi hostem victoriam insignem nuntiari contingeret.Ac inde in memoriam utriusque tam/praeclari divini misterii una die Romae relati Innocentius ipse et hanc basilicam cum Senatu devotissime visitavit et quotannis eam ipse die visitantibus plene indulsit primum Alleluja referens/contra bestiam babylonemque Mahumetem in ecclesia sanctorum iuxta Apocalipsim ea die fuisse decantatum.Inde vero vetustate murorum aut inhabitantium incuria fornice sacelli istius Hierusalem rui/nam minante et musivis figuris operis Valentiniani praeter canticum Ambrosianum quod in fronte descriptum fuit: omnino deletis R.mus D. Bernardinus Lupi Carvaial Epus Ostien. S.R.E. cardinalis/s.+ in Hierusalem patriarcha hyerosolymitan. et fornicem ipsum ac figuras musivas denuo ad instar prior.refecit.Intra ipsam quoque maiore basilic quae prim(us cardinalium)est titulus diversa alt(aria) nonnullis S.R.E. cardinalibus in cathalogo sanctorum anumeratis erexit atque dicavit. Claustrumque parvum et magnum intra domum ipsam patrum Carthusiens. chorumque institu(it maioris b)asilicae & utrumque descensum/et antecapellam ipsam ad perpetuam Christian.reipub. foelicitatem fundavit. +

The inscription on the door leading to St. Helen's chapel is as follows:

(O cru)x splendidior cuntis astris mundo celebris hominibus multum amabilis an (. . . .) universis que sola fuisti digna portare talentum mundi dulce lignum dulces clavos dulcia ferens pondera salva p͂ntem catervam hodie in tuis laudibus congregatam.

---

[1] Schrader's transcription is not entirely exact.

[2] Here Schrader's transcription abruptly stops.

MARIA VITTORIA BRUGNOLI PACE

Un modello antico e due disegni attribuiti a Michelangelo

Il problema del rapporto di Michelangelo con l'antico, puntualizzato sulla individuazione di quelle opere della statuaria ellenistica e romana che spunti e sollecitazioni poterono offrire all'artista in momenti diversi e successivi della sua attività, è tema ricorrente presso quanti si siano dedicati agli studi michelangioleschi. Un tema sempre stimolante poichè non si conclude nella indagine delle fonti di informazione figurativa dell'artista, ma può offrire un mezzo prezioso per giungere a precisazioni cronologiche, per penetrare nel difficile e complesso processo creativo di un'opera fino all'atto iniziale, là dove le esperienze figurative rifluiscono per risolversi in una immagine inedita e al tutto nuova.

E' qualità particolare di Michelangelo, e fin dai suoi primi disegni, quella di operare una scelta rigorosa dei propri modelli, una scelta presieduta da una coscienza nitidissima di quei valori umani ed universali cui egli intese dare espressione e forma per tutto il corso della sua lunga e operosa esistenza. Motivi e spunti suggeriti dalla pittura che lo precedette nel tempo, dalla statuaria antica cui rivolse la propria attenzione non soltanto negli anni della educazione artistica, appaiono pertanto trasformati e rifusi in termini nuovi e diversi quasi all'atto stesso del tracciarne il ricordo sul bianco di un foglio; ed è per ciò caso rarissimo—qualora si escludano i primi disegni da Giotto e da Masaccio—e del tutto eccezionale quello di poter individuare con persuasiva precisione i monumenti che furono oggetto di studio da parte dell'artista.

Per quanto riguarda la statuaria antica, il caso più fortunato può considerarsi senza dubbio quello della figura da fontana nel giardino Cesi a Roma, riconosciuta dal Panofsky e successivamente puntualizzata dal Tolnay nel disegno di Michelangelo al Louvre (688 recto) per un Mercurio.[1] E certamente intervengono con il loro peso, nella difficoltà di tali individua-

zioni, la dispersione che le opere di statuaria hanno subìto nel corso dei secoli e le nostre limitate conoscenze circa la effettiva consistenza delle collezioni di antichità nel '500; o comunque circa i prodotti della plastica antica a quell'epoca noti agli artisti ed al pubblico.

Può accadere così di circoscrivere la ricerca del rapporto di Michelangelo con l'antico a pochi esempi di statuaria classica, di più vasta risonanza e di più sicura acquisizione; e di causare per ciò anche delle forzature nelle conclusioni cronologiche e stilistiche circa l'opera michelangiolesca. Ciò è avvenuto, ad esempio, a proposito del "S. Matteo" dell'Accademia fiorentina, per il quale la ripetuta affermazione di un intervento del Laocoonte nella definizione della immagine michelangiolesca ha convinto a datare il marmo al 1506, ritardando di circa un biennio quanto suggerito ad evidenza dai documenti: la nota di pagamento contenuta nei registri dell'Archivio dell'Opera del Duomo, pubblicata dal Frey, sembra infatti non lasciar campo ad una datazione oltre il 1504; nè certo le lettere del Balducci e del Soderini—rispettivamente del 9 maggio e del 27 novembre del 1506—offrono argomenti tali da persuadere a non prendere in considerazione quanto si legge, e in modo sufficientemente esplicito, nel documento del 1504.[2] L'intervento del gruppo rodio, rinvenuto nel gennaio 1506, non appare del resto affatto condizionante per spiegare la nuova violenza espressiva del "S. Matteo" (fig. 1) qualora si tengano presenti, accanto al Menelao mutilo (il c.d. Pasquino) collocato sin dal 1501 presso il palazzo del Cardinal Carafa,[3] pezzi antichi come il torso nella

1. E. Panofsky, M.A. Literatur... in: *Jahrb. f. Kunstgesch.*, Wien, 1921–2, Buchbesprechungen, col. 23; Ch. Tolnay, *The Youth of Michelangelo*, Princeton, 1947, p. 70 e p. 182, n. 14. Un altro esempio di raffronto sufficientemente puntuale con l'antico può offrire il disegno di bambino seduto in basso a destra nel foglio Brit. Mus. 1887–5–2–117 *verso*: per esso cfr. la figura, probabilmente da un esemplare ellenistico del gruppo "fanciullo con l'oca", nel fol. 37 v. dei *Römische Skizzenbücher* dello Heemskerk, pubbl. dallo Egger, Berlino 1916. Un esemplare di tale gruppo esisteva a Roma "in vinea Colotii in hortis

Sallustianis". La collezione lapidaria di Angelo Colocci era già famosa nel 1521, allorchè si trovava nella casa in via in Parione (Lanciani, *Storia degli Scavi*, I, p. 203).
2. Per il rapporto tra il Laocoonte e il "S. Matteo" cfr. O. Ollendorf, Der Laokoon und Michelangelo's gefesselter Sklave, in: *Rep. f. Kunstwiss.*, 1898, p. 112 ss.; e, più recentemente, Ch. Tolnay, *op. cit.*, p. 170, e H. von Einem, M.A. und die Antike, in: *Antike und Abendland*, I, pp. 62–64. Per i documenti relativi al "S. Matteo" cfr. K. Frey, Studien zu M. A. Buonarroti... in: *Jahrb. d. K. Pr. Kunstsamml.*, 1909, Beiheft, pp. 112–13; A. Gotti, Vita di M.A., Firenze, 1875, II, p. 52. Sull'argomento vedi M. V. Brugnoli, Note sul rapporto Leonardo-Michelangelo, in: *Boll. d'Arte*, 1955, pp. 133–4.
3. Cfr. A. Grünwald, Über einige Werke M.A. in ihrem Verhältnis zur Antike, in: *Jahrb. d. Kunstsamml.*, Wien, 27 (1907–9), pp. 130–1.

collezione della Valle, collocato su un'alta base in un disegno del Cock (fig. 2) datato al 1553 ma che ripete certamente un disegno più antico.[4] Si tratta di un torso mutilo delle braccia e delle gambe, caratterizzato da un impeto ribelle nella accentuata torsione della testa e del busto, tale da poter impressionare Michelangelo al tempo del suo primo soggiorno romano, e al punto da indurlo a farne rivivere il ricordo nel marmo sbozzato dopo il ritorno a Firenze. Per quella violenza espressiva, il torso della collezione della Valle riporta a mente opere del tipo del Polifemo rinvenuto più di un secolo fa sulle rive del lago di Albano nel ninfeo della villa di Domiziano (figg. 3, 4);[5] un tipo statuario cui probabilmente apparteneva anche il Polifemo visto da Claude Bellièvre nel palazzo Rossi a S. Eustachio durante i primi anni del pontificato di papa Leone X e che il francese descrive con sufficiente efficacia nelle sue "Noctes romanae": "hec facies tam torva et crudelis est ut posset convertere hominem in fugam".[6] Il ricorso, per il "S. Matteo" dell'Accademia, al torso della collezione della Valle, e ad eventuali raffigurazioni del Polifemo note a Roma agli inizi del '500 ed oggi perdute, non vuole e non può essere—allo stato attuale delle nostre conoscenze—più che una ipotesi; ma forse varrà a suggerire, nella indagine delle "fonti" antiche della cultura figurativa michelangiolesca, la necessità di operare su un raggio più vasto di quello permesso dai superstiti prodotti della statuaria classica.

In tale senso, e in questo caso l'interesse esorbita dai termini del problema per incidere in un campo dei più discussi inerenti all'attività dell'artista, mi sembra utile tornare su un argomento cui ebbi altrove la possibilità di accennare solo di sfuggita e del tutto marginalmente.[7] Si tratta del disegno Casa Buonarroti 69 F recto e di quello Louvre 716, al primo strettamente legato per evidenti analogie figurative (figg. 6, 7). Il disegno Casa Buonarroti è oggi pressochè concordemente ricondotto agli anni del "Giudizio" nella Sistina e poche riserve sussistono circa l'autografia michelangiolesca;[8] più discusso il foglio Louvre, per il quale la trasposizione quasi puntuale della figura nel Cristo della "Pietà" dipinta da Sebastiano del Piombo

per Don Ferrante Gonzaga, e da questi inviata in Spagna e conservata nella chiesa di Ubeda, ha indotto più volte a proporre il nome del veneziano ma senza giungere a comporre, fino ad oggi, la divergenza di opinioni al riguardo.[9]

All'argomento, che si inserisce nel travagliatissimo tema del rapporto Michelangelo-Sebastiano, può portare un contributo non privo di aperture per ampie conclusioni il riconoscere in un pezzo di statuaria ellenistica la diretta fonte di ispirazione per il foglio Casa Buonarroti. Nella serie di disegni che il Poelenburg andò tracciando, in gran parte da statue antiche, durante il soggiorno romano del 1617-1623 e che venne data alle stampe nei "Paradigmata" che Episcopius pubblicò ad Amsterdam intorno al 1672, ci imbattiamo a tav. 27 della parte I in uno studio di un gruppo mutilo (fig. 5) segnato: "*Poelenburg delin. ex marm. antiq.*"[10] Si tratta dunque di un'opera di arte antica il cui modello veniva identificato dal Klein, nel 1907, nel gruppo di Atamante che sorregge il figlio Learco da lui ucciso in un impeto di follia; un gruppo bronzeo rammentato da Plinio che ne indica quale autore lo scultore rodio Aristonidas.[11] Del gruppo, e della sua copia marmorea di età romana, non resta oggi traccia, ma non v'è dubbio che a Roma ne esisteva un esemplare mutilo in marmo agli inizi del '600: il disegno Casa Buonarroti (fig. 7) ne testimonia anzi la presenza già nel quarto decennio del '500, poichè un raffronto tra il disegno di Michelangelo e la figura del giovane figlio di Atamante sembra dimostrare a sufficienza quale sia stato, in questo caso, il motivo figurativo che sollecitò la fantasia dell'artista.[12] Uno spunto rielaborato nella inversione parziale della figura, in

4. Cfr. *Röm. Skizz.*, cit., testo II, p. 56 ss.; tavv. II, 128—il torso è quello a sinistra nel disegno.
5. G. Lugli, Scavo fatto nel 1841 nel ninfeo detto Bergantino sulla riva del lago di Albano, in: *Bull. archeologico municipale*, 1913 (XLI), p. 89 ss., tav. X. Debbo alla cortesia dell'amico Enrico Paribeni la segnalazione di questa opera ellenistica e il suggerimento di un suo rapporto con il "S. Matteo".
6. Cfr. E. Müntz in: *Révue arch.*, 1882 (43), p. 35. Sulla collezione Rossi cfr. Lanciani, *op. cit.*, I, p. 176.
7. Cfr. M. V. Brugnoli, *Disegni di Michelangelo*, ed. Martello, Milano, 1964, p. 27, n. 51.
8. Per la bibliografia relativa, cfr. P. Barocchi, *Michelangelo e la sua scuola. I disegni di Casa Buonarroti e degli Uffizi*, Firenze, 1962, n. 143.

9. Per la bibliografia relativa cfr. Ch. Tolnay, *Michelangelo. The Final Period*, Princeton, 1960, n. 168, pp. 180-1; più recentemente, M. Hirst in: *Journ. of the Warburg and Courtauld Inst.*, 1961 (XXIV), p. 181, nota 119, attribuisce il disegno Louvre a M.A.; S. J. Freedberg in: *Art Bulletin*, Sept. 1963, p. 253 ss., a Sebastiano del Piombo. La "Pietà" di Ubeda si trova attualmente nella Casa di Pilatos a Siviglia (cfr. M. Hirst, A Late Work of Sebastiano del Piombo in: *Burl. Mag.*, April 1965, p. 177, nota 3).
10. Episcopius (Jan de Bisschop), *Paradigmata Graphices variorum artificum*, ed. Amsterdam s.a. Il disegno è stato ripubblicato di recente da E. Paribeni (Riflessi di sculture antiche, in: *Archeologia classica*, 1961, pp. 103–5) che lo poneva in rapporto con il Cristo nelle "Pietà" di Annibale Carracci.
11. W. Klein, Zu Aristonidas, in: *Österr. Jahreshefte*, Wien, 1907, p. 243 ss.
12. Di questo riferimento all'antico, da me segnalato a p. 27 dei "*Disegni di Michelangelo*", cit., dell'aprile 1964, leggo un richiamo a p. 188, n. 9, del volume *European Art and Classical Past*, di C. Vermeule, pubbl. a Cambridge (Mass.) nel medesimo anno 1964. Il Vermeule ricorda la fonte antica a proposito del disegno Louvre 716, che attribuisce a Michelangelo e di cui anticipa la datazione al 1519 circa, contro la più accreditata opinione dei critici; egli individua nel disegno Louvre un precedente per la composizione del "Cristo morto e angeli" del Museum of Fine Arts di Boston, firmato dal Rosso fiorentino e nel quale si vuole riconoscere—anche se con riserva—il quadro

controparte rispetto alla incisione fatta eccezione del braccio destro e del collo; soltanto accennato questo dal tratto sottile della matita ma quanto basta per farne supporre il proseguimento nella testa reclinata sull'omero. E sotto l'ascella destra, un groviglio di segni in ombra suggerisce il tracciato delle dita che, nel marmo antico disegnato dal Poelenburg, restavano a documentare la perduta figura del vecchio re che sorreggeva il figlio morto. Una composizione, quella concepita dallo scultore rodio, che Michelangelo ricostruirà nel risorto faticosamente sollevato a braccia nella zona inferiore a sinistra del "Giudizio" sistino; e ancora nella "Pietà" del Duomo di Firenze, o in quella da Palestrina. Ma risolvendola in termini al tutto nuovi per la tragica evidenza del corpo abbandonato del risorto e ancor più del Cristo, le cui membra, lungi dal comporsi nell'equilibrio della statua antica, scivolano senza presa sui piani di sostegno per la greve pesantezza di morte.[13]

Il modello ellenistico concorre dunque nei limiti di una semplice sollecitazione a definire la tragica immagine michelangiolesca, anche se in questo caso il monumento antico offriva più di un elemento affine alla tematica dell'artista. Il quale, forse per questo, sembra ricorrervi anche nei due studi del foglio Windsor 422 recto, ove l'abbandono della testa reclinata—un abbandono di morte più che di sonno per l'ombra che affonda le orbite, per la piega dolorosa delle labbra—suggerisce di individuarne la fonte di ispirazione nella figura del giovane Learco ucciso piuttosto che altrove.[14]

La trasposizione in termini di così dolorosa intensità

operata da Michelangelo sul modello, induce a forti riserve circa una attribuzione a lui del disegno Louvre 716 (fig. 6); una rielaborazione questo del foglio Casa Buonarroti, ma attraverso una rimessa a punto minuziosa sul pezzo ellenistico, per cui la indagata struttura anatomica del disegno Buonarroti viene ricondotta entro l'involucro epiteliale e la concisa definizione plastica sostituita con un modellare indugiante sul sottile trapasso dei piani, chiaroscurati oltre qualunque effetto traslucido di una superficie marmorea. E, nel disegno Louvre, il rapido tratto di matita che accenna al collo flesso nel disegno Buonarroti è completato dalla testa reclinata secondo una angolazione analoga alla statua antica, della quale ripete i caratteri fisionomici. Tanto studiosa attenzione al marmo romano impone già di per sè più che un sospetto circa l'attribuzione a Michelangelo del foglio Louvre, poichè solo eccezionalmente—e sempre in disegni del momento più giovanile—è dato constatare in lui una simile adesione a un modello.

L'autore del disegno Louvre inoltre va tramutando—mediante il tracciato delle ginocchia flesse, del panno gettato sulle gambe—la statua antica nella immagine del Cristo morto della "Pietà" di Ubeda, dimostrando di avere del tutto chiara alla propria mente la configurazione conclusiva, che gli suggerisce anche varianti insistenti specie per quanto riguarda il braccio destro, studiato in più aspetti nella posizione abbandonata lungo il fianco del disegno Buonarroti (e della statua antica) e infine risolto, nello schizzo in alto a destra, in una posizione flessa, che ne permetta una funzione di appoggio. Il Cristo di Ubeda infatti, anche se composto verticalmente in gruppo con la Madre, non trova in questa il proprio sostegno e il busto si mantiene eretto per il suo puntellarsi sul braccio destro, in una posa implicitamente energica e pertanto del tutto incoerente nei confronti del corpo privo di vita. Una soluzione questa cui certo non poteva aderire Michelangelo, il quale in ben altri termini, come si è accennato, configurava il medesimo spunto dall'antico nel risorto del "Giudizio" sistino o nelle "Pietà" di Firenze.

Alla conclusione che ormai va imponendosi, di identificare cioè in Sebastiano del Piombo l'autore del foglio Louvre, non contraddicono certo i caratteri e le qualità che qualificano il disegno, nei quali al contrario può riconoscersi più di un tratto in comune con i disegni di Sebastiano del periodo tardo; ad esempio con il disegno Louvre (n. 5051) per una "Visitazione", di recente e in modo del tutto persuasivo posto in relazione con la composizione già in S. Maria della Pace.[15] E tornerebbero qui a proposito molte delle

---

rammentato dal Vasari tra le opere eseguite dal Rosso durante il suo soggiorno romano.
Ferma restando—a parte l'attribuzione a Michelangelo o a Sebastiano del Piombo—una datazione al quarto decennio per il disegno Louvre, come per quello Casa Buonarroti ad esso strettamente collegato, gli eventuali rapporti tra il dipinto del Rosso e il torso ellenistico del gruppo di Aristonidas potranno venire concretamente impostati soltanto dopo che uno studio a fondo del quadro di Boston ne avrà permessa una persuasiva datazione: qualora si tratti in effetti dell'opera rammentata dal Vasari, il ricorso al pezzo antico non potrà infatti tener conto di mediazioni michelangiolesche; mentre queste ultime potranno assumersi quale fonte verosimile nel caso che il "Cristo morto" di Boston debba ricondursi—e per quanto può giudicarsi da una riproduzione fotografica ciò non sembra del tutto da escludere—all'ultimo decennio dell'attività dell'artista.

13. Per la "Pietà" del Duomo di Firenze, H. von Einem, art. cit., suggeriva un ricordo del Patroclo morto nel gruppo con Menelao e in un rilievo di una urna etrusca del Museo Archeologico di Firenze. Al gruppo c. d. di Pasquino, oltre che al Laocoonte, fa ricorso anche il Kleiner, *Begegnungen M.A.s mit der Antike*, Berlin, 1950, p. 49.

14. Nel catalogo dei disegni di Windsor (*It. Drawings of the XV and XVI Centuries*, p. 246) Popham-Wilde suppongono giustamente la esistenza di un modello plastico per i due studi di testa reclinata; un modello che suggeriscono però di identificare con il Cupido addormentato nel rilievo noto con la denominazione di "Letto di Policleto".

15. Cfr. M. Hirst, art. cit., in: *Burl. Mag.*, April 1965, p. 177 ss.

sottili osservazioni fatte da Michael Hirst su quell'argomento, circa la cura posta da Sebastiano disegna-
tore nel definire la immagine già nei precisi aspetti
della redazione finale, circa il faticoso studio di ricerca
tradito dai pentimenti e di cui un segno ripetutamente
inciso sottolinea la soluzione più soddisfacente.

Vorrei rammentare infine che nel percorso dell'attività
romana del pittore veneto una adesione così concorde
ad un modello antico non costituisce certo un fatto

eccezionale: e basti tener presente il fregio che delimita
in basso il bel ritratto di Andrea Doria, là dove i
motivi di ancora e di remo e di nave rostrata derivano
direttamente da un rilievo romano che alla fine del
sec. XV si trovava a San Lorenzo fuori le Mura e che
si conserva oggi nel Museo Capitolino.[16]

16. Dobbiamo tale identificazione a J. W. Crous, Ein antiker
Fries by Seb. del Piombo, in: *Mitt. d. deut. archäol. Inst.*, 1940
(55), p. 65 ss.

NORMAN W. CANEDY

The Decoration of the Stanza della Cleopatra

Among the projects which particularly interested Julius III during the early months of his reign was the decoration of the recently-constructed room at the end of Bramante's eastern corridor.[1] This room, square in shape, could be entered from any one of three sides. The main entrance, however, was clearly the one at the top of the flight of stairs leading from the eastern corridor, since a fountain was constructed as the focal point of the long passageway. Another doorway, opening onto Bramante's famous statue court, was found in the wall to the left of the main entrance, while a narrow door next to the fountain gave access to the Villa of Innocent VIII to the north. The Stanza della Cleopatra, which received this designation from the famous ancient statue originally positioned on the fountain, could hardly escape being seen by virtually any visitor to that part of the Vatican Palace.[2] It would appear that Julius took advantage of this strategic location when the program of the room's decoration was drawn up. As this paper attempts to show, by means of its decoration the room was transformed into a kind of rostrum from which were propagated the Roman pontiff's views concerning the topical and heatedly-contested subject of the legitimacy and supremacy of the Papacy.

Vasari records that Julius wanted to place a fountain '*in testa al corridore al Belvedere*', that is in the new square room at the head of the stairs.[3] Michelangelo, to whom the Pope first turned for suggestions, pro- posed a 'Moses Striking the Rock' which he would carve from marble. Giving as his reason the factor of time, Julius bypassed Michelangelo's idea in favor of the alternate plan submitted by Vasari, one which would utilize the Cleopatra still in its original niche in the adjoining statue court.[4]

An engraving by Cavalleri documents the appearance of the fountain complex with the antique statue in place[5] (Fig. 1). The figure was positioned on a rocky shelf which was supported in turn by a rectangular structure consisting of symmetrically balanced pilasters on either side, connected by a cornice. Superimposed on each pilaster was a terminus figure which supported the capital above. A grimacing male mask, winged and wearing a head covering, was centered on the cornice beneath the statue. At the base of the fountain, filling the entire space beneath the feet of the termini, lay a large sculptured scallop shell. These elements framed the entrance to a shallow grotto, the opening of which resembled a proscenium with the curtains hung at the sides.

From Vasari's account we learn that Daniele da Volterra, at Michelangelo's instigation, was given charge of the fountain but that he took so long with the *stucchi* and the paintings that these were the only parts he finished.[6] The authorship of the fountain design, therefore, remains unclear. It has been suggested that the fountain was indeed Daniele's design;[7] on the other hand, two architects of note, Vignola and Girolamo da Carpi, both of whom were in positions of authority for the Vatican Palace at that time, received payment for work on the Cleopatra fountain.[8] Since there is not sufficient evidence within Cavalleri's record to reach a satisfactory decision on the basis of style, attribution must remain in the realm of conjecture.

1. The premise that the Stanza della Cleopatra was a pro- grammed fountain room was first proposed in a term paper written for Professor Wittkower in December, 1959.
James S. Ackerman, *The Cortile del Belvedere* (*Studi e docu- menti per la storia del Palazzo Vaticano*, vol. III; Vatican City: Biblioteca apostolica vaticana, 1954), esp. pp. 77–78. (Hereafter known as *Ackerman*.) The plan of the room may be seen in *Ackerman*, Fig. 38. The room's decoration had been begun by October, 1550, approximately seven months after the election of Julius III. I am grateful to Dr. Hermine Speyer for having the paintings on the ceiling photographed for me.
2. Ludwig von Pastor, *The History of the Popes from the Close of the Middle Ages*, ed. Ralph Francis Kerr (St. Louis: B. Her- der Book Co., 1951), XIII, p. 367: 'Strangers were allowed to visit the Vatican in all its parts . . . ' (Hereafter known as *Pastor*.) Also on the Stanza della Cleopatra as an important passageway, see *Ackerman*, pp. 77–78, n. 3. This room has been designated in a variety of ways since the sixteenth century. It is presently known as the Sala del Torso since the Torso Belvedere is now its prime attraction.
3. Giorgio Vasari, *Le vite de' piu' eccellenti pittori, scultori ed architettori*, ed. Gaetano Milanesi (Florence: Sansoni, 1906), VII, pp. 58–59. (Hereafter known as *Vasari*.)

4. On the history of the statue, now generally regarded as a Sleeping Ariadne, see Walther Amelung, *Die Sculpturen des Vaticanischen Museums* (Berlin: G. Reimer, 1903), II, pp. 636 ff., no. 414, pl. 57.
5. J. B. Cavalleriis, *Antiquarum statuarum urbis Romae* (Rome: [n.n.] 1594), fol. 6. I am indebted to Mrs. Enriqueta Harris Frankfort and the Warburg Institute, University of London, for the photograph of the engraving. The fountain, altered during the reign of Paul V, was finally removed in the eighteenth century (*Ackerman*, p. 78).
6. *Vasari*, p. 59.
7. *Ackerman*, p. 78.
8. Alberto Serafini, *Girolamo da Carpi: pittore e architetto ferrarese, 1501–1556* (Rome: Unione editrice, 1915), p. 358, n. 2.

The fountain in the Stanza della Cleopatra has been said to owe its conception to the original Cleopatra fountain in the statue court.[9] In a general way this is true.[10] In addition to the substitution of the mantelpiece for the sarcophagus of the original setting, however, the winged mask, the termini supports, and the proscenium-like grotto entrance are all new attributes on the fountain in the Stanza della Cleopatra. This combination of motifs, as far as has been determined, is far from common on earlier fountains. These motifs, however, are often found together on another category of sixteenth-century monuments, the commemorative tomb. The semi-recumbent figure, the termini supports, and the winged, grimacing mask all appear in Michelangelo's designs for either the Medici or Julius tombs. A similar combination of attributes is also to be found on Guglielmo della Porta's slightly later funerary monument for Paul III.[11] Furthermore, several of the design elements used on the lower part of the fountain structure and their general arrangement have parallels on the reliefs of ancient grave altars.[12]

Attributes which are familiar from their use on both ancient and Renaissance funerary monuments, then, form an integral part of the Cleopatra design for the new fountain room. The question arises as to whether these additions to the design of the original setting retain whatever significance they are known to have had within the context of the funerary monument, or whether in transition from one class of monument to another they have been drained of their content. As we have come to anticipate when confronted with the decorated rooms of the Cinquecento, the various elements are to be ultimately understood as contributing to the programmatic significance within the sum of their parts.[13] While the fountain was the dominant feature of the Stanza della Cleopatra, it nevertheless was surrounded by an elaborate scheme of stucco and painted decoration which, in great part, may still be seen. It follows, then, that before attempting to answer

the question proposed above and others concerning the form and the purpose of the fountain, we should, through an examination of the other parts of the decoration, try to determine the character and relationship of the total decorative scheme.

When we turn to the painting of the lower zone of the room, the pilasters and the walls up to the cornice, we are confronted with problems of remodeling and restoration (Fig. 3). It is known that repainting and alterations were undertaken during the reign of Pius VI.[14] At that time a series of panels was painted for the soffit and embrasures of the window to the right of the main entrance and the walls hung with fictive draperies. Also, probably in the course of regularizing the wall after the removal of the fountain, the filling of the pilasters was changed. There are no known visual records which establish to what extent the present painting of the walls reflects the original design. Two drawings exist, however, which provide a record of the general appearance of the pilasters before the eighteenth-century changes, still to be seen, were made.[15] These drawings, both of which are in the Royal Library, Turin, show that the lower one-third or so of each pilaster was redesigned to include either female personifications seated under canopies or sphinxes, phoenixes, and armorial devices from the stemma of Pius VI. Originally, as the drawings reveal, there were two basic designs used on the lower part of the pilasters throughout the room, one a richly figurated urn surmounted by lions and the other a like urn surmounted by Phrygians. Other losses above these lower parts include winged *putti* caught within foliated scrolls which evolve from centered candelabra forms. Alterations have also been made on the motifs in the upper part of the pilaster which, by and large, still conform to the designs of the sixteenth century, but these changes seem to have been effected primarily for purposes of decorum. It is highly likely that the *grottesche* of the pilasters were composed to be read for meaning rather than to be seen simply as evocations of antique decoration, although we are without the evidence to specify what that meaning might be.[16]

9. *Ackerman*, p. 78.

10. See Elías Tormo y Monzó, *Os desnos das antigual has que vio Francisco d'Ollanda, pintor portugues* (Madrid: [n.n.] 1940), fol. 8 v, for F. d'Ollanda's drawing of the Cleopatra *in situ* in the statue court.

11. See Erwin Panofsky, *Tomb Sculpture: Four Lectures on Its Changing Aspects from Ancient Egypt to Bernini* (New York: Harry N. Abrams, Inc. [n.d.]), Fig. 438. See Charles de Tolnay, *Michelangelo* (Princeton: Princeton University Press, 1954), IV, for termini (esp. pp. 28 and 91) and masks (esp. p. 30) as symbols of death.

12. See the cinerary urn illustrated in Franz Cumont, *Recherches sur le symbolisme funéraire des romains* (Paris: Paul Geuthner, 1942), pl. XI. (Hereafter known as *Cumont*.)

13. We need only recall here the iconographical deciphering of the decoration of the Sala della Galatea in the Villa Farnesina, Rome, or of the Camera di S. Paolo in Parma.

14. Anthony M. Clark, 'Four Decorative Panels by Unterberger', *Worcester Art Museum Annual*, IX (1961), pp. 1–11.

15. One of these drawings is cataloged and reproduced in Aldo Bertini, *I disegni italiani della Biblioteca reale di Torino* (Rome: Istituto poligrafico dello Stato, Libreria dello Stato, 1958), p. 29, no. 107, Fig. 167, as Giovanni da Udine. The other is found in a portfolio of Girolamo da Carpi drawings, fol. 5 r, and is presently unpublished. It is included in my forthcoming study on Girolamo's Roman sketchbook.

16. One of Daniele's contemporaries, Pirro Ligorio, states that grotesque designs should be read for their meaning. On this, see David R. Coffin, 'Pirro Ligorio and the Decoration of the Late Sixteenth Century at Ferrara', *The Art Bulletin*, XXXVII, no. 3 (September, 1955), pp. 167–85.

Pervading these additive designs, however, is an apparent symbolization of facets of elemental or demonic nature, interwoven with devices from the Papal arms. Climaxing the pilaster filling is either a Fame or two youthful Victories connected with the del Monte laurel branch and triple monticules. It is tempting to interpret these crowning figures as an allusion to the eventual triumph of the Pope over inferior powers.

Above the cornice on each of the four walls is a lunette enframed by a double meander pattern alternating with the familiar triple monticules and laurel branch. In the center of each of these lunettes is a circular landscape fresco surrounded by a simple stucco molding on either side of which are found fabulous marine creatures or nereids on dolphins or sea centaurs[17] (Fig. 2). Whatever else these stucco figures may have been meant to convey, their appearance within the decoration seems in keeping with the general watery theme of the room.[18] In the lunette paintings as well, great emphasis has been placed on the element of water. The composition of each of these paintings is similar and includes the same kinds of elements: a deep ravine containing a pool of water which apparently is either the terminus or the source of a river whose winding path is the link between foreground and background, towering trees on one or both banks, ancient ruins in the middle ground, and hazy mountain ranges in the far distance. In each, as well, miniscule figures are included in the fore- and middleground.

The lunette paintings have much the same character as those which were used increasingly within decorative schemes in mid-sixteenth-century Rome.[19] Their inclusion here may well reflect a continuing tradition of the use of certain kinds of subjects which were felt to be apt for rooms of particular character. That codifier of much sixteenth-century practice, Giovanni Battista Armenini, states specifically that the decoration of fountain rooms should include, among other subjects, landscape paintings.[20] The figures within the paintings, however, raise the possibility that the intent was to create narrative scenes. A close examination of the circular painting below 'The Israelites Crossing the Red Sea', found in the ceiling over the window,

reveals an indistinct bearded figure on a high precipice which may be seen as Moses on the mountain. If the reading of this form is valid, it may be supposed that the other landscapes are instilled with a narrative content. Each of these landscapes, then, could conceivably be a kind of visual footnote or capsule summary of events which would precede the biblical passage illustrated in the oval paintings directly above them. Militating against this view is the fact that the figures are so minute as to be all but illegible except to the viewer anticipating, rather like an expected cliché, such a subject within this particular context. Furthermore, the loose calligraphic handling of the lights and darks in constructing the figural forms, while conforming to the period's goal of apparent ease and rapidity of execution, forfeits within this small format the sense of iconographical clarity. Due to the latter quality in particular, these river-landscapes may be regarded as intending to convey an additional significance within the context of the religious subject matter above. The appearance of four rivers in any Christian scheme of decoration would, because of their long typological history, recall the theme of the four rivers of Paradise.[21] The conventional meaning of the spirit of God as the Source, carried on these waters which flow out to all parts of the world and, inversely, lead back to the Giver of Living Waters, will be seen, it is hoped, to be particularly relevant to the conceptual program of the fountain room.

The ceiling is covered with an elaborate network of stucco bands which is designed in such a way that compartments of a variety of shapes and sizes have been formed (Fig. 4). These compartments serve as enframements for the major components of the ceiling decoration: the relatively large square painting in the center, the oval paintings in the vaults above the lunettes, the high-relief figures in tabernacles in the corners above the pilasters, and the small-scale *grottesche* filling the interstices throughout. As on the pilasters below, except for the seraphim, these grotesques represent either credible or demonic forms of nature—vegetation, foliated masks, and seated satyrs, for example—which are either surmounted by or otherwise associated with the name or armorial device of Julius III.

The spaces at the corners have been left 'opened', so to speak, since the vaults above the lunettes spring from the outer edge of the stepped-out cornice above the pilaster rather than from the more conventional corner abutment. Subsequently, the vaults are imbued with a gravity-defying aspect somewhat reminiscent of billow-

17. Of the four paintings, the one reproduced here is found beneath the oval ceiling fresco of 'The Israelites Crossing the Red Sea'.
18. On the proposed meaning of nereids and fabulous creatures of the sea in antiquity as aids to departed souls in reaching their paradisical goal, see *Cumont*, esp. pp. 166–70.
19. Parallels may be found, for example, in the small landscapes included in the decoration of the Casino of Pius IV. See Walter F. Friedländer, *Das Kasino Pius des vierten* (Leipzig: K. W. Hiersemann, 1912), esp. pls. XVI–XVII. (Hereafter known as *Friedländer*.)
20. Giovanni Battista Armenini, *De' veri precetti della pittura*, ed. Stefano Ticozzi (Pisa: Niccolò Capurro, 1823), pp. 220–2.
21. Lars-Ivar Ringbom, *Paradisus Terrestris: Myt, Bild och Verklighet* ('Acta Societatis scientiarum Fennicæ', Nova Series C, 1, no. 1; Helsinki: Tilgmann, 1958), esp. pp. 9–22.

ing sails, while the space reserved at the corners resembles the shape of a ship's hull seen from the end. Within the context of the scheme of decoration we need not dismiss these resemblances as merely fortuitous.

Each corner space is filled with *stucchi* in high relief consisting of a triton encircled by vines from which *putti* emerge. The triton, in turn, functions as an atlas, supporting the tabernacle above. Because the tabernacle both overlaps the vaults to left and right and is attached at its arc to the heavier molding which sets off the central space of the ceiling, it appears both to hover above and be riveted to the stucco lattice of the ceiling.

The tabernacle as it is used in the corners of the ceiling, however, changes its directional movement from concave to convex as it rises vertically. The ship analogy mentioned above in connection with the corner spaces now seems even more tenable, for combinations of similarly shaped enframements supported by tritons may be found among the decorated prows of the period.[22]

Within these tabernacles are stucco figures representing the three theological Virtues and Justice. In figural treatment, especially of the faces and the general proportions, as well as in the handling of the drapery, these Virtues evince a stylistic similarity to the Cleopatra of the fountain. The sense of forward movement which has been achieved through the undulation of the enframement is underscored by these graceful figures. Because of their nearly frontal positions and their wind-blown draperies, they appear as figureheads of ships being thrust forward in the room.

The tabernacles with their Virtues serve to link the vaults with one another. Centered within these vaults are the four biblical paintings of oval shape. Two of the oval frescoes are based on Old Testament passages, two on New Testament passages, and all are essentially concerned with water. To the left of the main entrance, over the doorway which originally allowed admittance from the statue court, is 'The Finding of Moses' (Fig. 5). The second Old Testament subject, 'The Israelites Crossing the Red Sea', is found in the opposite vault over the window (Fig. 6). Above the entrance from the corridor is 'The Baptism of Christ', while the pendant to the latter is 'Christ and the Woman of Samaria' above the fountain (Figs. 7–8).

The prototypes for the figures and composition of the first three paintings may be found in representations of the same subjects in Raphael's second loggia.[23] The fourth, 'Christ and the Woman of Samaria', is nearly a quotation, albeit reversed, of a well-known design by Michelangelo, now preserved only in drawings or prints.[24] While the general influence of Raphael and Michelangelo is obvious, there are changes in figural proportions, in costume, and in the scale of the figures which convert the more monumental models in the direction of the decorative trend of mid-sixteenth-century Rome. In these particular kinds of transformations and in the undisguised borrowings from famous earlier works, Daniele reflects an attitude toward style and source which is the prevalent one of the time. Equally as noticeable are the changes he imposes on setting and the handling of light. Whereas in the earlier works the human figure invariably dominated the scene, in Daniele's paintings it is nature manifest which is of at least equal importance. Moreover, the intense eerie light which both etches figural parts in sharp relief and dissolves their surrounding into insubstantial patches of matter, so pronounced in these vault paintings, is absent from the models. Daniele, then, on the one hand, has retained a sufficient number of features of the famous earlier composition to permit the viewer easy recall of those works. On the other hand, the alterations are distinct enough to establish a new mood, one in which nature seems enlivened by the power of supernatural light.

The four religious subjects can be recognized to have one common thematic denominator, salvation through water. Beneath the literal illustration of the Old Testament scenes can also be read the long-established typological correspondence between the history of Moses and the history of Christ, Moses, moreover, having long been considered not only a prefiguration of Christ, but also the 'St. Peter of the Old Law', the 'Hebraic Pope'.[25] All of these aspects of the oval paintings gain significance when considered in relation to the center painting of the ceiling.

Dominating the other parts of the ceiling decoration in size as well as position is the square painting in the center (Fig. 9). It serves as a nucleus or a climax for the entire room, for from all sides of the frame radiate straight stucco bands which in turn are the major connecting links for the total stucco web. At first

22. A close parallel is found, for example, on a foreground ship in Martin van Heemskerck's 'Rape of Helen' (Walters Art Gallery, Baltimore), reproduced in Jacques Bousquet, *Mannerism: The Painting and Style of the Late Renaissance* (New York: Braziller, 1964), pp. 276–7.

23. See *Tutta la pittura di Raffaello: Gli affreschi* ('Biblioteca d'arte Rizzoli', no. 27; Milan: Rizzoli, 1956), pl. 142 (above) for 'The Finding of Moses', pl. 142 (below) for 'The Israelites Crossing the Red Sea', and pl. 153 (above) for 'The Baptism of Christ'.

24. Charles de Tolnay, *Michelangelo* (Princeton: Princeton University Press, 1960), v, pp. 64–65, Figs. 334–6. (Hereafter known as *Tolnay*, v.)

25. Louis Réau, *Iconographie de l'art chrétien* (Paris: Presses Universitaires de France, 1956), II, pt. I, pp. 176 and 201.

glance the subject appears to be a virtual quotation of Giotto's *Navicella*, then in the atrium of old St. Peter's.[26] There is, in fact, no reasonable doubt that Giotto's work was the basis for Daniele's painting. The two are comparable in overall compositional scheme, as well as in such specific aspects as the buildings in the background, the form and position of the ship, and the relationship of Christ and Peter in the right foreground. A closer examination, however, reveals important modifications and additions to the prototype. One of the obvious compositional changes is of the same kind as that imposed on the models for the oval paintings. By placing the figure of Christ so that His back is turned to the spectator and by diminishing the size of the ship in relation both to the figures in the foreground and to the total area of the space, a new sense of pictorial depth is achieved. In so far as the water and the distant view of the horizon have gained in importance, the large painting conforms with the compositional effects achieved in the other paintings of the ceiling.

The *Navicella* of Daniele also conforms with the four oval paintings in another way. To a greater or lesser degree, the *Navicella* and the other ceiling paintings reflect compositions which, because of their location or the fame of their authors or both, may be presumed to have been sufficiently familiar that at least the *cognoscenti* would have had little difficulty recognizing the original within Daniele's frescoes. Daniele, of course, may have selected these famous works as his obvious models for no other reason than that the forms appealed to him. His approach, then, could be interpreted as reflecting the prevailing practice of artists working in Rome around the middle of the sixteenth century.[27]

There are, however, other probable reasons for these undisguised borrowings from venerable images such as Giotto's *Navicella* or from the works of the two most highly regarded masters of the Cinquecento. For one, these sources could be used with the confidence that even in small format and at some distance, as they are found on the ceiling, both the subject and the precedent would be recognized. For another, the expected recognition could presume the transference to the new work of those meanings indigenous to the original, in so far as the borrowing agreed with its model. From this, the degree to which the new work varies from its prototype could reasonably be seen to indicate an

intention to reveal or emphasize aspects of content absent or only latent in the exemplum. The probability that once the decorative program was decided upon, the artist turned to the well-known images for the reasons suggested here, gains credence when we consider the frequency with which such borrowings appear in the decoration of the room. To deny a positive value of this kind to the repeated use of undisguised appropriations is to imply a poverty of resourcefulness which seems in no way borne out in Daniele's total *œuvre* and is not consonant with the importance he is known to have attached to the commission.[28]

To return to Daniele's *Navicella*, if the relative position of Christ and Peter recalls that in Giotto's representation, the conception of their actual physical relationship has been drastically altered. Giotto has shown Christ standing on the waters, physically supporting the foundering Peter by taking him by the hand. In Daniele's picture there is no bodily contact. Instead Peter, who is immersed in the waters up to his knees, bends toward Christ with his hands clasped together in a prayerful attitude and as if he were genuflecting. Christ has lifted His outstretched arms toward the fisherman to draw him from the waters by spiritual power. While conveying a sense of divine magnetism, strongly reminiscent of Michelangelo's 'Creation of Eve' on the Sistine ceiling, their confrontation suggests the performance of an act of conference of authority.[29] An addition clearly of symbolic import is the book which lies at the feet of Christ, partially obscured by the strong shadow cast by His body.

Should there by any doubt that Daniele made these changes for reasons other than simple formal manipulation, it should be dispelled by the inclusion of the two bearded figures to the right of Christ. There are no precedents among *Navicella* portrayals for figures of this kind next to Christ nor can a textual source be cited. Because Giotto's conceptual scheme of this subject had remained all but unchallenged for three and a half centuries, one may suppose that however uncritical the contemporary viewer may have been before the subtle adjustment of meaning in the other frescoes, he would be provoked to question the intentions which underlay the transformations wrought on one of the most familiar of venerable Christian images.

26. Wilhelm Paeseler, 'Giottos Navicella und ihrs spätantikes Vorbild', *Römisches Jahrbuch für Kunstgeschichte*, v (1941), pp. 51–162, reproduces a number of facsimiles which provide better comparative material for our purposes than the restored original. (Hereafter known as *Paeseler*.)
27. Craig Hugh Smyth, *Mannerism and Maniera* (New York: J. J. Augustin [n.d.]), esp. pp. 22–23.

28. *Vasari*, p. 59.
29. It is not clear what the object Christ holds in His hands may be. If it is a scroll as it appears, the sense of delegation of authority would be heightened. The act would then recall representations of the *traditio legis* of early Christian art in which Peter, as the Moses of the New Covenant, receives the New Testament to fulfill the law of Moses. (*The Catholic Encyclopedia* [New York: 1913], III, p. 425.) (Hereafter known as *Catholic Encyclopedia*, III.)

That Daniele has again presented a familiar theme with some interesting variations indicates an attempt to enlarge upon aspects only suggested in the original. The new emphasis on the water, the changed relationship between Christ and Peter, and the addition of the book and the spectators, when taken together, extend the implications of the scene which still retained the proliferation of associations attached to the prototype. The meanings which had come to be attached to the *Navicella* were several.[30] Giotto's mosaic represents the ship or *navicella* of the Apostles caught in a storm on the Sea of Galilee, with Peter sinking in the waters before Christ. Within the text (Matthew 14:24–33) the relationship between Christ and Peter illustrates the passage in which Peter cries, 'Lord, save me!' and Christ replies, 'Man of little faith, why do you doubt?' Of the underlying meanings of the *Navicella*, perhaps the most familiar was that of the ship as the symbol of Christ and of the primacy of Peter as the head of the Church implied by Christ's support of the apostle on the waters. The *Navicella*, therefore, had been utilized in times of crisis for the Church to give visual witness to Christ's implicit conference of supreme authority on the first head of His church and consequently to Peter's chosen successors.[31]

To suggest why the *Navicella* was included in the decoration of the room in the place of first importance and why it exhibits modifications of the original, certainly with the approval and more probably at the suggestion of the Pope, we need look to the events which preoccupied Julius during the months in which he was planning the fountain room. Julius III had inherited the problems with the reformers of the North which had plagued Paul III.[32] One of the tenets of the Protestants which was reverberating most loudly and which would have the most devastating consequences for the Roman Church and especially for the Papacy was the reformers' denial of the conference of absolute authority on Peter by Christ. Julius turned to the traditional image of the *navicella*, as had certain of his

predecessors, in visual defense of this central doctrine of the Church. The changes made in the traditional portrayal may reasonably be seen as reaffirming this delegation of authority with emphasis on Peter and all the significance attached to the encounter with Christ, rather than the equal importance given to the apostle and the Ship of the Church in Giotto's work. That the book lies at Christ's feet, or more precisely, between Christ and Peter and therefore linking them, is apparently a reminder that the doctrine is based upon implications in the Scriptures. But that the book is veiled by Christ's shadow also can be seen as refuting another controversial position of the Protestants. Whereas the reformers of the North held that the Scriptures were the only source of Divine revelation, the Council of Trent in February, 1546—significantly, under the guidance of the future Pope Julius III—concluded that the tradition of the Church must be taken together with the Bible as the standard of supernatural revelation.[33] It is the illustration of the tradition concerning the legitimacy of Peter as head of the Roman Church which is the aspect of Daniele's *Navicella* emphasized at the expense of the obscured Written Word. In this context the logical interpretation of the two onlookers who appear so skeptical would be the personification of disbelievers who do not allow the decree of tradition in spite of their confrontation with the Divine Truth.

The *Navicella* was correctly oriented for anyone entering the room from the corridor. Lowering his glance from the center painting, the visitor would next see the vault painting of 'Christ and the Woman of Samaria'. Continuing to read downward, he would be confronted by the landscape and then the fountain complex in the lower zone of the room.

Superficially, any interpretation which proposed a meaningful programmatic relationship between these components of the decoration would appear to be mitigated by Vasari's account of the fountain competition. That Michelangelo and Vasari should have offered such apparently different suggestions for the subject of the fountain could be construed as meaning that the dominant motif was of little importance to the Pope. Following from this, it might be inferred that Julius chose the Cleopatra rather than the Moses because it had the obvious advantage of being ready-made and exceedingly close at hand. From what we know of Julius' impatience to begin artistic endeavors, it is likely that the factor of availability may well have been a decisive one.[34] This hypothesis, however, need not exclude the possibility that the Cleopatra could

30. *Paeseler*, pp. 150–60, and Howard Hibbard and Irma Jaffe, 'Bernini's Barcaccia', *The Burlington Magazine*, cvi, no. 733 (April, 1964), pp. 159–70.

31. Clement VII, for one, had used the scene on a medal. (Emile Mâle, *L'art religieux après le Concile de Trente* [Paris: Librairie Armand Colin, 1932], p. 51, n. 3.) (Hereafter known as Mâle).

32. Under Paul III, Giovanni del Monti, the future Julius III, was the first Cardinal-legate to the Council of Trent. As Julius III, he was determined that the work of the Council be continued and issued a Bull in November, 1550, in which arrangements for reassembling the Council were made (*The Catholic Encyclopedia* [New York: 1913], xv, esp. pp. 32–33). (Hereafter known as *Catholic Encyclopedia*, xv.) There is little reason to doubt that the problems involved in handling the reformers were uppermost in his mind during the period in which the program for the Stanza della Cleopatra was being evolved.

33. *Catholic Encyclopedia*, xv, p. 32.
34. *Vasari*, pp. 58–59.

serve as well or even better than the Moses within the programmed scheme which Julius presumably had in mind when he stipulated a fountain for the *stanza*.

'Moses Striking the Rock' had traditionally conveyed the idea of a miraculous spring of spiritual water, with its attendant meaning of the Waters of Salvation pouring forth from the Rock, a symbol of Christ (1 Corinthians 10:4). Moreover, since Early Christian times, Moses striking the Rock and the waters gushing forth was understood to be a prototype of Peter as mediator for the Christian springs of grace.[35] Consequently, the theme was inextricably associated with the basic beliefs of Christianity.

Although Vasari refers to the antique statue which was installed on the fountain as 'Cleopatra', there is little reason to believe that, in its new setting, the figure was intended to make any reference to the dying Egyptian queen. Over the years the Cleopatra exhibited in the statue court had come to personify the embodiment of the Nymph of the Fountain. In his engraving, Cavalleri instinctively supports that popular interpretation of the semi-recumbent sculpture by first designating it a nymph. It is doubtful whether any other statue of the sixteenth century could be understood so readily in its role of symbolizing the source of perpetually and mysteriously flowing waters. As Kurz has noted, there is an almost reverential tone used whenever the Nymph of the Fountain is referred to in the Cinquecento.[36] On the sensible level, to speak generally, the Fountain Nymph typified the element of water in nature with its innumerable ancient connotations derived from the essential or primordial character of the life-giving substance.[37]

While a fountain dominated by a nymph and one constructed around Moses striking the Rock could be expected to share the ability to signify the miraculous source of life-giving water, the Moses, as mentioned above, would obviously convey an overt, specifically Christian meaning foreign to the Nymph of the Fountain in the Renaissance. There is evidence implicit in the juxtaposition of the fountain with the particular paintings directly in line with it which indicates that ultimately the program utilized the relatively imprecise meaning embodied by the statue in a way advantageous to the room's total significance. Of the four smaller biblical illustrations included in the ceiling decoration, the one which appears above

the fountain, as discussed previously, is that of 'Christ and the Woman of Samaria', taken from the Gospel of John (4:5–15). Jesus had sat down on Jacob's well to rest when a woman of Samaria came to draw water. The woman was surprised when He asked her for a drink of water:

... How does thou, being a Jew, ask of me to drink, who am a Samaritan woman? For the Jews do not communicate with the Samaritans.

Jesus answered, and said to her: If thou didst know the gift of God, and who he is that saith to thee, Give me to drink; thou perhaps wouldst have asked of him, and he would have given thee living water.

The woman saith to him: Sir, thou hast nothing wherein to draw, and the well is deep; from whence then hast thou living water?

Art thou greater than our father Jacob, who gave us the well, and drank thereof himself, and his children, and his cattle?

Jesus answered and said to her: Whosoever drinketh of this water, shall thirst again; but he that shall drink of the water that I will give him, shall not thirst for ever.

But the water that I will give him, shall become in him a fountain of water, springing up into life everlasting.

It would be difficult to accept as simply fortuitous that the biblical illustration which contains a direct reference to a fountain was located above the fountain in the Stanza della Cleopatra. Moreover, the downward-pointing gesture which Christ makes with His left hand is easily understood as pertaining both to the Well of Jacob and to the actual fountain beneath. The contrast which Christ has drawn between the 'living water' which comes from Him and the 'living water' of Jacob's well, as the Samaritan woman initially understands him to mean, is equally applicable to the essential differences between the meaning conveyed by the biblical illustration and that of the Nymph of the Fountain as most often implied in ancient and Renaissance descriptions. In short, it is the difference between the continually flowing waters of Nature and that water transformed into the instrument of salvation by being imbued with the spirit of God.

Consonant with the other meanings of this passage from the Gospel of John is the one of invitation to the Samaritans, a schismatic people, to unite in the true faith represented by Christ. When this biblical illustration is viewed in relation to the *Navicella*, as it was obviously intended to be, the combination achieves a subtle but encompassing statement of dogma. According to Catholic doctrine, when Christ built His Church on Peter, as alluded to in the *Navicella*, He indicated

35. *Catholic Encyclopedia*, III, p. 426.
36. Otto Kurz, 'Huius Nympha Locis. A pseudo-classical inscription and a drawing by Dürer', *Journal of the Warburg and Courtauld Institutes*, XVI, nos. 3–4 (July–December, 1953), pp. 171–7, esp. p. 174.
37. The subject is fully treated in Floyd G. Ballentine, 'Some Phases of the Cult of the Nymphs', *Harvard Studies in Classical Philology*, XV (1904), pp. 77–119.

the essential unity of the Church and especially its hierarchical unity.[38] The Fathers had concluded that where Peter is, there is the Church, and where the Church is, there is no death, but eternal life; that outside the unity of the Church the means of salvation, Baptism, is invalidated, for the Holy Ghost is not communicated.[39] When juxtaposed with these paintings, the fountain motifs which are analogous to those on funerary monuments and which are absent from the original setting, underscore the idea of death inherent in the natural waters bereft of the saving grace of God within the unity of the Church. Or to put it in positive terms, the paintings viewed together with the fountain indicate how its natural waters may be transformed, through Baptism administered by the Church, into a medium by which death may be conquered. These paintings, therefore, act as catalysts to direct the thoughts of the viewer from the general aura of the earthly connotations of the fountain design (with its innate ambivalent possibilities) to the true 'Fountain of Life', the Catholic Church, specified in related illustrations above it. In this light it is not difficult to see the Cleopatra as more apt than Michelangelo's Moses for the total significance of the room.

The other biblical events depicted on the ceiling may also be seen as contributing to this prevailing idea of the essential hierarchical unity and depending as well on the authority of tradition for their rationale. Each of the paintings portrays the major characters of biblical history who are deemed the most important precursors of Christ and who are therefore the most significant representatives in that progression toward the establishment of the Heavenly Church on earth. Each plays his role in the predetermined scheme and, as it would be understood, delegates his authority to one who follows him, the tradition being climaxed, here in the *Navicella*, in Christ's conference of supreme authority on Peter. Similarly, the pilaster designs with their allusion to the superiority of the Papal emblems to symbols of natural powers, the Virtues in naval context with their self-evident implications, and the landscapes with their emphasis on flowing rivers in Nature suggestive of the traditional four of Paradise, may be seen as contributing to one or another of the inextricably linked themes of spiritualized waters and Papal primacy which have been proposed here as the determinants for the decoration of the Stanza della Cleopatra.

Throughout, the program of the fountain room has depended for its articulation on tradition, the tradi-

tional textual interpretations of the Church, and the images of the greatest masters which had by this time entered the stream of artistic tradition. In a programmatic scheme of this kind, originality would be held likely to shift the importance from the desired lucid expression of iconographical content to that of exclusive admiration of the new image itself. Since the program is so dependent on the forms of common currency for its impact, innovation, when it occurs in the paintings or the fountain design, is in degree rather than in kind and intrudes only in so far as a modification will emphasize a traditional aspect of the Church's doctrine. As limiting as these instructions probably were for the artist, he must have felt some compensation in the freedom allowed by the stucco system. While performing its almost dialectical function of compartmentalizing the components of the 'defense' and simultaneously establishing their sum in the climactic center painting, Daniele's stucco web is nevertheless an imaginative creation of high quality.[40] Julius III has been called the last of the Renaissance popes. In so far as he was willing to use one of the most famous and, in the eyes of sixteenth-century artists and writers, one of the most beautiful of all ancient 'pagan' statues in the fountain room, he betrays his adherence to the predominant thinking of his High Renaissance predecessors. And that the utilization of this pagan sculpture was made legitimate by being imbued with a moral significance reflects that ambiguous desire of later sixteenth-century ecclesiastics to possess the beloved antique while denying that this desire was justified by anything other than the work's didactic value, the only explanation sanctioned by the new time.[41] But this should not deter us from recognizing that in the early part of his reign Julius III, in part by his use of such carefully formulated visual decrees as those found in the decoration of the Stanza della Cleopatra, reveals himself as a precursor of those later popes of the Counter-Reformation who are embroiled in defending the doctrines of the Church. However futile he may eventually have come to feel were defenses of the kind expressed in the Stanza,[42] this monument remained to remind others of his early involvement in matters of doctrinal reaffirmation before the attacks of the reformers. And in a sense the Stanza's decoration may well have accomplished goals beyond Julius' immediate one, for its defensive program evidently gave impetus for the kinds of subjects

38. *The Catholic Encyclopedia* (New York: 1913), XIV, p. 529. (Hereafter known as *Catholic Encyclopedia*, XIV.)
39. *Catholic Encyclopedia*, XIV, p. 531.

40. *Friedländer*, p. 70, n. 3, observes that the ceiling decoration of the Stanza is highly remarkable.
41. Jean Seznec, *The Survival of the Pagan Gods* (New York: 1953), esp. p. 269.
42. *Pastor*, pp. 155-7, summarizes Julius' later lack of mastery of his office.

and the manner of portrayal favored by Julius' more relentless successors.[43] The value of Julius' fountain-room program must have been understood almost immediately, for the schema of the Stanza della Cleopatra was the basis for one of the important rooms in that most magnificent of all sixteenth-century fountain houses, the Casino of Pius IV.[44]

43. *Mâle*, pp. 48–58, discusses the visual defense of the Papacy after the Council of Trent.

44. *Friedländer*, esp. pp. 70–72, pls. XIII–XXI. Problems of iconological interpretation in the Casino remain. But it would not be surprising to find that the decorative scheme of the Stanza della Cleopatra was adapted for the first room of the Casino for reasons analogous to those proposed here for Julius' fountain room.

PHYLLIS PRAY BOBER

Francesco Lisca's Collection of Antiquities

Footnote to a New Edition of Aldroandi

Collectors of antiquities in Cinquecento Rome included many for whom historical, antiquarian interest in classical inscriptions or iconography was paramount, as well as others more concerned with decorative potentialities of highly restored statues and reliefs, frequently coordinated into programmatic ensembles. Within either group were surely to be found both status-seekers and genuine lovers of classical beauty, not to mention collectors like Girolamo Garimberti who displayed a magpie avidity for acquiring fossils, minerals and other marvels of nature in addition to *anticaglie*. What is most impressive is their sheer number. Ulisse Aldroandi's *Delle statue antiche, che per tutta Roma, in diversi luoghi, et case si veggono*,[1] written in 1550 just before the founding of a few of the most illustrious, describes ninety-three private collections without exhausting all the possibilities of lesser holdings and various *vigne*. Through the researches of Lanciani, Michaelis, Huelsen and Hübner, we are fairly well informed about some major collections, but works of art in those which were not liberally made accessible to sketching artists have survived only as disembodied titles in inventories or in lists set down by Aldroandi. Yet clues often do exist to permit partial reconstruction of even these most elusive collections. In the course of preparing a modern illustrated edition of Aldroandi, I have found it possible to identify a wealth of ancient sculptures not previously connected with his descriptions.

Consideration of the assemblage of antiquities he visited at the house of Francesco Lisca in rione Parione may serve as a case in point.[2] This included at least seventeen statues, two portrait busts, and many fragments which Aldroandi does not enumerate. Of a not inconsiderable collection, only two statues have been identified until now (nos. 13 and 15 below). Lisca, a wealthy Milanese merchant serving the Curia, had settled in Rome some time before his marriage to the daughter of Giacomo Cardelli in 1532, acquiring the house in the Via del Governo Vecchio as well as a *vigna* on the Aventine near Sta. Sabina and S. Alessio. The latter property, on the testimony of Ligorio, was the site where Lisca unearthed many columns, statues and other marbles.[3] Although it does not emerge from Aldroandi's text, we shall see that his collecting embraced both archaeological material and 'artistic' works for show-piece installation.

Aldroandi commences with an open *loggia* where thirteen statues plus a portrait head are symmetrically displayed. At the right-hand side stand three statues: (1) '*una vergine vestale in pie vestita à l'antica*'; (2) '*una Iulia togata*'; (3) '*un Pane mezzo ignudo in pie, ma non ha testa ne braccia: ha un montone à pie senza testa*'. Corresponding to these, at the left, are three more: (4) '*Pomona ... et ha il grembo pieno di frutti*' (under cover of an entrance portico); (5) '*Fama, ha le ale, e smorza una face accesa*'; (6) '*Diana vestita con una mezza luna in testa, ma non ha braccia.*'

Before the porticoed façade a Bacchic group is artfully arranged: at the center (7) '*Bacco ignudo in pie, poggiato con un braccio sopra un tronco, nell'altro tiene avolto un cappotto*'; at his left (8) '*un Silvano ignudo, sona una tromba; ha la coda, e le orecchie caprine, e si tiene presso à i piedi una pelle di capra avolta*'; and at the right (9) '*Arethusa ignuda dalle coscie in su, e con una mano s'acconcia le treccie in testa.*' It is clear to the modern reader that the image of 'Silvanus' is actually a Silene or Satyr, and the 'Arethusa' a well-known Venus type. Aldroandi is in all likelihood quoting the owner's appellation for these statues, and correctly notes that, according to Latin poets, *Silvani* were divinities of the woods, while Arethusa was the personification of a fountain near Syracuse. However inaccurate the iconography, there is an apparent intention to compose a coherent group of sylvan personalities.

Above the foregoing '*frontispitio*', applied to the upper

1. Published in Venice by Ziletti in 1556 as the second portion of Lucio Mauro, *Le Antichità della città di Roma*; second and third editions, with some alterations and additions, appeared in 1558 and 1562. See P. G. Hübner, *Le Statue di Roma* (Römische Forschungen der Bibliotheca Herziana, II), vol. I, Leipzig, 1912, pp. 29 ff., with earlier bibliography. A French, annotated abridgement was published by S. Reinach, *L'Album de Pierre Jacques sculpteur de Reims*, Paris, 1902, pp. 23–109.
2. Aldroandi,[1] pp. 179–82 (pp. 173–6, 2nd ed.). See R. Lanciani, *Storia degli scavi di Roma*, III, Rome, 1907, pp. 140 f., and Hübner, *op. cit.*, p. 103.

3. Lanciani, p. 141, cites the marriage document in which the house was mortgaged in exchange for the Palazzo di Firenze as a dowry guarantee, as well as appropriate references from Ligorio's Turin volumes.

wall, appears in the center an antique head said to be (10) '*Aventino, Re di Alba, che morendo sul colle Aventino li diede il nome*'; at the right (11) '*una picciola statua della dea Cibele madre di tutti li Dei*'; and at left (12) '*un Fauno, che con una mano tiene per la coda un Tigre, con l'altra alza un bastone per darli*' (no size indicated, but necessarily a smallish figure like the Cybele). Behind these statues (nos. 7–12), within the portico, stand two more: (13) '*Giunnone Lucina togata con tre penne in testa, e con la mano sinistra tiene un branco di rose*', and (14) '*Hebe . . . vestita, e sta in atto di versare acqua con un vase, che ha in mano.*'

Aldroandi proceeds to a little unroofed retreat ('*ritiretto*') entered through a portal ornamented with the head of '*Agrippina . . . madre del crudo Nerone Imperatore*', and containing (15) '*uno Apollo ignudo in pie, con capelli lunghi appoggiato in un tronco del marmo istesso, nel quale è un serpe avolto*'. The text concludes with passing reference to a small garden where many heads, torsi and other ancient fragments are to be found, including '*uno Hercole mezzo ignudo, ma senza gambe e braccia*' and '*un fragmento di Bacco con un mezzo cane à i piedi*'. This garden, then, held Lisca's antiquarian congeries. If it did not interest Aldroandi, its inscriptions on bases and funerary monuments fortunately drew the attention of Renaissance epigraphers whose evidence enables us to sketch the history of the collection as a whole.

Let us first consider the two sculptures (nos. 13 and 15) already identified in scholarly literature. H. Stuart Jones, in his catalogue of the Capitoline collections, recognized that specific details—three feathers on her head and the flowers incorrectly restored in her left hand—assures identification of 'Juno Lucina' with a Muse in the Museo Capitolino.[4] Hübner never published the second volume of his work on the ancient statues of Renaissance Rome, but apparently intended to include in his check-list three Lisca works whose general type is recognizable from Aldroandi's text as well as the Apollo (no. 15) 'drawn by Pierre Jacques, the only artist who seems to have visited the collection'. His reference is to folio 16 of the Album in Paris where, at the left, appears a statue conforming to Aldroandi's description in all respects save that the god rests his left arm upon a 'lyre'[5] which is itself propped upon the tree-trunk entwined by a serpent (Fig. 1). This portion of Pierre Jacques' model is

clearly a restoration, but must already have existed in Aldroandi's day. Although he does not mention the instrument specifically, its presence is implied by his notation that the statue in the retreat is thought to have been originally united in a group with a figure of Marsyas, vanquished and ready to be flayed, similar to the figure owned by Camillo Capranica (the famous della Valle Marsyas in the Uffizi). On the base of the Apollo, Pierre Jacques inscribes '*apresso mo(n)te giordano*', a topographic reference which accords perfectly with the situation of Lisca's house.[6] Reinach's publication of the sketchbook identifies the drawing with an 'Apollo Sauroktonos' formerly in the Hope collection at Deepdene.[7] Its present whereabouts is not known to me, but it is evidently Lisca's statue in a subsequent restoration, without lyre and with a different head. In actuality, only the torso is antique and belongs not to an Apollo but to a replica of the so-called Pothos of Scopas.[8]

Since provenance is in each case unknown, neither the 'Juno Lucina' nor 'Apollo' provides any possibility of tracing the fate of other Lisca sculptures. The first entered the Capitoline collection before 1687, but the date of its acquisition is not known; the second came to Deepdene with another Lisca piece (see no. 14, below) in the late eighteenth or early nineteenth century. Before turning to collateral evidence for the history of Lisca's epigraphic material that serves to close this gap, one further identification may be adduced on the basis of unsupported confrontation of Aldroandi's text with an extant sculpture. The Faun (no. 12) belongs to a widespread type, but the description is explicit about a detail (his hand holding the tail of a panther) which focuses attention upon one variant of the composition. A statue in Brussels, first recorded at the end of the eighteenth century in the Paris hôtel of Quentin Crawfurd (Fig. 2)[9] preserves this motif as well as the raised *lagobolon*. Its small scale also suits our deduction that Lisca's figure, as a counterpart to the *picciola statua* of Cybele (no. 11), must have been substantially under life size.

The three statues above would exhaust potential

4. H. Stuart Jones, *A Catalogue of Ancient Sculptures preserved in the Municipal Collections of Rome*, 1: *The Sculptures of the Museo Capitolino*, Oxford, 1912, p. 298, salone 35, pl. 73.

5. Hübner, *loc. cit.* Reinach, *op. cit.*, p. 118, pl. 16. I must thank Dr. Emanuel Winternitz for his confirmation of the fact that the 'lyre' is an utterly non-functional invention of the restorer.

6. Monte Giordano took its name from Giordano Orsini and the palace of the family stood in the Middle Ages on the mound of ruins in the ancient Campus Martius. Aldroandi describes '*In monte Giordano e presso*' the house of the Ardiccio family, and that of the dealer Stampa; his next heading '*In Parione*' commences with Lisca. Cf. note 11 below.

7. Clarac 476B, 905C; Michaelis, *Ancient Marbles in Great Britain*, Cambridge University Press, 1882, Deepdene, no. 2. The present head, which does not belong to the figure, lacks the long locks which appear in Pierre Jacques' drawing.

8. P. E. Arias, *Skopas*, Rome, 1952, pp. 132 f.

9. F. Cumont, *Catalogue des sculptures et inscriptions antiques* (Bruxelles, Musées Royaux d'Art et d'Histoire), Brussels, 1913, no. 19 (A1143); with earlier bibliography. Clarac 711, 693A. Height: 1.37 m.

identifications among Lisca's sculptures were it not for the fact that Renaissance epigraphers give clues to the history of his antiquarian holdings so slighted by Aldroandi.[10] Without examining all of the documentation in detail, it is important to summarize the testimony of syllogai as to the dispersal of Lisca's collection. Some of the cinerary urns or dedicatory bases cited in mid-century alternatively as '*prope monte Iordano*' or '*in parione in casa di M. Francesco Lisca*' appear in Statius (1560–1570) '*in casa di Ms. Ludovico Taberna, Milanese abbreviatore appresso il card. Puteo*'. Slightly later, the author of the Anonymous Chisianus in at least one instance gives the same inscription '*In domo Hugonis Boncompagni in via Parionis*'. If Lanciani is correct in his assertion that Lisca's house in the present Via del Governo Vecchio was later owned by Hugo Boncompagni (Gregory XIII), then some antiquities at least remained *in situ* toward the end of the sixteenth century. In any case, they remained in the immediate vicinity, since Boissard's topography of Rome gives the houses of the area in the following order: the palace of Paolo Giordani on Monte Giordano (subsequently that of the Taverna family), the house of the Ardicci, Vicenzo Stampa's domicile in the Piazza del Flisco (the tower which once adjoined the Palazzo Fieschi-Sora purchased by Gregory XIII in 1579), the palace of Cardinal Giacomo Puteo whose name reflects the *puteum album* at the *turris de Flisco*, and the house of Lisca followed by that of Cardinal Angelo Medici (domiciled in the Palazzo Sora for a period from 1552, before his election to the Papacy).[11] Inscribed funerary monuments which survived appear in the former

Giustiniani collection, in the Villa Albani, and in scattered locations in Florence.[12]
But the most fruitful 'lead' is afforded by another group of inscriptions set down as Lisca's in mid-century, then by the Anonymous Chisianus '*in domo Hieronymi Garimberti episcopi Galessi*' (Bishop of Gallese from 1562 until his death in 1575).[13] Notable is a child's sarcophagus with seasonal Erotes, now in the Seminario Spagnuolo in Rome, the erstwhile Palazzo Altemps.[14] In Aldroandi's day, Girolamo Garimberti's collection centered upon portraits and contained works of small scale and minor art as part of his *Kunst- und Wunderkabinett*. However, Cavalieri's latest series of engravings (published in 1594) reproduces a substantial number of sculptures '*in musaeo Garimberti*'.[15] With the knowledge that some antiquities did pass from Francesco Lisca to Garimberti, it is natural to turn to the statues recorded in these engravings to seek still others.
The quest is richly rewarded. Cavalieri's Bacchus (Fig. 3) agrees precisely with Aldroandi's description of our no. 7; his *Virgo* (Fig. 4) is clearly the 'Arethusa' (no. 9), nude from the waist up, arranging her tresses with one hand; Pomona (Fig. 6) is Lisca's statue of the same name (no. 4), the usual Renaissance designation for this type representing the Hora of Autumn; and a 'Bacchissa' (Fig. 7) so explicitly illustrates Aldroandi's 'Hebe' in the act of pouring water from a vessel (no. 14) that one does not require the added confirmation of its later presence in the Hope collection with Lisca's 'Apollo'.[16] The Venus-Arethusa,

---

10. *CIL*, VI, nos. 366, 410, 1192, 1757, 14193, 17122, 18833, 20502, 20645, 27806, among others; some also appear among the false, Ligorian inscriptions. A selection is represented in Boissard, *Romanae Urbis Topographia et Antiquitates*, Frankfurt, 1597–1602, V, pls. 51–57 (Stockholm manuscript fol. 85 verso ff.).
11. Boissard, *op. cit.*, I, p. 33; his description of Lisca's antiquities is excerpted from Aldroandi, having been prepared in the very year the latter text first appeared. His choice of Latin vocabulary implies only the following modifications to the original: the Vestal Virgin wears a *stola* (no. 1) which might connote any long garment differentiated from the toga; the Pan statue is indeed half-goat (no. 3) whereas Aldroandi often uses the designation for other Bacchic figures; the Faun seems in Boissard's eyes to threaten the 'tiger' (no. 12); and the Apollo (no. 15) leans his elbow upon the tree-trunk.
I have not been able to determine whether the 'Ludovico Taberna' cited by the epigraphers is identical with the Ludovico Taverna who became bishop of Lodi in 1580; in any case he must have been related to the founder of the Villa Taverna, Ferdinando, and to the Settecento owners of the Palazzo di Monte Giordano. On the brief tenure of the Palazzo Sora by Cardinal Medici, see Lanciani, II, 117.
Lanciani, *loc. cit.*, identified Lisca's house as no. 120 Via del Governo Vecchio; I have not been able to visit the site to check on possible numbering changes since the nineteenth century and whether it might not have been the Palazzo Turci (no. 123)

whose facing porticoes and pseudo-porticoes in relief conform to Aldroandi's scant data.
12. A cippus of Julia Procula, Giustiniani collection (*CIL*, VI, 20645); Villa Albani grave altar (*CIL*, VI, 14193); cinerary urn of Julia Helpis (*CIL*, VI, 20502), Palazzo Rinuccini; and an honorary inscription on a marble base in the Museum in Florence (*CIL*, VI, 1192) recorded both as Ludovico Taverna's and as Garimberti's.
13. Aldroandi describes Garimberti's collection, in the former palace of Cardinal Gaddi on Monte Citorio, pp. 195 f. (184 f., 2nd ed.); see Hübner, *op. cit.*, pp. 99 f.
14. G. M. A. Hanfmann, *The Season Sarcophagus in Dumbarton Oaks*, Harvard University Press, 1951, no. 491, Fig. 60; *CIL*, VI, 18833.
15. J. B. de Cavalleriis, *Antiquarum statuarum Urbis Romae ... liber III–IV*, Rome, 1594, with a total of twenty-six Garimberti sculptures, reproduced in reverse. Hübner (*op. cit.*, pp. 42 f.) was unnecessarily suspicious of the authenticity of many of the engravings in this volume, particularly those from the Garimberti collection '*von denen kaum eins nachzuweisen ist*'. Extant pieces appear in scattered locations in Naples, Vienna, Turin; cf. T. Ashby, 'Antiquae Statuae Urbis Romae', *PBSR*, IX (1920), pp. 107–58.
16. Michaelis, *op. cit.*, p. 288, no. 30; Reinach, *Rep. stat.*, V, 207, 2. Cf. Reinach, II, 405, 10, reproducing the Cavalieri print as well as Ashby's error concerning the figure's presence in the Palazzo Borghese (which derives in turn from the false reference to Cavalieri in F. Matz and F. von Duhn, *Antike Bildwerke in Rom*, Leipzig, 1881, vol. I, no. 1374).

on the other hand, seems to have found its way to Florence (Fig. 5),[17] and one would think the same true for Pomona were it not that the famous Florentine example was apparently already in that city in Vasari's day.[18]

Proceeding to less obvious correlations between Cavalieri's prints and Aldroandi's text, one discovers that the statue of winged *Fama* extinguishing a lighted torch (no. 5), which might have been hypothecated as a female figure from the text alone, is in actuality a clothed Amor of doubtful authenticity (Fig. 8). As a candidate for Lisca's small Cybele (no. 11) Cavalieri's plate 55 (Fig. 9) seems most likely, in view of Aldroandi's consistent recognition elsewhere of a turreted crown as the emblem of this goddess.

Further identifications are problematic. Garimberti owned a Diana running in hunting garb (Cavalieri plate 20), but it seems unlikely that it could be Lisca's armless, fully draped figure with a half-moon on her head (no. 6). On the other hand, the next plate in Cavalieri (Fig. 10) shows a Diana which would fit the description; the arms do appear to be restorations, but the inscription states '*in aedibus Farnesianis*'. Because it is not otherwise related to Farnese holdings and because discrepancies do occur in Cavalieri's indications of locale, this statue must at least be mentioned as a possibility.[19] Equally indeterminate must remain

the query whether Lisca's undescribed 'Vestal' (no. 1) and '*Iulia togata*' (no. 2) might not be recognized in an Isis priestess type called a Muse by Cavalieri and a Garimberti statue dubbed 'Pietas'.[20] Garimberti also owned a very suspect Pan statue, but it seems to bear no connection with our no. 3.[21] A Silene with caprine ears and goat-skin could represent the Lisca statue (no. 8) in a different restoration[22] were it not for ambiguities in Aldroandi's description; did the figure wear a skin which hung down further than the normal nebris or was he truly *ignudo* with the goat-skin wrapped near his feet? Finally, is there any possibility that the curious Renaissance bust reproduced as Cavalieri's plate 100 ('*Ignotus In Musaeo Garimberti*') might be the portrait of Aventinus (no. 10)?

Although there can be no clear-cut answer to these final questions, Francesco Lisca's collection regains substantiality through the addition of six or seven statues to its roster. It is not inconceivable that our safe attributions may even embrace works from an earlier and more famous collection, that of the dealer, Giovanni Ciampolini, who died in 1518. For he or his family and Mario Volterrano were the previous owners of Lisca's *vigna* on the Aventine and the little Seasons sarcophagus once stood in Ciampolini's house near the Piazza Giudea.[23]

---

17. G. A. Mansuelli, *Galleria degli Uffizi. Le sculture* (Cataloghi dei Musei e Gallerie d'Italia), Rome, 1958, vol. I, pp. 97 f., no. 65.

18. Mansuelli, p. 153, no. 124. Ashby (*loc. cit.*) states that the statue was later in the Villa Borghese and is 'very like' a similar figure in Berlin or the example in Florence. First certain reference to the sculpture in the Uffizi dates from 1591, but it is evidently '*una femmina con certi panni sottili, con un grembo pieno di varij frutti, la quale è fatta per una Pomona*' among the antiquities cited by Vasari in the Palazzo Pitti (1568 ed., III, 2; omitted in many editions, cf. L. Bloch, *RM*, 1892, p. 81). Because a number of the Garimberti plates in Cavalieri III–IV bear numbers other than their published sequence, it is possible that they were prepared at the time of his first issue of prints *c.* 1567, and that Garimberti presented his Pomona to the Medici in the same period.

19. In Cavalieri's first issue of fifty-two plates a group of Este

sculptures appeared as Farnese possessions. Note that Reinach (*Pierre Jacques*) suggests in his notes on Aldroandi that this Cavalieri Diana is probably a statue described in the Silvestri collection: '*Diana in pie vestita, ha il carcasso dietro le spalle* (of which there is no trace in the engraving) *et una saetta in mano, et ha le sue treccie ravolte vagamente dietro.*'

20. Cavalieri III–IV, pl. 49 ('*Arithmetica*') and pl. 48; cf. note 11, above.

21. *Ibid.*, pl. 78, either a forgery or a Renaissance pasticcio; Reinach, *Rép. st.*, II, 69, 1.

22. Pl. 79; Reinach, II, 781, 5. The figure is restored with a long staff in one hand and a vessel of curious design in the other.

23. See Lanciani, *op. cit.*, p. 141; cf. Hübner, p. 103. The sarcophagus with the inscription of Fyrmius Metras and Aelia Chrysotyche is recorded by Petrus Sabinus '*In domo nobiliss. civis qui habitat ante forum piscarium*' (the *Porticus Octaviae*). *CIL*, VI, 18833.

CECIL GOULD

Observations on the Role of Decoration in the Formation of Veronese's Art

Any visitor to an art gallery who gives thought to it will realize without difficulty that he is seeing the exhibits under different conditions from the original ones and probably from what the artist intended. But not many, in all probability, will make an attempt to consider the full extent and nature of these differences, and in consequence due allowance for them is unlikely to be made.

Even if we leave out of consideration the more subtle changes caused by *ambience*—the entirely different states of mind in which a visitor approaches a work of art in a church, in a museum or in a private house —the material differences are formidable enough. For example, top lighting is usual in an art gallery, yet few or none of the exhibits will have been made with this in view. As to the optimum *quantity* of light, much research remains to be done. If we consider the average church in Venice, for instance, our dominant memory of visits is liable to be the battle against the darkness. On stepping out of the sunshine we see nothing at all, and only gradually and with an effort can the outlines of forms be discerned and only later still and with a further effort do we make out something, a mere token in many cases, of the colours. How would a Renaissance painter have reacted to a commission for a picture for such a church, particularly if his reputation, and therefore his livelihood, depended, as was usual in Venice, on the vividness of his colouring? He would surely realize that his only chance of defeating the pervading gloom would be by brightening his palette —using colours which would seem too bright in a side-lit studio and much too bright with full sky-lighting. Even granted that the daylight in northern Europe is less bright than in Mediterranean countries and that it is now possible to control the intake of light in sky-lit galleries by means of shutters and lay-lights there remains the question of how much is the optimum. The painter may have had a dark church in mind and brightened his palette accordingly. But he may have done this as a kind of gesture of despair. He had done the best he could in circumstances not of his making or choosing. If he had had *carte blanche* would not the lighting have been somewhat brighter? But how much? Would Bach have preferred his clavier music to be played on a modern grand piano?

These are universal problems affecting the display of works of art in museums. But in the case of Veronese an additional factor arises to bedevil the museum official and Veronese's reputation. For a very large proportion of Veronese's surviving work was intended as immovable decoration which has in fact been moved to totally different settings. This added complication affects Veronese to a peculiar degree. In Italy outside Venice the problem hardly arises since decoration was normally carried out in fresco, though with Rubens, whose decorations, like Veronese's, were usually on canvas, a comparable problem arises, though less acutely. As to the other great Venetians, a far higher percentage of Tintoretto's decorations remain *in situ*, while Tiepolo contrived to work mainly in fresco, even in Venice. In the case of Titian, a very high proportion of his pictures were always intended as movable.

It is highly probable that Veronese's reputation has in fact suffered by such removals and certain that they have caused misunderstanding of his art. In wall decorations, for instance, Veronese's unit was a rectangle twice as long, or more, as it is high. A number of such paintings, separated, as they would originally have been, only by narrow bars, make up a continuous frieze. But when a single one is hung in a gallery it is clear that such proportions are quite contrary to the classical canon for cabinet pictures. In the case of his ceilings, when they are hung in a gallery we are actually looking at them from the opposite side to what was intended. When they are attached to a ceiling we have to stand back from them and look up at an angle. The top of the painting is then nearest our eyes and its base farthest from us. But when such paintings are hung vertically on the wall of a gallery at the optimum height it is the base which is nearest our eyes and the top which is farthest away. As to the misunderstandings which inevitably follow the removal of the immovable one example may suffice. In the National Gallery in London there are three works of Veronese of the first quality—the *Family of Darius*, the four *Allegories of Love* and the *Consecration of S. Nicholas*—together with a number of others. Only one of these—the last—can be precisely dated and the three works show extraordinarily different styles. It is rather difficult to believe—or it would be if the pictures were not as familiar as they are—that one artist was responsible for all, while the relative dating would be anybody's guess. It does not solve the problem when we realize the different functions of the three works as wall decoration, ceilings and altarpiece respectively. We may still be puzzled how the artist came to evolve three distinct styles for the three genres.

In the present writer's view these anomalies would be readily explicable if we could see an interior—particularly a church interior—totally decorated by Veronese, with ceiling paintings, a continuous frieze of wall decorations and a set of altarpieces still *in situ*. But this is not possible. Not only have many of Veronese's decorations been removed. The ideal, total example never existed.[1] There was never an equivalent for Veronese of the Scuola di S. Rocco. The church of S. Sebastiano in Venice which retains its nave and sacristy ceilings and its main altarpiece is deficient in wall decorations. The great *Feast* is no longer there[2] and there never was a continuous frieze. The wall decorations which remain in the church consist, apart from some damaged frescoes in the gallery and the organ shutters, merely of two large paintings in the choir. Similarly, in the Doge's palace the only complete Veronese ceiling is in the Sala del Collegio, and in this room only one wall—a short one—of the frieze is Veronese's.[3] Working on these, however, and from the inherent qualities of certain of the paintings which have been removed, it is possible to see that Veronese's system of decoration was strictly, indeed almost scientifically, logical. His starting point was the relation between the eye level of the spectator and the height above ground of the paintings. This led him to evolve distinct styles for wall decorations and ceilings, and these he applied indiscriminately to sacred decorations and secular ones. His altarpieces, being destined for a similar altitude to the wall decorations, shared certain characteristics with them for that reason. But by observing the inherent differences of form between the wide wall decoration and the lofty altarpiece, as well as the particular function of the latter in a religious sense, and by stressing in his altarpieces what he had minimized in his wall decorations Veronese evolved a third style distinct from both the others.

It had not been thus with Tintoretto. His output, too, consisted mainly of decorations which were intended to be immovable, and like Veronese he evolved several distinct styles. But with him the various styles correspond much less closely with the different categories of decoration. He paid little regard to a realistic eye level, and indeed seems at times to be set on destroying or confusing the basic co-ordinates of space, namely absolute horizontal and absolute vertical. His figures gyrate in space like aeroplanes in a wind tunnel, and it may be difficult to decide whether the occasional glimpses of a flat surface are to be taken as floor, wall or ceiling, and consequently for what setting the painting was intended. Tintoretto's different manners depend rather on his widely differing systems of lighting (which with Veronese does not vary greatly), and on the tremendous variety in ratio of size of figures to size of surround.

In those of Veronese's wall decorations which remain in position—the choir laterals at S. Sebastiano[4] or the *Apotheosis of the Battle of Lepanto*[5] in the Sala del Collegio of the Doge's palace—the base of the painting in each case is well above the head of the spectator—perhaps about ten or twelve feet from the ground. If the space in the painting which is supposed to stretch behind the base of it were imagined as perfectly horizontal it is obvious that at this height from the ground only the figures depicted on the front plane would be fully revealed. As they receded from it they would be increasingly cut off from the feet up. In the organ shutters of S. Sabastiano—which are considerably higher above the floor than the choir laterals—Veronese was content to let this happen. But the exclusion of space definition which this system involves was at other times clearly a tiresome restriction, and in consequence he evolved various methods of cheating with the eye level in wall decorations. Sometimes, as in the Martyrdom lateral at S. Sebastiano and the Lepanto apotheosis, he merely permitted himself to raise the eye level a fraction above the base of the painting even though it should strictly have been just below it. At other times he conceived the space not as horizontal but as rising or falling. In a landscape the ground is shown undulating up or down hill. In an architectural setting it is done with steps. A particularly ingenious device was to imagine the foreground, on which the principal figures stand and which is almost invariably parallel with the picture plane, as consisting of a terrace raised above the level of the background. We must imagine that a staircase descends from the back of the terrace in the foreground to a large piazza or other level space, at the back of which elaborate architectural elements are seen. In this way it is only the upper, and usually more interesting, portions of the buildings which are seen.

1. The frescoes at the Villa Barbaro at Maser are left out of discussion here as the subject only relates to decorations painted on canvas.

2. It was included in Napoleon's plunder in 1797 and on return to Italy was allocated to the Brera.

3. The three further wall decorations in the Sala del Maggior Consiglio are studio work.

4. Reproduced by Fiocco, *Paolo Veronese*, 1928, pls. XX and XXI.

5. Reproduced by Fiocco, *op. cit.*, pl. LXXIX.

The great advantage of this device is in the flexibility which it gives the decorator who still wishes to retain a realistic eye level. For the actual level of the frieze may well be higher than the optimum from the artist's point of view and by this means it may be made to seem lower. What Veronese in fact does on these occasions is to substitute multiple levels within the painting for a single one. An extreme example is the *Susannah and the Elders*[6] at Vienna (Fig. 1). Here the lower storey of the building in the background on the left is almost entirely truncated. We think at first that the eye level is well below the base of the picture. But the foreground—where, on the right, we are shown it—is not. It is within the picture space that we must imagine the ground as falling steeply, and it is noticeable that the Elders are stepping *up* on to the foreground. This system, like other decorative devices, was applied by Veronese to pagan subjects—for example the *Family of Darius*—as well as to sacred ones.

The removal of most of Veronese's wall decorations from their original settings renders it impossible to understand the full subtlety of his system. This is particularly the case with what must have been his most elaborate essay of the kind, namely the paintings from the Old Testament, Apocrypha and New Testament of which seven are at Vienna and an eighth at Washington.[7] These show very considerable variations of design, clearly intended to accord with the placing of the paintings in the building they were painted for. It is one of the anomalies of scholarship that this is not known. We do not know from what church or chapel or even from what city the paintings came.[8] In two of them, for example—the *Rebecca* (Washington) and the *Lot and his Daughters*—the figures are crowded towards the left of the long rectangle and were therefore probably intended for a right-hand wall. In two more —the *Susannah and the Elders* already mentioned, and the *Esther and Ahasuerus*—the figures build up towards the right and were therefore probably intended for a left-hand wall. In three others—*Christ and the Woman of Samaria, Christ and the Adulteress* and *Hagar and Ishmael*—the figures are symmetrically disposed on either side of the central vertical axis and may therefore have been intended to be viewed centrally—perhaps on a back wall. In the remaining painting—the *Captain of Capernaum before Christ*— the composition is likewise more or less centrally

planned, though less specifically than in the preceding three. As to the eye levels in the eight paintings there seems at first sight to be a considerable variation. *Susannah and the Elders*, for example, gives the impression of being intended for a higher setting than the *Christ and the Woman of Samaria*—perhaps on the tier immediately above. This may indeed have been the case. But at this late stage of his career Veronese was a master of tricks in this respect. His falling terraces and rising and falling slopes conceal the fact that there is really little variation in the eye levels—roughly about a quarter of the picture's height from the base. With the flexibility that this permitted from a decorative point of view it would be rash to try to work out the relative heights of the original settings.

To what an extent Veronese's different styles as wall decorator and as ceiling painter resulted from observing the eye levels may be gauged by comparing the Uffizi *Annunciation*[9]—which in this context counts as a wall decoration—with the ceiling of the same subject (Venice, S. Zanipolo, from the Umiltà alle Zattere)[10] (Figs. 2–3). In the oblong painting the eye level is the normal for wall decoration—about a quarter of the way up from the base. In the oval it is far lower. But the pictorial elements are more or less the same in the two pictures—the two figures, the cherubim and the forest of pillars, plain in the one, twisted in the other. In the oval canvas an extra touch of drama comes from the Madonna's extending her arms rather than folding them. But if the angel in either picture were seen from the eye level of the other one they would be much alike. Even the lighting is similar. It is the difference in eye level alone which is responsible for changing a classical composition into a proto-Baroque one.

The realistic approach to ceiling decoration which is implied by a very low eye level brought with it the same consequences as when it was used on wall decoration. If the figures are imagined standing or sitting on the level only the ones nearest the edge will be visible. In order to reveal more figures they must be thought of as arranged either vertically or else on a steep slant. Tintoretto, who habitually favoured a high eye level in all his work, and who in his wall decorations was normally not prepared to make concessions to the eye level of the spectator,[11] used the second of these methods—the main ceilings at S. Rocco and the Doge's palace presuppose that the spectator is at the foot of a steep hill, looking up it. This convention permitted Tintoretto to combine the advantage, for him,

6. Reproduced by Pallucchini, *Veronese*, 3rd ed., 1953, pl. 133.
7. The *Susannah*, the *Hagar* and the *Rebecca* are reproduced by Pallucchini, *op. cit.*, pls. 133, 130 and 132. The present writer does not know of an easily obtainable reference book which includes reproductions of all eight pictures.
8. They are first recorded together with two others in the Duke of Buckingham sale of 1648. Since this article was written the missing pictures have been identified at Prague.

9. Reproduced Pallucchini, *op. cit.*, pl. 11.
10. Reproduced Pallucchini, *op. cit.*, pl. 66.
11. In the wall decorations in the Scuola di S. Rocco, for instance, the eye level is far above that of the spectator. The low eye level in the *Pool of Bethesda* (church of S. Rocco) is exceptional.

of a high eye level, namely the high horizon, with a degree of verisimilitude appropriate to a ceiling, and Veronese himself used it in his two battle scenes on the ceiling of the Sala del Maggior Consiglio at the Doge's palace.[12] In his largest ceiling in the same room—the *Triumph of Venice*[13]—he adopted the alternative system. The figures are conceived in three bands which are meant to be disposed more or less vertically one above the other. The middle band consists of spectators on a terrace, below which are others, while deities are arranged on clouds overhead.

As in his wall decorations Veronese makes no modification of his system of ceiling painting in respect of different subjects. A religious subject such as the *Coronation of Esther* at S. Sebastiano[14] is very much the same in arrangement as the *Venice enthroned between Justice and Peace*[15] in the Sala del Collegio of the Doge's palace. Not only is the angle of vision similar. Even the design—with the enthroned figure top right and the kneeling one bottom left—is essentially the same. The general impression of opulent magnificence is also the same in the two works, which, moreover, illustrate a further characteristic of Veronese's art. For the Esther is an early work—it dates from 1556—while the other, though so similar in so many ways, was painted more than twenty years later. The third genre which Veronese approached from the point of view of the decorator was the altarpiece. Here the base is normally at a similar height from the ground to wall decorations. At S. Sebastiano the high altar is in fact slightly higher than the choir laterals, and on the evidence of the relative heights of eye level in the majority of his wall decorations and altarpieces this would have been normal. But the difference would usually not have been great. On the other hand the far greater height of an altarpiece itself in most cases, and its usually upright format, would have made it more difficult to fill, with a low eye level, than an oblong wall decoration. The lower the eye level in an upright picture the more difficult it is to fill the upper reaches. For this reason among others the tendency in High Renaissance altarpieces had been to adopt an unrealistic eye level around the middle of the picture's height.

But in another sense the consequences of a low eye level were more favourable to an altarpiece than to a wall decoration. In the latter, as we have seen, Veronese had evidently found it irksome that a subbase eye level should truncate all the figures but those in the extreme foreground and should largely nullify space. His method of obscuring the precise eye level, which we noted in that context, by means of a multi-level space in the painting is sometimes used in his altarpieces also. But here the negation of space and the premium set on the extreme foreground could be turned to advantage. A figure of a saint seen from below and shown standing on the very edge of an altarpiece towers hieratically above the altar—and seems, indeed, if the view point is sufficiently near, to come right out of the surrounding frame—with a vividness and an immediacy which is far more difficult to suggest with a higher eye level.

Mantegna seems to have been the first to realize the implications of this idea for altarpieces representing saints, and though he and other Paduanists such as Tura were normally compelled to dilute its force by a less than life-size scale, in at least one memorable instance—the Cà d'Oro *S. Sebastian*—Mantegna made heroic use of it. In the intervening years Titian had on occasion done something of the kind—the *S. Giovanni Eliminosinario* is an example. Veronese used it with tremendous effect in his S. Jerome at Murano (S. Pietro Martire)[16] which is one of his rare altarpieces with a single figure. In another work—the S. Pantalone of 1587[17]—the central figure is surrounded by three others. In this late altarpiece, in which Veronese achieved an urgency of religious expression which he had seldom reached earlier in his career, the saint seems to float upwards from an unseen base and outwards towards the congregation.

In his larger and more complex altarpieces which introduced an upper tier of figures Veronese remained faithful to the Mantegna-Titian tradition. It might well seem impossible to incorporate an upper tier of figures in an altarpiece when the lower tier is already above the eye level of the congregation. Any attempt at consistent foreshortening in such cases would speedily lead to the ludicrous. It was no less an artist than Masaccio who evolved the solution of genius to this problem. In his frescoed altarpiece of the Trinity in S. Maria Novella, Florence, three eye levels are used. The donor and his wife are on a level with the spectator. The Virgin and S. John, above them, are appropriately foreshortened from below. But the crucified Christ and God the Father, far higher still, are again shown from the level. Not only did this solve the problem pictorially. There was religious justification for it in the Omnipresence.

It was Mantegna, in this respect as in almost every other the most important of Veronese's spiritual forebears, who incorporated this device into the more nor-

---

12. One is reproduced by Fiocco, *op. cit.*, pl. xcvi.
13. Reproduced Pallucchini, *op. cit.*, pl. 149.
14. Reproduced Pallucchini, *op. cit.*, pl. 12.
15. Reproduced Pallucchini, *op. cit.*, pl. 114.

16. Reproduced in the catalogue of the 1939 Veronese exhibition, Cà' Giustinian, Venice, no. 46, p. 116.
17. Reproduced Pallucchini, *op. cit.*, pl. 150.

mal type of altarpiece of the Madonna enthroned with Saints. He had been developing it throughout his career, and in his late altarpiece from Veronese's native Verona (now in the Castello Sforzesco, Milan, from the Trivulzio collection) he realized it in the most uncompromising form (Fig. 4). The standing saints are seen from a sub-base eye level, but the Madonna and Child, above them, remain level with the spectator. Titian had used his own, diluted, version of this system in altarpieces such as the Frari *Assunta* or the Verona altar of the same subject, and Veronese regularly used it in his two-tiered altarpieces. In the most splendid of these—the *Martyrdom of S. George* in S. Giorgio in Braida, Verona[18]—he evolved a particularly personal version of it (Fig. 5). The magnificent palace seen in the background is of a piece with those in his *Feasts* and other wall decorations. But here there is no need to minimize the height by raising the figures on a terrace. The entablatures seen from far below dive downwards at a giddy angle towards the head of the saint. Even in his kneeling position he towers above us while the Madonna and Child at the summit are seen from nearer their own level. The essential characteristics of the style which Veronese evolved for a spectacular altarpiece may easily be gauged by comparing the *S. George* with the Louvre *Marriage at Cana* as a comparable work in the sphere of wall decoration. From similar components two totally different effects have been obtained.[19]

*   *   *

It is to be hoped that the foregoing observations, brief as they are, may help to clear away a little of the brushwood which has obscured a proper understanding of Veronese's art. None of the great Italians of the Renaissance, indeed, is still in need of such study as he or has been more neglected by able students. But even if we agree that the attention which he paid to the eye level of the spectator was the main element which conditioned the evolution of his distinctive styles as wall decorator, ceiling decorator and painter of altarpieces that is only the beginning. A fourth genre—cabinet painting—in addition to his work as decorator, has its own problems, and the varying extent of participation by his active studio is a question common to the whole of his output. The fact that within each genre his style developed relatively little does not mean that it did not develop at all. It merely makes the attempt to establish a precise chronology—by far the most important of the remaining tasks—more difficult. Nevertheless, there can be little doubt that the kind of prolonged application which enabled Denis Mahon fundamentally to revise the chronology of Nicolas Poussin[20] might succeed in defining stages in Veronese's development which are at present imperceptible.[21] The task is indeed of alarming proportions, but it is perhaps worthier than some others which have in fact been carried out.

18. Reproduced Pallucchini, *op. cit.*, pl. 74.
19. Attention may be drawn in this context to the system used by Raphael in the *Disputa*. Here no attempt is made at a realistic eye level from the spectator's point of view. The eye level is between the two tiers. We look down on the lower and up to the upper. But in the middle of the latter Christ and God the Father—and they alone—are drawn from level.
20. Cf. *Burlington Magazine*, CII (1960), pp. 288 ff., and Gazette des Beaux-Arts publication, 1962, entitled *Poussiniana*.
21. A start was made by Michael Levey's remarkable reading of a date—1548—on Veronese's *Christ in the Temple* (Prado), cf. *Burlington Magazine*, CII (1960), pp. 107 ff. This led him to consider the repercussions of the discovery on other early works.

WILLIAM S. HECKSCHER

Reflections on Seeing Holbein's Portrait of Erasmus at Longford Castle*

Quis tibi Mimus erit!

In the autumn of the year 1524, Erasmus of Rotterdam wrote to William Warham: 'I presume that you have received by way of tribute a painted rendering of my features so that, should God summon me from here, you might have a bit of Erasmus.'[1] As far as can be ascertained, the painting in question is Holbein's half-length portrait of 'Erasmus of Rotterdam with the Renaissance Pilaster', which bears the date 1523 (Fig. 1). The painting is in the Collection of the Earl of Radnor at Longford Castle near Salisbury.[2]

The recipient of the letter and of the portrait, William Warham (c. 1450–August 22, 1532), famous as lawyer, diplomat and orator, had become, in 1504, Archbishop of Canterbury and Primate of England and, a little later, Chancellor of Oxford. He was one of Erasmus's oldest and truest friends and benefactors. In 1524 when picture and letter were sent to him, he was a good-natured gentleman, tottering ('troubled with an old disease in his head') and somewhat spineless ('ira principis mors est'). Although around 1524 eclipsed by others, he was still very powerful. The only proof which we have that William Warham admired Holbein's Erasmus portrait lies in the fact that three years later, in 1527, he commissioned Holbein to paint his own portrait and to make it—compositionally speaking—a paraphrase of the 'Erasmus' of Longford Castle[3] (Fig. 2).

In 1524 Erasmus had every reason to wish to express his indebtedness to William Warham with as tangible and lasting a gift as could be had. Nothing could have been more personal and more expensive than a portrait painted by Holbein, at that time the *pictor imaginarius* of great promise. The archbishop, whom Erasmus addressed as 'optime Mecoenas', had just (as we learn from the letter) not only presented Erasmus with a horse—

> not so much handsome as it is good, with none of the mortal sins but for gluttony and sloth, otherwise graced with all the virtues of the true confessor in that it is pious, prudent, humble, shamefaced, sober, chaste and quiet, won't bite or kick

—but he had also augmented the already substantial pension of £20—'pro aucta pensione habeo gratiam'. This pension had come to Erasmus since 1512 from the income of the Rectory of Aldington in Kent.[4]

* My gratitude goes out to several friends and colleagues who have been helpful in many ways. In the first place it is my pleasant duty to thank the Rt. Hon. the Earl of Radnor for permission to reproduce the panel in his possession. Lord and Lady Radnor have been most generous in giving me every facility to examine the painting. For critical assistance I wish to thank Erwin Panofsky. I am painfully aware of my shortcomings in handling sixteenth-century Latin texts, which play an important part in my argument. Others who have put me under obligation with their help are Mlle Roseline Bacou (Paris), Max Burckhardt (Basel), Mrs. Virginia W. Callahan (Washington, D.C.), D. Courvoisier (Basel), Mrs. Enriqueta Frankfort (London), Horst Gerson (The Hague/Groningen), Miss C. Heckscher (London), Günther Heinz (Vienna), Werner Kaegi (Basel), Miss Martine Klapwijk (Utrecht/Amsterdam), Miss Karla Langedijk (Utrecht), Miss Beatrice Langer (Vienna/Pittsburgh), Michael Levey (London), Otto Prinz (Munich), Pieter Singelenberg (Utrecht), Wolfgang Schmid (Bonn), Jan Schouten (Gouda), and Craig R. Thompson (Haverford, Pa.).

1. 'Amplissime Praesul, arbitror tibi redditam imaginem pictam, quam misi vt aliquid haberes Erasmi, si me Deus hinc euocarit'; Basel, September 4, 1524, ed. P. S. Allen, *Opus Epistolarum Des. Erasmi Roterodami*, v, Oxford, 1924, no. 1488, pp. 534–6. This edition will be cited as Allen, followed by the numbers of volume and letter(s).

2. Most of the important literature on the painting, its migrations before it was acquired for Longford Castle by Lord Folkestone, its copies and the analyses in the critical literature, will be found under no. 172 on p. 201 of the Catalogue *Die Malerfamilie Holbein in Basel* (Ausstellung im Kunstmuseum Basel zur Fünfhundertjahrfeier der Universität Basel, June 4–September 25), Basel, 1960. Among Erasmus's contemporaries the Longford Castle portrait was the most popular. To this some seven copies of the sixteenth century bear witness; see Paul Ganz, 'Les portraits d'Érasme de Rotterdam', *Revue de l'Art Ancien et Moderne*, LXVII, 1935, pp. 3–24, Figs. 7–12 and 14 (at Hampton Court, showing Erasmus in the interior of a Gothic church). To its descendants belongs the Dutch 100-guilder note (1953)—at best a somewhat clownish paraphrase. See also following note.

3. The obvious compositional agreement between the portraits of Erasmus and William Warham was observed by Hans Diepolder, *Die Erasmusbildnisse von Hans Holbein d. J.*, Berlin [1949], p. 9. For William Warham see *The Dictionary of National Biography*, LIX, London, 1899, pp. 378–83. The year in which he became Archbishop of Canterbury was 1504, not 1503, as is often said; a Bull of Julius II of November 29, 1503, had made him archiepiscopus designatus.

4. For Erasmus's pension see entry 'Aldington (Kent)', *Opus Epistolarum Des. Erasmi Roterodami*, XII (ed. Barbara Flower and Elisabeth Rosenbaum), Oxford, 1958, Index III, p. 38. It matters little that Erasmus received the wrong horse, which—as he reports—made him lose his patience; see ep. 1488, p. 536, and Allen's note *ad* line 50.

The remainder of the letter is, as I hope to show, important for our understanding of Holbein's painting. The letter represents, in the first place, a kind of stock-taking of Erasmus's situation at that moment. It contains a carefully phrased catalogue of adversities, physical as well as spiritual, besetting the forever ailing humanist, who was then a *senex* in his late fifties. This catalogue of woes is balanced, however, by the enumeration of his reasons for, if not exultation, at least consolation. On the debit side we learn about Erasmus's ill-health, the Roman detractors, and the *Lutherani*; on the credit side, about the munificence of Clement VII, about 'regum amicitia', and work accomplished. Psychologically speaking, I believe that —whether he was aware of it or not—something of Erasmus's innermost ideas about Holbein's painting found expression in the thoughts and accounts he communicated to his correspondent, which, if seen merely on the surface, seem to have little enough to do with this work of art, let alone the iconographic program behind it. Letter and portrait have nevertheless, as I shall try to show, a specific mood in common; we can be even more specific by saying that both are characterized by a similar manner of interblending emotions. What we find in the letter is a mixture of quasi-humorous self-deprecation, of fully justified hypochondria caused by a variety of physical ailments, of real anxiety prompted by attacks launched and pressures exerted from without: attacks from members of the Roman Academy as well as the henchmen of Martin Luther stirring up, to use Erasmus's terminology, a *tempestas*; pressures requiring that Erasmus should take a stand, all of which threatened to upset his carefully guarded *tranquillitas*. A measure of consolation came from his awareness of being recognized in his own worth by the great of the earth, but to an equal extent from his confidence that what he was doing was right and of lasting importance.

In order to gauge the emotions and counter-emotions to which Erasmus was subjected at this point in his career, we must keep in mind that his letter to William Warham (as well as a number of other letters to English friends which are also of importance for our better understanding of the Longford Castle portrait) was composed in September 1524. In that month Erasmus's *Liberum arbitrium* had appeared in print. Its publication was a deed which ushered in, as Erasmus and his contemporaries fully understood, a determined stand on his part. It was a challenge of the first magnitude to the very basis of Luther's theological philosophy. With it Erasmus had entered, as he admitted himself, the arena of theological controversy. Our portrait (even though close to the two famous profile portraits, in the Louvre and at Basel, in which Holbein had stressed the delights of *vita contemplativa* of a man at the height of his productivity) shows the sitter curiously withdrawn, the embodiment of *vita solitaria* as it were, inactive and—as has frequently been pointed out (Erwin Treu)—cast in a distinctly representative character. Taken one by one, much of what Holbein's painting is meant to tell the beholder is contradictory to the point of being enigmatic. These paradoxical qualities were not the result of accident or incompetence but were meant to puzzle the way a riddle does. I will show this at the end of my discourse, and I shall try to make clear that a certain cerebral quality of the painting is not only an indication that Holbein's art was at the threshold of Mannerism but also that he must have laboured under the dictates of a most demanding model.

Noble and aloof as the portrait may be, a closer examination of the inscriptions shows that Erasmus did not wish to appear as the prince of humanists to the exclusion of aspects altogether different. Although in many respects the painting is an apotheosis of the scholar, Erasmus is presented at the same time as the tireless worker in the vineyard of the word who by serving others suffers irremediable injury, and earns little gratitude and much criticism from the very people whom his endeavours were meant to benefit and who were not worthy 'to hold a chamberpot out to him'. What we might call the *aliis in serviendo*-syndrome of Erasmus was fully justified in the years 1523–1524. Having been born on the fourth day after a new moon, Erasmus knew that there was little happiness in store for him; Hercules had shared the same fate, and his entire life was spent deprived of all pleasures and full of labour so that, without the slightest benefit to himself, he sweated to help others—'quarta luna nati, dicuntur qui parum feliciter nati sunt . . . propterea quod Hercules hac luna natus fertur, cuius omnis uita uoluptatum omnium expers, ac laborum plena fuit, . . . qui iuuandis alijs sudauit, sibi inutilis'.[5] Yet, we should not forget that in the sixteenth and seventeenth centuries this self-inflicted suffering for the benefit of others was—however true—often little more than a fashionable pose, surpassed in popularity only by that of the melancholic *penseur*.

It is tempting though hazardous to read physiognomic interpretations into early portraits. Our portrait, especially if we compare its expression with that of other portraits of Erasmus done about the same time,

5. For 'aliis in serviendo consumor', see W. S. Heckscher, *Rembrandt's Anatomy*, New York, 1958, chap. xvi, p. 120. For the chamberpot simile and its sources, see M. M. Phillips, *The Adages of Erasmus*, Cambridge, 1964, n. 1 on p. 195. For 'quarta luna nati', see *Adagiorum Chiliadis Primae, Centuria I*, ed. 1523, p. 47, and *Morias Encomium*, § 61, where Erasmus's portrait (1515) accompanies this *dictum*. See also note 12 *infra*.

makes the sitter look remarkably old, and seems to me indicative of patient endurance in the face of some kind of *Unbehagen*. I consider it not impossible that this absence of expression was intended although it was, at this point, within Holbein's range to reveal expression. Whereas the first truly intimate portraits of the fifteenth century had studiously avoided the registering of any traces of emotion,[6] we have evidence which indicates that from the sixteenth century onward artists began to observe, and did not hesitate to isolate and record, one of the varying moods of their sitters. Quentin Matsys for example would (in 1517) defer his sittings because Erasmus's facial expression had undergone a change as the result of some indisposition[7] (Fig. 4). In our painting, Holbein recorded a mood that might be described as controlled tranquillity. Although this tranquillity consisted of non-expression, it would yet have contained a highly significant physiognomic meaning to a sixteenth-century beholder who was a humanist.

Erasmus himself, as his writings amply prove, strove

above all for *tranquillitas*. The quintessence of his letter to William Warham is a plea for it. *Tranquillitas* describes a state of mind which becomes manifest through facial expression or rather lack of expression. This quest for a solitary life in tranquillity was not, as one might assume, equivalent to the modern fear of noise decibels, air pollution, over-population and similar manifestations of *Weltangst*. Nor was it the seeking of mere comfort of a man admittedly lacking in the kind of virility that distinguished some of his contemporaries such as Luther.

Tranquillitas to Erasmus was related to the postulates of the Stoics. With them already it meant being in complete harmony within oneself and with the world. The prerequisite of a solitary and therefore happy existence was Virtue; such existence could serve as fortress and safe port against the tempests of life— 'undique felix et tranquilla (scil. vita solitaria) et, ut proprie dicam, arx munita tempestatumque omnium portus est'.[7a] Tranquillity was for the privileged few. It marked the sovereign in rank and the sovereign thinker who in spiritual matters stood above the common crowd (Fig. 3). Tranquillity, in its strictest observance, aimed at arriving at the outward projection of an inner harmony and firmness. One could enter into the spirit of tranquillity ('recipere mentis tranquillitatem') only by discarding the four passions or *affectus*: *gaudium*, *spes*, *dolor* and *metus*. Like the four temperaments, the passions had entered the world with the Fall of Adam and, like the temperaments, they were pernicious to body and soul of Man. It was said that

'Joy turns exuberant'—'gaudium dilatat'

'Expectation (or: Desire) inflames'—'Spes (or: Cupiditas) inflammat'

'Pain stifles'—'Dolor angustat'

'Fear renders downcast'—'Metus dejicit'.[8]

Erasmus summed up the *affectus* as 'any kind of motion of the soul which is the opposite to the rational mind' 'affectus [est] omnis animi motus, & opponitur rationi'. By yielding to the *affectus* one exposed oneself to the wiles of Fortuna, whose attributes were the

6. I have lectured on this problem and am planning an article on the apathetic portrait in the Northern Renaissance. P. J. Vinken and E. de Jongh have shown how problematic all attempts at reading physiognomies remain, even in the portraits of the seventeenth century; 'De boosaardigheid van Hals' regenten en regentessen', *Oud-Holland*, LXXVIII, 1963, pp. 1–26. However the game of physiognomic analysis is not new. When Martin Luther was shown a portrait of Erasmus—most likely Dürer's engraving of 1526—he observed: 'Erasmus, wie die Gestalt seines Gesichts anzeiget, wird ein listiger, tückischer Mann sein, der beide, Gott und Religion gespottet hat' 'Erasmus et vultu et stilo prae se fert calliditatem (Quia ibi habebat eius imaginem). Irridet tantum et Deum et religionem'; recorded by Johannes Schlaginhaufen (January–March 1532), ed. *D. Martin Luthers Werke. Tischreden (1531–1546)*, II, Weimar, 1913, no. 1319, pp. 41 f.

7. Our testimonial is Erasmus's letter to Thomas Morus [Antwerp, May 30], 1517, ed. Allen, II, no. 584, p. 576: 'Petrus Aegidius and I are being painted on the same panel: before long we shall send it to you as a present. It was most inconvenient that on my return Petrus labored gravely under I don't know what kind of illness which was anything but innocuous. Not even now has he recovered completely. We ourselves were in good health when, I don't know why, my physician got the idea to order me to take some pills to purge my bile. Well, what foolishly he prescribed, even more foolishly I carried out. The sittings for the painting had begun. When, however, after having taken that medicine, I went back once more to the painter, he maintained that my expression [*vultus*] was no longer the same. For that reason the painting had to be discontinued for a number of days, until I was a little more lively' 'Petrus Aegidius et ego pingimur in eadem tabula: eam tibi dono breui mittemus. Verum incidit incommode quod reuersus Petrum offenderim nescio quo morbo laborantem grauiter, nec citra periculum; vnde nec adhuc satis reualuit. Nos belle valebamus, sed nescio quomodo medico venit in mentem vt purgandae bili iuberet me pilulas aliquot sumere, et quod ille stultus suasit, ego stultius feci. Iam pingi coeperam; verum a pharmaco sumpto cum ad pictorem redirem, negauit eundem esse vultum. Dilata est igitur pictura in dies aliquot, donec fiam paulo alacrior.' See: *In elegant. Laur. Vallae*, ed. Erasmus, *Opera omnia*, I, Leyden, 1703, col. 1072, for Erasmus's definition of the *affectus*.

7a. Petrarch, *De vita solitaria*, ed. *Opera omnia*, Basel, 1581, p. 236. An effect that can only be described as equivalent to instant Stoicism is apparently provided by the new drug Ag 246, discovered by Henri Laborit. It has the ability to suppress passions without interfering with the functions of the advanced centers; see *Time* magazine, November 12, 1965, pp. 46 f.

8. For the phrase 'gaudium dilatat', etc., see Petrarch, *Rerum memorandarum*, III, lxxxiv, 2. The *affectus* literature is enormous. The most convenient survey—*pace* the title of the book— is found in Klaus Heitmann, *Fortuna und Virtus. Eine Studie zu Petrarcas Lebensweisheit* (Studi Italiani 1), Cologne-Graz, 1958, esp. pp. 89–150. See also W. S. Heckscher, 'Sturm und Drang', *Simiolus*, II, Utrecht, 1966 (in print).

sail, the stormwinds of the sea, and the ever-revolving sphere.

Tranquillitas then, rather than being an escape, was a proud rallying of powers of the mind. He who partook of 'sublime tranquillity', and only he, was capable of exercising science and wisdom in a frame of mind which made him—be he ruler or sage or both—not unlike God: 'commodissima est tranquillitas, cum ad alia, cum ad scientiam, & prudentiae exercitationem: non cauponatiam & forensem dico, sed magnam illam, quae Deo similem reddit sui participem' (Plutarch).[9]

9. The word 'Stoicism' was not in currency before 1626. The first to restore the entire doctrine of the Stoics systematically was Justus Lipsius (1547–1606); see Jason L. Saunders, *Justus Lipsius. The Philosophy of Renaissance Stoicism*, New York, 1955. However, Erasmus, more than anyone else in the first half of the sixteenth century, was not only deeply influenced by the first great revival of Stoicism but was one of its prime movers; see Léontine Zanta, *La Renaissance du Stoicisme au XVIᵉ Siècle* (Diss. Paris), 1914, esp. pp. 88–91. Erasmus was never a Stoic in the all too rigid sense. Nothing suggests that he ever made an effort to stretch his desire for tranquillity to the point of Stoical apathy which, a seeming *contradictio in se*, often led to excesses: the classical personification of all Stoical ideals, Marcus Aurelius (Fig. 3), succeeded in cultivating the attitude of apathetic tranquillity only by resorting to ever-increasing doses of opium; see Thomas W. Africa, 'The Opium Addiction of Marcus Aurelius', *Journal of the History of Ideas*, XXII, i, 1961, pp. 97–102. *Tranquillitas* became the great fashion in the second half of the fourth century after Christ; see Richard M. Honig, *Humanitas und Rhetorik*, Göttingen, 1960, p. 105. Christ calming the storm at sea (Matt. 8:26) had furnished the key words of Christian Stoicism: 'Tunc surgens imperavit ventis et mari, et facta est tranquillitas magna' (see further below). Eutropius (writing in the fourth century) might say: 'Post eum M. Antoninus solus rem publicam tenuit, vir, quem mirari facilius quis quam laudare possit. A principio vitae tranquillissimus, adeo ut ex infantia quoque vultum nec ex gaudio nec ex maerore mutaverit. Philosophiae deditus Stoicae, etc., etc., etc.'; *Breviarium ab Urbe condita*, chap. xi, ed. Franciscus Ruehl (Bibliotheca scriptorum Graecorum et Romanorum Teubneriana), 1887, p. 58. Constantius II roused the admiration of the Romans when, on April 28, 357, he entered the City in complete immobility, for 'as if his neck were held in an iron vice, he looked straight ahead, glanced neither left nor right, wiped neither mouth nor nose, and kept his hands completely still . . .'; Ammianus Marcellinus, *Res gestae*, XVI, 10. Does not this passage (which Erasmus knew because he edited it) recall the pose of Erasmus in his portrait at Longford Castle? See for this passage also W. S. Heckscher, *In Memoriam G. I. Hoogewerff*, Utrecht, 1963, p. 6 and n. 7. The seventeenth-century German poet Paul Fleming would still say: 'Ie höher Einer ist vom Stande,/ie weniger bewegt er sich'; *Oden*, v, no. 18. Tranquillity, apart from being an attitude or pose of immobility, which the Stoical prince might adopt in public and in private, was also an imperial prerogative. It could finally become a title, not unlike 'Serenitas Vestra'. Thus we may encounter the phrase 'Tranquillissimi ac Christianissimi Domini nostri' in reference to the *augusti*; see DuCange, *Glossarium mediae et infimae latinitatis*, Niort, 1886, s.v. 'tranquillitas'. The given names Tranquillus and Tranquillinus occur between the years A.D. 286 and 580 about seven times among members of the higher clergy; see Ulysse Chevalier, *Répertoire des Sources Historiques du Moyen-Age. Bio-Bibliographie*, II, Paris, 1907, col. 4552. I know of no instance where these or related names occur in the high middle ages. Tranquillus as a given name turns up again in the Renaissance. For Tranquillus Molossus,

Erasmus (I shall come back to the utterance of powerful feelings of resentment) came to the conclusion that the kind of work he was doing 'was of such a nature that it provided others with the greatest possible advantages, while its author gleaned practically no

see note 25a *infra*. Tranquillus Parthenius Andronicus, Secretary to Ferdinand I (1543), appears as 'Parthenius' in Erasmus's 'Convivium poeticum' of the year 1523; as to the identity, see Craig R. Thompson, *The Colloquies of Erasmus*, Chicago and London, 1965, p. 159. For the moral implications of the pairs: tranquillity, constancy, rest vs. tempestuosity, passion, motion, see W. S. Heckscher, 'Goethe im Banne der Sinnbilder', *Jahrbuch der hamburger Kunstsammlungen*, VII, 1962, pp. 35–54; also, *idem*, 'Sturm und Drang. The Genesis of a Phrase', *Simiolus*, II, Utrecht, 1966; and W. Welzig, 'Constantia und barocke Beständigkeit', *Deutsche Vierteljahrsschrift*, XXXV, 1961, pp. 416–32. At the opposite end of *tranquillitas* we find *tempestas, intemperies*, or *fluctuatio*—all those and many others in the sense of 'iratus Neptunus'. Every Latin dictionary furnishes classical examples. St. Thomas Aquinas states: 'est autem tranquillitas quies maris' (*teste* Nani Mirabellio's *Polyanthea*). Hugh of St. Victor in his famous catalogue of virtues and vices, 'De fructibus carnis et spiritus' (Migne, *P.L.*, CLXXVI, col. 1003), lists 'requies' 'per quam menti quedam securitas ex contemptu perfunctoriae varietatis affertur'. That the medieval sources, down to the thirteenth century, yield relatively little new material under 'tranquillus' and 'tranquillitas', I learned from Dr. Otto Prinz of the Mittellateinisches Wörterbuch (letter of January 21, 1966). We should, however, not overlook the impact of the words 'tranquillitas magna', Matt. 8:23–27, by which Jesus calming the 'tempestas aquae' shows, as the *Glossa ordinaria* expresses it, the 'potentia Salvatoris'. Medieval art repeatedly illustrated the scene in which a naked figure in the pose of the *penseur* appears (opposite Jesus, who is shown standing in the *navicula*), an obvious personification of Tempestas (not unlike the awe-struck River Jordan in certain early representations of the Baptism of Christ). The Princeton Index of Christian Art lists about seven examples between the eleventh century and the year 1356: MS. London, B.M., Add. 39627, fols. 26 r and 161 r; cf. my *Simiolus* article, Fig. 1.

SAEVIS TRANQVILLVS IN VNDIS served as a Medici Impresa, designed by Vincenzo Borghini and by Paolo Giovio for the Medici. It was also the device of both Elizabeth I and William of Nassau and Orange (d. 1584). Device and impresa were almost invariably associated with the icon showing the nest of the Halcyon birds (Pliny and Ovid inspired). Cf. J. Dielitz, *Die Wahl- und Denksprüche*, Frankfort, 1884, p. 28, Karl Frey, *Der literarische Nachlass Giorgio Vasaris*, II, Munich, 1930, pp. 247–52, and the tailpiece to this article.

Shakespeare's *Tempest* ends in Prospero's promise of a kind of sublime tranquillity that terminates all strife and upheaval, physical as well as spiritual. In his last years, Pieter Brueghel expressed in his 'Tempest' something of man's desperate effort to gain control over the passionate waves. The vessel center stage is making attempts to distract the pursuing whale by discharging a barrel, the age-old motif of the 'Magic Flight'. Quite possibly the episode is related to the idea of 'pouring oil on troubled waters'; cf. C. G. Stridbeck, *Bruegelstudien* (Acta Universitatis Stockholmensis, II), Stockholm, 1956, pp. 230–4. 'Tranquillitas' vs. 'tempestas' remains a significant pair of contrasting opposites until the age of Enlightenment. Here, in opposition to that movement, we may encounter a complete reversal of values: Tempestuosity becomes the ideal of those worshipping untrained genius, nature, the sublime—in the arts, in politics, and in music. At the beginning of the 1760's the German literati launch a revolutionary movement which springs into eminence no doubt on account of its challenging anti-tranquillity title, 'Sturm und Drang', which should, literally, be translated 'Tempest and the Passions'; see W. S. Heckscher,

other benefit from it but that of a modicum of fame, accompanied by a maximum of envy—"plurimum inuidiae"'.[10] The letter to William Warham states specifically who those envious detractors were, when he speaks of 'certain people in Rome who are over-awed by heathen literature (Cicero), and who envy me in a scandalous fashion while their letters to me breathe nothing but friendship'. Those 'apes of Cicero' were the members of the Roman Academy whose manners shocked not only Erasmus alone—to him they were, in a magnificent understatement, that heathenish sodality of scholars, 'paganum illud eruditorum sodalitium'.[11] I shall come back to Erasmus's letter for other passages of relevance to our portrait.

*   *   *

'Sturm und Drang', *Simiolus*, II, Utrecht, 1966. A beautiful resolution we find where Wordsworth refers to emotion collected in tranquillity as 'a profound statement about what goes on in a poet's mind when he is composing'.

Erasmus cites: 'While the sea is smooth, anyone can play for captain' 'tranquillo quolibet gubernator est'; *Adagiorum Chiliadis Quartae, Centuria V*, xcvi, ed. 1523, p. 789. From this convention Erasmus's references to the Lutheran tempest must be understood: 'Sed nulli fremunt insanius quam isti qui se Lutheranos appellant, quum horum intemperias detestetur etiam ipse Lutherus!' Thus Erasmus to William Warham in the letter cited in n. 1, p. 535. How deeply familiar Erasmus must have been with the Stoical therapy of the mind beset with anxieties ('semper instabilis mobilisque') and self-doubt ('illud taedium et displicentia sui') becomes clear when we realize that there appeared in 1515 L. Annaeus Seneca's *Ad Serenum. De tranquillitate animi* (book IX of the *Dialogues*) as part of the *opera omnia* edited by Erasmus *s.t. Ioannes Frobenius verae philosophiae studiosis S.D. En tibi lector optime, L. A. S. sanctissimi philosophi lucubrationes omnes, additis etiam nonnullis, Erasmi Roterodami cura, si non omnibus, certe ab innumeris mendis repurgatae*, Basel (July), 1515, 'Ad Serenvm de Tranvillitate vitae [*sic*] Libri duo', pp. 134–53. Seneca in this long exemplary treatise preaches the placid state of mind, the ideal of Horace's *aurea mediocritas*, in which the spirit neither soars nor crawls—'sed placido statu maneat, nec adtollens se umquam nec deprimens; id tranquillitas erit' (chap. ii). In chap. iii Seneca advocates the withdrawal into the ivory tower, into the recesses of inner harmony: 'a foro quidem et publico recedendum est'; see note 7a *supra*. See also note 25 *infra*.

10. See note 21 *infra* and text.

11. It is not impossible that the rumour that in Rome Erasmus's effigy had been burned along with his works might have contributed to the tension under which Erasmus laboured in September, 1524. It turned out eventually that this false report had been launched maliciously at Antwerp; cf. Allen, v, ep. no. 1494, Basel (*c*. September, 1524), pp. 542 f. See also note 25 *infra*. Erasmus wrote to William Warham (letter cited in n. 1, pp. 534 f.): 'Rhomae quidam qui litteras ethnicas adamant, misere mihi inuident, quemadmodum litteris suis significant amici.' For a lucid discussion of these difficulties which, in 1529, caused Erasmus to answer with his *Dialogus Ciceronianus sive de optimo dicendi genere* (Basel, Froben, in two editions), see Margaret Mann Phillips, *The 'Adages' of Erasmus*, Cambridge, 1964, pp. 64 f., Auguste Renaudet, *Érasme et l'Italie*, Geneva, 1954, bk. iv, esp. pp. 202–5, W. S. Heckscher, *Sixtvs IIII*, The Hague, 1955, pp. 24 f. and n. 92, and Rudolf Pfeiffer, *Humanitas Erasmiana* (Studien der Bibliothek Warburg XXII),

Before going any further I must attempt a brief description of Holbein's painting (Figs. 1, 1a and 1b): Erasmus is placed, as we notice at first glance, in a composite interior, as a figure at half length. As in nearly all his portraits, he is shown standing,[12] not, however, at the usual work desk but behind a very plain stone parapet.[13] On the parapet lies a beautiful book in a luxurious reddish-leather binding with gold tooling. On this tome Erasmus rests his relaxed hands. While it might seem as if Erasmus were shown in this pose to indicate that he is resting from his Herculean Labours, the book is placed in such a way that it can only mean that it is being offered to the beholder. From the way it is placed, it is clear that it must be opened and that its pages must be turned from (the beholder's) right to left. The preciousness of the binding stresses that the book must have been meant to be proffered as it were to the recipient of the painting as a gift within a gift. Two of the four pairs of dark green ribbons, meant to tie the book, are visible. The trimmed edge of the paper shows, on the bottom of the book, facing the beholder, a prominent inscription in Greek capital letters: ΗΡΑΚΛΕΙΟΙ ΠΟΝΟΙ. The

Leipzig–Berlin, 1931, pp. 11 f. As early as February 15, 1517, Erasmus told Budaeus 'inter tot scriptorum species nullos minus fero quam istos quosdam Ciceronis simios'; ed. Allen, II, no. 531, pp. 470 f. On June 6(?), 1526, Erasmus wrote from Basel to Franciscus Molinius: 'Romae paganum illud eruditorum sodalitium iam pridem fremit in me', ed. Allen, VI, no. 1719, p. 354. Hand in hand with the anti-Ciceronian tendencies, we very often encounter in sixteenth-century humanist thinking a predilection for Seneca; see Jason L. Saunders, *Justus Lipsius. The Philosophy of Renaissance Stoicism*, New York, 1955, p. 15. The *Lutherani*, which are listed in the second place in the catalogue of miseries, were a sudden new menace materializing about 1522. Erasmus's answer, the *De libero arbitrio* διατριβή, appeared in three different places in four issues in September, 1524, so that when Erasmus addressed himself to William Warham he had just taken his definite stand; see also Pfeiffer, p. 19, and note 28 *infra*, where the problem of the danger from the various new sects is touched upon, which danger seemed to Erasmus to be embodied in that of the *Ciceroniani* as much as that of the *Lutherani*.

12. Holbein's first portrait of Erasmus originated, in about 1515, as one of the famous marginalia in Oswald Myconius's private copy (preserved in the Kupferstichkabinett of the Kunstmuseum at Basel); it shows Erasmus seated at a slanting desk, whose flank is inscribed 'Adagia Erasm.' Erasmus, as is well known, criticized his much too youthful appearance in this picture. Young Holbein was, at the time, obviously unaware of the fact that Erasmus worked in a standing position; see Basel, Kupferstichkabinett, Inv. 1662.166, sketch no. 64, and Erwin Treu, *Die Bildnisse des Erasmus von Rotterdam*, Basel, 1959, pp. 40 f. and Figs. 5 and 6. For the text here illustrated, see note 5 *supra*.

13. Here as elsewhere our reproduction is somewhat misleading. It cuts off a few mm on the sides, especially to the right and bottom. I am convinced that the parapet must, originally, have been considerably larger. This presumed stretching of the painting would help to explain the 'almost life-size' appearance spoken of in the older sources. Such a stone balustrade might well have carried an added motto.

fore-edge of this book carries the abbreviated name ERASM. ROTERO.[14]

The sitter's cloak is the *vestimentum clausum*, a kind of ideal balance between the festive academic garb, the dress of the secular clergy and that of the church dignitary attired *in pontificalibus*. It is held together by a carefully tied sash. Variants of this so-called toga with velvet *revers* appear also in Holbein's other Erasmus portraits of the years 1523–1524, but here there is added the miniver, the ceremonial fur of reddish-brown, fine-haired sable (at least I believe it to be the fur of *Mustela zibellina* since its hair is too soft and its hues are too delicate for fox). Generous pieces of it issue from the wide sleeves and cover the wrists. In addition the fur furnishes a full-length lining to the coat. It supplies a touch of subdued elegance which is less in evidence in the other portraits.[15] The face, looking right ahead, is seen, as is the rest of the body, in three-quarter view, turned to the beholder's left. No shirt or jabot is visible, stressing the black solemnity of Erasmus's appearance. One might speak of a riot of blacks. The only precious object shown is a discreet gold ring with a diamond which Erasmus wears on the ring-finger of his left hand.

Behind the figure, at the left, is the pilaster (actually a pair of pilasters placed at right angles to each other) which has given the portrait its name. Its capital is adorned with a typical Renaissance grotesque, a winged mermaid or siren whose double-tail sweeps up in foliate forms. The foil against which Erasmus's head and shoulders appear is furnished by a bottle-green curtain, suspended from a black rod by dark-brown

rings. The pilaster is grey over a reddish underpaint; its capital however shows a somewhat muddy yellow over the same underpaint. Curtain and curtain-rod lack the organization we would expect in an autograph work by Holbein. The actual structure of the wall, partly concealed behind the curtain, remains unintelligible in terms of a groundplan. One gets the impression of its having a cylindrical form. The right of the background is occupied by a small and rather high bookshelf, attached to a receding portion of the wall (Fig. 1a). On this shelf we notice three books and a glass vessel. Two of the books are lying on their sides. The one with a piece of paper stuck in it as a place marker is light red, while its edge is white. The book on top of it, supporting the carafe, is bound in white (either pigskin or parchment) and its edge is of a light-brownish ochre. The small brown leatherbound volume leaning at an angle of about 45° against the glass-carafe has two brown ribbons. It cannot fail to attract attention because it bears two inscriptions. In dainty black capitals there appears on its fore-edge the following distich, whose letters are spaced at irregular intervals, to accommodate the ribbons:

> ILLE EGO IOANNES HOLBEIN, NON FACILE VLLVS
> IAM MICHI MIMVS ERIT, QVAM MICHI MOMVS ERIT.

The leather binding of the same book bears the date .MD.XXIII.

The wall is of an uneven greyish hue; it shows cracks around the bracket supporting the bookshelf which are carefully rendered. The glass bottle, of a particular type to which I shall refer once more, is empty.

When seen in raking light, the silhouette of the figure stands out as if it were a raised island amidst the relatively flat area constituting the background, including pilaster and bookshelf.

Certain passages in the painting seem to have suffered at some point in the past through all too radical cleaning. The shadow part of the jaw looks as if it had been overpainted clumsily in an effort to make up for earlier damage. The craquelure shows it to be a later patchwork. I am not sure that the rather summary brushstrokes highlighting the grey wisps of hair framing the left temple have not also been added by a later hand. A similar, but much more detrimental, repair can be seen all around the fingers of both hands: the shadows have been gone over in oils causing pastose ridges, where Holbein undoubtedly would have worked with unobtrusive glazes (Fig. 1b). Barely visible in our reproduction but quite clear in the original is the pentimento of the right hand. Originally, as indicated by the bluish lines which reveal Holbein's original

14. I should not be surprised if the tome on which Erasmus has placed his hands were once more a copy of the *Adagia* (cf. note 12 *supra*). Here it would be an ornate author's or gift copy of the Basel folio of the year 1523. That book measures 9 × 12 inches. Cf. F. Vander Haeghen, etc., *Bibliotheca Erasmiana*. *Répertoire des œuvres d'Érasme*, I, ii, Gand, 1893, p. 2, and *Overzicht van de werken en uitgaven van Desiderius Erasmus aanwezig in de Bibliotheek der Gemeente Rotterdam*, Rotterdam, 1937, pp. 8 f. The I of ERASM[I] is uncertain; a genitive would help to stress the authorship of the 'Labours of Hercules', not the ownership.

15. The Inventory of Erasmus's belongings lists under 'Cleyder' as first item: 'ein schwartzen Rock mit Marder gefüttert'; see Emil Major, *Erasmus von Rotterdam*, Basel, *s.a.*, 'Anhang X', p. 52. The outer garment worn by Erasmus is the costume of the academics of Italy and England which derived from the modified dress of the secular clergy. The so-called miniver (see the *Great Oxford Dictionary*) constitutes properly speaking two ornamental facings of fur, a fashion which dates back to about 1490, but the fur worn by Erasmus is of the best quality and provides a full lining; cf. W. N. Hargreaves-Mawdsley, *A History of Academical Dress in Europe*, Oxford, 1963, p. 193 and glossary, s.v. 'Miniver'. Another humanist, Justus Lipsius (d. 1606), stipulated on his death-bed that his furred robes (his 'richest and most honoured possession') should be placed at the altar of St. Peter's at Louvain, 'as a symbol of his past glories'; see Jason L. Saunders, *Justus Lipsius . . .*, New York, 1955, p. 56.

design, the hand was more strongly foreshortened, above all the thumb; the ring-finger and pink were more noticeably bent than they are now. The hand was done in a more natural perspective at first and closer to the preparatory sketch for it which is preserved in the Louvre (Fig. 6).[16] Yet, I feel that those pentimenti help to show that the Longford Castle panel cannot have been a copy but must be the original in which Holbein himself had changed the design. The off-side of the pilaster as well as its capital show traces of what I suspect to be nineteenth-century overpaint with a rather coarse craquelure. The crown of Erasmus's *pileus* was once considerably higher. This is clearly indicated by the shadowy bit above its present outline against the curtain.

The weaknesses I have enumerated are almost all of a relatively minor order. I have also stressed in my description—and possibly overly so—the additive character of the picture. This is less noticeable before the original. Here the vivid contrasts and correspondences of ochres, reds, beige passages and a variety of deep blacks, with here and there touches of green and the handsome accents of deep-black lettering, the alternation between glazes and somewhat pastose areas, go far in pulling together those discrepancies. Nevertheless, there are two somewhat disturbing factors: the parapet, by being the most luminous passage in the entire painting, and the mermaid-capital, by being the most plastic one on account of its exaggerated shadows, tend to detract—at least on first acquaintance—from Erasmus's head and hands. Yet after some contemplation the figure itself, and above all the subtle face with its silent mouth and speaking eyes, manages to capture and hold our attention. The figure of Erasmus, who in real life was a tiny man, suggests in our painting monumentality on account of the great simplicity with which it is treated. The relaxed hands act as signposts compelling us to look at the basis of the composition, the parapet and the heavy tome with the Greek letters: ΗΡΑΚΛΕΙΟΙ ΠΟΝΟΙ.

Are we allowed to conclude from the prominence given to the two Greek words that 'The Labours of Hercules' are intended to furnish a title to the painting? In a sense we may answer Yes. There exists in Erasmus's *œuvre*, in the *Adagia* of the year 1508 *et sequentes*, an essay entitled 'Herculei labores.

'Ηράκλειοι πόνοι'. It is one of the dozen or so longish topical essays which Erasmus inserted here and there in his work, full of lively digressions into matters of personal concern to him.[17] The essay is a surprise. Its keynote is the damage done by professional envy which has to resort to baseless criticism on the part of the jealous imitator who has failed in his imitation. Of course, the *catalogue raisonné* of adversities found in Erasmus's letter to William Warham immediately comes to mind. Not every art historian discussing Erasmus's portrait has resisted the temptation to bow to common or horse-sense and to suggest that here we have the great humanist resting from his Herculean Labours. Far from it. The initial of the Greek 'H' in the *Adagia* edition of 1523 at the beginning of the 'Herculei labores', is historiated and shows HERCVLES squeezing the last breath out of ANTEVS. The choice of this scene must have been due to Froben's enthusiasm in having the alphabet-block of a Hercules-initial in stock. It is the *faux pas* which may have misled those consulting early editions of the *Adagia*.[18] For if we take the trouble to read the entire essay,[19] it soon becomes clear that the superhuman and heroic aspects of the ever-victorious *labores* are not under discussion, that 'Hercules and Anteus' are never once mentioned or alluded to, but that Erasmus carefully focuses on one deed only, namely Hercules's fight with the many-headed Hydra of the Lernean Swamp. It is right at the beginning of his essay that Erasmus sounds the keynote on which, I think, the program of Holbein's picture is based: 'Those are said to be "Herculean Labours" which are of such a nature that their author gleans practically no benefit from them, except for a modicum of fame, accompanied by a maximum of Envy' 'Herculei labores dicuntur, qui sunt eiusmodi, ut alijs quidem maximas adferant commoditates,

16. The two sheets of 1523 with studies of Erasmus's hands and face in the Louvre (Cabinet des Dessins, Inv. nos. 18.697 and 18.698) are now adequately reproduced and excellently catalogued by Arlette Calvet in the Catalogue issued by the Ministère des Affaires Culturelles, as 'Dessins du Louvre, Paris, Musée du Louvre', *Le XVIᵉ Siècle Européen*, Paris (October-December), 1965, nos. and Figs. 58 f. See our Fig. 6, showing the sketch of Erasmus's head (b) and right hand (a), being leaf 18.698. See also note 24 *infra*.

17. All of them will be found in English translations in pt. II of Mrs. Phillips's work cited in note 11 *supra*, pp. 169–380.

18. Cf. Froben's edition, Basel, 1523, p. 541. The large initials in this edition, of which the Hercules-Anteus is one, are the somewhat coarse woodcuts by Jacob Faber after Holbein's 'Alphabet with the Pagan and Biblical Scenes'; they had been used by Froben from 1520 onward. I am of course fully aware that on another occasion (1513) Erasmus might speak of the superhuman efforts of getting a new edition of the *Adagia* into shape in a matter of months by saying that it amounted to 'Herculean Labours': 'Porro cum iterum pararem editionem apud Venetos, haud tum quidem ignorabam argumenti suscepti pondus ac difficultatem, sed tamen totum hoc negocium intra menses plus minus octo confectum est, et tantum laborem quantum non vnum requirat Herculem vni homuncioni erat exhauriendum'; taken from the 'Ad Lectorem' for the edition 1515 which went, through someone's *felix culpa*, not to Venice but to Basel, where it fell into the hands of Johannes Froben; see ep. London, January 5, 1513, ed. Allen, I, p. 523.

19. The entire essay is now available in Mrs. Phillips's splendid translation, *op. cit.*, note 11 *supra*, pp. 190–209; *Adagiorum Chiliadis Tertiae Centvria Prima* (unnumbered), ed. Basel, 1523, pp. 541–9.

caeterum autori suo nihil ferme fructus adducant, praeter aliquantulum fame, plurimum inuidiae.'[20] From here Erasmus turns to the Lernean Hydra 'by which symbol the ancients wished to express Envy' 'cujus symbolo veteres inuidiam exprimere uoluisse' (Fig. 7). For this equation Erasmus can lean on the authority of Horace:

> He that engaged the cruel Hydra of horrid repute, in the task with which Fate had charged him, discovered that it was Envy which at the very end had to be subdued.

From the context of the allusion to this, Hercules's second deed, it becomes clear that Horace wishes us to understand that Envy destroys justified fame as is shown, e.g., in the fate of Rome's founding fathers, who were honoured only after their death.[21]

Next, Erasmus specifies what he understands by the kind of labours which deserve the adjective 'Herculean'. They are the ones that consist of bringing to light again the ancient and true letters.[22] If they (i.e. the envious critics) had a try themselves, they would study the learned efforts of others with more indulgence.

There is, of course, nothing two-fisted and heroic about this modern Hercules engaged in this kind of struggle. The hero whom Erasmus has in mind is inactive, myopic, suffering from insomnia and prematurely old. The way in which Erasmus describes him in his *Adagia*—evoking laughter amidst tears—leaves no doubt that it is Erasmus in person. We may, therefore, consider this self-ridicule as probably the first modern humoristic literary self-portrait (1508). It is composed moreover by the man who produced, as far as we know, the first modern humoristic self-portrait in art. Erasmus drew himself with his brachycephalic profile, long nose, thin lips, eyes pinched by myopia and conjunctivitis, in a number of doodles, some of which are reduced to conventional fools' heads while others (Fig. 8) amount to genuine caricatures, done in 1524 or some time earlier. They originated about seventy-five years before caricatured portraits of identifiable persons were *en vogue*. At the same time the self-ridiculing passage which here I shall quote furnished the libretto upon which both Erasmus and Holbein could base their portraits:

> Turn away from all social pleasures, neglect your personal affairs, show no regard for your outward appearance, nor for sufficient sleep or health. Let your eyesight calmly suffer, and thus invite premature *senium*, show disregard for all damage inflicted upon your life so that you will rouse the disdain of every one, invite the envy of the many, and carry away in triumph—as a reward for all your nights of exertion—a few hearty snores.[23]

20. *Adagia* as cited in preceding note, p. 541.
21. 'Diram qui contudit hydram,/Multaque fatali portenta labore subegit,/comperit inuidiam supremo fine domandam'; Horace, *Epistle*, II, i, 10. We find an interesting echo in one of Erasmus's letters where he compares himself and his own situation clearly to St. Jerome fighting heresies: 'Thus it came about that this most holy man had to battle, to the last day of his life, the "hydra" [*excetra*] of Envy' 'His rebus factum est vt sanctissimo viro vsque ad extremum vitae diem pugnandum fuerit cum excetra inuidiae'; Allen, IV, no. 1451, Basel, June 1, 1524, p. 466, to William Warham. Thanks to the *Adagia*, Horace's association of *invidia* with the Hydra takes root among the sophisticated writers of the Renaissance. Boccaccio (*Genealogia deorum gentilium*, XIII, 8 = 'numerosum malum') and Colucio Salutati (*De laboribus Herculis* (1406), III, v, who equates, among others, 'ydra' = 'sophystica', or 'concupiscentia', while Hercules = 'philosophus') treat the Lernean encounter *moraliter* but do not as yet identify the Hydra with Envy. Pierio Valeriano, when he sums up the new ideas in his *Hieroglyphica* (*ed. princeps*, 1556; ed. Lyons, 1602, p. 166), shows that it is anything but commonplace: 'INVIDIA. Nonnvlli ex peritioribus inuidiam per Hydrae speciem significari tradunt, ideoque in nullo alio monstro domitando Herculem magis laborasse . . .' To those initiates belongs Acchille Bocchi, who in his *Symbolicarum quaestionum libri quinque*, Bologna, 1555, III, XC, pp. CLXXXVIII f., shows Hercules battling with the Lernean monster (Fig. 7) under the motto 'Obrvit invidiam non vltio, sed benefacta', the emblem is dedicated to Ercole of Ferrara. Alciati's emblem LXXI 'Inuidia' (1548 ff.) shows, for the benefit of the artists, a hag 'eating her heart out'; in all its brevity it is, as we should expect, full of classical allusions; yet it makes no mention of Hydra or Hercules; it is in some respects a descendant of Giotto's 'inuidia' personified in the Cappella degli Scrovegni all'Arena in Padua. The medieval treatment of the theme of Envy is simply limitless inasmuch as Invidia is one of the seven deadly sins. I have come across only one afterglow of Horace in a medieval proverb (see below). St. Thomas of Aquino treats of 'Invidia' as 'tristitia de bono alterius, in quantum aestimatur diminuere gloriam propriam'; *Summa Theologiae*, Secunda secundae, quaestio XXXVI, *passim*. But the sentiment is classical; cf. Cicero's 'Invidentia est aegritudo ex alterius rebus secundis'; *Tusculan Disputations*, III. Hans Walther, *Proverbia Sententiaeque Latinitatis Medii Aevi*, Göttingen, 1964, lists in nos. 12,741–12,804 some 60 proverbs under 'invidia (etc.)'. Among this formidable array only one seems to be vaguely aware of the passage in Horace; it reads: 'Invidiam nemo domuit, nisi fine supremo'; Codex of St.-Omer, saec. XIII, no. 12,778, *ed. cit.* How original and how modern was the approach of Erasmus

becomes evident if we examine a circumstantial treatise on *defamatio*, the anon. *Purgatorium detractorum saluberrimum*, Cologne, October 23, 1509, which conventionally states: 'detractio est denigratio aliene fame'.
22. 'Quod si ullis hominum laboribus hoc cognominis debetur, ut Herculani dicantur, eorum certe uel maxime debere uidetur, qui in restituendis antiquae, ueraeque literaturae monimentis elaborant'; *Adagia*, ed. 1523, p. 542.
23. 'Abdica te communibus humanae uitae uoluptatibus, neglige rem familiarem, ne parce formae, ne somno, ne ualetudini. Boni consule iacturam oculorum: accerse praematurum senium: contemne uitae detrimentum, ut plurimorum odium in te concites, plurium inuidiam, ut pro tot uigilijs, ronchos aliquot auferas'; *Adagia*, ed. 1523, p. 543. Only the Cynic philosopher, Crates of Thebes, who had given away all his wealth, knew himself free from the Envy of others: 'Aiebat (Crates scil.) se Diogenis ciuem esse, qui nullis inuidiae patebat insidijs. Opes enim ac nominis splendor conciliant [engender] inuidiam'; cf. Erasmus, *Apophtegmatvm ex optimis scriptoribus libri octo*, ed.

Apart from the preparatory sketches which Holbein did of Erasmus's hands in the Longford Castle portrait, the Louvre also possesses a camera-obscura-type silverpoint drawing (more frontally seen than the finished product) which, in faint outline, traces head, and *revers* of the coat (Fig. 6). This sketch is in no way flattered. Erasmus appears gaunt and ailing. We can corroborate this with a verbal characterization of Erasmus of the year 1525, i.e. two years after the portrait was made:

> I've seen him personally. Now he is a dove-grey, dignified, aged man of small and delicate features, garbed in a long blue wide-sleeved coat, held by a sash.
> allda hab ich in [ihn] gesehen von person, nun ain tubgrawer, ersamer, alter und ain klainer und zarter mensch, in ainem langen, blawen, zusamengurten rock mit witen ermlen beklaidt.[24]

This is no longer the lover of festive moods and festive people. The Erasmus of 1523-1524 is disillusioned

through the conflicts with the humanists in Italy, forced against his innermost inclination to take a stand between the equally dissatisfying claims of the adherents of Reformation and Counter-Reformation, the innocent victim of pressures which reached a near-intolerable force around the year 1523 when the preparation of a stream of new publications and re-issues of works of all kinds claimed all his attention.[25]

Antwerp, 1564, p. 538. The adage appears under the heading 'tranquillitas'. See also note 9 *supra*.

I make reference to the remarkable self-caricatures—as yet insufficiently explained and not easy to date—which Erasmus produced as doodles or markers (?) (often where he had scratched out a passage) in the margin of certain manuscripts: MSS. Basel, Universitätsbibliothek C. vi. a. 68 (a gathering of miscellanea from the Amerbach legacy), pp. 143 and 146 (Fig. 8), and A. ix. 56 (i.e. the scholia to the letters of St. Jerome, containing the major part of the caricatures), fol. 18 and others. Our Fig. 8 can be dated with some assurance in the year 1523, the year of Holbein's profile portraits. It comes from the fragment of a scholium to the fourth letter of St. Jerome which appeared in print in 1524. See Erwin Treu, *Die Bildnisse des Erasmus von Rotterdam*, Basel, 1959, Fig. 3 on p. 21. Looking through the two MSS. at Basel, I found at least one instance where Erasmus's caricature is directly related to the text. He shows himself with a drop of liquid suspended from his nose as an old man suffering from a head cold. The text: '*pituita*. humor est superuacuans qui in senibus abundat', C. vi. a. 68, p. 143. For the Basel MSS. and their marginalia see: Fritz Husner, 'Die Handschrift der Scholien des Erasmus von Rotterdam zu den Hieronymusbriefen', *Festschrift Gustav Binz zum 70. Geburtstage* . . ., Basel, 1935, pp. 132–46; Emil Major, *Handzeichnungen des Erasmus von Rotterdam* (Jahresberichte 1932, Historisches Museum), Basel, 1933, pp. 35–44 (a complete iconographic cat. rais. of the 80-odd marginal drawings by Erasmus, illustrated. Of those drawings 23 constitute faces, 34 miscellaneous objects ranging from finger rings via cooking utensils to shoes, and 23 decorative elements, stars, pointing hand, banderoles with various inscriptions); Eduard His, 'Selbstkarikaturen des Erasmus', *Basler Zeitschrift für Geschichte und Altertumskunde*, xlv, 1946, pp. 211–14.

24. Johannes Kessler, as quoted by Emil Major, *Erasmus von Rotterdam*, Basel, *s.a.*, p. 20, and n. 1. I am inclined to disagree with the observation that the portrait sketch of Erasmus (our Fig. 6b) must necessarily have been a later 'tracé de mémoire'; it rather impresses me as a trial drawing (possibly with the aid or experience of the camera obscura) for the pose of the model which incorporates, in all its economy, sharp on-the-spot observation; with this opinion cf., however, the view cited on p. 30 of the splendid catalogue listed in note 16 *supra*.

25. Aided by Fr. Germain Marc'hadour's magnificent *L'Univers de Thomas More. Chronologie critique de More, Érasme, et leur époque (1477–1536)*, Paris, 1963, the student of Erasmus is aware at one glance of the 'rerum omnium vicissitudo' and its steady increase during the years under discussion. *1516*: Erasmus's *annus mirabilis*, brings the first contact with Martin Luther. May 30, *1519*: Erasmus, addressing himself to Luther, pleads for 'tranquillitas studiorum'; he turns against Luther's 'tumultus' (ep. ed. Allen, no. 980). November 13, *1520*: Luther has become, to Erasmus, 'magister erroris ac dux tumultus' (ep. Allen iv, no. 1844). In *1521*: Luther excommunicated (Bull: 'Decet Romanum pontificem'); *eodem anno*: February 16, Erasmus expresses the misery of his day in one sentence: 'O how I loved Hutten's festive spirit which now the Lutheran tempest has snatched away from the Muses!' 'amabam et festiuum Hutteni ingenium: id Lutherana tempestas Musis eripuit!' (ep. Allen iv, no. 1184, p. 443, from Louvain, to Gulielmus Budaeus; for the word 'Lutherana tempestas' see note 9 *supra*, for the Muses, see the 'Gardens of the Muses', note 28 *infra*. See also Werner Kaegi, 'Hutten und Erasmus. Ihre Freundschaft und ihr Streit', *Historische Vierteljahrsschrift*, xxii, 1925, pp. 200–78, 461–514; for Hutten's aversion to Erasmus's cult of 'tranquillity', pp. 270–2). *1523*: the year in which Holbein's Longford Castle portrait originates. It is a year of multiple anxieties. The attacks of the Ciceronians have wounded Erasmus deeply. Those false Ciceronians are to him above all a sect, like that of the *Lutherani*. Erasmus considered the greatest menace of the age the forming of ever-new sects; cf. Walter Rüegg, *Cicero und der Humanismus. Formale Untersuchungen über Petrarca und Erasmus*, Zürich, 1946, esp. pp. 118 f. The pressure exerted upon Erasmus by both *Lutherani* and anti-Lutherans increases, to come to a head in the following year, which sees two new threats, both from the Roman Catholic camp: the theologians of Louvain advise their students to avoid using the *Colloquia* of Erasmus and, end June 1524, the Sorbonne condemns for the first time certain ideas voiced by Erasmus. *1523-4* is also a year of anxieties for the ordinary people. It was known that 16,out of 20 conjunctions prognosticated for 1524 would be in the house of Pisces and therefore cause disastrous floods; cf. Aby Warburg, *Gesammelte Schriften*, ii, Berlin–Leipzig, 1932, pp. 508–11. Erasmus himself to be sure had little patience with the astrologers: 'Let others observe the stars if it pleases; I consider it important that we should search the earth to find what it is that makes us happy or unhappy' 'stellas observent alii, si lubet; ego in terris quaerendum existimo, quod nos felices aut infelices reddat'; ep. no. 1005, August 10, 1519. Yet the broad masses and not few of the intelligentsia were deeply influenced by such prognostications. The fact that in 1523-4 the Reformation made headway in Basel, that in particular Johannes Oecolampadius, once Erasmus's intimus, lectured in German on Theology and that public disputations were allowed on such themes as the right of priests to marry, can only have added to the anxieties besetting Erasmus.

With all this in mind, we must not forget that 1523 was also a year of stupendous productivity and creativity on the part of Erasmus. In 1523 some nine works of his appeared in about thirteen issues either in first editions or in issues radically revised and augmented. I mention, without claim to completeness:

Erasmus stood not alone in his awareness of living in a period which, being torn by strife and the clashing of incompatible ideas, was hostile to all creative impulses. A summing up of those feelings in a few melancholy words we find prominently recorded along the base of the tomb of Pope Hadrian VI (who died September 14, 1523 and was buried, almost ten years after, at S. Maria dell'Anima in Rome): 'Pity, how much depends on the period in which the virtuous intentions of even the best of men are sown' 'Proh dolor, quantum refert in quae tempora vel optimi cuiusque virtus incidat.' Stripped of its negative implications, we are here faced with an early instance of the historical awareness of the particular genius of a particular age.[25a]

*   *   *

JANUARY: a revised and amplified edition of the *Adagia* (Froben), Basel; *Precatio dominica* (in aedibus Conrad. Resch)
FEBRUARY: ed. of Divus Hilarius, *Lucubrationes* (Froben), Basel
MARCH: *Paraphrasis in Evangelium secundum Ioannem* (Froben), Basel
APRIL: *idem*; *Catalogus lucubrationum* (Froben), Basel
AUGUST: *Paraphrasis in Evangelium Lucae* (Froben); *idem* (Th. Volfius), Basel
SEPTEMBER: *Spongia aduersus aspergines Hutteni* [twice issued, 8vo and 4to] (Froben), Basel; *Adagia*, Cologne
OCTOBER: *Spongia*
NOVEMBER: *Adagia* (Robert Estienne), Paris; *Adagiorum epitome* (Io. Bruchenii *opera* ed.) (Simon Cobinaeus), Paris; *Bellum* (Ioannes Cnoblauch), Augsburg
DECEMBER: *Paraphrasis in Evangelium Lucae* (Th. Volfius), Basel

as well as the undated:

De contemptu mundi epistola (Nich. Hillenius); *idem* (Ioannes Soter), Cologne; *Adagiorum epitome* (Simon Colinaeus), Paris; *Bellum*; *Paraphrasis in Evangelium Marci* (Froben); *Precatio dominica* (Froben) & Paris (?).

Apart from these, some twenty-four re-issues of Erasmian writings appeared, some revised by the author. I only mention ten new *Colloquia* among which the incomparable 'Convivium poeticum'; cf. Craig R. Thompson, *The Colloquies of Erasmus*, Chicago and London, 1965, pp. 86–176.
25a. The history of the successive tomb-inscriptions of the Pope is complicated and, as far as I am aware, not completely resolved. The original inscription was more personal: 'Here rests Hadrian VI who considered nothing a greater misfortune than that in his lifetime he had to rule' 'HADRIANVS SEXTVS HIC SITVS EST, QVI NIHIL SIBI INFELICIVS IN VITA DVXIT, QVAM QVOD IMPERARET'. The 'Proh dolor' inscription seems to have graced only the definitive tomb (completed August 11, 1533) which was erected under the aegis of Cardinal Enckevoirt; we cannot be sure whether it was he or Tranquillus Molossus who composed the inscription; see Ludwig von Pastor, *Geschichte der Päpste (1513–1534)*, IV, 2, Freiburg i. Br., 1907, pp. 148–50 and esp. n. 2 on pp. 149 f., and p. 87, where it is suggested that the tenor of the inscription goes back to Hadrian himself. In Gracián's *Oráculo manual y arte de prudencia* (*c.* 1647) the sentiment is echoed in §20: 'Fueron dignos algunos de mejor siglo, que no todo lo bueno triunfa siempre' 'Some men have deserved a better age . . .', a maxim that deeply impressed Schopenhauer; cf. ed. B. L. Walton, *The Oracle* (Everyman's no. 401), London, 1963, note on p. 281. For the influence of this concept, cf. J. Kamerbeek, *Tenants et aboutissants de la notion 'couleur locale'*, Utrecht, 1962.

As we turn to the second inscription in the picture, we find that once more the Envy-theme is sounded:

ILLE EGO IOANNES HOLBEIN, NON FACILE VLLVS
IAM MICHI MIMVS ERIT, QVAM MICHI MOMVS ERIT

'That one am I, Johannes Holbein; no one will ever be my imitator as easily as he will be my denigrator.' The wording is new and, I believe, made *ad hoc* and not only because the artist's name has been woven into it. The sentiment, on the other hand, is old. It can be traced back to the older Holbein (1513) and from there to classical antiquity. The inscription CARPET ALIQUIS CITIUS [CICIVS] QUAM IMITABI[T]UR—'it is easier for anyone to belittle than to imitate', is found on one of the two pilasters framing the 'Madonna Montenuovo' by Holbein the Elder (which, owned by Baronesse G. Bentinck-Thyssen, is as far as I know preserved in the Collection Thyssen at Lugano). Thus we may safely assume that the composer of our distich revived a tradition of the Holbeins.

At first sight the distich found in the Longford Castle portrait has—prosodically speaking—little to recommend it. The first line does not scan properly. The 'a' in *facile*, as Professor Panofsky was kind enough to point out to me, is short and the final 'e' of this word would be elided by the first vowel in *ullus*. As to the exact legibility of the letters and words as well as punctuation marks in the painting as it stands before us today, there can be no doubt except for the initial letter of the second line. It could be TAM but looks more like IAM.[26] Consequently we must reckon with

26. E. Panofsky, in a letter of September 9, 1965; in a second letter, of September 24, Professor Panofsky deals with the curious 'erit . . . erit' which, in my ignorance, I had considered another flaw in Erasmus's distich: ' . . . the double *erit* is a legitimate refinement. There is a distich translated by Mörike which reads:

"Si, nisi quae forma poterit te digna videri,
Nulla futura tua est, nulla futura tua est.
(Wisse nur, dass, wenn ohne durch Schönheit
                    dich zu verdienen,
Keine die deinige wird, keine die deinige wird.)" '

Dr. I. Grafe kindly informs me that these lines are found in Ovid (or Pseudo-Ovid), *Heroides sive Epistulae, Sappho ad Phaonem*, XV, 39–40.
One is also reminded of Heinrich Heine's 'Und da keiner von den beiden/Wollte, dass der andere zahle,/Zahlte keiner von den beiden.'
Erasmus, in his poetry and in that of others, was, as can be shown, most critically conscious of correct quantity and of prosodic refinements; ample testimony is found in the 'Convivium poeticum' of the year 1523 and in Erasmus's own verse; for the latter see C. Reedijk, *The Poems of Desiderius Erasmus*, Leyden, 1956, p. 80 and *passim*.
When on August 23, 1965, I examined the painting, I was astonished to find that the two lines of the 'Ille ego' distich

the possibility that Erasmus (whose confusion when it came to names and their spelling was as notorious in an age which on the whole preferred to render names phonetically, as his acriby was keen and alerted when it came to dealing with prosody) may well have written Holbein's name, as he did on other occasions, OLPEIVS. Such atrocious spelling would have somewhat improved the scanning:

ILLE EGO IOANNES OLPEIVS, NON FACILE VLLVS.

It would have been understandable enough if Holbein, on the other hand, casting aside for a moment his innate respect for humanistic schooling, might in the end have preferred to change back to the proper spelling of his family name at the sacrifice of a tolerable meter. Here we may sympathize with the wish of the artist to be identifiable to the world at large.[27] As we ponder this somewhat difficult second inscription in our painting, two welcome data stand unassailably firm: the challenge to the envious critic and the attempt at classical verse. The former makes the inscription subsidiary to the message contained in the words ΗΡΑΚΛΕΙΟΙ ΠΟΝΟΙ. The latter, i.e. the fact that Erasmus cast the inscription into verse, points for his source of inspiration at Pliny's *Naturalis historia*, Book XXXV, 63. Pliny relates how Zeuxis of Herakleia made

> an athlete and he took such pleasure from the painting that he inscribed a verse underneath it which from then on has become famous to the effect that 'it is easier to envy someone than to imitate him'.

fecit . . . et athletam. adeoque in illo sibi placuit ut versum subscriberet, celebrem ex eo, 'invisurum aliquem facilius quam imitaturum'.

In spite of certain misgivings, I am inclined to continue regarding Erasmus as the *spiritus rector* of the second inscription. If, by using it, Erasmus transformed Holbein into Zeuxis, he turned himself, at the same time, into the 'Athlete of the Spirit'.[28] This transposition, apart from being flattering to both artist and model, fully agreed with the transformation of Hercules fighting the Hydra into Erasmus strenuously resisting the unfounded criticism of his enemies.

Apart from the verse-form, as a hint at taking Pliny's report literally, there occurs a verbal echo. Pliny's

28. See J. Overbeck, *Die antiken Schriftquellen zur Geschichte der bildenden Künste bei den Griechen*, Leipzig, 1868, no. 1648, p. 311; see also *ibid.*, no. 1645, p. 310, which relates on the authority of Plutarch (*De glor. Athen.*, 2) that 'Apollodorus of Athens used to inscribe on his portraits: "It is easier to exercise criticism than to imitate"' 'Ἀ. ὁ ζωγράφος ἀνθρώπων . . . μωμήσεταί τις μᾶλλον ἢ μιμήσεται.
For the commonness of the verbal pattern at the back of 'mimus–Momus', 'invisurum–imitaturum', see also the 'mirari–laudare' pair in the fourth-century passage cited in note 9 *supra*. Erasmus's *De libero arbitrio* (see note 11 *supra*) appeared in print September, 1524. That at this decisive point in his life Erasmus felt himself to be an athlete in his fight against Luther becomes evident from a letter to John Fisher, written on the same day on which he addressed William Warham: 'Thus my fates willed it that in my old day I should be made a gladiator, having been a musician' 'Sic erat in fatis meis, vt hoc aetatis ex musico fierem gladiator'; Basel, September 4, 1524, ed. Allen, no. 1489, p. 538. In Patristic Latinity the title athlete could refer to the Christian martyr. Erasmus may therefore have had in mind the *arena* in which the Christian martyr suffered; he may have thought of the 'agones, in quibus ipsi coronamur' (Tertullian, *De spectaculis*, Cyprian, *Ep.* 10, 4) or of the kind of noble fight celebrated in general (Aurelius Prudentius Clemens's *Psychomachia*). The opposite of the arena of the gladiator are the gardens of the Muses: 'I was only too well aware of how inept I would be in the gladiatorial arena, having spent all my time in the most delectable gardens of the Muses' 'non ignorabam quam essem ineptus harenae gladiatoriae, semper in amoenissimis Musarum ortis versatus'; to Henry VIII, Basel, September 6, 1524, ed. Allen, no. 1493, p. 541. On or shortly after September 6, 1524, Erasmus dispatched to England a pouch containing at least eight important letters—Allen, v, nos. 1486–94—which, of course, are filled with the same emotions and sentiments that characterized the letter to William Warham. For the technicalities of mailing in one so-called budget, cf. Allen's introductory remarks to no. 1486, p. 532; in this first letter Erasmus speaks of his own boldness in having published the *diatribe*, 'aedidi libellum De libero arbitrio, facinus audax in Germania'; Basel, September 2, 1524. In the letter to William Warham, Erasmus states: 'A Lutheranorum [h]arena lubens abstinuissem'; p. 535. See also note 11 *supra*. Colin Eisler, 'The Athlete of Virtue. The Iconography of Asceticism', *De Artibus Opuscula XL*, New York, 1961, pp. 82–97, has shown that even in classical times the athlete might be regarded as the embodiment of virtue and asceticism. Erasmus ideally represents 'the true athlete of the commands of Christ' who, in the words of Basil the Great, 'was distinguished by leanness of body and the pallor produced by the exercise of continency' 'nam virtus in infirmitate perficitur'; see Eisler, n. 47 and *passim*.

were completely intact and that the letters—one by one—were painted in flawless calligraphy. This is a mystery to me since I understand that the painting was merely varnished in preparation for the Basel exhibition of 1960. I have been unable to learn when and by whom the panel was cleaned the last time. There does not seem to exist an X-ray of it, nor truly good photographs.
It was Alfred Woltmann, whose *Holbein und seine Zeit*, Leipzig, 1874[2], p. 88, drew my attention to the Elder's 'Carpet aliquis' inscription. Since, however, his reference is anything but clear, I wish to express gratitude to Dr. Günther Heinz of the Gemäldegalerie im Kunsthistorischen Museum at Vienna who referred me to Fig. 4 of the Catalogue *Die Malerfamilie Holbein in Basel*, Basel, 1960, where the inscription is tolerably visible; see also Norbert Lieb and Alfred Stange, *Hans Holbein der Ältere, s.l.* [1960], Cat. nos. 35 f., p. 70, Fig. 109.
27. The authority for the OLPEIVS spelling is Erasmus's letter to Johannes Faber, Basel, November 21, 1523, ed. Allen, v, no. 1397, p. 349: 'Ex tua salutatione, quam mihi per Olpeium misisti, melius habui; erat enim accurata et veniebat ab amico et per hominem amicum.' See also *Opvs Epistolarvm Des. Erasmi Roterod.*, XII, Oxford, 1958, 'Index III', s.v. 'Holbein, Olpeius'. If, as I suppose it did, the Longford Castle painting bore the distich from the beginning, it would be Holbein's first signed painting.

facilius turns into Erasmus—Holbein's *facile ullus*. The differences on the other hand are great. Pliny introduces Envy *expressis verbis*. Erasmus disguises his message in the *mimus–Momus* pair of words. *Mimus*, of course, stands for imitation. *Momus*, a Greek word which, as Erasmus points out, means 'reprehension', here takes on the meaning of Envy and Criticism personified, much in the same way in which Erasmus expresses 'silence' with the word *Harpocrates*. Borrowing from a dialogue of the newly-discovered Lucian (one of Erasmus's favourites), Erasmus narrates in another part of the *Adagia*[29] how Minerva, Neptune and Vulcan competed with one another in the making of artificial contrivances. The three divinities summoned Momus (who himself was utterly incapable of producing any kind of artifice) and requested that he should act as their 'arbiter certaminis, et artis expensor'. In Vulcan's contribution—he had constructed a human being—Momus expressed disappointment because the *artifex* had failed to insert a window in man's breast through which the *antrum* containing the human heart could be observed.[30]

*   *   *

29. *Chiliadis Primae Centuria V*, lxxiiiij, ed. 1523, pp. 168 f., *s.t.* 'Momo satisfacere, & similia'. The story comes from Lucian's *Hermotimus* (chap. 20).
30. Cf. P. J. Vinken, 'H. L. Spiegel's *Antrum Platonicum*. A Contribution to the Iconology of the Heart', *Oud-Holland*, LXXV, 1960, pp. 125–42. For 'Momos', see W. Kroll's meagre entry in Pauly-Wissowa, *Real-Encyclopädie der classischen Altertumswissenschaft*, XXXI, Stuttgart, 1933, col. 42, curiously omitting the key passage in Cicero's *Ad Atticum*, v, 20, 6: 'in quo laboras, ut etiam Ligurino μῶμον satisfaciamus', ed. Loeb Library, I, p. 392. Needless to say Erasmus, in the article cited in the preceding note, has this passage. See also K. Tümpel, 'Momos', in W. H. Roscher, *Ausführliches Lexikon der griechischen und römischen Mythologie*, cols. 3117–19.
Nobody will deny, least of all Erasmus himself, that there exists an inner affinity between Erasmus and Momus (see also his article cited in the preceding note). Of course, we shall never know whether the Longford Castle painting—rigid and contrived, compared to the portraits in Basel and Paris—was the result of stern directives given by the model, who took the supremacy of the word for granted even though in the arts he was a rank amateur; see J. Huizinga, *Erasmus*, Haarlem, 1936, where in n. 1 on p. 17 the references to Erasmus's juvenile endeavours as a painter are collected, and Emil Major, 'Handzeichnungen des Erasmus von Rotterdam' (Jahresberichte Historisches Museum), Basel, 1932, pp. 35 f., citing Houbraken's *Groote Schouwburgh*. Such an assumption—casting Erasmus in the role of Momus—has much in its favour. It would invest the distich with a humorously self-criticizing hint and, while it was soothing for the artist's pride, it would remain intelligible only to the initiates. Martin Luther in his *Table-Talk* chided Erasmus with words of uncommon perspicacity, provided we remove from them the polemical undertones. In the first half of the 1530's he observed: 'Erasmus momus. Erasmus verus est momus. Omnia ridet ac ludit, totam religionem ac Christum, atque ut hoc melius praestet, dies noctesque excogitat vocabula amphibola et ambigua, ut eius libri etiam a Turca legi possint' 'Erasmi Weise oder Ingenium. Erasmus ist ein rechter Momus, der Alles spottet, auch die ganze Religion und Christum. Und auf dass ers deste bass thun könne, erdenkt er Tag und Nacht

I trust that by now the intention of the *circulus methodicus* of my argument will have become clear: Erasmus sends his portrait to William Warham, and he announces—whether intentionally or not we do not know—the program of Holbein's work, which is keynoted: Envy. The title or motto of the portrait points at Hercules's superhuman fight against Envy, personified in the Hydra. The second inscription not only corroborates the Envy-theme but in doing so elaborates it by proclaiming Holbein as a victim of envious critics in his admirable role of the 'new Zeuxis' who paints the 'Athlete of the Spirit', and that is of course the Erasmus of *De libero arbitrio*. Letter and portrait announced by it are obviously in close interconnection, q.e.d. The program of the painting at Longford Castle seems to be utterly consistent, in spite of its composite character. The second inscription strengthens the main title by sounding the same theme. I have been unable to trace any actual cause for protest against critics and imitators which might have annoyed Holbein at that time and which might have resulted in the need for such a defensive inscription, except for one source: Erasmus himself. We are free to speculate on the possibility of Erasmus apologizing, in a half pedantic, half humorous way as it were, for the role of Momus he had played to the *artifex* Holbein when he tried to impose upon him the rather cerebral program for this portrait. The sentiment of the Holbein inscription may well have been an inheritance from Holbein the Elder. At any rate, with the 'Ille ego Johannes Holbein' Erasmus had hit upon a felicitous formula by which he could reward, and possibly console, this *artifex satis elegans*, similarly to the way in which he would, in the year 1528, celebrate and comfort Albrecht Dürer (after some gentle prodding by Pirckheimer) when he called him the 'new Apelles'.[31] To Erasmus and his

Wankelwort, dass seine Bücher auch können von Türken gelesen werden'; recorded by B. Dietrich and N. Medler, ed. *D. Martin Luthers Werke. Tischreden (1531–1546)*, I, Weimar, 1912, no. 811, pp. 390 f.
31. For the 'New Apelles', see Erwin Panofsky, ' "Nebulae in Pariete"; Notes on Erasmus' Eulogy on Dürer', *Journal of the Warburg and Courtauld Institutes*, XIV, 1951, pp. 34–41. Certain epithets are there to be distributed more or less at will. That of 'Apelles' suited Dürer so well because he was not only painter but also art theoretician. If we can trust Christopher Scheurl, Dürer was addressed by the Italians of Venice and Bologna not only as 'alter Apelles' but also as 'Zeuxis'. The latter, because his dog had been observed kissing his master's self-portrait which Dürer had done with the aid of a mirror; this made him 'sicut Zeuxis, teste Plinii'; *Libellus de laudibus Germaniae et ducum Saxoniae*, Leipzig, 1508, Hans Rupprich, *Dürer. Schriftlicher Nachlass*, I, Berlin, 1956, pp. 290 f. For the conventional identification of Renaissance artists with those of classical antiquity, see also Ernst Gombrich, 'Landscape Painting', *Gazette des Beaux-Arts*, 1953, I, pp. 345 f.
The 'Ille ego' with which the distich begins, is a very typical *incipit* of Roman funerary inscriptions revived in the Renaissance, quasi hailing the passer-by in order to inform him as to

contemporaries, such verbal eulogy would have suggested uncommon generosity. The repeated not-naming of Holbein when discussing his own portraits would at the time it happened have been perfectly normal. Holbein after all was to Erasmus by no means an 'amicus' but merely a 'homo amicus'.[32]

*   *   *

The evocation of classical antiquity is so obviously present in the Longford Castle portrait that one is apt to set it aside without further commentary. A few observations have to be made nevertheless. Both inscriptions have something remarkably in common in that they both point back at the most venerable phase of antiquity as it could be found in Greek culture. This consideration helps to draw attention to the aspect of Erasmus's portrait which has been called representative. Book and inscription, on which Erasmus rests his hands with so much solemn emphasis, clearly speak of the rehabilitation of not just antiquity in general but they reveal the new stress which Erasmus had placed on Greek rather than Latin letters as the fountainhead of all culture. What Erasmus truly aimed at, however, was not an investigation, let alone a revival of Greek literary sources for their own sake, not even in the *Adagia* whose entries invariably begin with the Greek proverb; rather he stressed over again that he was anxious to bring about a conciliation between *humanae literae* and *literae sacrae*.[33]

The representative character of the painting was not the result of mere pride of achievement. Erasmus's portrait—like almost every fifteenth- and sixteenth-century portrait—was designed as a forceful move against the new menace of Death and concomitant Oblivion. Below I shall discuss the fact that also compositionally the Longford Castle portrait could be called a painted monument which was designed—above all—to make manifest for all times that which was immortal about its model, the *dignitas Erasmiana quae non moritur*.[34] Some of the inherent magic of

such a monument reflects necessarily also on its maker. Apart from the inscription, naming and extolling Johannes Holbein, there is in the painting an impressive allusion to the artist's meritorious contribution to the revival of classical learning. The capital of the pilaster, in spite of its obvious Renaissance quality, is an intentional quotation from Vitruvius and as such as bookish a quotation as that of the 'Labours of Hercules'. Holbein, as has been shown, copied the mermaid capital from a print, showing a Tuscan column, which served to illustrate the latest, most sumptuous and exciting edition of Vitruvius yet to appear: Como, 1521. The woodcut (Fig. 9) was designed by the Bramante disciple Cesare Cesariano (1483–1543). Cesariano, illustrator as well as translator into Italian of the *De architectura libri X*, was an Erasmian figure in the sense that he too strove to search for the roots of antiquity in both the Greek and the Egyptian (hieroglyphic) past.[35]

*   *   *

identity and state in life of the deceased; cf. Richmond Lattimore, *Themes in Greek and Latin Epitaphs*, Urbana, 1962, pp. 288 f. and *passim*. Compare Ovid's similar use of 'ille ego' in his *Tristia*, IV, 10.

32. Cf. the passage from Erasmus's letter, quoted in note 27 *supra*; this distinction has been observed by Aloïs Gerlo, *Érasme et ses portraitistes*, Brussels [1950], n. 10 on p. 66 and p. 42.

33. For this, cf. Pfeiffer's *Studie*, cited in note 11 *supra*, and H. C. Porter, *Reformation and Reaction in Tudor Cambridge*, Cambridge, 1958, pt. I, chap. ii, 'Erasmus in Cambridge', pp. 21–40.

34. See in general W. S. Heckscher, *Rembrandt's Anatomy*, New York, 1958, chap. XVI, for the influence of funerary monuments on portrait paintings. Also see notes 53–55 *infra*. For the *dignitas quae non moritur*, see Ernst K. Kantorowicz, *The King's Two Bodies*, Princeton, 1957, esp. pp. 423 f. The art work itself could be considered immortal because it went from

generation to generation—'ars enim transfertur ab homine in hominem et propterea ars non moritur'.

35. [L. Vitruvius Pollio, *De architectura libri X*] *Di Lvcio Vitruuio Pollione de Architectura libri dece* [sic] *traducti de latino in vulgare affigurati: commentati & con mirando ordine insigniti: per il quale facilmente potrai trovare la multitudine de li abstrusi & reconditi vocabuli a li soi loci & in epsa tabula con summo studio exposti & enucleati ad immensa utilitate de ciascuno studioso & beniuolo di epsa opera* (Gotardvs de Ponte; dedicated to Leo X; privilege of Francis I, June 5, 1521, at Milan; Colophon: 'Impressa nel amoena & delecteuola citate de Como M.D.XXI') (July 15), Como, 1521. Cf. Leonardo Olschki, *Geschichte der neusprachlichen wissenschaftlichen Literatur*, II, Leipzig, etc., 1922, p. 203, Heinrich Koch, *Vom Nachleben des Vitruv* (Deutsche Beiträge zur Altertumswissenschaft 1), Baden-Baden, 1951, pp. 30–33, Erik Forssman, *Säule und Ornament*, Stockholm, 1956, pp. 49, 56, and Rudolf Wittkower, *Architectural Principles in the Age of Humanism*, London, 1962, pp. 13–15. For the discovery (and illustrated demonstration) of Holbein's indebtedness for the capital of the pilaster, credit must go to Heinrich Alfred Schmid, *Hans Holbein der Jüngere*, Tafelband I, Basel, 1948, pp. 100 f. and Fig. 26. The woodcut which shows a column graced with the mermaid-siren-capital (here a male figure) (Fig. 9) occurs as illustration of Book IV (chap. vii) on fol. LXIII [the numbering, incidentally, is chaotic]; it bears the inscription 'Columna Thuscanica'. Three folios further down we find the hieroglyphic signs which Ludwig Volkmann, *Bilderschriften der Renaissance*, Leipzig, 1923, publishes as Fig. 22 on p. 33. The Vitruvius edition, Como, 1521, thanks to Cesariano's initiative, helped to usher in the new and deepened concept of classical antiquity in that here, for the first time in a printed publication with illustrations, Renaissance hieroglyphs were introduced as part of a scholarly effort. Cf. Volkmann, pp. 32 f. Seen in retrospect, Erasmus stood in the forefront of those who prepared the field for *ars emblematica* [cf. also notes 56 f. *infra*]. As early as 1508 he had written a hieroglyphic-emblematic article, the 'Festina lente', for his *Adagia* in which he explained Aldus Manutius's signet: anchor and dolphin; see M. M. Philiips, *op. cit.*, in note 11 *supra*, pp. 117–90. That art works and *tituli* as adornments of house and garden played an important part in the aesthetic existence of Erasmus and his fellow humanists, has been stressed by Craig R. Thompson in his Introduction to the 'Convivium religiosum' (1522), *The Colloquies*, Chicago and London, 1965, p. 47; see

The various books with their inscriptions, the pilaster and the curtain as well as the carafe, constitute the equipment of what Erasmus himself used to call his 'nest' or 'beehive'—*nidus, nidulus, alvearium*.[36] They are, taken one by one, his professional attributes. It was, however, above all the golden ring in which a diamond was set which was meant to stress in the first place the *dignitas* of the model and to show in the second place to the initiates that Erasmus stood under the magic protection of a *gemma* which was particularly suited to ward off the kind of aggression that lies at the programmatic basis of this painting. Among princes of the church and of the realm,[37] Erasmus rated in many respects as an equal. He was being honoured, as was customary among princes, by a profusion of gifts of a precious and expensive kind which invariably were keepsakes with associative values. Favourites among such princely gifts for princely

recipients were finger rings. The magic quality of rings infiltrated heraldry. The gold ring with diamond appears in the heraldic signs of the d'Este and Medici clans. Through the inventories we can trace, even today, some thirty individual rings which once belonged to Erasmus's *dactyliotheca*.[38] Among them we find with near certainty the Longford Castle ring, which is listed in Erasmus's *Nachlass* as 'ein guldin ring mit dem Dyamant'.[39] This ring had come to Erasmus in the year 1519 from England as a *mnemosynon* from Cardinal Lorenzo Campeggio (1472–1539). It had bestowed upon Erasmus a special honour because the Cardinal had removed this ring from his own hand—'anulum quem digitis tuis detractum misisti'. Erasmus on receiving the ring found elegant words to describe the intrinsic value which the gift possessed in his eyes, words which Joseph might have used when thanking the Pharaoh: 'The fiery radiance of the gold will forever be an emphatic symbol of your wisdom as a Cardinal, while the diamond's amenable light shall signify to me your glory, ageless forever.'[40] Apart from the exchange of such courtesies, ring and diamond conveyed certain symbolical meanings applicable to almost anyone who

also, for Geoffrey Tory's proto-emblematic *Aediloquium*, Paris, 1530, 'Emblem, Emblembuch', *Reallexikon zur deutschen Kunstgeschichte*, v, 1959, col. 151. If for a moment I may play Momus to Mrs. Phillips's *apparatus criticus*: on p. 176 she fails to indicate that the Chaeremon cited is most likely Francesco Colonna, author of the *Hypnerotomachia*, Venice, 1499, while on p. 175 she does not identify the *Hieroglyphica* of Horapollo. How deeply and how seriously Erasmus was imbued with hieroglyphic writing has been shown by Giehlow and Volkmann; see the latter's *op. cit.*, pp. 71–74.
In the second decade of the sixteenth century, the initiates among the lovers of Antiquity began to turn to Vitruvius with ever-increasing enthusiasm. In the North, Dürer was one of his proponents. Dürer certainly was right—in so far as the Carolingian epoch had evinced a very lively interest in Vitruvius—when on October 17, 1520, he recorded in his *Diary*: 'Zu Ach had ich gesehen die proportionirten sewln mitt ihren guten capiteln von porfit, grün und rot, und gossenstein, die Carolus von Rom [*sic*] dahin hat bringen lassen und do ein flicken. Diese sind wercklich nach Vitruvius' schreiben [libri III and IV] gemacht'; ed. Hans Rupprich, *Dürer. Schriftlicher Nachlass*, I, Berlin, 1956, p. 159, and H. Koch, pp. 36–38. That Vitruvius himself was against the use of *grotesche* by his contemporaries occupied the minds of the theoreticians of the Renaissance. It dampened in no way the enthusiasm with which artists appropriated matters such as Holbein's mermaid which, in the words of Vitruvius, 'nec sunt nec fieri possunt nec fuerunt'; VII, v, 4 (referring, however, to painted extravaganzas). For the art theoretical problems see Allan Ellenius, *De arte pingendi*, Uppsala and Stockholm [1960], p. 125; see also Forssman's *Säule* cited in note 48 *infra*.
36. 'De cubiculo tantum optem nidum aliquem probe defensum a ventis, et foco luculento' and 'alvearium aliquod tepidum [heated] in quod me condam hac bruma', see H. C. Porter, *Reformation and Reaction*, Cambridge, 1958, p. 30, nn. 4 and 5 —both being references to the winter 1511 at Cambridge. For the composition of the 'nest' see note 52 *infra*. See also W. S. Heckscher, *Shakespeare and His Nest of Clay*, Utrecht, 1965, n. 5 on p. 4. A woodcut of the year 1530 shows Erasmus at work, dictating to Gilbertus Cognatus in his study at Basel; see Emil Major, *Erasmus*, Basel, *s.a.*, Fig. 10.
37. Erasmus's letter to William Warham stresses his favourable position in regard to Pope as well as kings: 'Clemens septimus misit honorificum Breve...Regum amicitiam hactenus alui. Rex Galliarum Franciscus incredibili est in me affectu...Amat ac fauet Ferdinandus...Polonia mea est...' *ep. cited* in note 1, p. 535.

38. Cf. (a) the Inventory of Erasmus's rings, etc., *s.t. Elenchus pecunie presentis, anulorum et similium, Erasmi Roterodami, Nono Aprilis An.* 1534 (Freiburg im Breisgau) which forms 'Anhang VII' of Emil Major's *Erasmus of Rotterdam*, Basel, *s.a.*, pp. 38–40, P.S.A., 'Documents and Records, I, Erasmus's Money and Rings in 1534', *The Bodleian Quarterly Record*, II, 14, 1917, pp. 143 f., and (b) the Inventory made after Erasmus's death by the notary Adalbert Saltzmann, Basel, July 22, 1536, MS. Basel, Universitätsbibliothek C. VI, a. 71, fol. 102–6, Major, 'Anhang X', pp. 52–66.
39. Emil Major, cited in the preceding notes, 'Anhang X', p. 54 and n. 63 on p. 63.
40. The Cardinal wrote to Erasmus on July 4, 1519, from London: '...suscipies vnaque pignoris loco adamanta anulo inclusum, his literis insertum, quem mei μνημόσυνον tenebis'; only ten days later, Erasmus replied from Louvain: 'caeterum anulus quem digitis tuis detractum [alluding to Genesis xli:42] ceu quoddam [note that *pignus*, as Campeggio uses it in his letter, may also mean 'relic'] amicitiae nostrae μνημόσυνον, imo si tuis verbis vtendum est, fraternae charitatis pignus ad me misisti, adeo gratus est animo meo vt recusaturus sim vnum illum vel cum vniversis Attali [III, king of Pergamum, hence *attalica* = splendid garments, etc., worked with gold thread] gazis commutare. Igneus auri fulgor mihi tuae sapientiae prorsus Cardinaliciae symbolum semper erit, et adamantis gratissima lux nunquam antiquandam nominis tui gloriam repraesentabit'; cf. Major, *Erasmus*, cited in note 38 *supra*, n. 63 on p. 63, and ep. Allen, IV, no. 995, p. 6, and no. 996, p. 7.
Lorenzo Campeggio (Bologna 1472–1539 Rome) was in the year 1524 at the height of his prestige in England, a favourite of Henry VIII. Although an alien with a foreign law degree, he was allowed to sit as a judge with Wolsey, to hear the divorce suit of the King against Catherine of Aragon (1533); equally amazing, in 1524, Campeggio received the bishopric of Salisbury. For Erasmus to wear this particular ring in that year would therefore not only have impressed the Primate of England but other influential people in that country—until 1534 when Campeggio was booted out unceremoniously. See *Dictionary of National Biography*, VIII, London, 1886, p. 398.

wore such a ring, and besides certain specific qualities of a significance restricted to the few. Generally speaking 'adamas', in the words of the seventeenth-century symbolist Philippus Picinelli, 'durat [or: ornat] et lucet' (Fig. 10). The diamond, by being indestructible, served to express perseverance and, by being luminous, stood for the splendour of Divine Wisdom.[41] The ring, by being a ring, FINEM NESCIT, and thereby symbolizes True Virtue, whereas the souls of the just may be compared to the gold of which the ring is made, for they too are tested in the furnace by the Lord— 'tamquam aurum in fornace probauit illos'. More specifically taken, the apotropaeic qualities of the ring with diamond are particularly applicable to Erasmus's situation as I have tried to sketch it. In Gabriello Symeoni's *Dialogo pio et speculativo* (Lyons, 1560), the ring with diamond is mentioned as a sign of nobility and constancy amidst adversities.[42] Similarly, its talismanic power may help to secure the courageous independence of mind amidst the onslaughts of Fortuna. Thus Pierio Valeriano in the XLIst book of his *Hieroglyphica* (1553) claims that 'whoever wears a diamond sees his mind and spirit, on account of the diamond's reputedly inherent divine quality, liberated from all senseless fear so that he is capable of holding his own even against ruthless Fortuna' 'quinetiam id insitum diuinitus habere fertur Adamas, vt mentem animamque gestantis vano metu liberet, vt superbae etiam fortunae responsare suadeat'.[43]

*   *   *

The only item which remains to be discussed is the carafe-like vessel of glass on the bookshelf (Fig. 1a). It is of course a commonplace item compared to the rest. At home in every artist's workshop as in every reasonably well-to-do citizen's dwelling, it might serve to contain water, wine, or any other liquid. The art historian cannot fail to associate it, especially when as here it is empty, with a powerful theological symbol which—far beyond Erasmus's time—featured in painted scenes of the Annunciation. In such contexts it is the meaningful decanter, whose glass-walls catch and then release a ray of sunlight as it passes through them without depriving the light of its substance or suffering change themselves, which simile furnishes a symbolical hint at the Madonna's unimpaired Virginity. In the words of Picinelli: 'Bombylius crystallinus, solarem lucem in sinu suo recipiens, iterumque ex se transmittens, epigraphen sustinet ILLAESOS TRANSFUSA PER ARTUS [i.e. transmitted through unimpaired limbs].'[44]

While a disguised hint at virginity would not actually militate against the *raison d'être* of a carafe in a portrait of Erasmus, I believe that we should scrutinize closely his actual need for a carafe of this kind. It has been suggested that the carafe, so prominently displayed, might have been a hint at Erasmus's inordinate love of Burgundian wine (Erwin Treu). This I believe to be a perfectly reasonable suggestion. Erasmus's letter of September 4, 1524 began with the announcement that his portrait was *en route* and that it was meant to serve as a remembrance for the event that he should be summoned by the Lord. He continued by saying that he had been ill in the month of April, suffering from a cold. No sooner had he recovered than he had to endure an attack of gallstones, which was so severe that he actually hoped for an end to all this suffering. 'But now,' he adds, 'I feel more comfortable.'[45] It was the discomfort of such gallstone attacks which Erasmus had learned to alleviate and, as he believed, to actually overcome by consuming quantities of *vinum Burgundiacum*. In a letter to Marcus Laurinus, Erasmus describes how, at the beginning of 1523, he had, more or less against his will, accepted a quantity of red Burgundy from Nicolaus Diesbach (at the time *episcopus designatus* of Basel). At first the wine did not appeal to Erasmus's palate. However, the night that followed pleaded for its true character. His stomach was restored so quickly that he seemed reborn as a different human being—'vt mihi viderer renatus in alium hominem'.[46] In the same letter, Erasmus waxes increas-

41. Ph. Picinelli, *Mundus symbolicus*, ed. and tr. Augustinus Erath, Cologne, 1687, XII, ii, 20, p. 679. The authority is Isidorus of Seville, *Etymologiae*, XVI, 13, 2. 'The Smith holding the Diamond in Iron Tongs' appeared in *c.* 1388 in Franciscus de Retza's *Defensorium inviolatae virginitatis*, 55, as proof of Mary's perpetual virginity.
42. 'L'anello col Diamante conferma pure la nobiltà & constanza dell'huomo nelle cose auerse, sicome durissimo è il Diamante contro a ogni violenza . . .' G.S., *Dialogo pio et speculatiuo, con diuerse sentenze latine & volgari*, Lyons, 1560, p. 227.
43. Picinelli, XV, iii, 20, p. 16. For the gold, cf. *Liber Sapientiae* iii:6 and Dorothea Forstner, *Die Welt der Symbole*, Innsbruck-Vienna-Munich, 1961, p. 196. For the predominantly princely role of the diamond ring in the Renaissance, see the splendid article 'Diamant' in Guy de Tervarent, *Attributes et Symboles dans l'Art Profane. 1459–1600. Dictionnaire d'un Langage Perdu*, Geneva, 1958, cols. 147 f.

44. To which Picinelli adds: 'Mariam Virginem haec imago spectat, quae solem Divinum, absque integritatis virgineae offensa, in utero recepit ac enixa est'; XV, iv, 30, p. 534.
45. Allen, V, no. 1488, p. 534.
46. 'Primo gustu non admodum adlubescebat palato, caeterum nox arguebat indolem vini. Sic enim subito recreatus est stomachus, vt mihi viderer renatus in alium hominem'; Basel, February 1, 1523, Allen, no. 1324, p. 215.
The use of *renatus* here is quite remarkable, for Erasmus was reluctant to speak of rebirth wherever he could avoid it. In his translation of John 3:3 (Nicodemus visiting Jesus), Erasmus rendered the words 'nisi quis *renatus* fuerit denuo' by: 'nisi quis *natus* fuerit e supernis'; see his *Novum Testamentum Graece et Latine*. Panofsky has shown that Erasmus circumvents Melanchthon's *renasci* with *repullulascere* or *revivivscere*; *Renaissance and Renascences*, I, Stockholm, 1960, p. 38, n. 3. For certain exceptions, see J. Huizinga, *Erasmus*, Haarlem, 1936, p. 121.

ingly dithyrambic in his praise of this particular wine:

I have tasted certain wines grown in Burgundy on previous occasions, but they were fiery and harsh. This one had a most attractive colour, near to purple. Its bouquet was neither cloying nor harsh, but mild; neither chilly nor fiery, but moist and innocuous. By all this so gentle to the stomach that even greater quantities did no harm. O Burgundy, happy for your name alone, and surely worthy as well, as one who may claim to be called Mother of Mankind because she has such milk in her breasts! Little wonder that the ancients worshipped it as a gift from their gods, since by their own diligence they succeeded in adding something of great service to human existence . . . Does not she [i.e. Burgundy] give life rather than wine?[47]

With this eulogy in mind, we may ask whether the carafe was not indeed prominently displayed on the bookshelf as a promise of physical health and mental stability and as a pointer at a reasonably Christian form of Epicurean *joie de vivre* indulged with the explicit approval of the Stoical health-regimen. Erik Forssman has convincingly pleaded for the possibility that the *grotesche* were recognized as hints at a cult of Dionysus in the Renaissance of the early sixteenth century. Whether such associations, linking the Vitruvian mermaid-capital with Dionysus and therefore with the magic and restorative powers of wine, could have taken root in the Erasmus-Holbein circle at Basel as early as 1523, is difficult to determine, however suggestive such a hypothesis might be. The enjoyment of wine under the aegis of Epicurus was known to both Erasmus and Holbein as early as about 1515. Erasmus, in his *Praise of Folly*, could approvingly cite the last lines of Horace's Fourth Epistle, in which the satisfied poet refers to himself as the well-nourished pig of the Epicurean herd. Holbein could draw in the margin a self-portrait celebrating drink and love[48] (Fig. 11).

Our carafe would come near to what in sixteenth-century England was called a claret jug. Wine, especially when imported, came to the individual buyer in a variety of wooden kegs or vats.[49] It was consumed by Erasmus and his equals either out of an ornate beaker (*cantarus*) or simple pewter mugs.[50] The glass-carafe then played a decanter-like role, acting as the intermediary between keg and beaker. Only a bohemian—a role in which Holbein has cast himself very wittily—would dream of drinking his wine straight out of such a jug (Fig. 11).

*   *   *

If now we look at the composition as a whole, we find that Holbein has depicted Erasmus in a paradoxical state of existence—frozen and yet animated, hovering between health and illness, mortality and power of

47. To Erasmus applies the *dictum* 'Laudibus arguitur vini vinosus'. It is indeed difficult to read the passage quoted below without somehow suspecting that the choice of words and phrases is either meant to suggest the effect of wine upon the writer's expression or that it is the wine itself which is shown to be at work (or both). Note especially how the eulogy of wine ends in the alliterative 'vita . . . verius . . . vinum'. 'Gustarem et ante vina quaedam apud Burgundiones nata, sed ardentia et austera. Hoc erat colore gratissimo, pyropum esse diceres, sapore nec dulci nec austero, sed suaui; nec frigidum nec ardens, sed humidum et innoxium, stomacho sic amicum vt nec copia largior [see the following note] multum offenderet: . . . O felicem vel hoc nomine Burgundiam, planeque dignam quae mater hominum dicatur, postea quam tale lac habet in vberibus! Non mirum si prisci mortales pro diis colebant, quorum industria magna quaepiam vtilitas addita est vitae mortalium. Hoc vinum qui monstrauit, qui dedit, quanquam monstrasse sat erat, nonne vitam dedit verius quam vinum?' Same letter and place as in the preceding note.

48. For a lucid *exposé* of the attitude of the sixteenth century towards a permissible form of Epicureanism and hedonism, see Craig R. Thompson's introductory remarks to Erasmus's Colloquy 'Epicureus' in *The Colloquia of Erasmus Translated*, Chicago and London, 1965, pp. 535–7.
Erasmus's praise of wine should also be seen against the background of Seneca's health regimen which advocates the 'liberalior potio' for the very reason that it removes anxieties, moves the mind to its very depths and cures not only sicknesses but also depressions. Bacchus is called 'Liber' because he liberates man from the enslavement of anxieties and fortifies as well as stimulates, lending boldness to all actions—'mutata regio [i.e. travelling] vigorem dabunt convictusque et liberalior potio . . . eluit enim curas et ab imo animum movet et ut morbis quibusdam ita tristitiae medetur, Liberque non ob licentiam linguae dictus est inventor vini, sed quia liberat servitio curarum animum et adserit vegetatque et audaciorem in omnis conatus facit'; Seneca, *De tranquillitate animi*, chap. xvii, ed. Erasmus (Froben), cited in note 9 *supra*, p. 145. Our Fig. 11 was undoubtedly intended by young Holbein to show 'the glossy pig from the herd of Epicurus' 'nitidum Epicuri de grege porcum'. The sixteenth-century hand that inscribed the word 'Holbein' above the feasting couple was not that of Johannes the Younger himself. The legend of Holbein's dissolute life originated in the year 1676 and took its start from this marginal sketch and inscription; see Rudolf and Margaret Wittkower, *Born under Saturn*, London, 1963, pp. 214 f. and caption to Fig. 65. See also Curt Loehning, *Erasmus von Rotterdam, Hans Holbein d.J., Das Lob der Torheit*, Berlin, 1950, Cat. no. 113. For the Dionysiac implications of the grotesques, see Erik Forssman, *Säule und Ornament. Studien zum Problem des Manierismus in den nordischen Säulenbüchern und Vorlageblättern des 16. und 17. Jahrhunderts*, Stockholm, 1956, chap. II, 'Vitruv und die Groteske', pp. 96–102, esp. p. 99. See also note 35 *supra*.
49. See again Erasmus's letter to Laurinus, *ed. et loc. cit.* in note 46 *supra*, pp. 215 f., where methods of shipping are discussed and where the word used for wine-kegs is *vas*.
50. For such a beaker of silver gilt, datable around 1525 and inscribed CRATER DES. ERASMI ROTER., see Emil Major, *Erasmus von Rotterdam, s.a.*, Fig. 25, idem, 'Ein Becher aus dem Besitz des Erasmus von Rotterdam' (Historisches Museum), Basel, 1929, Figs. a and b, and idem, 'Handzeichnungen des Erasmus von Rotterdam' (Jahresberichte, Historisches Museum), Basel, 1952, p. 38 and pl. D, 12 (for one of Erasmus's drawings of a simple drinking vessel).

regeneration, between scholarly triumph on the one hand and on the other petty Envy opposing it frivolously, an existence alternating between the justified pride of the prince of humanists and the dependence of the freelance writer upon those who were pleased to support him so that he might live in style. If we look at the painting as if it were a musical composition, the magic words, ΗΡΑΚΛΕΙΟΙ ΠΟΝΟΙ, serve as a *basso continuo* whereas the theme is taken up by the distich on high, acting as a treble[51] showing that humanist as well as artist must join the same battle-order.

The Erasmian figure in its *nidulus* was by no means Holbein's *invenzione*. The Renaissance artists had in fact revived the type of the classical poet, dramatist, or philosopher which, in turn, had survived in representations of the Church Fathers in their cells as for example Tommaso da Modena's representations in the *duomo* of Treviso (1352), none more famous than Albrecht Dürer's engraving of 'St. Jerome in his Study' of the year 1514 (Fig. 12). As an iconographic type, Holbein's Longford panel belongs to the representations of St. Jerome in his study. Such an association must have been pleasing to Erasmus.[52]

51. Erasmus, in fact, uses the military term *acies* in his letter to William Warham, *loc. cit.*, p. 534. At times he uses *phalanx*. This quasi-military language occurs in many of Erasmus's letters (see note 28 *supra*). At first hearing, it seems to strike a discordant note in so peace-minded an author. I believe, however, that Erasmus assumes that his readers are familiar with Seneca's *De tranquillitate animi* (cited in note 9 *supra*). In chap. iv, Seneca advises the interlocutor Serenus that he who is in quest of tranquillity may, at times, have to resort to warlike actions although he must be prepared to withdraw, 'salvis signis, salva militari dignitate'. At the same time we should not overlook the influence of St. Paul's warlike 'Induite totam armaturam Dei . . . super omnia assumpto scuto fidei, quo possitis omnia jacula mali illius ignita extinguere' (Epistola ad Ephes. 6:11 ff. according to Erasmus's version). For the implications which this sixth chapter had in medieval secular thought, cf. Robert W. Ackermann, 'The Knighting Ceremonies in the Middle English Romances', *Speculum*, XIX, 1944, p. 305, n. 5.

In describing the harmonious interrelationship between the two inscriptions in our painting, I purposely referred to it in terms of the musical harmony, i.e. of 'the simultaneous disposition of the voices in a harmonious whole'. In this sense Holbein too (or, possibly, Erasmus as the supposed maker of the program) belonged to those *moderni* (to quote an Italian writer on music of the year 1523): 'che considerano insieme tutte le parti'; see the important paper by Edward E. Lowinsky, 'The Concept of Physical and Musical Space', *Papers of the American Musicological Society* (Annual Meeting), 1941, p. 67, where the author shows that apparently not before 1523 was this harmony possible: 'Pietro Aron was the first to note the change from the successive manner of setting the different voices in a polyphonic complex to the simultaneous disposition of the voices in a harmonious whole . . .' See also Colin Eisler's article cited in note 28 *supra*.

52. While the somewhat archaic character of the Longford Castle portrait results no doubt from what I have called its attempt at presenting a painted monument of Erasmus, we should not overlook that the period of Holbein's great single portraits emphasizing the atmosphere of the spatial shell encompassing the figure was yet to come. Compare for example

Holbein, in spite of parapet, pilaster and curtain, fails to suggest a true interior. The message he wished to convey (or was commissioned to convey) did not depend on the rendering of a particular atmosphere, suggesting to the beholder a given interior space in Holbein's Basel house. The placing of the model in front of a bookshelf was no doubt directly inspired by Quentin Matsys's double portrait of Erasmus-Aegidius. The visitor to Longford Castle, as he stands between Matsys's 'Aegidius'-wing of what was once the 'Erasmus-Aegidius' diptych (of the year 1517) (Fig. 5) and Holbein's 'Erasmus' of 1523 (Fig. 1), becomes aware of a paragone. It is to the modern beholder as if Holbein were losing out against Matsys and as if he had become indifferent, if not antagonistic, to the very qualities of mood, atmosphere and perspective organization of the animate being as well as the furniture that—as every reader of Panofsky's *Dürer* knows—accounted for the unified 'spiritual climate' of the 'St. Jerome in his Study'. Seen from here, the Matsys portrait is still part of the heritage of the classical Renaissance of the North. Holbein, if I may somewhat exaggerate the contrast, atomizes in his Longford Castle panel the visible, tangible, proportionate, measurable world. We may presume that he relies upon the superb craftsmanship of his brushwork and of his composition to achieve a semblance of harmony. It is only in the course of the subsequent period that he manages to come to a new form of organic synthesis which convinces the beholder of those later portraits so that he no longer feels himself confronted with re-assemblages merely held together by a sophisticated program. The unity of the Longford Castle picture is more of a conceptual than of a formal nature.

*   *   *

One touch which I have mentioned in passing should not be overlooked: the parapet taking the place of the more common writing desk. It is an element which *au fond* is an oddity within a representation which in all its other parts—however additively presented they may be—suggests reality. The parapet is a *topos* which in the fifteenth- and sixteenth-century portraits would lead the beholder to cogent associations. If we go back to earlier half-figure portraits of gentlemen resting their hands upon a stone parapet, we arrive at Jan van Eyck's 'Léal Souvenir' and from there we may end up in front of a Gallo-Roman tombstone. In other words, we are led along a long line of bust-size representations

with the Longford Castle picture, Holbein's 'Georg Gisze' in the State Museums, Berlin-Dahlem. For the iconographic type 'Hieronymus im Gehäuse', see *s.h.t.* Anna Strümpell, *Marburger Jahrbuch für Kunstwissenschaft*, II, 1925–6, pp. 173–252 (with 52 plates).

whose lower portion is taken up and terminated by a parapet. The half-size portraits with parapets belong, as I have tried to indicate, to Holbein's iconographic ancestry. What they have in common is that they are all invariably concerned with the idea of the triumph of Remembrance over Death[53] (Fig. 13). Even in Erasmus's own day, the formal stone parapet was a favoured device in memorial images. Erasmus's close friend, Dean John Colet, died in 1521. He was honoured—some time after his death—by a tomb memorial that was placed in St. Paul's Cathedral. Of a type very similar to many other memorials, the original was destroyed by the London Fire but is preserved in fairly early copies and descriptions. It is, as we can see, decidedly related to Holbein's composition. John Colet is shown frontally, as a hyper-realistic effigy of the type that Pietro Torregiano (the supposed maker of the monument) had successfully introduced into England. Colet appears within a shell-niche, standing behind a parapet. As if to explain its true message, underneath the parapet the Dean appears a second time as the *esca vermium*, a prone skeleton[54] (Fig. 14). If the iconographic function of such parapets —of which Dean Colet's tomb is only a variant among many—was to serve as a hint pointing at all that is ephemeral and moribund, *caducum et putre* about man, the rest of our painting, especially the monumental triangle containing the effigy of Erasmus with the wise suffering face (but also the creative hands, the apotropaeic ring, the precious fur, the scholarly cap

and, surrounding him, the books with their challenging inscriptions, the ancient capital and pilaster, and the carafe with its promise of making man new) would serve as a hint at that 'aliquid Erasmi' which, welded into an indestructible monument, will triumph forever over death and its companion oblivion (Fig. 13). And here the good services of the artist are the *conditio sine qua non*. The sitter has to trust the artist's *ingenium* when it comes to creating a true likeness (for which Erasmus uses the word 'effigies'),[55] while his ability as a craftsman, his *rara dexteritas*, must vouchsafe that the monument he has created will be able to withstand the tooth of time.

* * *

As our portrait must thus be considered the pictorial equivalent of a monument of marble and brass as well as a *léal souvenir* celebrating an Erasmus still very much alive, there is yet another aspect to it. This is an aspect which is lacking in all the other portraits Holbein made of Erasmus,[56] and which moreover is diametrically opposed to the tradition-bound character I have just described. I have in mind the pronouncedly emblematic quality of the picture by which things to come are boldly anticipated. We find here, at the very threshold of the emblematic development, all the necessary ingredients of an emblem proper:

1. The words 'Labours of Hercules' serve as the MOTTO of which the 'Ille ego' verse is merely a legitimate extension.

2. The *imago picta Erasmi* furnishes the so-called ICON. The *icon* (also known as *pictura*, *imago*, or *Sinnbild*) shows the emaciated features of the *Stubengelehrte*. The motto, on the other hand, conjures up the muscular Labours of Hercules. This

53. See Erwin Panofsky, 'Who is Jan van Eyck's "Tymotheos"?', *The Journal of the Warburg and Courtauld Institutes*, XII, 1949, pls. 20 and 30-e, p. 80, and *idem*, *Early Netherlandish Painting*, Cambridge, 1953, pp. 196 f.; for a summary of these problems, W. S. Heckscher, 'Niche Portraits', *Ancient Art and Its Echoes in Post-Classical Times* (Imago. Netherlands Classical Association), 1963, pp. 15 f. and Figs. 17 f. See also note 34 *supra* and text.

54. Cf. W. S. Heckscher, *Rembrandt's Anatomy*, New York, 1958, pl. XLII-51. On June 13, 1521, Erasmus sent from Anderlecht a 'written portrait' of Colet to Jodocus Jonas; Allen, IV, no. 1211. Here Erasmus refers to Dean Colet's tomb (though it is not quite certain that he has the finished product in mind): 'sepultus est ad australe chori latus in suo templo [i.e. St. Paul's], humili sepulcro quod in eum vsum iam ante annos aliquot delegerat inscriptione addita JOAN. COL.' It has been suggested that the elaborate inscription of the finished tomb had been composed by Erasmus himself. See Allen, *loc. cit.*, p. 519, and editor's note to line 386.

For the type of hyper-lifelike effigy, see e.g. a painted terracotta bust ascribed to Pietro Torregiano (1472–1528), the so-called 'John Fisher', in the Metropolitan Museum of Art. The undoubted prototypes of those realistic portrait busts were the wooden effigies of princes and prelates which were carried triumphantly in English funerary cortèges of the fifteenth and sixteenth centuries; their heads were, it seems, often carved or modeled after death-masks. In France all such masks were destroyed in the course of the Revolution. For a wax-mask of the year 1610, see the one of Henri IV taken on May 14, and preserved in the Musée Carnavalet, Paris.

55. This is the sense in which Erasmus interpreted 'effigies': '*Effigies* est ad exemplar aliquid exprimere. Monendi sunt scholastici, ut Ciceronis stylum studeant *effingere*. *Effigies*, signum ad alterius similitudinem factum'; Erasmus, *In elegant. Laurentii Vallae*, ed. *Opera omnia*, I, Leyden, 1703, col. 1090. Holbein portrayed Nicolas Kratzer on his forty-first birthday, stressing that the painting (Louvre, 1528) was an '*imago ad viuam effigiem expressa Nicolai Kratzen* . . . '

56. It is full ten years later, in 1533, that Holbein's dependence on *ars emblematica* can be proved beyond doubt, for the one broken string in his 'Ambassadors' at the National Gallery in London (1533) is Alciati-inspired. This connection was discovered by Mary F. S. Hervey, *Holbein's 'Ambassadors'*, London, 1900, pp. 228–32. Two later monographs on the same painting copied her findings badly—C excerpting B; it is worth going back to A! I should not be surprised if Holbein were also the first artist to respond to the *editio princeps* of Andrea Alciati's *Emblematum liber* (Steyner, Augsburg, 1531): the broken string of the lute appears in Alciati's second emblem, *s.t.* 'Foedera Italorum' on sig. A 2 verso f. For an excellent treatment of the motive of the broken string from Alciati onward (except that Holbein is missing), see John Hollander, *The Untuning of the Sky. Ideas of Music in English Poetry 1500–1700*, Princeton, 1961, pp. 47–50.

poses—as every proper emblem should—a riddle. How do these two elements relate? What message are they meant to convey?

3. There is present here, as in every proper emblem, a third element, whose function it is to answer the rhetorical question and to solve the riddle posed by *icon* and motto. This third element is, in the case of Erasmus's portrait, extraneous and yet part of the whole: Erasmus's dedicatory letter to William Warham as well as the text on the 'Herculean Labours' in the *Adagia*. The letter, if seen in the light of this essay, helps us in understanding the exact nature of Erasmus's Herculean struggle against the envy of his opponents in Rome, and the picture confirms what the letter only hints at: the ultimate victory of *tranquillitas* in the face of tremendous odds (Fig. 7).

The question remains in how far a work of art could manage to be emblematic in the year 1523. It was after all only in 1522 that Andrea Alciati made the first, very unofficial announcement of the fact that he had composed a small book of epigrams which he had given the name *Emblemata*. Most likely Alciati made reference to a first sketch in manuscript.

As a book, the *Emblemata* of 1522 remain a ghost. It is still a question to what degree the canon of the true emblem (consisting of motto, *icon*, explanatory epigram) as it had officially been launched with the publication in 1531 of Alciati's *Emblematum liber* at Augsburg, had been formulated by Alciati when in 1522 he reported to his friend, the printer and publisher Francesco Calvo, that with his *Emblemata* (literally, a mosaic-like patchwork) he intended to produce a work for all kinds of artists, and that he proposed to make use of signets such as were being employed by various printers. He mentioned by name the anchor and dolphin of Aldus Manutius, the dove and serpents of Froben, the elephant of Calvus himself.[57] Erasmus and Alciati were, in the year 1522, in confidential epistolary contact. They had an endless number of mutual friends. Their desire to communicate knew no bounds.[58] To what extent Erasmus was

informed of Alciati's emblematic plans is, nevertheless, impossible to tell. When Alciati pointed at the emblematic quality of anchor and dolphin, he owed this intelligence to no other source than Erasmus's lengthy article in the *Adagia* which bore the title 'Festina lente'.[59]

How Erasmus's portrait at Longford Castle came to be emblematic we cannot say with certainty. It is perhaps safest to state that the emblematic configuration, in which word and image were treated as equivalent, was in the air in the decade 1522–1531 in which Alciati's genius worked at bringing about the classical three-part canon of the Renaissance emblem. Of the ubiquity of this emerging emblematic spirit, Holbein's portrait is eloquent proof.

*   *   *

I am afraid the reader will be struck by the vast number of explanations and aspects which are offered where often a single one would have been quite sufficient and probably more persuasive. However, I do not believe that the art historian should try to emulate the lawyer pleading his case. On the contrary. I believe that in historical research any water-tight argument is *eo ipso* suspect. Of course, it was a temptation to omit what in the end proved to be marginal to the essential message of individual symbols as well as to the sum total of their presumed meaning when taken in groups. In spite of this I have retained the secondary and even the tertiary explanations because I believe that in this way I have come closer to the spirit of the sixteenth century, which, it seems, had a great tolerance for multiple and even for contradictory interpretations of a single symbol.[60]

57. Andrea Alciati writes from Milan, December 9, 1522, to his friend Francesco Calvo: 'Libellum composui epigrammaton, cui titulum feci *Emblemata*'; see Gian Luigi Barni, *Le lettere di Andrea Alciati Giurisconsulto*, Florence, 1953, no. 24, pp. 45–47. For the structure of the Renaissance emblem, see article 'Emblem, Emblembuch', *Reallexikon zur deutschen Kunstgeschichte*, v, 1959, col. 153, and our Fig. 7a and b. For Erasmus's detailed treatment of Aldus Manutius's anchor and dolphin, see note 35 *supra*

58. Alciati entrusted Erasmus with the MS. of his 'Epistola contra vitam monasticam', which he trembled to think might get into untrustworthy hands; cf. ed. Barni, *op. cit.*, in preceding note, pp. 41 f.
Erasmus called Alciati 'shining light of Learning, not only of Law' in his *Adagia*; cf. M. M. Phillips, *op. cit.*, in n. 11, p. 391.

59. Alciati's *emblema* CXLIII, *s.t.* 'Princeps subditorum incolumitatem procurans.'
60. It might be useful to end by listing, in alphabetical order, those elements which constitute the program of our portrait and which play, through their absence or presence, a major or minor part in it:

affectus (the four passions), pp. 130 f., notes 7–9
  (see also: apathetic; emotions; physiognomy; Stoicism)

'aliis in serviendo consumor', p. 129, note 5
  (see also: *invidia*)

'aliquid Erasmi' (which will survive Death), pp. 129, 145

antiquity evoked, pp. 140 f., notes 30 f., 33, 35
  (see also: Epicurean; rebirth of Antiquity)

anxiety (prompted by attacks, pressures, celestial conjunctions), p. 136, notes 9, 25

apathetic traits, note 5, Fig. 3
  (see also: *affectus*; emotions, Stoicism)

apotheosis of the scholar, p. 129
  (see also: monument)

archaic character, note 52
  (see also: monument)

arena (see: athlete; gladiator)

Quite in general I hope to have shown that the Longford Castle panel speaks of the humanist's self-denying suffering, that it reveals his constancy and tranquillity amidst tribulations, and that it proclaims the ultimate triumph of man's dignity in spite of all vagaries of Fortune. The qualities of being sad, frightened, self-assured, proud—all at the same time—would clash and result in disharmony, were it not for the presence of a new kind of humor which allowed Erasmus to

tumultus, note 25
    (see also: tempestas; tranquillitas)

virginity unimpaired, p. 142, notes 44, 46 f.

voluptatum expers (shared by Erasmus, Hercules), p. 129
    (see also: quarta luna nati)

smile at the foibles of the world, including his own. This newly found Lucianian humour[61] constituted Erasmus's charm for his circle of friends, among them William Warham, owner-designate of his portrait. It still helps to explain Erasmus's lasting appeal to the world at large.

61. See W. S. Heckscher, ' "Was this the Face . . . ?" ' *Journal of the Warburg Institute*, I, 1938, pp. 295–7.

NVMMVS CASTRENSIS

GVILHELMI PRINCIPIS AVRIA⸗
ci, Comitis Naſſovij, cuſus ſub ipſum (uti videtur) belli Belgici primordium. Anno Chriſti 1568.

Coin struck in 1568; *recto*: 'William of Orange and Nassau', with on the *verso* his motto: SAEVIS TRANQVILLVS IN VNDIS with the *icon* of 'Halcyone Approaching Her Nest'. The mailed first of AEOLVS (here identified as CHRS) issues from clouds and assures the seven days' truce with the stormwinds. From: Joannes Jacobus Luckius, *Sylloge numismatum elegantiorum quae diversi Imperatores . . . cudi fecerunt*, Augsburg, 1620 (*sine paginatione*).

FRANCES A. YATES

The Allegorical Portraits of Sir John Luttrell

One of the most puzzling of sixteenth-century English portraits is the picture at Dunster Castle, the seat of the Luttrell family, of a naked man wading in an angry sea (Fig. 1).[1] Behind him is a sinking ship from which boatloads of people are escaping; the face of a drowned corpse floats near him. He raises his right arm with clenched fist into a world of allegory, sharply separated from the scene of storm and desolation by the dark rim of the cloud within which it is set. A female figure bearing an olive branch of peace and surrounded by groups of other allegories, bends down to caress the arm of the determined character in the sea. The allegory in the sky seems to form a picture in itself which is only very clumsily linked by the incongruous gesture of the man in the sea with the picture of shipwreck and storm of which he forms a part.

On the hero's wrists there are narrow bracelets. These contain Latin inscriptions; on the right wrist, *Nec flexit lucrum 1550*; on the left wrist, *Nec friget discrimen*. 'Neither swayed by love of gain nor deterred by danger.'

More obvious are the inscriptions on the rock (Fig. 3a) which rises from the sea in the foreground. These are as follows:

More then the rock amydys the raging seas
The constant hert no danger dreddys nor fearys.
.SIL.
Effigiem renouare tuam fortissime miles
Ingens me meritum fecit amorq[ue] tui.
Nam nisi curasses haeredem scribere fratrem
Hei, tua contigerant praedia nulla mihi.
1591. G.L.
1550
HE

I wish to express my grateful thanks for permission to reproduce works of art illustrated in this article to the Director of the Courtauld Institute (Sir Anthony Blunt), Colonel Walter Luttrell, the Earl of Radnor, the Director of the Museum of Aix-en-Provence, the Director of the Victoria and Albert Museum, and the Public Record Office.
Photographs of the Dunster picture were kindly supplied by the Courtauld Institute. All of the photographs of the Courtauld picture were taken by Mr. O. Fein of the Warburg Institute. Sir Anthony Blunt kindly allowed the Courtauld picture to spend some weeks at the Warburg Institute when I was working on the allegories.

1. This well-known picture has frequently been seen at Royal Academy exhibitions; *British Art*, 1934 (*Commemorative Catalogue*, no. 19); *Works of Holbein and other Masters*, 1950–1951, catalogue no. 56; *British Portraits*, 1956–7, catalogue

The couplet in English at the top suggests the rock in the stormy seas as an emblem of the courage and determination of the man in the sea. The bottom inscription gives the date 1550 (also given on the right bracelet) and the monogram HE, composed of the letters H and E. The middle inscription in Latin, dated 1591, was added in that year by 'G.L.' or George Luttrell. A possible rendering of the Latin inscription of 1591 is as follows:

> SIL. (probably referring to 'Sir Iohn Luttrell')[2] Your great merit and my love for you cause me, brave soldier, to renew your portrait.
> For had you not taken care to make your brother your heir, none of your possessions would have become mine.
>
> 1591.   G.L. (George Luttrell)

Sir John Luttrell was George Luttrell's uncle; he left all his landed property by will to his brother, George Luttrell's father.[3] Hence there can be no doubt that George Luttrell's inscription refers to his uncle, Sir John Luttrell, through whose will the property has descended to him. And since he says that he is renewing or restoring the 'effigy' of this uncle, it is to be assumed that the subject of the picture, the man in the sea, is a portrait of Sir John Luttrell.

There is another version of this picture (Fig. 2), now in the possession of the Courtauld Institute. It was bought for Viscount Lee at Christie's on July 22nd, 1932, at the sale of property from Badmondisfield Hall in Suffolk belonging to the Bromley family.[4] Hence it reached the Courtauld Institute as one of Lee's pictures. The fact that a picture, usually described as a copy or replica of the Dunster picture, was in the possession of Lee and later of the Courtauld Institute has been generally known and is mentioned in catalogue entries concerning the Dunster picture. But no attempt was made to compare the two pictures until December, 1960, when, at my request, the Courtauld picture was subjected to a technical examination by Mr. Rees Jones, and was also technically compared with the Dunster picture, kindly

no. 18. The picture is discussed in its relation to the Luttrell family in H. C. Maxwell Lyte, *History of Dunster*, London, 1909, I, pp. 156 ff.
2. Maxwell Lyte, I, p. 159.
3. *Ibid.*, I, p. 166.
4. Information from the Courtauld Institute.

sent for examination by Colonel Walter Luttrell. It was thus possible to see the two pictures side by side in Mr. Rees Jones's studio, and possible for a technical examination of both to be made under the best conditions. It is through the kind co-operation of Colonel Luttrell and of Sir Anthony Blunt in arranging for the examination of the pictures that I am able to use for the first time in this article the evidence of the Courtauld picture in solving the problems of this strange allegorical portrait. Mr. Rees Jones's technical analysis of the two pictures is given in an Appendix[5] to this article, and is the basis of the following remarks.

The two pictures are on panels of approximately the same size but the technical evidence shows that they are not an original and a replica from the same workshop. They are not by the same hands. The Courtauld picture is the work of two painters. In the allegorical group in the Courtauld picture 'the paint has been used with the greatest assurance to model forms such as the nude'. The figure of Sir John Luttrell, however, 'shows techniques similar to English or Flemish sixteenth-century portraits in general'. In short, the allegorical group in the Courtauld picture is by a mannerist painter of considerable expertise; the rest of the picture is by another hand.

The Dunster picture, on the contrary, is quite homogeneous, painted throughout by one hand. When the Peace allegory in the Dunster picture is compared with the Courtauld version of it, it becomes apparent that the Dunster version has omitted several details and has, in general, lost the firm moulding of the forms and the high quality of the painting in the Courtauld version. The shift of the figures to the right in the Dunster version has involved a distortion of the torso of Peace. The colours in the allegorical group in the Courtauld picture are 'brilliant and in keeping with the mannerist style, whereas in the Dunster picture they are more subdued'. The conclusion to which the technical examination unmistakably points is that the Courtauld picture is the original and the Dunster picture a copy of it. The Courtauld picture is in bad condition, and the report suggests that 'it is not inconceivable that the onset of this deterioration at an early date led to the commission of the Dunster version in 1591, as the inscription suggests'. In short it is now evident that George Luttrell did not restore or 'renovate' the Dunster version of the picture. His renovation consisted in having a copy made of an already existing picture, painted in 1550, the picture now in the Courtauld Institute Gallery.

The inscriptions on the rock 'have been retouched in both paintings' but the Courtauld version of the rock

5. See below, pp. 159–60.

(Fig. 3b) shows only the English couplet at the top (which has been clumsily restored, introducing the mistake 'amlodys' for 'amydys') and '1550 HE' at the bottom. In the Dunster version (Fig. 3a) the space between the two inscriptions was utilized by George Luttrell for his inscription of 1591.

From the revelations made by the technical examination and comparison of the two pictures, it follows that, whilst the inscription of 1591 on the Dunster picture gives evidence of the identity of the subject as Sir John Luttrell, any investigation of the possible origins and meaning of this very curious allegorical portrait should be based on the Courtauld version.

The general level of subject painting in England in the reign of Edward VI was archaic. Through what combination of circumstances arose the phenomenon that an allegory in French Renaissance style, executed by a mannerist-trained hand, should adorn the portrait of an Englishman painted in the year 1550? The search for an answer to this question involves an excursion into history, into the dark and troubled era of the reign of Edward VI, with its ill-starred war in Scotland, its conflict with Henri II of France over the town of Boulogne, ending in the peace treaty of Boulogne in 1550.

*   *   *

In 1547, Edward VI became King of England and Edward Seymour, Duke of Somerset, was appointed Protector during his minority.[6] Amongst the vigorous steps which the Protector took in this year was the expedition, led by himself, to Scotland. Its ostensible object was to force a marriage between Mary, Queen of Scots, and Edward VI, a project which had been mooted in the preceding reign. A great army marched to the north, a mass of excited, fanatical adventurers who were to wreak great destruction on the churches and abbeys of the north. Their iconoclastic mood is vividly reflected in the diary of William Patten.[7] A member of this army was Sir John Luttrell of whom Patten speaks with approval as a brave captain.

The army was supported from the sea by a fleet of ships of which the admiral in command was Edward Fiennes, Lord Clinton. Clinton's navy made contact with the army at Berwick and thereafter moved up along the Scottish coast in close contact with the land forces.[8] On September 10, 1547, the English and Scottish armies met at Pinkie, or Musselborough, on

6. On Somerset and his policies, see A. F. Pollard, *England under Protector Somerset*, London, 1900.
7. W. Patten, 'The Expedition into Scotland in 1547', published in *Tudor Tracts*, ed. A. F. Pollard, London, 1903.
8. These movements can be studied in Patten's diary, *Tudor Tracts*, pp. 91 ff. See also J. A. Froude, *History of England*, London, 1856–70, v, pp. 49 ff.; article Clinton in the *Dictionary of National Biography*.

the Firth of Forth. In this battle, Luttrell distinguished himself as leader of a successful charge of three hundred men.[9] The victory of Pinkie-Musselborough was however due to 'combined operations' between land and sea forces. Clinton's fleet was drawn in close to the shore during the battle, and the guns of his men-of-war came into action. The Scots found themselves pinned between the land forces and the ships and the result was a resounding victory for the Lord Protector and his men. This victory was the foundation of Admiral Clinton's reputation, for, as Fuller says:

> The masterpiece of his [Clinton's] service was in Musselborough field, in the reign of Edward VI, and that battle against the Scots. Some will wonder what a fish should do on dry land, what use an admiral in a land fight. The English kept close to the shore, under the shelter of their ships, the ordinance from the ships at first did all.[10]

This metaphor of the 'fish on dry land' for the combined operations of the battle of Pinkie-Musselborough is worth bearing in mind, since this was the battle in which Sir John Luttrell distinguished himself—on dry land, not with the fishes.

The Protector did not follow up his victory, for owing to difficulties at home and abroad, he withdrew the main force of his army from Scotland, leaving only small bodies of men to garrison the places taken. Now began the misfortunes of Sir John Luttrell who suffered long sieges with his garrisons, first on Inchcolm Island in the Firth of Forth and later at Broughty Craig.[11] He was placed in command at Inchcolm Island a week after the battle of Pinkie-Musselborough. There was an abbey on the little island or 'rock' of Inchcolm, formerly inhabited by Augustinian canons, which now became Luttrell's headquarters. The idea of garrisoning this island was to control shipping in the Firth of Forth, but Luttrell and his men became a source of anxiety to the English commanders since they were besieged on the island by enemy forces and it was difficult to reinforce or provision them. Instead of being able to control the navigation in the Firth, Sir John Luttrell was harried by Scottish ships and boats. Eventually he and his men were evacuated from the island by a vessel of the fleet, the *Mary Hamborough*, and had a very stormy voyage in her to Broughty Craig where another siege, and further adventures, most of them unfortunate, awaited them. Later on, Luttrell was captured and imprisoned. He was still in prison in Scotland in March, 1550.[12]

Admiral Clinton, however, not long after the battle of Pinkie-Musselborough was moved from Scotland to other spheres. He was made governor of Boulogne. Boulogne had been captured by Henry VIII in 1544 as part of an offensive war against Scotland and France in which he was then engaged. But when the Protector sent Clinton to Boulogne, this was more in the nature of a defensive policy. His rash campaign in Scotland had aroused much ill-feeling in France; the young Mary, Queen of Scots, was sent abroad to the French court to safeguard her against English designs for her capture. The Protector's revolutionary measures at home had aroused violent opposition and were throwing the country into a state of utter confusion; it was because of these many dangers at home and abroad that he had been obliged to withdraw his army from Scotland. Henri II of France saw that England's embarrassments might provide an opportunity for the recovery of Boulogne and he began to make extensive preparations for attacking the town.[13]

In September, 1549, war with France broke out, and at about the same time England was further convulsed by the overthrow of Protector Somerset, which meant that the Boulogne garrison could expect little help. The French soon began to make heavy attacks on the town, which was closely invested. Clinton took his full share of the hardships, and held out during the winter of 1549–1550, though without reinforcements and faced by growing difficulties and dangers. On February 20, 1550, a truce was concluded and peace terms began to be discussed. By a treaty made with Henry VIII in 1546, it had been agreed that England was to retain Boulogne for eight years, or until the debt to Henry VIII incurred by Francis I had been paid. In 1550, there were still four more of these eight years to run, but the French were determined to have the town at once though they agreed to pay a sum of money for it. This sum was to wipe out all former debts and to end once and for all the English occupation of Boulogne.

On March 24, 1550, a treaty[14] was concluded between France and England, or rather between the kings of those countries, Henri II and Edward VI. The distinctive feature of the treaty was that Henri II agreed to pay four thousand crowns for Boulogne in two instalments. Half of this sum was to be paid immediately on the conclusion of the treaty; the remaining half in the following August. In return for this the English agreed to evacuate Boulogne within six weeks of the day of

9. *Tudor Tracts*, p. 121.
10. Thomas Fuller, *Worthies*, ed. Nuttall, 1840, II, p. 277.
11. Maxwell Lyte, *History of Dunster*, I, pp. 142 ff.
12. *Ibid.*, I, p. 155.

13. For an account of the French attack on Boulogne, see the preface to *Calendar of State Papers Foreign, 1547–53*, pp. viii–ix; Froude, *History of England*, V, pp. 220 ff.
14. The text of the Treaty of Boulogne is printed in T. Rymer, *Foedera*, London, 1713, XV, pp. 211–17.

the signature of the treaty, and to give up all the munitions of war which they had in the town.

Provision was also made in the treaty for the evacuation or razing of the fortresses and places held by the English in Scotland. This treaty therefore marked the end of the Scottish war, the only result of which was—in spite of its initial success—that the English had to give up all that they had gained there and, in addition, to surrender Boulogne to the French.

The kings of France and England sent commissioners to Boulogne to conclude the treaty. One of these was Gaspard de Coligny, representing the Duc de Montmorency who had led the war in the Boulonnais on the French side. This Coligny was none other than the man later to become famous as a Huguenot leader; at this date, however, he was not yet either a Protestant or an Admiral. The commissioners for the English side were John Russell, Earl of Bedford, Lord William Paget, Sir William Petre and Sir John Mason.[15] According to Grafton's *Chronicle*, Paget, Petre, and Mason crossed to Calais on February 7 and went on from there to meet the French commissioners at Boulogne where 'a certayne house was newly erected for the sayd treatie to be had'.[16] This suggests one of those temporary buildings erected for the meetings of monarchs and decorated by artists, and though the Boulogne meeting was ungraced by royalty, Grafton's remark indicates that some effort may have been made to give it dignity. The English present might have reflected on the fall of their country's prestige since the days of Henry VIII and the Field of the Cloth of Gold. The great triangle—France, England, and the Emperor—in which England had played an important part in those days not so long ago was represented at Boulogne for all these three were interested in the treaty (the Emperor Charles V at a distance[17]), but now England was a weak and defeated country surrendering Boulogne to the commissioners.

As always in such documents, the hard facts of the terms are masked in the treaty by a noble and inflated preamble. This is of importance, for it gives an idea of the kind of official imagery, or state allegories, in which this peace treaty was presented.

The kings of France and England, states the Treaty of Boulogne, are now to be joined in friendship, and peace is to be established between them throughout all ages to come. The evils and miseries of war will be banished eternally in this perpetual peace. *Pax, Amicitia, Confederatio, Unio, Liga,* and *Summa Concordia* will forever link together these two illus-

trious kings and their heirs and successors. These allegories are later repeated, and the treaty is throughout described as a treaty of *Pax* and *Amicitia*. Then come the hard facts. France is to pay 2,000 gold crowns down, and another 2,000 in August. England is to evacuate Boulogne within six weeks and to leave in the town all the munitions of war. The fortresses in Scotland enumerated are to be yielded or destroyed.[18] Boulogne was duly handed over on April 25, 1550, and the document which is the French receipt for the town exists in the Public Record Office.[19] It states that François de Montmorency and Gaspard de Coligny acknowledge having received the town of Boulogne and all the munitions of war in it from the hands of 'Messieurs Edouard Seigneur de Clincton, Richard Cotton, & Lyenard Bekoits,[20] & autres ayans Pouvoir specials du dit Seigneur Roy d'Angleterre'. Since Montmorency was not actually there (as the receipt states) and since Clinton as Governor of Boulogne would head the English commissioners in the transaction, it may be said that Coligny and Clinton were the chief actors in this drama.

Clinton probably left Boulogne, with the English garrison, on the day of its surrender and came over to England. There great honours and promotions awaited him, for it would seem that, although the surrender of Boulogne was actually a defeat, Clinton came out of it with honour because of his long and heroic defence of the town. On May 4, he was thanked by the Privy Council for his services, and taken by members of the Council into the presence of the king who also thanked him and decreed that he should be made Lord High Admiral of England and one of the Privy Council.[21] The office of Lord High Admiral was a great one, the powers and prerogatives of which had recently been redefined.[22] Clinton was to hold it, with one short intermission, through the succeeding reigns of Mary and Elizabeth until his death in 1585. He first achieved it in this hour of his triumph in 1550. On May 11, the Privy Council decreed that, since Clinton's income was not sufficient to maintain his new office, he should be given land and estates 'forasmuch as his service at Bulloigne deserved notable consideration'.[23] Clinton was the hero of the hour.

The subject of the Treaty of Boulogne remained much in the public eye all through the summer of 1550, as anyone who cares to read through the contemporary

---

15. These commissioners are all named in the treaty.
16. R. Grafton, *Chronicle; or History of England*, ed. of London, 1809, II, p. 524.
17. See Paget's letters in *Cal. S.P. Foreign*, vol. cited, pp. 40–45.

18. Rymer, vol. cited, pp. 211–12.
19. P.R.O., E.30/1060 (*Lists and Indexes*, XLIX, p. 92); Rymer, vol. cited, pp. 228–9.
20. Sir Leonard Beckwith.
21. *Acts of the Privy Council*, N.S., III, p. 24.
22. 'De officio Magni Admiralli', October, 1549, printed in Rymer, vol. cited., pp. 194–200.
23. *Acts of the Privy Council*, vol. cited, p. 29.

documents will discover. In June, French ambassadors, one of whom was Coligny, came to London to receive the ratification by Edward VI of the treaty. They were met by a galley and two pinnaces at the mouth of the Thames which conducted their ship up the river to their lodgings. The next day they were escorted to an audience with the king by notable personages, amongst whom was the new Lord High Admiral, and on the following day the king took the oath of ratification. Entertainments were provided for the ambassadors, hunting parties, banquets, and a spectacle on the river, and on their departure. they were given gifts of gold plate and jewels.[24]

Thus the year 1550, the date given on the portrait of Sir John Luttrell, was a year in which the Treaty of Boulogne was the major event. Eternal *Pax* and *Amicitia* linking the Kings of France and England was the official theme and the basic fact was the achievement of this Peace and Friendship by the payment of a large sum of money *in two instalments*. Moreover this Peace and Friendship was signalized by a French embassy to England for the ratification of the treaty. For a brief moment, the isolation from the continent of the England of Edward VI was broken.

This might surely be the moment in which the phenomenon of a Peace allegory in Renaissance style painted by a mannerist hand in the England of Edward VI could be accounted for by the historical situation. With this thought in our minds, let us now turn to examine in more detail the Peace allegory in the portrait of Sir John Luttrell.

*   *   *

An admirable comparison for the central figure of Peace was pointed out by R. Wittkower in *British Art and the Mediterranean*[25] where he illustrated a figure of Peace of the School of Fontainebleau (Fig. 5a), now in the museum of Aix-en-Provence, beside the Luttrell portrait (in the Dunster version). The graceful semi-nude figure of the School of Fontainebleau Peace bears in her left hand an olive branch; on her right a dove is perched. She wears a jewelled head-band, and a pearl drop hangs from her ear. Compare with this the semi-nude Peace of the Luttrell allegory, with her jewelled head-band and pearl ear-ring and bearing her olive

branch. The comparison becomes even more striking when it is made with the Courtauld version of the allegory (Fig. 4) with its more erect pose.

On either side of the Luttrell Peace are groups of other allegorical figures. The group on Peace's left contains a savage-looking horse into whose mouth a female figure is placing a bit. This bit, very distinctly painted in the Courtauld version, has been lost in the Dunster version. On Peace's right are two female figures, closely linked together by a loving embrace.

The group of the horse and the woman can be very easily explained as Venus curbing the wrath of Mars. The horse can often be the symbol of *Bellum*[26] and this particularly fierce horse looks particularly warlike. The half-reclining Venus is curbing his rage by placing the bit in his mouth, at the same time softening with her gentle influence the martial helmet and breast-plate on which she leans. The figures behind the Mars and Venus group seem to be Minerva (in the helmet) and the Three Graces symbolizing the return of peaceful cultural activities now that war is curbed.

The two ladies behind Peace's right shoulder are expressive of *Amicitia*. One places her right hand in loving friendship on the shoulder of the other, who looks back towards her. And this other has in her left hand a bag of money, whilst with her right hand she fumbles in a purse for more. *Two instalments.* The money which the King of France gave to the King of England for Boulogne was paid in two instalments. This detail of the two money-bags or purses, always noted as a puzzling feature of the allegory, is the detail which makes it absolutely certain that the Peace allegory here depicted refers to the Treaty of Boulogne. The theme of the allegory, as of the peace treaty, is *Pax* and *Amicitia*. The theme of *Pax* is stated in the central figure of Peace; *Amicitia* or eternal friendship between the Kings of France and England is symbolized by the two female figures linked in friendship, one of whom is paying the other a sum of money in two instalments. This Peace is eternally banishing war between the two countries, symbolized by the bridling of the war horse by the gentle hand of Venus. *Pax* and *Amicitia* are the theme of the whole allegory, linking the two women engaged in the money transaction, expressed in the dominance of Venus over Mars, whilst Peace herself, as she lets her left hand fall on the arm of the hero in the sea, passes on to him the current of peace subduing war which is running between all the allegorical ladies.

The Peace allegory is personal to Sir John Luttrell only in the sense that the peace treaty of Boulogne meant for him the end of the campaigning in Scotland

24. The description of the visit of the French ambassador comes from the report about it sent by the Privy Council to Sir John Mason, ambassador in France (briefly calendared in *Cal. S.P. Foreign*, vol. cited, p. 48). There is a copy of the letter in Sir John Mason's letter-book (S.P. 68, 9A, fols. 1–10). Most of it is printed in P. T. Tytler, *England under the reigns of Edward VI and Mary . . . illustrated in a series of original letters*, London, 1839, I, pp. 284–8. See also *Acts of the Privy Council*, vol. cited, pp. 30 ff.

25. F. Saxl and R. Wittkower, *British Art and the Mediterranean*, Oxford, 1948, p. 39.

26. See P. Valeriano, *Hieroglyphica*, ed. Cologne, 1614, p. 44.

in which he had been engaged. All its details can be explained as in no sense personal to him (various attempts have been made to explain the money-bags in relation to Luttrell). They can all be explained as an allegory of the Treaty of Boulogne, of the eternal peace and friendship established between the Kings of France and England by the payment by Henri II to Edward VI of four thousand crowns in two instalments.

The Peace allegory in the Luttrell portrait is probably an echo of official imagery about the treaty current in 1550 when all the talk was of this peace, and when French ambassadors came to England to ratify it with the English King.

There was a tradition about the official imagery for peace treaties between France and England and some study of the iconography of this tradition can throw further light on the allegory in the Luttrell picture.

The Treaty of Boulogne of 1550 was not the first treaty of the sixteenth century by which France and England had sworn to maintain an eternal peace. Such a treaty was made between Henry VIII and Francis I in 1527. There are two copies in the Public Record Office[27] of the ratification of this treaty by the French king, both of which are illuminated. One copy (Fig. 6a) shows in its top margin a graceful little figure of *Pax Eterna*, with her branch, standing between the royal arms of France and England which she is linking together in amity. In the side margin are emblems of peace and love; a dove, a peacock (the bird of Juno, goddess of marriages) with tail outspread, two mating birds. In the lower margin, shepherds are dancing with a maiden to the tune of a piper; flocks and herds, trees laden with fruit, illustrate the blessings of peace. In the other copy of the same treaty (Fig. 6b), another charming *Pax Eterna* stands between the two royal arms, and the capital F of 'Franciscus' (Francis I) is formed out of a crowned salamander. This creature was, of course, the badge or device of Francis I and appears in other Anglo-French treaties contracted by him.

Turning now again to the two ladies symbolizing the peace between France and England in the Luttrell allegory, we find certain details in them now explained from these earlier illuminated treaties. A peacock with outspread tail is shown behind France with the bags of money. The peacock with outspread tail in the margin of the 1527 treaty is there shown in a context of other emblems of marriage or peace between the two countries. This explains its appearance in the Luttrell allegory, where it does not mean that the lady beside it is Juno (she is not at all like a Juno). It appears as a

marriage emblem, a love and amity emblem, symbolizing the loving marriage between France and England in a *Pax Eterna*, just as it does in the 1527 treaty.

France with the money-bags in the Luttrell allegory has a crescent moon in her hair (the Dunster copyist left out this detail[28] which is so conspicuous in the Courtauld version). This may be explained, by comparison with the device of a salamander symbolizing Francis I in the 1527 treaty, as a reference to a French royal device. The device of Henri II was, of course, a crescent moon. The crescent moon in the hair of France with the money-bags relates her to the present King of France, Henri II, who paid the money to the King of England. The peacock of Juno and the crescent of Diana may also be intended to introduce allusions to those goddesses into the Olympian allegory as a whole, but the two female figures with whom they are associated are neither a Juno nor a Diana. They represent the Kings of France and England in amicable embrace. These two ladies engaged in their amicable money transaction are modern Renaissance allegories replacing the arms of the two kings or countries between which the *Pax Eterna* of the 1527 treaty stands. And how remarkably, too, *Pax Eterna* herself has been modernized, transformed from the still medieval and modestly clothed little Eternal Peaces of the 1527 treaty into a Renaissance nude! And the humble little rustic scene of happy shepherds enjoying the blessings of peace transforms into a Renaissance Mars and Venus allegory. But all the elements of a traditional Anglo-French treaty are present in the Luttrell picture though expressed in the new classicizing manner of the Renaissance.

The original of the Treaty of Boulogne, signed by Edward VI, exists in the Public Record Office;[29] also the ratification of the treaty by Henri II, with his signature.[30] If the precedent of 1527 had been followed, the latter document—the French ratification of the treaty—would have been illuminated with some figure of *Pax Eterna* and other allegories. But unfortunately the ratification of the Treaty of Boulogne is not illuminated though it is adorned with a magnificent impression of the royal seal of France which depends from it.

Nevertheless, the allegory in the Luttrell portrait strongly suggests that an official allegorical representation, or representations, of this new treaty of *Pax Eterna*, expressed in the style of the French Renais-

27. P.R.O., E.30/1110 and E.30/1111; see *Catalogue of Manuscripts and other objects in the Museum of the Public Record Office*, London, 1948, p. 13.

28. The Dunster copyist not only left out the crescent on this lady's head; he added a squirrel in her hair! How he could possibly have misunderstood the coils of hair in the original as a squirrel remains a mystery.
29. P.R.O., E.30/1054.
30. P.R.O., E.30/1058.

sance, probably existed. One may fancy behind the Luttrell allegory the ghost of some long-vanished picture, brought by the French ambassadors for presentation to Edward VI. The 'Peace' in the museum of Aix-en-Provence (Fig. 5a) is so extraordinarily close to the Peace of the Luttrell allegory as seen in the Courtauld version (much closer than to the Dunster version with which Rudolf Wittkower compared it) that one can imagine what such a presentation picture in the style of the School of Fontainebleau may have been like. And there seems good reason to suppose that the allegory in the Courtauld version of the Luttrell portrait is actually painted by a French or Italian artist, who had perhaps come to England with the embassy.[31]

Sir John Luttrell, when he induced a mannerist artist to reproduce on his portrait the official allegories of the Treaty of Boulogne, preserved for us an echo of the influence on art of the Anglo-French rapprochement of 1550 of which no other traces survive.

*   *   *

We have now to turn our attention to the main body of the picture, to this bearded man wading naked in the sea with his right arm upraised into the Peace allegory. We have the word of George Luttrell, in his inscription on the Dunster version, that this is intended to be a portrait of Sir John Luttrell. But why did this eccentric man choose to have himself represented in this extraordinary manner?

In the Victoria and Albert Museum there is a remarkable example (Fig. 5b, c) of one of those jewels or pendants formed of a large or 'baroque' pearl which were fashionable in the latter half of the sixteenth century. They are usually of Italian workmanship, though some are Flemish-Italianate. The specimen in the Victoria and Albert Museum was bought in India by George Canning, when he was Viceroy in the early nineteenth century, hence the name by which it is always known, 'The Canning Jewel'. Its history before Canning acquired it in India is unknown. There is no documentary backing for the legend that it was a gift from a Medici prince to one of the Mogul Emperors.[32]

The Canning Jewel represents a Triton, or merman, a figure with a bearded face whose body is formed by a single 'baroque' pearl, ending in a tail of coloured enamel. The head and arms are of white enamel, and an enamelled shield is held in the left hand. In his upraised right hand this pearly Triton holds a club in the form of a jawbone. On the wrist of the firmly clenched hand which holds the club he wears a narrow bracelet, and higher up on the right arm a wider bracelet, the function of which is to conceal the join of the enamel arm to the pearl body. The whole jewel is in the form of a pendant, with three large pearl drops depending from it.

The Triton of the jewel has affinities with those fierce sea gods, half horse and half fish, who wield fish-bone weapons in their conflicts, as depicted, for instance, in Mantegna's famous engraving of the 'Battle of the Sea Gods'. Nevertheless there is also in the jewel a combination of Samson with classical marine mythology. The jawbone weapon recalls the jawbone of an ass with which Samson smote the Philistines.[33] The shield in the form of an animal head with widely stretched jaws may allude to another of Samson's exploits, the rending of the lion's jaws.[34] The two exploits—the smiting of the Philistines with the jawbone and the rending of the lion—are very commonly alluded to in representations of Samson,[35] but I know of no other example of Samson exploits associated with a Triton. This curious mingling of Biblical and classical to form a strong man of the sea seems peculiar to the Canning Jewel. It might suit a successful naval commander or admiral, but since the early history of the jewel before it left Europe is so totally obscure no suggestion about for whom it might have been made can be hazarded.

Comparison of the man in the sea of the Luttrell portrait with the Canning Jewel causes a shock of surprise. The Canning Jewel has a bearded portrait face; so has the man in the sea. The Triton of the Jewel wears a wrist bracelet very like those of the man in the sea, whose knotted scarf is worn at the point on the arm where the Triton wears an arm bracelet, to conceal the joint of his arm with the pearl. The Triton's body anatomy is rather indistinct, owing to the convolutions of the pearl; so is the body anatomy of the man in the sea, rising pearly white from the waves. The latter's arm poses, too, are rather unnatural—more like stiff enamel arms jointed to a pearl than arms studied from the human form. The Triton of the jewel has a weapon

---

31. The fact that the allegory is unfinished might support this suggestion; if the artist was connected with the embassy he might have had to leave with it before he had quite finished his painting on the Luttrell portrait. The Three Graces are only roughly sketched in and there are other figures at the back too indistinct to discuss or identify—the apparently flying figure above France and the face above Minerva's shield.

32. See *100 Things to See in the Victoria and Albert Museum*, no. 85; H. Clifford Smith, *Jewellery*, London, 1908, p. 249 (the Jewel is reproduced in colour in the frontispiece of this book); Peter Stone, 'Baroque Pearls', *Apollo*, February, 1959, p. 33. There is a companion jewel of a mermaid which is reproduced in Peter Stone's article.

33. Judges 15:14–16.

34. Judges 14:5–6.

35. Many examples could be cited. A notable one is the bronze in the Boston Museum in which Samson rides on the lion, rends its jaws with one hand, and holds the jawbone in the other. See H. Swarzenski, *Monuments of Romanesque Art*, London, 1954, pl. 236.

in his clenched right fist. This must surely be the explanation of the raised clenched fist of the man in the sea, that it held an invisible weapon.

The fierce Old Testament weapon which the Triton of the Canning Jewel wields in his strong right hand—Samson's weapon wherewith he smote the Philistines—would very well suit Luttrell who had been one of the fanatically Protestant and image-smashing army which marched to Scotland under the Protector. However, owing to the indistinctness of the early history of the Canning Jewel, it is quite impossible to know whether Luttrell or his artist could have seen it in England in 1550. But something of the kind they surely must have seen, or known of, and the jewel explains the kind of allegorical character that Luttrell was aiming at for himself—a strong man of the sea. The man in the Luttrell portrait is not a wader in the sea; he is a creature of the sea with an invisible fish's tail, a Triton, naked with the allegorical nakedness of a water divinity.

Since Luttrell was a soldier, and not a sailor, a land captain and not a sea admiral, this marine role does not seem to suit him very well. The person whom it would have suited would have been Admiral Clinton, the hero of the land and sea battle of Pinkie-Musselborough, the 'fish on dry land' of those combined operations, the governor of Boulogne and rewarded with the office of Lord High Admiral of England for his services in its defence—the great hero of the hour at the time of the Treaty of Boulogne. One wonders whether Luttrell, who evidently had a flair for picking up public official imagery and applying it to himself, picked up some current allegorical glorification of Clinton and applied it to himself.[36] After all, he had fought at Pinkie-Musselborough, though on land not at sea, and his later operations on Inchcolm Island had been partly amphibious, involving minor naval engagements in the unsuccessful effort to keep the Firth of Forth open to English shipping.

At any rate, the striking similarities between the Canning Jewel and the Luttrell portrait give a new insight into that portrait as an allegory. We now understand that Luttrell presents himself as a fighting sea divinity, that he himself is an allegory, and one which he attempts to connect with the allegory in the sky through the raised right hand raised into the sphere of Peace. The hand has dropped its weapon and Peace's gesture is one of restraint, complementary to that of Venus as she bridles the horse of war and lays her restraining hand on the armour and the helmet. There are no Neptunes or water divinities in the allegory in the sky. This aspect of Olympus is represented by Luttrell himself. An attempt has been made to connect the Peace allegory with the allegorical portrait of Luttrell by representing him as a warlike water divinity restrained by the hand of peace.

Or, in other words, the Scottish war is over and Luttrell's part in it is over. The *Pax* and *Amicitia* of the Treaty of Boulogne put a term to his warlike efforts. Though the juxtaposition of the curious figure in the sea with the civilized goddesses in the sky has a barbaric and ludicrous effect, one can see that an effort has been made to integrate mythologically those parts of the picture which seem at first sight quite disparate—the peace allegory in the sky and the allegorical portrait.

But artistically there is no integration. As the eye travels from the competently painted torso of Peace to the vague anatomy of the man in the sea it becomes ever more evident that these two parts of the picture were painted by different hands.

*   *   *

We now come to the last of the three elements which make up the parts of the picture—the storm in the sky, the foundering man-of-war, the terrified crew leaving the ship in boats, the drowned man floating in the sea. These scenes may be partly reminiscent of real experiences in the Scottish war, and partly an allegory of the storms and disasters of War now ended by Peace. The ship flies the flag of St. George. She is therefore an English ship; her guns are clearly visible (Fig. 7a, b). One of the most terrible of Luttrell's war experiences must have been the evacuation of himself and garrison from Inchcolm Island in the ship *Mary Hamborough* during a frightful storm. The ship was not wrecked, as here, but the scene perhaps recalls the evacuation and some tragedy of drowning which accompanied it.[37]

36. Since nothing whatever is known of the origin and early history of the Canning Jewel, anything is possible and nothing could be proved. Could it have been made by a foreign jeweller in England and have belonged into an atmosphere and field of reference similar to that of the Luttrell portrait? The face of the Triton of the Jewel is remarkably like the portrait of Admiral Clinton in the National Portrait Gallery. Supposing that it was made for Clinton, fell later into the clutches of Queen Elizabeth, who used it as a diplomatic gift to an oriental potentate, and after long sojourn in the east was eventually found in India by Canning. It is as good a guess as any other in a field where everything would have to be guesswork. But the companion jewel of a mermaid (illustrated in Peter Stone's article) would have to be taken into account in guesswork about this problem.

37. Maxwell Lyte's interpretation of the picture is worth quotation: 'It is not necessary to suppose that Sir John Luttrell ever suffered actual shipwreck. The year 1550 witnesses the wreck of the English cause in Scotland. Sir John Luttrell, one of its chief representatives, is a prisoner, denuded of all that he values most. He does not, however, give way to unseemly grief. No offer of lucre can turn him from his duty; no danger can break his lofty spirit. In a sea of misfortune he stands erect. The rainbow of hope appears in the sky and the darkest cloud

(George Luttrell perhaps put some other meaning into the corpse in the sea since the Dunster version of the picture elaborates it into a portrait.[38]) If this is the experience reflected by the storm and the shipwreck, these would yet still be an allegory—an allegory of those disasters of the later part of the Scottish war, those useless attempts to hold the places taken with insufficient garrisons—efforts now terminated by the Treaty of Boulogne with its stipulation that the fortresses held by the English in Scotland are to be delivered up or destroyed.

The storms of war are over. Peace dawns with the Treaty of Boulogne. The hero's hand is empty of its weapon. Sir John Luttrell celebrates his part in the campaign with this extraordinary portrait in which personal reminiscence mingles with public and official allegory to form a remarkable record of the mood of the year 1550 in England.

> More then the rock amydys the raging seas
> The constant hert no danger dreddys nor fearys.

The eccentric, excitable, fanatical man has come through the storms of the dangerous years, and he celebrates his own rather small part in their events by a portrait in which he identifies himself with great state allegories.

*   *   *

The monogrammatist 'HE', who signs the Luttrell portrait on the rock, also signed, in the same year 1550, a portrait of Thomas Wyndham (Fig. 8) now in the possession of the Earl of Radnor at Longford Castle.[39] On the barrels of the gun slung over his shoulder are the sitter's initials 'T.W.' and the inscription 'Aetatis sui XLII. MDL. HE'.

shows a silver lining. The goddess of peace takes him by the arm and holds forth a sprig of olive symbolical of the treaty concluded between England and Scotland. Behind her stand satellites, ready to restore to the hero all that he has recently lost' (*History of Dunster*, I, pp. 158–9). This may be not far from the truth, except for lack of understanding of the peace allegory and of the allegorical meaning of Sir John's denudation.

38. In the Dunster version, the corpse in the sea has been turned into an allusion to a dead man in a coffin. George Luttrell may have meant this as an allusion to his own father, Thomas Luttrell, who served in the Scottish wars under his brother Sir John, died in 1571 and was buried at Dunster (see Maxwell Lyte, *History of Dunster*, I, pp. 166–71). Since the face in the coffin in the Dunster version floats just above the rock on which George Luttrell records that it was through Sir John's bequest to his brother (Thomas Luttrell) that the property has come to him, it seems likely that the face in the coffin refers to that brother. It was entirely for family reasons that George Luttrell had the portrait of Sir John Luttrell copied; for the same reasons he might also wish to record in his copy an allusion to Sir John's brother, his own father.

39. Exhibited at the Royal Academy, *Works of Holbein and other Masters*, 1950–1, catalogue no. 54; *British Portraits*, 1956–7, catalogue no. 17.

Wyndham and Luttrell were related, Wyndham being Luttrell's uncle.[40] And, like Luttrell, Wyndham had been through the Scottish campaign. In 1547, he was appointed vice-admiral, under Clinton, of the fleet which went to Scotland. He thus had some share in the glory of Pinkie-Musselborough. He distinguished himself also at the subsequent siege of Haddington, and by a good deal of destruction of abbeys and other ecclesiastical property. He was still in Scotland in March, 1550, negotiating for the release of Luttrell,[41] but returned to England later in the same year.

We have thus to picture these two, Luttrell and Wyndham, nephew and uncle, both just disbanded from the Scottish wars, both repairing to the 'HE' studio to have commemorative portraits of themselves painted, with results strangely different. The 'HE' portrait of Wyndham is a straight portrait and a good one. His exploits in the Scottish war are perhaps alluded to in the background scene, where the tents of a military camp seem to be stationed in the neighbourhood of some large church or abbey. But there is nothing allegorical in the solid presentation of this tough guy. How different from the marine fantasies of Luttrell and the allegories with which he linked them! The association between Wyndham and Luttrell continued after the peace and after the painting of their portraits, for they organized a privateering expedition to Morocco.[42] The expedition was ready to start in July, 1551, but on the 10th of that month Luttrell died at Greenwich of the sweating sickness, which was very prevalent in that year. He was about thirty-one years of age. His portrait was thus his swan song. Wyndham continued with the project and duly sailed from Portsmouth on this new adventure, but died on one of his later voyages in 1553.

*   *   *

Amongst the portraits listed in the Lumley Inventory of 1590, a list of works of art said then to be in the possession of Lord Lumley, are the following:

> Of Sir John Lutterel, who died of the sweat in K. Edw: 6 tyme.
> Of Mr. Thomas Wyndeham drowned in the sea returninge from Ginney.[43]

(These entries do not follow one another immediately, as given here.) The Inventory gives no name of artist for either of these pictures. The portrait of Wyndham

40. See Maxwell Lyte, *History of Dunster*, I, pp. 146 ff.; and on Wyndham's life and career the article in the *Dictionary of National Biography*.

41. Maxwell Lyte, I, p. 155.

42. *Ibid.*, pp. 161 ff.

43. Lionel Cust, 'The Lumley Inventories', *Walpole Society*, VI (1918), pp. 23, 25.

can be traced from the Lumley collection through subsequent owners to its present owner; it was therefore the portrait of Wyndham signed 'HE'.[44] No such definite history of the portrait of Luttrell mentioned in the inventory has been traced but it is assumed to be the allegorical portrait signed 'HE' in the version now in the Courtauld Gallery.[45]

In modern catalogue entries concerning the Dunster version of the portrait of Luttrell—the only version hitherto seriously considered—it is confidently stated that the picture is by 'Hans Eworth'. This statement rests on the dubious arguments with which Lionel Cust supported his assertion, in an article published in 1912,[46] that the monogram 'HE' represents the initials of a Flemish artist settled in England called Hans Eworth. Cust's article has been enormously influential and his explanation of the monogram has been accepted for more than half a century.

Cust noticed that three portraits listed in the Lumley Inventory are there said to be by 'Haunce Eworth'. He discovered by research among documents that a Flemish painter of this name, or of something like this name under various spellings, was consecutively in England from about 1545 onwards. He thereupon published his article of 1912 in which he asserted that all pictures signed 'HE' are by Hans Eworth. It is strange that the uncritical element in Cust's arguments was not noticed. Not one of the three portraits assigned

to 'Haunce Eworth' in the Lumley Inventory has been traced[47] (though one of them may be reflected in a seventeenth-century copy). There is therefore no work of art known to be by this artist from which his style can be known. When 'the style of Hans Eworth' is spoken of, this means the style of pictures signed 'HE' which Cust supposed to be by Eworth. He assumes that because some portraits in the Lumley Inventory are said to be by 'Haunce Eworth' therefore other portraits in the list are also by this artist. The Inventory mentions portraits of Wyndham and Luttrell but does not say that these portraits are by Eworth; it gives no name of artist for them. It was Cust's assumption that the Inventory means that these portraits are by Eworth because in the same list it names other portraits which it does state to be by Eworth. This is surely a very extraordinary argument. Once Cust's article is critically examined, it begins to fall apart at many points and it becomes evident that the whole question of the portraits signed with the monogram 'HE' requires to be tackled in an entirely new way, with detailed examination of all the pictures. This work is now being undertaken,[48] and until the results are published no statement can be made about the artist, or the artists, or the firm which used the monogram.

This article has not been concerned with the 'HE' problem but only with the meaning and origin of the allegories in one of the pictures signed with the monogram, the portrait of Sir John Luttrell in the Courtauld version, of which it can be confidently stated that it is by more than one artist.

This picture is a curiosity, some may think it a monstrosity, but it is historically important. It catches something of the feeling of the hour in England in 1550, a dark hour, fraught with anxiety. It reflects the rapprochement with France over the Treaty of Boulogne and the coming of the French embassy. No other French embassy was to come to England for thirty years, until the time of the proposed marriage of Anjou with Queen Elizabeth in the fifteen-eighties. The vision in the sky in the Luttrell portrait is a vision of the outside world of continental art which tries,

---

44. Lionel Cust, 'The Painter HE, Hans Eworth', *Walpole Society*, II (1912), p. 19.

45. Cust thought ('The Lumley Inventories', p. 24 note) that it was either the Dunster picture or the picture then at Badmondisfield Hall, now in the Courtauld Institute. The catalogue entry (no. 54) of the *Works of Holbein and other Masters* exhibition assumes that it was probably the Courtauld version that is mentioned in the Lumley Inventory.
It would now seem certain that it was the Courtauld version which was in the Lumley collection in 1590, since the Dunster version is a copy, not made until 1591. Did George Luttrell see the Courtauld version in the Lumley collection about 1590? The picture must have been accessible to his artist when the copy was made in 1591.
Any attempt to trace the later history of the Courtauld picture would presumably have to start with the Bromleys of Badmondisfield Hall, to whom it belonged when Lord Lee bought it in 1932, and work backwards. The ownership of Badmondisfield goes back from the Bromleys to a family called Warner who had inherited it from the Norths of Mildenhall (see A. Page, *History of Suffolk*, Ipswich, 1847, p. 904). The founder of the North family, Sir Edward North, had held important official posts in the time of Edward VI. It is thus possible that the North family might have been interested in acquiring from Lord Lumley the Courtauld picture with its historical associations. However, there is no reason to assume that the Courtauld picture necessarily descended with Badmondisfield Hall to its successive owners and so its history, after its appearance in the Lumley Inventory in 1590, really remains unknown. Since the picture was in such a bad state when Lord Lee acquired it, probably it had been little valued or understood by previous owners.

46. 'The Painter HE, Hans Eworth', *Walpole Society*, II (1912).

47. The three portraits are as follows:

Of Mr. Edw. Shelley slayne at Mustleborough feilde, drawen by Haunce Eworth.
Of Haward a Dutch Jueller, drawne for a Maisters prize by his brother Haunce Eworth.
Of Mary, Duchesse of Northfolke, daughter to the last old Earle of Arundel doone by Haunce Eworth.

See L. Cust, 'The Lumley Inventories', *Walpole Society*, VI, pp. 24, 25, 26; 'The Painter HE', *Walpole Society*, II, pp. 3–4.
It is of course not impossible that Hans Eworth may come into the HE problem in some way, but not in the form of the sweeping statements of Cust.

48. By Roy C. Strong.

awkwardly and unsuccessfully, to make contact with the sequestered world of the England of Edward VI. What is also interesting in the picture is its revelation of the psychology of a man of the age of Protestant iconoclasm. The images have been smashed, but they

come back in the form of the pagan imagery of the Renaissance. Amidst the storms of his turbulent life, Sir John Luttrell needs the kindly images of Peace and Friendship on which to call in the hour of shipwreck.

Note. This article was completed and out of my hands early in 1965; at that time little public attention had as yet been paid to the Courtauld version of the portrait of Sir John Luttrell. Later in that year, the inclusion of the picture in an exhibition held at the City of Leicester Art Gallery and the National Portrait Gallery from November 1965 to January 1966 aroused interest

in it and raised again the problem of the identity of HE; see R. C. Strong, 'Hans Eworth, A Tudor Artist and his Circle', printed with the catalogue to the exhibition; and 'Hans Eworth Reconsidered', *Burlington Magazine*, June 1966.
I wish to thank Miss Yvonne Hackenbroch of the Metropolitan Museum of Art, who is a specialist on Renaissance jewelry, for valuable consultations about the Canning Jewel.

APPENDIX

Report on the Dunster Castle and Courtauld Institute Versions of the Portrait of Sir John Luttrell

by S. REES JONES

The two paintings, which will be referred to as D and C, are on panels of approximately the same dimensions. C measures 43″ × 33″, and D is ¾″ longer. The composition however suggests that C might have been cut on the left with the loss of the elbow of the figure with the two purses and part of the peacock. The possibility of some loss on the right cannot be excluded judging by the look of the forearm and the bracelet. There is further evidence of cutting in the dimensions of the outer panel members; the widths of the four members are:

at the top,	7⅛″	8⅞″	9⅕″	7⅞″
at the bottom,	7¼″	8⅞″	9⅛″	7¾″

The panel of C, in oak with dowelled joints, is typical of Flemish and Northern painting generally; D is in elm, a wood far less commonly used for panels. This evidence suggests that the two works are not an original and a replica from the same workshop. They are certainly not by the same hand. The visual and X-ray evidence show that D is homogeneous in execution and has nothing in common with C which indeed might be the work of two painters. The X-ray photograph of the figure of Sir John Luttrell in C shows technique similar to English or Flemish sixteenth-century portraits in general. In the allegorical group on the other hand, the paint is thicker and has been used with the greatest assurance to model forms such as the nude for example. It thus becomes necessary to decide which of the two versions has the greater claim to be regarded as the original.

In support of the view that C is not a copy are the following points:
(1) The existence of a pentiment in the position of the dark band which separates the allegorical group from the sky.
(2) Several details occur in C and not in D; for example the crescent on the head of the figure with the purses, the flying figure, and the swirl of foaming water below the floating head. These details do not appear to have been lost in D through overpainting.
(3) There is a marked difference in tonality between the two paintings which is not entirely to be accounted for by the state of the varnish. The sea is green in C and brown in D; D has a greenish-grey peacock which is a bright 'peacock' in C; the colours in the allegorical group are brilliant in C, and in keeping with the mannerist style, whereas in D they are more subdued.
The scale is the same in the two works, but since D includes the elbow of the figure with the purses there is a shift of the figures to the right. This shift (which was measured with full-size tracing) is curious in that it involves a distortion of the torso of Peace.
It is difficult to draw positive conclusions about the inscriptions on the rock because they have been retouched in both paintings. In D the retouching is simply a strengthening of some of the letters which had become thin. In C the many losses have been crudely made good and the entire inscription repainted. There is no trace of the Latin quatrain followed by '1591.G.L.' in C. It is not possible to decide on the

technical evidence whether *renovare* implies restoration in the sense of picture conservation or whether the date 1591 gives the year in which the copy was made. The only restoration to be seen is modern.

The inscription on the left-arm bracelet in C is badly mutilated and has been restored to read NEC FECIT LUCRUM which also appears on the right arm. There is however under the repaint NEC FREGIT DISCRIMEN as in D.

The Courtauld Institute version has suffered much loss of paint through flaking. It is not inconceivable that the onset of this deterioration at an early date led to the commission of the Dunster version in 1591, as the inscription suggests.

HARALD KELLER

Entstehung und Blütezeit des Freundschaftsbildes

Über die dekadente Spätphase des Freundschaftsbildes in der deutschen Romantik besitzen wir ein ausgezeichnetes Buch von Klaus Lankheit.[1] Für Entstehung und Frühzeit dieser Bildgattung mussten wir uns bisher mit der einleitenden Übersicht zu diesem Buche begnügen.

Das Freundschaftsbild tritt zu dem frühest möglichen Termin auf, zu dem die Bedingungen für seine Existenz gegeben sind, nämlich an der Schwelle der Frührenaissance. Die Literatur war der bildenden Kunst um fast hundert Jahre voraufgegangen: in Petrarcas Sonetten und in seinen Epistolae familiares finden wir den Niederschlag eines geradezu zärtlichen Freundschaftskultes.

Die bildende Kunst konnte nicht eher folgen, bis die formellen Voraussetzungen einer solchen Bildnisgattung geschaffen waren. Das gemalte Porträt eines Fürsten in Halbfigur oder in Büstenform, durch einen Rahmen als autonomes Kunstwerk bestimmt und von aller mittelalterlicher Zuordnung zu einem Heiligen oder einer gesellschaftlichen Schicht befreit, hatte schon die Mitte des 14. Jahrhunderts ausgebildet (Porträt des französischen Königs Jean le Bon, gest. 1364, Paris, Louvre und des Herzogs Rudolf IV. von Österreich, gest. 1365; Wien, Erzbischöfl. Diözesan-Museum).[2]

Aber dem Trecento waren doch im Grunde nur weltliche und geistliche Fürsten und allenfalls städtische Magistrate um ihrer selbst willen als bildwürdig erschienen; die grossen Künstler, Dante und Petrarca, treten nur als Assistenzfiguren in vielgestaltigen religiösen Fresken in den Kapellen von Kirchen und Comunalpalästen auf. Eine der Grundvoraussetzungen des Freundschaftsbildes, nämlich die Aufhebung der Standesunterschiede, war im Trecento weder in der Literatur noch der bildenden Kunst gegeben: wie Petrarcas Freundeskreis nur aus Klerikern und Literaten, aus Humanisten bestand, so kannte die bildende Kunst nur das Fürsten- und Regentenbildnis.

Wenn also das Freundschaftsbild wirklich eine mittel-

alterliche Wurzel haben sollte, so kann sie nur in dem Standesbildnis der Gotik zu suchen sein. Der Ansicht Lankheits: "Wie das Einzelbildnis entwickelt sich auch das Gruppenporträt und in seinem Rahmen das Freundschaftsbildnis aus dem Kultbild"[3] vermögen wir nicht beizupflichten. Wir glauben vielmehr, dass das Freundschaftsbildnis als ganz neue Gattung in der profanen Luft des Frühhumanismus sich entfaltet hat. Auch von den Reihenbildnissen der uomini famosi, welche im italienischen Trecento die Darstellung der "neun guten Helden" der nordischen Gotik ablösten, führt im Süden kein Weg zum Freundschaftsbild.[4]

Soweit wir sehen, läuft nur eine recht schmale Entwicklungslinie vom Mittelalter in die Frührenaissance —vom mittelalterlichen Künstlerbildnis zu dem des Quattrocento. Gruppenbildnisse von Architekten hatten ja schon die Labyrinthe der französischen Kathedralen gebracht.[5] Dabei waren die stolzesten Ansprüche angemeldet worden. Wenn das Labyrinth nämlich das Wahrzeichen des Daedalus bedeutet, den das Mittelalter als den mythischen Baumeister des Altertums schlechthin verehrte, so gibt der gotische Architekt, indem er sein Bildnis in das Labyrinth setzt, die Meinung kund, dass seine Kathedrale den grossen Bauwerken der Antike ebenbürtig sei. "Die Erstarkung des Persönlichkeitsbewusstseins", die man so gern als einen stolzen Gewinn des Quattrocento ansieht, hat demnach im Künstlerselbstbildnis um die Mitte des 13. Jahrhunderts schon eine erstaunliche Höhe erreicht. Indessen kennt das 13. Jahrhundert auch Doppelselbstbildnisse von Künstlern, die nun durchaus nur als Handlanger oder Werkmeister Gottes verstanden werden wollen. Die Gedenktafel für zwei in voller Figur abgebildete Baumeister im Baseler

---

1. K. Lankheit, *Das Freundschaftsbild der Romantik* (Heidelberger Kunstgeschichtliche Abhandlungen, hrsg. v. W. Paatz, N.F. 1), Heidelberg 1952.
2. H. Keller, "Die Entstehung des Bildnisses am Ende des Hochmittelalters", *Römisches Jahrbuch für Kunstgeschichte*, III, 1939, p. 344 f. und p. 348 f.

3. Lankheit, p. 21.
4. Nur im Norden und erst im 16. Jahrhundert gibt es ausgesprochene Freundschaftsbilder, die sich aus den Triaden der "neun guten Helden" entwickelt haben: Freundschaftstempel mit Herzog Wilhelm IV. von Bayern, Ottheinrich und Philipp von der Pfalz unter der Gestalt Karls des Grossen, des Gottfried von Bouillon und des Königs Artus, gemeisselt von Hans Daucher (Schloss Neuenstein, Württemberg), vgl. Ph. M. Halm, *Studien zur süddeutschen Plastik*, II, Augsburg 1927, Abb. 177 ff.—E. F. Bange, *Die Kleinplastik der deutschen Renaissance in Holz und Stein*, München o.J. (1928), p. 24 und Taf. 14.
5. H. R. Hahnloser, *Villard de Honnecourt*, Wien 1935, p. 38 ff. —R. de Lasteyrie, *L'Architecture religieuse en France à l'époque gotique*, Paris 1927, II, p. 247 ff.—C. Enlart, *Manuel d'Archéologie Française*, 1. Architecture religieuse. Paris 1920, p. 814 ff.

Münster, um 1200 entstanden, bezeichnet die beiden als "Aula celesti lapides vivi titulantur hiduo templi huius quia structure famulantur."[6]

Das grosse Breitbild mit den Begründern der florentiner Renaissancekunst (Paris, Louvre) ist ein säkularisiertes Künstlergruppenbild.[7] Sind die Baumeister des Labyrinths von Amiens durch die vier Balken des Kreuzes Christi von einander getrennt, das in der Mitte des Labyrinths steht, so umweht die fünf Künstler aus dem florentinischen Quattrocento nun eine ganz profane Luft. Auch ist das "Fünf-Männer-Bild" kein reines Standesbildnis mehr, sondern steht in der Mitte zwischen Standes- und Freundschaftsbild. Die Dargestellten sind gar nicht mehr alle Künstler, Antonio Manetti ist ein hervorragender Gelehrter. Es sind aber auch nicht "die Erfinder der Perspektive" dargestellt—wie man das Bild sehr oft fälschlich genannt hat—denn Ghiberti und Masaccio fehlen. Ghiberti muss fehlen, weil er in der Frage der Einwölbung der Domvierung der schärfste Konkurrent Brunellescos gewesen war. Ein Freundeskreis schliesst sich nicht durch objektive Auswahl, sondern durch Zuneigung zusammen. Masaccio muss fehlen, weil er zu jung (mit 27 Jahren) starb, um in eine solche Männerfreundschaft hineinwachsen zu können! Das Freundschaftsbild entsteht also in den ersten Jahren der Frührenaissance und in Florenz—das heisst also, die Ausbildung dieser Gattung ist an die Entstehung des Humanismus auf Gedeih und Verderb gebunden und wird es noch über hundert Jahre bleiben. Diese Männer besitzen eine gemeinsame geistige Welt, und jeder ist bei seiner Lebensarbeit auf Hilfe der Freunde angewiesen. Giotto allein hatte hundert Jahre früher gelebt—aber seinem Werk fühlten sich alle als der Grundlage ihres eigenen Wirkens dankbar verpflichtet. Der Erhaltungszustand der Tafel ist derartig schlecht, dass nicht entschieden werden kann, ob man ein Original des Quattrocento oder eine Replik des 16. Jahrhunderts vor sich hat. Über eines aber besteht Einmütigkeit: dass das Bild keinesfalls eine ursprüngliche, für diesen Zweck erfundene Komposition darstellt. Man sieht sogleich, dass die Porträts, die gar nicht recht zusammen stimmen wollen, hier in Zweitverwendung erscheinen, dass diese Büsten also aus ganz anderen Vorlagen heraus kopiert worden sein müssen und hat dabei vor allem an Masaccios verlorenes Fresko mit der "Sagra del Carmine" gedacht,

in das—nach Vasaris Zeugnis—viele Künstlerporträts aufgenommen waren.[8] Dass dieser Vorgang keineswegs ungewöhnlich wäre, beweist ein Breitbild mit den Büsten dreier Künstler aus der Malerfamilie Gaddi (Florenz, Uffizien), dem Giulio Pesello zugeschrieben, bei dem die Figur des Agnolo Gaddi nachweisblich aus einem Fresko dieses Meisters in Santa Croce herauskopiert worden ist.[9]

Doch sind es zunächst nicht die Stadtrepubliken, sondern die fürstlichen Musenhöfe, wo das Freundschaftsbild gepflegt wird. Eine geschlossene Gruppe bilden die Doppelporträts, auf denen ein Fürst sich mit einem oder mit zwei seiner familiari darstellen liess. So malte Jean Fouquet, der sich zwischen 1443 und 47 in Italien aufhielt, in Rom das Leinwandbild Papst Eugens IV. (gest. 1447) mit zweien seiner Vertrauten. Das Werk ist verloren, wir wissen davon nur durch Filarete, der aus eigener Kenntnis und als Zeitgenosse urteilt: "Il quale fe a Roma papa Eugenio e due altri de' suoi appresso di lui; che veramente parevano vivi proprio. I quali dipinse insù uno panno, il quale fu conlocato nella sagrestia della Minerva. Io dico così, perché a mio tempo gli dipinse."[10] Auch Vasari, der den Künstler in der ersten Ausgabe richtig "Fochetto" nennt, dies aber in der 2. Ausgabe in "Foccora" entstellt, hat die Nachricht noch.[11]

Ein Doppelbildnis des Markgrafen Lionello d'Este von Ferrara mit seinem Günstling Folco di Villafora schuf 1449 ein Maler Andrea di Padova, der nicht unbedingt Andrea Mantegna sein muss.[12] Nach dem von Campori veröffentlichten Beleg[13] waren Fürst und Diener einander im Profil gegenüber gestellt (Lionello d'Este da un verso e Folco da Villafora dall'altro), natürlich nur als Halbfiguren, wie ja auch die Bildnisse Pisanellos und Jacopo Bellinis vom Ferraresischen Hof nur erst Halbfiguren geben.

Genau die gleiche Darstellungsform findet man mehrfach am Hofe von Urbino, dem glanzvollsten der Musensitze auf der der Adria zugekehrten Seite Italiens. Zunächst wird im herzoglichen Palast unter der Inventar-Nr. 806 ein Flachrelief aus Kalkstein in Form einer Lünette aufbewahrt, das ursprünglich

6. Abb. *Reallexikon zur deutschen Kunstgeschichte*, Bd. III, Artikel Denkmal (H. Keller), Sp. 1276 und Abb. 4.
7. Aus der sehr umfangreichen Literatur zum Fünf-Männer-Bild nennen wir nur die beiden jüngsten Publikationen: Jenö Lanyi, "The Louvre Portrait of five Florentines", *Burlington Magazine*, 84–85, 1944, p. 94 ff.—J. Pope-Hennessy, *The Complete Work of Paolo Uccello*, London o.J. (1950), p. 154 ff. und Taf. 103–8.

8. Vasari—Milanesi, II, p. 295. Brunellesco, Donatello und Masolino werden namentlich erwähnt.
9. H. Keller, *Römisches Jahrbuch*, III, 1939, p. 341 u. Abb. 302.
10. Ant. Averlino Filaretes Tractat über die Baukunst. Hrsg. von W. v. Oettingen (Eitelberger-Ilgs Wiener Quellenschriften, N.F. III), Wien 1890, p. 307.
11. Vasari—Milanesi, II, p. 461.—M. J. Friedländer spricht in Thieme-Becker's *Künstlerlexikon*, 12, 1916, p. 252 von einem Bildnis des Papstes mit zwei "Nepoten", wovon in der Quelle nichts steht. Von Friedländer hat P. Wescher, *Jean Fouquet*, Basel 1947, p. 26 den "Nepoten" übernommen.
12. P. Kristeller, *Andrea Mantegna*, Berlin 1902, p. 41, note 1.—E. Tietze-Conrat, *Mantegna*. Phaidon, Köln 1956, p. 250.
13. S. Campori, *Pittori degli Estensi*, 1886, p. 357 (Atti di Deputazione di Storia Patria, Modena 1886, 3, III, 2).

wohl in den Verband einer Türe, eines Kamins, einer Loggia oder dergleichen gehört haben wird. Es zeigt die einander zugekehrten Bildnisse des Herzogs Federigo da Montefeltre (rechts) und seines Sekretärs, des Grafen Ottaviano Ubaldini (links) in Halbfigur. Das Relief ist—sicher zu Unrecht—dem Francesco di Giorgio zugeschrieben worden.[14] Nun war dieser Graf Ubaldini zwar entweder der illegitime Bruder oder doch der unebenbürtige Vetter des Herzogs,[15] aber niemals würde es dem Sprossen einer alten erlauchten Dynastie in den Sinn gekommen sein, sich mit einem Bastard seiner Familie porträtieren zu lassen, wenn nur solche Bande einer illegitimen Verwandschaft die beiden verbunden hätten! Nein, es handelt sich vielmehr um ein echtes Freundschaftsbild, denn der Graf führte daheim in Urbino die Regierungsgeschäfte, wenn Federigo als einer der meist begehrten Condottieren seiner Zeit oder als Gonfaloniere der Kirche im Felde stand. In seinem Testament hat der Herzog den Ubaldino zum Vormund seines minderjährigen Erben eingesetzt, und dieser hat eine Regentschaft geführt, die dem jungen Guidobaldo seine Rechte nicht schmälerte.

Ganz daselbe Schema zeigt eine vatikanische Miniatur welche den Herzog mit einem der bedeutendsten Künstler seines Kreises darstellt, mit Francesco di Giorgio Martini (cod. Urb. lat. 508).[16] Die Tempera—Malerei gehört nicht in die Handschrift, der sie später beigebunden ist. Weller vermutet, dass sie ursprünglich das Titelblatt eines Exemplars der Handschrift des Trattato di architettura darstellte, den Francesco di Giorgio seinem Herrn gewidmet hatte. Da Weller die Illustration für eine eigenhändige Arbeit des Künstlers ansieht, so hätten wir hier ein Dedikationsblatt vor uns, das zum Freundschaftsbild geworden ist. Dargebracht wird hier gar nichts mehr, und der Künstler ist auch nicht mehr kniend und mit gebogenem Rücken dargestellt. Herr und Diener stehen in einem Fensterrahmen, über dessen Brüstung ein kostbarer persischer Teppich herabhängt, völlig gleichberechtigt nebeneinander, und nichts weist darauf hin, dass das aufgeschlagene Buch, das der Herzog mit beiden Händen vor der Brust ergreift, der ihm gewidmete Traktat sei.

Die venezianische Miniatur auf Pergament im Boymans-Museum in Rotterdam, welche dem Dogen Andrea Vendramin (1476–1478) in Halbfigur einen jungen Geistlichen im Profil gegenüberstellt, folgt genau demselben Bildaufbau wie das Widmungsbild des Francesco di Giorgio. Auch auf dem venezianischen Einzelblatt erscheinen die Dargestellten in einem Fensterrahmen und hinter einer Brüstung, von der ein kostbarer Teppich herabhängt, in dessen Mitte das Vendramin—Wappen erscheint. Wir müssen also annehmen, dass es sich ebenfalls um eine Widmungsminiatur handelt, die zum Freundschaftsbild geworden ist und dass Schenker und Beschenkter sich menschlich nahe standen.[17]

In den Kreis der urbinatischen Hofkunst gehört schliesslich noch das Tafelbild der Pinakothek in Neapel, das den grossen Mathematiker Fra Luca Pacioli hinter einem Tische stehend zeigt, auf dem Bücher, ein Winkelmesser, ein Kompass, ein Tintenfass mit Futteral und ein Polyeder aus Holz liegen. Etwas unorganisch ist an die Halbfigur des Mönchs die Gestalt eines jungen Mannes in weltlicher Tracht am rechten Bildrand herangeschoben, sodass nicht schwer zu erkennen ist, dass man hier eine spätere Hinzufügung vor sich hat.[18] Das Bild, welches auf einem cartellino die ungedeutete Inschrift trägt: "Jaco. Bar. vigennis. p. 1495" ist alter Besitz des urbinatischen Fürstenhauses, da es in den Inventaren dieses Hausgutes vorkommt, die 1631 bei Erlöschen der herzoglichen Familie Rovere angefertigt wurden. Auch kann ja gar kein Zweifel darüber herrschen, dass das Bild die Atmosphäre des urbinatischen Hofes aus der Spätzeit des Quattrocento festhält: in dem zweiten Polyeder, diesmal aus Kristall, der an einem roten Faden von der Decke herabhängt, spiegelt sich das Licht, das aus einer unsichtbaren Lichtquelle (also aus einem Fenster im Rücken des Betrachters) fällt und dabei werden Teile eines Gebäudes und von Bäumen

14. Von A. Venturi, *Arte*, 26, 1923, p. 204 und Abb. 7 als eine Replik nach Francesco di Giorgio veröffentlicht. Diese Zuweisung von A. St. Weller, *Francesco di Giorgio*, Chicago o.J. (1943), p. 335 f. mit Recht abgelehnt.
15. Über Ubaldini vgl. A. Schmarsow, *Melozzo da Forlì*, Stuttgart 1886, p. 87 f.—W. Bombe, *Florentiner Mitteilungen*, I, 1908–11, p. 133 mit 2 Abb.
16. A. Venturi, *Arte*, 28, 1925, p. 191 ff.—Die Identifizierung der zweiten Person mit Francesco di Giorgio aber erst bei A. St. Weller, p. 192 u. Abb. 51.

17. Burlington Fine Arts Club, 1912, *Early Venetian Pictures*, Nr. 70, p. 64, damals Giovanni Bellini genannt und in Sammlung J. P. Heseltine, Sunderland.—Bei A. Venturi, *Storia dell'Arte italiana*, VII, 4, p. 558 u. Abb. 343 als "Anonimo Belliniano".—Beste Abb: Italian Drawings exhibited at Burlington House, London 1930, London 1931, Nr. 159 u. Taf. CXXXVIII; damals in Sammlung Königs, Haarlem als "Venezianisch, 15. Jhdt."—Bei L. Servolini, *Jacopo de' Barbari*, Venedig o.J. (1944), p. 30 u. Taf. III dem venezianischen Miniaturisten Jacometto (nachweisbar zwischen 1472 und 1494) gegeben;—von F. Heinemann, *Giovanni Bellini e i Belliniani*, Venedig o.J. (1960), p. 240, v 150 in den Kreis des Gentile Bellini gerückt.
18. Die ältere Literatur über das Bild verzeichnet bei A. Colasanti, *Die Malerei des 15. Jahrhunderts in den italienischen Marken*, Florenz, 1932, p. 101 ff. u. Taf. 76.—Mostra di Melozzo da Forlì e del Quattrocento Romagnolo. Forlì 1938, Kat. Nr. 45, p. 36.—Bei Heinemann v 394, p. 274 dem Alvise Vivarini zugeschrieben. Dort auch die Nachricht, dass Röntgen—Untersuchungen ergeben hätten, dass die Signatur nicht ursprünglich sei.

in starker Verkürzung reflektiert. Wir haben hier demnach ein Zeugnis für die mathematisch—optischen Interessen des urbinatischen Musenhofes und einen Niederschlag der niederländischen Tafelmalerei, besonders der kleinen profanen Genrebildchen in der Art des Jan van Eyck, vor uns. Hingegen wissen wir immer noch nichts über die Persönlichkeit des Malers und des jugendlichen Dargestellten, der über die Schulter aus dem Bilde herausschaut. Dass die Signatur nicht—wie es so verführerisch wäre—in "Jacopo dei Barbari" aufgelöst werden kann, wissen wir seit Jahrzehnten. Für die Hinzufügung der Randfigur hat Roberto Longhi den Marco Palmezzano als Künstler vorgeschlagen.[19] In dem jungen Manne den Herzog Guidobaldo von Urbino erblicken zu wollen, hat man ebenfalls aufgeben müssen. Wir wissen also nicht, wer der junge Mensch ist, um dessentwillen das Porträt des Mathematikers von 1495 bald darauf zu einem Freundschaftsbild erweitert wurde.

Die Gattung des Freundschaftsbildes muss an der Schwelle der Hochrenaissance in dem Kreise um Giorgione geradezu die ideale Atmosphäre gefunden haben, wo sie gedeihen konnte. Rätseln wir schon ewig vergebens an der Entschlüsselung der Bildstoffe von Giorgiones mythologischen Gemälden herum. so sind seine Bildnisse erst recht mit dem Schleier des Geheimnisses umgeben. Von dem Porträt einer Kurtisane abgesehen, sind uns nur Bildnisse von schönen Jünglingen von der Hand Giorgiones überkommen. Niemand wird das für einen zufälligen Erhaltungszustand ansehen wollen: gewiss hat der Meister nur seine gleichaltrigen Freunde aus jenem esoterischen Kreise gemalt, dem er selbst angehört haben muss. Auf den gemalten Brüstungen, hinter denen alle diese Halbfiguren von Jünglingen erscheinen, sind die rätselhaftesten Embleme angebracht, die nur den Eingeweihten, den Mitgliedern dieser Sodalität, ihren Sinn erschlossen (Broccardo, Budapest).[20]

Doppelbildnisse von Giorgione sind nicht auf uns gekommen, aber durch Vasari literarisch bezeugt. Dieser kannte in Florenz das Bildnis des Giovanni Borgherini von Giorgione, eines Musikers, der einen Teil seiner Jugend in Venedig verbracht hatte, zusammen dargestellt mit seinem maestro, also wohl einem Musiklehrer.[21] Eines dieser Doppelbildnisse scheint uns aber in zwei Repliken erhalten zu sein, von denen das eine, dem Cariani zugeschrieben, sich im Louvre befindet,[22] während das andere neuerdings in das Museum of fine Arts von Houston (Texas) gelangt ist.[23] Beide Bilder besitzen hervorragende Provenienzen, das Pariser Stück, aus der Sammlung Vendramin in Venedig, ging durch die Sammlungen König Karls I. von England, Jabach, Ludwig XIV., ehe es seinen Platz in der Grande Galerie des Louvre fand. Das Bild in Houston kam mit der Sammlung Solly in der Romantik (1821) schon in die Berliner Museen, die es später veräusserten. Die Replik des Louvre ist vom jungen Degas um 1859–1860 kopiert worden.[24] Die beiden Repliken unterscheiden sich nur darin, dass auf dem Pariser Bild die Figuren ihre Plätze getauscht haben und dass der neutrale, dunkelbraune Hintergrund in Paris durch einen echt venezianischen Landschaftsausschnitt ersetzt wurde (Abb. 1).

Ein giorgioneskes Doppelbildnis, das Berenson und Fiocco dem Domenico Mancini geben wollten, kam als Legat des Principe Fabrizio Ruffo di Motta Bagnaia in das Museum des Palazzo Venezia in Rom. Auf der venezianischen Giorgione—Ausstellung von 1955 hat man es gar—einem alten Vorschlag von Roberto Longhi folgend—unter die eigenhändigen Werke des Meisters einreihen wollen.[25] Die Zuordnung der beiden Jünglinge, des Verträumten und des Energischen, zueinander schiebt den einen zu sehr in den Hintergrund, sodass man beinahe an die Darstellung eines Herrn und seines Dieners denken könnte. Indessen werden die Gründe für diese Gruppierung schliesslich doch nicht soziologischer, sondern formaler Natur sein. Bildnisse, bei denen die Komposition an einer stosskräftigen Diagonale in drastischer Verkürzung aus der Tiefe her oder in die Tiefe hin entwickelt wird, sind nicht stadt-venezianisch, sondern zumeist auf der Terra ferma beheimatet. Unter den Porträts von Lorenzo Lotto[26] oder von Savoldo[27] finden sich viele verwandte Beispiele. So möchten wir auch bei unserem Doppelbildnis, das dic liebevolle Charakterisierung des Verhältnisses der beiden Freunde zueinander einem äusserst wirksamen Bildaufbau opfert, für einen Künstler aus der Terra ferma als Maler plädieren.

Wendet man sich aus der Lagune nach Rom, so lässt

19. Mostra di Melozzo da Forlì, Kat. Nr. 45, p. 36.
20. Fr. Hartlaub, *Giorgiones Geheimnis*, München o.J. (1925), Abb. 5–7, 13, 15, 17.
21. Vasari—Milanesi, IV, p. 94.
22. L. Gallina, *Giovanni Cariani*, Bergamo 1954, p. 122 u. Taf.
LIX.—Fr. Heinemann, Abb. 600 u. Text p. 228, Nr. v 71 als Jugendwerk des Paris Bordone.
23. H. Posse, *Die Gemäldegalerie des Kaiser Friedrich-Museums*, I, 2. Aufl. Berlin 1913, p. 127 als "Vittore Belliniano (?)".—Gallina, *Cariani*, Taf. LIX, und p. 122. Fr. Heinemann, Abb. 539 Text p. 200. Nr. 804, um 1515 angesetzt.
24. P. A. Lemoisne, *Degas et son œuvre*, Paris o.J., II, Nr. 59.
25. Giorgione e i Giorgioneschi, Catalogo della Mostra Palazzo Ducale 1955, p. 80, Nr. 35.—G. Fiocco, *Rivista del R. Istituto d'Archeologia e storia dell'Arte*, I, 1929, p. 133.
26. Mostra di Lorenzo Lotto. Venezia Palazzo Ducale, 1953. Catalogo Uffiziale, Nr. 67, 68, 69, 70.
27. Ant. Boschetto, *Giovan Gerolamo Savoldo*, Milano o.J. (1963), Taf. 30.

man den Kreis schöner, undurchdringlicher Jünglings-
gesichter, die alle untereinander im geheimen Einver-
ständnis zu leben scheinen, hinter sich und tritt in die
Sphäre von Männern auf der Mittagshöhe des
Lebens. Unvergleichlich ist das Bildnis der beiden
venezianischen Dichter Andrea Navagero und Agostino Beazzano in Halbfigur von Raffael (Rom, Galleria
Doria-Pamphili).[28] Im März 1516 etwa muss das
Doppelporträt gemalt worden sein; damals weilte der
soeben zum Bibliothekar der Marciana ernannte
Navagero mit seinem Freunde in Rom. Wir wissen
aus einem Briefe Bembos, dass damals beide Vene-
zianer an einem Ausfluge nach Tivoli teilnahmen, den
Bembo mit Raffael und Castiglione veranstaltete. Das
Bild scheint auch für Bembo gemalt worden zu sein,
jedenfalls war er der erste Besitzer. In seinem Hause
in Padua sah der Anonimo Morelliano das Doppelporträt und erst in einem Briefe vom 29. Juli 1538
erklärt sich Bembo bereit, das Gemälde an Beazzano
abzugeben.[29] "Vielleicht führt kein Bildnis so tief in
den Kreis dieser humanistischen Gesellschaft mit ihren
Ansprüchen an Harmonie im inneren und äusseren
Gleichgewicht ein; es gibt eine Ahnung von der
geistigen Vielgestaltigkeit im Nebeneinander erlesener
Menschen. Und Raphael weiss zu deuten, wohin in
ihrem Auftreten und Verhalten zur Welt die Wünsche
gingen.... Sie blicken in die Welt wie mit *einem*
Augenpaar: der eine durchdringend und prüfend
das klare rechte uns zugewandt, der andere, mehr
schauend, bannt uns mit dem seelischen linken."[30]
Es ist nicht unmöglich, dass der neutrale Grund nicht
von Anfang an geplant war. Vielleicht verlangten die
beiden Auftraggeber zunächst vor einer echt venezianischen Landschaft mit Baum und Turm dargestellt zu
werden, die unter der Übermalung erkennbar bleibt.
Dann hätte Raffael sie vielleicht erst kurz vor der
Vollendung des Bildes zu der klassischen Folie beredet.
Die Zeiten, da man auch in dem Doppelbildnis des
Louvre "Raffael und sein Fechtmeister" ein Werk
dieses Künstlers oder eine Replik nach einem verlorenen Original Raffaels erkennen wollte, sind längst
dahin.[31] Das Werk ist von L. Dussler sehr entschieden

für Sebastiano del Piombo in Anspruch genommen
worden—und mit sehr guten Gründen.[32] Aber selbst
die Theorie, dass der Urbinate wenigstens hier porträtiert sei, die Oskar Fischel noch kurz vor seinem
Tode zu begründen versucht hat, ist von Dussler ange-
fochten worden. Der hervorstechendste Zug der Bild-
komposition ist zweifellos die sehr vergrösserte,
ausgestreckte Hand des vorderen Mannes, die aus
dem Bild herauszuragen und die Komposition nach
vorn hin zu öffnen scheint. Das kommt aber bei
Sebastianos Bildnissen immer wieder vor, es ist eine
Lieblingsform von ihm.[33] Auch das Verhältnis der
Figuren zum Rahmen, der Kontur der Büsten, das
Räumlichwerden der Körperdrehung findet sich in
vielen Bildnissen des Mönchs, aber auch in seinen
Altarblättern.[34] Das Sentiment des sogenannten
"Bravo" vorn kehrt ebenfalls mehrfach bei Sebastiano
wieder.[35]
Es bleibt merkwürdig, wie distanziert von einander die
beiden Freunde trotz der raumschaffenden Körper-
drehung des "Bravo" zu dem Partner hin bleiben.
Die en face-Figur nimmt diese Bewegung nicht auf
und wirkt wie angeschoben, vor allem aber blickt sie
aus dem Bilde heraus. Der formalen Geschlossenheit
der strengen Diagonalkomposition entspricht nicht
eine seelische Übereinstimmung des Freundespaares.
Wohl aber tritt dem Beschauer die Verschiedenheit
der beiden dargestellten Temperamente ins Bewusst-
sein.
Wir wissen von einem zweiten Freundschaftsbild des
Sebastiano del Piombo. Vasari berichtet von einem
Porträt des berühmten Kapellmeisters von San Marco
Verdelot, zusammen mit dem Sänger Obrecht, das sich
um die Mitte des 16. Jahrhunderts in Florenz im
Hause des Bildhauers Francesco da Sangallo befand
und heute verschollen ist.[36] Doch kann der Lebens-
daten der Dargestellten wegen das Doppelbildnis nicht
in Sebastianos venezianischer Jugendzeit vor 1511
entstanden sein, sondern erst während eines kürzeren
Aufenthaltes des Künstlers in der Vaterstadt 1528.[37]
Dem Giorgione-Kreis nicht allzu fern steht das
venezianische Halbfiguren-Bildnis aus der Zeit um
1515-1525, bei dem die reine Profilfigur eines Brief-
lesers mit einem diagonal aus dem Bilde heraus-
schauenden Manne konfrontiert wird (Berlin, Kaiser-
Friedrich-Museum). Roberto Longhi sah in dem
Gemälde ein frühes Werk des Tizian aus der Zeit um
1518-1520, eine Zuschreibung, die nirgends Anklang

28. A. Venturi, *Storia*, IX, 2, p. 295.—O. Fischel, *Raffael*,
Berlin 1962, p. 87.—I. A. Crowe u. G. B. Cavalcaselle, *Raphael,
sein Leben und seine Werke*, Leipz. 1885, II, p. 265 hingegen
halten das Bild nur für eine Kopie nach Raffael, deren Zustand
sie besonders ungünstig beurteilen.—Lankheit, p. 23 verkennt
den Sinn der Komposition ganz.
29. Die Belege bei V. Golzio, *Raffaello nei documenti, nelle
testimonianze dei contemporanei e nella letteratura del suo
secolo*, Città del Vaticano, 1936, p. 162.
30. Fischel, p. 88.
31. J. D. Passavant, *Raffael von Urbino und sein Vater Giovanni Santi*, II, Leipz. 1839, p. 424, 623; III, Leipz. 1858, p. 176.
—Crowe—Cavalcaselle, II, p. 471.—A. Venturi, *Storia*, IX, 2,
p. 327 u. Abb. 272, O. Fischel, p. 89 u. Taf. 157 f.

32. L. Dussler, *Sebastiano del Piombo*, Basel 1942, p. 61 f.;
p. 114, note 53; p. 138.
33. Dussler, *Sebastiano*, Taf. 31, 33, 44, 50, 53, 55, 57, 69.
34. Vgl. Dussler, Taf. 46 u. 77.
35. Vgl. Dussler, Taf. 53 u. 79.
36. Vasari—Milanesi, V, p. 565.
37. L. Dussler, *Sebastiano del Piombo*, p. 163, Nr. 134.

gefunden hat.[38] Die Berliner Museen besitzen ferner das Breitbild zweier Schachspieler in freier Landschaft, ein signiertes Werk des Paris Bordone.[39] Beide Herren sehen den Betrachter an, bleiben aber durch das Schachbrett zwischen sich (auf dem der eine gerade einem Zug tut) mit einander gleichwohl verbunden. Der eine Spieler erscheint vor der ungeformten Natur einer offenen Waldlandschaft, während dem anderen eine kostbare Säulenloggia im Hintergrund zugeordnet ist—ohne dass diese Verschiedenheit für die Charakterisierung der Dargestellten ausgenützt würde. Echt venezianisch ist der untere Bildabschluss: es handelt sich weder um ein "Kniestück", noch ist der untere Bildrand wirklich architektonisch akzentuiert.

Im florentinischen Manierismus ist das Freundschaftsbildnis vielleicht nicht weniger beliebt gewesen als in Venedig. Die Reihe beginnt mit dem Halbfigurenporträt zweier jüngerer Männer im Hochformat, das sich 1956 noch in der Sammlung des Marchese Paolo Guicciardini in Florenz befand, inzwischen aber in den Besitz des Conte Cini in Venedig übergegangen ist.[40] Es ist ein Werk des Pontormo aus der Zeit zwischen 1520 und 1525. Sobald wir die Lagune verlassen, gewahren wir, wie auch in der Gattung des Freundschaftsbildnisses die übrigen italienischen Kunstlandschaften dem venezianischen Breitformat während des Manierismus das so viel aktivere Hochformat vorziehen. Da Vasari in seiner Vita des Pontormo nur ein einziges Doppelbildnis erwähnt, so werden wir dies ja wohl vor uns haben. Dargestellt sind zwei von des Malers allernächsten Freunden, von denen der eine der Schwager des Becuccio Bicchieraio war, während Vasari den Namen des anderen jungen Mannes noch weniger weiss.[41] Es dürfte schwer zu entscheiden sein, ob Pontormo die Porträtierten durch das Medium seiner eigenen grüblerischen Natur sieht oder ob das

Freundespaar tatsächlich aus zwei solch überwachen Charakteren bestand. Grossartig ist der Gegensatz zwischen dem scharfen Denker und dem gemütstiefen Träumer herausgearbeitet. Man versteht sehr gut, dass solch extreme Naturen sich gegenseitig anziehen mussten.[42]

Das Kniestück zweier Architekten im Palazzo Venezia in Rom, das am Tischbein "MDLVI" datiert ist, wird heute dem Maso da San Friano gegeben (der eigentlich Tommaso Manzuoli heisst, 1536–1571) und wäre somit das Werk eines Zwanzigjährigen.[43] (Abb. 2) Die beiden Kollegen werden durch eine momentane Handlung einander verbunden—der eine greift mit dem Stechzirkel die Masse auf einem Grundriss ab, der auf dem Tische ausgebreitet liegt, da tritt der Ältere heran und verlangt nach dem Zirkel, um seine Gegenargumente zu erklären. Die steilen Figuren werden zwar nicht durch die Rahmungen von Tür und Kamin umgriffen, aber diese straff tektonische Aufteilung des rechten Bilddrittels verleiht doch der Figurengruppe eine strenge, leicht beengte Vertikalfügung.[44]

Wendet man sich dem Norden zu, so macht man auch dort sogleich die Beobachtung, dass das Freundschaftsbildnis in Humanistenkreisen entstand und dort seine früheste Pflegestätte fand. Ernst Buchners Corpus des "Deutschen Bildnisses der Spätgotik und der frühen Dürerzeit"[45] hat erwiesen, dass aus dem ganzen 15. Jahrhundert in Deutschland uns kein einziges Freundschaftsbild überkommen ist. Alle Doppelporträts stellen Verlobungsbildnisse, ganz gelegentlich auch Bildnisse von älteren Ehepaaren dar. Das früheste erhaltene deutsche Freundschaftsbildnis

38. Roberto Longhi, *Vita artistica*, II, 1927, p. 224.—Vgl. ferner H. Posse, *Die Gemäldegalerie des Kaiser Friedrich Museums*, I, p. 182, Nr. 152.

39. H. Posse, ebda I, p. 181, Nr. 169—Giordano Canova, *Paris Bordone*, Venezia 1964, p. 54 u. 74.—Die Berliner Museen besitzen ein zweites Bildnis zweier Schachspieler aus der späten Tintoretto—Zeit, entstanden um 1590 (Posse, p. 191, Nr. 1665). Indessen handelt es sich um ein reines Genre-Bild und nicht um ein Freundschaftsbild. Das eine der beiden Gesichter vor der kostbaren Ledertapete ist nur im verlorenen Profil zu sehen und scheidet also als Porträt aus.

40. Die gesamte Literatur über das Bild bis 1956 verzeichnet bei: Mostra del Pontormo e del primo Manierismo fiorentino. Firenze, Palazzo Strozzi 1956, Sec. Ediz. Nr. 39 u. Taf. xxx. Seither: Jeanet Cox Rearick, *The Drawings of Pontormo*, Cambridge (Mass.) 1964, Kat. Nr. 193, p. 207 u. Abb. 182 u. 184 mit Abb. einer Skizze für die linke Hand des Mannes links. Diese Zeichnung war zuerst veröffentlicht worden von O. H. Giglioli, *Dedalo*, VII, 1926–7, p. 777 u. Abb. p. 784.

41. Vasari—Milanesi, VI, p. 260

42. Es wäre sehr wichtig, ja vielleicht ein Schlüssel zu dem Gehalt des Bildes, den Text auf dem Briefe entziffern zu können, auf den der eine Dargestellte so nachdrücklich hinweist. Leider ist mir die Entzifferung dieses lateinischen Textes auch mit Hilfe von Dr. Hans Martin Freiherr von Erffa in Florenz nicht gelungen.

43. Über Manzuoli vgl. H. Voss, *Die Malerei der Spätrenaissance in Rom und Florenz*, Berlin 1920, I, p. 191.—A. Venturi, *Storia*, IX, 5, p. 282 ff. In beiden Publikationen unser Bild nicht erwähnt. Solange das Gemälde noch der Galerie von Neapel gehörte, hiess es Bronzino, vgl. A. Ippel u. P. Schubring, *Neapel*, Leipz. 1927 (Berühmte Kunststätten Bd. 77/78, p. 297 ff. mit guter Abb. 222).

44. Bei dem Doppelbildnis eines Musikers und eines älteren Mannes in der Kapitolinischen Galerie in Rom, das früher G. B. Moroni hiess und das man heute dem Bartolomeo Passarotti zuweist, wird es sich wohl eher um Vater und Sohn, als um zwei Freunde handeln.—Ganz bei Seite müssen auch die nicht seltenen Bildnisse bleiben, die einen Kardinal mit einem Kaplan oder Sekretär, der sich bescheiden im Hintergrunde hält, oder einen weltlichen Fürsten mit einem Rat oder Vorleser zeigen. Vgl. etwa Pulzone da Gaetas Doppelbildnis des Kardinals Niccolò Gaetani (Bei F. Zeri, *La Galleria Spada in Roma, Catalogo dei dipinti*, Firenze 1952, Nr. 102, p. 42 u. Abb. 21, allerdings der bolognesischen Schule des 16. Jahrhunderts zugewiesen.

45. Berlin 1953, Taf. 195 ff.

kommt aus einem ganz anderen Bereich. Es wäre von ihm nicht viel Aufhebens zu machen, wenn man seine absoluten Masse unbeachtet liesse, denn zumindest in der Photographie wirkt das Bildnis des Rektors der Universität Greifswald im Kreise von sechs anderen Professoren in Amtstracht unter dem Schutze der Madonna doch wie irgend eines unter den Hunderten von erhaltenen Epitaphien aus der deutschen Spätgotik. In der Tat hat das Votivbild seinen Platz in der Nikolaikirche in Greifswald niemals verlassen, es gehört noch ganz der sakralen Sphäre an. Erst wenn man sich klar macht, dass die aus sechs Eichenbrettern zusammengefügte Tafel eine Höhe von 1,50 m und eine Breite von 2,16 m hat, dass die Gestalten also fast lebensgross erscheinen, begreift man, dass diese Figuren dem mittelalterlichen Epitaph schon im buchstäblichen Sinne entwachsen sind. Das Bild ist gestiftet von Heinrich Rubenow, dem eigentlichen Initiator und ersten Rektor der Universität Greifswald, der zugleich auch der Bürgermeister dieser Stadt war —von der Gründung der neuen Hochschule 1456 bis zu seiner Ermordung 1462 die zentrale Gestalt aus der Frühgeschichte der Universität.[46] In der vordersten Zone kniet allein der Pedell der jungen Hochschule mit dem Universitätsszepter. Den unteren Rand des Epitaphs schliesst eine lateinische Versinschrift in leoninischen Hexametern ab, die Rubenow wahrscheinlich selbst verfasst hat und in der Christus der Heiland gebeten wird, den Dargestellten zu vergönnen, in sein himmlisches Reich einzugehen und sie nicht im Abgrund des Todes umkommen zu lassen. Von den sechs Freunden des Rubenow, mit denen er hier vor das Antlitz der Gottesmutter tritt, waren vier Professoren von Rostock, zu denen Rubenow seit 1437 in enge Beziehungen trat, als die mecklenburgische Hochschule vorübergehend in Greifswald eine Wirkungsstätte fand, weil über die Stadt Rostock Acht und Aberacht des Reiches und Bann und Interdikt der Kirche verhängt worden waren. Übrigens blieben diese vier Kollegen in Greifswald, als die Universität Rostock 1443 in ihre Heimatstadt zurückkehrte. Alle sieben Professoren halten lange Spruchbänder in Händen, die sich untereinander verschlingen und auf denen Namen und akademische Würden der Freunde verzeichnet sind. 1460, im Jahre der Entstehung des Epitaphs, waren alle sechs Freunde schon tot—und dies bestimmt die Stellung des Stifters im Bilde: in der Mitte, versammelt um die Mandorla der Gottesmutter, die sechs Toten, am linken Bildrand aber der lebende Stifter. Das älteste Freundschaftsbildnis nördlich der Alpen entstand also ebenfalls in Humanistenkreisen—aber anders als in Italien wächst es aus einer sakralen Bildform heraus. (Abb. 3.)

Die Namen der sieben Greifswalder Freunde sind heute vergessen. Aber im Jahre 1517 liessen sich Erasmus und sein Freund Peter Gilles, der Stadtschreiber von Antwerpen, in einem Diptychon von Quentin Massys malen, das für Thomas Morus, den dritten dieses Freundschaftsbundes bestimmt war.[47] In dem Begleitbrief zu diesem Geschenk, den Erasmus am 8. September 1517 an Morus sandte, heisst es: "Da schicke ich Dir die Tafeln, damit wir immer bei Dir sein mögen, auch wenn wir einmal nicht mehr sind." ("Mitto tabulas, quo tibi utcunque adsimus, si qua sors nos ademerit.")[48] Erasmus war damals wohl 51 Jahre alt (wenn man sich unter den möglichen Geburtsjahren für das wahrscheinlichste, 1466, entscheidet), Peter Gilles jünger. Die beiden Tafeln besitzen zwar jede ihren eigenen Rahmen, doch versetzt der Maler die beiden Freunde in einen fiktiven einheitlichen Bildraum; die Horizontalen des Bücherregals im Bildhintergrund und der Tischkante vorn laufen einheitlich durch beide Flügel des Diptychons durch. Die Bildform des Gelehrtenporträts hatte sich im Laufe des 15. Jahrhunderts aus der Darstellung des Hieronymus im Gehäus entwickelt. So bleibt der Erasmus an seinem Schreibpult auch hier noch ganz für sich, in das Geschäft des Schreibens vertieft. Er arbeitet an seiner Paraphrase des Römerbriefs und nimmt über sein Pult hin nicht den Kontakt zu dem Freunde auf. Die Beziehungen der drei Humanisten zueinander werden vielmehr von Massys ganz äusserlich motiviert: Peter Gilles hält einen Brief des Thomas Morus in Händen, dessen charakteristische Schriftzüge Massys genau nachzuahmen verstanden hat, denn Morus muss am 6. Oktober 1517 in einem Briefe, in dem er den Empfang des Diptychons bestätigt, gestehen: "Unser Quentin hat wirklich alles vollendet gut gemacht, doch scheint er mir vor allem ein hervorragender Fälscher zu sein; denn er hat die Unterschrift meines Briefes an Dich so geschickt nachgeahmt, dass ich selbst sie nicht so nachmachen kann. Daher bitte ich Dich, mir den Brief zurückzusenden, wenn er

46. V. Schultze, *Geschichts- und Kunstdenkmäler der Universität Greifswald*, Greifswald 1906, p. 9 ff. u. Taf. I–II.— W. Paatz, *Sceptrum Universitatis* (Heidelberger Kunstgeschichtliche Abhandlungen, N.F. 2), Heidelberg 1953, p. 24 f., bes. Anm. 36.—R. Schmidt, "Die Anfänge der Universität Greifswald", in *Festschrift zur 500-Jahrfeier der Universität Greifswald 17.10.1956*, I, p. 13 mit Abb. 2 u. p. 37 f.

47. *Opus epistolarum Des. Erasmi Roterdami*, ed. P. S. Allen, II, Oxonii 1910, Nr. 584 v. 30.V.1517.—M. J. Friedländer, *Die altniederländische Malerei*, VII. Quentin Massys. Berl. 1929, p. 41 ff. u. 120, Taf. XXXIV u. XXXV.—W. Cohen, *Studien zu Quentin Metsys*, Bonn 1904, p. 85.—Jean de Bosschère, *Quinten Metsys*, Brüssel 1907, p. 108 ff.—H. Brising, *Quinten Matsys und der Ursprung des Italianismus in der Kunst der Niederlande*, 2 Aufl., Leipz. o.J. (1908), p. 37 ff.

48. *Opus epistolarum*, III, 1913, Nr. 654.

für Dich und Massys nicht mehr nötig ist. Neben das Bild gehalten, wird er das Wunder um das Doppelte erhöhen."[49] Gilles scheint über den Inhalt des Schreibens nachzudenken. Die Finger der Rechten des Stadtschreibers ruhen auf des Erasmus Werk "Antibarbari", auf dem Bücherbord aber liegen—durch Aufschriften an der Schnittfläche genau gekennzeichnet—die Hauptwerke des Erasmus vor 1517. Und doch ist es dem Künstler wohl um mehr gegangen, als um die Beschwörung eines humanistischen Fluidums durch den Einblick in die traute Stille einer behaglichen Gelehrtenstube und durch das Aufreihen von Büchertiteln. Schon Hans Diepolder hat in der Gegenüberstellung des versonnenen Gelehrten und des agilen, blitzgescheiten weltkundigen Verwaltungsmannes "dieses sehr pointierte Gegenüber einer vita contemplativa und activa" erkannt.[50] Somit wäre hier ein echtes Freundschaftsbild der Hochrenaissance entstanden, bei dem der besondere Fall ins Allgemeingültige emporgeläutert wäre. Der mit dem Diptychon Beschenkte, der dritte im Bunde, Thomas More, war jedenfalls voll Dankes: "seine Eitelkeit sei befriedigt, denn er wisse nun, dass Briefe, Bücher und Bilder die Nachwelt daran erinnern würden, dass er der Freund des Erasmus gewesen."[51]

Im Original ist offensichtlich nur die rechte Tafel, das Bildnis des Gilles in Longford Castle, erhalten. Von dem Erasmus—Flügel hingegen besitzen wir vier Repliken, von denen wahrscheinlich keine—auch nicht die der Galleria Colonna in Rom—den Anspruch erheben darf, das Original zu sein.

Den grössten Gegensatz zu diesem intimen Geschenk für Thomas Morus bildet Hans Holbeins d.J. Doppelbildnis der beiden Gesandten (London, Nat. Gallery). Es ist das einzige Freundschaftsbildnis monumentalen Formats aus der nordischen Renaissance, das wir besitzen (Holz, 2,06 × 2,09 m) und es ist zugleich ein sehr offizielles Bildnis, obwohl es niemals in Renaissance oder Barock öffentlich zu sehen war, vielmehr unmittelbar nach seiner Entstehung in dem französischen Provinzschloss eines der beiden Porträtierten verschwand, wo es 232 Jahre lang ein recht vergessenes Dasein führte. Über die Lebensläufe der beiden Dargestellten, des Gesandten Jean de Dinteville und des Bischofs von Lavaur, George de Selve, wissen wir erstaunlich viel, wie wir auch über die Umstände der Entstehung des Bildes überraschend gut unterrichtet sind, dank dem ausserordentlichen historischen Spür-

sinn einer englischen Dame.[52] Zunächst einmal erweist sich nach den Ergebnissen M. Herveys der Titel des Bildes "die beiden Gesandten" insofern als missverständlich, als zwar beide Porträtierte als Diplomaten tätig waren, niemals aber gemeinsam zu einer Mission entsandt worden sind. Vielmehr empfing Jean de Dinteville, als er 1533 als dauernder Gesandter König Franz I. in London akkreditiert war, sich krank fühlte, das englische Klima nicht vertragen konnte und sich selbst als "den melancholischsten Gesandten, der je gelebt hat", bezeichnete, den privaten Freundesbesuch des Bischofs von Lavaur. Diese Visite in der Fastenzeit des Jahres 1533 war alles andere als ein öffentlicher Staatsakt, vielmehr berichtet Dinteville darüber in einem Briefe an seinen Bruder: "Monseigneur de Lavor hat mir die Ehre erwiesen, mich zu besuchen, was für mich keine geringe Freude war. Es ist nicht notwendig, dass der Kanzler etwas davon erfährt." Also ein reines Freundschaftsbild! Wie uns die Menschen des Mittelalters und der Renaissance auf ihren Bildnissen stets viel älter erscheinen wollen, als sie in Wahrheit sind, so würden wir niemals vermuten, zwei noch nicht Dreissigjährige vor uns zu haben. Aber als Holbein sie malte, war Dinteville 29 und der Bischof von Lavaur 25 Jahre alt!! Dass die Attribute, welche die Dargestellten charakterisieren sollen, allzu stark unsere Aufmerksamkeit beanspruchen, sind wir von vielen Holbein-Porträts her gewohnt. (Kaufmann Georg Gisze von 1532; Berlin, Kaiser Friedrich Museum.) In unserem Falle sind fast alle diese Geräte —Erdglobus, Himmelsglobus, Kompasse, Sonnenuhr, Richtscheit, Zirkel u.s.w. der Welt des Laien zuzuordnen, während nur die beiden geistlichen Bücher, auf die er den rechten Unterarm legt, die Atmosphäre des Bischofs bezeichnen sollen.

Indessen gibt es unter diesen Instrumenten einige signa, die sich auf beide Freunde beziehen, und auf sie vor allem wird es den Auftraggebern angekommen sein, als sie den Maler anwiesen, die Zeichen des "memento mori" so aufdringlich in den Vordergrund des Bildes zu rücken. Wie so viele Porträts und auch Doppelbildnisse aus Spätmittelalter und Frühmanierismus in Deutschland[53] und Italien[54] stellt auch unser Freundschaftsbild die beiden Porträtierten unter den Schatten des Todes—nicht nur durch den

49. *Opus epistolarum*, III, 1913, Nr. 684, p. 107.
50. H. Diepolder, "Hans Holbeins d.J. Bildnisse des Erasmus von Rotterdam", *Der Kunstbrief*, Heft 57, Berlin 1949, p. 5.
51. Morus an Erasmus aus Calais unter dem 7. Oktober 1517. *Opus Epistolarum* III, Nr. 683, p. 104.—R. W. Chambers, *Thomas More*, deutsche Übersetzung München 1946, p. 191.

52. Mary F. S. Hervey, *Holbein's Ambassadors. The picture and the men*. London 1900.—C. G. Heise, "Die Gesandten von Hans Holbein", *Der Kunstbrief*, Nr. 22, Berlin 1943.—P. Ganz, *The Paintings of Hans Holbein*, first complete edition, London 1956, Cat. Nr. 74, p. 241 ff.
53. E. Buchner, Textabb. 8 (p. 59), 9 (p. 60), 45 (p. 172), 46 (p. 174).
54. Lorenzo Lotto, Männerbildnis, Rom Galleria Borghese, Spätwerk (B. Berenson, *Lorenzo Lotto*, Köln 1957, Taf. 287)— Jacopo Ligozzi, Handzeichnung (A. Forlani, *I Disegni italiani del Cinquecento*, Venezia 1964, Taf. 103) usw.

rational gar nicht genugsam zu erklärenden Vexier-spiegel mit dem Totenkopf, dessen Basierung und Stellung im Raum unklar und beunruhigend bleibt, sondern auch durch die Laute mit der gesprungenen Saite und durch die beiden davor liegenden Bücher, von denen das aufgeschlagene Johann Walthers "Geistliches Gesangbüchlein", 1524 in Wittenberg gedruckt, ist und das Noten und Text des Liedes "Komm Heiliger Geist Herre Gott..." und die Paraphrase über die zehn Gebote "Mensch wiltu leben seliglich" sehen lässt. Dies memento mori—das sicherlich keine Idee Holbeins ist—muss als Grund-stimmung durch viele Freundesgespräche gegangen sein. Und so wird der Tod sie vorbereitet gefunden haben, als er den Bischof schon mit 32, den Dinteville nach Schlaganfällen mit 51 Jahren abberief.

Dieser sich vordrängende Hinweis auf die Gebrech-lichkeit alles Irdischen lässt allzu leicht darüber hin-wegsehen, dass in dem intimen Diptychon des Massys und in dem lebensgrossen repräsentativen Doppel-bildnis Holbeins die beiden Freundespaare gleichwohl auf sehr ähnliche Weise gruppiert sind—denn auch der Bischof von Lavaur ist als eine stille, in sich zusam-mengenommene Gestalt dem weit ausladend sich dar-bietenden Weltmann gegenüber gestellt; Sinnender und Handelnder dürfen auch hier als Vertreter von Vita contemplativa und Vita activa betrachtet werden.

Ganz kürzlich erst ist in englischem Privatbesitz das Bildnis zweier junger Burschen in Halbfigur unter einer Arkade aufgetaucht, das mit den vier Initialen des flämischen Malers Crispin van den Broeck signiert ist. (1524 bis wahrscheinlich 1591).[55] Die Form des Rahmens macht es nicht unwahrscheinlich, dass das Bild in eine Serie solcher Doppelbildnisse gehört haben könnte. Von Lebensangst, vom Versagen der physischen Kraft, die Kämpfe des Lebens zu meistern, von dem bitteren Bodensatz früher Lebenserfahrung, wovon die florentinischen Jünglingsbildnisse aus dem Manierismus so deutlich Zeugnis ablegen, weiss dieses tüchtige, vergnügte Freundespaar allerdings nichts.

Im siebzehnten Jahrhundert ist das gesellschaftliche Ideal nicht mehr der Humanist, auch nicht mehr der Cortigiano, sondern der honnête homme. Das berühmte Freundschaftsbild des Palazzo Pitti, das unter einer Büste des Seneca um den einen Text auslegenden berühmten Philologen Justus Lipsius, "den zweiten Seneca", seine Schüler Jan Wowerius und Philipp Rubens, dazu den Maler des Bildes Peter Paul Rubens vereinigt, ist das letzte, bedeutende Freundschaftsbild des Humanistischen Zeitalters. Ist es auch nicht mehr in Rubens italienischer Zeit ent-standen, wie man früher annahm, sondern erst zu Beginn des zweiten Jahrzehnts, so gehört es doch jedenfalls noch an die Schwelle eines Jahrhunderts, in dem das Ideal des honnête homme das des Humanis-ten verdrängte.[56]

Dieses französische Leitbild ist keineswegs nur für die Angehörigen des Adels erreichbar, es wendet sich durchaus an "la cour et la ville". "Es ist sogar bezeichnend für die honnêteté, dass sie nicht nur von allem Ständischen, sondern überhaupt von allen jeweils gegebenen lebensmässigen Bindungen absieht. Jeder konnte sie erwerben, der auf seine innere und äussere Pflege im Geiste der Zeit Sorgfalt zu verwenden willens und fähig war, und das Resultat war eben dieses: dass der Betreffende von jeder besonderen Qualität gereinigt wurde, nicht mehr Zugehöriger eines Standes, eines Berufes, eines Bekenntnisses war, sondern eben honnête homme. Freilich ist damit, gerade damit, das Kennen und Beachten der Abstände verbunden; zum honnête homme gehört notwendig auch das se connaître."[57]

Für unsere Fragestellungen sind zwei Eigenschaften der honnêteté und deren Genesis besonders wichtig. Eine Reaktion nämlich wendet sich "gegen das Pedantische in der humanistischen Gelehrsamkeit, gegen das Hypertrophe des die schöne Menschlichkeit zerstörenden Bücherdaseins und Gelehrtenwesens."[58] Von hier aus wird das Verschwinden des humani-stischen Freundschaftsbildes verständlich. Zum andern kann es bei der damaligen politischen Konstellation, die von dem Kampf um die Hegemonie über Europa zwischen Frankreich und Spanien bestimmt ist, nicht Wunder nehmen, dass der honnête homme die Partei des französischen Geschmacks gegen das spanische Pathos nimmt. Frankreich und die Niederlande wer-den also Freundschaftsbilder dieser Art hervorbringen: Italien aber scheidet aus der Entwicklung ganz aus.[59]

---

55. Le triomphe du Maniérisme européen de Michel-Ange au Gréco. 2. Ausstellung des Europarats, Amsterdam 1955, Katalog Nr. 29, p. 54.—*Kunstchronik*, 8, 1955, Abb. gegenüber p. 344.

56. *P. P. Rubens, Des Meisters Gemälde* (Klassiker der Kunst, Bd. v), 4. Aufl. v. R. Oldenbourg, Stuttgart 1921, Abb. 45 u. p. 456, datiert 1611–12.—L. van Puyvelde, *Rubens*, Paris u. Brüssel 1952, p. 114 gar erst um 1614–15.

57. E. Auerbach, *Vier Untersuchungen zur Geschichte der französischen Bildung*, Bern 1951, p. 38 f.

58. Carl J. Burckhardt, "Der honnête homme", in: *Gestalten und Mächte*, München o.J. (1941), p. 82.—Aus der sehr umfangreichen Sekundärliteratur über den honnête homme verweisen wir nur auf das grundlegende Werk von M. Magendie, *La Politesse Mondaine et les Théories de l'Honnêteté en France aus XVIIe Siècle, de 1600 à 1660*, Alcan 1926, 2 Bde. Ferner P. Bénichou, *Morales du Grand Siècle*, Paris 1948.

59. Wir vermögen allenfalls ein einziges italienisches Freund-schaftsbild des Seicento zu nennen, und auch dies ist nur ein verkleidetes Bildnis. Im Prado in Madrid und im Berliner Kaiser Friedrich-Museum befinden sich zwei Repliken eines monogrammierten Halbfigurenbildes der beiden Apotheker-Heiligen Cosmas und Damian von dem neapolitanischen Barockmaler Giov. Batt. Caracciolo, unter welcher Gestalt sicher die Porträts zweier Ärzte aus der Stadt am Vesuv zu

Natürlich kann der Wandel vom Humanisten und vom Cortegiano zum honnête homme nicht allein einleuchtend das Verstummen Italiens für unsere Gattung begründen. Ein ebenso wichtiger Grund dafür besteht in der Tatsache, dass Italien im Seicento zwar das schöpferische Land für Architektur und Plastik bleibt, seine Führerrolle in der Malerei aber nach dem Tode Caravaggios (1610) an die nordischen Länder abgibt. Dass die Geschichte des Freundschaftsbildes sich fortan in den nordischen Ländern vollzieht, entspricht demnach dem allgemeinen Verlauf der Entwicklung der Barockmalerei.

Bleibt das Ideal des honnête homme auch strenge an die französischen Einrichtungen gebunden, an das Königshaus, an die gallikanische Kirche, an das Heer, an die robe, an den salon, ist es also nicht in eine andere Nationalkultur des grand siècle übertragbar—in den Doppelbildnissen, die van Dyck vom englischen Hochadel malte, findet sich gleichwohl ein Widerschein dieses französischen Vorbilds.[60] Heisst der Maler aber nicht mehr van Dyck, sondern ist nur irgend ein flämischer oder englischer Dutzendmaler, so wird das Freundschaftsbild fast zum Jagdstück und von einer inneren Verbundenheit der Porträtierten untereinander ist nichts mehr zu spüren.[61] Nun ist aber auch wenigstens ein Freundschaftsbild von zwei Bürgerlichen von der Hand van Dycks erhalten, das den Theaterdichter Thomas Killigrew gemeinsam mit einem anderen Manne darstellt, in dem man neuerdings den königlichen Kammerdiener William Murray erkennen möchte.[62] Hier, wo der Aufwand der Prunkgewänder durch die schlichte Kleidung ersetzt ist, wo die kostbaren Waffen, wo Schärpen und Ordensbänder nicht mehr die Aufmerksamkeit von den Gesichtern weglenken, verbreiten die beiden Freunde um sich Intimität, Vertrauen, Stille, kurz jene Atmosphäre, in der das Zwiegespräch glaubwürdig wird.

Diese Tonart findet man nun auch in zwei Doppelporträts von Künstlern durchgehalten. Sehr viel Beachtung hat in der letzten Zeit um der beiden Dargestellten willen das Doppelbildnis zweier Bildhauer gefunden, das sich seit 1690 im Statens Museum for Kunst in Kopenhagen nachweisen lässt.[63] (Abb. 4.)

K. Feuchtmayr hat den älteren, bärtigen Mann mit François du Quesnoy, den jüngeren mit Georg Petel identifizieren wollen, und in der Tat scheint das Bildnis des jungen Oberdeutschen von van Dyck in der Alten Pinakothek in München einer solchen Bestimmung nicht zu widersprechen. Leider aber ist das Bildnis der Residenz-Galerie in Salzburg (aus der Sammlung Czernin in Wien), das bisher den Beleg dafür bot, dass der Partner von Petel eben du Quesnoy sei, kürzlich als ein Werk des vierzehnjährigen Charles Le Brun erklärt worden, der hier seinen Vater, den Bildhauer Nicolas Le Brun porträtiert habe.[64] Der Kupferstich mit dem Porträt des du Quesnoy, in Büstenform, von einem Medaillon umschlossen, vor seiner Vita in Giovanni Pietro Belloris Vitenwerk,[65] den dann Sandrart im Gegensinne in seiner "Teutschen Academie" wiederholt,[66] bleibt bei der Schilderung der Physiognomie so im Allgemeinen, dass dieses Blatt die Theorie von Charles Sterling allein nicht umzustossen vermag. Falls die Profilfigur wirklich du Quesnoy darstellen sollte, so können die beiden Künstler sich nur in Rom getroffen haben, wo du Quesnoy 1618 eintraf, während Petels Aufenthalt in der ewigen Stadt wahrscheinlich vor 1623 anzusetzen ist, weil der Bildhauer in diesem Jahre sich in Livorno nachweisen lässt, sich also offensichtlich schon auf der Rückreise befand. Das Kopenhagener Doppelporträt muss also um 1620–1622 entstanden ein. An der Autorschaft hat man viel herumgerätselt. Die alte Bezeichnung der Kopenhagener Museums-Inventare von 1690 und 1737 "Gratschini" (= Saraceni)[67] geht sicher in die Irre; der vorgeschlagene Historien- und Genremaler Bernhard Keil (genannt Monsù Bernardo, 1624–1687) war zur Zeit der Entstehung des Bildes gewiss noch nicht geboren; Roberto Longhi denkt an einen flämischen Caravaggio-Nachahmer aus der Zeit von 1615–1630.[68] Die meiste Überzeugungskraft besitzt die Zuweisung an Adam de Coster, doch weiss man leider nicht, ob dieser Künstler sich Anfang der Zwanziger Jahre des Seicento in Rom aufgehalten hat.[69]

Die Stimmung, die über dem Bilde liegt, ist mit den Mitteln beschworen, die Caravaggio in die Malerei

---

erblicken sind. (H. Voss, *Jahrb. d. preuss. Kunstsammlungen*, 48, 1927, p. 131.)

60. *Van Dyck, Des Meisters Gemälde* (Klassiker der Kunst XIII), hrsg. von G. Glück, 2. Aufl. Stuttgart 1931, Abb. 401, 435, 440.—Lankheit, p. 32.

61. M. Gheeraerts zugeschrieben (gest. 1635/6), Prinz Henry von Wales, der älteste Sohn James I (der schon 1612 mit 18 Jahren starb), zusammen mit Robert Devereux, 3. Earl of Essex. Hampton Court. *Catalogue of the Pictures at Hampton Court*, ed. C. H. Collins Baker, 1929, p. 65.

62. *Klassiker der Kunst*, Abb. 451.

63. Th. Müller u. A. Schädler, *Georg Petel, Katalog der Ausstellung im Bayerischen Nationalmuseum*, Sommer 1964, p. 18, Kat. Nr. B. Dort die gesamte Literatur.

64. *Katalog der Residenz-Galerie Salzburg*, Salzburg 1962, Nr. 15, p. 35 u. Umschlagbild.—Ch. Sterling, "Les peintres Jean et Jaques Blanchard", *Art de France*, I, 1961, p. 100.

65. Giovanni Pietro Bellori, *Le vite de pittori, scultori et architetti*, Roma 1672, p. 267.

66. J. von Sandrart, *Accademia nobilissima artis pictoriae*. Noribergae et Francoforti 1683, Abb. NN gegenüber p. 328.

67. H. Olsen, *Italian Paintings and Sculpture in Denmark*, Amsterdam 1961, p. 88.

68. Roberto Longhi, "Monsù Bernardo", *La Critica d'Arte*, III, 1938, p. 124.

69. B. Nicolson, "Notes on Adam de Coster", *Burlington Magazine*, 103, 1961, p. 185 ff.

eingeführt hat, und an deren Anwendung und künstlerischer Steigerung die Nordländer, besonders die Flamen und Holländer, viel interessierter waren als die Italiener. Die tonige Gebundenheit, die das Nachtstück zu entwickeln erlaubte, die reiche Abstufung der Helligkeitswerte, die das offene und flackernde Kerzenlicht der Palette gewährte, haben Honthorst und Baburen, Terbrugghen und Georges de la Tour ganz anders gepflegt als die Italiener. Und so liegt denn die Atmosphäre des Traulichen und Geborgenen, aber auch der Hingegebenheit an eine Sache über den beiden Bildhauern zwischen ihren Modellen und Bozzetti.

In die Helligkeit des Tageslichts gehört ein Freundschaftsbild eigener Art, auf dem zwei junge Maler sich gegenseitig dargestellt haben. Die äusseren Bedingungen sind also hier ideal, das fremde Gegenüber des neutralen Beobachters und Künstlers fällt ganz fort— jeder der Freunde malt den andern so, wie sich ihm dessen Wesen im vertrauten Umgang erschlossen hat. Kein fremdes Medium vermag hier die gemeinsame Welt des Freundespaares zu verfälschen. Auf dem Leinwandbild des Museum Boymans in Rotterdam sitzt links vor seinem Zeichenbrett Jean Baptiste de Champaigne (1631–1681), ein Neffe des berühmten französischen Malers Philippe de Champaigne, ihm gegenüber Nicolas de Platte Montagne (eigentlich Plettenberg, 1631–1706), der sein Cello zwischen den Knieen hat, in der Linken einen grossen Schlapphut hält, und mit der geöffneten, ausgestreckten Rechten auf den Freund hinweist. (Abb. 6.) Das Bild ist bezeichnet links "N. Montaigne pinxit me", rechts "I B de Champaigne me fecit." Auf der Schriftrolle, die in der Mitte des Bildes vom Tische herabhängt, steht gross die Jahreszahl "1654". Beide Maler waren also, als sie einander porträtierten 23 Jahre alt.[70] Von den beiden, die sich hier unter der Büste des Seneca zusammengefunden haben, besitzt das Cabinet des dessins des Louvre noch einmal zwei Porträtskizzen in schwarzer Kreide und Rötel mit Lavierungen und Höhungen in Weiss auf gelbem Papier.[71] Da auf dem Bildnis des Platte—Montagne die Jahreszahl 1658 steht, so sind—wenn diese Datierung ursprünglich ist —die beiden Blätter erst vier Jahre nach dem Rotterdamer Bild entstanden. Dafür sprechen nun tatsächlich Physiognomik und Gesichtsausdruck des Freundespaares. Die jungen Herren sind nun sehr viel selbstbewusster und weltläufiger geworden. Die treuherzige Offenheit, die zarte Empfindung, die das

Antlitz der beiden in dem Rotterdamer Bildnis mit dem Flaum der Jugend beschenkt, ist nun ganz verschwunden. Übrigens haben die beiden Maler in den Pariser Zeichnungen sich nicht noch einmal wechselseitig porträtiert, beide Blätter stammen nun von der Hand des Jean-Baptiste de Champaigne.

Das bekannte Doppelporträt des Louvre, das zwei Männer in der Tracht des mittleren 17. Jahrhunderts in Halbfigur hinter einer Balustrade zeigt, trägt auf dieser Brüstung das Datum 1656 und bezeichnet den Dargestellten zur Linken als "Mansard", den zur Rechten als "Perrault" worunter man von jeher natürlich den berühmten Architekten Claude Perrault verstand. An der Ursprünglichkeit der Inschrift sind nun Zweifel aufgestiegen, und Hélène J. Adhémar war zudem aufgefallen, dass keine Porträtähnlichkeit mit den gesicherten Bildnissen dieser beiden grossen Baumeister bestünde, und dass beide Dargestellte, falls sie Architekten wären, doch wohl mit den Attributen ihres Berufes dargestellt sein müssten (Zirkel, Winkelmass, Bauplänen u.s.w.).[72] Sie schlug dann vor, in den beiden anstatt Claude Perrault lieber dessen Bruder Charles zu sehen, und anstatt Mansart den Literaten Jean Desmaretz de Saint-Solin, zwei der Führer in der querelle des Anciens et des Modernes. Sollte das Datum unseres Bildes, 1656, sich behaupten, so würde Madame Adhémars Deutung hinfällig sein, da die Querelle erst am 27. Januar 1687 ausbrach.

Neuerdings hat nun Bernard Dorival in der auf dem Bilde als "Mansard" bezeichneten Persönlichkeit den Präsidenten Jean Perrault erkennen wollen, der 1647 Präsident der Chambre des Comptes wurde.[73] Sein Partner sei sein Schwager Abraham Girard, mit dem zusammen Perrault als Güterverwalter bei Henri II. von Bourbon, dem Prinzen von Condé, tätig gewesen war. Die These steht schon deshalb auf ungewöhnlich schwachen Füssen, weil wir ein Bildnis dieses Girard, das die Kontrolle erlauben würde, gar nicht besitzen. Im Louvre befindet sich übrigens ein offensichtlich als Gegenstück gearbeitetes Doppelbildnis von Rigaud, das Le Brun und Mignard zeigt, das auch in den Massen mit dem eben besprochenen Bild von Champaigne übereinstimmt.

Sind im Grand Siècle unter den Freundschaftsbildnissen diejenigen noch in der Minderzahl, welche den Künstlerfreundschaften gelten und also Künstlerselbstbildnisse enthalten, so stellen sie seit dem Ende des 18. Jahrhunderts fast die Regel dar. Aus den Zweier- und

---

70. Museum Boymans, Rotterdam, *Gids, Schilderkunst und Beeldhouwkunst*, 1951, p. 132, Nr. 81.

71. Musée du Louvre. *Inventaire général des dessins des écoles du Nord.* Fr. Lugt, Ecole Flamande, I, Paris 1949, Nr. 528 u. 529.

72. H. Adhémar, "The so-called Portrait of Mansart and Claude Perrault by Philippe de Champaigne", *Journal of the Warburg and Courtauld Institutes*, XII, 1949, p. 200 ff.

73. Bernard Dorival, "Essai d'identification de quelques modèles de Philippe de Champaigne", *La Revue des Arts*, I, 1951, p. 223 ff.

Dreier-Gruppen befreundeter Maler wächst dann schliesslich die malerische Wiedergabe von zahlreichen Vertretern einer bestimmten künstlerischen Strömung hervor in grossen Kompositionen, die schon ihrer Vielfigurigkeit wegen sich eher an die niederländischen Regentenstücke des 17. Jahrhunderts anlehnen, als dass sie die Traditionen des alten Freundschaftsbildnisses aus Renaissance und Barock fortführten. (Fantin-Latour, L'atelier à Batignolles [hommage à Manet], 1870—Cézanne, Apothéose von Delacroix, 1894.—Maurice Denis, Hommage à Cézanne. 1901.—Ernst Ludwig Kirchner, Die Künstler der Brücke, ein Erinnerungsbild, da erst lange nach der Auflösung dieses Kreises, 1925, gemalt.) Zuweilen ist es der Mäzen, der in den Mittelpunkt des Kreises der Künstler tritt, die er beschäftigt. Am meisten hat sich in dieser Rolle der Sammler von Montpellier, Alfred Bruyas gefallen (Auguste Barthélémy Glaize, L'interieur du Cabinet de Bruyas, 1848, Montpellier, Musée Fabre). Aus diesem Kreise ist dann das eigenartigste Freundschaftsbild des 19. Jahrhunderts hervorgegangen: Courbets "Bonjour, Monsieur Courbet" (1854, Montpellier, Musée Fabre). Bei seiner ersten Reise in den Süden ist dem Fusswanderer der Mäzen mit seinem Diener ein Stück entgegengefahren, und auf der staubigen Landstrasse vor Montpellier begrüssen sich die beiden unter dem blassblauen Himmel der Provence. Niemals ist Künstlerstolz mehr darauf bedacht gewesen, sich vor den Augen des Mäzens nichts zu vergeben. Er naht als der Schöpfer und der Schenkende.[73a]

So hat es wirklich den Anschein, als sei das Freundschaftsbild im 19. Jahrhundert auf Künstler und allenfalls noch deren Mäzene beschränkt geblieben. Welche Verengung! Aber zwei grosse und stolze Einsame haben dem Freundschaftsbild noch einmal seinen ursprünglichen Sinn zurückgewonnen: Hans von Marées und Degas. Im Kreise um Conrad Fiedler knüpften sich die Bande der Freundschaft zwischen Künstlern und Laien, weil ein gemeinsames Bildungsideal noch für alle Angehörige dieses Bundes verpflichtend war. So besass Anton Dohrn den Mut, einen Saal seiner Zoologischen Station in Neapel mit Fresken

von Marées schmücken zu lassen, in dem die Biologen aus allen Ländern, die hier arbeiteten, aus den Schranken der Naturwissenschaften entrückt werden, wo sie den Blick von der Enge des Mikroskops zu grossen Wandkompositionen erheben sollten.[74] Hier hat im Sommer 1873 Marées unter anderen Fresken auch das von der "Pergola" gemalt, wo Dohrn, dessen Mitarbeiter Kleinenberg, Charles Grant, Marées und Hildebrand um den schlichten ungedeckten Tisch einer ländlichen Osteria versammelt werden. Dieses Fresko ist unter den strengen Kompositionen des Saales die strengste. Fast will es scheinen, als drücke das unerbittliche Gitter der das Bild ganz durchziehenden Vertikalen und Horizontalen den Freundeskreis beiseite. Aber es bezieht ihn auch in eine grosse Ordnung ein. Es bewahrt ihn vor dem "Anekdotischen", das Gruppenbildnissen des 19. Jahrhunderts so leicht anhaftet. Die Freunde gestikulieren nicht, sie sind sich ohnehin einig. Indem Anton Dohrn das Gewicht seines schweren Körpers zur Seite kehrt, bewahrt er die Gruppe vor der Erstarrung in der Orthogonalen.[75]

Bei Degas bezeugt das Freundschaftsbild nicht die Zugehörigkeit zu einem Kreise gleichgesinnter junger Männer und bedeutet es formal nicht die Frucht einer Jahrzehnte langen Auseinandersetzung mit den Kompositionsgesetzen der Freskenwelt des Südens. Die Bildgattung des Freundschaftsbildes ist für Degas einfach ein geglücktes psychologisches Experiment. Er ist vom Familienbild zum Freundschaftsbild gekommen. Gleichheit und Verschiedenheit von Geschwistern, gar von Zwillingen, haben den Psychologen in Degas beschäftigt und den Künstler zur Darstellung gereizt. Schon mit etwa 23 Jahren malt er das Doppelbildnis zweier kleiner Mädchen, der Schwestern Beauregard.[76] Als dann zwischen 1858 und 1860 das grosse Familienbild seiner nahen Verwandten, der Bellelli aus Neapel in Florenz entsteht, beschäftigt den Künstler die schon so ausgeprägte Verschiedenheit der Charaktere seiner beiden Cousinen, von denen Giovanna 1858 zehnjährig, Julie siebenjährig war. In immer neuen Zeichnungen, Ölskizzen auf Papier und Leinwandstudien hat er das stille und in sich gekehrte Wesen der Älteren der temperamentvollen, kecken und originellen Art der Jüngeren gegenüber gestellt.[77] Auch fünf Jahre nach Vollendung des grossen Familienbildes des Louvre hat

73a. Diese Doppelbildnisse von Künstler und Mäzen sind seit dem 17. Jahrhundert bereits üblich. Vgl. etwa Guercino und der Cavaliere Manzini, Halbfigurenbild im Museo Civico in Cento, oder Watteau und der Kunstsammler Jean de Jullienne, der Herausgeber des "Œuvre gravé de Antoine Watteau". Wenn Kurfürst Max III. Joseph von Bayern sich mit dem Intendanten seines Hoftheaters, dem Grafen Seeau, von Georges Desmarées malen liess, so gehört dies eher in die Reihe der Protektoren- als der Freundschaftsbildnisse, wie schon allein die Zuordnung der Figuren zueinander beweist, denn der Graf hält das Tablett in der Hand, auf dem er soeben dem Kurfürst eine Tasse Schokolade serviert hat (Abb. 5).

74. J. Meier-Gräfe, *Hans von Marées*, I, München 1910, p. 245, bes. p. 268 ff.—II, München 1909, p. 158 ff. mit Abb. 217 ff.
75. Vgl. auch H. von Marées Doppelbildnis von A. von Hildebrand und Charles Grant in der Kunsthalle in Mannheim aus derselben Zeit. Kunsthalle Mannheim, *Verzeichnis der Gemälde- und Skulpturen-Sammlung*, 1953, Nr. 94 u. Abb. 22.
76. Lemoisne, II, Nr. 45.
77. ebda II, 19, 19, 63–66, 68.

Degas die beiden Schwestern noch einmal in der Gegensätzlichkeit ihres Wesens gemalt.[78]

Bei solchen Studien muss Degas zu der Überzeugung gekommen sein, dass man den Charakter eines Porträts am besten durch Kontrastierung mit einer sehr verschieden gearteten Natur zur Darstellung bringen könne. So hat er sich um 1864 zusammen mit seinem Freunde Evariste Bernardi de Valernes gemalt[79] (Louvre) und sein eigenes grüblerisches Antlitz dem selbstsicheren und weisen des um 14 Jahre älteren Kollegen gegenüber gestellt. Die Spannung zwischen dem verhangenen Ausdruck des Halbkreolen und dem Gesichte des Freundes, das in seiner Nuanciertheit aller Dumpfheit so fern wie möglich ist, macht den Zauber des Bildes aus. Solange das Porträt im Mittelpunkt von Degas' Interessen und Schaffen stand—das heisst also bis zur Reise nach New Orleans 1873 und bis zur Entstehung des "Baumwollkontors"—reiht sich die Kette der herrlichsten Freundschaftsbildnisse. Um 1869 schuf Degas das Porträt seines Vaters zusammen mit dem des spanischen Gitarrespielers und Volkssängers Pagans (Paris, Louvre), in seiner Art der Charakterisierung wohl das reifste dieser Doppelbildnisse. Wie hier volle Manneskraft und Greisentum, vitales und reflektierendes Leben, der Spielend-Singende und der Lauschende, tätig-offene und ruhend-geschlossene Hände, der Kopf vor der dunklen Wand und das Antlitz vor dem weissen Notenheft miteinander kontrastiert werden, wird kein Betrachter je vergessen.[80] Auch nach der Reise in die Vereinigten Staaten entstehen noch solche Doppel-Porträts wie das zweier bekannter Künstler des Impressionismus, des Marcel Desboutin und des Grafen Lepic von etwa 1876 beweist.[81] Gemessen an der scharfen, hellen Luft, in der solche Porträts entstehen, erscheint das Freundschaftsbild von Marées in der Zoologischen Station in Neapel noch wie ein Spätling der deutschen Romantik.

Wie schade, lieber Rudi, dass wir beide uns nicht vor 35 Jahren in Rom zusammen malen liessen. Gewiss würde die Hertziana ein solches Bild gern im Vestibül des Palazzo Zuccari aufhängen! Nun ist es zu spät dafür. Erhalten Sie mir Ihre Zuneigung, so lange es Tag ist—auch ohne Freundschaftsbild!

78. ebda II, 126.
79. ebda II, 116.

80. ebda Nr. 256, 257, 287, 288, 345.
81. ebda Nr. 395.

RICHARD KRAUTHEIMER

A Christian Triumph in 1597

In the spring of 1596 Clement VIII pressed Cesare Baronio under threat of excommunication to accept a cardinal's hat.[1] On June 20, the learned member of the congregation of S. Filippo Neri gave in. As his title church he requested and obtained the *titulus Fasciolae*, SS. Nereo ed Achilleo on the Via Appia near the Baths of Caracalla. He was a poor man and the title church he asked for was the poorest of the twenty-five cardinals' titles, then in Rome. The income was practically nil and the church, built by Leo III about 814 in place of the old titulus and remodelled by Sixtus IV in 1475, was in disrepair; Ugonio, in the 1580's, saw but fragments of Leo III's mosaic in the apse and found the narthex in ruins.[2] The pope teased Baronio about his choice. After all, he said, Baronio was the richest among the cardinals and it was only fair for him to have a title church which would require continuous repairs.[3] But Baronio stood fast. Just because it was so poor and neglected, he wanted that particular church. The pope would help him he trusted, and if not, he himself would go into debt and pay the promissory note back within a year.[4]

The reasons for Baronio's insistence were, of course, more deeply rooted. Ever since he had started on his scholarly work in the late 1550's he had focused his indefatigable energy and his amazing erudition on one single aim: to establish sound historical foundations on which to rest the claims of the Apostolic Church revived by the Council of Trent. Of his *Annales Ecclesiastici*, long prepared, the first two volumes had appeared—the first in 1588, the second in 1594—covering the time from the beginning of Christianity to the beginning of the fourth century. His *Martyrologium Romanum*, commissioned by Gregory XIII, and first published in 1584, had been reworked, approved in 1585, and published in revised form in 1588.

Against this background of a retrospective militancy of the Church, it was but natural for him to claim the title of SS. Nereo ed Achilleo: 'an ancient church in ruins, its tottering walls in disrepair and filled with rubble...'; a church moreover, '... where once Saint Gregory addressed a homily to the people, and where in ancient times our forebears had erected the *titulus*, formerly called *Fasciolae*'. Long before his elevation to the purple he was fascinated by the thought of once being able to restore it and through it, the Church to their ancient glories. '... What are the heretics to say', he exclaimed, 'about the dilapidation of these churches, they who daily come to the city and slander us all over? You know, Lord, what I would do if I had the power.'[5]

Thus he claimed and obtained the title and in the course of a few months he had the church repaired and redecorated. The ruins of the narthex were removed, except the lateral walls, and the site converted into a shallow plaza, provided with benches. In front of the plaza, facing the road, a column was set up, resting on a porphyry base and carrying a capital with lion and bull protomae, surmounted by a cross.[6] Inside the church, the fifteenth-century windows in the earlier clerestory were blocked and replaced by three rectangular windows. The pavement was repaired and the last remains of the ninth-century mosaic in the apse were removed after a careful copy and reconstruction in tempera had been made.[7] In their place a fresco was painted in the apse vault showing the martyrs flanking the jewelled cross, the men to the left (that is, the liturgical right), the women to the right, led by the titular Saints, Nereus and Achilleus and by their fellow martyr, Domitilla. Below, on the wall of the apse, another fresco shows Saint Gregory preaching to a large crowd his homily XXVIII which tradition linked to this church rather than to the catacomb church of the saints on the Via Ardeatina, where it was really delivered. Angels were painted in the spandrels of the arcades, scenes from the legend of the

1. The principal sources for Cesare Baronio's life and work are H. Barnabeus, *Purpura sancta seu vita Cardinalis Baronii*, Rome, 1651, and R. Albericus, *Venerabilis Cesaris Baronii ... Epistolae et opuscula*, 3 vols., Rome, 1770. On the church of SS. Nereo ed Achilleo, see A. Guerrieri, *La Chiesa dei SS. Nereo ed Achilleo* (Collezione 'Amici delle Catacombe', XVI), Città del Vaticano, 1951; R. Krautheimer and S. Corbett, *Corpus Basilicarum Christianarum Romae*, III, Vatican City, 1967, pp. 135 ff.
2. P. Ugonio, *Schedario*, Barb. Lat. 2160, fol. 196 v.
3. Barnabeus, *op. cit.*, pp. 62 f.
4. Letter of Baronius to Fr. Antonio Talpa, February 22, 1597 (Albericus, *op. cit.*, III, Epist. LXIII, pp. 79 f., particularly p. 80).

5. Barnabeus, *op. cit.*, p. 62; Albericus, *op. cit.*, I, 88; Guerrieri, *op. cit.*, p. 67.
6. G. Carletti, *Memorie ... di S. Silvestro in Capite*, Rome, 1794, p. 21, note b, and G. Marangoni, *Delle Cose Gentilesche e Profane*, Rome, 1744, p. 20, both with reference to Villalpando, *Commentarius in Ezechielem*, Rome, 1604, II, p. 86.
7. G. B. De Rossi, *Musaici Christiani ...*, Rome, 1883, text to SS. Nereo ed Achilleo; Guerrieri, *op. cit.*, pp. 116 ff.

titular Saints and their companions between the clere-story windows, the martyrdoms of the Apostles in the aisles. The glorification of the titular Saints decorates the entrance wall, while the two altar paintings in the aisles represent, the one Domitilla and a group of female martyrs, the other Nereus, Achilleus, and other male saints. Baronio, in a letter dated February 22, 1597, described what was then finished of this painted decoration.[8] In the same letter he listed in detail the new furnishings of the church: '*Si e' fatto nella chiesa restituita degno loco per loro* (*scil.* the martyr's relics), *cioè un Altare tutto di pietre nobilmente lavorate che senz' altro paliotto è bellissimo e se si coprisse di broc-cato, non sarà così bello. Ho avuto le pietre in dono dall'Abbate di S. Paolo, quali servivano alla confes-sione, dove si tengono le reliquie sotto l'Altare di maravigliosa bellezza. Ho fatto e benaccconcio il presbiterio e la sede presbiteriale, amboni per l'Evan-gelio, e epistola; candeglieri nobilmente lavorati ed ornati, ed acciò niente manchi all'antiquità si è fatto un bellissimo Cereo paschale molto magnifico . . .*' Presumably later, since they are not listed in this letter, he added a pulpit, placing it on a porphyry base, and erected a canopy over the altar.

The furniture of his church was apparently of signal importance to Baronio, and for good reasons. It was to conform to old custom (*che niente manchi all'anti-quità*) in every detail. That is, it was to have all the fittings which Baronio believed to be essential for services in an early basilica and it was to have them in the right place: an altar provided with a *confessio* and surmounted by a canopy; a chancel site (*presbiterio*) with a cathedra in the apex of the apse; screens in front of the altar enclosing the chancel site; ambones for the reading of the scriptures; a pulpit for the ser-mon, candlesticks, finally a huge candelabrum for the Easter candle. Such were the fittings and the placing in Roman churches he had reason to consider Early Christian: S. Clemente, S. Pudenziana, S. Maria in Cosmedin, S. Pancrazio, S. Giorgio in Velabro; a belief shared by scholars as late as the nineteenth century.[9] Baronio would feel on safe ground: not only his own studies in the history of the early Church, but also his intimate association with Onofrio Panvinio and Antonio Bosio, the learned Christian archeologists, had prepared him for the task. None could know, after all, that in these buildings the placing of the furniture and in the majority of cases the furniture itself and at times even the structure dated from the twelfth and

thirteenth centuries. In Baronio's eyes, SS. Nereo ed Achilleo, while rebuilt by Leo III, took the place of the *titulus Fasciolae*. It was an old church and it was only proper that he should provide it with fittings as of old or, to put it into the words of a contemporary, that 'he took care to restore it (*ridurla*) as far as pos-sible to the ancient form (*modello*) in which the *memorie* of the martyrs were formerly built'.[10] One cannot help suspecting that the new cardinal wanted to set an example for those among his contemporaries who saw in a return to the customs of old the best chance for a renewal of the Catholic Church. He opposed the innovators, such as the abbot of S. Paolo who remodelled the confessio of his basilica '*alla moderna*', and he went on record in favour of retain-ing at least the nave of Old St. Peter's, against the churchmen and architects who were about to demolish its last remains.[11]

Nor was it by chance that the fittings he provided for SS. Nereo ed Achilleo were composed of fragments of old church furnishings and of other spoils: the cathe-dra, a twelfth- or thirteenth-century lions' throne framed by the remnants of a ciborium dating about 1300; the altar and its confessio, composed of a cosma-tesque antependium, a fourth-century *cancello*, a twelfth-century cornice and, in the rear, a piece of Roman coffering; the ambones, built up from two cosmatesque screens, as they customarily separated sanctuary and church nave in thirteenth-century Rome;[12] the candlesticks, cosmatesque colonnettes; the pulpit, apparently of sixteenth-century date placed on a Roman porphyry base and with cosmatesque fragments set into the cheek of the stairs and into the newel post;[13] the Easter candelabrum adapted from a huge banister, one of a set of six in the church, either of Roman or, what is more likely, of fifteenth-century workmanship, but in Baronio's eyes certainly Roman.[14] Some of these fragments may have been in SS. Nereo

10. O. Panciroli, *Tesori nascosti* . . . , Rome, 1600, p. 63.

11. L. Pastor, *History of the Popes*, xxvi, St. Louis, Mo., 1937, p. 381, n. 1.

12. Such screens, though no longer extant, were to be found, for instance, at S. Pudenziana, S. Pancrazio, S. Sisto Vecchio, S. Sabina; see Krautheimer-Corbett, *Corpus Basilicarum*, iii (as above, note 1), pp. 162, 299, and iv (in the press).

13. It is generally assumed that the pulpit came from S. Silvestro and is of Roman or Early Christian workmanship; see G. Giacchetti, *Historia della . . . Chiesa di S. Silvestro in Capite*, Rome, 1629, p. 43, and Guerrieri, *op. cit.*, pp. 93 ff.; Ilaria Toesca in I. S. Gaynor and I. Toesca, *S. Silvestro in Capite* (*Le Chiese di Roma Illustrate*, 73), Rome, 1963, p. 64, n. 27, quotes the receipt of the mason who at S. Silvestro dismembered '*il pulpito dove si diceva l'Evangelio*'. But I doubt that this refers to the pulpit now in SS. Nereo ed Achilleo. I should pre-fer to link the passage to the cosmatesque pulpit at S. Cesareo; see below, and note 18.

14. Guerrieri, *op. cit.*, pp. 90 ff.; Krautheimer-Corbett, *Corpus Basilicarum*, iii (as above, note 1), p. 142 and note 3.

8. Letter of Baronio to Talpa, see above, note 4.

9. P. Sarnelli, *Antica Basilicografia*, Naples, 1680, frontispiece and *passim*; G. Piazza, *Gerarchia Cardinalizia*, Rome, 1703, pp. 774 ff., and still H. Holtzinger, *Die Altchristliche Archi-tektur* . . . , Stuttgart, 1889, pp. 114 ff.

ed Achilleo itself. But the major part Baronio gathered from all over: from S. Paolo, the plaques for the altar;[15] from S. Silvestro, the capital of the column in front of the church and either the pulpit or possibly one of the choirscreens used as ambones and the lecterns placed on them.[16] The porphyry base of the pulpit, if the tradition is correct, came from the Baths of Caracalla.[17] Other pieces could have come from S. Sisto Vecchio, just across the Via Appia, where the thirteenth-century church was remodelled in 1582; or from S. Pudenziana where the cosmatesque furniture was removed between 1588 and 1599; or from any of the numerous other Early Christian and Romanesque churches which were remodelled during these decades. In fact, Baronio apparently bought wholesale a set of cosmatesque furniture, far larger than he required for SS. Nereo ed Achilleo; the rest, comprising a set of cosmatesque fragments exactly corresponding to those at SS. Nereo ed Achilleo and a beautiful ambo with lectern, went to S. Cesario, a few hundred yards to the south, which was remodelled between 1597 and 1600 under his supervision.[18] Whether Roman or medieval (and thus in his eyes Early Christian) Baronio received them as gifts or through barter. Even when he had to buy them, they presumably cost him little; medieval church furniture in the last decades of the sixteenth century went cheaply all over Rome. The need to economize, no doubt, was one of the reasons for Baronio's eagerness to acquire such discards. Also, in recomposing and adapting them, as he did, he acted like any antiquarian and collector of antiques of the latter sixteenth century. But he obviously had other reasons as well. To the moderns the Roman and medieval fragments were worthless rejects; to him they were precious reminders of the past: a past when the Church, sprung in Rome from a pagan ambient, had formed itself, still one and undivided and untouched by the modern heresy, Protestantism. To fit together these fragments into furnishings, at once new and old, coincided with his broad concept of history in which the past, whether Roman or Christian, formed the basis of present and of future Rome.

This concept becomes even clearer in the arrangements made for the translation of the relics of the titular saints into his church. The remains of Saints Domitilla, Nereus and Achilleus had originally been buried on the Via Ardeatina in the catacomb church, which

bears Domitilla's name. Later legend had made her into a Flavian princess and Nereus and Achilleus into her servants. Their remains had been brought in 1228 to the church of S. Adriano, formerly the *curia senatus* on the Roman Forum.[19] A papal breve dated February 14, 1597, granted Baronio permission to transfer them to his titular church.[20] This he did on the vigil of the feastday of the Saints, May 11, 1597, with the greatest solemnity. In the morning the pope visited both S. Adriano and SS. Nereo ed Achilleo.[21] In the evening the translation itself took place. The procession moved from S. Adriano first to the Gesù where, at an altar set up in front of the church, the relics were greeted with church music. From there the procession ascended the Capitoline Hill passing between the statues of the Dioscuri and came to a halt at the statue of Marc Aurel. Descending the east slope of the hill it passed successively under the three triumphal arches, 'once erected for the triumphs of the various emperors': the Arch of Septimius Severus, the Arch of Titus, and the Arch of Constantine, proceeding thus along the Via Sacra. Turning south it passed by S. Gregorio Magno and ended up at SS. Nereo ed Achilleo where honorific arches of perishable material had been set up decorated with the trophies of the martyrs. The procession of the relics then was essentially cast in the form of a Roman triumph as described by the ancients. All the elements are present, though not in the original sequence: the visit to the Capitol, the march along the Via Sacra, the return to the house of the triumphators—their church and final resting place.[22]

Of course, the procession of May 11, 1597, was not just a Roman triumph revived, an ecclesiastical masquerade as it were. It was carefully planned and its real meaning becomes clear even more than from the descriptions of the procession, from the inscriptions which were set up at the successive stations of its path: at the Dioscuri flanking the entrance to the Capitol; at the three triumphal arches, two inscriptions at each; at the honorific arch of the martyrs near their church. Antonio Galliano has transcribed them.[23]

15. See above, p. 175 and note 8.
16. See above, note 13, and below, note 18.
17. Guerrieri, *op. cit.*, p. 95, quoting Ficoroni, *Vestigia di Roma*, Rome, 1774, I, p. XIII.
18. G. Matthiae, *S. Cesareo 'de Appia'*, Rome, 1955, pp. 25 ff., 35 ff., and 53 ff. The ambo I suspect to be the '*pulpito dove si diceva l'Evangelio*' purchased from S. Silvestro in Capite, see above, note 13.
19. V. Forcella, *Iscrizioni delle Chiese ... di Roma*, II, 1869 ff., p. 49; Baronius, *Martyrologium Romanum*, Venice, 1630, pp. 283 f., Maii 12.
20. Baronio's letter to Talpa, as quoted above, note 4.
21. Baronio's letter to Talpa, May 16, 1597 (Albericus, *op. cit.*, III, *Epistola*, LXVII, pp. 86 f.).
22. The procession is described in detail by Baronio himself in his *Martyrologium Romanum*, *op. cit.*, Maii 12, notes, pp. 283 f.; by Panciroli, *op. cit.*, pp. 625 ff., and by A. Galliano, *Relazione della traslazione delle sacre reliquie ...*, Rome, Bibliotheca Vallicelliana, G. 99, fols. 14, 14 v, 16, 16 v; see also Guerrieri, *op. cit.*, pp. 70 ff.
23. *Bibl. Vallicelliana*, G. 99, Antonio Galliano, Vitae sanctorum et alia diversi generis.

The Capitol, so the first sign ran, burnt and twice restored by Domitilla's relations, Vespasian and Domitian, but returned to the old superstition, has been cleansed from the cult of the daemons by Domitilla's self-sacrifice at the stake as a Roman martyr. At the Arch of Septimius, facing the Capitol, Senate and People of Rome proclaimed that the three martyrs, their fellow citizens, had won through their blood for the Christian Republic the peace of Christianity and through their glorious deaths had brought glory to the name of Rome. On the opposite side, the inscription praised them as an ornament to the city they had glorified through their shining testi-mony to the Christian faith. On the Arch of Titus, one inscription rededicated to Domitilla the arch once dedicated to Titus who had revenged Christ's death through destroying Jerusalem; the other reminded the reader that she, more gloriously than Titus, had avenged Christ's death through giving her blood and life. On the Arch of Constantine, facing the Colosseum, one inscription again stressed how on the Via Sacra where the Roman emperors had celebrated their triumphs over subject provinces, the three martyrs had triumphed over the triumphants. On the opposite face of the arch, Domitilla was singled out for having brought greater glory to Rome than the Imperial family and the twelve Caesars by renouncing for Christ's sake both Empire and life. Finally on the honorific arches in front of their church, the martyrs were welcomed back to their old residence, once deserted but now restored.

The theme then is clearly set forth and it was carefully planned. The learned circles of Rome took it up with enthusiasm. Just as it dominates the inscriptions, it runs through a volume of poems presented to Baronio at the time of the transfer by the Collegio Romano and others. They are awkward poems on the

Fol. 14. Ad Fornicem Septimi ab ea parte, quae respicit Capitolium

S. P. Q. R.

SS. FLAVIAE DOMITILLAE, NEREO, ET ACHILLEO,
OPTIMIS CIVIBUS SUIS
OB NOMEN ROMANUM GLORIOSA MORTE ILLUSTRATUM,
PARTAMQUE CHRISTIANAE REIP. PROPRIO SANGUINE
TRANQUILITATEM

Ab ea verò parte que Forum spectat

S. P. Q. R.

SS. FLAVIAE DOMITILLAE, NEREO, ET ACHILLEO
INVICTISSIMIS IESU CHRISTI MARTYRIBUS
OB URBEM PRAECLARO CHRISTIANAE FIDEI TESTIMONIO
DECORATAM ORNAMENTUMQUE.

Fol. 14 v. Ad Fornicem Titi ab ea parte, quae spectat Hortos Palatinos Farnesiorum

S. P. Q. R.

TRIUMPHALEM HUNC ARCUM, OLIM TITO FL. VESP. AUG.
OB TUMULTUANTEM IUDAEAM IMP. PO. RO. RESTITUTAM
DECRETUM ET ERECTUM
S. FL. DOMITILLAE EIUSDEM TITI NEPTI,
OB CHRISTIANAM RELIGIONEM PROPRIA MORTE AUCTAM,
PROPAGATAMQUE,
MULTO FOELICIUS NUNC DECERNIT, CONSECRATQUE

Ab ea parte quae respicit Amphitheatrum

S. FL. DOMITILLAE VIRG. ET MART. ROM.
TIT FL. VESP. AUG. NEPTI
QUOD IESU CHRISTI MORTEM, AB EODEM TITO, EVERSIS
HIEROSOLYMIS
DIVINO CONSILIO VINDICATAM,
IPSA, SANGUINE, VITAQUE PRO EIUS FIDE PROFUSIS
GLORIOSIUS CONSECRAVERIT
S. P. Q. R.

Ad Fornicem Constantini in Fronte ea in parte, quae respicit Amphitheatrum

SS. FLAVIAE DOMITILLAE, NEREO, ET ACHILLEO
VIA SACRA, QUA PLURES RO. IMPP. AA.
DE SUBACTIS IMP. PO. RO. PROVINCIIS TRIUMPHARUNT
DE IPSIS TRIUMPHATORIBUS, QUANTO FORTIUS SUPERATIS
TANTO GLORIOSIUS TRIUMPHANTIBUS.
S. P. Q. R.

Ex altera verò parte item in Fronte quae respicit Septizonium Septimii

S. FL. DOMITILLAE VIRG. ET MART. ROM.
QUOD GENTEM FLAVIAM, URBEMQUE A. XII. RO. IMPP. AA.
GENTILIBUS SUIS
REBUS PRAECLARE GESTIS DECORATAM,
UNA IMPERIO, VITAQUE PRO CHRISTO TRADITIS,
OMNIUM PRAECLARISSIME ILLUSTRAVERIT,
S. P. Q. R.

Fol. 16. Visebantur praeterea ibidem ad equos marmoreos eiusmodi inscriptiones maximis literis exaratae

S. FLAVIAE DOMITILLAE VIRGINI ET MARTYRI RO.
OB CAPITOLIUM AB INFELICI DEMONUM CULTU
FELICIUS EXPURGATUM QUAM AB EIUS
GENTILIBUS FLAVIO VESPASIANO ET DOMIT. AA.
PRISTINAE SUPERSTITIONI RESTITUTUM
S. P. Q. R. S. FLAVIAE DOMITILLAE VIRGINI
ET MARTYRI RO. QUOD MAIOREM URBI GLORIAM
ATTULERIT INCENDIO IPSA PRO CHRISTO FIDE CONSUMPTA
QUAM UTERQUE FLAVIUS VESPASIANUS ET DOMITIANUS
AUGUSTI GENTILES SUI CAPITOLIO BIS
INCENDIO CONSUMPTO PROPRIIS SUMPTIBUS
RESTITUTO
S. P. Q. R.

Fol. 16 v. Non longe autem ab ecclesia arcus seu fornices honoris causa ad tempus, martyrum trophaeis ornati, erecti erant, Basilicae parietibus vel his proximis carmina quamplurima quae suis quibusque locis exscribentur affixa extabant, ubi etiam et inscriptiones aliquot his verbis notatae

S. FL. DOMITILLAE VIRG., ET MART. RO.
A.B. CLEMENTE PAPA IESU CHRISTO CONSECRATAE CORPUS
AB EIUS SUCCESSORE CLEMENTE VIII, PRISTINAE SEDI
HONORIFICENTISSIME RESTITUITUR.
SS. FLAVIA DOMITILLA, NEREUS, ET ACHILLEUS
PROPRIAS AEDES, IAM COLLAPSAS, AC DESERTAS,
RESTITUTIONE
SS. FL. DOMITILLAM, NEREUM ET ACHILLEUM
VETERES PATRONOS SUOS, AEDES ANTIQUAE RECIPIUNT
ET QUORUM CORPORIBUS SPOLIATAE IACEBANT, RESTITUTIONE
EORUMDEM MODO FELICISSIME EXTOLLUNTUR ET
ILLUSTRANTUR.

Guerrieri's transcriptions from Galliano's MS. (*op. cit.*, pp. 70 ff., n. 29) are unfortunately full of misreadings and omissions. I have checked the manuscript and I am grateful to Mr. R. M. Stapleford for rechecking it for me.

whole, and one gets the impression that those presented by the Collegio Romano were for the better part written by schoolboys, each required to compose six lines on the given theme.[24] But the theme itself, as expressed both in the inscriptions along the processional road and in the schoolboy exercises, has grandeur: the martyrs were Romans; through their blood they have brought new glory to the name of Rome; they have triumphed over those that formerly had trod the same path for worldly glory; they have thus defeated paganism and made Rome into a Christian city. Within this framework it becomes clear why Domitilla whose relics tangibly were the least important was so conspicuously singled out by the authors of the inscriptions. Her legendary position as a Roman princess made her the ideal figure to set off the new triumph of Christianity against the old triumphs of her pagan Imperial ancestors. The obvious simplicity of the contrast was bound to appeal to the average

24. *Bibl. Vallicelliana, Q. 60.*
Carmina Collegii Romani Societatis Jesu et aliorum in Translatione SS. Martyrum Nerei Achillei et Flaviae Domitillae Ad Caesarem Baronium Cardinalem ... MDXCVII.

Fol. 2. Urbe triumphata Divos agitare triumphos
         Viderat aetherea Praeses ab arce Petrus
         I nunc et veteres his, inquit, confer honores
         Et quos iactabas, Martia Roma, Duces
         Si Superis Reges aequas pompam aspice utramque
         Illam homines dicas hanc statuisse Deum.

Fol. 4. Ut Divum cineres Capitolia ad alta triumpho
         Vectari omnipotens vidit ab arce Pater
         Hisque arcus veterum Regum monumenta sacrari;
         Risit et ad superos talia versus ait
         Cernitis, ut cedat Romana potentia coelo
         En quos calcavit, Roma superba colit.

Fol. 18. Aspice quam dignus devicto ex hoste triumphus
         Ducatur quantum vivat in urbe decus
         Occubuit victor, victusque perculit hostis
         Qui superest lata ex morte triumphat honor
         Mors felix tales victor de more triumphos
         Numque ducturus, ni periisset, erat.

mind and inevitably it became the *leitmotif* of the procession when described by the *ciceroni*, witness Panciroli's guide-book. To the planners of the procession, on the other hand, it was but one element among many and perhaps not its most important. To them, the meaning underlying the triumphal transfer of the Roman martyrs to their church was more all-embracing: the Rome of old, in its defeat, had been integrated into the new, the Christian Rome.

It is but legitimate to view Cesare Baronio as the leading spirit planning the procession of the relics to his church. The motifs of the triumph of the new over the old Rome, the integration of both and the concept of an essentially Roman Christianity recur throughout his scholarly work. They are likewise reflected, it seems to us, in the refurnishing of his church with fittings as recomposed from fragments both classical and medieval but always Roman. After all similar concepts had pervaded the work of Roman scholars and churchmen throughout the last third of the sixteenth century: of Panciroli who had written on Roman emperors, on Roman triumphs, on Roman Christian basilicas; of Ugonio who had published the *Stationi di Roma* in 1588; of Sixtus V who had set up the old obelisks, christianized by inscriptions, exorcisms, and crosses, and had placed the statues of Saints Peter and Paul atop the triumphal columns of Trajan and Marcus Aurelius; of Bosio who had first entered the catacombs. This same spirit, the triumph of the Church over Paganism—and implicitly also over Heresy—was no doubt responsible for Baronio's placing into the newly created atrium-plaza of his church a column surmounted by a capital with animal heads which he would interpret as representing pagan daemons and surmounting it by a cross. But rarely are all these concepts as succinctly spelt out in words as in the inscriptions that interpreted the Christian triumph of the martyrs to SS. Nereo ed Achilleo.

GIULIO CARLO ARGAN

Il valore critico della "stampa di traduzione"

Nei secoli XVII e XVIII, fino alla scoperta della fotografia, la cultura artistica europea si è in gran parte sviluppata attraverso le riproduzioni di opere d'arte per mezzo dell'incisione su rame. E' quindi necessario stabilire quale tipo di esperienza e d'insegnamento figurativo venisse comunicato e diffuso con questo mezzo. La riproduzione a stampa non è, infatti, una sottospecie della replica e della copia, ma implica una problematica affatto diversa e non priva di qualche importanza per la storia della teoria e della critica dell'arte. La replica e la copia presuppongono semplicemente il pensiero che un determinato procedimento operativo che ha prodotto un certo risultato possa essere ripetuto dando luogo all'identico risultato; se poi la qualità della replica o della copia appare inferiore a quella dell'invenzione iniziale, ciò si imputa alla scarsa abilità o accuratezza dell'esecutore e non al principio che l'opera d'arte sia, per la propria natura stessa, irripetibile. Il concetto che la ripetizione, anche se fatta dallo stesso artista, sia sempre e necessariamente inferiore alla prima invenzione appare solo nel Settecento, nella teoria della critica del Richardson; e come difesa contro le contraffazioni da cui era invaso il mercato artistico inglese.

Nella riproduzione all'incisione il procedimento tecnico è completamente diverso da quello dell'originale; e il risultato è una figurazione iconograficamente similie a quella dell'originale, ma di dimensioni ridotte e priva di quell'elemento visivo fondamentale che è il colore. Evidentemente si ammette, almeno in linea di principio, che il valore o alcuni componenti del valore artistico siano indipendenti dalla dimensione, dal collocamento, dalla destinazione e perfino dal colore; oppure si ritiene che il valore intrinseco dell'opera possa essere conservato e trasmesso integralmente, sebbene a una scala diversa, dal foglio stampato. Poichè alla fine del Cinquecento, con i Carracci e specialmente con Agostino, l'incisione assume la dignità di una tecnica artistica autonoma, è chiaro che vale la seconda ipotesi: si ammette cioè che la stampa non trasmette soltanto l'immagine o il soggetto ma, sia pure a un livello diverso e attraverso una certa serie di passaggi, il valore integrale dell'opera originale. Questo convincimento può in parte spiegarsi con il concetto di "disegno", così com'è stato formulato dai teorici del Manierismo: nel senso cioè che l'incisione ricostruisca e riproduca una "idea" formale precedente alla sua realizzazione mediante la tecnica della pittura e, per il suo carattere universale, ugualmente realizzabile mediante altri procedimenti tecnici. Ma sta di fatto che lo stile incisorio carraccesco si forma in tutto un altro ambito di cultura e specialmente attraverso lo studio del Correggio e dei veneti, cioè di opere in cui l'elemento disegno è inseparabile dal colore. In realtà, quando Agostino riproduce opere del Tintoretto o del Veronese, non soltanto non tiene alcun conto della distinzione tradizionale tra il disegno romano e il colorito veneziano, ma cerca di cogliere il disegno di quegli artisti proprio in quanto esso è espresso mediante il colore. Il Malvasia fornisce, su questo punto, indicazioni assai importanti. Non considera Agostino, a causa della sua preminente attività incisoria, un artista inferiore ad Annibale. V'è differenza di carattere ("Agostino timido nell'arte e guardingo, Annibale coraggioso e sprezzante"), ma si tratta di una "gran diversità di genio in non diversa elezione di studio e di professione". Non esclude che la "carta stampata" possa essere perfino "più intesa ed aggiustata" dell'originale dipinto. Le opere del Tintoretto sono state intagliate da Agostino "con più diligenza, per non dir miglioramento"; e il Dürer non aveva esitato a riconoscere le incisioni di Marcantonio Raimondi "tanto de' suoi originali migliori". Si trattava, in quest'ultimo caso, di una correzione della durezza "gotica"; ma, senza l'esperienza viva delle incisioni di Agostino, difficilmente il Malvasia sarebbe arrivato ad affermare che una riproduzione a stampa può essere migliore dell'originale. D'altra parte il merito che il Malvasia riconosce a Marcantonio è, in definitiva, di avere tradotto le opere di Dürer dal tedesco in italiano: ciò che dimostra com'egli considerasse la riproduzione a stampa alla stregua di una traduzione o trascrizione e non di una ripetizione o copia.

La ragion pratica della diffusione mediante riproduzioni a stampa di opere di soggetto religioso è nota: la Chiesa cattolica rivaluta le immagini che la Riforma aveva screditato e proibito; incoraggia il formarsi e il diffondersi di una nuova iconografia sacra, che fornisse a tutti i fedeli gli stessi oggetti e gli stessi simboli per una devozione di massa; si serve delle stampe figurate come di un mezzo potente di propaganda religiosa. Ma il procedimento di trascrizione è evidentemente lo stesso quando si tratta di opere di tema profano e perfino erotico. Ciò che interessa dunque

[179]

non è tanto il nuovo mezzo per la divulgazione di una tematica devozionale, ma lo sviluppo di una tecnica di comunicazione culturale in una larghissima area. Si vuole che l'istruzione alla vita devota sia anzitutto educazione dei sentimenti; nè si mira all'espressione di un sentimento religioso popolare, ma alla diffusione nel popolo di una religione colta che ha (anche per questo si distingue dalla religione riformata e dalla sua attesa della grazia) un fondamento nella storia. Se la riproduzione a stampa di opere di soggetto religioso ha un'efficacia educativa, l'ha proprio in quanto comunica, insieme all'immagine, il valore estetico che le è connesso, cioè la grandiosa concezione del mondo che gli artisti esprimono in immagini. Il Malvasia fa dire ad Annibale che desidera di copiare il Correggio per "far con lui un pane, che ogni un ne possa mangiare".

Abbiamo detto, però, che l'opera riprodotta a stampa si presenta molto diversa dall'originale: ciò che determina, ovviamente, un diverso modo di fruizione o di consumo. Un affresco o una grande tela d'altare sono ridotti alla dimensione di un foglio di carta, che può essere tenuto in mano e guardato da vicino; il suo aspetto, in bianco e nero, è simile a quello di una pagina scritta; la tecnica con cui l'immagine è realizzata è più affine a quella dell'impressione tipografica che a quella della pittura; spesso la figurazione è accompagnata da uno scritto in margine o inserita, come illustrazione, in un libro. A rigore, la riproduzione a stampa delle opere d'arte avrebbe potuto provocare, nel campo dell'arte figurativa, la stessa rivoluzione che l'invenzione di Gutenberg aveva provocato nel campo della cultura letteraria e scientifica; e indubbiamente la grande diffusione delle riproduzioni a stampa è un fenomeno che rientra nel grande piano secentesco di una profonda riforma sociale fondata sulla cultura d'immagine e sullo sviluppo delle tecnologie relative. Il fatto più importante, però, è che lo affresco o il grande quadro vengono contemplati e ammirati proprio per le qualità che inevitabilmente scompaiono nella riproduzione a stampa: il rapporto con un'architettura "monumentale", le dimensioni imponenti, lo splendore dei colori. La riproduzione a stampa, invece, non forma oggetto di contemplazione o ammirazione, non ha alcun carattere monumentale, la sua forza di appello visivo è assai limitata. Piuttosto che contemplata o ammirata viene letta e riletta; il suo messaggio è diretto al singolo individuo e il fatto culturalmente importante è proprio che lo stesso messaggio sia ricevuto singolarmente da ciascuno.

Il principio della "lettura" dell'opera figurativa è tipicamente secentesco; i dipinti "di genere" sono oggetti di lettura molto più che elementi decorativi; nelle quadrerie principesche e cardinalizie i quadri sono allineati sulle pareti come i libri negli scaffali, pronti per la consultazione; l'Agucchi, il Giustiniani, il Mancini, ma specialmente il Bellori, leggono e descrivono, più che non celebrino con discorsi ammirativi, le opere dei loro contemporanei. Indubbiamente la riproduzione a stampa tende a rendere leggibile e ad offrire alla lettura le opere figurative; e in questo senso rientra nel fondamentale tema barocco dell'equivalenza, in termini di valore, dell'opera figurativa e dell'opera letteraria. *Ut pictura poesis*; ma non soltanto nel senso di una uguale facoltà immaginativa concessa al pittore e al poeta, bensì nel senso di una versione testuale dell'opera figurativa "da contemplare" in un'opera figurativa "da leggere". Qual'è il processo della trasformazione del valore da contemplare in un valore da leggere? E poichè l'incisore, mediante la propria tecnica, proceda ad una lettura analitica dell'originale e la riproduzione è offerta come un "modello di lettura", vi sono canoni o regole per la lettura esemplare? Come si spiega che la lettura rapida e vivace di Annibale venga considerata diversa ma altrettanto valida che la lettura studiosa e diligente di Agostino?

E' già notevole che, riconoscendosi nella lettura il miglior modo di accostarsi all'opera d'arte e di intenderne il valore, si ricorra a "modelli di lettura": ciò significa che la giusta interpretazione dell'arte è quella che ne dà l'artista e che, dunque, la riproduzione a stampa ci dà l'opera riprodotta come arte veduta dall'artista, cioè dallo specialista. Ma il metodo della buona lettura o della giusta interpretazione deve essere cercato nella metodologia operativa dell'incisore, cioè nella sua tecnica. La prima difficoltà che si presenta all'incisore è quella della dimensione. Per non rendere meschina, fastidiosamente minuta una grande composizione che viene ridotta alle misure di un foglio di carta bisogna compensare il fattore dimensionale con la giustezza delle proporzioni, quindi mettere in opera un complesso sistema di rapporti dei valori. La riduzione dei colori al bianco e al nero, e alle loro graduazioni intermedie, è indubbiamente un limite inerente alla tecnica incisoria, e un limite che incide fortemente sulla fedeltà della riproduzione. Ma è anche una condizione essenziale per la riduzione dell'opera a un sistema di rapporti di valori o alla proporzione: una riproduzione colorata in piccole dimensioni ridurrebbe l'originale senza compensare la perduta grandezza, senza darne l'equivalente proporzionale. Ma per ottenere l'equivalenza o l'equilibrio dei valori non basta neppure operare una semplice riduzione al chiaroscuro: questo potrebbe forse (e, ancora, con molte riserve) valere per un dipinto di scuola romana, il cui impianto strutturale fosse chiaroscurale; ma non potrebbe valere per un dipinto veneziano, il cui impianto strutturale è tonale o coloristico. Ne risulterebbe gravemente alterata la struttura stessa della forma e il dipinto sarebbe letto in una chiave decisamente falsa. Si pone quindi il problema di tradurre in valori di chiaro e di scuro le specifiche qualità dei colori in quanto elementi costruttivi della forma. I mezzi di cui l'incisore dispone, almeno nella prima fase della storia della riproduzione a stampa, sono limitati: il tratto e le possibilità di ripetizione e combinazione dei tratti. Il tratteggio sul fondo bianco della carta determina un alternarsi di linee nere e bianche e quindi una vibrazione luminosa la cui frequenza muta con il mutare della frequenza dei segni. La sostanza in cui l'incisore opera è dunque una sostanza intrinsecamente luminosa ed è a questa che devono ridursi tutti i valori coloristici dell'originale. Per la determinazione plastica della forma l'incisore ha un mezzo facile ed efficace: segue con il bulino l'andamento dei piani guidando così l'occhio del lettore lungo i risalti, i declivi, gli avvallamenti della forma: dove l'ombra è più densa e la struttura plastica dei piani meno evidente incrocia i segni togliendo loro ogni indicazione di direzione. Ma proprio perchè i valori plastici risultano nell'incisione anche più chiaramente definiti che nell'originale la questione del colore diventa più grave: un modello di lettura in chiave plastico-chiaroscurale non può essere, in ogni caso, un modello di lettura di validità universale. Non rimane, dunque, che trasformare la graduazione chiaroscurale continua in una gamma di ben distinte qualità coloristiche, cioè tradurre la scala di grigi che va dal bianco al nero in una serie di tonalità grigie singolarmente individuate. E' precisamente quello che si fa differenziando le zone tratteggiate non soltanto con la maggiore o minore frequenza dei tratti paralleli (orizzontali, verticali, obliqui), ma incrociando i tratti e talvolta sovrapponendo un reticolo di tratti obliqui ad uno di verticali e orizzontali, e perfino rompendo il breve spazio bianco tra i tratti incrociati con altri piccoli segni (punti d'impasto). Le differenze qualitative del tessuto segnico stanno per le differenze qualitative tra i colori; l'incisore si serve così dei diversi tipi di tessiture segniche esattamente come il pittore si serve dei colori disposti sulla tavolozza. Rimangono infatti, di mano di Annibale, prove di tratteggio (a tergo dei rami), che equivalgono alle prove di colore che fa il pittore dopo avere impastato un tono e prima di applicarlo sulla tela.

Si tratta tuttavia di diverse quantità tonali isolate, differenziate e assunte come qualità coloristiche: dall'incisione non si potrà mai risalire alla reale qualità dei colori dell'originale perchè, naturalmente, non esiste una corrispondenza costante tra un determinato modo di tessitura segnica e un rosso, tra un secondo e un azzurro, tra un terzo e un giallo. L'incisore non traduce nel tessuto chiaroscurale della stampa i singoli colori, ma si limita a individuare per ogni valore di

quantità un corrispondente coefficente qualitativo: il suo compito consiste insomma nell'individuare e sviluppare, come principio strutturale della figurazione, un preciso rapporto di quantità e qualità. In altri termini, il modello di lettura è in chiave di valori o, propriamente, tonale; e questo vale anche nel caso di un originale il cui impianto sia strettamente chiaroscurale, trattandosi evidentemente di un caso particolare in cui i termini di qualità e quantità coincidono.

Nella storia della critica (intendendo per tale non soltanto la critica verbalizzata o scritta, ma tutti i processi di accostamento, interpretazione e fruizione dell'opera d'arte) la riproduzione a stampa segna una svolta quanto mai importante: se prima, specialmente con il Vasari, l'arte romana forniva lo schema interpretativo e valutativo anche per la pittura veneziana (di cui infatti si lodava il colorito, lamentando la mancanza di disegno), ora è la pittura veneta che, come pittura tonale o di valori, fornisce attraverso l'incisione lo schema interpretativo e valutativo anche per la pittura romana. La stessa tecnica dell'incisione "di traduzione" è modellata sul procedimento tecnico della pittura veneziana, che, dando un'importanza predominante al colore, non può evidentemente prescindere dalla materia dell'impasto coloristico. L'incisione non è un disegno al tratto di penna; il segno è scavato dal bulino in una materia dura e viene impresso dal torchio in una materia soffice come la carta. Il frequente ritorno su zone già tratteggiate con altri strati di tratteggio, che rimangono visibili come reticoli sovrapposti, è singolarmente simile alle successive stesure di velature sovrapposte, tipiche della pittura veneziana. Con il procedere dell'esperienza, al finire del secolo XVII si passa, com'è noto, dall'incisione al tratto o al bulino alla cosiddetta "maniera nera", che consiste nel brunire tutta la superficie della lastra e nel ricavare successivamente, per abrasione, i chiari; eliminando così quasi completamente il tratto e riducendo l'immagine ad una misurata giustapposizione di "valori".

Se ora si considera che tutta la pittura barocca può definirsi una pittura "di valori", non soltanto risulta chiaro come la incisione "di traduzione" debba ritenersi un vero e proprio "genere" pittorico, ma come proprio la larghissima diffusione di questi "modelli di lettura" secondo i valori, e il loro impiego come materiale di studio negli *ateliers*, abbia contribuito a determinare una pittura "di valori", essenzialmente preoccupata di concertare le singole qualità coloristiche nel "tono generale". In questo senso, la riproduzione a stampa non appare soltanto come un rigoroso metodo critico per la lettura interpretativa delle opere d'arte, e quindi come un procedimento valutativo o di giudizio, ma anche come primo impegno della critica nello sviluppo operativo storico dell'arte.

P. A. TOMORY

Profane Love in Italian Early and High Baroque Painting

The Transmission of Emotive Experience

'The transmission of emotive experience was the main object of Baroque religious imagery . . .',[1] it was also the principal aim of Baroque secular imagery and it is evident that while secular imagery of this period did not wholly rise to the artistic heights of its religious counterpart, it nevertheless played an important part in the Baroque movement.

By examining the imagery of profane love in relation to the literary and sociological environment, it may be shown that the artists of Early and High Baroque not only continued the examination of the human condition started in the Renaissance, but by centring their attention on the emotive collisions of the sexes, made a pictorial contribution to the establishment of a '. . . modern conception[s] of a sexual love that relies on itself, deriving no sanctions from Platonic idealism or religion'.[2] It would be tedious to list all the subjects of male and female pairs which abound in the period under discussion and which Pigler[3] has noted so exhaustively, but we find such subjects drawn from the Testaments, from mythology, from ancient and contemporary history and literature and, importantly, from life. This is common knowledge,[4] but it is worth noting that the incidence of these subjects is highest during the period spanning Early and High Baroque. For instance, *Esther and Ahasuerus* was painted by Tintoretto, Veronese, Crespi, Salimbeni, Spada, Domenichino, Guercino, Artemisia Gentileschi and Cavallino (Fig. 1), amongst many other lesser artists between 1580 and 1654. Another interesting feature is the variety of the emotional exchanges taking place and the range of conditions of the participants. As Lee[5] has pointed out, in relation to Tasso's *Gerusa-lemme*, the painters '. . . chose for the most part [only] those amorous and idyllic episodes wherein the lyric element is strong. . . .' This was also the general rule

in regard to other sources. This overwhelming interest in the human passion of love has been examined,[6] but it is hoped to show that this interest occurred at a critical point in the development of the humanist conception of love between the sexes. Thus the whole gamut is run from the erotic dalliance of pagan gods through open sensual desire and conquest to the unspoken declaration of love between man and woman.

One has to return to the early Renaissance to find the source of this development, for as in other things, the Baroque inherited a great many of its views from medieval times.[7] One could do no better to point up the difference in the relationship of the sexes between the thirteenth century and the mid-sixteenth century than quote lines from the verse of the two periods. Guido Guinzelli (*c.* 1235–1276) wrote 'non credo che nel mondo sia cristiana/si piena di beltate e di valore',[8] while Torquato Tasso (1544–1595) wrote 'Io v'amo sol perchè voi siete bella':[9] again Guido Cavalcanti (*c.* 1255–1300) wrote 'Angelica sembianza/in voi, donna, riposa',[10] while Gaspara Stampa (1523–1554) wrote 'Io non v'invidio punto, angeli santi'.[11] The teachings of the medieval church exerted sufficient influence even on thirteenth-century poets concerned with declaring their earthly love that this love should be seen 'as a reflection of the divine'.[12] Tasso however can say quite simply that he loves the girl because she is beautiful, while Gaspara Stampa goes on in her poem to liken her enjoyment of her lover's face, to that of the angels of God's—their only advantage is that their enjoyment is eternal! This, of course, was no

1. R. Wittkower, *Art and Architecture in Italy, 1600–1750*, London, 1958, p. 92.
2. J. M. Cohen, *The Baroque Lyric*, Hutchinson University Library, 1963, p. 59.
3. A. Pigler, *Barockthemen*, Budapest, 1956, 1.11.
4. R. W. Lee, 'Ut Pictura Poesis, the Humanistic Theory of Painting', *The Art Bulletin*, XXII, 1940, p. 261.
5. R. W. Lee, *op. cit.*, p. 242.

6. E. Panofsky, *Studies in Iconography*, Harper Torch Books ed., 1962, pp. 129 ff., and sources quoted.
7. R. G. Cox, 'A Survey of Literature from Donne to Marvell', *From Donne to Marvell* (ed. Boris Ford), Penguin, 1956, p. 44.
8. G. Kay, *The Penguin Book of Italian Verse*, London, 1958, p. 53. 'I do not believe that in the world there is a Christian girl so full of beauty and worth.'
9. G. Kay, *op. cit.*, p. 188. 'I love you simply because you are fair'.
10. G. Kay, *op. cit.*, p. 57. 'The likeness of an angel is in you, my lady'.
11. G. Kay, *op. cit.*, p. 177. 'I don't envy you in the least, holy angels'.
12. J. M. Cohen, *op. cit.*, p. 52.

sudden development as will be shown, but these comparisons show that even by the middle of the century, earthly love was conceived only as a temporal, if often a temporary, situation, and that within the ambience of love there was equality between the sexes, exemplified in the tone of Gaspara Stampa's 'Credete ch'io sia Ercol o Sansone/a poter sostener tanto dolore'.[13] It is also true that there is a distinct division between Dante's vision, Beatrice, whom he worships, after her death, as being at the right hand of the Virgin Mary (religious belief and secular love being thus equated), and Petrarch's, who wrote his *Rime* on Laura at a more mature age than Dante had his *Vita Nuova*. He could recognize the central dilemma, for 'With the praise for Laura's beauty and the recognition that she points the way to heaven, there is also the confession of his desire as sensual, and this the path to hell.'[14] Thus by the mid-fourteenth century, and certainly within the intellectual van of the Renaissance, a critical point had been reached in 'the conflict between the worldly will to life and the Christian sufferance of life'.[15] Amongst the prose writers, this same problem was engaged from a lower level. For in the several groups of novelle published in the same period, endless variations on the theme of erotic love are played. The dissemination of these stories would certainly have had their abrasive effect on contemporary social conventions, but perhaps no more than this. But we may recognize in Boccaccio, Petrarch's friend, a writer who was not content only with his narration of the plot, but gained verisimilitude for his stories, with his acute observations of people, places and language. His stories were not only true to life, but, as Auerbach puts it, developed '. . . a distinct, thoroughly practical and secular ethical code rooted in the right to love. . . .'[16] As an instance, there is a passage in the seventh story of the third day where a lady is explaining to a pilgrim (her lover disguised) why she had forsworn him. A friar, to whom she had confessed her love and intimacy, had warned her that she would fall into the abyss of hell if she did not give up her lover. To this her disguised lover replied, 'As soon as he became yours, you became his. Had he not been yours, you might have acted as you had thought fit, . . . 'twas conduct most disgraceful, to sever yourself from him against his will.'[17] Here indeed was a secular code of love and

stated directly in opposition to the teaching of the church.

Nevertheless, the conflict between the demands of the church and the demands of passion continued unabated in the greater part of Italian society. It was not, however, this conflict that the Platonists wished to resolve so much as the human conflict itself—between the spirit and the flesh. Admittedly, victory for the spirit, for platonic love, would correlate with the moral teachings of the church. The Platonists were if nothing devout men. Devoutness apart, the platonic solution was an intellectual revulsion against the common prurience of the time. Similar intellectual solutions have been proposed since, our own time not excepted. These well-established facts are to introduce the third book of Castiglione's *Il Cortegiano*, published in 1528, but as many have pointed out, exerted an influence well into the seventeenth century. Its main tenets are too familiar to require repetition, but one or two observations by one or other of the participants are highly relevant. Giuliano proposes that no man can be called the male that has no female, nor woman be called the female that has no male. This is the central proposition of equality between the sexes in the territory of love. Central to the theme here is Giuliano's statement that the eyes are the harbingers of love, and by them the lover discloses his passion for the beloved. Giordano Bruno, in the second half of the century, repeats this in his *Il Candelaio*:[18] 'L'esser fascinato d'amore adviene, quando . . . un occhio con l'altro . . .' and concludes with '. . . e cossi commuoveno amatorio incendio'. It is left to Burton in his *Anatomy of Love* (1621)[19] to name the source—Plotinus—when he repeats the same message, while John Donne several years earlier in his *Extasie* had written 'Our eye beams twisted, and did thread/Our eyes upon one double string'. Referring to the paintings reproduced here, it is quite obvious that painters, too, were more than familiar with the 'eye beams twisted' theme. It might be pre-supposed, therefore, that this message of love was carried, uncomplicated, into the seventeenth century. But this was not so. There is, for instance, a somewhat revealing doubt raised in *Il Cortegiano* where Bembo has suggested that the mature older man can experience love without desiring the sensual pleasures, but Morello, answering him, avers that love without the body is pure fantasy. This is also restated quite firmly by Benedetto Varchi, later in the century, in discussing

13. G. Kay, *op. cit.*, p. 188. 'Do you believe that I am Hercules or Samson to bear so much grief'.
14. J. H. Whitfield, *A Short History of Italian Literature*, Penguin, 1960, p. 30.
15. E. Auerbach, *Mimesis*, Doubleday Anchor Books ed., 1957, p. 198.
16. E. Auerbach, *loc. cit.*
17. G. Boccaccio, *The Decameron*, Everyman ed., trans. J. M. Rigg, 1930, I, p. 195.

18. G. Bruno, *Il Candelaio*, I, x. Quoted by M. Praz, *The Flaming Heart*, Doubleday Anchor Books, 1958, p. 197, n. 14. Praz also refers to the same theme in Petrarch's sixty-third sonnet.
19. R. Burton, *The Anatomy of Love*, 4 Square Classics (D. George ed.), 1962, p. 56.

the question—'Se nell'onesto si sentono passioni'[20]— where he comes to the conclusion that true love depends on the feeling of the body and the power of the mind combined together. This happy equation may have appeared conclusive to a Florentine Acade- mician, but the dilemma remained, for those en- gaged both in profane *and* sacred love, as to which was the primary motivating force, the spirit or the flesh.

Nowhere was this dilemma engaged so fervidly than in the Spiritual Exercises of Ignatius Loyola, for through them the exercitant was expected to develop a highly sensitive field of spiritualized emotions based on real sensory experiences. This was the religious counterpart of Ronsard's line 'L'esprit incorporé, devient in- genieux'.[21] Sypher[22] has well described the rapture attained as 'precarious', for Donne, that truly experi- enced religious, turns the dilemma in the other direc- tion with his lines 'So must pure lovers soules descend/ T'affections and to faculties,/Which sense may reach and apprehend'.[23] Thus, when Sypher[24] goes on to remark that in Baroque art and piety, the spirit was transfused with the flesh, rather than the flesh with the spirit, he is spelling out the fact that the idea of platonic love could no longer be subscribed to, and consequently, that human love could no longer be seen as a reflection of divine love. For to preserve this unity was to preserve the dilemma. Rather was it better to see human love as a unity in itself, where the passion of the spirit and the passion of the flesh could interact in perfect balance. Without, necessarily, overstressing their importance, it is possible to see in the general pattern of Bandello's *Novelle* (first edition 1554) this balance of spirit and flesh. For although there are stories of carnal desires, there are others of devoted love. Where one story may tell of violent retribution, another, dealing with the same circumstances, will tell of liberal forgiveness. For instance, one records how Niccolo d'Este, finding his son in adultery with his stepmother, has them both beheaded on the same day at Ferrara. Another, however, tells how Seleucus, find- ing that his son is dying of love for his stepmother, cedes her to him (Fig. 2). This case of ancient liberality correcting contemporary violence is often found in Bandello's pages. For Bandello is immensely interested

in contemporary or near-contemporary events,[25] and if he has not Boccaccio's gift of mimesis within the narrative, at least in his prefaces he enables the reader to understand that his stories are true *about* contem- porary life, if not true *to* it.[26] The prefaces apart, Bandello will often support his account of a contem- porary action by recounting one from ancient history. As an example, he retells Castiglione's story[27] of the simple working girl, Giulia of Gazuolo, who, having been raped, drowns herself in the Oglio. This story is almost straight reportage. However, in his story of Tarquinius and Lucretia, he not only records a similar action by a noblewoman, but through the mouth of his heroine, gives the reasons, in terms of contemporary reality, why *any* woman should prefer death to dis- honour. For Lucretia asks how her innocent soul can continue to exist with her dishonoured body, for although her reason might reject her ravisher, her senses and body could not resist taking pleasure from the act. It is the dishonourable nature of this pleasure which makes it impossible for the woman to live with herself. The connection between these two stories is even more pointed, for the preface of the latter is dedi- cated to Lucrezia Gonzaga of Gazuolo, and Bandello tells her that he had heard the story from Castiglione himself in the presence of her grand aunt, Isabella Gonzaga. As the obverse to womanly honour, Bandello recounts the story of the continence of Cyrus, a variant of the more popular account of the continence of Scipio, which appears in Castiglione. The latter also relates how Xenocrates resists the blandishments of a woman for a whole night. These improving stories are evidence of the influence of liberal humanism, leading to a greater sensibility between the sexes, even though this may have been restricted to the upper strata of society.[28] Mention should also be made of those great sources of romantic love, Ariosto's *Orlando Furioso* (first edition 1532) and Torquato Tasso's *Gerusalemme Liberata* (completed 1575) which Lee has discussed;[29] while an important influence would have come from the numerous plays of the *Commedia del Arte*. Refer- ence has already been made to Bruno's *Il Candelaio* and Stechow[30] has shown that the story of Antiochus and Stratonice was the subject of plays in Spain, Italy and France during the sixteenth and seventeenth

20. B. Varchi, *Lezione sopra alcune quistioni d'amore*, quoted by M. Y. Hughes, 'The Lineage of the Extasie', *Modern Language Review*, xxvii, 1932, p. 4.
21. P. de Ronsard, *Sonnets pour Hélène*, L. Stanza quoted in full by J. M. Cohen, *The Baroque Lyric*, Hutchinson University Library, 1963, p. 62.
22. W. Sypher, *Four Stages of Renaissance Style*, Doubleday Anchor Books ed., 1955, p. 168.
23. J. Donne, *The Extasie.*
24. W. Sypher, *op. cit.*, p. 189.

25. T. G. Griffith, *Bandello's Fiction*, Blackwell, 1955, p. 62.
26. T. G. Griffith, *op. cit.*, p. 129.
27. B. Castiglione, *Il Cortegiano*, bk. iii.
28. R. and M. Wittkower, *Born under Saturn*, Weidenfeld & Nicolson, 1963, pp. 167–8.
29. R. W. Lee, 'Ut Pictura Poesis, the Humanistic Theory of Painting', *The Art Bulletin*, xxii, 1940, pp. 242 ff., discussing Rinaldo and Armida.
30. W. Stechow, ' "The Love of Antiochus with Faire Stratonice" in Art', *The Art Bulletin*, xxvii, 1945, pp. 225–6.

centuries. It would be unwise to overemphasize the influence of the theatre on the artists, as it manifestedly had in the middle ages, but it seems possible, since so many of these plays were performed in the open air, that many of their dramatic situations must have exerted, at least, a visual influence in the grouping and positioning of the characters on the passing artist, thus providing him with additional 'real' evidence for the themes suggested to him by his intellectual patrons.[31]

This brief survey of the literary background and the psychological changes in the human condition of love it reveals, will now allow a discussion of the pictorial imagery associated with it. There can be no doubt that the principal source of this imagery was Venice. In political and sociological terms alone, there could hardly be any other source in the last decades of the sixteenth century. It is well known that Venice was the city least influenced by the *diktats* of the Council of Trent, for secular control of the church, there, extended to the nomination of bishops by the Senate, priests had to be of Venetian birth and the traditional privileges of the Holy See were controlled by the secular authorities. Neither the Jesuits nor the Inquisition ever established a strong foothold there. Due also to the northern trade routes, there was the significant influence of Protestantism. Commercial success and wealth also enabled the Venetians to colour their politics with a materialistic indifference to moral, ethical or religious persuasion, unless, of course, it happened to suit them. Hazlitt[32] gives the instance of Bianca Cappella, daughter of a noble Venetian house, who ran away to Florence with a book-keeper of the Salviati bank. There, she became the mistress of Francesco de' Medici. In 1578 after his wife had died, Francesco married Bianca, whose husband had been removed by assassination on his orders. Despite the protestations of the Vatican, the Venetian Senate had little difficulty in proclaiming Bianca a 'true and particular daughter of the Republic'. Venice could be called, to use a modern phrase, 'freedom-loving'—in all things. It occupied a similar position for the emancipated as Paris did in the 1890's. Morris[33] records that at the end of the sixteenth century there were 11,654 courtesans listed on the tariff sheets maintained by the Senate, and Bandello[34] gives a vivid and enthusiastic description of this side of Venetian hospitality. Artistically progressive, Venice was a pioneer in secular

drama and its professional companies were noted throughout Europe. While Giovanni Gabrieli[35] (1557–1612) was an innovator of orchestral composition, the great Monteverdi became director of music at S. Marco in 1613 and the first public opera houses were opened in the city. Thus Venice, with a combination of commercial wealth, political independence, creative fertility and *la dolce vita*, could offer a freedom of expression, attitude and behaviour obtainable nowhere else in Italy.

The essence of the Venetian ambience is to be seen in the Bassano detail (Fig. 3), where a sophisticated conversation between the sexes takes place. The arrangement of the figures provides a triangle of forces, while the space between the man and woman on the far side of the table, acting like a true Mannerist vortex pulls the figures together rather than forcing them apart. This use of the space between, as a potent, dynamic vacuum through which the eyebeams twist, occurs constantly with greater or lesser significance throughout this period. The most explicit example of the theme itself is to be found in Garofolo's *An Allegory of Love*[36] where the centre couple—Pulchritudo—gaze into each other's eyes. The general theme of his painting—the growth of love—had been more poetically interpreted by Titian (*Sacred and Profane Love*) and exemplified by the young couple in the same artist's *Three Ages of Man*. But it is probable that while these earlier 'dialogues of love' and the mythology manuals[37] provided the iconological source, the real compositional prototype was a sacred subject—Christ and the Woman of Samaria.

As Lee[38] has said, the painters continually broke the rules laid down by the critics and patrons and yet this was not irrelevantly done. For we know[39] that mythology was used allegorically, even for Christian themes; Marino, the poet,[40] considered that the ancient gods had been sent to the Greeks as angelic messengers. It seems not unreasonable that the painters should borrow from sacred compositions in order to give their secular subjects both a painterly and intellectual significance and continuity.

31. J. Seznec, *The Survival of the Pagan Gods*, Harper Torch Book ed., 1961, p. 258.
32. W. C. Hazlitt, *The Origin and Rise of the Venetian Republic*, Black, 1900, II, pp. 207 ff.
33. J. Morris, *Venice*, Faber & Faber, paperback ed., 1964, p. 68.
34. M. Bandello, *Novelle*, Flora ed., pt. III, Novella 31.

35. E. Panofsky, *Studies in Iconography*, Harper Torch Books ed., 1962, p. 248, n. 69, referring to the connection between music and the Venetian painters.
36. National Gallery, London. C. Gould, *The Sixteenth-Century Italian Schools*, 1962, p. 65. Also E. Wind, *Pagan Mysteries of the Renaissance*, Faber & Faber, 1958, p. 126, pl. 36.
37. J. Seznec, *The Survival of the Pagan Gods*, Harper Torch Books ed., 1961, bk. II, chaps. I, II, III, discussing the manuals and their influence.
38. R. W. Lee, 'Ut Pictura Poesis, the Humanistic Theory of Painting', *The Art Bulletin*, XXII, 1940, p. 243.
39. J. Seznec, *op. cit.*, p. 271, n. 42.
40. J. S. Ackerman, 'Gian Battista Marino's Contribution to Seicento Art Theory', *The Art Bulletin*, XLIII, 1961, p. 333.

The subject of Christ and the Samaritan woman lent itself very well to the painters' purpose. Its informality; it presents a brief encounter between apparent equals; yet the Jews did not speak with the Samaritans, but Christ reveals Himself as the Messiah to a woman who is living in sin. Between them is the well of water.[41] It does not seem impossible that the worldly eyes of the Venetian artists could see this subject as an approximation of Sacred and Profane Love or rather at the end of the sixteenth century as an allegory of the balanced, yet opposed, forces of the spirit and the flesh, in love. Besides, the outward curve of the well served excellently as a piece of Baroque compositional machinery. Hence it appears constantly in such subjects as Elieazar and Rebecca and Jacob and Rachel, both popular subjects through the Baroque period, for not only do they exemplify the Baroque concept of true love, but probably served as betrothal or wedding pictures. To return to the original composition, we find it informally treated as early as Catena (Honolulu Academy of Fine Arts, Hawaii) in Venetian painting. Recognition of the later Venetian interpretation of this subject can be achieved by comparing Palma Giovane's work (Verona, Museo Civico)[42] and Annibale Carracci's well-known painting (Kunsthistorisches Museum, Vienna). The former is wholly Baroque in composition; the well has become a wheel about which the two figures revolve. Christ '... con occhi immensi, di magnetica tristezza ...'[43] looks straight into the eyes of the woman. The spirit infuses the flesh. The latter is proto-Poussinesque and full of a classical restraint, and yet, in a more subtle way than Palma, Annibale conveys the same interpretation, for as Rouchès has observed, 'La physiognomie, l'attitude de ces personnages sont humaines ... le "Christ et la Samaritaine" ... sont des êtres vulgaires dans le sens primitif du mot.'[44] The Bolognese work reveals the influence of Tridentine demands for clarity, for if the Venetians were for plain speaking in their allegories,[45] it was their visitors, like Annibale and Furini (Fig. 2), who could transmit the emotive experience of the theme with greater depth and understanding. Even in mythological subjects, this is apparent, for again Palma Giovane and Annibale

may be compared. The former's *Mars and Venus*[46] shows the pair in uninhibited love play, with Venus as the protagonist, i.e. Love subduing Force. This plainly erotic contest is eschewed by Annibale (Fig. 4),[47] who shows Jupiter and Juno symbolizing marriage. The expressive communication between them confirms a tenet of the *Cortegiano*, that true love must find its consummation in marriage. The flesh infuses the spirit. Turning now to the Scarscellino (Fig. 5) (Uffizi), there again is reason to suggest that this compositional type (Cavallino, Fig. 1) has a sacred source, namely, the Noli me tangere; and Titian's work (National Gallery, London) may serve as a prototype, although Scarscellino's composition has more direct painterly affinities to Bassano's *Susannah and the Elders* (Musée de Beaux Arts, Nîmes) and Veronese's *Venus and Adonis* (Landesmuseum, Darmstadt). The Noli me tangere source is by no means irrelevant or irreverent, since in the sixteenth century Diana had even been equated with the Virgin Mary.[48] Basically, the Scarscellino is a continuation of the growth-of-love theme, for through the contemplation of beauty comes love, and the eyes are the harbingers of love. That love is also fleeting is given a melancholic gloss in the same subject by Poussin (Institute of Arts, Detroit), where the lovers, gazing into each other's eyes, part at dawn. But the true connection between sacred and profane is that Christ indicates by His words to Mary Magdalen that love must find permanence in the spirit and not in the body. This theme of the growth of love through the contemplation of beauty to the attainment of true love is a central idea in the seventeenth century and the three examples reproduced here (Figs. 1, 2, 6) give evidence of the high seriousness with which the theme was interpreted. Drawn from the Testaments, ancient history and contemporary life, they show how comprehensively the painters of the High Baroque matched their interest and interpretation with the literature and attitudes of contemporary life. For these three works were executed within the period 1625–1650 (Vouet 1626: Furini c. 1630–1635: Cavallino c. 1640–1650). It is patently evident that in the latter half of the century, this high seriousness evaporates. Not only because the artists were of lesser calibre, but because that miraculous balance of intellect and emotive expression of the High Baroque could not be sustained. For in each case, these

41. E. Wind, *op. cit.*, pp. 124–5, describes the fountain in Titian's *Sacred and Profane Love* as containing the water of pure love. While in Christian symbology, the well indicates Baptism or Rebirth.
42. I. Fenyó, 'Contributo ai Rapportai Artistici tra Palma Giovane e Bernardo Strozzi', *Acta Historiae Artum*, v, 1–2, 1958, pp. 143–4, discusses these two paintings in another context.
43. I. Fenyó, *loc. cit.*
44. G. Rouchès, *Les Carrache*, Paris, 1913, pp. 221 ff. and 229. Quoted by D. Mahon and D. Sutton, *Artists in 17th Century Rome*, Wildenstein, London, 1955, pp. 28–29.
45. J. Seznec, *op. cit.*, pp. 303 ff.

46. National Gallery, London. A painting of the same subject by Palma was owned by Marino, the poet, *vide* C. Gould, *Catalogue of the Sixteenth-Century Venetian School*, 1959, p. 57.
47. A reduced easel version of the fresco in the Palazzo Farnese. The general theme of the fresco cycle being, of course, Sacred and Profane Love. The composition is derived from Veronese's *Venus and Mars* (Galleria Sabauda, Turin).
48. J. Seznec, *op. cit.*, p. 266.

three works referred to lie within the tradition of composition and concept established by the innovators of the Baroque and they preserve the allegorical equation of sacred and profane love. Perhaps due in part to a new generation of patrons, unversed in the subtleties of this equation, the painters of the Late Baroque could catch only the literary and often vulgar substance of the subject. The comparison, alone, of Furini and Cagnacci as Waterhouse has made,[49] makes this point clearly.

Complementary to the principal theme with which this study is concerned, are those subjects like Lucretia, Susannah and the Elders, Joseph and Potiphar's Wife and The Continence of Scipio which allude to the moral and honourable behaviour of either sex in the face of carnal desire or demand. Lucretia, in fact, undergoes a secular canonization during this period from Titian's Roman mystery figure of *Lucretia Stabbing Herself* (H.M. the Queen) to Guido Reni's *Lucrezia* (Galleria Spada, Rome), who, with her eyes turned to Heaven, becomes a female saint.

The recipient of this Festschrift has remarked that '. . . la distinzione tra esposizione verbale ed emblema, tra parola ed immagine e estremamente tenue nell'eta barocca'.[50] The distinction between sacred and profane imagery, in form and content, is as tenuous. By manipulating this delicate distinction, the painters of Early and High Baroque were able to transmit the emotive experience of a modern conception of human love.

49. E. K. Waterhouse, *Italian Baroque Painting*, Phaidon, 1962, p. 101.

50. R. Wittkower, 'Il Barocco in Italia', *Manierismo, Barocco, Rococo*, Convegno Internazionale (1960), Accademia Nazionale dei Lincei, Rome, 1962, p. 325.

JULIUS S. HELD

Rubens' *Het Pelsken*

While in art history the writings of scholars may not always make a contribution towards the understanding of works of art, they always throw a light on the personal interests and idiosyncrasies of the art historians themselves. The two problems, indeed, are obviously connected with each other. The more we perceive how art history is affected by the specific attitudes and prejudices of the writers and the thought patterns current at the time, the greater will be our reluctance to accept their verdict without qualification. Today it is easy to recognize typical nineteenth-century attitudes in much of the art historical writing produced at that time. But it is equally certain that those who follow us will know to what extent our own studies are colored and our own image of history distorted by the tastes, pet theories, and popular scientific notions to which we have fallen heir.

In the meantime, we may derive a bit of innocent merriment from the examination of our ancestors' pitfalls in art scholarship.[1] In the beginning of the present paper, I should like to examine the views expressed in art historical literature on an illustrious example of Flemish seventeenth-century painting: the portrait by Rubens of Hélène Fourment, preserved in Vienna and commonly known as *Het Pelsken*, or *La Petite Pelisse* (Fig. 1).

The title of the picture goes back to Rubens himself. In his will[2] he stated that the painting known as *Het Pelsken* should go to his wife 'sonder iet daervore te geven oft intebrengen'.[3] Although the pedigree of the Vienna painting does not go back further than a painted inventory of 1730,[4] no one has ever questioned that it is indeed the painting referred to in Rubens' will and I, too, consider the identity established as beyond any reasonable doubt.

Ever since its appearance in the Vienna Collections, the painting has occupied an honored place in Rubens' work. No serious biographer has ever failed at least to mention it, and it also figures frequently in popular writings. To the best of my knowledge, it has never been taken for anything but a somewhat unusual, possibly daring, portrait of Hélène Fourment. Most writers have praised the beauty of colors and the sympathetic portrayal of young womanhood, but they have disagreed in a number of points. In the older literature (John Smith,[5] A. van Hasselt,[6] C. G. Voorhelm Schneevoogt,[7] E. R. v. Engerth,[8] Jacob Burckhardt[9] and Louis Hourticq[10]) she is generally described as going to the bath. Others (Michel,[11] followed by Hope Rea,[12] W. von Bode[13] and L. van Puyvelde[14]) maintain that she is coming from the bath. Although they differ on whether it was before or after the bath, both Hourticq and van Puyvelde agree that Rubens surprised Hélène on her way and painted her while the impression was still fresh. Gustav Glück[15] is sure that she is neither going to, nor coming from, the bath, 'as is occasionally assumed'—for which woman would wrap herself in a fur coat on such an occasion? Yet he, too, believes that we owe this masterwork to a lucky accident: 'during a pause between modeling, Hélène may have wrapped herself into a fur coat in order to get warm. This may have aroused in Rubens a recollection of ... Titian's girl in a fur coat, now also in the Vienna gallery.... The accidental view of the magnificent youthful body brilliantly standing out from the soft background of the dark fur and the red carpet combined with that recollection of Titian's half-length picture, may have given Rubens the idea

---

1. For the romantic interpretation of van Dyck's portrait of Charles I in the Louvre (*Le Roi à la Chasse*), see my article in the *Art Bulletin*, XL, 1958, pp. 139 ff.
2. See J. Denucé, *De Antwerpsche 'Konstkamers'*, Antwerp, 1932, p. 80, CVI.
3. The legal terms mean that she receives the painting free of any obligation towards the estate.
4. Storffer, *Gemaltes Inventarium*, II, 1730, no. 101, now preserved in the Direktion of the Vienna Gemäldegalerie.

5. John Smith, *A Catalogue Raisonné of the Works of the Most Eminent Dutch, Flemish, and French Painters*, II, London, 1830, p. 94, no. 300.
6. A. van Hasselt, *Histoire de P.-P. Rubens*, Brussels, 1840, p. 331, no. 1035.
7. C. G. Voorhelm Schneevoogt, *Catalogue des Estampes Gravées d'après P.-P. Rubens*, Haarlem, 1873, p. 165.
8. Eduard R. v. Engerth, *Kunsthistorische Sammlungen des Allerhöchsten Kaiserhauses, Gemälde, Beschreibendes Verzeichnis*, II, 1884, p. 402, no. 1181.
9. Jacob Burckhardt, *Recollections of Rubens*, London-New York, 1950, p. 40.
10. Louis Hourticq, *Rubens*, New York, 1918, p. 132.
11. Emile Michel, *Rubens, His Life, His Work, and His Time*, London-New York, 1899, II, pp. 175-6.
12. Hope Rea, *Peter Paul Rubens*, London, 1905, p. 107.
13. W. van Bode, *Die Meister des Holländischen und Vlämischen Malerschulen*, Leipzig, 1923, p. 332.
14. Leo van Puyvelde, 'Les Portraits des Femmes de Rubens', *Revue de l'Art Ancien et Moderne*, LXXI, 1937, pp. 1-24.
15. Gustav Glück, *Rubens, van Dyck, und ihr Kreis*, Vienna, 1933, p. 128.

of painting his Hélène once entirely for his own pleasure.' Who would not recognize in the theory that credits the genesis of *Het Pelsken* to a lucky visual accident a characteristic late nineteenth-century concept about the purely sensory character of artistic inspiration common to artists and art historians alike?[16]

Writers have disagreed on other points. Rooses, who thought that this may have been the very first portrait painted by the master of his bride, describes her breasts as 'young and firm'.[17] This may have been an implied retort to Michel's statement that Hélène's flesh 'lacks its former firmness'. Since he dated the painting rather late (*c.* 1638), Glück, too, sees the flesh as 'ein wenig schlaff', and suggests that the breasts need the support of the arm. (He also thinks that Hélène here appears slenderer than in earlier portraits, and attributes her loss of weight to her many pregnancies.) Several authors (Michel, Verhaeren[18]) dwelled on the marks left above the knees by the garters as signs of Rubens' unsparing realism. Rooses thought her feet deformed, from wearing shoes that were too tight.[19] Madame J. Bouchot-Saupique[20] recognizes Rubens' 'objectivity', which prompts him to render 'des détails anatomiques peu esthétiques'. Leo van Puyvelde sees in the picture Rubens' 'swan song' though this image is slightly blurred when he calls the work 'un cri vigoureux d'amour', and, yielding to no-one for colorful writing, describes 'ces plis de chair lymphatiques, ces fossettes grassouillettes, ces genoux gonflés'. Occasionally Rubens is even accused of a 'positive depravity in taste', for seeking beauty in ugliness.[21]

Writers were sometimes troubled by the artist's willingness to paint his wife in a rather intimate view. Rooses could not help reproaching Rubens for a certain indelicacy, but justifies the portrayal by the husband's pride (did he think of the story of ill-fated Candaules?) in letting others see and appreciate the treasure he himself possessed.[22] By contrast, he recognizes in Hélène's face a somewhat bashful expression ('l'expression un peu gênée'). This again is almost like an answer to Michel's statement that Hélène shows no sign of embarrassment or shame;[23] Verhaeren tries to have it both ways for he sees in her expression a mixture of modesty and immodesty. Cammaerts,[24] aware of the gulf between Rubens' painting and official English taste, believes that the beholder needs 'racial sympathy', in other words, some Flemish gusto, to appreciate fully the Vienna canvas. At any rate, most scholars are relieved to know that the picture was never meant to be sold, but was willed by the master to Hélène as her personal property.

While most writers of the late nineteenth and early twentieth centuries are concerned with the outward appearance of Hélène, frequently giving descriptions that are literally no more than skin-deep, and, as did G. Vanzype,[25] justify this approach on the basis of the supposed shallowness of Hélène Fourment, a somewhat different attitude is taken by Evers.[26] He finds in the picture something comparable to the feminine 'Zauber' and 'Unergründlichkeit' of Leonardo's Mona Lisa. His is a poetic description of Hélène's appearance: she cradles her breasts in her arms like a child; her legs are covered with the artist's tenderness, a necessary attitude of the painter in view of the fact that Evers, too, believes that Hélène was basically a homely woman. At any rate, Evers was the first specifically to reject the 'surprise'-theory when he states: 'Surely such a picture is not due to improvisation, but matured slowly.' Even he, however, fails to ask whether the painting is really no more than an intimate portrayal of Hélène Fourment.

Such a question involves a simple iconographic problem: whether or not the Vienna panel is unique in the choice of its subject. Before examining this problem, it is useful to stress one observation that as far as I can see, is mentioned nowhere in the literature. All descriptions and especially those based on the 'surprise'-theory tacitly assume that Rubens painted Hélène indoors, either in a room near the bath (though we may wonder if Rubens' house had a special 'bath'-room), or in the studio. This assumption is contradicted by the evidence of the picture itself. On the right we see, if only vaguely, the forms of a fountain with water gushing from a lion's mouth. At the left are horizontal streaks of light which seem to indicate a sky. Hence, despite the pillow and the carpet, the setting is out-of-doors.[27] (All old photos as well as the

16. See, for instance, Emile Zola, *L'Œuvre*, Le Livre de Poche, pp. 16–17.
17. Max Rooses, *L'Œuvre de P.-P. Rubens*, IV, Antwerp, 1890, no. 944, pp. 166–8.
18. Emile Verhaeren, *Rubens* (tr. by Stefan Zweig), Leipzig, 1913, p. 51.
19. Max Rooses, *Rubens, Sa Vie et ses Œuvres*, Amsterdam-Antwerp-Ghent, 1903, p. 502.
20. Madame J. Bouchot-Saupique, *Hélène Fourment*, Paris, 1947.
21. Hope Rea, *op. cit.*, p. 108.
22. Rooses, *op. cit.* (*Sa Vie* . . .), p. 502.

23. *Op. cit.*, p. 175.
24. Emile Cammaerts, *Rubens, Painter and Diplomat*, London, 1932, p. 257.
25. G. Vanzype, *Pierre-Paul Rubens*, Paris-Brussels, 1926, p. 74.
26. Hans Gerhard Evers, *Peter Paul Rubens*, Munich, pp. 451 ff.
27. Our photo renders the painting without the later lateral additions, which are still seen in Oldenbourg's edition of the KdK of 1921, pl. 424.

graphic renderings such as the one by Paul Gleditch[28] show a uniformly black background, which makes understandable the failure of all interpreters to see this important detail.)

With the setting plainly characterized as out-of-doors, all the romantic notions about the genesis of the picture (including van Puyvelde's sentimental 'il peint une dernière fois sa chère Hélène') fall to the ground. A portrait of a nude Hélène standing near a fountain out of doors makes no sense unless the true meaning of the picture can be shown to be structured in a more complex fashion. We must ask whether, besides being a portrait of Hélène, it may also render another type of subject.

Three themes, all of them frequently rendered in art, qualify for the basic iconographic elements of the canvas: Bathsheba, Susanna, and Venus. An unknown artist of Rubens' school (possibly J. van Egmont) indeed used the theme of a nude figure draping herself in a fur coat for a Bathsheba (Fig. 2). She is identified beyond any doubt by a young Negro messenger who is handing a letter to her. Rubens' painting has no such detail, nor does the setting suggest the vicinity of a palace, from which the woman could have been seen. The Bathsheba story, hence, is a rather unlikely literary base for *Het Pelsken*, and can safely be eliminated.

It is a different case with Susanna. Contrary to Bathsheba, Susanna is a proverbially chaste figure, so that Hélène's pose of modesty would not be inappropriate. The choice of Susanna as a disguise for Hélène would even make a certain psychological sense, considering the age difference between Hélène and her illustrious husband, comparable to the one between Susanna and the Elders. Moreover, there exists a print by J. Collaert after Marten de Vos (Fig. 3),[29] and probably known to Rubens, which renders Susanna in terms surprisingly similar to those of *Het Pelsken*. Like Hélène, Susanna stands before us in full length, and largely nude, only flimsily covered by a bit of a shirt and an elegantly trimmed fur-lined coat draped over her shoulders. (It is perhaps worth while noting that the fur coat in *Het Pelsken* is not made like a modern coat with the fur worn outside. The coat is clearly a dark velvet coat *lined* with fur.) The sleeves of this coat hang down on either side of the figure as they do in *Het Pelsken*, and Susanna's head, like Hélène's, is turned toward the right shoulder. Thus it is quite possible that de Vos'

print played a role in the formal genesis of the Vienna painting. Iconographically, however, there remain considerable differences. De Vos' figure is the image of chastity and with her hands folded in prayer, and her heavenward glance, a symbol of confidence in God. Hélène, by contrast, is worldly and seductive, and there is no hint of any impending danger.

There remains the classical theme of Venus, and all the evidence indeed points to it as the correct identification. While it is not always easy to establish Rubens' familiarity with specific ancient works of art, there is no doubt that he knew thoroughly all that ancient writers, above all Pliny, had to say about the creations of the great masters. Like other artists of the Renaissance and the Baroque, he was influenced not only by what he had seen of ancient art, but also by what he read about it. It is fortunate that we have his own words for this aspect of his study of the ancients. On August 1, 1637, he wrote to Franciscus Junius (1589–1677), who had sent him a copy of his book *De Pictura Veterum*, that a similar book ought to be written about the Italian painters.[30] He maintains that things which can be seen physically make a deeper impression than those 'which can be perceived only in the imagination, like dreams, and imperfectly outlined by words; apprehended in vain, they elude us often (like Eurydice's image Orpheus) and thwart our hopes'.[31] He then continues, 'I speak from experience. For how few of us, trying to reconstruct for the sake of its dignity, a famous work, by Apelles or Timanthes, graphically described by Pliny or other authors, will not produce something tasteless or foreign to the majesty of the ancients? Each one following his own talent will offer a new wine for that bittersweet *Opimianum*' (a celebrated wine of the vintage of A.U.C. 633 when Opimius was consul) 'and will do an injustice to those great souls whom I follow with the highest veneration; and while I adore their vestiges, I am not ingenuous enough to claim that I could equal them, not even in thought.'

No wonder that a good many subjects treated by Rubens can be linked to themes listed by Pliny as the works of ancient artists. The theme, often painted by Rubens, of nymphs surprised by satyrs evokes Pliny's reference to a picture by Nicomachus, showing Mainades with Satyrs stealing upon them (XXXV, 109:

28. See Rooses, *op. cit.* (*L'Œuvre*), IV, pl. 289. It is possible that in the nineteenth century the background details were hidden under a layer of old varnish. Rooses actually described the background as a 'fond de noir opaque', *op. cit.*, p. 166.

29. Icones Illustrium Feminarum Veteris Testamenti A Philippo Gallaeo Collectae atque Expressae, no. 19.

30. See Rooses-Ruelens, *La Correspondance de Pierre Paul Rubens*, V, Antwerp, 1909, p. 179, and R. Magurn, *The Letters of Peter Paul Rubens*, Cambridge, 1955, p. 407. The letter was first printed, contrary to the statement by Rooses, in the Dutch edition of Junius' book published in 1641 in Middelburgh. The following quotations deviate in minor ways from the translation given by Miss Magurn.

31. Rubens characteristically uses here a quotation from Virgil's *Aeneid* (2.794): *ter frustra comprensa manus effugit imago.*

Nobiles Bacchas obreptantibus Satyris). In a lost painting, for which we have, however, a magnificent drawing, Rubens painted the Death of Hippolytus—the same subject Antiphilus is said to have painted (xxxv, 114: *Hippolytum tauro emisso expavescentem*). Another classical subject, treated by Rubens, is mentioned by Pliny as the theme of a work of Athenion of Maroneia (xxxv, 134: Achilles in the guise of a maiden at the moment of detection by Ulysses).

When he painted Count Lerma on horseback, showing both rider and horse *en face*, he may have remembered paintings by Pordenone and possibly El Greco. Yet without Pliny's mention of a painting by Apelles showing Antigonus in armor, advancing with his horse (xxxv, 96) Rubens might not have thought of applying to a portrait a compositional scheme that had hitherto been used only in narrative context.

According to Pliny, Parrhasius had painted a picture of two boys 'whose features express the confidence and the simplicity of their age' (xxxv, 170: *pueros duos in quibus spectatur securitas et aetatis simplicitas*). This indeed seems to be the theme of the portrait of Rubens' two sons in the Liechtenstein collection. One might even go so far as to say that Rubens depicted more *securitas* in the older boy, more *simplicitas* in the younger.[32]

32. In a short report submitted at one of the sessions of the XX International Congress of the History of Art held in New York in 1961, I listed a number of paintings which may have been inspired less by actual works of ancient art than by Pliny's report about them. Thus in Giotto's Ognissanti Madonna both the Virgin and the Christ Child show their teeth, a detail mentioned by Pliny as having been introduced into art by Polygnotus of Thasos (xxxv, 58); a whole series of paintings by Bassano, El Greco, Rubens, Jordaens and Honthorst, among others, can be traced to Pliny's statement (xxxv, 138) that Antiphilos 'was praised for his picture of a boy blowing on fire, and for the reflection cast by the fire ... on the boy's face'; the so-called *fruttaiuolo* by Caravaggio brings to mind Zeuxis' famous boy carrying grapes (xxxv, 66); the gorgon-pictures of Leonardo (mentioned as unfinished by Vasari), Caravaggio and Rubens dealt with a subject for which Timomachus of Byzantium had been praised (xxxv, 136); even in works of Frans Hals, who hardly was an avid reader of Pliny, we find themes made famous by ancient artists, such as 'a [Thracian] nurse with an infant in her arms' and 'two boys whose features express the confidence and the simplicity of their age', both by Parrhasius (xxxv, 170); Jordaens' young Satyr in Amsterdam recalls a picture by Protogenes (xxxv, 106); Aetion's picture of Tragedy and Comedy, known only from Pliny (xxxv, 78), may have been in Reynolds' mind when he painted his canvas of Garrick between these personifications; and the striking manner, finally, in which Pluto's hand is impressed on Proserpina's flesh in Bernini's famous sculpture has its classical analogy—and probably literary 'model'—in a Pergamene sculpture by Cephisodotus described by Pliny (xxxv, 197). For all quotations from Pliny see K. Jex-Blake, *The Elder Pliny's Chapters on the History of Art*, London, 1896. A corollary of the interest artists took in works which they knew only from description by ancient authors is the frequent comparison of 'modern' artists with Greek masters. For this complex of problems see especially Charles Sterling, *Still Life Painting*, Paris, 1959, pp. 11–12, and E. H. Gombrich, *Norm and Form*, London, 1966, pp. 6 f. and

In the light of this evidence, it is certain that Rubens knew well Pliny's reference to that work which 'excelled all works of art in the whole world' (xxxvi, 20), the Cnidian Aphrodite of Praxiteles. Its powerful attraction had been described tellingly in the *Erotes* (formerly attributed to Lucian), and witty poems in its honor were still written at a later date.[33] Though he may not have had a very correct idea of her appearance, Rubens surely knew that she was standing and undressing to take a bath.[34]

If *Het Pelsken* was indeed stimulated by what Rubens knew about the Cnidian Aphrodite, it is also obvious that at least in regard to the position of her arms, his notion of the figure was influenced by other, more familiar classical Aphrodite types, such as the Venus Medici (Uffizi, formerly in the Villa Medici), or the Capitoline Venus.[35]

The theory that the painting renders Hélène Fourment in the role of Aphrodite finds support in a composition known to me in two nearly identical versions. One of them, apparently the better of the two, is in the Gallery at Potsdam-Sanssouci (Fig. 4). The other belonged, in 1949, to the Conde de Adanero in Madrid (Fig. 5). The paintings, reminiscent of the style of Sustermans, portray a lady very much as Rubens had portrayed Hélène Fourment in *Het Pelsken*. Here, too, the model is naked and only lightly draped in a fur-lined coat and she also looks at the beholder, though we see her from the left instead of the right. The picture is obviously a portrait of a definite individual, and there is a slight possibility that she is Vittoria della Rovere of Tuscany (1622–1694), the wife of Grand Duke Ferdinand II.[36] Whoever she was, one thing is obvious: she is unmistakably cast in the role of Venus, since she is accompanied by Cupid, complete with wings and arrow-filled quiver, playfully tempting a fuzzy lapdog with some titbit. Moreover, the mirror standing on a table at the right is often, as we shall see, an object associated with Venus.[37]

112 ff.; see also E. Panofsky, *Renaissance and Renascences*, Stockholm, 1960, p. 115.

33. See Antologia Graeca, I, 97, 1 and I, 104, 6, as cited by Heinrich Bulle, *Der schöne Mensch im Altertum*, Munich, 1922, p. 108.

34. See Christian Blinkenberg, *Knidia*, Copenhagen, 1933, *passim*, but especially pp. 21, 37, and 56.

35. Bulle, *op. cit.*, pls. 156 and 158.

36. This identification rests primarily on a comparison of the model with a painting by Sustermans of St. Margaret in the Uffizi which Pierre Bautier, *Juste Suttermans, Peintre des Medicis*, Brussels-Paris, 1912, reproduced (pl. xvi) and discussed as a portrait of Vittoria della Rovere. The connection between the St. Margaret and the authentic portraits of Vittoria (see Bautier, pls. vi and vii) is, however, not sufficiently close to make this identification completely convincing.

37. For the use of Cupid in conventional portraits of ladies see A. v. Dyck, Mary Duchess of Lennox, North Carolina Museum of Art, Raleigh, N.C.

That the 'Sustermans'-painting is derived from *Het Pelsken* no one can possibly doubt, though Rooses clearly went too far when he called it a copy.[38] The picture, at any rate, proves that the meaning of Rubens' painting, Hélène Fourment in the guise of Venus, was perfectly understood by contemporaries.

If it is reasonable, on the basis of the foregoing discussion, to give both de Vos' engraving of Bathsheba and Praxiteles' Cnidian Aphrodite (and some of her derivatives) a place in the genesis of *Het Pelsken*, we must consider yet another source. It has always been realized that Rubens' painting had been decisively influenced by Titian. Titian, more than once, had increased the glamour of a lovely female body by using a fur-lined garment as a coloristic relief. The picture closest to *Het Pelsken* is Titian's *Woman in a Fur Cloak* in Vienna, a painting which was in the collection of Charles I and in Rubens' time hung in his Privy Lodging Rooms.[39] Undoubtedly, Rubens had seen it during his extended visit to London in 1629–1630. The motif of the nude body enshrined, as it were, by a fur coat, also occurs, however, in the painting by Titian now in Washington (formerly in the Hermitage), showing Venus as she admires herself in the mirror, held by Cupid. Rubens painted a version of this theme that is clearly derived from such a Titianesque prototype, though not necessarily from the picture in Washington. That canvas is now in the Thyssen Collection in Lugano, and is probably identical with a painting listed as no. 48 in the inventory of Rubens' estate, as the last of eleven pieces which Rubens had copied after Titian: 'Venus qui se mire avec Cupidon'[40] (Fig. 6).

The painting at Castle Rohoncz was dated by Ludwig Burchard *c.* 1610–1615, which seems to me much too early. It could hardly have been done before the 1620's. Rubens, however, had indeed dealt with the theme of Venus looking into the mirror at an early period in a painting in the Liechtenstein Collection at Vaduz (KdK 101).[41] That painting, of which Velasquez may have had some knowledge when he painted the Rokeby Venus in London, brings us back once more to *Het Pelsken*.

In the Liechtenstein picture Venus, sitting at the right, is seen from the back, and the mirror is held in such a way that we see her face reflected in it slightly turned to the left. If Venus were actually looking at her own face, it would have to appear in the mirror turned to the right rather than the left. Actually, Venus is not looking at her own reflection. Rather, she uses the mirror to glance at and communicate with somebody outside, whoever he may be.

In a brilliant discussion of English eighteenth-century portraiture,[42] Edgar Wind commented on the difference between English eighteenth-century portraits 'in disguise' and Rubens' use of Hélène Fourment as a model for a Saint Cecilia or an Andromeda. He claims that our knowledge of the true identity of his model is hardly indispensable for a proper understanding of such works by the master. Yet it is dangerous to generalize. In the case of *Het Pelsken* the knowledge that Hélène Fourment was painted in the role of Venus certainly gives a richer meaning to the painting than straight portrayal would have. Hélène Fourment was, after all, not only 'the perfect, if mortal, representative of a certain type of beauty' (Wind) but the artist's young wife. He could hardly express his affection for her more aptly than by painting her in the role of the goddess of love and of beauty. It was obviously a 'natural' disguise, and Hélène appears more than once in this role, especially in the great painting of the Judgment of Paris in Madrid (KdK 432), a fact duly appreciated by the Cardinal Infant Ferdinand when he wrote to the king: 'Venus in the center is a very good likeness of his (Rubens') own wife, who without doubt is the most beautiful woman in this city' (que sin duda es lo mejor de lo que ahora hay aqui).[43]

As Venus had done in the early Liechtenstein panel, Venus-Hélène looks out of the canvas called *Het Pelsken* but without recourse to the subterfuge of a mirror. Frankly facing the beholder, we may well imagine that she found herself mirrored in the loving and admiring eyes of her devoted artist-husband.

38. Rooses, *op. cit.* (*L'Œuvre*), p. 167.

39. See Margaret Whinney and Oliver Millar, *English Art 1625–1714*, Oxford, 1957, p. 5, n. 4. According to Hans Tietze, *Tizian, Leben und Werk*, Vienna, 1936, II, p. 317, Titian used the same model for the so-called Bella in the Pitti Palace and the Venus of Urbino in the Uffizi.

40. See *Sammlung Schloss Rohoncz*, Catalogue by Rudolf J. Heinemann, Lugano, 1958, no. 358a. Heinemann misunderstood the entry in Rubens' inventory, and thought that Rubens had actually owned the Titian original.

41. The mirror in that painting has the same octagonal shape as the mirror in the Sustermans picture(s) discussed earlier.

42. Edgar Wind, *Humanitätsidee und Heroisiertes Porträt in der Englischen Kultur des 18. Jahrhunderts*, Vorträge der Bibliothek Warburg, 1930–1, p. 192.

43. Max Rooses, *Correspondance de Rubens*, VI, Antwerp, 1909, p. 228, February 27, 1639.

WOLFGANG STECHOW

On Büsinck, Ligozzi and an Ambiguous Allegory

Many years ago, while doing some research on the chiaroscuro woodcuts and other works of Ludolph Büsinck, I happened to discover that the data on this interesting if somewhat provincial German artist had been badly confused during the last century or so; that his first name was not Ludwig but Ludolph (Ludolf), that he did not hail from Minden, München or Mannheim but from Münden (in southern Hanover), and that his woodcuts were not all made in France but partly in his native town, where he resided as a painter from about 1630, became a collector of customs about 1647 and died in 1669.[1] I could have saved myself much effort and circuitous proof if at that time I had known a chiaroscuro woodcut of his that (for reasons about which I shall venture a guess later on) seems to have survived in one impression only: the dedication copy proper, now preserved in the Kassel Print Room (Fig. 1).[2] It is not mentioned in any list of Büsinck's works, including my own, and it would have escaped my attention even now but for a brief note by the late Rudolf Hallo.[3]

It is a chiaroscuro woodcut from three blocks (line block and two-tone blocks), printed in brown, and bears the inscription: 'Illustrissimo principi ac Domino, Domino Wilhelmo Landgravio Hassiae Cassell.' and 'Jacobus Ligotius Veronensis inven. 1565—de nove [sic] tagliato in legne [sic] Oper Ludolf Büsinck Mündensem [sic] Anno 1646.' This is the only work that Büsinck signed with his full Christian name; it is also by far his latest-dated print, there being no other known after 1630, and no chiaroscuro after 1625.[4] At first sight, it is perhaps somewhat disappointing that

this should be no more than a clever copy after another chiaroscuro print (Fig. 2).[5] However, such copying is something of a rarity, and it is interesting to observe the details of Büsinck's translation of the older work into his own unmistakable and more fully baroque technique, and the method of his reducing a four-block chiaroscuro print into a three-block one; furthermore, I shall try to show that the same composition served two quite different purposes.

The original from which Büsinck worked is one of the earliest prints of Andrea Andreani; its inscription reads: 'Francisco Medici Serenissimo Magno Ethrurie Duci Andreas Andreanus Incisit ac Dicavit/Jacobus Ligotius Veronensis invenit ac Pinxit' and 'In Firenze 1585. Lettere Vocale figurate A. Amore. E. Errore. I. Ignoranza. O. Opinione. V. Virtù.' As already indicated, this print[6] was done from a line block and three tone blocks; it expressly mentions a painting by Ligozzi as its source (Büsinck's less specific formulation: 'Jacobus Ligotius Veronensis inven. 1565 [sic]' is hardly more than a faulty abbreviation of Andreani's). If, however, 'pinxit' can be taken to refer to one of those carefully worked-out wash drawings in which Ligozzi excelled, rather than an oil painting, the original may well have been a slightly altered version of the drawing in the famous Praun collection in Nuremberg which Maria Katharina Prestel reproduced in a chiaroscuro aquatint dated 1777 (Fig. 3).[7]

The subject of Ligozzi's painting (or drawing) is just what one might expect of this highly original Italian

1. *Neues Göttinger Jahrbuch*, IV, 1933-4, pp. 5 ff.; *The Print Collector's Quarterly*, XXV, 1938, pp. 393-419, and XXVI, 1939, pp. 349-59.
2. Inv. no. 5314; 470 × 328 mm. Photograph from the Staatliche Kunstsammlungen Kassel through the kind offices of Dr. Lisa Oehler.
3. Rudolf Hallo, *Das Kupferstichkabinett und die Bücherei der Staatlichen Kunstsammlungen in Kassel*, 1931, p. 11.
4. *The Luteplayer* (ordinary woodcut), St. no. 26. The chiaroscuro with the *Holy Family in an Oval Frame* after G. Lallemand (St. no. 3) is dated 1623, not 1633 or 1643; the *St. James Minor* of the Apostle series (St. no. 8) is inscribed on the stake: 'Paris 1625', a fact which I overlooked in my catalogue of 1939. It is not probable that Büsinck made the chiaroscuro print of 1646 in Münden; the complicated presses used by him in Paris had certainly remained there after his return to Münden (see my article of 1938, p. 399). His large altarpiece with the *Crucifixion*, now in the Catholic Church in Göttingen, still the only painting identified so far, was done in 1636.

5. Photograph, after the impression of the Staatliche Graphische Sammlung in Munich (inv. no. 61.626), through the courtesy of the late Dr. Peter Halm. The Boston Museum of Fine Arts also owns an impression.
6. Bartsch XII, Clair-obscurs des maîtres italiens, pièces allégoriques, no. 9, 1; L. Kolloff, in his article on Andrea Andreani in Julius Meyer, *Allgemeines Künstler-Lexikon*, I, Leipzig, 1872, listed this print (and state) as no. 25, II. See also note 27.
7. Nagler, *Künstlerlexikon*, s.v. M. C. Prestel, no. 15; Le Blanc, *Manuel*, no. 20. See also Nagler s.v. Ligozzi. Our Fig. 3 reproduces the impression in the Print Room of the Städelsche Kunstinstitut in Frankfurt, printed in yellow-brown and grey-brown tints; the photograph was kindly provided by Dr. K. Schwarzweller. Maria Katharina Prestel also made a print after Ligozzi's allegory of *Truth Triumphing over Envy* in the Albertina in Vienna (cat. 1926, I, no. 213; Heinrich Leporini, *Die Stilentwicklung der Handzeichnung*, Vienna-Leipzig, 1925, no. 163). This print, dated 1781 (Nagler no. 16), proves that the Vienna drawing comes from the Praun collection in Nuremberg.

mannerist.[8] His allegory of Virtue conquered by the Vices seems to be based on the punning *concetto* of the Five Vowels rather than on any 'orthodox' or even clearly defined iconography. However, the characterization of the Vices is not entirely without parallel in manneristic practice. *Amore* (Cupid) is of course blindfold; but instead of being punished himself by being bound to a tree by wrathful women[9] he is here, by a clever twist, shown helping to tie up a helpless Virtue. *Errore* is described as blindfolded by Cesare Ripa;[10] Ligozzi (Fig. 2) extended the bandage over his entire face (a feature seemingly misunderstood by Büsinck, whose *Errore* looks gagged rather than blindfolded). It is not even quite clear which of the two remaining figures stands for *Ignoranza* and which for *Opinione*, although off-hand one would prefer to see the A-E-I-O-U-cycle continued in the figure reclining on the ground.[11] The bat-like wings attached to the head of the standing woman may be Ligozzi's own version of the live bat which according to Ripa should accompany the personification of *Ignoranza*:[12] 'Si dipinge presso à lei il Pipistrello, overo Nottola, perche, come dice Pierio Valeriano lib. 25, alla luce simiglia la sapienza e alle tenebre, dalle quali non esce mai la Nottola, l'Ignoranza', which should also be 'brutta di faccia' and 'cieca', as she is in Ligozzi's depiction (the gesture of the left hand seems to indicate blindness). On the other hand, the ass's ears, which form the only clearly recognizable attribute of the lying figure, are also a traditional feature of ignorance (see Fig. 4) as expressly stated by Ripa (after Valeriano) under *Vulgo, overo Ignobilità*[13] and under *Arroganza*;[14] and the

pose of this figure may well bring to mind the occasional characterization of *Ignoranza* as lame.[15] But it should be noted that Ripa himself did not exactly require ass's ears for *Ignoranza* proper, and it is just possible that by the same method by which Ripa imparted this ornament to *Arroganza* and *Vulgo*, Ligozzi, before him, connected it with *Opinione*; the latter sometimes shares the element of instability with *Occasione* and *Fortuna*,[16] and could have been interpreted by Ligozzi as something like fickleness (or else opinionatedness), while Ripa treated her with chivalrous objectivity.[17] The whole idea of Virtue chained to a rock by vices and exposed, Andromeda-fashion, is very remarkable, even beyond the punning device (about which more in a moment); nevertheless, Ligozzi was here able to hark back to a quattrocento tradition, namely the concept of *Virtus Deserta* or *Despecta*.[18] This motif seems to have originated in an early, pseudo-Lucianesque work by Leone Battista Alberti, called *Virtus et Mercurius*, in which Virtus, persecuted by Fortuna, takes refuge, first with Jupiter, and after having been spurned by him for fear of Fortuna's wrath, with Mercurius, to whom she complains, again in vain, that being so despised she 'would rather be a tree trunk than a Goddess'. An outright identification of this *Virtus Deserta* with Daphne occurs in works by Mantegna (the famous studiolo painting in the Louvre and the engraving attributed to Zoan Andrea), Lorenzo Leombruno (as part of a *Calumny of Apelles*), and Peter Vischer the Younger (drawing in the Louvre);[19] in Lodovico Cigoli's drawings in the Uffizi, Virtus stands naked in a copse, now victorious over a snaky but impotent *Invidia*.[20]

The question inevitably arises: what reason did Ligozzi and/or Andreani have for choosing the device of the Five Vowels when they dedicated to Francesco

8. This facet of Ligozzi's art has received very little attention after the pioneering summary by Hermann Voss, *Die Malerei der Spätrenaissance in Rom und Florenz*, Berlin, 1920, pp. 413 ff. On Ligozzi see further: Adolfo Venturi, *Storia dell'arte italiana*, IX, VII, 1934, pp. 462 ff.; M. Bacci and A. Forlani, Catalogue of the *Mostra di disegni di J. Ligozzi*, Florence, 1961; Mina Bacci, 'A Portable Altar by Ligozzi', *Allen Memorial Art Museum Bulletin*, XX, 1963, pp. 47 ff.; and *eadem*, 'Jacopo Ligozzi e la sua posizione nella pittura fiorentina', *Proporzioni*, IV, 1963, pp. 46 ff.

9. Guy de Tervarent, *Attributs et symboles dans l'art profane*, Geneva, 1958–9, I, cols. 17 (*L'Amour châtie* after Ausonius) and 19. On Cupid tied to a tree symbolizing 'anterotic' virtues see Erwin Panofsky, *Studies in Iconology*, New York, 1939, p. 127 and Fig. 95; it is interesting that there should be exactly four female witnesses here, including a drastic 'derrisio'.

10. *Iconologia*, Venice edition, 1645, p. 180; illustrated on p. 181.

11. However, this order was not accepted in the caption of the Prestel print (Fig. 3).

12. *Iconologia*, p. 270. The wings in the Prestel print (Fig. 3) may conceivably refer to 'nottola' in the sense of 'owl' rather than 'bat'.

13. *Iconologia*, p. 655: 'L'orecchie d'asino denotano Ignoranza essendo che i sacerdoti dell'Egitto dicono (come narra Pierio Valeriano nel lib. XII. de i suoi Geroglifici) che questo animale è privo d'intelligentia, e di ragione....' See also Dora and Erwin Panofsky, *Pandora's Box*, New York, 1956, p. 48, n. 22.

Even *Errore* may have been depicted with donkey's ears; see the *male* figure (πλάνος) in the engraving after Mantegna mentioned below.

14. '... con ragione si dipinge con l'orecchie dell'asino, nascendo questo vitio dall'ignoranza, e dalla stolidezza' (*op. cit.*, p. 44).

15. Dora and Erwin Panofsky, p. 47, n. 22.

16. Guy de Tervarent, II, cols. 360 f.

17. *Op. cit.*, p. 453.

18. On the following see: Richard Foerster in *Jahrbuch der preussischen Kunstsammlungen*, XXII, 1901, pp. 78 ff.; Julius Schlosser, *Praeludien*, Berlin, 1927, pp. 296 ff.; Wolfgang Stechow, 'Apollo und Daphne' (*Studien der Bibliothek Warburg*, ed. Fritz Saxl, XXIII), new ed. Darmstadt, 1965, p. 20, n. 4; Edgar Wind, *Bellini's Feast of the Gods*, Cambridge, Mass., 1948, p. 18; Arthur M. Hind, *Early Italian Engraving*, V, 1948, Mantegna no. 22; D. and E. Panofsky, pp. 43 ff.; Guy de Tervarent, I, cols. 142 f., and II, cols. 232 ff.

19. Louis Demonts, *Musée du Louvre, Inventaire général des dessins des écoles du Nord, Écoles allemande et suisse*, Paris, 1938, II, no. 353, pl. CXIV.

20. Two drawings in the Uffizi: *Mostra del Cigoli e del suo ambiente*, San Miniato, 1959, nos. 85 and 86, pl. LXVI; see also below, p. 196.

de' Medici an allegory on the harassing of Virtue by vices?

The five vowels appear as representatives of theological concepts, virtues and human conditions in late medieval thought; Johannes Gerson (1363–1429), late heir of a very ancient tradition which involves the seven Greek vowels and with them the musical scale,[21] identified the letter 'a' with 'gaudium' and 'Dei magnificentia', 'e' with 'spes' and 'munificentia', 'i' with 'compassio' and 'misericordia', 'o' with 'timor' and 'justitia', 'u' with 'dolor' and 'nostra miseria'.[22] There seems to appear a kind of sarcastic reversal of such an order in Ligozzi's print, and I suspect that this was occasioned by a political matter.

Ever since the days of Frederick III of Hapsburg, the five vowels have been connected with a whole arsenal of political punning devices which use them, 'notarikon'-like, as beginning letters of a five-word motto;[23] it is said that there exist more than three hundred of them. The most famous are 'Austriae est imperare orbi universo' and 'Alles Erdreich ist Oesterreich untertan'; but these are late interpolations of the plain letters as they appear in Frederick's diary of 1437,[24] in which he may originally have entered them as part of a gnostic figure game or as an amulet-like device (he had just returned from the Near East). When Frederick actually interpreted them somewhat later he did so in self-defence; after an opponent had given them the meaning 'Aller erst ist Oesterreich verdorben', the emperor had his ghost-writer, Nicolaus Petschacher, use the rebuttal: 'En, amor electis injustis ordinor ultor/Sic Fredericus ego mea jura rego.' There is still no imperialistic dream involved in this. However, what the emperors did not indulge in (Maximilian never referred to the device at all) their courtiers did. In 1567 we find: 'Austria extenditur in orbem universum'; by 1584, interpretations were being collected *en masse*.

Now it so happens that Francesco de' Medici was involved in a troublesome relationship with the Austrian dynasty. For strictly political reasons he had married Johanna of Austria, the sister of Emperor Maximilian II, in 1565, but he continued to see Bianca Cappello, who had been his mistress after 1563. The Austrian princess, pious but proud, jealous and unattractive, died in 1578 and Bianca promptly replaced her as Grand Duchess; however, Francesco's personal (though not political) standing at the Austrian court had inevitably suffered from the contempt which he and Bianca had shown for the Hapsburg princess ('L'altera sposa', as Francesco had irreverently called her)[25] and about which she had reported in detail to her brother, the emperor.[26] It seems quite possible that Ligozzi, still a newcomer in Florence in 1578, the year of Johanna's death, intended to ingratiate himself with Francesco and his new wife Bianca Cappello ('Virtù'!) through a sarcastic—and now safe—allusion to the Hapsburgs, an allusion whose somewhat scurrilous subtlety seems to go very well with many other allegorical conceits of this extraordinary artist. That the drawing (or 'painting') was not cut in wood until 1585 is easily explained by the fact that Andrea Andreani first appeared in Florence in 1584.[27]

Ligozzi, some of whose works show an intimate knowledge of German art of the early sixteenth century,[28] seems in turn to have made quite an impression on northern artists and art lovers of the seventeenth and eighteenth centuries.[29] But surely, Büsinck must have had a very special reason for making his outright copy after Andreani's chiaroscuro—an outright copy, that is, but for the elimination of the topical Five Vowel pun, and the rededication to Landgrave William VI of Hesse.

Ligozzi's composition bears a certain resemblance to

21. Franz Dornseiff, *Das Alphabet in Mystik und Magie*, Leipzig-Berlin, 1922, pp. 35 ff. Prof. W. S. Heckscher kindly called my attention to this book.

22. See the quotation in J. J. M. Timmers, *Symboliek en Iconographie der Christelijke Kunst*, Roermond-Maaseik, 1947, no. 1955. This kind of thing is parodied to perfection by Goethe's 'Teufelchen A' (*Faust, Parerga*, scenes for Prince Radziwill, 1814–19; strangely misquoted by F. Dornseiff, p. 51):

> 'Den Laffen [Amor!] müssen wir erschrecken.
> A, a! E, e! I, i! O! U!'

23. C. W. King, *The Gnostics and their Remains*, London, 2nd ed., 1887, p. 234; F. Dornseiff, p. 51; Alphons Lhotsky, 'AEIOV. Die "Devise" Kaiser Friedrichs III. und sein Notizbuch', *Mitteilungen des Instituts für Österreichische Geschichtsforschung*, LX, 1952, pp. 155 ff.

24. See the facsimile *ibid.* and in the catalogue of the exhibition 'Maximilian I, 1459–1519', Vienna, 1959, pl. 1.

25. Conte Paolo Galletti, *Poesie di Don Francesco dei Medici a Mad. Bianca Cappello*, Florence, 1894, pp. 62 f.

26. Guglielmo Enrico Saltini, *Bianca Cappello e Francesco I de' Medici*, Florence, 1898, pp. 208 ff. See also the report on the dramatic encounter between Johanna and Bianca on Ponte Trinita (Galletti, p. 65) and Johanna's bitter answer to a person seeking Francesco's favor through her: 'Amico, avete sbagliato porta, bussate invece a quella della Bianca' (Saltini, p. 185).

27. On letters written by Ligozzi to Bianca Cappello in that very year 1584 in connection with his work for embroidery see Nina Bacci in *Proporzioni*, IV, 1963, p. 47. Andreani's print exists in a state without the letters and their interpretation. Bartsch considered this the second, Kolloff (see note 6) the first state. One could make only guesses as to the reasons for either of these sequences.

28. A drawing in the Morgan Library in New York (Fairfax Murray Coll., I, no. 91) is a variation on Burgkmair's chiaroscuro woodcut with *Death and the Lovers*; see J. Byam Shaw, 'The Prototype of a Subject by Giacomo Ligozzi', *The Art Quarterly*, XIX, 1956, pp. 283 f. (Shaw overlooked that this relationship had already been pointed out by Hermann Voss [see note 8], p. 422, n. 1). Ligozzi's passion for Dürer is well known.

29. For the prints by Katharina Prestel see note 7; there is also one by Johann Theophilus Prestel, 1781 (Le Blanc 72).

the ill-fated *Porta Virtutis* with which in 1580–1581 Federigo Zuccari intended to take revenge on his Bolognese detractors (Fig. 4).[30] However, there exists a significant basic difference between these two allegories. Ligozzi's, while topical, does not involve the artist's own personal sensitivities; Zuccari's does. Beginning with an adaptation of Apelles'-Lucian's *Calumny* (1572) and proceeding to the greater freedom and daring of the *Lamento della Pittura* (1579) and finally the *Porta Virtutis*, he inserted his artistic grievances into the mainstream of his activities, while on the 'positive' side, he made his late brother's artistic career the subject of a lovely and loving cycle which foreshadows both in content and style nineteenth-century fantasies on 'Künstlers Erdenwallen'.[31] How much Zuccari's self-defence impressed other impartial artists can be deduced from Cigoli's aforementioned *Invidia* which was clearly designated by the artist himself as a (more mild-mannered) rebuff of the critics of his altarpiece for St. Peter's (1604).[32]

In this light, the difference between Ligozzi's original of 1585 and Büsinck's copy of 1646 takes on special significance; while the composition remains unaltered the intrinsic meaning changed from elegant flattery to anxious self-defence, though still addressed to a princely court. In other words, I am convinced that by appropriating Ligozzi's design, Büsinck reinvoked, as it were, Zuccari's widely publicized critical suggestions regarding his fellow-artists—or at least one of them. Rudolf Hallo has already suggested[33] that with this print, Büsinck may have wanted to recommend himself to his landgrave, who was not only an art patron of considerable rank but also a draughtsman of some merit. It now appears equally significant that in the very year 1646 in which Büsinck's woodcut was made, a certain Moses Goldschmidt (alias Wilhelm Friedstadt from Frankfurt) was appointed to the court as drawing instructor.[34] It may not be accidental after all that this chiaroscuro woodcut has survived in one single impression only—nor that one year later Büsinck gave up his artistic activity altogether and became a collector of customs. He may have been just as unsuccessful in defending himself against his colleagues as Zuccari had been in spite of his plea 'che alli pitori non deba esare imputtato l'intrinsicho del animo loro, quando nelle loro piture non vi siano ritratti ne nominati in scritto persona alchuna'.[35] One is reminded of the story about the index of a learned book. It contained the name of Professor X with reference to a page which fails to mention the professor by name but does sport the line: 'Only a thorough fool can maintain that . . .' This is fun but it does not always succeed.

30. Preserved in three slightly different drawings: Frankfurt (H. Voss, p. 460 and p. 596, Fig. 245); Oxford, Christ Church (Exhibition at the Matthiesen Gallery, London, 1960, no. 80); Collection Janos Scholz, New York (J. Bean and F. Stampfle, *Drawings from New York Collections, I: The Italian Renaissance*, New York, 1965, no. 141). Mr. Scholz kindly provided the photograph for our Fig. 4 and called my attention to the account of the story in Gaudenzio Claretta, *Il pittore Federigo Zuccari nel suo soggiorno in Piemonte e alla corte di Savoia*, Turin, 1895, p. 13. See further D. Heikamp, 'Vicende di Federigo Zuccari', *Rivista d'arte*, XXXII, 1957, pp. 175 ff., especially pp. 189 ff.; *idem*, 'Ancora su Federigo Zuccari', *ibid.*, XXXIII, 1958, pp. 45 ff. (where the author accepts the drawing in the Scholz Collection as an original, p. 46, n. 7, without reference to his previous listing as a copy, 1957, p. 191, n. 48).
31. D. Heikamp (1957), pp. 200 ff.
32. See the elaborate inscription of the first of the two drawings mentioned in note 20 and the comment in the catalogue cited there.

33. R. Hallo (see note 3), p. 11.
34. *Ibid.* (to nobody's surprise, this particular information was eliminated in the 1933 edition of the booklet).
35. D. Heikamp (1957), p. 191.

EDOARDO ARSLAN

Disegni del Mola a Stoccolma

Mi sono occupato del Mola molti anni fa in un modesto articolo che trattava soltanto le opere romane.[1] Sono passati, ripeto, molti anni e sono seguiti, da allora, molti pregevoli contributi sul pittore ticinese; la riedizione delle vite del Passeri da parte dello Hess,[2] i due volumi del Waterhouse,[3] la pubblicazione, da parte di Charles Sterling, di un "Guerriero Orientale", firmato e datato 1650, acquistato dal Museo del Louvre,[4] l'eccellente articolo della Montalto,[5] le nutrite osservazioni del Wibiral,[6] l'ottimo saggio del Martinelli,[7] e altri sparsi ai quali accenneremo. Nè va dimenticata la bella mostra dei disegni romani del '600 organizzata nel 1959 al Louvre,[8] e la notizie sui Mola di Coldrerio presenti a Roma dal primo Cinquecento alla metà del Settecento, pubblicate dal Martinola.[9] Nè può essere dimenticato, a questo punto, il cenno, puntualissimo, fatto dal nostro Wittkower nel suo eccellente *Art and Architecture in Italy*;[10] seguito dall'articolo, non del tutto persuasivo, della Sutherland.[11]

Ne è uscita, sempre più, l'immagine di un artista di straordinario interesse, di qualità varia, estrosa, ma sempre molto alta e viva; superiore direi, a un Pietro da Cortona. Un pittore, quest'ultimo, che si colloca con pieno diritto in uno dei filoni maestri della pittura italiana e di cui nessuno negherà la grandissima importanza; se è vero che il Berrettini ha la discendenza che tutti sappiamo e gli è debitrice addirittura, attraverso

Giordano, parte della pittura europea del Settecento. Il seguito del Mola, invece, è esiguo; e lo si deve alla qualità incostante di una pittura che si volge a registri sempre diversi, ma sovente giunge al capolavoro; o, meglio ancora, all'opera unica, irripetibile, che non trova imitatori. La carica figurativa del Mola è quasi sempre, vorrei notare, molto intensa; più intensa sulla tela e nel disegno che non nell'affresco (che egli eseguiva, lo sappiamo ora con certezza, un pò *obtorto collo*).

Sarebbe veramente molto meritevole lo studioso che si occupasse in una monografia del pittore ticinese. Non lo invidieremo certo: a suo tempo il Waterhouse lo aveva definito "una personalità piuttosto proteiforme il cui percorso di stile è arduo da tracciare"[12] e non sembra strano che, anche recentemente, lo Zeri lo abbia qualificato un artista "instabile".[13] Tanto dovrebbe bastare per scoraggiare chi cerca facili imprese; e pungolare invece chi è alla ricerca di un tema arduo e affascinante.

Pubblico, per onorare l'amico Rodolfo Wittkower, una serie di disegni trovati nel Museo di Stoccolma che, confido, non saranno del tutto inutili per chiarire questo lato dell'attività (e della personalità) dell'artista, anche se la mancanza di una conoscenza, il più possibile completa, dell'opera grafica del Mola o, anche, soltanto, il ricordo dei notevoli gruppi di disegni esistenti nelle raccolte europee ed americane (sul qual ricordo è, come risaputo, incauto fidarsi, sopra tutto quando è passato qualche anno), può rendere provvisoria questa prima sistemazione.

I disegni di Stoccolma sono diciotto: alcuni molto belli, altri un pò meno, altri ancora forse non del tutto sicuri. Non li pubblichiamo tutti.

Al 1641 circa, anno dei bellissimi affreschi (tanto poco conosciuti) nella chiesa del Carmelo a Villa di Coldrerio, stupendamente densi di colore, coi bellissimi ritratti dei committenti, e così diversi da ogni cosa coeva lombarda, va riferito un grande studio a

1. "Opere romane di P. F. Mola", *Bollettino d'Arte*, Agosto, 1928.
2. J. Hess, *Die Künstlerbiographien von G. B. Passeri*, Lipsia-Vienna, 1934, p. 367 ss.
3. E. Waterhouse, *Baroque Painting in Rome*, Londra, 1937; *Idem, Italian Baroque Painting*, Londra, 1962.
4. *Bull. des Musées de France*, 1950, p. 33 ss. Il dipinto figurò nella mostra del "Seicento Europeo" a Roma (*Catalogo*, 1956-7, p. 187) e vi apparve manifesto il timbro guercinesco di quegli anni. Lo pubblica anche il Waterhouse (1962) a p. 67. Altri dipinti importanti del Mola figurarono in quell'occasione, tra cui lo splendido "San Bruno" della raccolta Incisa della Rocchetta.
5. L. Montalto, "Gli affreschi del Palazzo Pamphilj a Valmontone", *Commentari*, VI, 1955, p. 267 ss.
6. N. Wibiral, *Bollettino d'Arte*, Gennaio-Giugno, 1960, pp. 143, 150, 151, 158, 164 (con ampia bibliografia).
7. V. Martinelli, "Nuovi ritratti di G. Abbatini e P. F. Mola", *Commentari*, IX, p. 99 ss.
8. Musée du Louvre, Dessins romains du XVII siècle, Parigi, 1959, p. 35 ss. Il gruppo parigino è notevolissimo; e degno di più attenti studi e confronti.
9. G. Martinola, *Le maestranze d'arte del Mendrisiotto in Italia nei secoli XVI-XVIII*, Bellinzona, 1964, p. 85 ss.
10. Londra, 1958, p. 215.
11. Sutherland, "Pier Francesco Mola—His visit to North Italy and his residence in Rome", in *The Burlington Magazine*, CVI, 1964, p. 363 ss.
12. Waterhouse, 1937, p. 82.
13. L'aggettivo è F. Zeri (La galleria Spada in Roma, Firenze, 1954, p. 99). Anche la critica più scaltrita si dimostra ancora molto cauta, e talora un pò imbarazzata, nella cronologia dei disegni (cfr. Blunt-Lester Cooke, *The Roman Drawings of the XVII and XVIII centuries*, etc., *at Windsor Castle*, Londra, 1960, p. 70 ss).

sanguigna per l' "Agar e Ismaele" (fig. 1) e, forse, un foglio, a penna e acquarellato in nero, con una "Flagellazione" (fig. 2) di gusto nettamente guercinesco che attesta le singolarissime capacità di assimilazione del Ticinese.[14]

Quando avvenne che il Mola "imparò in Roma dall'Albano" e "tanto s'imbevè di quella bella, e vaga maniera, ma un poco più tinta che i suoi quadri sono in gran stima" come scrive l'Oretti[15] e confermano altre testimonianze? E'difficile dirlo con tutta precisione, ma si può credere di quel tempo con una certa sicurezza un grande foglio come questo (fig. 3), a sanguigna e inchiostro acquarellato, figurante "Cristo e la Vergine con una santa in ginocchio". Il disegno si può credere del sesto decennio; e la riprova potrebbe darla un disegno di Windsor per il noto affresco di palazzo Costaguti[16] che è, stilisticamente, quanto mai affine a quello svedese. E' però difficile stabilire di qual tempo sono queste caricature (fig. 4), certamente del Mola (un capriccio che l'artista spesso si concedeva, e ne abbiamo altri esempi). "Si vedono—anche l'Oretti ce lo conferma—molte caricature alla Carraccesca di sua mano, e molte in Casa di suo nipote in Roma"[17] I primi contatti col cortonismo si possono cogliere nella bellissima testa barbuta a sanguigna (fig. 5), forse raffigurante l'Eterno (che rivedremo più tardi anche nel Baciccia); e si accusano nettamente in un dipinto del Museo dell'Università di Notre Dame (USA) con l' "Apostasia di Salomone"[18] e nel bellissimo dipinto con "Erminia e Tancredi" del De Young Memorial a San Francisco.[19]

Come si è visto, gli elementi albaneschi non danno ancora una sicurezza assoluta nei riguardi della cronologia. L'opera del Mola, anche nel campo grafico, è infatti così varia, e oscillante tra poli opposti (Guercino e l'Albani; i ricordi veneziani—Veronese e Bassano— e quelli genovesi; il Berrettini e spunti chiaramente caravaggeschi;[20] Gaspare Dughet e i suggerimenti formali raffaelleschi) che soltanto uno studio di tutti i suoi disegni raccolti in tante collezioni europee ed americane, potrà, alla fine, dare un più sicuro assestamento ai singoli pezzi. Ricordiamo quelli delle raccolte italiane (Roma, Firenze, Venezia), i bellissimi gruppi del Museo Britannico, del Kupferstichkabinett di Berlino, di Leningrado ecc. ecc.; un materiale imponente di cui soltanto una minima parte è stata vagliata (il Parker per Oxford, il Blunt e il Lester Cooke per Windsor) ma dove è chiaro—sia detto con tutto il rispetto per gli esimi studiosi che se ne sono occupati— che la critica procede ancora, per forza di cose, incertissima. Proseguendo l'esame del bellissimo gruppo di Stoccolma, non si possono disconoscere elementi genovesi, richiamanti il Castiglione, e precorrenti il Gaulli, nei disegni 563, 557, 555 (fig. 6, 7 e 8) che potrebbero anche essere (il 563 specialmente) di tempo più inoltrato. Il 557 e il 563 sono condotti a sanguigna e inchiostro (o matita nera), che mira a effetti dichiaratamente coloristici.[21]

Pure a sanguigna e inchiostro acquarellato è il disegno (fig. 13), finalmente sicuro come tempo, fatto per il bell'affresco del Quirinale con Giuseppe che accoglie i fratelli, e quindi del 1657.[22] E un altro disegno di sicura identificazione, quanto all'opera cui si riferisce, è il grande foglio della raccolta svedese (fig. 14), studio evidente per la nota pala di San Barnaba in S. Carlo al Corso,[24] di qualche anno posteriore al 1652, a inchiostro acquarellato, in biacca e matita nera. I due bei ritratti, a inchiostro (fig. 9), se raffrontati a quelli pubblicati dal Martinelli[24] si potrebbero ritenere anteriori, ma, anche qui, non potremmo giurarvi: non si può tuttavia non pensare ad analoghi saggi dello stesso Bernini in una tecnica che ci sembra, però, affine a quella, tanto sottile, del Testa.

14. Il disegno delle "Tre fanciulle", pubblicato dal Grassi (*Il disegno Italiano*, Roma, 1956, fig. 133) palesa questo gusto guercinesco, ma è forse dell'ultimo tempo, come lo è pure il disegno allegorico per un soffitto reso noto dal Grassi medesimo (*Storia del disegno*, Roma, 1947, p. 146). Di epoca invece più giovanile è il bel disegno con la Madonna e santi del Museo di Varsavia, pubblicato da M. Mrozinska (*I disegno del codice Bonola del Museo di Varsavia*, Venezia, 1959, p. 116). Vedi anche, ivi, a p. 122 e 123 le schede per due altri disegni del Mola, nati certamente insieme: ma così diversi di tecnica. Prossimo al disegno di soffitto pubblicato dal Grassi (per restare sempre in quest'ordine di idee) mi sembra il n. 578 della Biblioteca Reale di Torino (A. Bertini, *I disegni italiani della Biblioteca Reale di Torino*, Roma, 1958) più che il n. 577; ambedue ascritti al Mola.

15. M. Oretti, *Vite di pittori, etc.*, Bibl. Comunale di Bologna, MS. B 95, f. 497.

16. Cfr. Blunt-L. Cooke, *Roman Drawings*, p. 70, fig. 50.

17. Oretti, v, p. 497. Caricature del Mola sono anche nella Witt Collection (cfr. A. Blunt, *Hand-list of the Drawings in the Witt Collection*, Londra, 1956, n. 79) all'Ashmolean (cat. del Parker, numeri 915 e 916), nel Gabinetto delle Stampe di Berlino (dove sono svariati disegni del Mola degni di attento studio), nel Museo di Worcester, Mass. (*Worcester Art Museum*, vol. vi, 1958, n. 30–31 (Vey)).

18. Vedi: Dwight C. Miller, *Seventeenth and Eighteenth Century Paintings from the University of Notre Dame*, Krannert Art Museum, University of Illinois, Urbana, 1962.

19. Illustrato nel Catalogo della raccolta Kress in quel Museo, edito nel 1955 a p. 60–1.

20. Un dipinto come il San Pietro liberato dal carcere della Borghese era stato dato al Ribera, dopochè, già nel Settecento, era stato fatto correttamente il nome del Mola (cfr. Paola della Pergola, *Galleria Borghese, I dipinti*, II, Roma, 1959, p. 106).

21. Dell'ascrizione al Mola della Ninfa con Satiro del Fogg Art Museum (A. Mongan, *Drawings in the Fogg Art Museum*, Cambridge, Mass., 1946, II, fig. 138) mi sentirei di dubitare. La diversità dai 3 disegni summenzionati di Stoccolma è, infatti, notevole.

22. Vedilo riprodotto in: Wibiral, cit., fig. 32. Un altro disegno per lo stesso affresco è nel British Museum (1853, 10–8–10).

23. Un'eccellente riproduzione a colori del dipinto, che dà ragione veramente a una datazione intorno al 1660 è in: *Via del Corso*, Roma, 1961, tavola III.

24. Opera citata.

Lasciamo per ultimi tre bellissimi disegni, due di puro paesaggio (fig. 11 e 12) e uno con un S. Giovanni Battista (fig. 10) che, se non c'inganniamo, vanno ascritti ad settimo decennio. A inchiostro acquarellato il n. 568, a matita nera il n. 567, i grandi fogli di notevoli dimensioni palesano, specie il primo (ma dovettero nascere insieme), il gusto delle belle, vaste frappe arboree, lo scenario boschereccio così lontano ormai da quanto in Roma si era fatto, dai Carracci e dall'-Elsheimer in poi, nel pur bellissimo paesismo romano del Seicento, fedele o meno ai prototipi di Paolo Brill (qui ormai completamente dimenticati), del Dòmenichino, del Tassi, di Claudio: nessun dubbio che qui il ticinese, si richiama al paesismo tardo di Paolo Veronese, scavalcando nettamente mezzo secolo di pittura romana di paesaggio.

Davanti allo stupendo Battista, grande foglio in sanguigna acquarellata in rosso, non si può esitare nel riconoscere un prodotto degli anni più tardi, vicino al San Giovannino di Santa Anastasia:[25] l'impostazione ancora un pò carraccesca della figura è riscattata dal gusto eccellente dell'inquadratura (che fa del disegno un vero quadro), dalla meravigliosa vivacità del tronco, degli arbusti.[26]

ELENCO DEI DISEGNI ATTRIBUITI A P. F. MOLA NEL MUSEO NAZIONALE DI STOCCOLMA

N. 555/1863   Battesimo di Cristo (cm 19,6 × 34,7). Inchiostro e acquarello.

N. 556/1863   Flagellazione (due studi) (cm 22,5 × 32,7). Inchiostro e acquarello.

N. 557/1863   Angelo e Tobiolo (cm 22,5 × 32,7). Matita nera e sanguigna.

N. 558/1863   Cristo, la Vergine e Santa (cm 32 × 22,8). Sanguigna acquarellata a inchiostro.

N. 559/1863   Putti con uno scudo (cm 17,8 × 25,3). Sanguigna.

N. 560/1863   Santo Apostolo (cm 85 × 135). Sanguigna e inchiostro.

N. 561/1863   Studi per un San Girolamo (cm 15,4 × 18,7). Inchiostro acquarellato.

N. 562/1863   Studio per il S. Brunone (mm 319 × 196). Inchiostro acquarellato con matita nera e biacca.

N. 563/1863   Allegoria fluviale, satiri e ninfe (cm 13 × 19,3). Sanguigna e inchiostro.

N. 564/1863   Studi vari di nudo (cm 12,4 × 20). Inchiostro.

N. 565/1863   Studi di figure (cm 13,1 × 25,3). Inchiostro acquarellato e sanguigna.

N. 567/1863   Studio di albero (cm 30 × 20,2). Matita nera.

N. 568/1863   Studio di alberi (cm 31 × 20,2). Inchiostro acquarellato.

N. 569/1863   Studio per l'Agar (cm 22,1 × 33,8). Sanguigna.

N. 570/1863   Testa di un padre Eterno (cm 10,3 × 98). Sanguigna.

N. 572/1863   San Giovanni Battista (mm 340 × 279). Sanguigna, acquarellato in rosso.

N. 573/1863   Caricature (mm 165 × 199). Inchiostro.

N. 1633/1875   Scena con più figure (cm 35 × 49,9). Inchiostro acquarellato e biacca.

Devo le indicazioni contenute nella suddetta lista al Dr. Patrik Reuterswärd del Museo Nazionale di Stoccolma che vivamente ringrazio; gli devo anche l'informazione che i disegni dal n. 555 al 570, e i n. 572/3 provengono tutti dalla proprietà dell'architetto Carlo Gustavo Tessin e che probabilmente fecero parte di 21 disegni, attribuiti al Mola, acquistati dal Tessin alla vendita Crozat, Parigi, 1741, n. 276. L'ultimo disegno n. 1633 proviene dalla collezione dello scrittore J. T. Sergel (1740–1814). Quest'ultimo disegno va negato recisamente al Mola: si tratta, forse, di un veneto seicentesco. Quanto al n. 564 (Studi di nudo) sono anche un pò perplesso. Sicuri mi sembrano invece i restanti tre non illustrati (nn. 559, 560, 561).

16. 1. 1967

25. Di quest'ultimo tempo, se proprio non inganna la riproduzione, dovrebbe essere il "Ragazzo con colomba" del Museo di Toronto (Art Quarterly, Estate, 1959, p. 183). Ma si impone qui una necessaria cautela. Dell'ultimo Mola si può ben credere invece lo stupendo paesaggio con due certosini di propr. Mahon a Londra (G. Briganti, "The Mahon Collection of Seicento Paintings", in The Connoisseur, vol. 132, agosto 1953, p. 15) affine a un disegno dell'Ashmolean (no. 910; K. T. Parker, Cat. of the Collection of Drawings, etc., Oxford, 1956, II). Sempre a questi ultimi anni (1660–5) lo Zeri dà tre dipinti della Gall. Pallavicini (La Galleria Pallavicini in Roma, Firenze, 1956, numeri 311, 312 e 313), il migliore dei quali è, senza dubbio, il 313 (Testa di vecchia).

26. Il gusto per il paesaggio boschivo, per i tronchi incrociati, per la frappa che rende (quasi auditivamente) lo stormire del vento è certo degli ultimi tempi. Nulla di simile seppe mai escogitare il paesismo romano del Seicento, sempre ligio ad altre formule, del tutto diverse (e pure di gusto elettissimo); uno dei meno noti paesaggi del Mola, tra Dughet e i bolognesi è quello della coll. Brown a Newport (R.I.) pubblicato dal Tietze (European Master Drawings in the United States, New York, 1947, n. 53).

DONALD POSNER

The Picture of Painting in Poussin's *Self-Portrait*

In the background of the *Self-Portrait* in the Louvre that Poussin painted for his dear friend and great patron, Paul Fréart de Chantelou, there are several framed canvases (Fig. 1). The nearest one is unpainted and it serves as a neutral ground for the gold lettering of the inscription at the right: EFFIGIES NICOLAI POVSSINI ANDELYENSIS PICTORIS. ANNO ÆTATIS. 56. ROMÆ ANNO IVBILEI 1650. Just behind this canvas is what appears to be a finished painting. Only a small part of it is visible at the left. A woman with a classical profile, wearing a crown with an eye inset, seems to embrace and to receive the embrace of another figure, whose bare forearms and hands alone are seen. The sun, hidden behind a mountain, casts a dim light on the landscape in the background. The dark blue sky extends across the width of the strip of canvas visible at the top.

Poussin's friend and biographer, Giovanni Pietro Bellori, explained this enigmatic painting within a painting as a 'dedication' that complements the 'tavola del nome' (the canvas with the inscription): 'Dietro nell'altra tavola contraria è figurata la testa di una donna in profilo con un'occhio sopra la fronte nel diadema: questa è la Pittura, e v'appariscono due mani che l'abbracciano, cioè l'amore di essa pittura, e l'amicitia, à cui è dedicato il ritratto. Così egli espresse le lodi, e l'affetto verso quel Signore, che sempre lo favorì per la sua nobile inclinatione.'[1]

Many later critics have been sceptical of Bellori's interpretation. Indeed, anyone who has consulted an edition of Ripa, or looked at some of the numerous demonstrable pictures of 'Painting' from the seventeenth century, knows that Dame Painting should hold or have near her brushes, palette, or some of the other instruments of her art. She may wear a golden chain with a pendent mask inscribed *imitatio*, or even have wings on her head to signify her intellectual flights,[2] but a one-eyed crown is not one of her traditional attributes. If Poussin's figure is Painting it is probably unique in the history of art—but who or what else could the lady be?

Even if we suppose that Poussin has given us a glimpse of a real painting in his studio at the time,[3] instead of an emblematic image, the figure (and in that case, the event too) would still have to be explained. While many scholars have been non-committal and have merely recorded Bellori's identification, others have proposed alternatives: for instance, Smith opted for Thermutis, the Egyptian princess who found the infant Moses; Tolnay proposed Hera 'of the oxen eyes', embracing Zeus on her wedding day (as symbolic of Poussin's own marriage); Kauffmann argued for 'Theory', coupled with the 'naked arms' of 'Practice'. However, these suggestions prove to be supported by no more evidence than has been found for Bellori's interpretation, since the unusual headdress cannot be found in art or literature adorning either Thermutis, Hera, or 'Theory'.[4]

There exists, however, an example of an identifiable allegorical figure who wears a crown with an eye on it. Hitherto unnoticed in this connection, it is a picture of 'Providence' from Rubens' great decorations for the entry of the Cardinal Infante Ferdinand into Antwerp in 1635. The painting, preserved in the Lille Museum, is inscribed 'PROVIDENTIA REGIS'. It shows Providence with a globe, a rudder, and a crown with a very prominent eye (Fig. 2). The rudder and globe traditionally symbolize Providence's role as the 'helmsman of the world'. The eye on the crown, however unusual in art, is easily understood in association with a figure of Providence. The crown is a traditional symbol of supremacy.[5] The eye, as Gevaerts' text accompanying van Thulden's engravings after Rubens'

1. G. P. Bellori, *Le Vite de' pittori . . .*, Rome, 1672, p. 440.
2. See, for instance: Ripa's description of Painting (*Nova Iconologia*, Padua, 1618, pp. 416–17); Pietro Aquila's etching after Carlo Maratta showing 'Annibale Carracci reviving Painting' in *Galeriae Farnesianae Icones*, Rome, 1673; Francesco Lopez's etching of 'Painting with the Muses' in V. Carducho, *Dialogos de la Pintura*, Madrid, 1633.

3. B. Dorival, 'Les Autoportraits de Poussin', *Bulletin de la Société Poussin*, I, 1947, p. 42. It is, by the way, most unlikely that such a painting made by Poussin around 1650 would not have been recorded in either his letters, the contemporary literature, copies, or prints.
4. G. Kauffmann, in *Poussin-Studien* (Berlin, 1960, pp. 92–93), cites and summarizes the earlier literature on the problem. I agree with Kauffmann that the eye connotes 'insight' or 'intelligence' and refers to the theoretical aspect of painting, but there seems to be no evidence that the figure is Theory and that the picture is an allegory of 'Theory and Practice'. For the traditional representation of Theory (which has a compass, not a crown with an eye, on her head) see Kauffmann's Figs. 11 and 16. Practice may be represented bare-armed (although in Ripa she has long sleeves [*op. cit.*, p. 613]), but so may 'Muta Poesis' and 'Conceptus Imaginatio' (see Bellori, *op. cit.*, pp. 104, 201, 289).
5. G. de Tervarent, *Attributs et symboles dans l'art profane*, Geneva, 1958–9, I, p. 126.

decorations explains, means 'Providence'. The ancient Egyptians combined it with a scepter in a hieroglyph denoting their Lord and ruler Osiris: scepter=power; eye=providence.[6]

It would be relatively easy, but I think imprudent, to construct an interpretation of Poussin's picture based on the assumption that the woman, like Rubens' figure, represents Providence. Like all other modern interpretations it would conflict with Bellori's unequivocal statements, and this is more serious than some writers have supposed. Bellori apparently began his *Vite* long before Poussin's death and, since he was a close friend of the artist, his material for Poussin's biography is mostly first-hand.[7] There is no reason to doubt that Bellori saw and discussed the *Self-Portrait* with Poussin when it was being painted, and that his published explanation is essentially the one the artist gave him. Bellori, of course, knew very well how Painting was generally represented,[8] and he also knew that a woman crowned by an eye could be Providence, for he had, in fact, seen and read Gevaerts' *Pompa Introitus Ferdinandi*.[9] Yet, the erudite Bellori was satisfied that Poussin's figure is Painting.

The eye on the crown of Rubens' figure of Providence was apparently an iconographic innovation.[10] It is easily understood because the figure's other attributes and, of course, the inscription localize its meaning. However, an eye has a number of symbolic possibilities. Most of its meanings are closely related to Providence. Thus, as a Renaissance hieroglyphic, for instance, an eye can signify 'God' or 'Godly', the 'guardian of Justice', and 'Prudence' as well as 'Providence'. By extension, it can have such meanings as 'foresight', 'attention', and 'cognition'. It can be an attribute of Modesty (because Modesty 'hà occhio di non cascare in qualche mancamento') and, in the context of an emblem or devise, its possibilities are innumerable. Combined with a compass, for instance, we find it signifying 'reason', 'l'œil de la pensée'.[11]

From this small sampling of eye iconography it should be evident that the eye worn by Poussin's figure is not in itself a sufficient clue to her identity. In fact, the whole 'picture' at the left in the *Self-Portrait* is remarkable for its iconographic indistinctness. It confronts us with the problem of discovering its 'spirit' or emblematic meaning through an examination of its 'body', the visual apothegm, without reference to its 'soul', the accompanying verbal aphorism. For it is in the nature of the emblem—and I think we must understand Poussin's picture as an emblematic image —that icon and epigram reciprocally interpret each other. Poussin told Bellori that his figure is Painting, and his explanation of the picture must have supplied, like an emblematic epigram, verbal clues which, in conjunction with the eye, make a specific statement about Painting. Bellori did not pass these clues on to us, but there is some evidence that makes it possible, I think, to understand the image without them.

Certainly, the eye refers to the cognitive or rational faculty of Painting. It is not entirely impossible that Poussin was making a somewhat recondite allusion by means of an association of the prudential eye with Minerva, the goddess of Prudence, who is also protectress of the Arts. However, some well-known remarks of the artist suggest another explanation. In a letter of 1642, Poussin speaks of two ways of seeing objects: (1) simply, which 'n'est autre chose que recevoir naturellement dans l'œil la forme et la ressemblance de la chose veûë'; (2) by considering the object with

6. J. C. Gevaerts, *Pompa Introitus Ferdinandi*, Antwerp, 1641, p. 25. Gevaerts gives the classical sources: Plutarch, Diodorus Siculus, and Macrobius. See further, Tervarent, *op. cit.*, II, p. 287.
The scepter with an eye is, of course, frequently found in seventeenth-century art. For instance, in Andrea Sacchi's fresco in the Barberini Palace to express the providential rule of Divine Wisdom.

7. Bellori probably met Poussin in the 1630's. For his relationship to the artist, and for the chronology of his *Vite*, see K. Donahue, ' "The Ingenious Bellori"—A Biographical Study', *Marsyas*, III, 1943–5, pp. 115–16, 132, n. 35; and further, Donahue, *Notes on Gio. Pietro Bellori* (unpublished M.A. thesis), New York University, 1942, pp. 46–47.

8. On Bellori as an iconographer see Donahue, *Notes on . . . Bellori*, pp. 58–68.

9. Bellori discussed the publication in his biography of Rubens and he described two of Rubens' figures of Providence (*op. cit.*, pp. 238, 241). He did not mention the eye on the crown in our Fig. 2 because it is not visible in van Thulden's engraving, and it is not described in the accompanying text (Gevaerts, *op. cit.*, pp. 108A, 112–13). However, Bellori describes the second, winged Providence, who doesn't wear a crown, but does have an eye on top of her head (in Gevaerts, opp. p. 25): 'la Providenza alata con l'occhio sopra la fronte, e col mondo in mano'. It is most likely that Poussin, too, knew Gevaerts' book.

10. Ripa, for instance, offers seven different personifications of Providence, including one with a globe and rudder, but none of them have an eye. (*Op. cit.*, p. 427.)

11. Examples of most of these symbolic uses, and others, can be found easily in L. Volkmann, *Bilderschriften der Renaissance*, Leipzig, 1923. See also Tervarent, *op. cit.*, II, pp. 286–7. For Alberti's famous winged eye see R. Watkins, 'L. B. Alberti's Emblem', *Mitteilungen des Kunsthistorischen Institutes in Florenz*, IX, 1959–60, pp. 256–8. For 'cognition' see G. P. Lomazzo, *Trattato dell'arte della pittura . . .* (Milan, 1584), Rome, 1844, II, p. 395; for Modesty see Ripa, *op. cit.*, pp. 346–7; for 'reason' see L. Lalanne, *Le livre de Fortune. Recueil des . . . dessins inédits de Jean Cousin* (1568), Paris, 1883, pl. LXXXIV (I am indebted to Eugene Carroll for this reference); for Prudence see C. C. Malvasia, *Felsina Pittrice*, Bologna, 1678, I, p. 416. (Professor and Mrs. Richard Krautheimer kindly called my attention to a drawing in the Victoria and Albert Museum for the Fonte Gaia in Siena that shows an allegorical figure with three eyes, one of them on her forehead. The figure may represent Prudence, as Professor Krautheimer has suggested in an article in the *Metropolitan Museum of Art Bulletin*, X, 1952, p. 270.)

attention, so that 'l'on cherche avec une application particuliere les moyens de bien connoistre ce mesme objet'. The first, 'le simple aspect', is a natural operation. The second, 'ce que je nomme le *Prospect* est un office de raison que dépend de trois choses, sçavoir de l'œil, du rayon visuel, et de la distance de l'œil à l'objet'.[12] This rational, attentive seeing, bent on understanding the world through a knowledge of the physiology and mathematics of vision is, of course, 'perspective seeing' (*Prospect* = *Prospetto* or *Prospettiva*).[12a] There is good reason to believe that Poussin (who certainly regarded brushes and palette merely as the technical accessories of his profession) adopted the eye of Perspective to denote the intellectual and creative vision which is the supreme characteristic of Painting. In the first place Perspective actually has an eye, although Ripa makes her wear it as a pendant on a golden necklace rather than on a crown.[13] In the second place a woman wearing a crown with an eye on it appears in art, one year after Poussin finished his portrait, in a context that unmistakably has to do with perspective. Moreover, she appears in a book illustration for a volume that was partly dependent on Poussin and much indebted to the efforts of his patron, Chantelou.

Leonardo da Vinci's *Trattato della Pittura* was published in Paris in 1651, simultaneously in an Italian edition and in a French translation by Chantelou's brother, Fréart de Chambray. The book is based on the manuscript that Chantelou brought to France from Italy, and Poussin, to whom the French edition is dedicated, made many of the drawings for the engraved illustrations used in both editions. Three plates, however, illustrating Leonardo's chapters on drapery, were apparently designed by Charles Errard.[14] Errard put his draped figures in architectural settings and he added accessory details in order to make 'pictures' rather than mere drapery diagrams. Furthermore, he extended their meaning so that they are at once illustrations of different problems in the representation of drapery and also symbolic vignettes of essential parts of the art of Painting. The first and third pictures apparently refer to Proportion and Invention respectively.[15] The second picture (Fig. 3) illustrates Chapter CCCLXII, entitled 'Delle pieghe de' panni in scorcio'. The problem of representing drapery folds in foreshortening is, of course, in the province of Perspective, which is the general subject of the picture. At the lower right one sees a tablet with a perspective diagram, showing an eye and the 'visual rays' connecting it to an object. The fact that there are two women represented may very well be fortuitous. The additional drapery of a second figure is useful for the perspective demonstration. However, the contrast of a woman with a classical profile, whose stance is dignified and commanding, and a figure who is quite humble in appearance and dress might suggest that the Theory and Practice of perspective are represented here. In any case, the 'noble' woman wears a crown with an eye on it. In the context of the print this eye can only be the noble, rational eye of Perspective. The figure, of course, is derived from Poussin's painting, whose meaning Errard would have known from Chantelou.

Poussin's figure then, can be understood as Painting, characterized by her supreme asset—an intellectual vision or *Prospect*, which is not a function of 'ordinary seeing'.[16] It is possible that the landscape, barely visible in the faint light of the sun, which is hidden behind the mountain, also has a specific meaning in this connection. Against this dark landscape the eye-crowned figure may illustrate the kind of metaphorical statement that Ripa makes in his discussion of 'Cognition', where he explains that corporeal eyes need light to see, but 'l'occhio nostro interno, che è l'intelletto . . . fa mestiero dell'istrumento estrinseco de' sensi'.[17] Poussin's insistence on this intellectual characterization of his art in his *Self-Portrait* for Chantelou was perhaps not without motive. There had been a moment when Chantelou needed reassurance about the quality of the work that the master sent to him. In 1647 Poussin wrote his famous letter on the 'modes', in which he admonished his patron to remember that the art (and consequently the criticism) of painting is a high and difficult intellectual pursuit.[18] The artist reiterated this idea of Painting in the *Self-Portrait*, while quite sincerely thanking Chantelou for his friendship and loving patronage. Bellori's explanation that the hands

---

12. C. Jouanny, *Correspondance de Nicolas Poussin*, Paris, 1911, p. 143.

12a. See C. Goldstein, 'The Meaning of Poussin's Letter to De Noyers', *Burlington Magazine*, CVIII, 1966, especially p. 234, n. 8.

13. *Op. cit.*, p. 426.

14. Cf. W. Friedlaender and A. Blunt, *The Drawings of Nicolas Poussin*, London, IV (1963), pp. 26–30.

15. The first (on p. 110 of the Italian edition of the *Trattato*) illustrates Chapter CCCLX, on the form or structure of drapery folds. It shows a grave old man surrounded by the attributes of Mathematics and Geometry. The third (p. 112) illustrates Chapter CCCLXIV, which deals largely with the adjustment of drapery to the action and attitude of the figure. It shows a pensive woman with an open book on her knee and symbols of the Fine Arts at her feet.

I should like to thank Miss Frances I. Duck, Librarian of Stevens Institute of Technology, for her kindness when I consulted Stevens' fine collection of 'Vinciana', and especially for her help in procuring the photograph for Fig. 3 (from p. 111 of the *Trattato*).

16. A nice parallel is found in Lomazzo: 'l'occhio insieme con l'intelletto umano, regolato con l'arte della prospettiva, ha da essere la regola, la misura, ed in una parola il giudice della pittura'. (*Op. cit.*, II, p. 9.)

17. Ripa, *op. cit.*, p. 85.

18. Jouanny, *op. cit.*, pp. 370–5.

in Poussin's picture, seen embracing the figure of Painting, refer to friendship and love can easily be accepted, if for no other reason than that metaphors like 'a friendly hand', 'love's embrace', '*prestare mano a*', '*être en bonnes mains*', are commonplace in all languages.

The story of Poussin's *Self-Portrait* is well known.[19] The artist made it, despite his dislike for painting por-

traits, to express his great friendship and gratitude to Chantelou.[20] The pictorial dedication that he included is evidently a private statement of Poussin's idea of Painting, and also of the debt that he and his art, owed to Chantelou.

19. The painting was mentioned frequently by Poussin in his letters to Chantelou. See the discussion in *Exposition Poussin* (Paris, 1960, pp. 119–20), where the references to Jouanny are given.

20. The diamond ring worn by Poussin in the painting is possibly an allusion to the strong friendship between him and Chantelou. Kauffmann has discussed the various emblematic meanings of a diamond (*op. cit.*, pp. 88–91), and Blunt, in his review of Kauffmann's book, has emphasized the particular relevance of the idea of 'constancy in friendship' (*Burlington Magazine*, CIII, 1961, p. 285).

MARIO PRAZ

Francesco Pianta's Bizarre Carvings

Visitors to the Scuola di San Rocco in Venice, not unreasonably attracted by the major artist, Tintoretto, often forget, in the upper room, to cast a glance at the frames of those huge canvases. But whoever deigns to pay attention to the carvings of Francesco Pianta cannot fail to be struck by their enigmatic strangeness and by the mixture of violence and refinement in their technique. Flasks, guns, chains, hampers, books, masks, a donkey's head here, a severed human foot there, reading-desks, sieves, brushes, ropes and hammers, jugs, musical instruments, what is the meaning of all this odd assortment accompanying figures of athletes and dons, of people naked or else wrapped in their cloaks, of lusty fellows or maimed wretches, all carved in a mellow, glossy, worm-eaten wood? No doubt this work belongs to the seventeenth century; in any other epoch of the past, this would have been the work of a madman. But in the seventeenth century, in the century of Don Quixote and of Manzoni's Don Ferrante, there was a *razón de la sinrazón*, a method in madness. If instead of Tintoretto's paintings there had been Greco's, we might have thought that this series of puzzling telamons had been suggested by the lucubrations of one of the pale and melancholy gentlemen of the painter of Toledo.

Francesco Pianta (who lived about 1630–1690) belonged to the successive generation to that of Emanuele Tesauro, the theorist of abstruse wit, and equally considered emblems and hieroglyphs a science. The learned and scientific assumption is blazoned in the long scroll displayed by Mercury (Fig. 1) at the very entrance door: the scroll is of wood imitating vellum (further on, in the deception of a shelf full of vellum bindings, with all their rumpled and indented appearance, Pianta nearly makes us gasp with admiration), but the writing is in ink. It runs:

Ai Lettori.—Dell'origine e del progresso dell'Iconologia. Iconologia deriva da due parole greche, *icon* che significa immagine e *logia* parlamento; sicché altro non vuol dire Iconologia che ragionamento di immagini, perché in quella si descrivono infinite figure esplicate con saggi e dotti discorsi dai quali si rappresentano le bellezze delle virtù e le bruttezze de' vitii affine che questi si fuggino e quelle si abbraccino. Ché però gli filosofi vanno rivelando in quanti modi la filosofia distinguer si possi cosicché

gli Egittii occultarono la filosofia sotto oscuri velami di favole e geroglifici secreti. Pittagora la vestì con un drappello d'oscuri simboli, Empedocle con enigmi, Protagora con intricati commenti, Platone con sensi mistici, Gorgia con bizzarri, fallaci e contrari argomenti che tutte le cose sono e non sono, Zenone l'istesso con possibili ed impossibili esperienze, Aristotele con termini oscuri e difficile testura di parole, sicché tutti unanimi e concordi si appigliano a quel detto di Marco Tullio nel primo dell'Oratore nel quale dice: *Philosophia in tres partes est distributa; in naturae obscuritatem, in disserendi subtilitatem, in vitam atque mores.*

Whoever is acquainted with the copious literature of devices and emblems produced during the sixteenth and the seventeenth centuries will at once recognize some of its commonplaces in the wording of Pianta's scroll. In fact the very words with which Pianta's speech opens[1] occur in the printer's address to the readers introducing the *Iconologia*[2] by Cesare Ripa from Perugia (which, printed in Rome in 1593 and 1603, went through numberless editions): this work, which supplied so many decorative motifs to baroque art,[3] suggested to Pianta not only the text of the long scroll held by Mercury, but also some of the figures (Furore, Spia), and inspired him with others of his own

1. Enrico Lacchin, in his study *Di Francesco Pianta junior, bizzarro e capriccioso scultore in legno del Barocco veneziano e dei suoi 'Geroglifici' nella Scuola di San Rocco*, Venice, Libreria Emiliana Editrice, 1930, though tracing most of Pianta's allegories to Ripa, omits to call attention to the source of the foreword to the readers, and quotes the form 'fuggino' as an instance of Pianta's solecisms, whereas it is found in the source.
2. The latter portion of the foregoing speech is found under the item 'Filosofia', on pp. 208–9 of the 1645 Venice edition (publ. by Cristoforo Tomasini) of the *Iconologia*: 'Tullio nel primo dell'Oratore: *Philosophia in tres partes est distributa, in naturae obscuritatem, in disserendi subtilitatem, in vitam atque mores* . . . li Filosofi fin da tempi antichi hanno avuto costume di addombrarla con sofisticarie obscure. Gli Egitij occultarono la filosofia sotto oscuri velami di favole, & Geroglifici segreti. Pitagora la vestì con un drappello d'oscuri simboli, Empedocle con Enigmi, Protagora con intricati commenti, Platone con sensi mistici, Gorgia con bizzarri, fallaci, & contrarij argomenti, che tutte le cose sono e non sono, Zenone l'istesso con possibili, & impossibili esperienze, Aristotele con termini oscuri & difficile testura di parole.'
3. See E. Mâle, *L'Art religieux après le Concile de Trente*, pp. 383 ff., and on the subject of emblems in general my *Studies in Seventeenth-Century Imagery*, London, the Warburg Institute, 1939, 2nd ed. Rome, Edizioni di Storia e Letteratura, 1964.

invention. But while Ripa's figures are based on classical learning,[4] those which Pianta contrived in his bizarre imagination partake of the same nature of both his Latin and Italian styles: that is, they are rather confused and odd, even if we take into account that the brain which gave them birth was that of a man of the seventeenth century. No doubt Manzoni's humour would have been stimulated by Pianta's 'explanations' of his symbols!

But the closely written explanations contained in Pianta's scroll are bodily lifted from Ripa's *Iconologia*. Let us examine the figures one by one together with the inscriptions which accompany them. And first of all let us consider the order in which they occur:

1. Malinconia. 2. Honor. 3. Avaritia. 4. Ignoranza. 5. Scientia.
Diceria nel riquadro.

6. Distinzione del bene dal male.
Speculazione nel secondo riquadro.

7. Furore.
Magnificenza nella libreria.

8. Spia o curiosità. 9. Scandalo o scrupolo. 10. Piacere onesto. 11. Cicerone in difesa della Scultura.
Vigilanza nel riquadro.

12. Giacomo Robusti per la Pittura. 13. Abbondanza. 14. Stratagemma esempio. 15. Biasimo vizioso.
Geroglifici sotto le finestre.

This list of subjects leaves us rather puzzled: we seem to hold in our hands a set of ill-assorted tarots; if this is to be a cycle, what is its key? Pianta says nothing of the reasons of his choice, and therefore Cicero and Giacomo Robusti, i.e. Tintoretto, who are peering out (and with what attributes!) from the disorderly troop of vices and virtues, have all the appearance of sallies of a lunatic.

Ripa represents Melancholy in the shape of a 'sad and sorrowful old woman, poorly clad'. Pianta has instead an old man wrapped up in a cloak, with a stupefied face. It has been remarked[5] that as a rule Pianta substitutes male figures to Ripa's female ones, going so far as to represent Abundance as an old man, and what an old man, as we shall see! It does not seem to me that this may be due to his inability to carve female figures. I would not be surprised, instead, that an odd brain like his should have been a misogynist's or worse: the naked chests of the impersonators of his allegories are treated with a remarkable sensuality, and often

surrounded with cords or chains. Apparently he never married; we do not want however to insinuate that he was another Monsieur de Charlus (who, besides, was a widower). But although Pianta has not taken inspiration from the woodcut of Ripa's Melancholy, he has nevertheless transplanted several passages into his text, as is shown by the following comparison:
Ripa, p. 385:[6]

Fa la malinconia nell'huomo quegli effetti istessi che fa la forza del verno ne gl'alberi, & nelle piante, li quali agitati da diversi venti, tormentati dal freddo e ricoperti dalla neve appariscono secchi, sterili, nudi, & di vilissimo prezzo . . . ben disse Virg. nel 6: *Pallentes habitant morbi, tristisque senectus.*

Pianta:

Melancolia come ben disse Virgilio (Eneide 6) *Pallentes habitant morbi tristisque senectus*—fa la malinconia nell'huomo quegli effetti istessi che la forza dell'inverno negli alberi & nelle piante, li quali agitati da diversi venti, tormentati dal freddo e ricoperti dalla neve appariscono secchi, sterili, nudi e di vilissimo prezzo.

One would vainly search in Ripa for the attributes of Pianta's Melancholy: the dial, bellows, fire. Pianta says that the melancholiac has the clock by him, an instrument which 'se falla, o battaglia o suona fuori tempo o dà quattro botti quando doveva darne due, subito tutti si ammirano e mormorano di chi n'ha cura e di chi l'ha fatto—così il melancolico è ammirato e borbottato da tutti'. This very clock we find in Ripa, but surprisingly enough as an attribute of Prelatura (Office of Prelate, p. 499):

Se poi un horologio falla una volta, o suona fuor di tempo, o dà quattro botti, quando doveva darne due, subito tutti s'ammirano, e mormorano di chi n'ha cura, e di chi l'ha fatto.

Ripa concludes by saying that prelates are like clocks in the world, and must be careful to strike right because they serve as a rule and an example to others. The symbol, which in its proper place in Ripa has a meaning, becomes incongruous in Pianta, who continues thus: '[Il Melancolico] porta seco il foco che sicome dal foco ne esce la fiamma, così tra sé pensando ne uscisse buoni consigli perché con caldezza & prestezza far l'opera sua, consumando quel che bisogna per mantenere nell'essere suo il proprio splendore.' This passage does not yield much sense, be it a defect of the text or of Lacchin's transcription, but in Ripa,

4. See E. Mandowsky, *Ricerche intorno all'* Iconologia *di Cesare Ripa*, Florence, Olschki, 1939 (in *Bibliofilia*, vol. XLI).
5. By Lacchin, *op. cit.*, p. 15.

6. Quotations from Ripa are after the 1645 Venice edition (Tomasini).

under Sollecitudine (p. 581) we read: 'Et la fiamma significa la sollecitudine, perché con caldezza, & prestezza fa l'opera sua, consumando quel che bisogna, per mantenere nell'esser suo il proprio splendore.' Finally Pianta mentions a further attribute:

> Reca seco il mantice perché la perturbazione nasce dall'inequalità come col vento soverchio desta la calidità del fuoco e maggiormente l'accende, però la mescolanza dei colori mostra la confusione delle passioni.

Ripa, under Perturbatione (p. 484), has:

> Dunque la perturbatione nasce dall'inequalità, il che si mostra col Mantice, che col vento soverchio desta la calidità del fuoco, & maggiormente l'accende & ove non sono motivi contrarij non può esser perturbatione, però la mescolanza de' colori mostra confusione delle passioni.

As one sees, Pianta's method was the same which Gabriele d'Annunzio was to use two centuries and a half later;[7] but of course he was no d'Annunzio; while the poet is always able to elicit a new order from the passages of other authors he fits together, Pianta only brings in confusion and produces a heap of ill-fitting parts.

He represents Honour as a handsome youth with little wings in the place of arms; one of them clings to a hanging flag: he has his loins girt with a necklace and a laurel wreath (Fig. 2). Pianta explains:

> Honore secondo S. Tomaso secunda secunde 129 Art. 4° dice: *honor est cuiuslibet virtutis praemium* —si che si fa giovane bello, perché per se stesso senza ragione o sillogismi alletta ciascuno e si fa desiderare: ancora è nome di possessione libera e volontaria degli animi virtuosi attribuito a l'huomo per fermezza contro qualsivoglia sinistro incontro.

Ripa, s.v. Honore (p. 258):

> Honore è nome di possessione libera, & volontaria degl'animi virtuosi, attribuita all'huomo per premio d'essa virtù, & cercata col fine dell'honesto; & S. Tomaso 2.2.q.129, art. 4 dice che *honor est cuiuslibet virtutis praemium*. Si fa giovane, & bello, perche per se stesso, senza ragioni, o sillogismi alletta ciascuno, & si fa desiderare.

Pianta goes on:

> L'asta o bandiera significa la cagion principale per

la quale perpetuamente la scienza, sebbene fa immortale la fama di chi la possiede, non di meno non si acquista senza molta fatica & sudore.

Ripa (p. 258):

> l'hasta, & il Cornucopia, & la Corona d'Alloro significano le tre cagioni principali, onde gl'huomini sogliono essere honorati, cioè la scienza, la ricchezza, & l'armi, & l'alloro significa la scienza, perche come questo albero ha le foglie perpetuamente verdi, ma amare al gusto, così la scienza, se bene fa immortale la fama di chi la possiede, nondimeno non si acquista senza molta fatica, & sudore.

Pianta has abridged in this case, but to the detriment of sense.
Pianta:

> Il setro dassi ad intendere che le Muse tutte honorano quello che per mezzo delle molte fatiche, è arrivato alla scienza delle cose, & all'immortalità del suo nome.

Ripa:

> Però disse Esiodo, che le Muse gli havevano donato uno scettro di lauro, essendo egli di bassa fortuna, per mezzo delle molte fatiche arrivato alla scienza delle cose, & alla immortalità del suo nome.

Pianta:

> La corona & colana significano come queste erano insegne degli antichi re così per premio davansi da romani a chi di tal virtù era possessore & perfine le armi significano l'onore essere figliuolo della vittoria, e così conviene che sia ornato dell'insegne della madre.

Ripa, apropos of another representation of Honour, as a 'huomo d'aspetto venerando, & coronato di palma, con un collaro d'oro al collo & maniglie medesimamente d'oro alle braccia, nella man destra terrà un'hasta, & nella sinistra uno scudo':

> Si corona di Palma, perche quest'Albero . . . è segno di Vittoria . . . & essendo l'Honore figliuolo della Vittoria . . . convien che sia ornato dall'insegne della madre. L'hasta, & lo scudo furono insegne degli antichi Re, in luogo della Corona . . . Le maniglie alle braccia, & il collaro d'oro al collo, erano antichi segni d'Honore, & davansi da Romani per premio a chi s'era portato nelle guerre valorosamente. . . .

Pianta represents Avarice as an old man with a visored cap which, together with his beard and the unbuttoned coat, gives him a curious family air with the soldiers of the Italian Risorgimento or of the American Civil

---

7. D'Annunzio's way of borrowing from various sources has been illustrated by me in the chapter 'D'Annunzio e "l'amor sensuale della parola"' in my book *La carne, la morte e il diavolo nella letteratura romantica*, Florence, Sansoni, 1948 and 1966 (fourth edition) (this chapter is omitted in the English translation of the book, *The Romantic Agony*).

War; but instead of a cartridge belt he carries round his waist an inkstand and books of accounts, as crumpled and life-like as all the wooden books of this sculptor, besides money-bags, pincers, and a sponge.

> Avaritia è uno sfrenato appetito d'aver, come dice S. Agostino lib. 3 de libero arbitrio: *ut parcas opibus tibi quid non parcis an unquam*—si rappresenta ora homo & alle volte donna, se gli dà il cappello in testa perché non cessa mai di coprire il viso alla ragione & con disusata forza spezza il freno della temperanza e, non avendo riguardo a virtù alcuna, trasmuta i cuori pietosi in crudeli e si fa universal guastatrice delle virtù. . . .

Ripa describes five different ways of portraying Avarice. In the third one (p. 52):

> L'Avaritia è uno sfrenato appetito d'havere, come dice S. Agost. libr. 3 *de libero Arbitrio*, che non cessa mai di coprire con grosso velo il viso alla ragione & con disusata forza spezza il freno della temperanza, & non havendo riguardo a virtù alcuna trasmuta i cuori pietosi in crudeli, & si fa universal guastatrice delle virtù.

The Latin verse quoted by Pianta without indicating its source comes from an epigram of Maffeo Barberini (Urban VIII) cited by Ripa in the second of his allegories of Avarice.[8]

Pianta:

> Si fa con la borsa o sacchetti serrati godendo più nel guardare i denari come cosa dipinta per diletto, che in adoperarli come utile per necessità e virtù.

Ripa (second allegory, p. 51):

> Si fa con la borsa serrata, godendo più nel guardar i denari, come cosa dipinta per diletto, che in adoperarli come utile per necessità.

Pianta:

> Li libri danno ad intender essere come una tenaglia che siccome detto istromento stringe e tira sempre a sé, così è la perversa natura dell'empio avaro il quale non lascia mai occasione che non faci il medesimo effetto non guardando né stato, né conditione di qualsivoglia persona.

Ripa (fifth allegory, p. 53 wrongly numbered 69):

> La tenaglia, che tiene con la destra mano mostra, che si come detto stromento stringe e tira sempre a sé, così è la perversa natura dell'empio avaro, il quale non lascia mai occasione, che non facci il medesimo effetto non guardando né stato, né conditione di qual si voglia persona.

As for the inkstand and the sponge, possibly they lurk in Ripa's *Iconologia*, but let us grant, until we get evidence to the contrary, that Pianta, no less fond of writing than of carving, may have drawn them out of his own experience.

Ignorance (Fig. 3) has the face of an elderly, bald man with side-whiskers, who, but for the disproportionate ears, might even remind us of Alessandro Manzoni; a hamper, a wig, and a donkey's head (Fig. 4) hang from his belt, next to a pair of tongs. The text runs:

> Gli antichi Egittii per dimostrare un ignorante di tutte le cose, facevano una figura col capo dell'asino che guardava la terra perché al sole della virtù non s'alza mai l'occhio degli ignoranti, & li greci, come racconta Isidoro (*Soliloquiorum* libro 2°, capo 17) l'ornavano con questo verso '*Summa miseria est nescire quo tendas*' dove porta la testa dell'asino atacata ad una molletta istromento da foco, sicome quella col continuo esercizio suo non si abbrucia, né si converte in fuoco ma si consuma, così l'ignoranza può star ben sempre accompagnata con la sapienza.

Ripa represents Ignorance as a woman, and deals of her in six little chapters. In the one on Ignorance of everything, one reads (p. 271): 'Gl'antichi Egitij, per dimostrare un ignorante di tutte le cose, facevano una imagine col capo dell'asino, che guardasse la terra, perche al Sole della virtù non s'alza mai l'occhio de gl'ignoranti.' In the chapter that follows (the fifth): 'Ignoranza dipinta da' Greci . . . però disse Isidoro Soliloquiorum lib. 2 cap. 17: *Summa miseria est nescire quo tendas*.'

But the symbol of the tongs, which is rather odd, is not found in the *Iconologia*, and is perhaps a further evidence of the incoherence of Pianta's imagination. He goes on by saying: 'Mai leverà quel puerile ingegno nudo affatto di ogni ornamento virile, abbrucciando[9] quella goffaggine, cioè levando quelle cose rette da senso che sono più grosse che non l'asino.'

Ripa (fifth chapter):

> Fanciullo e nudo si dipinge per dimostrare, che l'ignorante è semplice, & di puerile ingegno, & nudo d'ogni bene . . . con questa pittura volevano i Greci occultamente significare, che l'Ignorante era di

8. Strangely enough Lacchin in his explanation refers to this epigram and other learned allusions of Ripa without mentioning their source or drawing parallels between Ripa's text and Pianta's: he does not venture beyond a general statement (p. 14): 'Ricercato e avuto quel libro [Ripa's] fra mano, abbiamo constatato che da esso il Pianta avea preso gran parte dei concetti per la formazione e per la spiegazione dei suoi gerogli-fici, gran parte, ma non tutto, perché alcuni tratti, i più deficienti per espressione, ma sempre originali di pensiero, devono essere interamente suoi.'

9. Lacchin's reading; perhaps: 'abbracciando'?

semplice, & di puerile ingegno, nudo affatto d'ogni ornamento virile, retto dal senso, che è più grosso, che non è un asino.

One cannot certainly say that Pianta has improved on Ripa's text. Pianta again:

> Porta seco la sporta davanti il che ci dimostrò Esopo quando figurato ogni uomo con due sacchi uno avanti il petto, l'altro di dietro, in quello avanti poniamo i mancamenti d'altri, in quello di dietro i nostri & particolarmente chiaro si vede esser radicato nella mente degli ignoranti di conoscer li diffetti d'altri e non li suoi. Ha nella cintura un cappello a modo di peruga perché quando volevano i Romani dare libertà ad un servo dopo averli raso i capelli li facevano portare il cappello e questo lo facevano per dar ad intender che quello non era buono per loro.

The attribute of the hamper comes from Phaedrus's ninth fable: *Peras Juppiter imposuit nobis duas*; Ripa speaks of it under Amor di se stesso (pp. 28–29):

> Che offusca il senso, talche innamorati di noi medesimi scorgiamo si bene i mancamenti de gli altri per leggieri che siano, ma non conosciamo li nostri, ancorche gravi, il che ci dimostrò Esopo, quando figurò ogni huomo con due sacchi, uno avanti il petto, l'altro di dietro, in quello davanti poniamo i mancamenti d'altri, in quello di dietro i nostri, perche dall'Amor di noi medesimi non li vediamo, si come vediamo quelli de gl'altri.

The attribute of the hat 'a modo di peruga' is taken from what Ripa says under Misura (p. 407): '[I Romani] quando volevano dare la libertà ad uno schiavo, lo radevano & gli ponevano in testa un capello [*sic*]: della [*sic*] nobiltà non si portava in Roma, ancorche Marziale lib. xj epig. 7 chiami Roma pileata.' Science is represented by Pianta as an elderly scholar, his head covered with a cap, reading a book laid on a reading-desk (Fig. 5); the book, as usual, is rendered to perfection in the crumpled aspect of its pages: the same may be said of the pile of books (Fig. 6) lying in front of the scholar's knees, and of the hanging parchment written all over which comes down his shoulder not unlike the leaf of a banana-tree. Pianta states:

> Platone diceva con brevissima sentenza lib. *De Scientia* così dicendo—*Scientia est Opinio vera cum ratione*—La scienza secondo l'istesso Platone nel libro intitolato *litigiosus* è una vera strada & potenza a la felicità il che ne dimostrano quelli tre nomi della felicità assegnati dai greci antichi cioè Eodemonia—Eutichia & Eufragia. Il primo significa la

cognizione del bene, il secondo l'esecuzione di esso, il terzo l'uso, il che tutto dipende dalla Scienza.

All this is bodily taken from Ripa (p. 553):

> . . . diffinitione . . . brevissima ne dà Platone libro *de Scientia* dicendo: *Scientia est opinio vera cum ratione*. La scientia secondo l'istesso Platone nel libro intitolato *Letigiosus* è una vera strada & potenza alla felicità, il che ne dimostrano quelli tre nomi assegnati dalli Greci antichi cioè Eudemonia, Eutichia, & Eufragia; il primo significa la cognitione del bene, & il secondo l'essecution di esso, il terzo l'uso, il che tutto dipende dalla Scienza.

From another passage of Ripa (under Dottrina, p. 166: 'Il libro aperto, & le braccia aperte parimente denotano essere la Dottrina liberalissima da se stessa') there comes what follows in Pianta: 'Il libro aperto denota essere la dottrina liberalissima da se stessa.' The next allusion of the sculptor is more difficult to trace, so much so that Lacchin (*op. cit.*, p. 23) credits him with its invention: 'E qui il Pianta mostra cervello fino perché prendendo a paragone la stimata scuola di retorica di Isocrate, chiama il sapere officina dell'eloquenza.' However Pianta does not invent anything himself even here; he only combines together higgledy-piggledy various passages from the *Iconologia*. This is what he writes:

> Il tripode o lettorino [i.e. the reading-desk] significa la fucina dell'eloquenza essendo dove del continuo concorrono a lavorare fabbri di gran valore e donde alla giornata vi escono opere di tutta perfetione—si può dir casa ove sempre sono chi va & chi viene che però il principe della Romana eloquenza diede alla cattedra di Isocrate giusto nome così dicendo *Domus Isocratis quasi ludus quidam atque officina dicendi*.

Ripa states under Scienza (p. 552) that 'il deschetto overo tripode, è inditio della Scienza'. Under Poesia (p. 492) he praises the Accademia degli Insensati and Cesare Crispoldo in particular:

> Gentilhuomo di rara Dottrina, & varia disciplina, nella nobil Casa del quale, come già i Platonici nella Villa d'Academo, gli Academici Insensati si radunano, & ben si potrebbe alla sua casa dare quell'Epiteto, che il Prencipe della Romana eloquenza diede alla casa d'Isocrate Illustre Orator d'Athene: *Domus Isocratis quasi ludus quidam atque officina dicendi*. . . . Si come dunque è stata tenuta la casa d'Isocrate fucina dell'eloquenza, così hora la casa del Crispoldo è tenuta fucina d'eloquenza, & d'ogni arte liberale, ove concorrono a lavorare fabbri di gran valore & d'onde alla giornata n'escono opere di tutta perfettione, & eccellenza.

Pianta, having thus maltreated the syntax of this passage from Ripa, concludes: 'Porta la cartella perciochè siccome in quella si scrive e con la spongia si leva il scritto, così l'ignoranza essendo coperta da oscuramento viene a levar & nettar quella negrezza per via degli studi come una spongia.' One may feel sure that this incoherent speech is Pianta's own. Ripa only says under Dottrina: 'Lo Scettro con il Sole è inditio del Dominio, che ha la Dottrina sopra li horrori della notte dell'ignoranza.'

The 'diceria' (saying) in the 'riquadro' (panel) is the word FORNITO formed by capital letters scattered and interwoven in the decoration of the panel. Pianta gives the following explanation: 'Fidia antico & nobilissimo scultore disegnò l'occasione con diversi geroglifici, ma sopratutti mi serve di notare quello con darli le ali a i piedi.' Here he is shortening Ripa's passage (Occasione, p. 449): 'Fidia antico, & nobilissimo scultore, disegnò l'Occasione; Donna ignuda, etc. . . . con piedi alati . . .' The Venetian sculptor goes on: 'Onde Ausonio poeta, sopra questa statua quasi interrogando dice: *Quid talaria habes? volucris sum. Mercurius quae.*' Ripa had written: 'Onde Ausonio Poeta sopra questa statua di Fidia, il quale vi scolpì anco quella della penitenza, come che spesse volte ci pentiamo della perduta occasione, a dichiaratione dell'una, & l'altra statua fece questo bell'epigramma.' The whole text of Ausonius's epigram follows. Pianta continues: 'Sicché intendeva l'accennato poeta che l'occasione si deve prevenire aspettandola al passo & non seguirla per pigliarla quando ha volte le spalle; perché passa velocemente con piedi alati.' Ripa: 'L'occasione si deve prevenire, aspettandola al passo, & non seguirla per pigliarla quando ha volte le spalle; perché passa velocemente; con piedi alati posasi sopra la ruota, che perpetuamente si gira.' The sculptor concludes on his own account: 'Io per stendardo mi appiglio a questo & vedendo che l'occasione per me già se ne era andata non volse corrergli dietro altrimenti ma volsi farlo sapere che se ne era sfuggita dicendo: FORNITO.' Lacchin explains this 'fornito' as a synonym of the present-day 'servito' ironically used ('serves you right!'). The same panel has the inscription: *Famam estendere factis est virtutis opus.* One finds it in Ripa under Attione virtuosa (p. 50): '*sed famam extendere factis, hoc virtutis opus*, dice Virgilio nel decimo dell'Eneide'.

The following hieroglyph represents a naked youth seen from behind; a rope fastened to a big nail and hooks twists behind his head and behind his waist, at which point a hammer is inserted; below, a loaf and a jug (Fig. 7). Is this the image of a miner, a prisoner, a man under torture? The back of the youth is riddled with wormholes, almost as Saint Sebastian's chest with

arrows. We learn to our astonishment from the accompanying speech that Pianta intended to represent here the Distinction between Good and Evil. In Ripa the Distintione del Bene, & del Male, is symbolized by 'una donna d'età virile, vestita con habito grave con la destra mano terrà un crivello, & con la sinistra un rastrello da villa'. Ripa explains: 'Pierio [Valeriano] prese il Crivello per geroglifico dell'huomo di perfetta sapienza, perche uno stolto non è atto a sapere discernere il bene dal male, né sa investigare li secreti della natura, onde era questo Proverbio appresso Galeno, *Stulti ad cribrum*.' Pianta's speech begins from this point: 'Era per proverbio appresso Galeno: *Stulti ad cribrum*, il che si vuole inferire per geroglifico dell'uomo di perfetta sapienza perché uno stolto non è atto a discernere il bene dal male né sa investigare li secreti della natura & è con occupazione continua nelle vili, & ne' pensieri biasimevoli.' The last portion of Pianta's sentence is taken from the allegory of Accidia (Ripa, p. 6), but the sculptor has fitted it badly, because the words 'nelle vili' lack a proper reference. To find it out one has to have recourse to the text of the *Iconologia*:

> Accidia: Donna che stia a giacere per terra, & a canto starà un asino similmente a giacere, il qual animale si soleva adoperar da gl'Egittij per mostrare la lontananza del pensiero dalle cose sacre, e religiose, con occupatione continua nelle vili, & in pensieri biasimevoli, come racconta Pierio Valeriano.

The attribute of the rope is also taken from the *Iconologia*: 'Accidia: Donna vecchia, brutta, che stia a giacere, con la mano tenghi una corda. . . . La corda denota, che l'Accidia lega, & vince gl'huomini, e li rende inhabili ad operare.' Pianta: 'La corda che seco tiene volta si dimostra che l'accidia lega & vince gl'huomini & li rende inhabili ad operare.' He goes on:

> Il martello & il chiodo significano che la necessità è l'essere della cosa in modo che non possa stare altrimenti dicendosi volgarmente, quando non è più tempo da terminare una cosa con consiglio, esser fitto il chiodo; intendendo la necessità delle operazioni che è il voltargli le spalle.

Ripa, s.v. Necessità (p. 432):

> Donna, che nella mano destra tiene un martello, & nella sinistra un mazzo di chiodi. Necessità è un essere della cosa in modo, che non possa stare altrimenti, & pone ovunque si ritrova un laccio indissolubile, & per ciò si rassomiglia ad uno, che porta il martello da una mano, & dall'altra li chiodi, dicendosi volgarmente quando non è più tempo da terminare una cosa con consiglio, essere fitto il chiodo: intendendo la necessità dell'operationi.

The phrase 'che è il voltargli le spalle' (i.e. to fly) which follows in Pianta, is one of his usual ill-suited additions. Indeed if Pianta's speeches had to be transformed into marble sculptures, one would have as a result jumbles of unrelated parts, like ancient statues badly restored, or a game of consequences. A characteristic, this one, which ought to recommend him to the surrealists. Let us continue reading him: 'Il pane significa qualsivoglia opera operata a buon fine non restando mai infruttuosa.—Et il vaso denota che l'allegrezza per lo più non si cela & volentieri si communica come proprio è per la bontà del vino.' This last sentence is in Ripa s.v. Allegrezza (p. 17): 'Il vaso di christallo pieno di vino vermiglio . . . dimostra che l'Allegrezza per lo più non si cela, & volentieri si communica.' It is difficult to see how this confused allegory of Pianta's should symbolize the Distinction between Good and Evil.

Round the following panel one reads the motto ET ITERUM carved in Gothic letter; the explanation runs:

> Quel grande padre di eloquenza, Cicerone, quasi specchio di sentenza con breve motteggiare apre la bocca dicendo: *Et iusta omnia decora sunt, iniusta contra*. Qui ne volse dar ad intender che ad un animo eccelso & invitto in ogni cosa che si fa & si dice con ordine & modo, nel quale vi è la modestia e la temperanza & ogni mitigazione di perturbazione di animo nelle quali cose si conviene[10] il decoro, si cavino con la lanterna a modo di Diogene cercando e prevedendo.

Ripa, s.v. Decoro (p. 134):

> [Il Decoro & l'honesto nasce . . .] o dalla grandezza, & fortezza d'animo eccelso, & invitto in ogni cosa, che si fa & si dice con ordine, & modo, nel quale vi è la modestia, la temperanza, & ogni mitigatione di perturbatione di animo, nelle quali cose si contiene il Decoro. . . . Onde Marco Tullio. . . . *Et iusta omnia decora sunt iniusta contra ut turpia sic indecora*.

Pianta adds: 'Non è però lecito ad un uomo savio che la lingua sia più veloce della mente (*Linguam praeire animo non permittendum*) diceva Omero.' Here the sculptor has been misled by a wrong interpretation of Ripa's text, who under Decoro, p. 135, after having quoted Thersites as an instance of a voluble tongue,

10. Such is Lacchin's reading. But Ripa has 'contiene'. Lacchin remarks: '[Il Pianta] dà saggio di sua erudizione dicendo proprio a questo luogo, non ne sappiamo la ragione, che le cose giuste sono decorose e che così non è delle ingiuste: parole tolte da Cicerone.' The erudition is not Pianta's, but Ripa's, and it is not the first time that the reason of Pianta's allusion escapes common sense.

and his contrary, Ulysses, measured and cautious in his language, says of the latter:

> conoscendo egli, come saggio, & accorto, che per osservare il Decoro d'un huomo savio, la lingua non deve esser più veloce della mente, devendosi pensare molto bene, come si habbia a ragionare. *Linguam praeire animo non permittendum*. Disse Chilone Lacedemoniese, & molto ben pensare ci si deve, etc.

That full stop after the Latin quotation (the five volumes edition, Perugia 1765, of the *Iconologia*, vol. II, p. 128, has correctly a comma) has misled Pianta who has attributed the quotation to Homer, who had been referred to before, without thinking that Homer wrote in Greek, not in Latin, and that Ripa used to quote Greek texts in the original, as he does further on, on the same page. However at last Pianta appears to have something personal to say: 'Adunque se prima non si sarà fatto l'opera non devo dir se non ET ITERUM come sta là attorno, dico, principio un'altra volta.'

The figure of Furore is one of the most powerful of Pianta's: a frantic youth, his eyes blindfolded, his chest lashed by a chain (Fig. 8), seems on the point of bursting like the cannon which together with a bundle of arms and a flask (Fig. 9) (which one would imagine containing gunpowder, instead of vinegar, as Pianta specifies), forms his support. This figure offers the best illustration of that violence of conception and execution which redeems many imperfections of this artist. Fixed to the wall like a nailed hawk, this youth breathes a grim and sombre beauty in his agony, the beauty of Milton's indomitable fallen angel, majestic though in ruin:

> Dark'n'd so, yet shon
> Above them all th'Arch Angel; but his face
> Deep scars of Thunder had intrencht, and care
> Sat on his faded cheek, but under Browes
> Of dauntless courage, and considerate Pride
> Waiting revenge. . . .

The mouth, with lips tightly stretched on clenched teeth, seems to roar like a wild animal's. The wood, which on the ribs of the youth simulates a swollen sea, is elsewhere roughly cut, split on the right shoulder, riddled with wormholes, and worn with age, so that this figure has all the appearance of a weather-beaten figurehead of a ship doomed to founder. The commentary on this symbol is, as usual, taken from Ripa, to whose illustration Pianta is this time closer than on other occasions:

> Mentre andava Virgilio versiferando e avendo posto la punta della penna in carta lancia con mano così scrivendo: *Iamque faces, saxa volant, furor arma*

ministrat. Il furore non è altro che cecità di mente del tutto priva del lume intellettuale, che porta l'uomo a far ogni cosa fuor di ragione. Si lega per dimostrare che il furore è una specie di pazzia la quale deve esser legata o unita dalla ragione. Ha la fascia legata agli occhi per mostrare che s'arresta l'intelletto quando il furore prende il dominio nell'anima. Posa sopra un monte di armi di più sorte quasi che in tempo di discordia le somministri a coloro in diversi modi che hanno l'animo acceso alla vendetta. E' orribile nell'aspetto perché un uomo uscito di se stesso per subito impeto dell'ira piglia natura e sembianza di fiera o d'altra e più spaventevole cosa, e tanto maggiormente quando voria vendicarsi e non può massime contro la virtù che non teme niuno per grande che sia.

Ripa (p. 233):

> Furore, Huomo che mostri rabbia nel viso, etc. La fascia legata a gli occhi mostra, che privo resta l'intelletto quando il Furore prende il dominio dell'anima, non essendo altro il Furore, che cecità di mente del tutto priva del lume intellettuale, che porta l'huomo a far ogni cosa fuori di ragione. . . . Il Furore è ministro della guerra, come accenna Virgilio in quel verso, *Iamque faces, & saxa volant, furor arma ministrat.* E perciò il medesimo altrove lo dipinse sedente sopra un monte d'armi di più sorte, quasi che in tempo di guerra le somministri a coloro, che hanno l'animo acceso alla vendetta. Si lega per dimostrare, che il Furore è una specie di pazzia, la quale deve esser legata, e unita dalla raggione. E' horribile nell'aspetto, perche un huomo uscito di se stesso, per subito impeto dell'ira, piglia natura, e sembianza di fiera, o d'altra cosa più spaventevole.

This last sentence is linked by Pianta with a recollection of what Ripa says s.v. Virtù (p. 671), who 'non è mai abbattuta da qual si voglia avversario'. He gives attributes to Furore which are not listed by Ripa under that personification:

> Si gli da il vaso a foggia di fiasco pieno d'aceto per segno d'amaritudine e dolore essendo & vedendo essere conosciuto & ci si rabbia quasi in sdegno e ne muore a somiglianza del serpe.—Et il cristallo del vaso significa l'allegrezza che hanno certune faccie che sono con cristallo e vetro significati.[11]

Ripa mentions as an attribute of Amaritudine (p. 20) 'un favo di mele, dal quale si vede germogliare una pianta d'Assentio': it would indeed be impossible to give an idea of vinegar with a figure. Allegrezza in

11. Such is Lacchin's reading.

Ripa (p. 17) holds a crystal vase in her right hand. One fails to understand how Pianta's passage may be appropriate here, because one does not see the crystal, as the flask is wickered, and on the other hand there is little occasion for mirth in this case. One finds however in Ripa the snake which dies of rage (p. 234, and especially p. 235 under Furore implacabile: 'nessun Furore si può comparare a quello dell'aspido, il quale subito, che si sente tocco, così bestialmente s'infuria, che non si satia fin che non habbia avvelenato col morso chi l'ha offeso, overo di rabbia non si muora come dice Euthimio'). We find in Ripa (p. 235) also the 'rotte catene che dalle braccia, & dalle gambe gli pendono' which we see in Pianta's carving: they 'denotano che il furore è indomito, & poche sono quelle cose che a lui facciano resistenza'.

The figures of Furore and Spia are on either side of what Pianta calls 'Magnificenza nella libreria': a *trompe-l'œil* of such brilliant execution, down to the smallest details of the vellum, the paper, the inkstand, the quill and the spectacles, that we cannot refrain a gasp of admiration (Fig. 8).

> Magnificenza è una virtù la quale consiste intorno all'operare cose grandi e d'importanza come nell'edificar tempi, palazzi & altre cose di maraviglia, tra quelle mirabile & commendata nelli Tempi Antichi fu quella di Ptolomeo Filadelfo Re d'Egitto desideroso dunque di raccogliere tutti i libri che si trovavano nel mondo & acquistare ogni volume degno d'industria non guardando ad alcuna spesa sì che alla prima instruttione raccolse 20.000 milla volumi, di lì poco tempo arrivò alla somma di 50.000 milla oltre tanti altri che sono stati portati dalla Giudea & interpretati dalli 70 huomini di Hebreo in greco. Dove che potiamo dir quel verso: *Vose literata & articulata debito modo pronunciata, gloriosa dappertutto.*

The beginning of this passage is taken from Ripa (Magnificenza, p. 383): 'La Magnificenza è una virtù, la quale consiste intorno all'operar cose grandi, e d'importanza . . . l'effetto della Magnificenza è l'edificar tempi, palazzi, & altre cose di maraviglia.' Ripa quotes as an instance Augustus who found Rome brick and left it marble. But of the Library as a symbol, and of the one collected in Alexandria by Ptolemy Philadelphus we find mention only in the additions of the abate Cesare Orlandi to the 1764 edition of *Iconologia* (vol. I, p. 249), so that Pianta must have got from elsewhere the after all common information about the Library of Alexandria; and as to the quotation which concludes this section, it has a sufficiently popular character to allow us to see in it a personal trait.

Also the figure of the Spy coincides with that of Ripa; Ripa's is the idea of a man muffled in a cloak, his hat lowered over his eyes, with the lantern and the felt shoe, which Pianta has carved very skilfully, as if the same furious wind swept over the wrapped figure shrinking within the cloak and the raving one which writhes naked on the other side. This portion of Pianta's decoration is one of the most telling examples of the Baroque spirit, for its realism and its vehemence of feelings and attitudes: the figure of the Spy is almost Goyesque (see a similar one in the crowd of the *San Isidro Pilgrimage* in the Prado).
Of Spia and Curiosità Pianta says:

Grande fu quell'anagramma riferito dall'intrepido Filopono accademico: *Virtutem et vitam alterius livore mormordet* [sic] *pallentique suo virus in ore terit.*—Dice adunque che tutto il suo studio non consiste in altro se non di tradire & di assassinare qualsivoglia amico quantunque caro gli sia, & questo proprio è di coloro i quali non curano né stimano l'honore loro e questo procede da un sfrenato desiderio di curiosità che cercano saper più di quello che devono; tiene coperto il viso perché chi fa tale esercitio se ne va incognito posiaché da se stesso si arroscisse né si lassa conoscere da niuno & però si suol dir di quelli i quali risplendono di onorata & chiara fama che possono andar con la fronte scoperta.

Ripa, under Spia (p. 591):

Huomo vestito nobilmente, tenghi coperto quasi tutto il viso col capello [*sic*], & con la cappa, o ferraiolo che dir vogliamo, il quale sia tutto contesto d'occhi, orecchie & lingue, terrà con la sinistra mano una lanterna: i piedi saranno alati . . . tiene coperto il viso, perche chi fa tale esercitio, se ne va incognito, ne si lassa conoscere da niuno, per poter meglio essercitar l'offitio suo . . . non curano né stimano l'honore loro, & non hanno riguardo di tradire, & assassinare qual si voglia amico, quantunque caro gli sia; come anco potiamo dire che il tener coperto il viso, dinota che essendo la spia huomo vituperoso, & infame, non può come gli huomini d'honore tenerlo scoperto, & però si suol dire da quelli, i quali risplendono di honorata, & chiara fama: posso andar con la fronte scoperta . . . simili costumi acconciamente descrive l'Intrepido Academico Filopono in questo suo Anagramma . . . *Virtutem, et vitam alterius livore mormordet* [sic], *Pallentique suo virus in ore terit.*

Pianta has inserted also a passage taken from the chapter on Curiosità (p. 129): 'La Curiosità è desiderio

sfrenato di coloro, che cercano sapere, più di quello che devono.'

La lanterna che seco porta—*Pianta explains*—significa che il curioso non solo cerca di sapere di giorno ma ancor la notte, pure sarebbe da lodar se questi tali facessero a modo di Diogene per cercar buoni costumi andassero vagando in ogni tempo.

Ripa (p. 594):

La lanterna . . . significa che non solo si fa la spia di giorno, ma anco di notte: se Diogene portava la lanterna di dì per cercare un huomo, lo spione cerca gli huomini di notte.

Pianta:

La scarpa alata dinota la diligente & presta cura di coloro in veder & saper questo & quello dappertutto che però gli dà le ale ai piedi come a Mercurio, che secondo la finzione dei poeti conduceva l'anime dannate alle infernali pene così essi con le sue parole conducono le genti a varii precipitii.

Ripa (p. 594):

I piedi alati dinotano, che alla spia conviene essere diligente, & presta, altrimente non farebbe profitto se non fosse sollecita, & veloce come Mercurio alato, il quale secondo la fintione de Poeti . . . conduceva l'anime dannate alle infernali pene, così li spioni conducono li rei al supplitio mediante le parole.

The next allegory, Scandalo e Scrupolo, blends two of Ripa's symbols, taking inspiration from the first of them for the carving. Ripa says that Scandolo is represented in the aspect of 'un vecchio con bocca aperta con i capelli artificiosamente ricciuti, & barba bianca, l'habito vago, & con ricamo di grande spesa, terrà con la destra mano in atto publico un mazzo di carte da giocare, con la sinistra un leuto, & alli piedi vi sarà un flauto, & un libro di musica aperto': all these characteristics we find in Pianta's gay old dog (Fig. 10), who however, instead of the legs and the left hand, has repulsive stumps. Pianta begins thus:

Andava pensando Seneca un giorno tra sé & dopo lungo pensiero stava soprapreso non volendo così a bell'agio dar sì arguta sentenza eppur se ne stava per proferir la parola & ecco però sopraggiunge un suo cordialissimo amico Hippolito e dice: 'Olà Seneca', in questo atto non rispose, sopraggiunse l'amico, o Maestro Seneca, all'hora sentendosi in questo atto pungere di obbligo, voltossi dicendo: 'al giovane l'allegrezza, al vecchio si convien severo il ciglio': *Laetitia iuvenem frons decet tristis senem.*

A strange anecdote that Pianta has embroidered over a

quotation made by Ripa s.v. Scandolo (p. 551).[12] I shall now give in their proper order Ripa's passages, and then I shall continue with Pianta:

Ripa:

> Si dipinge vecchio lo Scandolo, percioche sono di maggior consideratione gli errori commessi dal vecchio, che dal giovane.... Il tenere la bocca aperta significa, che non solo con i fatti, ma con le parole fuor dei termini giusti, & ragionevoli, si dà grandemente Scandolo, & si fa con esse cadere altrui in qualche mala operatione, con danno, & con ruina grandissima, come ben dimostra S. Tomaso in 2.2. quaest. 43, art. primo dicendo, che Scandolo è detto o fatto meno dritto, che dà occasione a gl'altri di ruina. I capelli ricciuti, la barba bianca artifitiosamente acconcia, l'habito vago, & gli stromenti sopradetti dimostrano che nel vecchio è di molto Scandalo il metter in disparte le cose gravi & attendere alle lascivie, conviti, giuochi, feste, canti & altre vanità.... Perche sì come dice Seneca in Hippolito atto 2, 'Al giovane l'allegrezza, Al vecchio si convien severo il ciglio. *Laetitia iuvenem frons decet tristis senem.*' Il tenere, ch'ogn'un veda, le carte da giocare è chiaro segno come habbiamo detto di Scandolo, e particolarmente nel vecchio, essendo che non solo non fugge il giuoco, ma dà materia, che li giovani faccino il medesimo ad imitatione del suo male essempio.

Pianta, after the Seneca quotation, goes on:

> Dando ad intendere secondo la condizione ognuno deve andar contrappesato e S. Tommaso 2.2 questione 43 articolo primo dicendo che scandolo è detto o fatto meno dritto che dà occasione agli altri di ruina. Si forma vecchio lo scandolo percioché sono di maggior considerazione gli errori commessi dal vecchio che dal giovine. Il tener la bocca aperta significa che non solo con i fatti ma con le parole fuor dei termini giusti & ragionevoli si dà grandemente scandolo.—I capelli ricciuti e la barba artificiosamente acconciata, l'abito vago e gli stromenti musicali dimostra[13] che nel vecchio è di molto scandolo metter in disparte le cose gravi & attender alle lascive come giuochi, feste, canti e altre vanità. Il tenere che ognun veda le carte da giocare è chiaro segno come s'è detto[14] di mal esempio e particolarmente nei vecchi dando materia agli giovini di far il simile.

12. These are words of the Nurse to Hippolytus while exhorting him to a more youthful behaviour. Lacchin remarks: '*Tutto ciò puoi leggere nel secondo atto dell'Ippolito di Seneca*': obviously he has not grasped Pianta's licence.
13. Lacchin's reading; but it ought to be 'dimostrano'.
14. Ripa, not Pianta, had said it; but Pianta copies mechanically.

At this point Pianta joins up with what Ripa says under Scropolo (pp. 556-7): 'e da qui nasce il scrupolo essendo che chi ha qualche rimorso di conseguenza[15] sempre ha timore della giustizia di Dio che non gli dia condegno castigo'.

Ripa:

> [Scropolo] si dipinge timoroso essendo che chi ha qualche rimorso di Coscienza sempre habbia timore della Giustizia di Dio, che non li dia il condegno castigo.

As for Scrupolo's attribute, the sieve, Ripa says:

> Tiene il crivello essendo un istromento che separa il buono dal cattivo... a guisa della Synteresi quale va considerando, & eleggendo le artioni buone, & virtuose dalle cattive & vitiose, restando le cattive nel ventilabro della conscienza.

Pianta:

> Porta il crivello il scrupolo, essendo un istrumento che separa il buono dal cattivo sicché a guisa della synteresi va considerando & eleggendo le attioni buone e virtuose dalle cattive & vitiose e si vede il scandolo esser chiompo[16] per il ventilabro della conoscenza.[17]

Finally Pianta adds a rope in order to bind together his ill-contrived symbols: 'la fune che tiene legato il crivello via del mezzo dassi ad intendere che il scandolo e il scropolo quasi sempre sono uniti'.

Next symbol shows an abbé with long hair and a skullcap who is looking from behind a broken lattice window; a guitar, a little flask, a crumpled book (Aristotle) complete this baroque figure which is meant to stand for Piacere Onesto.

Ripa represents Piacere Honesto in the aspect of Venus dressed in black (p. 487):

> Per significar il Piacer honesto, Venere vien chiamata da gl'Antichi Nera, non per altra cagione, secondo che scrive Pausania nell'Arcadia, se non perche alcuni piaceri da gl'huomini si soglion pigliar copertamente, & honestamente di notte, a differenza de gl'altri animali....
> Dipingesi col cingolo, come è descritta Venere da Homero in più luoghi dell'Iliade, per mostrare, che Venere all'hora è honesta, e lodevole, quando sia ristretta dentro a gl'ordini delle leggi.

Although a few phrases of this passage recur in

15. Thus Lacchin, but if Pianta has followed Ripa's text, the reading should be 'coscienza'.
16. In the Venetian dialect *chiompo* stands for *ciompo, cionco, monco*, maimed.
17. Thus Lacchin, but Ripa has here: 'conscienza'.

Pianta's speech, his symbol is altogether different. Pianta says: 'Anticamente in più luoghi dell'Iliade quel grande Homero & anco come scrive Pausania nell'Arcadia fingevano il piacere honesto niente esser molto dissimile di differenza dagli altri piaceri & è lodevole quando sia ristretto dentro agli ordini della legge.' But for the image and the rest of his speech Pianta has turned to the symbol of Diletto in Ripa (pp. 150 ff.); we find there the figure of a 'giovinetto di età di sedeci anni, di vago & bellissimo aspetto . . . in capo haverà una ghirlanda di rose . . . & al collo una collana d'oro . . . terrà con la sinistra mano una lira appoggiata al fianco sinistro, & la destra alzata con il plettro . . . dalla parte destra vi sarà un libro intitolato *Aristotelis*, & un libro di musica aperto'. But Pianta has had recourse also to that part of *Iconologia* which deals with the ages of man (p. 185), and particularly to the passage dealing with old age (the fourth age) because this one takes delight in virtue. 'La quarta età', Ripa says, 'è regolata dal Sole per haver lui il quarto loco nel mondo, & perche questo è il Pianeta più perfetto, & di maggior valore amatore dell'honestà, & d'ogni altra attione virtuosa.' By kneading together Venus and an abbé, a young man and an old one, we get as a result this singular cento:

> et posiaché il nome di piacer si dia ad ogni sorta di gusto, non di meno non operandosi con quel diletto della virtù che si deve nelle operationi nostre & non riusciscono, & questo si vede chiaro che la quarta età è regolata dal sole per aver lui il quarto loco nel mondo e perché questo è il pianeta più perfetto & di maggior valore, amatore dell'honestà e di ogni altra atione virtuosa. Così parimente deve essere cosa perspicace il piacer di essa sendo in questo temperata.

As for the lyre, Pianta writes: 'Seco porta la lira per la sodezza del suono percioché chi attende a cose virtuose deve haver un sodo & accordato rimbombo, operatione che per l'incostanza molte volte si conviene il detto di David: *Mei autem pene moti sunt pedes.*' Ripa sees in the lyre the symbol of hearing, and Pianta combines this allusion with what he has found under Piacere on p. 486:

> L'Arpa, per la dolcezza del suono, si dice haver conformità con Venere, e con le Gratie. . . . Gli stivaletti d'oro convengono al piacere, per mostrare che l'oro lo tiene in poco conto, se non gli serve per sodisfarne gli appetiti, overo perche pigliandosi i piedi molte volte per l'incostanza, secondo il Salmo, *Mei autem pene moti sunt pedes*, si scuopre, che volentieri s'impiega a novità, & non mai stima molto una cosa medesima.

The explanation offered by Pianta for the book of Aristotle differs from Ripa's under Diletto (p. 154: 'Il libro intitolato *Aristotelis* significa il gusto, & il Diletto del Filosofare, etc.'). Pianta writes: 'Il libro di Aristotele significa sicome quello è oscuro & dificile per la testura di parole da esser inteso così la virtù per via del piacere con la tessitura di composizioni deve esser ventigliata & ornata.' Here Pianta has put to use a passage from the symbol of Filosofia in Ripa (p. 209): '. . . quasi che non bastasse, che la Filosofia nelle cose occulte di natura fosse per se stessa oscura, se anco non le aggiungevano maggior oscurità con difficile testura di parole . . .' And a little before, in a passage we have already seen utilized by Pianta in the foreword: '. . . Aristotele con termini oscuri, & difficile testura di parole'. The broken lattice window is explained thus: 'Gettar a terra & spezzar il balcone significano chi attende a cose virtuose rompe qualsivoglia vizio che è come finestra o muraglia in habitatione della virtù & contrastato come un leone per la magnanimità e fortezza dell'animo suo contro chi essersi voglia.' This is a cento of Ripa's commonplaces: (p. 50, Attione virtuosa) 'il virtuoso con l'attioni sue è sempre contrario, & combatte continuamente con il vitio suo perpetuo nimico'; (p. 671) [la Virtù] 'abbatte continuamente il vitio'; (p. 134) 'la pelle di Leone simbolo del valore della virtù e fortezza d'animo, la quale assegnar soleano a quelli che . . . si fossero mostrati generosi, forti, e magnanimi' (see also p. 240, the lion compared to a generous man). Pianta concludes rather incoherently that the lattice windows (a symbol of vice!) 'danno ad intender la chiarezza che ha con sé la virtù & è risplendente come un cristalo' (Ripa, p. 50: 'l'Attion virtuosa fa che l'huomo sia chiaro & risplendente', p. 485: 'gioventù . . . come un nuovo & mondo cristallo'). 'Il collare qui è segno di animoso difensore & dà indizio di esser sollecito & pronto a zuffarsi senza tema in difesa del suo onore.' Ripa, on the symbol of Roma, p. 317: 'alli piedi davanti un cane . . . con un collare al collo. . . . Il cane . . . sarà qui segno d'animoso Defensore . . . il collare essendo armatura difensiva del cane dà inditio che l'Imperadore stava provisto sempre, & pronto azzuffarsi con lupi famelici senza tema del morso loro in difesa della Romana Chiesa.'
As one sees, Pianta rambles from one into another vice, from one into another virtue, and recollections from Ripa throng in his head and create a confusion which is all but a labyrinth.[18] And what about the flask?

---

18. Lacchin may be excused if in this confusion he has taken a dog's collar for a collar of lace, 'un collare di pizzo, distinzione tutta propria del cavaliere, che è sollecito e combatte in difesa del suo onore'. But no collar of lace is to be found in the carving; perhaps he has seen one in the abbé's bands, or else he has mistaken the ornament under the window for one.

Pianta fails to account for its presence, so we may as well give up trying to find an explanation ourselves.

And who is that preacher who, while holding a mask in his right hand, points his finger in the direction of an hourglass, and has before him what seems a joint from a cannibals' long-pig, a severed human foot, under which we read in a stone: *Inventor et sculptor idem Planta faciebat*? This signature, and the foot, has led imaginative but ignorant guide-books to see here a portrait of the artist. But this telamon which is also a tarot is intended instead to represent 'Cicerone in difesa della scultura', and his canting arms is not the foot, but the wart on the right cheek, Cicero's chick-pea (Fig. 11).

It is Cicero who speaks in the attitude Eloquence has in Ripa (p. 175): 'nella man destra tien un libro, con la sinistra mano alzata, & con l'indice, che habbia il secondo dito dell'istessa mano steso, & presso a'suoi piedi vi sarà un libro, & sopra esso un horologio da polvere'. Cicero, however, speaks as a ghost, because he begins by alluding to an event which took place a few centuries after his death:

Cominciando Emiliano a guerreggiar da putto, fu capitano di Decio imperadore in Mesia, scacciò gli Sciti, dopo la vittoria fu chiamato imperadore dall'esercito, scrisse al Senato di esser stato eletto imperadore, promise di liberar la Tracia, la Mesopotamia e di recuperare l'Armenia, intanto i soldati Alpini elessero Valeriano—l'esercito di Emiliano udito ciò per non distruggersi in guerra civile tra loro l'ammazzarono verso Spoleto. Io Marco Tullio al paragone di questo fatto sin da putto nell'eloquenza e nell'oratoria sottigliai l'ingegno e come guerriero & capitano servii, ma a chi non uno solo come Emiliano. . . .

We find the anecdote in Ripa, under Roma Eterna, an image derived from a 'medaglia di Caio Giulio Emiliano Imperadore col titolo *Roma eterna* posta da Adolfo Occone sotto l'anno del Signore 254' (p. 309):

Cominciò Giulio Emiliano a guerreggiar da putto, fu Capitano di Decio Imperadore in Mesia, scacciò gli Sciti, doppo la vittoria fu chiamato Imperadore dall'esercito, scrisse al Senato d'essere stato eletto Imperadore, promise di liberar la Tracia, la Mesopotamia, di recuperar l'Armenia, intanto i soldati Alpini elessero Valeriano; l'essercito d'Emiliano udito ciò, per non distruggersi in guerra civile l'ammazzò verso Spoleto.

In Pianta's speech Cicero draws a parallel between Æmilianus's career and his own. Let us resume the quotation:

. . . come guerriero & capitano servii, ma a chi non uno solo come Emiliano, ma la mia servitù fu tale che la repubblica romana mi elesse principe & padre dell'eloquenza, vedendomi così honorato promisse di guerreggiar la Tracia cioè debellare li errori dei filosofi antichi, render vinta la Mesopotamia, il discorso retorico, & recuperar dalli sconciamenti della lingua latina per l'Armenia. Altri oratori non io solo volsero levare il principato. Come dunque non potrò come guerriero dell'eloquenza difendere una regina sì grande come è la scultura? Non mi tenessero superbo per lodarmi poiché la troppa umiltà diventa vizio. La pratica non consiste solo per l'operazione ma anche per l'intelligenza delle cose, essendo dunque come due estremità la teorica e la pratica si congiungono, non differiscono, in un mezzo e punto solo che è cognizione.

We have little doubt that other portions of this speech must have been put together with fragments from Ripa, as this latter one is: (Ripa, Pratica, p. 495) 'La Pratica versa intorno all'operationi. . . . Essendo dunque come due estremità la Teorica, e la Prattica si congiungono nondimeno insieme in un mezo, e punto solo che è la cognitione del bene, vero, o non vero, maggiore o minore. . . . Onde è la verità de i pareri fra gli uomini dotti, & ignoranti, nobili, & plebei, servi, e liberi, ricchi, e poveri, vecchi, e giovani, huomini, e donne credendosi da una parte alle sentenze de'sapienti, dall'altra a i proverbij del volgo, etc.' We shall see further on how Pianta puts this last passage to wrong use. After the words: 'e punto solo che è cognizione', Pianta proceeds to the symbol of Sculpture. He says: 'Gli antichi formavano la scultura una donna di età matura, con gravità nel volto poiché l'arte tiene in se stessa imperial maestà come ancora non poteva niuno scolpire se non era cittadino romano.' Ripa describes Scultura as a 'giovane bella'; it is rather Architecture he represents as a 'donna di matura età', and art in general as 'di età consistente', 'di età virile', 'perché un artefice giovane non può havere esperienza di molte cose': and s.v. Arte he speaks of painting and sculpture 'arti nobilissime'. This may explain Pianta's incoherence, for he adds immediately after the preceding passage:

La significavano giovane bella con l'acconciatura di testa semplice e con vari istrumenti necessari per l'esercizio suo; ma poco ornato perché mentre con la fantasia l'uomo s'occupa in conformare le cose dell'arte con quelle della natura non può impiegarsi molto nella cura delle cose del corpo. Il ramo del lauro che nella severità del verno conserva la verdezza, così la scultura nell'andar degli anni si conserva bella e viva contro la malignità del tempo.

Il vestito d'oro significa per il diletto e si mantiene per magnificenza.

All this more or less follows Ripa (Scoltura, p. 555):

Giovane bella, con l'acconciatura della testa semplice, & negligente, sopra la quale sarà un ramo di lauro verde, si farà vestita di drappo di vago colore, con la destra mano sopra al capo di una statua di sasso, nell'altra tenghi varij istromenti necessarj per l'essercitio di quest'arte, co' piedi posati sopra un ricco tappeto. Si dipinge la scoltura di faccia piacevole, ma poco ornata, perche mentre con la fantasia l'huomo s'occupa in conformare le cose dell'arte con quelle della natura, facendo l'una, & l'altra somigliante, non può impiegarsi molto nella cura delle cose del corpo. Il ramo del lauro, che nella severità del verno conserva la verdezza delle sue frondi, dimostra, che la scoltura nell'opere sue, si conserva bella, & viva contro alla malignità del tempo. Il vestito di drappo di vago colore, sarà conforme alla scoltura stessa, la quale essercita per diletto, & si mantiene per magnificenza.

The dress of cloth of gold belongs in Ripa to Magnificenza.

Pianta adds the mask among the attributes placing it in Cicero's hand in the same way in which Imitatione holds it in Ripa (p. 273) in her left hand, whereas she holds a bunch of brushes in her right: these latter signify the imitation which is proper to painting, while the mask signifies the imitation of human actions in comedy. But Pianta thinks of the mask that Fraude holds in the same hand and in the same position in Ripa (p. 232), the mask which indicates that 'la Fraude fa apparire le cose altrimenti da quel che sono', and writes: 'la maschera significa che la pittura a paragone della scultura è Buggia e la scultura la Verità'. It is an obvious case of *Cicero pro domo sua*. Pianta goes then back to Ripa's text on Scoltura in order to explain that human foot which is combined with the effigy of Cicero in such a surrealistic way:

Il piede che tiene appresso significa che sebene la scultura è principalmente oggetto degli occhi può medesimamente dal tatto esser giudicata. Onde Michel Angelo Buonarotti lume e splendore di essa essendogli in vecchiezza per lo continuo studio mancato quasi la luce soleva al tatto palpeggiando le statue e antiche e moderne dar giudizio del prezzo, e del valore.

Ripa (p. 555):

La mano sopra alla statua dimostra, che se bene la scoltura è principalmente oggetto de gli occhi, può

esser medesimamente ancor del tatto.[19] ... Onde sappiamo, che Michel'Angelo Buonarotta, lume, e splendore di essa, essendogli in vecchiezza per lo continuo studio mancata quasi affatto la luce, soleva col tatto palpeggiando le statue, o antiche o moderne che si fossero, dar giuditio, & del prezzo & del valore.

Pianta introduces also a curious attribute, a little table: 'Il tavolino significa il tribunale dove secondo le ragioni dei dotti giudicar si deve.' According to Ripa (p. 369) Law 'siede in Tribunale perche nelli Tribunali sedendo, secondo le leggi da' dotti Leggisti giudicar si deve'.

He mentions then, as Ripa for Scoltura, the carpet: 'Il tappeto fassi intender che dalla magnificenza vien sostenuta la scultura.' Ripa (p. 555): 'Il tapeto sotto i piedi, dimostra come si è detto, che dalla magnificenza vien sostenuta la scoltura.' Pianta proceeds: 'L'orologio significa che le parole sono strumento dell'eloquenza le quali però devono esser adoperate in ordine & misura di tempo—come denotò veramente Platone.' Ripa, under the allegory of Eloquence (p. 175): 'Il libro, & l'horologgio ... è inditio, che le parole sono l'istromento dell'eloquente: le quali però devono essere adoperate in ordine, & misura del tempo.' This 'misura del tempo' has caused Pianta to rehearse what Ripa says about Misura in a moral sense (p. 413): '... noi parimente dobbiamo ponere il Livello [misura] sopra le nostre opere, & con giusta mira bilanciare, & misurare la nostra conditione, e lo stato nostro': this is a test 'se ella è retta, giusta & eguale'. Then it seems to him that the moment has come to insert that passage of Ripa's discourse on Prattica, where he talks of 'verità' as we have seen; and the result is the following *cadavre exquis*: 'Essa sola [i.e. Misura] è bastante a rappresentare la verità dei pareri di uomini dotti, & ignoranti, nobili e plebei, poveri e ricchi, uomini e donne e stato loro' (these last two words from Ripa's passage on p. 413, quoted above). Also the mirror ('Il specchio significa il disegno appartenente a quell'organo interiore dell'animo, il quale fantasia si dice, luogo dell'immaginazione') comes from Ripa (p. 159, s.v. Dissegno): 'Lo specchio significa come il Dissegno appartiene a quell'organo interiore dell'anima, quale fantasia si dice, quasi luoco dell'immagini, percioche nell'immaginativa si serbono tutte le forme delle cose, etc.' Pianta concludes, and we wonder at last whether in his own words: 'Se mi fosse concesso trasmutarmi in tutte le lingue non sarebbero sufficienti in raccontare le sue lodi e grandezze. Vale.'

The following panel shows a ribbon with the inscription: 'Iustitia et judicium correptio sedis eius.' The

---

19. The 1645 text has wrongly 'dal tatto', hence Pianta has completed with 'giudicata'.

'Vigilanza nel riquadro' contains a text which, according to Lacchin, bears witness to the character of the artist: Pianta, who must have been a very active person, 'lo volle indicare lasciandoci un pensiero sulla vigile operosità'. This document is, needless to say, another cento of passages from Ripa:

> Zelante Salomone negli studi & componendo le sue sentenze e *in cantica* respirando dice: *ego dormio et cor meum vigilat.* E il grande filosofo Demostene interrogato come aveva fatto a diventare valente oratore rispose che aveva usato più olio che vino intendendo con quello la vigilanza negli studi. Sicché debonsi intendere nel libro nel quale apprendendosi le scienze si fa l'uomo vigilante e desto a tutti gl'incontri che però Apuleio giura per l'occhio del Sole e della Giustizia significando che l'uomo giusto per propria elettione è operatore e dispensatore così del bene e del male fra sé & altri o fra altri & altri secondo le qualità o di proporzione geometrica ovvero aritmetica. La verità vien detta onnipotente sapiente[20] come quella che rappresenta il giusto ornando la strada per incontrare la giustizia e con la lucerna accesa della vigilanza si viene a far retto giudizio. *Ego sum via et veritas et vita.*

Ripa, s.v. Vigilanza (p. 668):

> Donna con un libro . . . & una lucerna accesa . . . l'una, & l'altra vigilanza, & del corpo, & dell'anima, vien dimostrata dalla presente figura, quella dell'animo nel libro, nel quale apprendendosi le scienze si fa l'huomo vigilante, & desto a tutti gl'incontri della Fortuna . . . però del corpo e dell'animo s'intende il detto della Cantica: *Ego dormio, & cor meum vigilat.*
> (p. 669) E però si legge, che Demostene interrogato, come haveva fatto a diventare valente Oratore, rispose di havere usato più olio che vino intendendo con quello la Vigilanza de gli studij, con questo la sonnolenza delle delitie.

Pianta supplies from Ripa's passage on Giustizia (p. 245):

> Onde Apuleio giura per l'occhio del Sole & della Giustitia insieme. . . . Et perciò potiamo dire che la Giustitia sia quell'habito secondo il quale l'huomo giusto per propria elettione, è operatore, e dispensatore, così del bene, come del male fra se, & altri, o fra altri & altri secondo le qualità o di proportione Geometrica, overo Aritmetica.

He inserts also the following quotations from the allegory of Verità (p. 665): 'Bachilide chiama la

Verità onnipotente sapienza'; 'Si può anco dire, che riguarda il Sole, cioè Dio, senza la cui luce non è Verità alcuna; anzi egli è l'istessa verità, dicendo Christo Nostro Signore, *Ego sum Via, Veritas et Vita.'* The carving (Fig. 12) is usually described as a caricature of Tintoretto; Lacchin, however, sees in it a heroic portrait. It is a racy sculpture which makes one think of one of the gnomes decorating the misericord under the seat of a Gothic choir stall: indeed one is reminded more of the Gothic than of the Baroque by the outline of the composition and the type of realism (there is no jumble of symbols here, but a precise representation of the utensils of a painter's studio, brushes, colour-grinder, roll of drawings, book of rules on which the painter's finger energetically points at a sentence: 'il disegno è il padre della pittura e della scultura e della architettura'). The speech relating to this effigy of 'Giacomo Robusti per la pittura' curiously begins in a key of personal recollection:

> Non potevano far di meglio li scultori quanto trovar quello che ne manco perdonò a sua figlia & l'occasione mi suggerisce a memoria. Dice Petrarca libro II° trattato 3 Cap. XV:[21] sebbene è già gran tempo che ho letto questo ancora che non studiai nel Bò di Padova tuttavia quello che lessi da giovane sempre a memoria la[22] tenevo, così il Petrarca.

This sounds odd, if one bears in mind that Pianta merely was copying from Ripa (s.v. Decoro, p. 142, wrongly numbered 242):

> Alle donne sì che si conviene la gravità nell'andare . . . ma l'huomo deve camminare virilmente col passo maggiore delle donne: Marco Tullio (sì come riferisce il Petrarca, nelle opere Latine lib. 2, trattato 3, cap. 3) vedendo che Tullia sua figliuola caminava un poco più forte che non si conveniva al Decoro d'una donna, & per lo contrario Pisone suo marito più lentamente che non si conveniva ad un huomo, tassò ambedue con un medesimo motto, dicendo in presenza di Pisone suo genero alla figliuola, o così camina da huomo. *Ambula ut vir.* Volendo inferire, che ella doveva caminar piano da femina, & Pisone più presto da huomo.

Exactly like Pianta, whose memory faithfully repeats, not Petrarca however, but Ripa:

> Cicerone vedendo che Tullia sua figliola camminava un poco più forte che non si conveniva al decoro di una donna e per lo contrario Pisone suo marito più

---

20. Should be 'sapienza' in conformity with Ripa's text.

21. Such is Lacchin's reading, but one should read (as Ripa has it correctly) cap. 3 of the Second Book of *Rerum memorandarum.*

22. Thus Lacchin; one would expect 'lo'.

lentamente che non si conveniva ad un huomo tassò ambedue con un medesimo motto dicendo in presenza di Pisone suo genero: *Ambula ut vir*, volendo inferire che essa doveva camminare piano da femina e così cammina—va da uomo e non da donna.

He adds: 'Questo l'ho detto per far stare un poco allegri.' It was high time that there should be a little mirth, after so many soporific explanations of allegories! The bright interval is however soon over. The text is instantly overcast by the mass of clouds of iconographical erudition:

Ma torniamo al ponto della ragione. Due sono le questioni principali: l'una è se dobbiamo fondarsi sopra la filosofia morale o naturale ovvero sopra il loro capriccio, l'altro è se habbiamo da fondarsi sopra la comparazione dell'una e dell'altra, torno a replicare se si[23] fondiamo sopra il capriccio, il quale termina in favola o in Bugia gli è più fastidio a sentire li suoi argomenti che a fare una figura a concorenza da due valenti uomini una di pittura e l'altra di scoltura. Io nell'arte di aringare per difender non ci intro voglio difender la mia arte con questo che porto in giudicio e darò ad intender che cosa è la pittura con li suoi geroglifici.

There follows an anecdote taken from Pliny, Book 35, ch. 10,[24] which I have not found in the *Iconologia*, or else it has escaped me.

Vi fu Apelle che faceva cose inaudite & aveva giudicio retto perché si vede che nel far la faccia di Antigono il quale era cieco di un occhio l'ha volto in tal modo che diverso quel difetto vedevasi se in scultura havaria niuno per grande huomo che fosse ancora sia come un Fidia o Prassitele, sia antichi come moderni potuto coprir quel difetto scolpendo o in legno o in pietra o in bronzo, questa distinzione per la pittura ha dell'infinito.

After having said: 'Voglio seguitar a dar ad intender cosa sia la pittura & voglio contrastar contro Cicerone nel discorso detto della rettorica', Pianta copies what Ripa says s.v. Pittura (pp. 490–1):

Il pittore diceva impara dal maestro ma con una sola cosa ne apprende molte venendo per la conformità & similitudine congionte & incatenate insieme, dico dunque li antichi dicevano che la poesia tace nella pittura & la pittura nella poesia ragiona. Si dipinge in figura di donna bella la pittura con capelli negri grossi e ritorti per significar che la

23. Lacchin's reading.
24. See Carlo Dati, *Vita de' Pittori Antichi*, Florence, 1667: *Vita di Apelle*. In the 1806 edition (Classici Italiani), pp. 163 and 215 ff.

bellezza nota nobiltà. Li capelli della testa si fanno neri & grossi, figurando il pittor in pensieri continui della imitazione della natura & dell'arte viene a prendere molta cura & melanconia che i medici chiamano adustione. Le ciglia inarcate mostrano maraviglia & veramente il Dipintore operando per aiuto dell'arte sua ne acquista stupore & maraviglia. La bocca è ricoperta & indica che non è cosa che giovi al pittore quanto il silenzio e la solitudine. Tien la catena d'oro onde pende una maschera per mostrare che l'imitazione è congiunta con la pittura inseparabilmente. Gli anelli della catena mostrano la conformità di una cosa con un'altra & la congiunzione, la qualità dell'oro dinota che quando la pittura non è mantenuta dalla nobiltà facilmente si perde. La veste cangiante mostra che la varietà particolarmente diletta l'occhio a sublimare.

Ripa, Pittura:

Donna bella, con capelli negri, & grossi . . . con una catena d'oro al collo, dalla quale penda una maschera, & habbia scritto nella fronte, *imitatio*. Terrà in una mano il pennello, & nell'altra la tavola, con la veste di drappo cangiante, la quale le cuopra li piedi, & a' piedi di essa si potranno fare alcuni istromenti della Pittura, per mostrare che la pittura è essercitio nobile. . . . Si dipinge questa imagine molto bella, & che la bellezza noti nobiltà. I capelli della testa si fano neri, & grossi, perche stando il buon Pittore in pensieri continui dell'imitatione della natura, & dell'arte . . . viene per tal cagione a prendere molta cura, & malinconia, che genera poi adustione, come dicono i Medici. . . . Le ciglia inarcate mostrano maraviglia, & veramente il Dipintore si estende a tanta sottile investigatione di cose minime in se stesse per aiuto dell'arte sua, che facilmente n'acquista maraviglia, & malinconia. La bocca ricoperta è inditio, che non è cosa che giovi quanto il silentio, & la solitudine. . . . Tiene la catena d'oro, onde pende la Maschera, per mostrare che l'imitatione è congionta con la Pittura inseparabilmente. Gli anelletti della catena mostrano la conformità di una cosa con l'altra & la congiuntione, perche non ogni cosa, come dice Cicerone nella sua Rettorica, il Pittore impara dal Maestro, ma con una sola ne apprende molte, venendo per la conformità, & similitudine congionte, & incatenate insieme. La qualità dell'oro dimostra, che quando la Pittura non è mantenuta dalla nobiltà, facilmente si perde, & la maschera mostra l'imitatione conveniente alla Pittura. Gli antichi dimandavano . . . essendo vero quel detto triviale, che la poesia tace nella Pittura, & la Pittura nella poesia ragiona. . . . Ha bisogno dunque la Pittura della imitatione di cose reali. . . .

La veste cangiante mostra, che la varietà particolarmente diletta.

Here are, according to Pianta, the appurtenances of his figure:

Li disegni significano che tutte le cose fatte dall'arte si dicano più & meno belle a seconda che hanno più & meno disegno, li penelli mostrano l'effetto loro nella fabbrica della pittura così medesimamente gli scodelli & altre cose. La pietra & macinino significano che l'una ha bisogna dell'altra & sole mai non possono far l'opera di macinare il colore. Anco il pittore per se stesso non può riuscir perfetto se anco l'Idea in suo aiuto vi sia nelle operazioni e perfine il libro significa che il pittore deve essere grandemente dotto nel componere & questa essendo pratica acquistata per via dello studio per accostarsi al reale delle cose.

The last three allegorical telamons are less conspicuous and involved. One of them represents an emaciated old man with bare chest and an apronful of fruits tied to his belt: one would think him a kind of Tantalus tormented by the sight of unattainable things, so downcast are his looks as if gasping for utter exhaustion. 'Tale geroglifico', Lacchin writes, 'è interamente uscito dalla fantasia del Pianta', and contrasts it with Ripa's description of Abundance, as a graceful woman, her forehead wreathed with flowers, holding the horn of plenty, and so on: all being characteristics of 'cosa buona e desiderata da ciascheduno, quanto brutta, & abominevole è riputata la carestia, che di questa è contraria'. Who else indeed but a man of the seventeenth century, accustomed to feed his imagination on out-of-the-way pastures, could hit on the idea of representing Abundance as her opposite, Famine, in the garb of an old peasant worn by the toil in the fields and wasted away 'dall'abbondanza dei suoi sudori'? Also this time Ripa has given the cue; for Pianta writes:

Ovidio scrivendo sopra le trasformazioni ed aggiungendo volume a volume non stancandosi mai per l'abbondanza eccellente delle sue imagini causate dall'Idea sua serena: mentre facendo le ottave carte di carmi piene nel nono libro ecco la memoria sua feconda gli suggerisce di Acheloo sotto figura e manifesto segno di abbondanza e con volto novello dice lietamente: *Naiade;* (libro nove) *hoc pomis et floris odore repletum—sacrarunt, divesque meo bona copia cornu est*—or perché l'abbondanza si dice Copia, per mostrarla così. . . .

In the text of the 1645 edition of Ripa there is a mis-

print: instead of *Naiades hoc*, etc., one reads *Naiade: hoc*, an error which Pianta has reproduced.[25]

Ripa, s.v. Abbondanza (p. 1):

Il corno della dovitia per la favola della Capra Amaltea . . . & per quello che Ovidio scrive del detto Acheloo . . . nel lib. 8 delle Transformazioni, è manifesto segno dell'Abbondanza, dicendo così: *Naiade; hoc pomis, & floris odore repletum Sacrarunt, divesque meo bona copia cornu est*. Et perché l'Abondanza si dice Copia, per mostrarla, così la rappresentiamo. . . .

. . . per mostrarla così [Pianta goes on] formiamo un vecchio e degno padre come avendo seco altre figure di età provette come consigliere, perché si deve prestar più fede ad uno che è di età senile che a un giovane e ciò per dire tutti gli accidenti praticati & come l'esperto agricoltore porta le dovizie di fiori e frutti colti dall'abbondanza delli suoi sudori e per questo è cinto da corda per non perder quello che godiamo per via dell'abbondanza sia giusto e ragionevole non torto pieno di errori & unito da falsità come per il più fa la corda in tutte le operazioni.

Ripa, under Aiuto (p. 16) says that better than a young man 'il vecchio può dar consiglio per l'esperienza delle cose del tempo passato', and under Consiglio (p. 106) he expatiates on this idea, quoting Saint Ambrose in *Hexameron: Senectus est in consiliis utilior*. To an old peasant, then, Pianta transfers the attribute of the 'corno della dovitia pieno di molti & diversi frutti', and the flowers which Ripa calls 'messagieri dei frutti'. The symbol of the rope and the speech referring to it are confused and contradictory: the result of a defective rumination of the *Iconologia*.

The figure of Stratagemma, the trunk of a warrior girt round with a chain and having winglets in the place of arms, has this illustration called Stratagemma Esempio:

Parmenione capitano di Alessandro Magno esortava Alessandro che assaltasse all'improvviso i nemici di notte, questi rispose che era brutta cosa ad un capitano rubbare la vittoria e che ad un Alessandro si conveniva vincere senza inganni, *Victoriam furari, inquit, turpe est; manifeste ac sine dolo Alexandrum vincere oportet*. Fassi ad intender però con questo geroglifico che la principale sapienza che deve aver uno che professa di esser savio è certamente con stratagemma senza periglio acquistar la vittoria, imperciocché in tutte le cose la temerità e l'ardire

25. It is even more surprising that Lacchin, in his paraphrase of Ripa's text, should give the quotation thus: 'NAIDE: *hoc pomis et floris*, etc.', as if Naide was a speaker in a dialogue.

devono esser congiunte con la prudenza e col consiglio. Per contrario chi vuole servirsi solo del suo, perde o per il più resta perdente sicome nell'incatenata figura si vede e per questo lo strattagemma si scolpisce così per darsi ad intendere che con la sua poca prudenza incatenò se stesso.

Ripa (p. 604, Stratagemma militare):

Pingasi un huomo armato. . . . Questa figura è totalmente contraria al parere di Alessandro Magno, il quale abborrì oltrammodo la Stratagemma, & perciò essendo egli persuaso da Parmenione, che assaltasse all'improvviso li nemici di notte, rispose che era brutta cosa ad un Capitano robbare la vittoria, e che ad un Alessandro si conveniva vincere senza inganni. *Victoriam furari, inquit, turpe est: manifeste, ac sine dolo Alexandrum vincere oportet,* riferisce Arriano non ostante questo altiero detto considerando, che Alessandro Magno fu nelle attioni sue precipitoso, & hebbe per l'ordinario più temerità, & ardire, che virtù di fortezza, la quale vuole esser congiunta con la prudenza, & col consiglio . . . [Dice Polieno Macedonio] che la principal sapienza de' singulari Capitani, è certamente senza periglio acquistar la vittoria.

Pianta's conclusion is, as usual, inconsequential.
Although having the same title as Ripa's allegory, Biasimo Vizioso has not its characteristics. The sculpture represents a soldier whose chest is bitten by a snake issuing from beneath his abdomen. This is a traditional image of sin, which is seen for instance in the lectern of Salerno cathedral.[26] The scroll states:

Benché dagli scrittori vien commendata la fedeltà del cane si vede però che Plinio nel libro 25 capitolo 8 lo tassa di malignità, in tal modo dice: *invidus alterius macrescit rebus optimis* & dice che sentendosi il cane un poco di male per ricuperare la sanità mangia una certa herba insegnatali dalla natura e per non mostrarsi prenderla per bisogno guarda di non esser veduto dagli uomini. Così il biasimo vizioso, significa di bassa sua viltà perché per il più questo difetto genera in persone vili. Guarda con l'occhio torto in disparte per non mostrare il piacere e l'allegrezza per il male altrui, che porta con sé il biasimo. La serpe dà ad intender il rammarico, che ha sempre al cuore l'invidioso del bene altrui e si fa di color livido per mostrare che il livore nasce comunemente dal freddo e l'invidia è fredda & ha spento in sé ogni fuoco di carità.

This is a mosaic of passages from Ripa's (pp. 298–9) explanation of the allegory of Invidia:

Donna vecchia . . . di color livido, haverà la mammella sinistra nuda, e morsicata da una serpe. . . . Invidia non è altro, che allegrarsi del male altrui. . . . L'esser di color livido, dimostra, che il livore nasce communemente da freddo, e l'invidia è fredda, & ha spento in se ogni fuoco, & ardore di carità. La serpe, che morsica la sinistra mammella, nota il ramarico c'ha sempre al cuore l'invidioso del bene altrui, come dice Horatio nell'Epistole, *Invidus alterius macrescit rebus opimis*[27] . . . Donna vecchia . . . con gli occhi biechi . . . haverà appresso un cane magro, il quale come da molti effetti si vede è animale invidiosissimo, e tutti gli beni degl'altrì vorrebbe se solo, anzi racconta Plinio nel lib. 25, cap. 8 che sentendosi il cane morso da qualche serpe, per non restar offeso mangia una certa herba insegnatagli dalla natura, & per invidia nel prenderla guarda di non esser veduto dagli huomini . . . questo vitio ha luogo particolarmente fra gli huomini bassi, e con la plebe.

We see under the windows a decorative motif of leaves of the peach-tree which surrounds the figure of Hope. This and the other figures of the theological virtues, which do not depart from conventional iconography, are accompanied with Latin inscriptions. Hope: *Quasi Sol ego sculptura exaltata sum in mundo*; Faith: *Virtus virtutum gloriarumque Michaelangelus Florentinus sculptor et coelis extollere laudibus coronatus* (all round, entwined with the decoration: *Ubi Virtus ibi Honor ubi Labor ibi Gloria*); Charity: *Pictores venite et iam gaudium accipite in delineanda varietate formis Iacobi Tintorecti Veneti.* Finally: *Stupite caeli videntes laurum coronator regum exaltator triumphantium.* A speech accompanies also these hieroglyphs: 'Questa è quella virtù che nel geroglifico del persico congiunto ad una delle sue foglie vien rassembrata e ciò affine di insinuarci che la lingua mai sempre deve accoppiarsi col cuore.' Although Lacchin says apropos of this sentence: 'Come è bello quel pensiero, e tutto suo', we find it in Ripa, s.v. Silentio (p. 570): 'Nella sinistra tenghi un persico con le foglie . . . ha le foglie simili alla lingua humana, & il frutto rassomiglia al cuore: volsero forse significare, che il tacere a suoi tempi è virtù, però l'huomo prudente non dee consumare il tempo in molte parole vane, & senza frutto, ma tacendo ha da considerare le cose prima, che ne parli.' Pianta continues by saying: 'Quel grande Peripatetico (in tercio de anima) la chiama intelletto dell'immagina-

---

26. 'Cette image qui n'est pas rare, mais qui est assez équivoque', remarks Roger Peyrefitte in *Du Vésuve à l'Etna*, Paris, Flammarion, 1952, p. 138.

27. Pianta, with his customary confusion, gives Pliny as the author of this passage, as well as of the further passage on the dog.

tione; l'agente è quello che fa le cose. *Potentia intel-ligibilis actualiter intellecta.*' We read in Ripa s.v. Imaginatione: 'L'Imaginatione dice Aristotele tertio de Anima che è un moto[28] fatto dal senso attualmente, cioè una cognitione di quello che gli altri sensi . . . hanno sentito. . . . La potentia imaginativa riceve le fantasme di qual si voglia oggetto presentateli dalli sensi esteriori . . . potentia sì in ricevere dette fantasme, come anco in presentarle all'intelletto.'

Pianta's speech relates to the Aristotelian distinction between potential intellect and acting intellect, but is far from clear, and possibly derives from another passage of Ripa which I have been unable to trace. I have not found in Ripa either the source of the classical reference in what follows:

> se in pretiosa gemma di lucido saffiro scolpito havea quel Eminentissimo scultore Fidia Ateniese a sem-bianza di leggiadrissime Donzelle la statua dell'Amo-re e dell'Onore, hora che bisogna per prender licenza con onorati corsaletti difender e honorar la madre pittura & con l'Amore la mia Arte scultura, né però devo partirmi sì tosto e nemmeno indagare con molto lume, ma con grande amore & honore, in pegno gli lascio il core.—*Idem Planta sculpebat et ad intelligentiam idem Franciscus facebat.*

There rises between two windows a naked man with powerful arms and legs and a long and slim chest round which a scarf is tied; the dead white of his eyes and of the eyes of the sun he brandishes in his left hand (while his right holds behind his head a shrunken head which looks like the trophy of a head-hunter) cause

28. The text has actually 'motto'.

this apparition to look somehow spectre-like and formidable, as of a human snake which from a dark corner should cast a mysterious spell (Fig. 13).

The sun is like the one the figure of Verità brandishes in Ripa 'per significare che la Verità è amica della luce; anzi è luce chiarissima, che dimostra quel che è'. The small head this giant holds behind his back is perhaps that of the skin of the lion of Nemea, there-fore this image is thought to stand for Hercules. Be it as it may, this snake-like wizard who lurks between two windows is far from inspiring confidence, and the general impression of this congregation of strange telamons and head-figures reminds one of worn-out galley-slaves. This Venice of Pianta's seems closer to Otway's gloomy play, *Venice Preserved*, with spies, treasons, furies and dejections, than to Tintoretto's paintings, which nevertheless so dominate the room that few visitors, as I was saying at the beginning, are aware of the strange caryatids.

The requisites Winckelmann (*Essay on Allegory*) demanded from allegory, that it should be self-explain-ing, so as to need no interpreter, were never so much ignored as by Pianta. The arrows of irony Winckel-mann aims at laboured allegories would have found in those of the Scuola di San Rocco (had Winckelmann heard of them) an ideal target. Just imagine how the German aesthete would have judged Pianta if he was able to say of Ripa: 'It is impossible to imagine any-thing more ridiculous than some of his thoughts, and I am sure that if he had thought of the Italian adage *pisciare nel vaglio* to mean waste of time and labour, he would have expressed even this pretty thought through figures.'

HANS KAUFFMANN

Der Werdegang der Theresagruppe von Giovanni Lorenzo Bernini

Wie in der Beurteilung der Theresakapelle Bewunderung und Ablehnung miteinander streiten, so sind der Karmeliterorden und die italienische Kongregation der Unbeschuhten während des 17. Jhs. durch inneren Zwiespalt und von aussen kommende Anfeindungen beunruhigt gewesen. Unter Wetterleuchten ist Berninis Cornarokapelle zustande gekommen, und zuweilen möchte man sich fragen, ob sich etwas von dem Widerstreit in und zwischen den Kongregationen auf die Beurteilung des Kunstwerks ausgedehnt, aufs Ästhetische übergegriffen und sich darin fortgesetzt hat. Doch soll an dieser Stelle nur von der Genese der Altargruppe im Anschluss an Rudolf Wittkowers Forschungen[1] die Rede sein. Sie wirkt wie aus einem Guss, ist aber nicht ein Geschöpf der ersten Stunde. Zwar sind, um den Werdegang vollständig zu rekonstruieren, zu wenige Vorarbeiten auf uns gekommen. Sie lassen jedoch, weil sie von der endgültigen Gestaltung recht weit abliegen, erkennen, dass Bernini erst nach Umwegen sein Ziel klar vor sich gesehen hat (Abb. 1).

Die von Carlo Maderno zwischen 1608 und 1620 errichtete Kirche war dem Heiligen Paulus geweiht, bis schon 1621 nach der Schlacht am Weissen Berge "Sta. Maria della Vittoria" zur Patronin erhoben wurde.[2] Indes blieb der linke Querhausarm Pauluskapelle, bevor er dem Kardinal Federigo Cornaro für die Einrichtung einer Kapelle der Heiligen Theresa überlassen wurde. Das Altarbild hatte 1618 Gerard Honthorst gemalt: es zeigt, in die Sakristei übertragen, "Pauli Entrückung in den Himmel"; Kardinal Scipione Borghese, ein Förderer der Karmeliterkirche, hatte es in Auftrag gegeben.[3] Das ziemlich seltene Thema

war schon von Ludovico Carracci[4] behandelt und von Domenichino in seiner für Giovanni Battista Agucchi 1604–1607 vollendeten Komposition (Louvre) auf eine Höhe gebracht worden, die vierzig Jahre später für Poussin vorbildlich wurde[5]—zu der Zeit als Bernini den Theresaaltar heranbildete. Ist es ein Zufall, dass nun auch diese Heilige in einer Szene der Entrückung dargestellt wurde, zu der ihre Ikonographie bisher noch nicht vorgedrungen war? Sowohl dem Auftraggeber wie dem gestaltenden Künstler kann der Gedanke vorgeschwebt haben, der Sphäre der Paulusentrückung im Theresaaltar nahezubleiben, und etwas von den damals schwebenden Rivalitäten könnte sich darin niedergeschlagen haben.

Indes lassen die beiden vermutlich frühesten uns erhaltenen Vorzeichnungen, nur grosszügig umrissene Kopfstudien mit sparsamer, klärender Schattierung (Rötel) offen, wie der Gesamtzusammenhang gedacht, ob schon eine Himmelsszene vorgesehen war. Sie nehmen sich wie Varianten des Brustbilds der "Maria Raggi" aus, und die Ausdruckslage der früheren Heiligenstatuen des Meisters "Bibiena" und "Longinus" bleibt lebendig. Theresa wird frontal gezeigt, bei zurückgelegtem und zu ihrer rechten Schulter geneigten Kopf das Antlitz einmal mehr, einmal weniger verkürzt, und die Mimik erprobt, auch eine Profilansicht skizziert. Das etwas grössere Blatt (Br.-W. 24a) ist präziser durchdacht, einen Schritt weiter (Abb. 2). Eine Inszenierung des Ganzen ist denkbar, die der schon eingebürgerten Ikonographie der Pfeilvision noch

1. R. Wittkower, *G. L. Bernini*, London, 1955, 28 ff. und 207 ff.
2. Zum Sieg in der Schlacht am Weissen Berge vor Prag (18.11.1620) hatte mit Hilfe des Gnadenbildes der Maria P. Dominicus à Jesù Maria aus dem römischen Karmeliterkloster im Gefolge des Heerführers, des Herzogs Maximilian von Bayern, Rühmliches beigetragen; S. Riezler, *Der Karmeliter P. Dominicus à Jesù Maria und der Kriegsrat vor der Schlacht am Weissen Berge*, Sitzungsber. Bayer. Akad. d. Wiss. phil.-histor. Klasse, 1897, 423 ff.
3. In situ erwähnt von P. Totti, *Ritratto di Roma moderna*, Roma, 1638, 268 f.; F. Sapori, *Rass. d'Arte*, 18, 1918, 7 ff.; J. R. Judson, *Gerrit Honthorst*, 's Gravenhage, 1956, 33 f. und derselbe: *Gerrit Honthorst*, 's Gravenhage, 1959, 34 ff. und 172 f. Cat. Nr. 57. Über die Konflikte zwischen den spanischen und italienischen Kongregationen und die durch ein Breve von Clemens VIII. 1608 veranlasste Gründung einer dritten Kongregation unter dem Namen des Apostels Paulus, weiterhin die spätere Verlegung dieser Kongregation von S. Maria della Vittoria nach S. Pancrazio fuori le mura vgl. P. Helyot, *Histoire des ordres religieux*, vol. I, Paris, 1721, 357 ff., chap. XLVIII.
4. R. Wittkower, *The Drawings of the Carracci in the Collection of Her Majesty the Queen at Windsor Castle*, London, 1952, Nr. 47 Abb. 16: "The Ascension of St. Paul the Hermit" um 1605–10.
5. Über seine beiden Fassungen für Chantelou 1643 und für Sarron 1650 vgl. den Katalog der Poussin Ausstellung, Paris, 1960, Nr. 67 und 92, und W. Friedländer, *The Drawings of N. Poussin*, London, 1939, 37 Nr. 72 und A 17. Lebruns Erläuterung des Poussinbildes (L. Réau, *Iconographie*, III, 3, 1044 f.) kann auch für Berninis "Theresa" verwertet werden. Natürlich steht Raphaels "Ezechielvision" hinter den Gestaltungen der "Paulusentrückung".

ähnlich sah: Theresa auf dem Boden knieend[6] und während sich der Pfeil nähert, mit zurücksinkendem Haupt von Engelhand gestützt. Es mag genügen, um die Ausbreitung dieser Darstellungsform zu vergegenwärtigen, an Bilder von Cagnacci und Gerard Seghers zu erinnern. In ebenso zahlreichen wie noch wenig differenzierten Gestaltungen hatte die Bildkunst, auch die niederländische, Theresa und ihre Verzückung seit ihrer Heiligsprechung im Jahr 1622 vorgeführt.[7] Unverkennbar ist, dass die Szene in Analogie zu Ekstasen anderer Heiligen aufgebaut wurde. An Prägungen vergleichbarer Legenden orientierte sich die neue Aufgabe, thematische Verwandtschaft empfahl eine entsprechende Fassung. In erster Linie scheint sich die Ekstase des Hl. Franziskus angeboten zu haben, sogar eine typenprägende Rolle scheint ihrer Formulierung zugefallen zu sein, sodass weitere Themenkreise von ihr inspiriert worden sind. Von der Jahrhundertwende an reihten sich in Rom Bilder der Franziskus-Ekstase von G. Baglione und Cesare d'Arpino, von Annibale Carracci und Domenichino aneinander.[8] Art und Mass ihrer Ausstrahlung wird an der Assimilierung erkennbar, die etwa der Reue-Verzückung der Hl. Magdalena in Darstellungen von Simon Vouet und Domenico Feti zuteil geworden ist[9] und dadurch Gruppierungen der Franziskus-Ekstase wiederspiegelt. Ihre Ausdrucksform und ihr Helldunkel-Diesseits sind auch für die Theresa-Verzückung in jenen, Berninis Erfindung vorangehenden Gestaltungen vorbildlich geworden. Legitimierte doch auch von ihrer Persönlichkeit her die sehr eindringliche Franziskusverehrung der Theresa die Angleichung der Bilder. Kein Wunder, dass wir in S. Maria della Vittoria die Merendakapelle dem Heiligen von Assisi geweiht finden (1629) und Domenichinos Altarbild der "Erscheinung der Maria vor dem Hl. Franz" von den beiden Wandbildern begleitet sehen, deren eines seiner Ekstase vorbehalten ist.[10]

Bernini näherte sich diesem Bereich gegen Ende der 30er Jahre mit seinem Entwurf der "Franziskusverzückung" für den Altar der Cappella Raimondi (Abb. 5).[11] Zwei jugendliche Engel sind dem von der Vision überwältigten, im Knieen schwankenden Heiligen zu Hilfe gekommen, der eine um ihn von der Seite zu stützen, der andere um ihn von oben her aufzurichten. Dem wie im Traum nach vorn taumelnden, sein Antlitz schräg nach oben kehrenden Heiligen kann der Franziskus des Annibale Carracci, der vor der Maria hinsinkt, während ein Engel ihn von hinten her stützt, zunächst an die Seite gestellt werden:[12] dies wäre ein weiteres Zeugnis hoher Wertschätzung, mit der Bernini bis in seine späten Jahre des vorbildlichen Bolognesen gedacht hat. Freilich liess er Franziskus noch aufgelöster hinsinken, den Mund wie stöhnend geöffnet. Vor allem aber griff er höher und über alle bisherigen Darstellungen hinaus, indem er die Gruppe vom Boden gelöst vor Himmelsgrund in der Schwebe gehalten zeigte. Bernini hatte kurz zuvor an den Vierungspfeilern von St. Peter die Passionsreliquien verherrlicht, indem er sie von auffahrenden Engeln emporgetragen vor eine Wolkenfolie stellte[13]—Züge einer Apotheose, mit der er nun auch die Franziskus-Ekstase erhöhte.

So war er vorbereitet, als die Theresavision ihn zu fesseln begann. Die "Entrückung Pauli", Honthorsts Altarbild, der dem Theresaaltar Platz machen sollte, brauchte ihm nicht erst den Weg zu weisen, konnte ihn aber auf dem Weg bestärken, den er in der "Franziskus-Ekstase" eingeschlagen hatte.[14] Sollen wir uns danach die beiden Kopfstudien Berninis, dieses phantasiemächtigen, dem Ausserordentlichen zustrebenden Geistes, in Gedanken zu einer Kniefigur in einer schattigen Klosterzelle ergänzen, die der gewohnten, in der Kunst schon eingebürgerten Situation ähnlich blieb? Selbst Honthorsts "Paulus", erst recht Berninis "Franziskus" erweist, dass die Kopfstudien zur Theresa mit einer Entrückung in den Himmel sehr wohl vereinbar sind. Diese Zeichnungen machen uns

---

6. Nicht nur aus physischer Schwäche, sondern auch zum Zeichen der Verehrung und der Askese. Vgl. die Worte der Hl. Theresa zur Würdigung des Pedro d'Alcantara (−1562) bei L. Cristiani, *Histoire de l'Eglise*, vol. 17, St. Dizier, 1948, 445.
7. Auch schon vorher, z.B. Lanfrancos um 1612–13 für die Karmeliter von S. Giuseppe (Capo le Case) gemaltes, von Bellori (*Le Vite . . .*, Roma, 1672, 368 f.) gepriesenes Bild "Theresa empfängt von Maria und Joseph Kette und Gewand ihres Ordens" nach der unter anderen von M. Lépée, *Ste Thérèse mystique* (Paris-Bruges, 1951, 180) wiedergegebenen Visionsschilderung. Auch an Rubens' 1614 für die Brüsseler Karmeliterkirche gemalte "Vision des Hl. Geistes" (M. Róoses, *Rubens*, Philadelphia, 1904, 180 f., und L. Burchard im Katalog der Rubensausstellung der Gall. Wildenstein in London 1950) sei erinnert. Vgl. ferner Mar. Salinger, "Representations of St. Thérèse", *Bull. Metrop. Mus. New York*, N.S., 8, 1949–50, 97 ff.
8. Dem Baglionebild gegensinnig höchst ähnlich die Komposition von Guglielmo Caccia (Turin vor 1625) in der Gall. Spada-Rom (Zeri, Catalogo 48, Nr. 290 um 1610); Widerholung in Turin, Gall. Sabauda. Cesare d'Arpino, Brera Nr. 580.
9. Simon Vouet Hl. Magdalena, Musée des Beaux Arts, Besançon und Vorzeichnung im Louvre; W. R. Crelly, *The Painting of Simon Vouet*, 1962, Nr. 9; Dom. Feti, Rotterdam Mus. Boymans Nr. 140.

10. J. Hess, *Die Künstlerbiographien von G. B. Passeri*, Leipzig-Wien, 1934, 54 f.; Bellori, *Vite*, 1728, 200. Das dem Ippolito Merenda ("Caesenat. Jurisconsulti") von Kard. Francesco Barberini nach Berninis Entwurf gestiftete Epitaph befindet sich in S. Giacomo alla Lungara (Wittkower, a.a.O., 203 f.).
11. Wittkower, a.a.O., 205 ff.
12. Das im Besitz von Pope-Hennessy befindliche Kupferbild: Mostra dei Carracci, Bologna, 1956, Nr. 91; ein zweites Exemplar (Leinwand) in Detroit.
13. An Lanfrancos Hl. Margarethe von Cortona ist mit Recht schon öfter erinnert worden.
14. M. Florissone, *Esthétique et Mystique d'après Ste. Thérèse d'Avila et St. Jean de la Croix*, Paris, 1956, 40 und 47 (über die Paulusverehrung der Hl. Theresa).

also mit einem Anfangsstadium der Arbeit bekannt, das die Himmelskonzeption nicht ausschliesst, und ich sehe keinen Grund, mit einer früheren, andersartigen Bildidee zu rechnen.

Und nun kann es nicht zweifelhaft sein, findet sich auch bei Brauer und Wittkower vermerkt, dass sich die gewichtigere und eingänglicher durchgearbeitete Gewandstudie (Br.-W. 24b) dieser selben Arbeitsstufe einfügt, ja dass die Kopfstudien mit dieser Gewandstudie zusammen erdacht sind, mit ihr zusammengehören. Auf der Rückseite der grösseren, genauer durchgearbeiteten Kopfstudie, statt in Rötel in schwarzer Kreide ausgeführt, bringt sie eine "Modellaufnahme" der Sitzenden, die den Kopf auslässt, um die Pose und die Lagerung der Kutte durchzuklären (Abb. 3). Der Oberkörper ist nahezu frontal, der Unterkörper fast ins Profil (nach links) gestellt, man sieht den unbekleideten linken Fuss der unbeschuhten Karmeliterin hinunterhängen, ihr rechtes eingeschlagenes Knie— wie wenn sie kniete—an einen Wolkenumriss gestützt. Ihre rechte Hand greift quer über die Brust, ihre linke ist schreckhaft erhoben und uns entgegen gespreizt. Fast ebenso lehnten sich schon die Engel über dem Hochaltar von St. Agostino (1626–1628) an ihre schrägen Wolkenbänke an. Von dieser Formulierung machte der Meister für die Himmelssituation der Theresa wenigstens in dieser Anfangsphase Gebrauch, hatte er sie doch auch bei "Franziskus" beibehalten. Ihm blieb er nahe. Denn die offene Ansicht, das Bewegungsbild des länglich gestreckten Körperbogens mit der schrägen Begrenzung vom linken Fuss zum rechten Knie, dazu das Hochnehmen der Hände in erregter und ausladender Gebärde: bis in die unruhige Affektlage ist diese Studie von der Erinnerung an den Hl. Franziskus der Cappella Raimondi durchdrungen und bestätigt noch einmal, dass Bernini eine Gestaltung ins Auge fasste, die seine Franziskuskomposition weiterbildete.[15] Rötel- und Kreidezeichnung, d.h. Vorder- und Rückseite dieses Blattes (Br.-W. 24a und b) auf den gleichen Massstab gebracht, lassen sich zu einer vollständigen Figur zusammensetzen: Theresas Kopf zurückgelehnt und ihrer rechten Schulter zugeneigt, die breite Brust mit quergerichteten Armen, die Abkehr der Beine ins Profil—über den "Franziskus" hinweg ist selbst noch von der "Assunta" des Pietro Bernini ein ferner Nachklang zu vernehmen (Abb. 4).[16]

Keine so bestimmte Vorstellung ist von ihrem Engel zu gewinnen. Immerhin ist deutlich, dass die ihn vorbereitende Kreidezeichnung (Br.-W. 25) der Gewandstudie für Theresa korrespondiert: wie diese auf der Rückseite der grösseren Rötelstudie, befindet sich jene auf der Rückseite der kleineren, sodass wir an keine andere Phase zu denken brauchen. Nur ein Unterkörper, beschwingt nach rechts ausschreitend, von parallelen Linienschwüngen einem Wasserfall ähnlich umflossen; einer Andeutung nach war ein etwas vorgeneigter Oberkörper beabsichtigt. Aber wie war die Gruppierung mit der Hauptfigur gedacht? Sollte dieser Engel vor der Brust der Theresa vorbeigreifen, um mit dem Pfeil auf ihre linke Herzseite zu zielen? Allein schon wegen des Quergriffs ihrer rechten Hand eine nicht recht befriedigende Vorstellung. Oder könnte Bernini der Komposition der "Franziskusentrückung" sogar soweit gefolgt sein, dass er wieder an eine Dreiergruppe dachte: Theresa einigermassen frontal zwischen dem links herantretenden und einem rechts nahenden Engel mit dem Pfeil, dessen Kommen das weggezogene Gewandstück über Theresas linkem Arm anzeigt? Sicherheit haben wir nicht.

Wir haben keinen Grund zu bezweifeln, dass diese Studienblätter auf eine statuarische Gruppe, nicht mehr auf ein Relief ("Franziskusentrückung") abzielen, jedoch bleibt unentschieden, ob der Zeichner schon an eine Beleuchtung von oben her dachte. Wie nicht selten Bildhauerzeichnungen, lassen diese eine folgerichtige Lichtführung vermissen: Oberlicht würde noch an anderen Stellen Schatten erzeugen, doch wirkt sich auch Seitenlicht nicht konsequent aus, und so bleibt im Zweifel, ob Bernini schon in dieser ersten Phase einen Kapellenschrein mit Eigenlicht aus der Höhe im Sinn gehabt hat.

Wann sich der neue schöpferische Impuls einstellte, mit dem er sich von seiner Konzeption der "Franziskusekstase" freimachte, und die Erfindung der endgültigen Gestalt ihm eingegeben wurde, wissen wir nicht. Vorbereitende Arbeiten sind uns von nun an nicht mehr zur Hand, aber wir nehmen eine Evolution wahr, die durch Berninis eigene Formenwelt ausgelöst wurde. Vielleicht waren es noch zwei Schritte bis zur abschliessenden Lösung. Denn ein neues Ausdrucksmotiv ergriff von ihm Besitz und eine neue Komposi-

---

15. Die Wichtigkeit des "Franziskus" der Capp. Raimondi in der Vorgeschichte der "Theresa" ist schon von M. Reymond, *Le Bernin*, Paris, 1911, 63 bemerkt worden. Eine den Engeln auf den Giebelschrägen des Hochaltars von S. Agostino ähnliche Stellung hat A. Sacchi seinem auf der Altarstufe knieenden, zur Maria aufschauenden Hl. Bonaventura gegeben (Sta Maria della Concezione, "schon 40er Jahre", H. Posse, *Andrea Sacchi*, Leipzig, 1925, 99 ff.).

16. Dass sich das Kopftuch Theresas linker Schläfe anschmiegt,

gegenüber freier hängt und offener ausbreitet, entspricht den asymmetrischen, zu ihrer Rechten steiler absinkenden Schultern. Für die Gestalt im ganzen mag ein Hinweis auf Tintorettos Bild: Die Hln. Ludwig, Georg und die Königstochter (E.v.d. Bercken, *Jac. Tintoretto*, München, 1923, II, Abb. 49) und auf des Tommaso Amantini Bozzetto erlaubt sein (L. Planiscig, *Die Estensische Kunstsammlung*, Wien, 1919, I, 95, Nr. 142: "ging 1648 nach Rom"; A. E. Brinckmann, *Barockbozzetti*, I, 126 ff.).

tionsidee stieg mit zwingender Kraft auf, und es könnte sein, dass in dem geheimnisvollen Prozess der Bildwerdung das Eine das Andere nach sich gezogen hat.

Im Licht des Theresathemas wurde der dreissig Jahre zurückliegende Barberinische "Sebastian" aufs neue aktuell. Erstaunlich genau leben die Ausdrucksmotive des schmerzlich erliegenden Märtyrers im Marmorwerk der Theresa wieder auf—nur in den Gegensinn gewendet. Scharfer Kontrapost[17] rückt das zurückgelehnte Antlitz der hochgedrängten Schulter nahe; darunter hängt der Arm schwer hinab, und das Bein gleitet schräg ab, weil sein Fuss keinen sicheren Halt findet, während das andere aufruht. Gegenüber stuft sich die weniger gedehnte Köperseite bestimmter gewinkelt ab, und die Hand haftet, wie unbewusst nach oben geöffnet, locker auf einem über den Schoss herübergenommenen Tuch. Der Mund lässt mit heruntergezogenen Winkeln die obere Zahnreihe sehen; selbst die asymmetrische Gesichtsumrahmung, durch die erkennbar wird, wie heftig der Kopf zur Seite gesunken, findet sich vorgebildet (Abb. 6).

Dass das Theresathema die Sebastiansgestalt wachrief, ist nicht unverständlich. Beide werden von Pfeilen, zwar sehr verschiedenen, getroffen, beide erliegen ihnen nicht, sondern ermatten bis zu todesähnlicher Ohnmacht. Beiden kommen Engel nahe, dem Sebastian in der Weise der Engelpietà und in Angleichung an sie, und beide erfahren eben darin die Nähe Christi. Die Sebastian-Ikonographie kennt sogar eine der Engelvision Theresas genau entsprechende Pfeilverwundung: an den Baum gefesselt und erschöpft wird er von einem Engel mit einem Pfeil in der Brust verletzt. Ein solches Bild von Daniel Seghers ist von Paul Pontius gestochen und der Widmung an den Bischof von Ypern D. George Chamberlain die Erläuterung hinzugefügt worden: "S. Sebastianus divini Amoris magis quam Barbarorum telis saucius . . .

    Vulnera feci Amor hostili licet hausta pharetra
    Ille sed ut curem: pungit ut ungat Amor."[18]

Mit den inhaltlichen Gemeinsamkeiten haben sich künstlerische Bestrebungen verbunden. In Bernini scheint der Gedanke gereift zu sein, die Heilige dürfe nicht zum Objekt der Handlung werden. Franziskus musste mit sich geschehen lassen, was ihm angetan wurde, und Bernini hatte anfänglich eine ähnliche Reaktion der Theresa ersonnen. Seitdem jedoch das Einzelbild des Sebastian fruchtbar wurde, wuchs der Gestalt der Mystikerin ein höherer Personenwert zu. Sie wurde beruhigt, verselbständigt und zum Subjekt

des Bildes erhoben. Das gesammelte Wesen einer in sich gegründeten, aus sich heraus lebendigen Persönlichkeit trat zutage. War Berninis "Sebastian" das erste und auf lange hinaus einzige monologisch introvertierte Menschenbild seines Meissels gewesen, so liess er eben diese Wesensart und seelische Verfassung auf Theresa übergehen. In ihr sind die bestimmenden, für Berninis Schöpfung konstitutiven Ausdruckswerte angelegt: die Versunkenheit, die Stille und Vereinsamung einer auf sich selbst zurückgeworfenen Seele.[19]

Es ist, als habe Bernini erst durch den "Sebastian" einen persönlichen Zugang zur "Theresa" gefunden; durch die Vermittelung, um nicht zu sagen in der Gestalt des Vertrauteren eignete er sich das Fremdere an. Und so änderte er an seinem vorangehenden Theresa-Entwurf. Kein Glied mehr sollte sich in einer Willenshandlung regen, und es gab keine Überschneidung mehr. Das rechte Bein, vorher z.T. versteckt, bekommt eine ruhige Normalhaltung und ist übersehbar; neben ihm gewinnt der herabhängende linke Fuss an Eindruckskraft: ohne eigenes Zutun wird die Heilige von der Wolke emporgehoben. Die Randlage aller Glieder, ihr Schwerwerden und Hängenlassen trägt zum Ausdruck der Ermattung Wesentliches bei und die zuvor äusserlich motivierte Reaktion wich einer ganz verinnerlichten Erschütterung. Auch über den "Sebastian" hinaus wurde eine bedeutende Weiterbildung erreicht. Die grosszügiger entworfene Gestalt der Nonne hebt sich mit geklärten Umrissen von der Umgebung ab, ihr Haupt bildet den Gipfel, während das des "Sebastian" von dem Laub und dem Baumstamm gesondert werden muss, an die es sich anlehnt. "Sebastian" hat an allen Stellen Halt, sämtliche Glieder sind festgelegt.[20] Theresa hält sich ohne jede Stützung im Sitzen aufrecht, lässt Hand und Fuss ins Leere hängen, sie spürt keinen Boden unter sich. Des Sebastian stabilen Zustand auf dem Felsensitz hat Bernini in eine Schwebelage übergeleitet, deren die Heilige gleichsam tastend innewird, und in der sie ermattend sich mit einer Anspannung geradehält, die sich vor allem in dem mühsamen Hochdrang der Schulter ausprägt. Trotz des unerhörten Formenreichtums, der über die ganze Komposition ausgegossen ist, setzt sich ihr gross gebautes Antlitz als das

17. Seit der "Daphne" war er Bernini nicht mehr interessant gewesen, nun greift er ihn wieder auf.

18. J. Linnik, "Tableaux inconnus de G. Seghers à l'Ermitage", *Jahrb. d. Ermitage in Leningrad*, I, 1956, 167 ff.

19. Das Körperbild lässt auch an Bilder der "Mater dolorosa" (z.B. Girolamo Siciolante da Sermonata, "Beweinung", Mus. Posen, H. Voss, *Spätrenaissance*, I, 104 ff.) denken, am ehesten an die ausdrucksverwandten Marienfiguren in Annibale Carraccis Gemälden der Pietà. Eine Vergleichbarkeit mit dem Christus der Michelangelo-Pietà in St. Peter kommt schon bei Berninis "Sebastian" in Betracht und wäre demnach durch ihn in die Theresa eingegangen.

20. Durch den Ast, an den sein Arm gefesselt und an dem sein Körper gleichsam aufgehängt und hochgehalten wird, wird Sebastian durch eine Aussenstütze vorm Zusammensinken bewahrt—Theresa dagegen durch eine eigene Anstrengung.

Ausdruckszentrum durch. Sebastian bleibt sogut wie stumm, man könnte ihn für einen Schlafenden halten; ein lebendig atmender, von einem Schmerzenskrampf berührter,[21] doch in sich ruhender Organismus. Theresa ist intensiver ergriffen, und wenn wir die Ausdruckstypen hinzunehmen, die wir bei Lebrun gezeichnet und erläutert finden, so lesen wir aus der Mimik der Theresa eine Mischung von "Vénération" und "Ravissement" mit "Tristesse" wahrhaft exemplarisch heraus; neigt sich doch auch der Kopf—entgegen den ersten Zeichnungen—zu ihrer linken Schulter hin dem Herzen zu, zum Zeichen der Demut, die im "Ravissement" beteiligt ist.[22]

Schliesslich verlangte die Umsetzung der Akt- in eine Gewandfigur eine schöpferische Erfindung. Die Dispositionen der Vorzeichnung wurden von Grund auf neu durchdacht; dort war die Gewandung einfacher geordnet und der von innen andrängende Körper prägte sich verfolgbarer mit deutlicheren Artikulationen aus. Im Marmor fügt sich das Gewand keinem Kanon, der Körper wirkt wie zugedeckt, nichts Schwellendes hebt sich hervor. Wo sich stellenweis Motivierungen regen, besitzen sie eine intensive Ausdruckskraft: das zusammengeschobene Kopftuch im Halswinkel—mit dem Übergang von den eingebuchteten Flächen über Stirn und Wange zu der Schulterwölbung[23]—und, höchst kunstvoll, die Stauung des Ärmels, aus dem die linke Hand trotz der angehobenen Schulter umso länger hervorkommt. Sonst aber scheint das Körperleben wie verhängt. Sehr anders hatte Bernini die zuseiten des Epitaphs für Carlo Barberini lagernden Allegorien (1630, S. Maria Aracoeli) mit antikisch leichten Gewändern umkleidet, die mit den Gliedern mitgehen, und wenn das Thema passend erscheint, kommt er auch später darauf zurück.[24] Theresa liegt unter mehreren Schichten auflastenden Stoffs, und weil der Mulde, der Konkaven jede Stelle überlassen zu sein scheint, wirkt der Organismus wie eingesunken, zurückgezogen, ohne pulsierendes Leben, gleichsam des Atems beraubt. Beim "Longinus" hatte Berninis Gewandkunst zum ersten Mal innerlichen Regungen nachgegeben, war für Affekte und einen speziellen Ausdrucksmodus empfindlich geworden.[25] Aber des "Longinus" expansivem Pathos ist der Theresa schwindendes Körperleben entgegengesetzt: eine Hülle über einem bewegungslosen Körper, dem die Kraft zum Aufstehen fehlt. Gegenüber dem "Sebastian", der seiner Fesseln ledig sich erheben könnte, gelang am Gewand der Theresa eine völlige Neuschöpfung: Entkräftung durch eine gleichsam negative Gegenwart des Körpers.

Der Engel ist ein Gewächs aus dem Geschlecht der grossen Engelgestalten auf dem Bronzebaldachin unter der Peterskuppel. Die Majestät dieses Raumes, die Dimensionen des Tabernkels geboten ein Heldenmass; mit höfischer Gelassenheit umstehen sie die Tabernakelbekrönung, nehmen die Lorbeerranken mit wiegender Gebärde auf und reichen sie weiter. Schon der Kreideentwurf für den Theresaengel knüpfte mit seinem strömenden Gewand[26] hier an und die Marmorfigur wächst daraus hervor. Allerdings jugendlicher, noch nicht ganz erwachsen ist er in seiner correggiesken Schönheit auf die persönliche Intimität seines Auftrags eingestimmt: darin einzigartig in Berninis Schaffen und deshalb ein Zeuge für des Künstlers genaues Bedenken, welcher "Modus" dem jeweiligen Thema wesensgemäss ist. Aber das doppelseitige Öffnen der Arme mit schräger Neigung zu dem aufmerksam beobachteten Blickziel hin, das Gegenspiel der nach rückwärts ausholenden, nur mit den Fingerspitzen zugreifenden Hand und des zur anderen Schulter sich überneigenden Kopfes[27] sind vom Tabernakel her Bernini ein Besitz gewesen, dem er in dem sublimeren Geschöpf der Traumsphäre um Theresa neuen Odem eingehaucht und den flüchtigeren Wolkenschritt mitgegeben hat.[28] Seinem Antlitz sind die Züge des "Amour simple" im Sinn der Mimiktypen Lebruns aufs genaueste aufgeprägt: strahlende Augen, geschwellte und locker geöffnete Lippen mit lächelnd hochgezogenen Winkeln, ein Antlitz voll Gelöstheit und Wärme und das Haupt zum Partner hingeneigt.[29]

---

21. Ganz anders die kraftgeschwellte Muskulatur des sich anhebenden "Laurentius" in dem frühen Marmorwerk.

22. *Conférence de Mr. Lebrun ... sur l'expression générale et particulière enrichies des figures gravées par B. Picart*, Amsterdam, 1698, pl. 6, 8 und 30; *Conference of Mr. Lebrun ... upon Expression general and particular*, translated from the French and adorned with 43 copper plates, London, 1701, Nr. 6 und 22.

23. Nicht zu übersehen die Differenzierung der Stoffe, des dünneren Kopftuchs gegenüber dem dichteren Ärmelgewebe.

24. Beispielsweise die Zeichnung zur Hl. Ursula für S. Maria del Popolo (Br.-W. Tfl. 41).

25. H. Kauffmann, "Berninis Longinus", *Gedenkband der Bibliotheca Hertziana*, 1962, 366 ff.

26. In welcher Weise Antikes hereinspricht, mag durch eine der Niobiden-Florenz angedeutet werden.

27. Man wird nicht unterlassen, die Christusfigur des "Pasce Oves"-Reliefs in der St. Petervorhalle (Vorzeichnungen Br.-W. Tfl. 12 f.) zu vergleichen bis hin zu dem weggeneigten Kopf mit der asymmetrischen Frisur. Vgl. übrigens den Engel in O. Gentileschis "Hl. Cäcilie" (Gall. Corsini-Rom).

28. Das den Körper umfliessende Gewand vibriert noch züngelnder und hebt durch Kräuse die glatte Haut nebenan noch lichter hervor, ein raffiniertes Meisterstück, in dem im Wetteifer mit antiken Beispielen; ich begnüge mich mit dem Hinweis auf Marg. Bieber, *Griechische Kleidung*, Berlin, 1928, Tfl. VII 2 (eine der Nereiden von Xanthos), VIII 2-3 (Aphrodite im Thermenmuseum), IX 2 (die nur wie Pezschwänzchen ansetzenden Falten, mindere Qualität). Im römischen Thermenmuseum notierte ich mir die Ceres Nr. 11, ferner Nr. 14. In Berninis eigenem Schaffen ist das leichte Gewand der Justitia am Grabmal Urbans VIII. das nächste Vergleichsstück.

29. *Conférence de Mr. Lebrun ...*, 1698, pl. 18; der Begriff "Amour simple" bedarf möglicherweise einer philologischen

Die Komposition bekam ihre endgültige Form, als der Künstler sich für die Profillage der Hauptfigur entschied. Er hätte der Statue des "Sebastian" verschiedene Aspekte abgewinnen können, denn man kann schwanken, ob dies Frühwerk auf eine bevorzugte Ansicht angelegt war.[30] Die Wendung der Theresa ins Profil bedeutete nicht nur eine Abkehr von der zuvor beabsichtigten Frontalität und eine Neuerung in der Ikonographie der spanischen Mystikerin. Nimmt man die ihrer Art nach heraldischen Allegorien am Epitaph für Carlo Barberini (1630), desgleichen den frühen "Laurentius" aus, dessen Lagerung auf dem Rost nicht auszuweichen war, so griff Bernini im Ringen um die Theresa zum ersten Mal und aus freier Wahl zu der in Seitenansicht hingelagerten Gestalt. Seitdem kann die Szene kaum mehr anders gedacht werden, so zwingend ist die Kraft dieser neuen Erfindung. Die Alternative zwischen Front- und Profilansicht hat den Künstler in diesen Jahren auch bei anderen Aufgaben beschäftigt und wie es scheint beunruhigt. In den Vorzeichnungen zur "Veritas" erprobte er beide Möglichkeiten und entschloss sich—umgekehrt zum Werdegang der "Theresa"—in der Marmorausführung zu dem breit auseinander gelegten Kontrapost in Vorderansicht. Der Umschwung in der Entwicklung des "Vierströmebrunnens" hat etwas in hohem Grade Fesselndes. Noch in dem stattlichen, scheinbar fertig abgerundeten und zur Ausführung bestimmten Bozzetto blieb es bei dem Vertikalismus der vier Flussgötter an den vier Kanten des viergeteilten Felsens, den vier Engeln vergleichbar, die überm Bronzebaldachin (St. Peter) vor den vier geschweiften Bügeln seiner Bekrönung aufgerichtet stehen. Ebenso kehren sich am Brunnenmodell die Flussgötter radial nach aussen, bevor sie im Monument auf der Piazza Navona in Breitenansicht quer gelagert werden und ein neuer

Rhythmus eingreift: statt der vier gleichwertigen Seiten entstanden zwei Hauptfronten und zwei subordinierte Flanken. In Zukunft ist Bernini zu der früher bevorzugten Frontalität nicht wieder zurückgekehrt, bis zur "Lodovica Albertoni" und bis zu dem Grabmal Alexanders VII.—zum Unterschied von dem Grabmal Urbans VIII.—wirkt die Wendung der späteren 40er Jahre fort. Die Genese der "Theresa" bekam durch die neue Konzeption ihre bestimmende Richtung.

Mehrere Formwerte waren darin eingeschlossen. Die Lagerung macht schon beim ersten Anblick die körperliche Schwächung evident. Die Gestalt kann breiter, ausladender zur Wirkung kommen, und eine grössere Richtungsvielfalt ermöglicht ein reicher abgestuftes und markanteres Bewegungsbild. Wie tief auch der Kopf zurücksinkt, verliert er nicht durch Verkürzung an Gewicht, mimischer Ausdruckskraft noch Würde. Der Künstler kann konzentrieren: nicht beide Arme müssen zu sehen sein, und durch die Verschmälerung der Brust verstärkt sich die Uberlegenheit des Kopfes. Ausdrucksorgane rücken zusammen und ihre Wirkung wird verdoppelt wie sich hier Kopf und Schulter qualvoll bedrängen, darunter die senkrechte Bahn den Arm überlang und wie gelähmt erscheinen lässt. Rechnet der Künstler mit Oberlicht, so bietet eine seitlich gelagerte Gestalt ausgedehntere Beleuchtungsflächen dar, sodass die Figur zum grössten Teil dem Licht ausgesetzt ist. Am "Longinus" und seiner Beleuchtung von der Peterskuppel aus hatte Bernini Erfahrungen gemacht. Am Gewand der Theresa räumte er dem von oben einfallenden Licht Querfalten möglichst aus dem Wege; flächige, meist senkrecht abgleitende Bahnen walten vor, an denen die Beleuchtung aus der Höhe entlangstreift. Nur strichweis zeichnen sich Schatten ab—anders die Wolken mit ihren breiten und dunstigen Dunkelzonen. Infolgedessen liegt über der Heiligen nahezu schattenlose Helligkeit gebreitet.[31] Als eine Lichtgestalt oder als Erleuchtete ist sie anzusehen inmitten der tieftonigen Farbigkeit der Architektur, und dem matten Grau der Wolken überlegen.[32] Eines der Beispiele, bei denen

Interpretation, denn nachdenklich stimmt mich G. Etchegoyen, *L'Amour Divin, Essai sur les sources de Ste Thérèse*, Bordeaux, 1923, 53. Zum Thema und zur Definition des "Amor divinus" nehme ich hier Bezug auf V. Cartari, *Imagini dei Dei*, zuerst Vendig 1556 (die Ausgabe Venedig 1647 ist dem Neudruck Graz 1963 mit Einleitung von Koschatzki zugrunde gelegt); auf einen Stich von Hieronymus Wierix: "De goddelijke liefde overwint de aardse liefde" (Knipping, *Ikonographie der Gegenreformatie*, I, 65, Abb. 40); die Kritik des Orazio Gentileschi an Giov. Bagliones "Amore sacro" und die dadurch veranlasste zweite Fassung des Themas von Baglione (H. Voss, *Jahrb. d. preuss. Kunstsammlungen*, 1923, 93 ff., und A. Bertolotti, *Artisti lombardi a Roma*, Milano, 1881, II, 62 f., 14.9.1603); Guido Renis "Amore sacro e profano" Genua, über das Exemplar in Pisa der Katalog der Guido Reni—Ausstellung 1954, Nr. 24, um 1625; dazu das Beispiel des Sebastianbildes von Ger. Seghers mit dem Stich von P. Pontius (s.o. Anm.).

30. Man hat die Wahl zwischen den recht entgegengesetzten Aufnahmen bei A. Riccoboni, *Roma nel Arte, La Scultura...*, Roma, 1942, Tav. 230 ("Duquésnoy") und bei R. Wittkower, a.a.O., Tfl. 5, ausserdem noch Zwischenstufen wie der bei V. Martinelli, *Bernini*, Verona, 1953, 20, Abb. 4 gezeigten. Der Abbildung bei Riccobono möchte ich den Vorzug geben.

31. Der Tonbozzetto in Leningrad (47 × 42 cm, herausragende Endigungen, auch der Engelkopf leider verloren)—vgl. G. Matzulewitsch, "Tre Bozzetti di G. L. Bernini all'Ermitage di Leningrado", *Boll. d'Arte*, 48, 1963, 67 ff.—steht doch wohl nicht auf der Höhe eines Originals, hat nicht die Frische der saftigeren verlässigen Werke seiner Hand. Dazu wirkt das Gesicht der Theresa puppenhaft unentwickelt. Nähme man ihn ernst, so würde man vermerken, dass sein krauseres Gewoge im Marmorwerk geglättet, Knäuel entwirrt, die Oberfläche gleitender behandelt worden ist.

32. Die Art der Aufrauhung—durch den Abdruck eingepresster Stricke—hat Nicodemus Tessin 1673 bemerkt und ausführlicher notiert; O. Sirèn, *Nicodemus Tessin D.Y.S. Studieresor*, Stockholm, 1914, 163.

nicht fraglich ist, dass Bernini das Marmorweiss nicht als Farblosigkeit, sondern als einen echten positiven Farbwert angesehen und angestrebt und in seine Rechnung aufgenommen hat. Profillage und Oberlicht gehen also zusammen, jene kann dieses herausgefordert haben, wenn Bernini nicht schon vorher die Eigenbeleuchtung des Sacellums—über den Franziskusaltar der Cappella Raimondi hinaus—vorgesehen hatte.

Bedenken wir weiter den Einfluss der Profilstellung auf die Bildform, so bringt sie eine Distanzierung gegenüber dem Beschauer mit sich. Frontalität schlägt zu ihm eine Brücke ("Äussere Einheit"), jene verharrt dagegen in ihrer Tiefenschicht und weicht in eine objektivere Sphäre zurück.[33] Was an Stille, Heimlichkeit, Einsamkeit der "Theresa" Gruppe innewohnt, liegt hauptsächlich in dieser ihrer Absonderung von der Beschauerzone begründet, ist also erst auf dieser fortgeschrittenen Entwicklungsstufe in sie eingezogen. Der Gegensatz zu den ganz auf "äussere Einheit" hin komponierten Seitenreliefs der Herren aus dem Hause Cornaro konnte so erst volle Schärfe bekommen.

In diesem Stadium besitzen wir die Gewissheit einer Zweifigurengruppe. Theresas Profilstellung drängte auf ein einfaches Gegenüber in einem innerbildlichen Geschehenszusammenhang. Nach Theresas Schilderung hätte der Engel mit dem Pfeil auf der anderen Seite, ihr zur Linken erscheinen müssen. Nicht nur um der Links-Rechts-Gravitation willen, wird Bernini davon abgewichen sein, sondern auch die Sichtverhältnisse in der Weise bedacht haben, dass der im Langhaus sich Nähernde zuerst Theresa zu Gesicht bekommen und sie nicht vom Rücken her wahrnehmen würde.

Die Gruppe lebt von der Beschränkung auf die Zweizahl. Die "Verherrlichung der Passionsreliquien" in den Reliefs der Kuppelpfeiler von St. Peter und die "Franziskusentrückung" waren von Puttenengeln umspielt. Wie schlicht, ohne jeden Aufwand spielt sich dagegen das Geschehen im Theresaaltar ab! Bernini hätte darauf hinweisen können, dass das Wenige und Grosse der klassizistischen Forderung nach dem Bedeutenden bei geringer Figurenzahl angemessen war. Seit die mit "Aeneas und Anchises" einsetzende faszinierende Reihe seiner Marmorgruppen in der "Daphne" ihren Gipfel und ihr Ende erreicht hatte, war Bernini nicht wieder mit einem Thema befasst worden, bei dem er seine Kunst des Gruppierens hätte erweisen oder weiter fortbilden können. Man hat

gesagt, nur psychisch nicht formal seien die Partner auf einander eingestimmt.[34] Sehen wir aber klar genug, was Bernini unter Gruppierung verstand, wie er ein Zusammenspiel oder einen Rapport organisierte?

Berninis frühe Gruppen lassen sich als Entfaltungen eines und desselben Leitbildes begreifen und zusammensehen.[35] Ob die beiden Akteure über- oder nebeneinander geordnet sind, Parallelismus geht durch, und Umkehrungen, rückläufige oder reziproke Aktionen binden ein Figurenpaar aneinander, schliessen es zusammen und von der Umwelt ab. Die "Daphne"-Gruppe empfängt ihren Einklang und ihre konfliktgeladene Spannung aus der Verdoppelung der "figura serpentinata" bei gegenläufiger Rotation den Säulenwindungen des Bronzetabernakels gleich; der Verfolger und die Verfolgte korrespondieren in scharf durchdachtem "vice versa". Zu einer Figur wird eine zweite hinzuerfunden und als ein Gegenbild ihr zugesellt. Beide agieren zugleich aufeinander zu und voneinander weg, ein Hinüber und Herüber in einem ausschliesslich bilateralen Widerspiel der ganzen Leiber. Eben darin liegt die höhere Einheit oder die Ganzheit der Gruppe: Gedanken an eine Erweiterung der Szene durch Hinzutritt noch anderer Personen kommen nicht auf. Indem jede Figur auf die andere rückbezogen ist, tritt der Gegensatz und der Gradunterschied im Ausdruck der Affekte ans Licht, und das Figurenleben wird in ein rhythmisch gesteigertes, auf eine Kulmination hindrängendes Formenspiel gefasst. Diesem aus dem Manierismus fortwirkenden Formalismus war Bernini zur Zeit der Theresa-Gruppe entwachsen. Keine dieser beiden Figuren hätte sich von der anderen aus ersinnen lassen, beide sind von verschiedenen Vorformen aus in das Thema und in ihre Rollen eingetreten. Für das Persönliche, Individuelle, für die beseelte Gebärde suchte Bernini das treffende, ausschöpfende Körperbild auf gesonderten Wegen, sowohl für Theresa wie für den Engel. Die Anspannung der Kausalität, die augenblickliche Zuspitzung derart, dass die Heilige in plötzlichem Erschrecken die Hände schützend oder abwehrend hochnimmt, hat der Künstler nur als eine anfängliche Durchgangsphase seiner Entwurfsarbeit angesehen und überwunden, in ihrem einfachen Entgegenharren hat der Künstler den tieferen Ausdruck gefunden. Zuletzt mässigt der Engel sein Tempo, richtet sich auf und nimmt Abstand, sein Ausholen mit dem Pfeil gleicht dem Innehalten in der Umkehr. Beide verweilen, als stände die Zeit still.

33. Es gibt keine Verkürzung eines herausgerichteten Gliedes, wie es sich ergeben hätte, wäre die Heilige nach der Gewandstudie mit der Gebärde ihres linken Arms ausgeführt worden.

34. R. Pane, *Bernini Architetto*, Venetia, 1953, 115 f.; vgl. andererseits A. Blunts Bemerkung über einen möglichen Einfluss der Theresagruppe auf Poussins "Verkündigung" (Nat. Gall., London): *Bull. de la Société Poussin*, 1947, 18 ff.
35. H. Kauffmann, "Die 'Aeneas und Anchises'—Gruppe von G. L. Bernini", *Festschrift für Theodor Mueller*, München, 1965, 281 ff.

Das Ensemble fügt sich nicht mehr dem Vertikalismus, der in den frühen Gruppen dominierte und sie emporsteilte. Allein, wie ähnlich gravitiert auch jetzt wieder das Zusammenspiel! Von links her wird der Beschauer hereingeleitet: wie Apollo lässt der Engel den Raum hinter sich, aus dem er gekommen ist. Dagegen wird rechts wieder eine Grenze gesetzt, über die es bei "Theresa" wie bei "Daphne" nicht weitergeht: links der offene, rechts der bündig geschlossene Umriss, der senkrecht abstürzt und in seinem unteren Verlauf zur Mitte zurückgebogen ist. Man kann die Anordnung nicht umkehren. Wieder sind in der Theresagruppe die Beiden um eine halbe Armlänge voneinander entfernt oder miteinander verschränkt. Mit diesen Zügen ist Berninis Vortragsstil aus seiner Frühzeit in das Altarwerk seiner hohen Reife übergegangen, und doch ist das Ganze, schon durch den Mittenbezug anders gestimmt. Ein Gefälle geht von links nach rechts. In einer aufsteigenden Diagonalen schwebten die Engel mit den Passionswerkzeugen in den Ädikulen der Kuppelpfeiler von St. Peter vor dem wolkenähnlichen Marmorgrund empor, der als Himmelssphäre hinter ihnen wie hinter der Theresa ausgespannt ist. Dagegen ist im Theresaaltar zu fühlen, dass der Engel aus der Höhe niedergestiegen ist. Jede Aktion bekommt ihr Mass durch eine behutsame Angleichung aller Grössen. Ein Parallelogramm in Gestalt einer verzogenen Raute liesse sich der ganzen Gruppe umschreiben, und geht man das Gefüge durch, so wird man wahrnehmen, dass ein übereinstimmendes Grössenmass in den Hauptstücken wiederkehrt und kein Übermass oder Übergewicht die Vergleichlichkeit durchbricht.[36] Dadurch ist dem Beisammen die Balance gesichert. Das leichte Engelgeschöpf vermag die hohe Gestalt der Heiligen aufzuwiegen, und die feine Rechnung soll nicht übersehen werden, mit der eine Partie der Kutte wie zufällig über die Knie der Theresa herübergeholt und doch gerade so gelegt und bemessen

36. Die Spannweite der Arme des Engels gleicht der Höhe seiner Gestalt, der Strecke von Theresas Scheitel bis zu den Fingerspitzen ihrer rechten Hand, ihrer Breite (wagerecht in Höhe von Theresas rechtem Knie), schliesslich noch der unteren Schräge vom Fuss zum Knie und der oberen von Kopf zu Kopf.

ist, dass der Engel darüber sie fortsetzt, als wäre es ein Gewandstück von ihm und gehörte zu ihm. Und so gemässigt und ausgewogen werden die Kontraste fühlbar. Der agile, die Arme ausbreitende Engel und die wie gelähmte Heilige, ihr dichtes, beim Steigen der Wolke angedrücktes Gewand und sein schleierartiges, beim Herabkommen luftfangendes Kleid, seine offene und gedehnte, von hellem Licht beschienene Schulter und die hochgestaute der Heiligen. Jedes ein Ausdrucksmotiv und kennzeichnend für die Person, und das eine antwortet auf das andere und gewinnt dadurch an unverwechselbarer Prägnanz. Durch die ganzen Gestalten geht ein kunstvolles Widerspiel: beider Unterkörper im Profil, aber der Engel dreht sich zu uns heraus, Theresa von uns weg, doch in den parallel gestellten, vor- und zurückgelehnten, beidemal zur Herzseite geneigten Köpfen wechselt es um, kehrt sich der Engel ins Profil, zeigt Theresa ihr Antlitz nahezu voll. Der zielende Blick des Engels bindet dies Hin und Her noch ausdrücklich zusammen. Wie früher einigen die Korrespondenzen das Paar, doch greifen sie nicht mehr so taktmässig wie die genau regulierten Aktfiguren der Frühzeit ineinander. In dem einfacheren Gegenüber kommt die dramatische Spannung nicht zur Entladung, sondern wird in der Schwebe gehalten. Hier ist die Gruppierungsweise der Spätkunst über den Vierströmebrunnen bis zur Kathedra Petri angelegt. Allein, der Meister der "Daphne"-Gruppe ist in der "Theresa" noch wiederzuerkennen. Im Grad der Formendichtigkeit, in der Pracht und Leuchtkraft steht keine der anderen nach, und die Zusammenschau mit der Naturwelt, in die die Menschengestalten hineinwachsen oder gebettet sind, macht es nicht schwer, von der Schöpfung der Jugendjahre zu derjenigen aus der hohen Reifezeit überzugehen. Im kühnen Wagnis, dort die Metamorphose, hier das Wolkenschweben zu bewältigen, sind beide einander gewachsen.

Der hohe Anspruch und das subtile Ausformen haben an der Vollendung der Theresagruppe zusammengewirkt. Auf dieser Grundlage wäre das Verhältnis zwischen Berninis Bildwerk und dem Text der "Vida della Madre Teresa de Jesus" zu erörtern.

ANTHONY BLUNT

Two Drawings for Sepulchral Monuments by Bernini

The two drawings which are the subject of this article are of totally different kinds, but each has a certain interest in connection with well-known sepulchral monuments by Bernini. The first (Fig. 1) is a rapid sketch for the tomb of Countess Matilda in St. Peter's; the second (Fig. 2) is a highly finished drawing for the tomb of a doge which does not appear to have been executed, but which contains ideas used by the artist in some of his later works.

The study for the tomb of Countess Matilda[1] is in the small but regrettably neglected collection of Italian drawings in the Musée des Beaux-Arts, Brussels, and comes, like most of the drawings in the museum, from the collection formed by de Crez in the later part of the nineteenth century. It is unfortunately cut, with the result that the head of the statue is incomplete, and the whole of the arch which encloses it is missing. The main features of the tomb as it stands today are already traceable in the drawing: the sarcophagus, the inscription flanked by two figures, and then the statue of the Countess standing in the niche, flanked by concave panels. There are, however, important differences. On the tomb the inscription is flanked by two putti, but the drawing shows in their place allegorical figures of Religion and Justice, easily recognizable by their attributes. The figure of the Countess, though only indicated in a few rapid pen strokes, is different in its pose and in its relation to the niche. It stands on what appears to be a rather elaborate pedestal, quite different from the simple plinth that it has today. The figure is smaller in relation to the niche than in the actual tomb and is entirely contained within the opening. The main movement of the drapery is in the opposite sense, and the arms have different poses: the right hand holds the sceptre, as in the statue, but in an upright pose, while the left arm appears to be stretched out, perhaps holding the keys, but certainly not the tiara. The sarcophagus is decorated with a bas-relief showing the submission of Henry IV to Gregory VII, of which the main outlines are already fixed, but it stands on lion's feet and is topped by scrolls leading up to the inscribed cartellino, which is considerably more elaborate than in the executed monument.

The drawing is no doubt one of the small sketches specifically mentioned in the document of 1644, in which Bernini sets out precisely what he himself has contributed to the execution of the whole tomb.[2] In character it is typical of Bernini's more sketchy drawings of the 1640's, such as those for the *Pasce Oves meas* and the tomb of Urban VIII.[3]

The second drawing[4] is a design for the tomb of a doge. It follows the Venetian tradition in that the monument is designed to surround a door, presumably leading from the church into a family chapel. The doge is shown kneeling on a sarcophagus; below him, in a panel immediately over the door, is a skeleton holding an hour-glass and a scythe; above is a coat-of-arms, unhappily not filled in, carried by two trumpeting angels; and on either side are figures of Charity and Fortitude.

There is no evidence to show that Bernini ever erected a monument to any of the doges; nor indeed were his connections with Venice at all close. According to Baldinucci he made busts of Cardinals Agostino and Pietro Valier, which survive in the Seminario Patriarcale in Venice,[5] but these are both very early works and, although he might have been invited to design a monument for the Doge Bertucci Valier, who died in 1658, there is no reason to suppose that he continued in touch with the Valier family after his early years.[6] He also had some share in the tomb of Cardinal Gerolamo Dolfin, designed by his father for

1. The drawing is in pen and brown ink and measures 21 × 13.8 cm.

2. Cf. R. Wittkower, *Gian Lorenzo Bernini*, London, 1955, p. 196.
3. H. Brauer and R. Wittkower, *Die Zeichnungen des Gianlorenzo Bernini*, Berlin, 1931, pls. 12 ff., 18.
4. The drawing measures 42.3 × 30 cm, on paper without watermark. The ground plans at the bottom, the arch at the top, and the string-course continuing the entablature of the upper order across the wall are drawn in a black chalk so faint that they are almost invisible in a reproduction. The rest of the monument is drawn and washed with brown ink, apparently without underdrawing in chalk. In certain areas, particularly down the right-hand side of the monument, the paper has been worn away and the drawing has been retouched: the right-hand console, the end of the upper entablature, and parts of the drapery of the figure of Fortitude are the parts principally affected.
5. R. Wittkower, *op. cit.*, p. 190, no. 25.
6. The doge is in fact commemorated by a statue on the tomb erected by his successor, Doge Silvestro Valier (d. 1700), in SS. Giovanni e Paolo, to the design of Andrea Tirali.

the church of S. Michele all'Isola,[7] but in this case also there is no reason to think that he worked for other members of the family, and there was no Dolfin doge during the remainder of the artist's life.

With one Venetian, however, Bernini must have been in close contact over a number of years, namely Cardinal Federico Cornaro, who was in Rome from 1644 till his death in 1653, and who commissioned Bernini to decorate his chapel in S. Maria della Vittoria during that period. The Cardinal's younger brother, Francesco, who was elected doge in 1656, only held the office for a few weeks, but their father, Giovanni, had been doge from 1625 to 1629, and there is evidence to show that projects for erecting a monument to his memory were being made just at the time that the Cardinal was in Rome and in contact with Bernini.

In 1654 Francesco Cornaro made a will,[8] in which he explained that he had been prevented from putting up a monument which he had planned for his father in his chapel in the Theatine church of S. Nicolò da Tolentino, but that he had collected the marbles and other material for it, and he instructed his son Federico to undertake the erection of the monument within two months of his death. The chapel was completed according to his instructions and is described in Giustiniano Martinioni's *Aggiunte* to Sansovino's *Venetia Città Nobilissima*, which appeared in 1663.[9] After mentioning that the chapel contains the tombs of both Giovanni and Francesco Cornaro, Martinioni continues: 'A questi degni Principi sono eretti due ben ordinati Depositi dalle parti del loro Altare, l'uno incontro all'altro, fatti simili, di questa forma: Sopra la base che liga con li pilastri della Chiesa, vi è un Quarisello con sua cimasa, e regolon di sopra, che tuol sù le basi delle colonne di ordine Corinto; nel spatio de mezzo sono posti li sepolcri, e sopra essi li loro ritratti scolpiti in marmo. Sopra le colonne vi è la cornice con suo rementato, due Quariselle et alette, che tolgono su un'altra cima di ordine composito, il tutto di marmi fini benissime lavorati, et intagliati.' These monuments were apparently destroyed in 1720

by the second doge, Giovanni Cornaro, who is responsible for the chapel as it now stands.[10]

From all this we learn that Federico Cornaro's brother, Francesco, was planning in the early 1650's to erect a tomb to his father in his chapel in S. Nicolò da Tolentino, and, though it is clear from Martinioni's description that what was finally carried out bore no relation to the design shown in Bernini's drawing, it is quite possible that the latter may represent a project sent from Rome by the Cardinal, in the hope that his brother might be persuaded to employ the great Roman artist who had just attained such superlative results in the chapel designed for him in S. Maria della Vittoria.[11]

The Cornaro chapel in S. Nicolò da Tolentino is in fact the south transept, the end wall of which contains an elaborate marble altar with a *Virgin in Glory* by Palma Giovane. It is not easy to imagine that the church authorities would have allowed a monument to have been constructed which would have protruded so far into the crossing as would have been the case with Bernini's project—and indeed this may have been the reason why it was never carried out—but the dimensions appear to fit almost exactly. The drawing has on it a scale which has no unit indicated but which is almost certainly in palmi, and on this assumption the width of the whole monument would have been 33.5 palmi, that is to say, 7.37 metres, which is almost precisely the width of the transept, if it is assumed that the monument would have come in front of the pilasters which face east and west at its entrance.[12]

Stylistically the Venetian design takes its place quite logically at this stage in Bernini's development. In its basic form the design is close to the tomb of Cardinal Pimentel in S. Maria sopra Minerva, designed by Bernini soon after 1653.[13] In each design the base consists of a straight central section, flanked by two concave side bays; above this is a stepped zone, supporting allegorical groups, two of which, Charity and Fortitude, occur in both schemes; and in each case the design culminates in the figure of the dead man kneeling on a sarcophagus.

There are, of course, many differences in detail. The Venetian design is much taller in its proportions; in the middle of the base it has an open door with a skeleton above it; it has only two, instead of four,

7. R. Wittkower, *op. cit.*, p. 183, no. 16.
8. The will is in the Archivio di Stato, Venice (Testamenti G. Paganazzi, 806, no. 187). I am very grateful to Mrs. F. Vivian for tracing and copying this will for me. It is dated June 25, 1654. The relevant part of it reads as follows:
'Quando in vita non havesi fatto per le grave spese della casa, il deposito del q. Ser^mo mio Padre nella mia cappella in chiesa de' Padri Teatini nelle due ali dell'una e l'altra parte, conform'al disegno, per il qual effetto ho di già comprato le pietre et li si ritroveranno nella mia bottega di tagliapietra a San Mauritio, ordino e comando che doppo due mese dalla mia morte sia principiato a fabricare e si continui con ogni celerità a perfezionare.'
9. P. 208.

10. Cf. A. da Mosto, *I Dogi di Venezia*, Venice, 1939, p. 227.
11. The portrait of the doge appears at the extreme right of the relief of the Cornaro family to the left of Sta Teresa in S. Maria della Vittoria, where he is shown with the same square beard as in the drawing (cf. R. Wittkower, *op. cit.*, p. 209, Fig. 58).
12. Cf. the plan in *Le Fabbriche più cospicue di Venezia*, published by the Accademia di Belle Arti, Venice, 1815-20, II, pl. 99.
13. R. Wittkower, *op. cit.*, p. 217, no. 56.

allegorical groups at the middle stage; the figure of the dead man is shown frontally and not in profile; there is no architectural setting for the central figure, and there are no trumpeting angels; but all these features of the Venetian design which are not to be found in the Pimentel monument are taken up in the design for the tomb of Alexander VII, begun before his death in 1667 and erected under the pontificate of his successor, Clement IX.[14]

The first design for this[15] has a central convex bay with an inscription flanked by two concave bays containing doors. Above this is the kneeling figure of the pope, set against a sarcophagus and flanked by four groups of figures reminiscent of those on the Pimentel tomb, and the whole design culminates in a pair of trumpeting angels. A variant of this scheme[16] shows the figure of the pope kneeling on the sarcophagus, an arrangement directly related to the Venetian scheme.

These designs were made when it was planned to erect the tomb in S. Maria Maggiore, and when the site was changed to one in St. Peter's the scheme was radically altered; but even in the form in which the tomb was eventually erected in this new position certain fundamental elements of the Venetian design were preserved.

Of these the most important is the fact that the monument is planned around a door. This had long been a normal manner of tomb design in Venice, but it does not seem to have been used in Rome before this time. The idea of placing a skeleton over the door is also unusual, and though it is introduced with much more dramatic effect in the tomb of Alexander, where it draws back the curtain leading to the grave, the basic *concetto* is the same in the two projects.

It seems likely, therefore, that, when Bernini found himself compelled to design the tomb of Alexander VII for a site in St. Peter's over a door, he bethought himself of Venetian tombs. In this way the commission to design a tomb for a Venetian doge—even if the design was never executed—may have had an important influence on one of Bernini's most famous tombs.

The exact status of this drawing is not easy to determine. At first sight the obvious weakness of the architectural drawing, particularly in the two lateral concave bays, would lead one to conclude that it was the work of a studio assistant, but similar weaknesses occur in a drawing for the tomb of Alexander VII, which is accepted by Professor Wittkower as an original,[17] and it might even be maintained that Bernini's studio assistants, being often architectural specialists, are sometimes more competent than the master in this particular field.[18] Moreover, the drawing of the figures, notably those of the doge and the skeleton, is extremely vivacious, and is comparable both in manner and in quality with originals by Bernini, such as the study for the tomb of Alexander VII already referred to and, more unexpectedly, with sketches for St. John preaching, in Leipzig.[19] In execution it is strikingly similar to the Windsor studies for a chariot designed for Agostino Chigi, which are classified by Professor Wittkower as studio works,[20] but which, I have elsewhere ventured to suggest, may well be originals.[21] Even certain technical tricks, such as the flicked-in touches representing the inscription, have their parallels in Bernini's work, witness the design for a catafalque in honour of the Duc de Beaufort, in the British Museum.[22]

When the drawing was shown in an exhibition at the Courtauld Institute Galleries in 1964, I catalogued it as 'Attributed to Bernini', but was reproached by several experts on Roman drawings for my timidity. I should still like to leave the question open, because the borderline between genuine and studio drawings is in my opinion exceptionally difficult to define in the case of Bernini; but I confess to a greater feeling of optimism that this drawing may fall on the right side of the frontier.[23]

14. *Ibid.*, p. 238, no. 77, and Brauer and Wittkower, *op. cit.*, pp. 168 ff.
15. Brauer and Wittkower, *op. cit.*, pl. 129a.
16. *Ibid.*, pl. 129b.
17. *Ibid.*, pl. 129a.
18. Cf. even the feeble drawing for the monument of Alexander VII in Siena Cathedral (*ibid.*, pl. 160a and b).
19. *Ibid.*, pl. 106b and c.
20. *Ibid.*, p. 137.
21. A. Blunt and L. Cooke, *Roman Drawings at Windsor Castle*, London, 1960, p. 25, nos. 50, 51.
22. Brauer and Wittkower, *op. cit.*, pl. 121.
23. Since this article was written Professor Wittkower has published both drawings in the second edition of his *Gianlorenzo Bernini* (1966), pp. 201, 216, accepting both as originals.

ANDREINA GRISERI

Una fonte "retorica" per il Barocco a Torino

La fonte appartiene al Tesauro, che a più riprese è stato indicato come efficiente anche per l'iconografia delle arti figurative; ma come interferisse su di un piano non solo di suggerimenti iconografici, anzi per tutta una struttura, appunto retorica, vorrei chiarire dopo gli accenni che ne ho fornito in occasione della Mostra recente del Barocco a Torino, nel 1963.[1]

Indicando con maggior precisione un referto ampio, fonte preziosa (e nei riguardi delle arti figurative finora non considerata), a documentare i soggetti e il contesto iconografico della pittura e della decorazione in Palazzo Reale: così emerge dal testo delle *Inscriptiones* dettate dal Tesauro e raccolte nell'edizione del 1666 dall'erudito Panealbo,[2] ad una data molto

1. Vedi A. Griseri, in *Catalogo Mostra del Barocco Piemontese*, Sezione Pittura, in Prefazione a pag. 6–7; schede a pag. 57–64; e nell'*Itinerario per Palazzo Reale*, pag. 29 segg. Il rapporto di Tesauro con l'ambiente figurativo di Palazzo Reale è stato in seguito messo in risalto, per quanto riguarda il teatro e le feste, nel testo di M. Ferrero-Viale, *Feste delle Madame Reali di Savoia*, a cura dell'Istituto Bancario San Paolo in Torino, 1965. Queste mie pagine rientrano ora nel capitolo III° di una sintesi dedicata al Barocco in corso di stampa presso l'Editore Einaudi, Torino, che molto vivamente ringrazio.

2. Riporto il frontespizio di questa seconda edizione con aggiunte (neppure la prima è finora stata considerata); e in base a queste "Iscrizioni" occorrerà rivedere la cronologia di molte opere in Palazzo Reale, Venaria, ecc.

"D. EMMANUELIS THESAURI
Comitis & Maiorum Insignium Equitis.
INSCRIPTIONES
Quotquot reperiri potuerunt
Opera et diligentia

EMMANUELIS PHILIBERTI PANEALBI,
In Augustotaurinensi Alma Universitate,
Sacrorum Canonum Interpretis Primarij.

Cum eiusdem Notis et Illustrationibus.

EDITIO SECUNDA.
Ab Impressionis Primae innumeris mendis
Authoris manu expurgata.

Multisque Inscriptionibus aucta.

TAURINI, M.DC.LXVI.

Typis Bartholomaei Zappatae
Superiorum permissu."

(p. 141)

REGII PALATII
TAURINENSIS
ORNAMENTA.

Nihil his in Aedibus est, quod non rapiat oculos; Regiamque Caroli Emmanuelis eo Nomine Secundi, Magnificentiam, vel

importante per Torino, che allora cresceva tra il Palazzo Reale e la Venaria.

tacendo, non eloquatur, Plurimus hic Auri nitor, pretiosa supellex, admirabiles Sculpturae, nobilis Pictura, nobiliores Historiae, immemorabilis aeui memoriam revocantes. Atqui, cum singulae Picturae suis inscriptionibus animentur; *omnium tamen argumenta unius Emmanuelis Thesauri ab ingenio atque calamo manare voluit optimus Princeps.*
Aedium igitur Porticum ingressis, in primo scalarum ascensu, "Equestris Statua" se profert "Victoris Amedei": quam aere fusili, marmoreo in equo sedentem, utroque artis miraculo; quasi domesticum Larem, locique Praesidem, gratissimus Filius collocavit, cum hac "Inscriptione" in anteriore Basis fronte.

D. VICTORIS AMEDEI
BELLICAM FORTITUDINEM,
ATQUE INFLEXUM IUSTITIAE RIGOREM,
METALLO EXPRESSUM VIDES.
TOTUM ANIMUM VIDERES,
SI VELOX INGENIUM,
FLEXILEMQUE CLEMENTIAM,
EXPRIMERE METALLUM POSSET.

(p. 142) Opposita in Basis fronte.

D. VICTORI AMEDEO
QUOD UNUM RAPERE FATA POTUERUNT,
REGIAM ORIS MAIESTATEM,
AETERNA VINDICAT HAEC IMAGO.
IN REGIAS VIRTUTES, ET HEROICA GESTA,
IUS NULLUM FATIS RELIQUIT FAMA.

*   *   *

AULAE REGIAE ORNAMENTA.

[Sala delle Glorie Sassoni o della Guardia Svizzera: cfr. C. Rovere, *Descrizione del Reale Palazzo di Torino*, Torino, 1858, che riporta la descrizione degli affreschi e le iscrizioni senza indicazione di provenienza—Vedi inoltre bibl. cit. in *Catalogo Mostra del Barocco Piemontese*, Torino, 1963.]
Maxima haec "Aula" conquadrata; ad summum scadentibus prima panditur; quam SAXONICAE GLORIAE nuncupare, Auctori nostro visum est: nulla enim visuntur emblemata vel ornamenta, quae insigne aliquod decus Saxonicae Domus, unde Sabaudae origo, non adumbrent. Superne, ubi multiformis aurearum trabium precursus multa in spatia rotunda & angulosa, contignationem distinguit: mediano in aequore apprimè spatioso, appictus Iupiter alte sedens, armatae Viragini, quae Saxonia est, de stemmate noscenda, sceptrum porgit: "Fatumque" astans, Diphteram, hoc est Amaltheae Caprae pellem, ubi futura omnia descripte continentur, ostendit; atque in ea grandibus literis fatidicum legitur carmen:

"His ego, nec metas rerum, nec tempora pono."
IMPERIUM SINE FINE DEDI.

Sub pedibus itaque Iouis, supta deiectam Matam "Tempus" asternatur, passis alis, fracta clepsydra, retusa falce.
....
Locum ipsum, veluti statuariam officinam, occupant informes lapides; illaborata Simulacra; marmorea Saxonum Stemmata; acuendorum scalprorum Rotae, Mallei, aliaque lapicidarum instrumenta.

E vorrei procedere oltre; ad un livello che superata la precisazione filologica indicasse come il sottofondo, (non solo figurativo), fosse intuitivamente evocato:

Reliquae Contignationis Areae, varios Trophaeorum Fasces, suis Titulis insignes, continent; ad Heroum Saxonum aeternum decus appensos. Primum Trophaeum barbarico priscorum armorum, ac gestaminum genere coagmentatum; Vandalico insigni, nempe "Aureo Leone", cruentis Clypeis insculpto; in alligata tabella Titulum gerit: SIGUEARDUS SAXONUM REX, VANDALIS EIECTIS. Primus enim Sigùeardus e Scandia in eam Vandaliae Provinciam profectus; delefrimam Gentem ab ijs sedibus expulit, Regnumq. Saxonicum fundavit.
Aliud "Trophaeum" ex diversis Christianorum Templorum, atque Altarium insignibus congestim colligatis. VIDECHINDO MAGNO, OB RELIGIONEM PROPAGATAM. Hic enim primus ab Ethnica superstitione, ab synceram Christi Religionem versus, Regnum totum convertit.
Aliud ex Navalibus armamentis. VERTEGIRUS ANGLIAE DUX, BRITANNIA SUBACTA. Nam primus felici Classe, victricia Arma in Britanniam traiecit, ut subinde dicetur.

Segue pag. 144 e segg. con descrizione degli affreschi e delle epigrafi.

[Segue la Sala delle guardie del Corpo e Dignità. Preziosa la descrizione dei soffitti: es. quello dello stesso Salone degli Svizzeri ora distrutto, e quello della sala delle Dignità.]

(p. 149)

AULA INTERIOR

Hanc "Dignitatum Aulam" vocavit Author, quod in omni ornatu praecipua Sabaudi Principatus Decora, & accrementa Comprehendat. Celsa igitur in contabulatione, aureo veluti Caelo, IMPERATORIA MAIESTAS, Mitrata, paludata, Coronas, Apices, Sceptra, Equestria signa distribuit. [Cfr. opera esposta alla mostra del Barocco 1953, scheda u. 47.] Infraque volitans Fama, buccis turgentibus geminas inflat Tubas. Sinuoso in limbo Horatianum legitur dictum, AD ORTUS SOLIS, AB HESPERIO CUBILI. Ex Ode 15. libri 4.

> Per quas latinum Nomen, & Italae
> Creuere Gentes, Famaque, & Imperi
> Porrecta Maiestas, AD ORTUS
> SOLIS, AB HESPERIO CUBILI.

[I dipinti erano di C. Dauphin e B. Caravoglia, ora perduti.] Imperialium enim Principum Dignitas, aeque in Eoo, atque Occiduo Imperio, ab Augusta Maiestate, veluti a fonte promanavit.
Mediam igitur hanc Tabulam, geminae altrinsecus Tabulae intercipientes, utranque Sabaudorum Principum Dignitatem insigniorem ostendunt: Occidentalis nempe Imperij "Perpetuum Vicariatum": & Orientalis Imperij "Perpetuum Electoratum".
Dextra ergo in Tabula "Conradus Imperator" in Procerum consessu Gladium, perpetui Vicariatus Insigne, Amedeo Secundo Sabaudiae Comiti committit. Ad Tabulae ornatum, in imo assidet "Roma" rerum Domina; & "Tiberis" Pater, flavam ex Urna effundit lympham: Rem attingit Inscriptio.

....

(p. 152)

ANTERIUS CONCLAVE
Ad Meridiem.
[Sala degli Staffieri.]

Pulcherrimum hoc, & Dignitatum Aulae contiguum Conclave, REGIIS VIRTUTIBUS merito nuncupavit Author: nam Dignitas fine Virtute, indignitas est.
Summo igitur in lacunari "Virtus" emicat, amazonica specie candido cultu, tricipitem ferrea catena cohibens, ac rutila face diverberans "Chimeram": quo Monstro Vitium omne monstratur, "Pallas" autem sublimis, Virtutem coronat; addito

una provocazione fantastica che segna il vero allargamento, oltre la tematica del manierismo del Marino, dei pittori di turno nella Galleria, e dello stesso Carlo di Castellamonte.

Maniliano dicto: CUM VIRTUTE POTESTAS. [Opera esistente, di C. Dauphin.]
Toto vero parietum ambitu Duodecim "Virtutes Regiae", totidem Tabulis visuntur expressae; suis quaeque Symbolis atque insignibus iconice distinctae. Singulis autem Tabulis appicta est consentanea Virtuti Historiola ex vetustis Sabaudorum Principum monumentis (nam recentia per se coruscant) ut quo quaeque inn Principe Regia Virtus excelluerit, imitatrix posteritas sentiat. Historiarum porro argumenta Inscriptionibus demonstrantur, non temporum, neque Principum, sed virtutum ordine servato. Prima igitur Regiarum Virtutum Regina sedet.

....

(p. 159)

INTERIUS CONCLAVE
Ad Meridiem.
[Sala dei Paggi.]

Cum nobilissimus Virtutis fructus Victoria sit; congrue noster Autor, quod Virtutum Conclavi iungitur, VICTORIARUM CONCLAVE censuit nominandum. Nec ullus sane dignior est Regiarum Aedium ornatus, quam qui res fortissime in bello gestas, ante oculos ponit. Aureo igitur in lacunari, quo nihil magnificentius, "Victoria" palmigera ipsa, palmas atque coronas donat: "Famaque" Aeneatrix, Victorum videtur nomina laudesque circumsonare; adscripto Virgiliano hemistichio: HABET VICTORIA LAUDEM. [Autore lombardo, Recchi; vedi Cat. 1963, pag. 30.]
Circa maiorem hanc Tabulam, minora spatia in orbem flexa, alites "Genios" continent; qui singuli, singula Coronarum genera, quibus Victores donabantur, ostentant, suisque distinguunt Titulis. [Per gli autori dei dipinti: C. Dauphin, A. Prelasca, ecc. vedi Cat. 1963, pag. 31.] "Laurea" hoc Titulo insignitur REDUCI TRIUMPHATORI. "Graminea", OBSIDIONE SOLUTA. "Robustea", CIVIUM SERVATORI. "Myrtea", OVANTI DECUS. "Olea", AUSPICIIS VICTORI. "Muralis", ex auro Murorum pinnas imitante, MURUM ASSILIENTI. "Prostrata", aurea, navalium rostrorum specie, NAVALI VICTORIAE. "Vallaris", item aurea ad Castrensis Valli imaginem; Lucani verbis, AUSO TRASCENDERE VALLUM.
(p. 160)
Parietes vero circumuestiunt duodecim illustriores Sabaudorum Principum "Victoriae", expressim depictae, brevique elogio declaratae: quarum tamen ordinem Fabrum incuria perturbatum nos ita corrigemus, ut verum atque historicum ordinem sequamur quilibet autem ex Elogio fabrilem inscitiam possit arguere.

PRIMA TABULA

REDIMAT SACRA LAURUS HUBERTUM:
QUI GODEFRIDO BULLIONO
PREALIORUM COMES, ET PRAEMIORUM,
REDEMPTORIS SEPULCHRUM REDEMIT.

*   *   *

Hic est Hubertus II. Amedei Primi Filius, Sabaudiae Comes, quem "Transmarinum" vocant.

II.

AD ARAM HANC
CRUENTO SUSTITIT FERRO AMEDEUS STATOR.
LAUREA DIGNUS, ET AUREA.
HOSTITUM TRIUMPHATOR, ET SUI.

*   *   *

Hic est Amedeus II. Humberti II. Filius; qui Gebennenses, absente Principe Sabaudiam populantes, ut redijt, internecioni dedit; neque a fugacium destitit caede, usquedum ad locum

Valutato dal Croce e ancora dalla critica più attuale,[3] di recente il procedimento (linguistico e fantastico) del Tesauro è stato analizzato entro una parabola di affinità elettive, in un senso di continuità (una "longue durée"), giungendo a prolungare quegli anni labirintici fino a Apollinaire, a Jean Paul (l'ingegno è l'anagramma giocoso della natura), a Eliot. In questo senso gli studi di Hocke sono riusciti davvero stimo-

hunc pervenit, quem Victorie metam esse voluit; atque Ara primum mox nobili Coenobio sacravit; cui corruptum adhuc "Stamedei" nomen haeret; quod ibi, steterit Amedeus; vel quod Gebennensium fugam stiterit. Non absurde igitur Amedeum Statorem vocat Author, uti Iovem Statorem vocavit Romulus; quod Romanorum fagam, & Sabinorum Victoriam progredi vetuisset. [Seguono le iscrizioni degli altri scomparti del fregio.] 3. Del Tesauro (1592–1675), passato giovane a Cremona nel 1619 per tenere una cattedra di retorica, vanno ricordati in questa occasione i viaggi a Napoli del 1622, il soggiorno a Roma, e dal 1624 a Milano fino al 1630. Ma già allora erano frequenti le puntate a Torino, e appartengono a questo periodo panegirici declamati in questa città dal 1626 al 1628. Fin da quegli anni egli attende alla stesura di un trattato dell'arte dell'argutezza, che poi diverrà l' "Idea dell'arguta e ingegnosa elocuzione" del *Canocchiale aristotelico*. Legatosi a Tomaso di Carignano, eletto predicatore della duchessa Cristina alla corte, divenne la personalità letteraria più in vista e più originale, interferendo direttamente nella vita artistica e suggerendo soggetti e allegorie per le decorazioni del Palazzo Reale. Dopo aver celebrato la nascita di Vittorio Amedeo I°, un libello lo costringeva a lasciare la Compagnia e riducendosi secolare passava in Fiandra presso Tomaso di Carignano come diplomatico e poi storiografo militare. Sono di questi anni i *Campeggiamenti ovvero istorie del Piemonte*, 1643-5, con incisioni del Boetto. Al ritorno, precettore presso i Carignano dal 1642, attese alla sistemazione del *Canocchiale*, steso nel 1654. Dopo il 1666 il Municipio di Torino lo incaricava della stesura di una Storia della città, incompiuta, e tra il 1669 e il 1674 apparivano i volumi da lui curati dell'opera omnia presso l'editore Zavatta. In onore del futuro Vittorio Amedeo II°, ottuagenario stese una *Filosofia morale*. Ma l'opera più rappresentativa resta tuttavia il citato *Canocchiale*, edito in una prima edizione dedicata al card. Maurizio di Savoia nel 1655 e poi, dopo varie edizioni, nel 1670 presso lo Zavatta: "Il canocchiale aristotelico o sia Idea dell'arguta e ingegnosa elocuzione che serve a tutta l'arte oratoria, lapidaria e simbolica esaminata co' principii del divino Aristotile dal conte e cavalier gran croce d. Emanuele Tesauro patrizio torinese. Quinta impressione", in cui sono presupposti per tutta la pittura decorativa che in quegli anni si svolgeva in Palazzo Reale. Per il sepolcro del Tesauro conosco un disegno acquerellato alla Bibl. Naz. di Torino. Per la bibl. vedi: L. Vigliani, *Emanuele Tesauro e la sua opera storiografica*, in "Fonti e studi di storia fossanese", R. Dep. Sub. di St. Patria, 1936; B. Croce, *I trattatisti italiani del concettismo e Baltasar Graciàn*, 1899, in "Problemi di estetica, ecc.", Bari, Laterza, 1945; Id., in *Saggi sulla letteratura italiana del '600*, Bari, Laterza, 1948; G. Marzot, *L'ingegno e il genio del Seicento*, Firenze, 1944; Samuel Leslie Bethell, *Gracian, Tesauro and the Nature of Metaphysical Wit*, in "Northern Miscellany of Literary Criticism", Manchester, 1953; G. Pozzi, *Note prelusive allo stile del Canocchiale*, in Paragone, 1953; C. Vasoli, *Le imprese del Tesauro*, in "Retorica e Barocco", Milano, 1955; E. Raimondi, *Ingegno e metafora nella poetica del Tesauro*, in "Il Verri", 1958; Id., *Grammatica retorica nel pensiero del Tesauro*, in "Lingua nostra", 1958, ora in *Letteratura Barocca*, Olschki, 1961, con ampia bibliografia; J. Rousset, *La littérature de l'âge baroque en France, Circé et le Paon*, Parigi, 1954; G. R. Hocke, *Die Welt als Labyrinth: Manier und Manie in der europäischen Kunst*, Amburgo, 1957; Id., *Manierismus in der Literatur,*

lanti, come sintesi di un'atteggiamento poetico.[4] Qui rientra Tesauro e la sua presa di posizione a Torino. In Palazzo Reale il Tesauro rappresenta fin dal 1660 una forza d'urto. L'intervento di lui non va limitato alle iscrizioni e all'impegno iconografico; il procedimento ha una portata più vasta: si estende alla cornice, e al significato più profondo di quella decorazione, come elemento primario, vitalistico. Il procedimento metaforico, come suggerimento di nuove argutezze (Tesauro è contro il luogo comune della metafora), tocca in senso fantastico il nuovo modo linguistico e l'apertura della decorazione, ricostruita come contesto architettonico. La pittura[5] al confronto è smorta, come risultato: per emblemi (erano di moda in tutta Europa), che raffiguravano ad uso fumetto un pensiero letterario; la cornice emerge al confronto come nuova ed esaltante

Amburgo, 1959; E. Raimondi, in *Trattatisti e narratori del '600*, Ricciardi, 1960. Va aggiunta ora la traduzione italiana, con aggiunte, dell'opera di G. R. Hocke, *Il manierismo nella letteratura*, ediz. Il Saggiatore, Milano, 1965. Per la letteratura emblematica che ha molti punti di contatto non solo iconografici ma di struttura con la pittura del Palazzo Reale nei fregi delle stanze del primo piano, vedi: M. Praz, *Studies in XVIIth Century Imagery: a Bibliography of Emblem Books*; Robert J. Clements, *Picta Poesis, Literary and Humanistic Theory in Renaissance Emblem Books*, Roma, 1960; W. Sypker, *Four Stages of Renaissance*, New York, 1956. Per la posizione del Tesauro a Torino, e del Marino, di fondamentale importanza le indagini, che andranno tenute presenti per le arti figurative, edite dai Congressi recenti: Terzo Convegno internazionale di Studi umanistici—Retorica e Barocco, Venezia, 1954; Secondo Congresso internazionale di Studi italiani su la Critica stilistica e il barocco letterario, Venezia, 1956; Convegno internazionale del 1960, con Atti presso l'Accademia Nazionale dei Lincei, Roma, 1962: *Manierismo, Barocco, Rococò: Concetti e termini*—con ampi esaurienti saggi di E. Raimondi, *Per una nozione di manierismo letterario (Il problema del manierismo nelle letterature europee)*, e di G. Weise, di cui andranno valutati anche i precedenti contributi: *Vitalismo, animismo e panpsichismo e la decorazione nel Cinquecento e nel Seicento* in Critica d'Arte, 1960. I° e II°. Sulla retorica del barocco, che tocca ampiamente il Tesauro vedi: P. Francastel, *Le Baroque* in Atti del V° Congresso di Lingua e Letteratura Moderna, Firenze, 1951; G. Getto, *La polemica sul Barocco*, in Letteratura e critica nel tempo, Milano, 1954; G. C. Argan, *La retorica e l'arte barocca* in Retorica e Barocco, III° Congresso Internazionale Studi Umanistici, Venezia, 1954 e Roma 1955; A. Chastel, *Le Baroque et la mort*, ibid., 1955; A. Hauser, *Storia sociale dell'arte*, Einaudi, Torino, 1955; V. L. Tapiè, *Le Baroque et la Société de l'Europe moderne*, Atti del II° Congresso Cristianesimo e ragioni di Stato, Roma, 1955. 4. Il citato testo di Hocke, nella traduzione italiana, discute fra l'altro anche la più recente bibliografia e rimando perciò a quelle stesse note. 5. Le singole biografie per i pittori attivi in Palazzo Reale (dal Demaret al Dauphin, al Caravoglia, al Dufour, fino al Miel, con molti minori), sono inserite nel *Catalogo della Mostra del Barocco* del 1963 e rimando a quella mia indagine filologica. Vorrei ora avvertire che la datazione di alcuni soffitti andrà riveduta con il testo delle "Inscriptiones" del Tesauro, datato 1666 (II edizione).

e fa piazza pulita del corrente manierismo. Un modo sincero, concreto, nella sua inclinazione retorica: in questo senso fornirà materiale all'età barocca, per convinzione intesa al piacere visivo come alla persuasione.

Mediatore di quella poetica della meraviglia, quale si esplica figurativamente nelle sale del primo piano, il Tesauro ne dilata ogni possibilità espressiva, e in quella traduzione ne ricerca il modo più idoneo e chiaro.

Liberandosi dal Castellamonte, ad opera del Tesauro l'oratoria del manierismo si innesta all'oratoria barocca, come nuovo modo della visione, ricuperato intanto nella sincerità del sentire.

Il "Canocchiale aristotelico" (o sia idea delle argustezze heroiche vulgarmente chiamate imprese. Et di tutta l'arte simbolica, et lapidaria, contenente ogni genere di figure e inscrittioni espressive di arguti e ingeniosi concetti. Esaminata in fonte co' rettorici precetti del divino Aristotele, che comprendono tutta la rettorica, e poetica elocuzione, Torino, Gio. Sînibaldo 1654), alludendo, ben oltre il concettismo, a una nuova astronomia poetico-emblematica, si protende su di un mondo aperto alle metafore dell'ingegno e della fantasia: la metafora con i nessi di una lingua dinamica, allusiva, "fa travedere in una sola parola più di un obietto", come "per un istraforo di prospettiva".

Questa non è solo strumento per l' "homo ludens" del manierismo, ma passa alla scoperta dell'oggetto in metamorfosi: nasce la decorazione a inserti naturali, e, quel che conta, una morbida concitazione, una inquietudine barocca: il pittoresco è sostenuto con qualità (non solo formali), eccellenti.

Come la metafora sfrutta le possibilità semantiche del vocabolo nel suo carattere lirico, "legando organicamente la pura terminologia con l'invenzione", ritrovando una lingua immaginosa che avvicina il Tesauro al Graciàn, così in Palazzo Reale il nuovo contenuto implica procedimenti formali, nei riguardi della cornice decorante, con uno sperimentalismo e un'entusiasmo degni di una vera e propria avanguardia. Una carica che è ormai molto vicina al barocco; e basti confrontare quegli intagli con gli stucchi precedenti del Castello del Valentino.

Il risultato in Palazzo Reale non va perciò inteso come prodotto di un edonismo epidermico, ma come una nuova proposta capace di riassumere e di indurre a nuove emozioni. Gli artigiani sembrano ora contrapporre alla fissità giocosa della grammatica manierista la mobilità naturale e rischiosa, vitale, di una lingua inedita. Un'accezione che, passando attraverso le mani degli intagliatori,[6] ricorda il procedimento di un dialetto che assurge a lingua letteraria.

Quella del Tesauro non si presentava solo come una nuova ipotesi grammaticale. Il suo intervento non limitandosi a iconografie, sia pure nuove di tono e di contenuto, ma avallando un nuovo montaggio scenico. Alla base, a riscattare tanta letteratura, erano una convinzione e una perizia artigianale così addestrate da interpretare i nessi di quella logica fantastica come nuova struttura linguistica; ancora intorno a Guarini, e nel '700 con Juvarra, non sarà difficile riconoscerne il seguito efficientissimo.

Il capitolo che riguarda il Tesauro interessa in questo senso l'utilizzazione, per la parte figurativa, di un procedimento letterario determinante. Rifiutato ogni criterio empirico, il concetto della rappresentazione artistica e della decorazione risulta fissato da un pensiero letterario-fantastico (volto non solo alla celebrazione dei fasti e delle virtù sovrane).

Tesauro e gli artigiani del legno, che ora non procedono con immagini prefabbricate, assumono consciamente la retorica come "forma simbolica", entro una dimensione aperta,[7] in uno spazio non prospettico ma certo anti-naturalistico (e perciò barocco); una relazione oltre le grandezze umane, vivificata dalla forte impressione materica, alle origini di un "Kunstwollen" inedito: la storia di questa volontà d'arte e della modificazione che ne seguirà a contatto con Guarini, e poi con Juvarra, come s'è detto, costituisce l'ossatura di un filone tutt'altro che astratto o di poco conto.

Sottratta alla convenzionalità, la metafora entra in ambito di magico artificio, con empito emozionale; l'ingegno e l'immaginazione si inseriscono in un nuovo problema dell'espressione come "presentimenti di territori da conquistare"; una strada libera alle "argutezze", le stesse che oggi si riscoprono nei nessi dinamici allusivi della poesia ingegnosa e hanno trovato nuova attenzione critica.

La struttura si identifica ora con un'idea nuova, quella del Tesauro e della sua preoccupazione retorica: una "folle deformazione" che trapassa in nuova poesia; investe "l'assemblage" in un tipo di visione universale, che è il carattere del nuovo barocco a Torino. Dove non manca nè la ricca orchestrazione nè l'illusione della massa pittorica propria del barocco autentico; con inserti ricavati dal gusto classico (inerente alla stessa cultura del letterato). Non si tratta di una mera officina verbale: la "dissociation of sensibility", in mano degli artigiani di turno, si con-

6. Per gli artigiani del legno attivi in Palazzo Reale si vedano le schede relative agli scultori nel Catalogo citato del 1963, a cura di L. Mallé. Agli scultori lignei si affiancavano gli architetti-ingegneri Michelangelo e Carlo Morello.
7. Vedo che questa analisi coincide con la definizione di **Hocke**, che propone a proposito dei rovesciamenti della metafora del Tesauro (op. cit. traduz. ital. pag. 110) il concetto di "prospettiva illusionistica linguistica".

creta validamente; la visione mutevole dell'ornato manierista acquista solidità.

La tecnica muta il modo di vedere: e questo tiene il passo con il nuovo rapporto instaurato dalla metafora come discorso aperto. Di qui la nuova morsura strutturale e l'eloquenza come imprevedibile emersione dell'oro-simbolo materico. Il simbolo è rivestito di nuova forza come onda ritmica: incorporato nella struttura decorante: in più l'allegoria e la metafora dominano i modi della decorazione con equivalenze di fantasia e di significato.

L'ornato assume valore preciso; intende essere persuasivo e suscitare emozioni. L'oro è modellato con una fondamentale sapienza coloristica, un "continuum" spaziale, fino a superare ad oltranza le posizioni del Castellamonte. Anche l'artificio è dunque proposto come oggetto di contemplazione, al massimo significante.

Il nuovo illusionismo risulta aperto a soluzioni di ripresa naturale. Le foglie d'acanto, a cespi veri, seguono un disegno che si riconosce tratto dai motivi che serviranno ai giardini in opera alla Venaria, come a Racconigi.

Ma su tutto scorre una tensione, un gusto della magìa, per cui la parte lignea risulta avvampante, rilevata con vitalità immaginifica, per sbattiti cupi. Superati i rovelli del manierismo (e siamo ormai, occorre riscontrarlo a tutte lettere, in clima barocco), la decorazione acquista naturalezza di inscenatura e animismo fortemente allusivo, prima del marmo nero scelto dal Guarini.

La mediazione del Tesauro era dunque preziosa; prima ancora dell'intervento del Guarini. Serviva a sbloccare da modelli e schemi di manierismo abusato; a dare un contenuto preciso, smuovendo le acque di strutture sorpassate; preparava le maestranze alle esigenze di autentico barocco, come saranno proposte dal Guarini.

Oltre le "istruzioni al pittore", il Tesauro propone dunque, per analogia fantastica, la metafora come strumento di conoscenza e di ricerca. In più i soffitti procombenti, prima della Sindone, portano avanti l'esigenza comunicativa di uno stile che avalla ragioni di interiorità; e la stessa morfologia ora si identifica con queste ragioni: suscitando le voci di un inconscio collettivo, sul punto di scoprire una realtà ultra sensibile, ben oltre le ragioni celebrative della casa regnante.

E' a questo punto che la metafora, di significato ad oltranza così ridotto alle apparenze, assume nuovo contenuto: quell'oro che tiene ancorati i simboli letterari alla cornice decorante riesce a legarli alla realtà delle cose, in virtù del nuovo significato interno della materia, proposta figurativamente con risultati di animismo intenso.

Gli intagli ora sono come i chiodi a cui gli artigiani attaccano le loro idee. La nuova generazione contrappone la sua nuova fatica, non solo con calore umano, ma con una presa di posizione che si riscontra in una inedita vitalità. L'intaglio procede a groppi, a viluppi serrati, con coerenza di struttura: questa coincide con una sostanza emozionale e raziocinante. Un antidoto che riesce a conferire fascino e comunicativa anche alle metafore e ne annulla il timbro arbitrario e sofisticato, interpretando il valore autentico di quel procedere, come "arguzia fantastica".

Capire Tesauro e i suoi rapporti effettivi con gli artigiani e i pittori attivi in Palazzo Reale, significa dunque render ragione, dall'interno, dello svolgimento dell'arte decorativa a Torino fra il 1660 e l' '80, prima dell'intervento del Seyter, aggregato alla routine del cortonismo romano.

Quel che conta, tra luci e ombre, in un magma materico, ancora come nel Della Valle e nel Cairo,[8] quasi a indicare, oltre il costume delle esigenze encomiastiche, quanto sia mutevole il "gioco delle apparenze": un dubbio non pure sulla gloria, ma sulla validità delle cose umane. Quella che era l'aspirazione celebrativa della corte trovava suggello fantastico, ma anche critico, ancora per forza della retorica.

Il "memento" raggiungeva il suo culmine nei balletti e in quelle feste a lungo metraggio che erano i funerali dei regnanti: come li conosciamo non solo dai disegni per apparati, ma pure dai libri che ne illustravano per mano di pittori, incisori (il Dauphin,[9] primo fra tutti) e architetti, il fasto da dimostrarsi oltre la morte; teatro destinato non più ad una stretta cerchia di letterati-cortigiani, ma ora a un largo giro, a un pubblico vasto. Lo stesso che tra poco alzerà lo sguardo nella Sindone alla nuova "ostensione" per opera del Guarini.

8. In altra occasione mi sono soffermata sul rapporto Cairo-Della Valle. In più i soggetti del Cairo vanno affiancati e quelli del Vinta (La regina Iliadia, Venezia 1605); Paccaroni (Romilda, Venezia 1626); De Ferrari (La Rosilda, 1625); Cicognini (La forza del Fato, over il matrimonio nella morte, Bologna, 1663); Bonicelli (Lugretia romana violata da Sesto Tarquinio, Venezia fine sec. XVII); più manierista ma certo con soggetto "lombardo", La Reina Esther' del Cebà, Genova 1615. E con soggetti che ancora riscontriamo puntualmente nel Cairo Il teatro poetico del Casoni (Virginia trafitta, Artemisia, Lucrezia romana ecc. Venezia 1625); sempre del Casoni la "Passione di Cristo" con strofe composte in modo da comporre la forma degli strumenti della Passione, può essere paragonata al quadro del Cairo con il "Cristo nell'orto con i simboli della Passione" di recente entrato al Museo Civico di Torino.

9. Incisioni del Dauphin compaiono a Torino in numerose occasioni celebrative. Inoltre va ricordato il contributo del pittore-incisore all'opera del Frugoni, "Del Sacro Trimegisto descritto nella vita di S. Massimo vescovo di Torino", Torino 1666; una storia dell'incisione in Piemonte dovrebbe includere ripetutamente, anche l'opera del Miel gia attivo per i frontespizi di Daniello Bartoli, a Roma, circa il 1650–60.

Tagliando i ponti con il Tesauro, ma non del tutto estraneo a quella stagione, anzi più comunicante di quanto non appaia a prima vista, Guarini finirà per ancorare quella poetica (retorica) dell'ingegno e della fantasia, alla ricerca geometrica.

Quanto al Tesauro, al di fuori del clima celebrativo, quei soffitti sembrano ricondurci ad un passato anch'esso "preso" nella nostra sorte inquieta.

Il passaggio dal manierismo al barocco, che non si configura certo con un taglio netto, dall'oggi al domani, include dunque fortemente, dopo gli esperimenti validissimi del Marino,[10] dei calligrafi di turno,[11]

anche il Tesauro e la sua metafora assunta come concetto fondamentale. In più il mezzo della comunicazione si arricchisce e si complica entro un crescere barocco, con un'accensione unitaria che resiste tuttora; e che, nella lettura difficoltosa del '600 in Palazzo Reale, resta come uno dei fatti-guida, ora corredato anche dalle "Inscriptiones" del 1666.

10. Per il Marino: alla bibl. recente, per accenni all'ambiente figurativo di Carlo Emanuele I, in una precedenza attuale per il Tesauro, vanno ora aggiunti i contributi di M. Guglielminetti, "Tecnica e Invenzione nell'opera di Giambattista Marino", Napoli 1964; e singolarmente l'edizione delle "Dicerie sacre ecc." a cura di G. Pozzi, Einaudi, Torino 1960, che insiste sulla

definizione decisamente manieristica per il Marino, invalidando la distinzione secentismo-barocco. Anche per il Marino, piuttosto che una ricerca intesa alla Galleria o ai soggetti iconografici forniti ai pittori, ancora potrà essere utile una lettura della lingua di lui in rapporto a quella dei pittori dell'*ultimo* manierismo, non solo in Piemonte.

11. Per i calligrafi alla corte va fatto il nome del Tiranti, autore del "Laberinto de groppi" nel 1656. Sui calligrafi é ora una precisa bibliografia in S. Morison, C. Marzoli, "Calligraphy, 1535–1835", Milano 1962; verrei aggiungere la citazione di testate e finalini decisamente calligrafici presenti nell'ediz. del 1613 edita a Parma per le "Quaestiones" di Ottavio Farnese.

JANOS SCHOLZ

Drawings by Alessandro Magnasco

It seems strange that among the extremely important holdings in the United States of drawings by the illustrious eighteenth-century Italian painters, one of the most spectacular personalities, Alessandro Magnasco, for many years was hardly represented at all either in our public or private collections. The study of the great Venetians, Piranesi or even a so-called minor like Amigoni, cannot be seriously pursued without taking stock of the wonderful sheets by these artists which are spread all over this continent. A few years ago it would have been quite difficult to select a drawing or two from U.S. holdings for an exhibition by the elusive Genoese.

Luckily, like many things in life, the appearance of drawings on the horizon seems to happen seriatim, too. At the time of the Diamond Jubilee of the Philadelphia Museum, that institution acquired the fine example of Magnasco's religious art, shown then in their memorable exhibition of drawings. A few years later the Metropolitan bought its first Magnasco sheet; about the same date another slipped quietly into the cabinet of the Kansas City Museum. A few eager private collectors secured here and there a sheet by Lissandrino whenever a chance arose (Mrs. Richard Krautheimer; Mr. David Daniels). The lovely *Flight into Egypt* at Cleveland and the superb example acquired by Ambassador and Mrs. Robert Woods Bliss in Stockholm, 1936, for Dumbarton Oaks were, up to quite recently, the only fine large figure compositions to compare favourably with the well-known groups in the Uffizi and Genoa.

Recently, however, marked changes took place. The Art Institute of Chicago bought the quite extraordinary, spectacularly fine pair of drawings which had been introduced to New York during the exciting Wildenstein exhibition, October 1963. And Miss Felice Stampfle discovered the enchanting *Peepshow* hiding under the guise of Fragonard, of all names! Needless to say, the latter quickly joined the holdings of the Morgan Library as the first example by Magnasco in that great collection.

Quite recently other drawings attributed to him have entered American collections. The first of these (Fig. 1) representing the *Eruption of a volcano*, with five frightened figures,[1] is a very fine standard example by the artist to be compared with the Santarelli series in the Uffizi, or the group in the Palazzo Bianco and the Prefumo collection, Genoa. The present owner, Mr. William T. Hassett, Jr., an ardent collector of drawings, found this in Washington a few years ago. The drawing, as far as it is known, has no previous provenance. The number 3 in the upper left corner of the sheet would indicate that it belonged to a similar album like the ones in the above-mentioned Italian collections. The next drawing (Fig. 2) is that of a *Monk seated in a landscape,* reading a book, with putti above him in the clouds.[2] The arched top of the composition and also the indication for a tabernacle in the foreground would suggest this to be a project for an altarpiece. There are inscriptions on the drawing in two different eighteenth-century hands reading *B. Augustinu novelli* and *B. Augustinus nouellus Panormitanus*. The sheet is mounted on an old, Mariette-type blue mat with a cartouche in the lower middle containing again an inscription *B. Agost. Novelli Panormitanus*. No collectors' marks are discernible and there is no other indication for provenance except that the drawing passed through the London sales rooms attributed to one of the lesser-known members of the Novelli family, prolific and pedestrian painters working in Sicily.

That we are confronted here with a strong example of Magnasco's art is evident. Compared with originals in Italy it can be dated rather late, after 1735. Quite a few drawings are known which can be connected with his existing religious works, most of them though, in his bozzetto-type technique of bold washes and heightenings, recalling Castiglione. In this work the artist adheres rather to his free-figure drawing style, while the composition and structure of the scene well combine all the rules of good baroque religious art without becoming weak or sentimental.

As for the subject, the old writings give a clue which could be valid. The various writers marking the drawing seemingly have been better versed in names of

1. Brush, brown ink heightened with lead white over preliminary work in red chalk. On light brown paper measuring 12½ by 8⅝ inches (318 × 220 mm). Collection of Mr. William T. Hassett, Jr., Hagerstown, Maryland. The writer is most grateful to the owner for permission to publish this drawing.
2. Brush, brown ink over slight preliminary work in black chalk, heightened with lead white. On light brown paper measuring 10¼ by 8⅜ inches (206 × 212 mm). The oxidation of the lead white has been skilfully treated by Mr. A. J. Yow in the laboratory of the Pierpont Morgan Library. Collection Janos Scholz, New York.

painters than in commonplace abbreviations in manu-script. For the capital *B* stands for *Beato*, therefore the *B. Augustinus Novellus* mentioned at once turns out to be the famous Augustinian, born into a noble family in Tarano (Sabina) during the thirteenth century. Through some error Agostino Novelli has been called 'from Palermo' (Panormitanus); actually he left his home early for Bologna where he became an Augus-tinian. After a few years spent in convents near Siena he went to Rome where he was ordained. Brilliant scholar and theologian, Novelli became one of the co-authors of the *Constitutions* of his order. Elected General of the order in Milan, 1298, he spent two years in Lombardy but soon retired to the hermitage of S. Leonardo near Siena. Agostino died 1309 and was buried in the church of S. Agostino, Siena. He was beatified by Clemens XIII in 1759.

All this leads to the assumption that some members of the order of St. Augustine asked Magnasco while in Milan to submit an altar-project to honour their revered brother. Probably the slow process of the beatification was initiated there too, and this would account for a proposed altarpiece which, as far as the writer could ascertain, was never completed.

The third drawing introduced in these lines is some-what of a problem. As it represents a subject up to now quite unknown in Magnasco's *œuvre*, the writer would like to put forward this attribution with the utmost caution, as an attractive and rather persuasive pos-sibility. The arguments put forth will support one fact which is quite manifest: that the drawing is of a quality worthy of a very good hand. The picture (Fig. 3) is that of a *Landscape* with buildings in the distance, ruins at the left and a man in the center leading a heavily-loaded mule down a path towards a river.[3]

There are two kinds of analytical approach towards a plausible solution for the authorship of this item: positive proof or elimination of possibilities. Let us start by eliminating possibilities. Obviously from the first third of the eighteenth century, this sheet shows a marked mixture of trends: a leaning in an ever-so-gentle way towards the Bolognese world of the seven-teenth, especially Guercino and Domenichino, but with a whispering *sfumato* alien to those two. The Veneto comes in for its share with trees reminding us of Marco Ricci, but again without the firmness and scraggy shapes of the alpine world. To complicate matters, this painter must have known the Roman Campagna of Claude and Poussin and, besides, the world of Casti-glione. All this would add up to a personality of marked talent, strong backbone and conviction, who not only

looks but sees without giving in too much to outside influences or impressions. It would point to a man who is, above all his considerable intrinsic talent, a thorough-bred painter.

Old inscriptions on drawings always have certain value and should be considered along with our critical con-templations. In this instance, there are two hands writing the same name on the verso: *Alessandrino*. Both are of the eighteenth century—one rather coarse and bold, the other written with a fine quill in an extremely fluid way. Studying the Geiger volume of Magnasco drawings, the writer remembered a sheet with an old inscription belonging to the Ambrosiana, Milan. It was that of the nickname of the Genoese, Alessandrino; or, as they called him when he was young, Lissandrino. Comparing the Milan hand with the one on the drawing under discussion, it became immediately clear that the same fine hand marked the two during the eighteenth century. At once a new path of reasoning opened up. The Milan drawing was also in red chalk and assumed to be a self-portrait of the young Magnasco. But this was just one of the en-couraging factors; more were to come later.

The bold hand on the back turned out to be quite akin to the writing on a Magnasco drawing in the Hamburg Kunsthalle. As there are no straight landscape compo-sitions in any of the collections containing traditionally accepted drawings by this master the writer examined many reproductions of paintings, besides the available originals, to assemble bit by bit (in a rather Morellian manner, alas!) enough positive proof to tranquillize almost all hesitancy or doubt. It would be going much too far to enumerate even part of this; the elements compared range from the bark of the trees and the fluffy Corot-like foliage to the half-submerged flat roofs or the theatrical side-wing effects so ably accom-plished in the trees and the classical ruin on the left. One main trend though is imperative: the composi-tional scheme of this drawing and many of the classical landscapes with or without the usual monks, brigands, smugglers or whatever they may be, are not only super-ficially but very much organically the very same. The horizon, placed little lower than the middle, a custom to which the painter adheres in most of his landscapes, is much in evidence in the drawing too: observe the strong dig of the red chalk in the tree on the left, the accent in the ruin on the same level, or the similar effect arrived at in the anticlimactic tenderness of the rooftops, so gently drawn and suggesting the infinite space behind, leading to the far-away horizon.

The man walking down the path behind his plodding mule, however, can be considered almost as a signature of the painter. The writer had this little group enlarged just to be able to look deeper into the construction of

3. Red chalk on white paper measuring 7⅞ by 11⅛ inches (200 × 283 mm). WM: *Anchor in circle*, letters C D (?) below. Collection Janos Scholz, New York.

the lines and their play with light and shade. The result was quite remarkable. As in so many instances with good art, it is the omissions which make the figures live and vibrate more than do the actual lines on the paper. In the collection of Conte Francesco Mattei,[4] there is a painting showing a group of traveling merchants with horses carrying heavy loads. The similarities between those and the mule on our drawing are astonishing. Only a person who observed very closely beasts of burden would know this strange concentration with which they follow their road, secure but fully conscious of the weight of the packs, so properly placed forward towards the shoulder to remove pressure from the back to the fore-legs. Only a sensitive painter sees and is able to re-create this kind of subtlety, especially on a small scale as in this drawing.

4. B. Geiger, *Magnasco*, Bergamo, 1949, pl. 81.

To conclude, in the writer's opinion all these arguments could add up to an attribution of this landscape to Magnasco. Some two hundred years ago others thought so too. But all this is not enough, for our own critical approach must be convincing to a degree which satisfies—if possible—every query. With that in mind the writer submits this item for the time being more for consideration and discussion than as a positive identification of Magnasco's drawing manner in landscape art.

Note. An additional group of important autograph drawings by Magnasco are in the Art Museum, Princeton University, Princeton, N.J. Five sheets with figures, like Mr. Hassett's example reproduced here, came to the museum in 1959, while the *Penitent Monk* published by Jacob Bean in 1966 entered with the drawings from the Dan Fellows Platt Collection in 1947 (J. Bean, Italian Drawings in the Art Museum, Princeton University, cat. no. 73).

LUIGI MALLÈ

Traccia per Francesco Ladatte, scultore torinese

Francesco Ladetti o Ladetto—che francesizzò il nome in Ladatte quando visse a Parigi—nacque a Torino il 9 dicembre 1706 (non come sosteneva il Paroletti, nel 1707, a Parigi) e morì a Torino il 18 gennaio 1787. Esplicite notizie documentarie sui modi delle prime prove mancano. Stando al Dussieux, Francesco tentò i primi passi nella scultura (e pare anche nella pittura) ancor bambino se, quando il padre, addetto alla corte del principe Vittorio Amedeo di Savoia-Carignano, presentò al suo protettore varie opere del figlio, questi aveva solo dodici anni. Fu allora, nel 1718, che il principe trasferendosi a Parigi da Torino, prese con sè ritenendolo meritevole d'aiuti allo studio il piccolo Ladatte. Questi aveva avuto a compagno, alla stessa corte dei Savoia-Carignano, il quasi coetaneo Carlo van Loo, amicizia destinata a riannodarsi più tardi a Parigi, con analogie, anzi comunanza di situazioni culturali nelle due carriere artistiche pur nelle divergenze di linguaggio e temperamento.

La breve nota del Dussieux prosegue sommaria o generica—il Ladatte "ne tarda pas à se perfectionner sous la direction des excellents maîtres qu'on lui donna"—e forse non sempre precisa nei dati, tuttavia interessante per alcune indicazioni; se il soggiorno a Roma e la seconda sosta parigina (che registrò anche le nozze dell'artista con una francese) sono appena accennati senza circostanziati riferimenti di date e durate, troviamo che il "Triomphe de la Vertu" (anche detto della Fama e che vedremo meglio precisato poi come "trionfo delle arti liberali" in una citazione di documento torinese), gruppo in terracotta firmato e datato 1744, che è ora agli Arts Décoratifs di Parigi, si trovava a fine '700 a Torino in proprietà del genero dello scultore, il pittore paesaggista Vittorio Amedeo Cignaroli, marito di Rosalia Ladatte ed era considerato la prima opera compiuta da Francesco al ritorno in Torino dal secondo soggiorno parigino; che le "Quattro Stagioni" in piombo al giardino della reggia torinese (Giovanni Battista Boucheron le precisò invece, al chiudersi del '700 e cioè all'incirca quando giunsero in Francia le notizie che servirono poi al Dussieux per le sue citazioni, come i "Quattro Elementi") erano successivi a quel gruppo e che all'Accademia reale torinese di pittura e scultura erano conservati, a fine secolo, un "Ratto di Proserpina" e un "Fanciullo con cigno" di cui non ci rimane alcun ricordo; opere, queste due ultime, che pure il Bou-

cheron gli assegnava e specificava eseguite in pietra, materia che Ladatte aveva trattato qualche volta in giovinezza e nella prima maturità (anche Ignazio Nepote lo loderà per lavori in marmo) anche se "le circostanze non gli permisero di attendere molto alla pietra; si rivolse pertanto alli lavori di bronzo e d'argento". La citazione d'un "ratto di Proserpina" è importante; e se esso risultava d'immediato seguito al ritorno definitivo da Parigi, potè esser veduto da Ignazio Collino prima della partenza per il tirocinio a Roma.

Non sappiamo esattamente con chi studiasse Francesco appena giunto a Parigi nel '18 e anni subito successivi, perfezionandosi per un decennio fino a concorrere con successo ai premi dell'Accademia di Francia. Ma tra il '18 e il '29—durata del primo soggiorno—ci è facile ricostruire ragionevolmente se non i precisi contatti materiali e gli effettivi corsi seguiti, il clima d'influenze subite e di suggestioni più spontaneamente accolte. Ormai prossimo a scomparire il Coysevox, ma lasciando un'eredità fondamentale, che Ladatte non ignorò, erano in pieno fervore Nicolas e soprattutto Guillaume Coustou, le cui opere del '20-30 lasciano segni anche sull'intervento di Francesco alla corte di Torino nel '32; ed erano in fama, e nello stesso giro aulico, René Frémin e Robert Le Lorrain (più severo e classicistico) nonchè J. B. Lemoyne I, il cui nipote Jean Baptiste II, che avrà poi a dare impulsi anche al Ladatte tardo, sarà proprio coetaneo di questi, essendo nato nel '04. Coetanei pure e pieni di slancio nelle prime prove parigine, gli Slodz (Paul Ambroise e Michel-Ange, nato quest'ultimo nel '05) e i lorensi impulsivi Adam: in particolare Lambert-Sigisbert e Nicolas-Sébastien, con i quali, nel periodo '30-50, il Ladatte segna molti e patenti paralleli. Non erano ancor di scena Pigalle e Falconet, in avvio solo dal '40 circa, nè i più giovani ancora Caffieri e Pajou, in avvio dal '50 circa, i quali tuttavia non ancor personalità riconoscibili neppure ai giorni della seconda sosta parigina del Ladatte, avranno da partecipargli valori utili nella sua fase tarda, dopo il '60. L'esperienza dell'Académie fu comunque fondamentale per il torinese. Ventiduenne, nel '28, Ladatte vi ottenne il secondo premio di scultura col bassorilievo "Joram e Naaman" e nel '29 colse il primo premio col bassorilievo "Joachim re di Giuda distrugge il libro di Geremia". Ladatte interruppe allora la dimora parigina per l'agognato soggiorno di studio a

[242]

Roma fornitogli dal premio e là nell'ambiente dell'"Académie de France a Rome" ritrovava artisti francesi già conosciuti a Parigi o anche piemontesi che vi si stavano perfezionando. Quando vi giunse nel '30 se non forse ancor nel '29 stesso, vi lavorava tuttora Claudio Beaumont torinese, già affermato alla corte sabauda e residente a Roma da un settennio (ed era già per lui un secondo soggiorno); e vi era l'amico Carlo Andrea van Loo, avviatosi alla pittura fin dall'adolescenza con un'educazione romana; v'era inoltre il francese Boucher (e tutti e tre questi artisti vi sarebbero rimasti fino al '31, il primo, e al '33 i due altri) mentre se n'era forse appena allontanato il Natoire.

In quel clima raffinato dalle sottili commistioni e fusioni di classicismo romano e di classicismo francese, il primo già per più versi venato di grazie e purismi francesi, assaporati per discendenze dirette o mediate, il secondo giungendo nell'Urbe carico d'una secolare eredità tanto profondamente nutrita di succhi romani, il giovane Ladatte tra i suoi ventidue e i venticinque anni maturò decisamente: le opere immediatamente successive per la reggia torinese sono dimostrazioni eccellenti d'una elezione lungamente epurata di gusti, d'una coerenza stilistica lucidamente controllata, d'un carattere vigoroso al di là delle grazie gentili, d'una perizia tecnica eccezionale. E veramente, nella sua città natale, il Ladatte ormai così maturo nonostante l'ancor giovane età, poteva rappresentare a quel momento un richiamo nuovissimo e affascinante, un filone di cultura più aulico ma al tempo stesso più brillante, ricercato, spiritoso ed elegante di tutto quanto il Piemonte da tempo conoscesse, orientato com'era in scultura su direzioni più strettamente locali e in buona parte d'accenti popolareschi: fossero le tante sculture devozionali lignee o fossero gli stucchi diffusi e ricchi anche nelle residenze aristocratiche o alla stessa reggia, ove permaneva calcato un sapore di doviziosa artigiania provinciale perfino nei ricchi intagli lignei, solo al chiudersi del '600 trovando accenti più raffinati, più brillanti e anche tecnicamente ingentiliti e impreziositi ma con densità e foltezza ancor tanto estranee ad una sbrigliatezza rocaille ormai scapricciante in pittura, con squisitezze salottiere e divagamenti amabili.

Certo, di fronte alla fama affermata e profondamente radicata in un gusto regionale, d'una scultura religiosissima e severa del Plura (apprezzato anche a corte e dallo stesso Juvarra), nome allora predominante nella capitale e negli altri maggiori (o più vivi) centri piemontesi, anzi anche di fronte alle composizioni sapienti dei forestieri romanizzanti invitati da Juvarra, come il Legros, il Baratta, il Cornacchini, il Cametti (nativo piemontese di Gattinara), di fronte a tutti questi (figs. 1–5), operanti da tempo oppure proprio allora arrivati di persona o invianti opere, il Ladatte dovette segnare, nel '32, un entusiasmante rinnovamento di gusti e di vitalità. Anche dinanzi a quegli ultimi, variamente modulanti una eredità berniniana su corde sensibilmente accademizzanti—e il Cornacchini e il Cametti, essi stessi, non senza consonanze, almeno, con certe soluzioni francesi—e tuttavia ancor piuttosto complicati e appesantiti da residui secenteschi, il Ladatte introduceva un fiotto di più libera vita, di spigliato linguaggio in cui la cultura sottile faceva tutt'uno con la sottigliezza d'una poetica preziosa e con una vena fresca di "coquetteries", sempre trattenuta sul filo della innata compostezza che lascia le cadenze "rocaille" slanciarsi, impuntarsi, impigliarsi ma le trattiene ora fuori di gravezze e complicazioni (non sfuggite, invero, in fase tarda) ed esclude sofisticazioni. E si può notare che se quel gruppo di romanizzanti, in cui rientrò anche Simone Martinez, ebbe sulla scultura piemontese largo e duraturo ascendente toccando la vecchiaia del Plura, la maturità del Tantardini e poi influendo largamente sul Perucca, sul Bernero e sul Clemente, di fronte a quella corrente il Ladatte costituisce un apporto particolare, il più vivo e moderno ma che fu, per l'ambiente plastico locale, meno fruttuoso e venne a costituire piuttosto un fatto essenziale considerato sotto il punto di vista della scultura decorativa d'interni, in ciò dando luogo a un capitolo primario, squisitamente collegato alle regie di Juvarra e di Benedetto Alfieri o, come nel caso di Vicoforte, di Francesco Gallo e alle collaborazioni con i più esperti argentieri o intarsiatori o ebanisti della corte di Torino. Ladatte inoltre venne così a presentarsi come l'unico scultore in Piemonte vivamente allineato con le più moderne, colte, preziose correnti di pittura aulica nella regione, suscettibile al pari di queste di assumere un timbro "internazionale" in perfetta aderenza al clima europeo della metropoli torinese in splendente ascesa.

E poichè s'è nominato il Martinez (figs. 6–8), vogliamo —senza sottintendere proposte di specifici nessi— notare come nel '37 a Torino, in S. Teresa, Simone scolpisse a bassorilievo "putti in gloria" e putti reggi Ghirlando uscenti da una cultura respirata a Roma in ambienti frequentati anche dal Ladatte; ed è già ben segnato—pur attraverso qualche parentela—il netto divergere da parzialmente comuni fonti da parte del più tradizionalista Martinez e del più fresco, brillantemente "internazionale" Ladatte. Ciò è sottolineato dal seguito del Martinez (ma la sua "Fontana della Nereide" a Palazzo Reale, pur con certe grossolanità, è l'unico esempio di scultura monumentale a Torino che traduca in grande certo gusto di gruppi decorativi di tipo ladattiano, o più genericamente romano-parigino, con timbri che vanno dal rustico al galante) come ad esempio nei "putti" delle consolles dell'armeria Reale, verso il '50 o nel prossimo basamento triangolare con "putti danzanti", al palazzo reale, dove il romanismo di più stretta eco berniniana accademizzata è evidente, non però escludendo qualche nota, non sfuggibile specie alla corte di Torino, di tenerezze e capricciosità francesi. Ma riprendiamo il corso dell'attività del Ladatte.

Nel 1732 Ladatte lasciò Roma per Torino dove trascorse un primo periodo d'attività per la corte; nel novembre era pagato—in una successione di rate per un cospicuo ammontare attestante l'importanza dell'incarico—per "metalli zisellati . . . per ornamento delle scrivanie cioè coffano forte per Sua Maestà"; il Rovere informa che "i lavori di bronzo dorato e cesellato a figure e ornati" delle scansie intarsiate dal Piffetti (figs. 9 e 10) nel gabinetto di toeletta della regina "furono fatti nel 1732 da Francesco Ladatte" e pagati lire 4612. Lavoro per noi fondamentale, questo, che fa constatare nel ventiseienne bronzista una piena maturità tecnica ed espressiva, un gusto compiutamente orientato; di qui il Ladatte in logica successione trascorrerà, solo ampliando e irrobustendo le forme (e più tardi appesantendole), alla "Giuditta" del Louvre, al citato "Trionfo delle arti liberali", al tabernacolo di Vicoforte, al pendolo col "Tempo". V'è, nei bronzi applicati agli stipi del gabinetto di toeletta, minor complicazione o ammassamento di elementi, minor turgore e spessezza di forme che, pur nella plastica corposa, manifestano più arioso e macchiato pittoricismo e—perfino mostrando qualche gentile gracilità—avviano una vicenda chiaroscurale palpitante, intenerita che cederà, più avanti, a luci e ombre più fisse, tese. Se elegantissimi e preziosi, pur nel compatto sboccio, sono i bustini di donne-arpie, a tutto tondo, deliziosi appaiono i bassorilievi leggeri, alitati, dei pannellini incorniciati da palme e "rocailles", con puttini (le Stagioni) e i motivi di nastri e trofei dal morbidissimo cesello.

E' anche un momento eccezionale diaccordo tra intarsiatore e bronzista; non più ripreso in tali termini. Quando Piffetti eseguirà lo stipo ora al Quirinale non gli sarà accanto un bronzista ma un intagliatore per le due belle, grandi cariatidi in legno dorato. Ma ci chiediamo se un pensiero per queste non venisse dal Ladatte, non potendosi supporre per le due figure scivolanti, tese (come nate da mente di bronzista) un'invenzione da parte d'alcun altro scultore piemontese del tempo.

Può essere inserito a questo punto il cervo bronzeo (fig. 11) coronante l'edificio della Palazzina di Stupinigi. Il primo a citare il cervo alla sommità del "cupolino" fu nel 1770 Ignazio Nepote, amico dello scultore, vivente quest'ultimo. Tuttavia il Vesme nel produrre i

documenti sul Ladatte non ne avanza alcuno relativo al cervo e solo in appendice riprende senza commento l'attribuzione, poi tradizionalmente accolta. Stilisticamente il cervo rientra bene nell'opera del Ladatte con caratteri che legano piuttosto a un momento di prima maturità che non a un periodo tardo. Il Bernardi lo pone in rapporto con disegni di Juvarra, "pensieri per finimento delle porte del salone della palazzina di caccia di Stupinigi", raffiguranti gruppi di cervi su basamenti, destinati a traduzione in bronzo per fungere da sovrapporte e che agli anni sul '32–34 non si saprebbe a quale altro scultore in bronzo in Torino, il Juvarra potesse affidare se non al Ladatte. Il fatto che sul cupolino sia stato posto effettivamente un cervo di questi mentre le sovrapporte del salone rimasero senza i gruppi previsti (accogliendo solo un trentennio appresso sculture marmoree di corrente dei Collino) autorizza a pensare che Ladatte sia stato incaricato del cervo grande appena giunto a Torino da Roma nel '32; ripartito per Parigi due anni dopo, cadde il progetto juvarriano per le sovrapporte del salone; al ritorno del Ladatte nel '44 il Juvarra era scomparso da tempo e del suo primo pensiero non fu più questione.

Nel gennaio 1733 Ladatte era testimone a Torino, in San Filippo, alle nozze di Carlo van Loo con Cristina Somis; nel febbraio 1734 veniva pagato "per due puttini di metallo con cascate di conchiglie e foglie in aqua" e per "altri lavori per il nuovo appartamento di Sua Maestà" nonchè per un "modello in cera fatto per una pendulla". Poichè dopo questa data cessano le menzioni nei conti della Real Casa, è giusto pensare che fin dall'inizio del '34 Ladatte fosse rientrato a Parigi. Del resto un certo periodo di attività già svolta colà dopo l'assenza, rende più logico il fatto ch'egli venisse accolto—"agrée"—all'Accademia parigina il 29 gennaio 1736; la nomina ad accademico seguì il 30 dicembre 1741 dietro presentazione—come "morceau de réception"—d'una Giuditta in marmo ora al Louvre, tema più volte trattato dallo scultore se la lettera di sua nomina ad accademico, firmata da Cristophe da Largilierre e da Oudry, accenna esplicitamente a vari esemplari: "les divers ouvrages en marbre de ronde bosse représentant une Judit tenant la tête d'Holopherne". La nomina a professore aggiunto ebbe luogo il 28 settembre 1743. In questo secondo periodo parigino Ladatte ritrovava gli amici. Boucher era rientrato a Parigi nel '33; Natoire faceva il suo ingresso all'Accademia parigina nel '34; Carlo Andrea van Loo tornava nel '34, diventando professore all'Accademia nel '37; Giovanni Battista van Loo insegnava alla medesima dal '35 al '38; Jean Baptiste Lemoyne il giovane, presto salito alla celebrità e già noto al Ladatte dagli anni dei premi giovanili, esponeva dal '38 al Salon dell'Accademia insieme a lui e diveniva professore aggiunto in essa dal '40. Le tangenze e le curiosità reciproche fra tutti erano dunque continue.

Non è puro piacere di spuntare annotazioni cronachistiche il seguire dal 1737 al 1743 le esposizioni al Salon dell'Accademia di Parigi cui Ladatte prese parte con opere che quasi tutte rimangono oggi note solo per la citazione di allora; il Ladatte vi presentò: nel 1737 un Luigi XV in gesso bronzato (bozzetto al Salon; statua già sullo scalone della Borsa—Palais des Consuls—di Rouen), un gruppo in bronzo di Rinaldo e Armida, già eseguito nel '36 e che gli varrà più tardi la nomina a professore aggiunto (tale bronzo è perduto), tre terrecotte e precisamente una Flora e i gruppi di Andromeda e dell'Educazione d'Amore; nel successivo 1738 un bassorilievo di materia imprecisata con due figure sotto una arcata, un S. Paolo in terracotta e una statua di Giuditta pure in terracotta; nel 1739 di nuovo una Giuditta in terracotta (che dalle citazioni potrebbe non sembrare la medesima del '38 se quella reggeva la testa d'Oloferne e questa invece vi si appoggiava) di cui la traduzione in marmo è firmata e datata 1741 e corrisponde con la Giuditta presentata per la nomina ad accademico; nello stesso anno 1738 egli esponeva una Madonna col Figlio, bozzetto in creta (rimasto al Salon) e una testa di S. Paolo in terracotta; nel 1740 le terrecotte di uno stemma reale con due putti e di un S. Agostino, una terza terracotta a bassorilievo con Plutone, Proserpina e la ninfa Oxiana, tema, questo "ratto", che sembra sia stato caro a Ladatte se poco più tardi lo riprese in un gruppo, da ritenere ridotto alle due figure di Plutone e Proserpina, al ritorno a Torino; nel 1741 il gruppo in terracotta di Diana uscente dal bagno con due ninfe, due putti e un cane; nel 1742 un bozzetto d'altare con tre scene figurate, rispettivamente costituite da due gruppi e un bassorilievo, simbolizzanti la Religione con un cherubino, fulminante l'Eresia; un angelo e un cherubino che calpesta l'amor profano; Clodoveo, Clotilde e l'Arcivescovo di Reims; e sempre nel '43 una terracotta allegorica con una donna su naviglio naufragante, un gruppo in terracotta con l'Abbondanza e l'Amore; nel 1743 il bozzetto per il mausoleo al Cardinal de Fleury a seguito di concorso indetto dal re, partecipandovi Lemoyne, Sebastien Adam, Vinache e Bouchardon che fu poi il prescelto.

Era stato esposto nel '38 al Salon il bozzetto in terracotta del "Martirio di S. Filippo" la cui realizzazione in bronzo (non in marmo come scrissero Auvray e Bellier) per la Cappella del Castello di Versailles ove è tuttora, fu compiuta solo nel 1746 dai bronzisti Slodtz (collaboratori anche di Lemoyne). In quel periodo Ladatte eseguì pure i gessi d'una Madonna col Figlio (da modello in terracotta del '39) e di S. Genoveffa

per la Chiesa di S. Luigi a Parigi; le figure e gli ornati marmorei per l'altare della Vergine alla cattedrale di Reims (1742); il Bachaumont parla anche di sculture per il giardino dell'Hotel Dufour a Parigi e dell'Hotel de la Popelinière (un altro ratto di Proserpina) a Passy. Un decennio, dunque, fittissimo; e la varietà e dislocazione degli incarichi provano che Ladatte, in una Parigi ricca di scultori e di fama, primeggiava. Sostiamo ad alcune fre le opere sopra citate. La statua di Luigi XV al Palais des Consuls di Rouen, che poteva dimostrare le attitudini dell'artista nella scultura aulica monumentale, andò distrutta. Ma la storia di questa statua può valere un indugio offrendo dati interessanti sullo scultore. Infatti, al Palais des Consuls edificato a Rouen negli anni 1704–1741 su disegni di François Blondel, l'architetto, pensando ad un imponente ed aulico elemento plastico per lo scalone, invitò il Ladatte. Se è scomparsa la statua del sovrano, rimane tuttora in situ il basamento in pietra, ornato con attributi allusivi alla Forza: capo e spoglie d'un leone e clava d'Ercole, oltre a trofei di lance e bandiere; e tale basamento reca la data dedicatoria del 1735. È perciò da credere che il Ladatte—onorato di gran stima se otteneva questo incarico ufficiale fin dai primi tempi del suo soggiorno parigino, anteriormente alle più fortunate sue esposizioni al Salon—abbia iniziato proprio il monumento dal piedestallo se solo nel 1737 lo vediamo presentare al Salon un bozzetto in gesso (verniciato a finto bronzo) figurante Luigi XV, da cui fu tratta poi la statua grande per lo scalone, certo non sistemata prima del '41 se non addirittura intorno al '50 quando i lavori di architettura erano del tutto compiuti. Ma l'incarico da parte del Blondel non s'era limitato alla statua regale. Ladatte, pagato 2600 lire per il Louis XV (e 538 per trasporto e posa del medesimo) ricevette inoltre 8950 lire per altre sculture ornamentali: frontone dell'edificio verso la rue Nationale; tre medaglioni con iscrizioni relative alla giurisdizione consolare, alla Camera e alla Borsa, ed emblemi del Commercio e della Giustizia su due facciate laterali (su rue des Charrettes e nella "Bourse Découverte"); e vari fregi interni.

Ma il 5 ottobre 1792 i rivoluzionari roannesi distrussero gli emblemi, pittorici o plastici, della regalità e della costituzione; e con sculture del Jadoulle e degli Slodtz anche il Louis XV di Ladatte andò in frantumi. Nel 1820 una statua (di Jean Baptiste Lemoyne) in marmo, di Luigi XV, fu destinata dal Ministero Francese dell'Interno a rimpiazzare il perduto Ladatte; ma tal statua troppo grande e costringente a rimaneggiamenti alla base dello scalone del Palais des Consuls, non vi fu mai sistemata, restando all'Hotel de Ville di Rouen; di qui forse derivò il più tardo equivoco d'un Luigi XV di Ladatte situato in tale secondo edificio.

Nel 1854 infine, al Palais des Consuls, sul primo basamento fu posto un calco in gesso del Luigi XV marmoreo di Nicolas Coustou esistente al Louvre. Sfortunato anche questo, poichè andò distrutto col Palazzo dei Consoli in bombardamento del 1944 che annientò anche il basamento del Ladatte di cui resta pallida memoria nella fotografia inclusa in un articolo del Geispitz (1901), dove si riconoscono grandi volute angolari compresse, quasi d'un ornatismo neosecentesco e un modo di serrare il grande piedestallo che risponde ad un principio adottato più tardi anche nei grandi elementi e modanature incornicianti il Sacro Pilone di Vicoforte e l'altare argenteo al Duomo di Torino, seppure, a Rouen, in termini di più massiccia compattezza, legando gli elementi strutturali del basamento strettamente ai trofei quasi ricoprenti le quattro facce.

Maggiormente ci trattiene la "Giuditta". Il tema stava a cuore a Ladatte: una terracotta al Salon nel '38, un'altra al medesimo nel '39 (entrambe, statue) non necessariamente la stessa; e nel '41 il marmo come "morceau de réception", certo traduzione del precedente o d'uno dei due precedenti bozzetti. Il marmo ora al Louvre (fig. 12) è d'alta qualità; i frutti del recente soggiorno romano si scoprono, dai riattacchi berniniani rivissuti attraverso le discendenze più baroccheggianti e le più accademiche, compenetrate e, anche qui, si vorrebbe avanzare una parentela di cultura fra il Ladatte sul '40 e un Simone Martinez degli stessi anni. Patetica e respirante questa Giuditta, in recitatissima posa, minuziosa nel prezioso dettaglio su carni e panneggi, frusciando come una dama o dea dipinte da van Loo e da Boucher, pezzo di virtuosismo ma di spontanea grazia. Si notino certe sottigliezze: il gioco di pieghe alla vita, il panno attorno e sotto la spada, marezzato dalle ombre come per tremuli tocchi di colore, la gracile spalla nuda nel ricamato scollo. I legami son chiari con i bronzi torinesi del '32; e si può, nella testa d'Oloferne, trovare elementi per assegnare al Ladatte, come faremo più avanti, un bozzetto del "ratto di Proserpina" inedito, colliniano alquanto ma più ancor ladattiano; e giova fin d'ora sottolineare come in Ladatte, sul '40, siano ferme le basi per la giovinezza e tutta la prima fase d'Ignazio Collino che il suo, sia pur non lungo, alunnato presso il bronzista, dovette trascorrerlo intorno al 1746–1747.

Un bozzetto della "Giuditta" (fig. 13) in terracotta dorata (Torino, Museo Civico) risponde nell'impianto al marmo; non vi rispondono alcuni particolari nella esecuzione che nel bozzetto è più risentita, più disegnativa, priva delle vibrazioni pittoriche morbide del marmo e che nel bozzetto si attenderebbero più mosse e calde. Gli attributi, le vesti, l'acconciatura, sono più rigidi e ricercati; ad esempio sul capo, invece del

libero nodo che è nel marmo, c'è un diadema. Più che supporvi uno dei precedenti bozzetti del Ladatte (che poi la doratura più tarda aggravò ancora) propendiamo a ritenerlo "d'après Ladatte", salvo miglior lettura consentita dalla rimozione della doratura o, almeno, ridoratura.

Il bassorilievo in bronzo all'altare della Cappella del Castello di Versailles, con il "Martirio di S. Filippo" (fig. 14) è uno dei punti più alti della attività ladattiana; ma ciò che soprattutto fa stupire dell'oblio in cui è caduta un'opera di così alta qualità e di così insigne ubicazione, è che essa è fra le cose migliori prodotte dalla scultura a Parigi intorno al '40. Al formato molto allungato, splendidamente s'adegua la ricca legatura narrativa del discorso, fitta nei due raggruppamenti laterali e sapientemente spaziata nel moto sospeso attorno al nodo compositivo del carnefice. Una ritmatura complessa, dalle moltiplicate riprese e annodature interne, sorregge la stesura dell'episodio trattato, direi, con un calcolo d'adesione marcata ed eloquente ad un testo "letterario", tanto è elaborato e cesellato il periodare. E nello schema generale, così come nel suo riassumere i moduli di gruppo o di figura singola, un'accademia romana sembra non rifiutare qualche eco veneta ("romanisante" essa stessa, s'intende). Se c'è qualche convenzione, qualche particolare generico, la scena è però tutta sostenuta da un'alta tensione, che non è solo di ordito strutturale dalle ben chiare trame geometriche in profondità e in superficie, ma è anche di nervosità del ductus—se pur tenuto sul filo d'una parlata aulicissima e risonante—e di pulsazione chiaroscurale. Ma sarà necessario puntare sui berninismi, filtrati attraverso una lunga serie di meditazioni romane compiute da francesi, quali proprio in questo torno di tempo, però, è Ladatte a riassumere e fissare in moduli che ritroveremo, e certo con più autorità di configurazione, più leggerezza e volo di tratto e più ornativo capriccio, in Coustou e nei due più noti Adam, che di prove del genere ne daranno dopo il '50 e oltre, con più fluide dissolvenze pittoriche. Il Ladatte, nel carnefice, sembra voglia del resto ritrovare idealmente, se non i valori formali, la posa del David berniniano mentre lo stesso scorcio quasi paradossale del Santo è un richiamo a classicismi d'una Accademia romana ancora ossessionata da spericolatezze barocche secentesche che alcuni più giovani scultori di Parigi sapranno più facilmente eludere.

Il ritorno definitivo di Ladatte a Torino avvenne il 18 luglio 1744. L'8 gennaio 1745 il re gli assegnava un annuo stipendio di lire 800 come "scultore in bronzi di Sua Maestà" con l'impegno, oltre a svolgere la sua professione negli incarichi per la corte, di "insegnare l'arte sua a quegli imprendizzi che gli venissero destinati". Nel corso dell'anno era pagato per "24 paia griglie da fuoco di bronzo dorato" per la reggia. Negli anni 1747–1750 eseguì "placche di metallo dorato a forma di girandole per la Galleria del Daniel e Gabinetto attiguo", una cornice per ritratto sabaudo, altre 22 griglie da fuoco; inoltre, in argento, piatti, candelieri e "surtout". Gli incarichi erano molteplici e vari: dalle "guarniture" in cartapesta per una illuminazione di gala al Teatro Regio ai bassorilievi per ornamento d'una nuova teca della SS. Sindone.

Ma rifacciamoci indietro al tempo del rientro in Torino. Il gruppo in terracotta citato, col "Trionfo della Virtù" o delle "Arti liberali" (fig. 15), firmato, e che si pone intorno al '44 è certo uno dei punti più alti della carriera del Ladatte. La materia vi è modellata con grazia spiritosa, tenerezza carezzante, preziosismi, soffici aliti pittorici e se nei tipi c'è molta aria di Boucher e quasi un anticipo di Falconet, nel capriccio delle involuzioni rococò, di continuo impuntate, c'è la vivacità e bizzarria d'un "décor" tra Germain e Caffieri (quest'ultimo, a tal data, ancor novizio e che in ogni caso potrà dare qualche spunto più tardi ad un Ladatte più anziano); e la vezzosa, insinuante allegoria, dalle civetterie da sopramobile—avorio, porcellana—viene a inserirsi nella Torino 1744 ad un culmine d'un gusto che aveva assorbito anche Crosato (Veneri, sorelle di questa "Virtù") e Giaquinto e da cui De Mura già fuoriesce.

A questo superbo esito avvicinerei, per stile, finezza e data, due gruppi di putti in terracotta (fig. 16) al Museo Civico di Torino, cui alluse il Vesme, identificandoli come allegorie dell'"Acqua" e del "Fuoco" e ritenendoli bozzetti per due dei quattro gruppi gettati in piombo dal Ladatte dopo il 1744 e situati attorno alla vasca del giardino reale, poi scomparsi. Se Giovanni Battista Boucheron citava quei gruppi—coppie di putti—come "Elementi", il Dussieux li disse allusivi alle "Stagioni". Le due terrecotte del Museo s'accordano meglio al secondo tema, genericamente interpretato; il Museo stesso conserva tre terrecotte minori, ognuna con una coppia di puttini, due delle quali corrispondono esattamente alle due maggiori; si tratta dunque d'una più piccola serie, già di quattro gruppi, confermanti la tematica delle Stagioni, però di esecuzione piuttosto rigida, mentre i maggiori sono di tenerissimo e luminoso modellato. Ci chiediamo se tali bozzetti amabili non siano stati tradotti anche in bronzo; in ogni caso costituiscono, proseguendo lo spunto dei putti nel gruppo degli Arts Décoratifs, un punto importante per il confronto—convergente e divergente—con i putti bronzei più tardi del Ladatte.

Vorremmo, a questo punto, accennare alla statua in marmo d'un putto (Torino, collezione V. e F. Giacosa) di significato allegorico non facile a individuare; è un Cupido con specchio e dardo, avvinghiato da serpe.

Lo stile invita a situarlo in prossimità del Ladatte, del quale tuttavia esulano le modulate ricerche chiaroscurali, sostituite da più tese forme; a meno che non sia questo uno dei rari casi, finora sfuggenti alla ricerca, di marmi del Ladatte, indotto dalla materia per lui insolita a una trattazione più ferma e fredda. Rapporti possono instaurarsi sia con i putti precedenti, sia, in direzione opposta, con i putti bronzei autografi, tardi, alla Chiesa del Carmine, certo più fluidi nello scorrer di luci sul metallo. In ogni caso, se l'attribuzione si possa accettare, il marmo citato in questo punto per comodità d'esposizione, dovrebbe esser avanzato nella data, di qualche anno e considerato, in ogni caso, meno raffinato della Giuditta. Questo Cupido, o consimili opere, non fu senza eco nell'ambiente piemontese se, ad esempio, un altro Cupido in marmo, per fontana (Torino, collezione V. e F. Giacosa), di buona qualità, fa trasparire, sotto un velo di mestizia, accenti ladattiani, peraltro allontanandosi maggiormente dai canoni del maestro, in cui il precedente più strettamente rientra.

Proponiamo, al nome del Ladatte, una terracotta del Museo Civico di Torino, col "Ratto di Proserpina" (fig. 17), fine, mosso, pittoresco, specie nel Plutone, più liscio e lucente nella Dea, con timbri francesi e tuttavia contatti forti con l'ambiente pittorico e plastico della Torino 1750 circa, cioè al punto d'incontro tra la piena maturità del Ladatte, ancor impregnato delle soste parigine (ma già orientantesi verso una sua maniere più larga e robusta, non sempre altrettanto vibrante e sensuosa) e le prime esperienze di Ignazio Collino che fu suo allievo tra il '46 e il '48 e che anche quando andrà nel '48—e fino al '64—a classicizzarsi a Roma, non dimenticherà il Ladatte e non mancherà di arieggiare ancora grazie francesi alla Pigalle (e risalendo all'indietro, fino a Coysevox che ricorderà ancora dopo il ritorno a Torino) o alla Falconet, dimostrando di conoscere anche gli Adam e Caffieri stesso. Il "ratto" in questione, che attaglia ad una data 1748–1750, si connette con i due scultori, parendo però troppo vibrante e caldo per Ignazio. La conoscenza, per documenti, dell'esecuzione del Ladatte d'un "Ratto di Proserpina" nel periodo parigino, e d'un altro dopo il rientro a Torino (e a fine '700 esposto all'Accademia delle Scienze), induce a ritenere questa terracotta bozzetto per uno di quei gruppi (ch'erano in marmo), in relazione, in tal caso, forse col secondo, compiuto verso la fine del quinto decennio e non col primo che raffigurava, oltre ai due dei, la ninfa Oxiana.

Nel 1748 o almeno in data prossima—così ritiene il Vesme in base al soggetto—Ladatte aveva anche disegnato, accompagnadovi una spiegazione delle allegorie esaltanti le glorie del sovrano, una fontana monumentale che egli vagheggiava per piazza San

Carlo. Di essa rimane appunto la lunga descrizione manoscritta dell'autore che espone l'origine del progetto, non dovuto ad incarico ma spontaneamente pensato per "mostrare che anch'io partecipo della comune contentezza per le continue gloriose vittorie da Sua Maestà poco fa ottenute" (e che il Vesme pensa siano in relazione con la battaglia dell'Assietta) e per abbellire "l'Augusta metropoli" sì che "ne resterebbe ad un'hora quella bellissima piazza maggiormente e più magnificamente adornata". Doveva formarne il centro la statua stante del sovrano in paludamento romano, appoggiato ad un timone, incoronato dalla Fama, affiancato dall'albero della Vittoria (una palma carica di trofei) e da una prora di vascello alludente al porto di Savona, quest'ultima apparendo più in basso in figura di donna che porge le chiavi al re mentre un uomo simbolizzante la Città di Finale, liberandosi dalle catene genovesi, si offre alla potestà del sovrano. Il basamento doveva portare due iscrizioni e due bassorilievi con battaglie nonchè elementi naturalistici (rocce allusive alle Alpi), il Po e la Dora, trofei d'armi.

Nel febbraio 1749 Ladatte ideava "una macchina" con cineserie per la mascherata di carnevale in via Po; la mascherata raffigurava l'ingresso dell'imperatore della China e la "macchina ... inventata dal signor Francesco Ladatte scultore di sua Maestà e virtuoso di S.A. Serenissima il Principe di Carignano e sottoprofessore dell'Accademia di Parigi", rappresentava "il trionfo della Pagotta, idolo dei cinesi, in mezzo a due torri con altri ornamenti".

Il 30 dicembre 1749, insieme all'orafo Andrea Boucheron, Ladatte si obbligava con l'Amministrazione Civica di Mondovì per i lavori del Sacro Pilone del Santuario di Vicoforte (figs. 18–19) secondo il disegno dell'architetto Francesco Gallo, utilizzando bronzo e argento donato dai fedeli; i lavori erano compiuti in due anni, il collaudo fu fatto nel '51 dal Vittone. L'opera monumentale e sfarzosa, legata alla necessità di formare tabernacolo o meglio edicola al pilone antico—il tutto sviluppandosi sotto l'architettura del baldacchino alla romana—risolve le materiali imposizioni con eccezionale fantasia; e nel capolavoro orafesco dei due maestri, il bronzista e l'argentiere, la struttura architettonica dell'edicola quadrilatera, di per sè costrittiva e massiccia, è superata come tale risolvendosi in mossi ed esuberanti valori decorativi con mensoloni a volute che smussano i lati, girali, fogliami, conchiglie, modiglioncini "rocaille", teste d'angelo, mazzi di fiori. Mentre al Boucheron spettano i due finissimi bassorilievi in estrosi medaglioni rococò con l'Annunciazione e lo Sposalizio della Vergine, condotti con squisitezza di sbalzo, grazia, respirante levità pittorica, al Ladatte spettano le cornici medesime

di quei medaglioni, le ghirlande, le teste angeliche accoppiate e i trofei che li circondano, le teste, volute, mazzi sui contrafforti angolari, il fregio formante cornicione, le grandi "rocailles" sventaglianti alla sommità e gli splendidi putti ai quattro angoli superiori.

Anche Andrea Boucheron portava nel lavoro alla teca un'educazione stilistica ed una perizia tecnica nutrite di forti succhi francesi; egli infatti aveva studiato a Parigi con il celebre orafo Thomas Germain. La collaborazione di Ladatte e Boucheron a Vicoforte costituisce un'alleanza di perfetta armonia inventiva ed esecutiva, con superbo esito, pur nella divergenza dei temperamenti, così delicato, vibrante, soffiato nei chiaroscuri in tenere modulazioni il Boucheron, squisitamente aderente ad una sensibilità di sbalzatore (e quasi pittore) in materia cedevole, così robusto invece il Ladatte, vigoroso, fermo nella definizione disegnativa delle forme e nella loro corposa, densa plasticità sviluppata sotto tese luci o sotto giochi pittorici marcati, sottolineando sempre la gravità compatta e sonora dei bronzi. E di fronte alle dilatazioni atmosferiche del Boucheron, il Ladatte oppone le sue forme colme, legate, meditatamente contrappesate in ogni valore in vista d'una potente sintesi compositiva. Qui lo stacco del Ladatte dalle più dolci e morbide forme del periodo giovanile è già assai marcato.

Ladatte compiva, occasionalmente, anche lavori di destinazione militare, ad esempio nel 1751 dava disegni per due cannoni. Nel 1752 era pagato 3700 lire dal Capitolo della Metropolitana di Torino per un "gran trono d'argento per l'esposizione del SS.mo Sacramento che portava operato di cesello un magnifico bassorilievo rappresentante il miracolo eucaristico, dodici grandi candelabri e quattro statue", lavoro dunque importante e certo dei suoi più complessi, non sopravvissuto nella sua interezza, forse sacrificato ad una fusione in tempi di crisi finanziaria dello stato sabaudo. Ma il "trono", che intendiamo come paramento per altare, sia pur non più completo di tutte le sue parti figurate, sussiste col "miracolo dell'ostia" a bassorilievo, al Duomo di Torino (fig. 21) e se il pagamento avvenne solo nel '52, la figurazione reca inequivocabile, assieme al punzone del mastro argentiere Paolo Antonio Paroletto, la data 1741. Come risolvere il distacco d'undici anni, in sè non impossibile come dilazione d'un pagamento ma imbarazzante per la implicazione d'una improbabilità di richiesta del disegno, da parte del Capitolo, ad un Ladatte allora a Parigi? Dobbiamo ritenere che Ladatte negli anni '50 avesse da occuparsi d'un "trono" per cui si utilizzasse un bassorilievo d'argento già da altri inventato dieci anni innanzi? O non piuttosto conviene connettere l'intervento del Ladatte per un'opera orafesca come il "trono" con l'attendere, all'incirca negli stessi anni, all'opera orafesca dell'edicola al Santuario di Vicoforte ed ai riflessi della sua plastica su opere d'argenteria, dimostrati alla mostra torinese del barocco in Piemonte del 1963, dalla stupenda "paiola" in vermeil dello Oesterreichisches Museum für angewandte Kunst di Vienna (fig. 20) e dal calice in argento dorato con putti a tutto tondo e medaglioni squisiti a rilievo, del Duomo di Vercelli, nelle quali due opere, seppur l'argentiere sia Lorenzo Lavy, come ha provato il Bargoni (e forse il Lavy stesso diede il disegno, sebbene il modellatore della paiola sembri essere Stefano Tamiatti) mi pare chiara l'influenza del Ladatte, nei tipi, nel modellato, nei pittoricismi del rilievo, e proprio d'un Ladatte del quinto decennio; così da sentirci indotti a chiederci se una solida fama acquisita dal nostro bronzista fin dagli anni dei deliziosi piccoli rilievi e dei bustini del Gabinetto della Regina a Palazzo Reale, e cioè dal '32, non avesse fatto scegliere proprio lui dal Capitolo del Duomo (dietro al quale sarà bene vedere il consiglio della corte) per il "trono" ancorché, al momento, egli fosse lontano. E ciò spiegherebbe anche il perchè, pur nella qualità e vitalità plastico-pittorica del "trono", appaiano accenti, nei tipi e nell'esecuzione, che inducono perplessità ad accogliere il nome del Ladatte come pienamente risolutivo di invenzione ed esecuzione (il Bargoni ritiene la partecipazione sua come probabile), la quale ultima ricadde sull'argentiere Paolo Antonio Paroletto che, in ogni caso, avrebbe dovuto essere esecutore anche qualora Ladatte si trovasse a Torino, causa la materia—l'argento—di trattazione al Ladatte non specificamente familiare.

Nella splendida coppia di zuppiere d'argento (fig. 22) di collezione privata torinese, punzonate da Paolo Antonio Paroletto, il Bargoni ha proposto il Ladatte come autore del disegno. Condividendo la proposta pensiamo, per la datazione—stando ai marchi di G. B. Carron e di C. Micha, assaggiatori alla zecca di Torino rispettivamente dal 1753 e dal 1759—ad un'esecuzione intorno al '60; ma il pittoricismo fresco e vibrante potrebbe far indietreggiare il disegno a qualche tempo prima.

Nel 1756 Ladatte ricevette un pagamento per "una portella di metallo dorato alla custodia dell'oglio sánto della Cura Regia" che ancora sussiste con bronzi di buona fattura, pur non fra le cose più fini del maestro, provveduta d'un rivestimento ad intarsi del Piffetti (Cristo nell'orto).

All'agosto 1757 una lettera del Marchese di Sartirana, ambasciatore sabaudo, da Parigi alla corte di Torino, informando della supplica d'un modellatore di porcellane della manifattura di Chantilly desideroso di venire a far prova a Torino, fa sapere che questo artefice—in verità non precisato col nome—aveva già lavorato a Torino "en qualité de sculpteur" proprio con il Ladatte, ciò che conferma l'effettivo costituirsi presso di questi d'una bottega vivace di scultura decorativa; in essa dovevano immancabilmente pullulare disegni del maestro per ogni genere d'oggetti da chiesa, da palazzo e da collezione, nonchè veri e propri tipici disegni esemplari per decorazione, come nei grandi ateliers dei celebri "ornemanistes" parigini o dei colleghi inglesi. E quando nel marzo '64 il Ladatte, infermo, stenderà il suo primo testamento, egli legherà a Simone Dughé (Duguet) appunto quel prezioso patrimonio d'invenzioni e di motivi: "tutti li modelli, forme, carte e disegni esistenti nel suo laboratorio che si trova nella corte laterale al maneggio della Reale Accademia": patrimonio poi andato disperso.

Nel 1760 è registrato un pagamento "per aver modellato in creta una figura grande al naturale entro il quale sono riposte l'ossa del Beato Amedeo in Vercelli ed altro fatto per il corpo del Beato"; e nel '65 per "tre pezzi d'ornati d'argento previsti per il di dietro dell'altare della SS. Sindone", pagamento seguito da vari altri con lo stesso riferimento.

Per il lavoro destinato a Vercelli, scomparso, sembrerebbero oggi difficili precisazioni stando al documento dei conti di corte, dai termini non netti. Dal Casalis però apprendiamo qualche notizia su quanto avvenne nel settecento nella Cappella del Beato Amedeo al Duomo vercellese. Vittorio Amedeo I, nel '19, aveva ordinato la traslazione, nella nuova cappella dedicata al Beato, delle ossa in una cassa d'argento già fatta eseguire da Carlo Emanuele I. Ma poi Carlo Emanuele III, dopo aver fatto rivestir di marmi la cappella nel '39, "fece porre accanto all'altare le due tombe in cui riposano le ossa dei Duchi Carlo III e Vittorio Amedeo I . . . e donò una più vasta cassa d'argento riccamente ornata per riporvi le sacre spoglie del Beato. La cappella del Beato fu depredata, come pure l'urna che racchiudeva le venerate reliquie, nelle vicende accadute sul finire del secolo XVIII". Crediamo in base a ciò di poter individuare la situazione d'allora e l'inserirvisi del Ladatte: questi, in data non sappiamo quanto posteriore al '39 ma anteriore forse di qualche anno al '60, modellò in creta una statua (giacente certo) del Beato, come vero e proprio simulacro devozionale contenente i sacri resti; tale figura non più sistemabile nella vecchia urna atta a rinchiudere sole reliquie, rese necessaria la fattura "d'una più vasta cassa d'argento" cioè della nuova urna che può appunto rispondere all'"altro"—come dice il pagamento di corte—fatto non per reliquie ma per il "corpo" cioè per la statua in creta. Tanto più si rimpiange la scomparsa, in quanto tale lavoro monumentale doveva presentare elementi decorativi notevoli, a rilievo e forse in parte anche a tutto tondo.

Per gli ornati ad arricchimento dell'altare della Sindone, il documento del '65 è laconico e generico; il prezzo di lire 1815 sembra tuttavia indicare una certa importanza, tanto più aggiungendovisi pagamenti successivi. L'altare o meglio il monumento—cella—reliquiario marmoreo era stato disegnato, certo non senza tener conto di pensieri del Guarini, dall'architetto biellese Antonio Bertola ed era pronto nel 1694; la "gloria" eseguita a coronamento da Francesco Borello resta in situ ed a lui spettano i pregevoli angeli in legno dorato ai lati della teca e i quattro, meno fini (forse di aiuti), putti sopra la teca, forse già reggenti festoni o piccole lampade. Altro non doveva gravare il monumento concepito come severa struttura saliente per gradi come a rievocare il "passo" della cupola e ribadendo le profilature delle pareti. Cosa avvenne dopo? D'una presenza del Ladatte, sia pure in parti secondarie, non appare oggi traccia. Il silenzio dei documenti settecenteschi, il carattere unitario delle aggiunte ottocentesche (balaustrata con putti; lampade angolari) fanno credere che l'altare avesse nel '700 mantenuta la sua espressiva nudità, anche nei giorni del "rocaille", non concedendo ad alcuno interventi di rilievo nè tali dovettero essere gli ornati applicati dal Ladatte, forse scomparsi nelle spoliazioni di fine '700 (e forse mal arieggiati da chi fece il nuovo scadente tabernacolo ottocentesco in argento?).

Nel 1763, alla chiesa juvarriana del Carmine in Torino era stato eretto, su disegni di Benedetto Alfieri, l'altar maggiore con la partecipazione di Giovanni Battista Parodi genovese per le sculture in marmo e di Francesco Ladatte per quelle in bronzo. L'altare però subiva già un rimaneggiamento nel 1770, quando per incarico di Carlo Emanuele III l'architetto Birago di Borgaro sostituiva il tempietto sul tabernacolo con altro fornito di nuovi bronzi. Riteniamo che alla data di quell'altare originario si colleghino comunque i due grandi putti portacero in bronzo (fig. 23), già ritenuti scomparsi a seguito dei bombardamenti del 1943 e fortunatamente invece ora rivedibili sulla balaustrata dell'altare e che sono fra le cose più note del Ladatte. Stilisticamente, per la pienezza e maggior gravità di forme, essi possono stare appunto ad una data intorno al '63; il "rocaille" già va acquietandosi attenuando le divagazioni lineari e ritmiche (che il Ladatte serberà ancora scapriccianti in lavori di puro carattere ornamentale) ma il modellato mantiene ancora una morbidezza che stacca nettamente queste gentili e dolci figure dalle forme più levigate e sfreddate d'un decennio appresso. Anche questi putti trovano richiami, prevalentemente tematici, ma a volte con qualche nota di affinità di gusto e di stile, con tutta una serie di

creazioni francesi, di cui costituiscono anelli, ad esempio, i putti portacero eseguiti intorno al 1709–1713 da Claude Le Fort du Plessy al Palazzo Daun-Kinsky di Vienna o quelli poco più tardi del 1721–1724 al Palazzo del Belvedere nella stessa città; putti qui veduti dall'architetto svedese Karl Gustav Tessin che forse, dirigendo a Stoccolma più tardi i lavori a Palazzo Reale, fu lui a richiederne di analoghi a Jean Philippe Bouchardon nel 1752 (con fusione più tarda) per lo scalone; e si tenga conto che il Bouchardon in un viaggio europeo del 1750–1751 aveva toccato anche Torino. Richiami, ripeto che qui si propongono più che altro su un piano di diffusione d'un tema e d'una sua esteriore trattazione ma comunque culturalmente validi e significativi, situando anch'essi nettamente il Ladatte in un gusto che in quel periodo diramava da Parigi a Vienna a Torino alla Svezia a Pommersfelden a Salisburgo e che trova ancora esiti, per il tema di putti portalanterna, in quelli del Defernex allo scalone del Palais Royal di Parigi, già posteriori ai ladattiani, toccando il 1768.

In prossimità di tempo sta la partecipazione del Ladatte all'altar maggiore della chiesa del Sudario e Misericordia di Carignano, disegnato dall'architetto Agliaudi di Tavigliano e per il quale il bronzista eseguì i putti del tabernacolo; il disegno dell'Agliaudi per l'altare, con edicola sovrastante al tabernacolo, è del 1752; i bronzi decorativi (fregi e putti) del Ladatte stanno qualche poco più oltre. I putti, che attorniano e sormontano la cupola dell'edicola-tempietto, sono memori della modellazione di quelli di Vicoforte; non è da escludere che l'incarico al bronzista e quindi almeno i primi pensieri per i putti seguissero a poca distanza l'ideazione architettonica del '52, restando più vicino quindi ai putti di Vicoforte che a quelli del Carmine di cui non hanno la densità formale, anche se poi l'esecuzione tardò. Riteniamo comunque che qui non si abbia uno dei momenti migliori del Ladatte, la cui presenza è d'altronde—per quanto al culmine dell'altare—attenuata dall'evidenza della monumentale "mostra" architettonica nitida e severa e dalle due belle anonime statue d'angeli laterali, uno dei più tardi ma più vibranti casi di recezione del ritmo e del patetismo di derivazione berniniana nel '700 piemontese, in modi in parte paralleli a quelli del tardo Tantardini e del tardo Martinez ma più fluidi ed espansivi.

Documentati al 1770 da pagamenti per serie di arredi vari da tavolo e da parata, grandi candelieri con scene di caccia sul piede (fig. 24), rimasero poi trascurati a favore del celebre, ricchissimo ma non così fine di gusto anche se abilissimo e squisito di fattura, pendolo con "il Tempo e la Gloria militare" posteriore di cinque anni. Questi candelabri sono in numero di sei, sui camini della "Galleria del Daniel"; sul camino centrale due analoghi ma più piccoli candelabri, pure del Ladatte, sono ora accompagnati—aggruppati su un unico piedestallo—con una pendola a figure la quale non appartiene al Ladatte ed è più tarda (si notino, lungo le pareti della "Galleria del Daniel" le appliques a ornati "rocaille" (fig. 25) collegate nel gusto ai candelabri, e risalenti al Ladatte, non però tutte in quel torno di tempo, ma anche di un ventennio prima, sul 1747-1750). Per i due esemplari maggiori, sulla montatura di base, combinante un giro di ovuli a giorno con volute "rocaille", s'innalza il corpo dei candelieri realisticamente inteso come un nervoso e capriccioso tronco d'albero, svettante da un cumulo di terra e diramato in tre branche suddivise nei rametti portacero. Ai piedi degli alberi, cani azzannano selvaggina. Lo spunto descrittivo e la tesa vivacità dell'episodio si fondono mirabilmente all'alata e fervida fantasia decorativa. Il Fleming avanza un richiamo—per accordo fra opulenza ornamentale e realismo—con candelieri di Claude Vallin del 1742 e collega le basi con quelle di alari eseguite dal Pitoin nel 1772 per Madame du Barry (Louvre). Ciò che riconferma l'estensione della cultura del Ladatte e l'importanza fondamentale della sua educazione francese dagli esiti persistenti anche dopo il definitivo abbandono di Parigi, seppure forse, agli ultimi anni di vita, questa consonanza e risonanza del clima parigino acquisti alcunché di statico e, pur nel fervore e nell'opulenza, qualcosa di arcaico, come sarà in opere ancor più tarde, mentre i candelieri rimangono creazione tutta spontaneità ed eleganza, che gli artifici sottili del "rocaille" rendono più estrosa.

Firmato e datato 1773, in relazione all'assunzione al trono del personaggio, il busto eccellente di Vittorio Amedeo III al Museo Civico di Torino, in bronzo (fig. 27), traduce un tipo di ritratto di corte divenuto tradizionale nella scultura francese dagli inizi del regno di Luigi XV, secondo un gusto di piccolo oggetto soprammobile che, nelle diminuite proporzioni, nulla perde di maestà e di piglio volitivo e molto acquista in eleganza e vivezza e meglio si concede alle preziose abilità tecniche del cesellatore. L'impianto può anche richiamare ad una ritrattistica regale in voga a Parigi, per mano particolarmente di Jean Baptiste Lemoyne il giovane, ma se qualcosa qui resta di uno schema, ne è superato l'atteggiamento stilistico, più pittorico in Lemoyne pur se con valori di segno acuti e incisivi, a favore d'un plasticismo più liscio e compatto (ad esempio i piani lucenti della corazza e il risvolto con i nodi di Savoia) e d'una organizzazione del busto più calibrata anche nei riguardi della fissazione di carattere, balzante immediato e impavido in Lemoyne, più riflessivo e statico in Ladatte. Rilevante

la modellazione elaboratissima del volto. Squisito il basamento barocchetto-classicistico che da un lato inclina verso passate delizie boucheriane, dall'altro è in parentela con elementi decorativi di precedenti opere colliniane giovanili, come la base inghirlandata della "Vestale".

Nel 1772 Ladatte riceve il saldo per "uno ostensorio a raggio ed altro fatto e provisto per la Real Chiesa di Superga" (sottratto durante l'occupazione francese); nel 1777 poi, con un primo quinto del prezzo stabilito di lire 5000, per una "custodia di pendula di bronzo dorato istoriata, rappresentante la Verità scoperta dal Tempo (fig. 29), collocata nel gabinetto d'udienza di Sua Maestà", opera tuttora esistente e datata 1775; e in tutti questi anni avevano fatto seguito oggetti vari come caffettiere, piatti, vassoi, posate, crocifissi, acquasantiere, candelieri, vasi da fiori, cornici, alari, ornati per camini.

Già nel '34 Ladatte era pagato a corte per un modello in cera per una "pendulla". Del modello, imprecisato nel tema, non è comprovata una traduzione in bronzo. Per il '34, nel modello—e nell'eventuale bronzo derivato—l'accento francese doveva essere particolarmente pronunciato e la trattazione piuttosto mossa e pittoricamente fluida, come si vede nelle opere ladattiane del quarto decennio. Illustri esempi di pendole egli aveva trovato a Parigi e ne riflesse caratteri fino al tardo esemplare del '75; altri esempi parigini egli poi ritrovava nella stessa reggia torinese, così il pendolo con aquile nel gabinetto cinese o il pendolo col Tempo nel gabinetto delle miniature, quest'ultimo tuttavia in spiccati nessi col Ladatte stesso sì che, piuttosto che riferire entrambi quegli esemplari ad un francese sul '50, vorremmo ora proporre per il secondo un momento arretrato anche al '35-'40 e se non spingerne l'assegnazione al Ladatte, almeno considerarlo come uno dei riferimenti francesi più prossimi per il suo gusto. Circa il pendolo del '75 è da discutere il soggetto raffigurato. Il documento esplicitamente parla di "Verità scoperta dal Tempo"; in realtà, la raffigurazione come si presenta va al di là del tema richiesto al Ladatte. Poiché l'identificazione del pezzo è indiscutibile, conviene pensare che l'artista si sia comportato con estrema libertà poiché le figure non esprimono esattamente il soggetto assegnato. Il "Tempo" in alto, appare del tutto indipendente dalla figura femminile campeggiante in basso, vestita come mai nessuna "Verità" apparve, reggente per di più l'attributo di un disco raggiante e antropomorfizzato, presentandosi piuttosto come una "Fama" o equivalente allegoria; e attorno ad essa i trofei d'armi e bandiere e il piccolo guerriero con la spada brandita ribadiscono un significato allusivo ad una "gloria militare", fulgente e irruente, sotto il segno inesorabile del "Tempo".

Dal punto di vista tecnico la "pendulla" del Tempo è forse l'opera più virtuosistica e d'effetto del cesellatore ma non con la grazia squisita e lo spontaneo equilibrio fra forma e forma e tra pieni e vuoti, quali Ladatte dimostrava in precedenza, ad esempio in capolavori come i bronzi montati negli stipi di Piffetti (1732–1734) a palazzo reale, nel Gabinetto di toeletta della regina, o già assai più tardi nei putti e nei motivi decorativi di fiori, trofei e "rocailles" al Tabernacolo del Sacro Pilone al Santuario di Vicoforte (1750). Sulla cassa del pendolo la figurazione allegorica è fittissima e perfino carica, d'estrema eleganza componendo un "décor" sontuoso di grande parata: un pezzo da salotti di Versailles d'un buon trentennio prima; ciò che fa dire al Fleming che, al 1775, nella Parigi di Louis XVI esso sarebbe apparso "vieux jeu", ciò che non ne sminuisce la qualità superba di cesello, la magistrale distribuzione delle parti in cui il contrasto un po' troppo forte tra le luci sulle emergenze plastiche calcate e le ombre improvvisamente ritagliate, lascia brillare una esuberanza e una preziosità degne d'un Caffieri.

Al pendolo col "Tempo" è da connettere il bellissimo calamaio in bronzo col "Tempo" (fig. 28) della collezione Fila di Biella, che rientra nel gruppo delle prestazioni tarde. Grandioso nell'impianto e negli elementi singoli, porta sul vassoio, incorniciato da vigorose "rocailles" i due vasetti portainchiostro e portapolvere in cui si ripropone la tipica compiacenza per l'accostamento di liscie lucentissime modanature e carnosi sviluppi di ornati, in questo caso fogliami e scaglie. Sul vassoio è semidisteso il "Tempo", di impeccabile cesello. Il nesso col pendolo del '75 è scoperto; tuttavia il calamaio potrebbe porsi qualche poco in antecedenza, nel corso del quinquennio e più vicino al '70.

Nel 1778 Ladatte fu nominato professore alla Reale Accademia di pittura e scultura allora fondata in Torino ma dall'80 la sua salute era sempre più precaria; aveva rinnovato il testamento nel 1777, rivedendolo nell'80 e lasciado poi, con codicillo dell'84, erede universale la figlia Rosalia sposata al pittore Vittorio Amedeo Cignaroli; ciò spiega il trovarsi, più tardi, cose del Ladatte in proprietà della famiglia Cignaroli. Ladatte morì, dopo anni d'inattività, il 18 gennaio 1787.

Il segretario dell'Accademia di Parigi, Cochin, richiese con lettera del 27 febbraio notizie precise sul decesso al Cignaroli, e probabilmente molte notizie pubblicate poi dal Dussieux hanno per fonte il pittore. Un documento del 28 febbraio 1787, firmato da Ignazio Collino, Giovanni Battista Bernero e Filippo Collino (colleghi di Ladatte all'Accademia) e conservato dagli eredi Cignaroli ancora a fine '800, contiene una stima

d'un "gruppo in terracotta fatto dal fu F. Ladetti scultore" raffigurante il Trionfo delle Arti Liberali con la Fama incoronata da due geni e attorniata da tre puttini con gli attributi delle arti maggiori: gruppo corrispondente con quello ora agli Arts Décoratifs di Parigi e che dovette esser molto caro all'autore se lo conservò sempre presso di sè.

Ricordiamo alcune attribuzioni al Ladatte, parte accettabili, parte da escludere. Alla "Galleria Beaumont, Armeria Reale, spettano al bronzista i capitelli e le basi in bronzo delle colonne, lavoro pregevole pur se di effetto decorativo assorbito nell'insieme degli ornamenti di vario tipo e materia della Galleria. Al Santuario della Madonna degli Angeli in Cuneo, spetterebbe al Ladatte, secondo il Vesme, l'urna del Beato Angelo. Non ci constano documenti più antichi riferenti un impegno del Ladatte nè sappiamo se il Vesme attingesse l'attribuzione da fonti non citate o puramente a tradizione orale. L'urna non sembra però ammettere un intervento ladattiano.

Il Bartoli, disse del Ladatte gli ornati in bronzo della terza Cappella nella chiesa anteriore della Consolata di Torino. Anche qui mancano appoggi documentari all'attribuzione; e quegli ornati hanno un carattere generico, più di clima ladattiano che di personale presenza.

Il Nepote nel suo poemetto—ed egli era contemporaneo e amico dello scultore—assegnò al maestro il gruppo in cartapesta dipinta della Risurrezione di Cristo alla Basilica Mauriziana (fig. 30). Obiezioni possono essere sollevate: non risulta che il Ladatte mai trattasse quel materiale, nè che dedicasse la sua attenzione a tal tipo di scultura devozionale, processionale, teatralmente popolare. Nè i personaggi del veramente notevole gruppo rispecchiano tipi strettamente ladattiani, sembra piuttosto ravvisare un timbro alla Plura. E tuttavia osserveremo che i gruppi figurati devozionali del Plura non ebbero mai, nè quella grandiosità d'impianto nè quella complessità di relazioni interne, nè quel balzante dinamismo. Il panneggiato stesso è qui più libero e organico di quanto non sia di solito nel Plura. D'altronde, poichè l'asserzione del Nepote risale ad anni di attività ancor vitalissima e lucida del Ladatte che avrebbe potuto controbatterla se inesatta e poichè le figure del gruppo dimostrano una energia e una tensione al di là delle invenzioni del Plura e possono riflettere una sensibilità di scultore in metallo, ci chiediamo se fu possibile che il Plura, esperto in gruppi devoti e patetici da processione, abbia qui eseguito su disegno di Ladatte che fu spesso, in Torino, soprintendente alle esecuzioni di "macchine" per manifestazioni ufficiali. Ma ciò implicherebbe un disegno ladattiano anteriore al '37, anno di morte del Plura e quindi in tempo di assenza di

Ladatte. Forse piuttosto il suo disegno fu assai più tardo, affidato per l'esecuzione ad un buon plasticatore di cerchia del Plura? La "Risurrezione" rientrava in una serie di cinque gruppi in cartapesta (unico superstite) già conservati alla Basilica Mauriziana, ove un misero dipinto anonimo trasmette la testimonianza delle processioni con i cinque gruppi portati su carri.

Difficile oggi appurare la partecipazione del Ladatte in parte dei circa 150 vasi in piombo con stemmi e ornati, già al giardino della reggia (ora in altre parti di essa o, alcuni, dispersi) che il Rovere disse compiuti da Simone Boucheron per un gruppo più antico, e dal Ladatte.

Bellissime le due "ventole" in bronzo (fig. 26) con putti, rocailles, rametti e mazzetti al Museo Civico di Torino, di recente attribuite dal Viale. Il disegno elegantissimo e d'alta fantasia è sul piano del tardo Ladatte, tra Vicoforte e il Carmine di Torino; qualche aggravio nel modellato dei putti fa pensare a collaboratori. Le appliques in bronzo nella sala di ricevimento alla Palazzina di Stupinigi sono invece da escludere anche da una generica cerchia, denotando altro gusto, già classicistico.

I bronzi dorati di due vasi cinesi in celadon (coll. privata) comparsi alla mostra del Barocco a Torino, 1963, con vaga designazione ladattiana ma già ivi considerati meglio di generica cerchia di Andrea Boucheron, lasciano incerti sulla stessa origine picmontese.

Un "leone accucciato" in terracotta—già dipinta a finto bronzo nel tardo '800—al Museo Civico di Torino, con firma e data "Ladatte 1745" è cosa più tarda; l'iscrizione fu aggiunta dopo la cottura.

Ringrazio vivamente per gentile concessione di fotografie il Dr. Vittorio Viale, direttore dei Musei Civici di Torino, M. Michel Faré, conservateur en chef du Musée des Arts Décoratifs di Parigi, M.me Sylvie Béguin e M.me Odette Dutilh, Departement des Peintures du Louvre, M.me Nament, Service Documentation Photographique de Versailles. Esprimo particolare riconoscenza a M. Fr. Blanchet, Directeur des Services d'Archives de la Seine Maritime, Rouen, per la sua rara sollecitudine nella ricerca e comunicazione di tutti i dati sul perduto monumento ladattiano a Louis XV.
Il presente studio non può essere che una prima proposta per un riesame completo dell'attività del Ladatte. Non mi sono stati per ora possibili definitivi accertamenti sulla sopravvivenza o meno di lavori del Ladatte per la Cattedrale di Reims e per S. Louis-en-l'île di Parigi; ne è quindi escluso ogni discorso, fuor dalla citazione pura e semplice degli incarichi o di eventuali bozzetti.

BIBLIOGRAFIA

1748—F. Ladatte, Descrizione manoscritta di progetto di fontana, in manoscritti del Vernazza, Accademia delle Scienze, Torino, F. VI, 15.

1749—Raccolta de' giornali stampati in Torino, l'anno 1749 n. 9.

1770—I. Nepote, Poesia inedita, in mss. alla Pinacoteca Sabauda, Torino.

1776—F. Bartoli, Notizie delle pitture e sculture, etc., Venezia.

1778—I. Durando di Villa, Ragionamento sulle belle arti, etc., Torino.

1800 c.—G. B. Boucheron, Serie degli artisti che hanno lavorato in metallo, etc., opuscolo in unico esemplare, Torino, Bibl. Reale.

1819—M. Paroletti, Turin et ses curiosités, Torino.

1° quarto dell'800—P. Zani, Manoscritto 3623, Biblioteca di Parma.

1821—C. F. Pastori, Storia della Real Basilica di Superga, Torino.

1826—Lettres sur Rouen, Rouen.

1851—G. Casalis, Dizionario storico, geografico, etc., degli Stati Sabaudi, Torino.

1854—L. Dussieux-Soulié . . . , Mémoires inédits sur la vie et les ouvrages des membres de l'Académie Royale, etc., Tomo II, Parigi.

1858—C. Rovere, Descrizione del Real Palazzo di Torino, Torino.

1873—G. Bessone, Nuova guida del Santuario di N.S. di Mondovì, Mondovì.

1877—G. Claretta, La campana ducale, etc., e la famiglia Boucheron, in Atti Soc. piemont. Arch. e Belle Arti, Torino.

1879—G. Claretta, I marmi scritti di Torino e suburbio, etc., in Atti Soc. Piemont. Arch. e Belle Arti, Torino.

1881—D. Guilmard, Les maitres ornemanistes, Parigi.

1887—T. Chiuso, La chiesa in Piemonte dal 1797 ai giorni nostri, Torino (Speirani e Arneodo), vol. I.

1893—G. Claretta, I Reali di Savoia in Miscellanea di Storia Italiana, Deputazio di Storia Patria, Torino.

1893—A. Baudi di Vesme, I van Loo in Piemonte, in Archivio Storico dell'Arte.

1901—H. Geispitz, La statue de Louis XV au Palais des Consuls à Rouen, Rouen (Lecerf).

1901—Inventaire général des richesses d'art de la France, vol. III, Parigi.

1905—M. Demaison, Le musée d'Arts Décoratifs, in Les Arts, n. 48.

1910—G. Rodolfo, Notizie . . . sulle antichità scoperte e Carignano . . . , Torino.

1911—P. Toesca, Torino, Bergamo.

1911—S. Lami, Dictionnaire des sculptures de l'Ecole Française au XVIII siècle, vol. II, Parigi.

1922—H. Barbet de Jouy, Musée National du Louvre, Description des Sculptures, vol. II, Parigi.

1925—A. Lindbloom, J. Ph. Bouchardon, in Gazette des Beaux Arts, vol. I.

1928—voce (redazionale) F. Ladatte in Thieme-Becker Künstlerlexikon, vol. XXII, Lipsia.

1934—L. Rosso, La pittura e scultura del '700 a Torino, Torino.

1950—M. Charageat-M. Beaulieu, Catalogo esposizione "Louis XV et rocaille", Parigi.

1958—J. Fleming, F. Ladatte, an Italian ciseleur, in The Connoisseur.

1958—R. Wittkower, Art and Architecture in Italy 1600-1750, London.

1959—M. Bernardi, Il Palazzo Reale di Torino, Torino.

1960—L. Mallè, Scultura, intaglio, intarsio del '700, in Storia del Piemonte, vol. II, Torino.

1961—L. Mallè, Le arti figurative in Piemonte dalle origini al periodo romantico, Torino.

1963—L. Mallè, La scultura barocca in Piemonte, in Catalogo della mostra del Barocco piemontese, Torino.

1963—A. Bargoni, Le argenterie barocche piemontesi, in Catalogo della mostra del barocco piemontese, Torino.

1963—V. Viale, I mobili, in Catalogo della mostra del barocco piemontese, Torino.

1963—Y. Avenel, . . . Une statue de Louis XV détruite en 1792 au Palais des Consuls, in "Paris-Normandie", 18-8-1963.

1964—L. Mallè, Alcune revisioni per la scultura del '600 e '700 in Piemonte, in Studi in onore di Wart Arslan, Pavia (in corso di pubblicazione).

JOHN FLEMING and HUGH HONOUR

Giovanni Battista Maini*

Writing of the generation of sculptors born between 1680 and 1700 and working in Rome, Professor Wittkower remarked that 'four names stand out by virtue of the quality and quantity of their production: those of Agostino Cornacchini (1685–after 1754), Giovanni Battista Maini (1690–1752), Filippo della Valle (1697–1770) and Pietro Bracci (1700–1773)'.[1] Studies have been devoted to each of these sculptors,[2] with the exception of Maini[3] who, it must be admitted, is the least exciting member of the quartet. Maini was, however, the author of a few outstanding works—the statues of Clement XII and Cardinal Neri Corsini in the Lateran, two statues of founders of religious orders in St. Peter's and a very handsome statue of Benedict XIV—which have encouraged us to gather together a check list of his documented œuvre.

It is perhaps significant that the only two contemporary accounts of Maini appear as appendices to biographies of his much greater master, Camillo Rusconi.[4] As he worked under Rusconi for some twenty years—nearly half his career—it is hardly surprising that he never entirely shook off his influence (which was, of course, felt to some extent by all other early eighteenth-century sculptors in Rome). He was a carver and modeller in stucco of considerable ability but one feels that he lacked invention and it would hardly be surprising to discover that he derived the designs for all his best works from other artists.

Giovanni Battista Maini was born at Cassano Magnano in Lombardy on 6 February, 1690.[5] He presum-ably received his earliest training in Milan, perhaps under Giuseppe Rusnati. In 1708 or 1709[6] he went to Rome and joined Rusconi's studio where he appears to have remained until his master's death in 1728. In 1728 he was elected to the Academy of St. Luke of which he became *Principe* in 1746. Little is known of his private life save that he married Margherita, daughter of one Giacomo Scaramucci, with whom he lived in the parish of S. Andrea delle Fratte.[8]

His earliest independent work is, in all probability, the attractive terracotta relief of St. Francis of Paola in the Accademia di S. Luca, perhaps presented as his *morceau de réception*. His earliest work in marble is the monument to Innocent X in S. Agnese in Piazza Navona, which was probably, as Baldinucci remarks, executed after a model by Rusconi and certainly shows his influence (Fig. 1). Rusconi's ghost also hovers behind the two reliefs which he contributed to the cupola of SS. Luca e Martina in 1731. Immediately afterwards he carved the statue of St. Francis of Paola for St. Peter's, availing himself of a design provided by the Genoese painter Pietro Bianchi who performed a similar service for several contemporary sculptors in Rome. At about the same time he carved two heroic-scale statues for that great repository of early eighteenth-century Italian sculpture, the Basilica at Mafra. Here the sources of inspiration were rather more distant: the statue of the Archangel Gabriel is derived from Bernini's angels in S. Andrea delle Fratte and the Archangel Michael is little more than a marble version of Guido Reni's famous picture in S. Maria della Concezione, Rome. In 1732 he sat on the committee appointed to choose a design for the façade of S. Giovanni in Laterano and two years later carved a low relief for the portico which had been built to Alessandro Galilei's design. His most famous, and probably his best, works were also executed for the Lateran: the bronze statue of Clement XII and the

---

* Documentation for the sculptures by Maini mentioned in the text of this article is given in the catalogue of works.

1. R. Wittkower, *Art and Architecture in Italy 1600–1750*, Harmondsworth, 1958, p. 291.

2. For Cornacchini see: H. Keutner in *North Carolina Museum of Art Bulletin*, Winter 1957–Spring 1958, pp. 13–21, and Summer 1958, pp. 36–42, and R. Wittkower in *Miscellanea Bibliotecae Hertzianae*, Munich, 1961, pp. 464–73. For Filippo della Valle, V. Moschini in *L'Arte*, XXVIII (1925), pp. 177 ff.; and H. Honour in *The Connoisseur*, November, 1959, pp. 172–9. For Bracci, K. von Domarus, *Pietro Bracci*, Strasbourg, 1915, and C. Gradara, *Pietro Bracci*, Milan-Rome, 1920.

3. There is a life in Thieme-Becker, *Künstler Lexikon*, vol. XXIII (1925), p. 578. T. von Wahl appended a brief list of works by Maini to his article in *Rep. f. Kunstwiss.*, vol. XXXIV, II, p. 16. An undocumented list of works is in A. Riccoboni, *Roma nell'Arte*, Rome, 1942, pp. 286–8.

4. L. Pascoli: *Vite de' Pittori, Scultori...*, Rome, 1730, vol. I, p. 270. F. Baldinucci, *Vite di Pittori* (*c.* 1732), Bib. Naz. Florence, MSS. Palat. 565, vol. I, fol. 70 v.

5. The date of birth is given by Pascoli, *op. cit.* The S. Andrea delle Fratte *Stato delle Anime* register describes him as 'figlio di G.B.'

6. Pascoli states that he was eighteen when he arrived in Rome, Baldinucci says he was nineteen.

7. Riccoboni, *op. cit.*, states that he left Rusconi in 1725 when he began work on the Chapel of St. Teresa in S. Maria della Scala but in fact this work is much later (see cat. no. 15). No documented works by Maini date from before 1728.

8. *Stato delle Anime* register for S. Andrea delle Fratte from 1733. He lived in the Vicolo della Purificazione.

marble monument to his nephew, Cardinal Neri Corsini, both of which owe a clear debt to Rusconi. The figure of the pensive Cardinal has a noble grandeur rare in early eighteenth-century Roman sculpture and unique in the work of Maini. Indeed, one can hardly believe that he was entirely responsible for its conception. A single hand seems to have guided all the various sculptors employed in the Corsini chapel and to him most of the credit is due for the success of this masterpiece of carefully integrated sculpture and architecture.

There is a lacuna in Maini's documented works between 1735, when the Corsini chapel statues were completed, and 1739 when he carved the figures of Justice and Religion, added as an afterthought to Fuga's Palazzo della Consulta. In 1741 he modelled a figure of Neptune for the Trevi fountain—the model has not survived and it cannot now be determined whether it was similar to that eventually carved (after Maini's death) by Pietro Bracci.[9] He was employed between 1741 and 1743 to provide a statue and a large low relief for the new portico of S. Maria Maggiore. The statue is now badly weathered, but the relief is a handsome work, if rather overcrowded with figures of obscure significance. Shortly afterwards he joined Filippo della Valle and Slodtz in decorating the chapel of St. Teresa in S. Maria della Scala.

Maini's next dated works are the statue of Benedict XIV in the cloister of S. Agostino, which he began in 1747, and the monument in S. Maria in Publicolis to Scipione Santacroce who died in that year. The statue is among his best works, very grandiose in conception though perhaps a little coarse in execution. In 1748 he finished a statue of Charles III of Naples for the Abbey of Montecassino and contributed a relief of the Death of the Virgin to the Chigi chapel in Siena Cathedral. In 1750 he was apparently at work on one of the squinches for the cupola of S. Luigi dei Francesi and

9. *Il Settecento a Roma*, Rome, 1959, p. 264.

the altar of St. Anne in S. Andrea delle Fratte. In the same year he carved a copy of the Callypigian Venus for Wentworth Woodhouse, Yorkshire—and one wonders whether he did not execute some of the other copies after the antique which were produced in such quantity in eighteenth-century Rome and provided many a sculptor with his 'bread and butter'. Shortly afterwards he was commissioned by Lord Charlemont to execute a series of busts, presumably after the antique, but he had not begun them before he died, and Lord Charlemont had difficulty in retrieving the 'advance' that he had paid.[10] He died on 29 July, 1752, and was buried in the church of S. Andrea delle Fratte.

The following catalogue is restricted to the works of G. B. Maini mentioned in the mid-eighteenth-century guides to Rome and other contemporary sources. Few scholars have been tempted to attribute further works to him on stylistic grounds.[11] And it would, indeed, be rash to hazard any such attributions until more has been discovered about his still more obscure contemporaries such as Giuseppe Lironi, Bartolomeo Pincellotti, Giuseppe Rusconi, Antonio Montauti, Bernardino Ludovisi and Carlo Tantardini who contributed statues or reliefs to various decorative schemes on which he was employed.

10. M. J. Craig, *The Volunteer Earl*, London, 1948, p. 264.
11. Thieme-Becker and Riccoboni credit him with the monument to Marchese and Marchesa Santacroce in S. Maria in Publicolis, in fact by L. Ottoni. Riccoboni gives him a vast and clumsy plaster group of *St. Augustine Casting Down Heresy* in the cloister of S. Agostino, which is undocumented and unlikely to be by him. A. E. Brinckmann, *Barock Bozzetti*, 1923, vol. i, p. 155, ascribes to him a terracotta which, however, W. Hager, *Die Ehrenstatuen der Päpste*, Leipzig, 1929, p. 70, ascribes to Cornacchini. The only other terracotta attributed to him appears to be the statuette of St. Gregory in the Palazzo Venezia (A. Santangelo, *Museo di Palazzo Venezia: Catalogo delle Sculture*, Rome, 1954, p. 79). This work, erroneously given to Bernini by Brinckmann (*op. cit.*, pl. 40/2), may well be by Maini but it is not a study for a documented work and as no terracottas certainly by Maini are known the attribution must remain doubtful.

Catalogue of Works

WORKS IN ITALY

FOLIGNO

1. Duomo. Silver statuette of St. Feliciano. G. B. Maini provided the model which was cast 1732–1733 by Francesco Giardoni (the silversmith of the Rev. Camera Apostolica) and Filippo Tofani.
Bibl.: Costantino G. Bulgari: *Argentieri Gemmari e Orafi d'Italia*, Rome, 1958, vol. i, p. 533.

MONTECASSINO

2. Abbey. Marble statue of Charles III King of Naples, carved in Rome and sent to Montecassino 17 May, 1748; destroyed in Second World War.
Bibl.: A. Bertolotti: 'Esportazione di Oggetti di Belle Arti' in *Archivio Storico Artistico Archaeologico e Letterario della Città e provincia di Roma*, Spoleto, 1877, vol. ii, fasc. i, p. 59.

ROME

3. S. Agnese in Piazza Navona. Marble monument to Pope Innocent X, 1729. F. Baldinucci attributed the model to Camillo Rusconi: 'ha lavorato sopra di se [G. B. Maini] col modello del Maestro il bel deposito d'Innocenzo decimo . . .', but *Roma Antica e Moderna* makes a point of saying that it is 'opera ed invenzione di Gio. Battista Maini'. The former statement is more probably correct, though the model may have been no more than a rough sketch. Ercole Ferrata had originally been commissioned to execute the monument immediately after Innocent X's death, but his design proved too costly for the avaricious Camillo Pamfilij and Donna Olimpia.
Bibl.: F. Baldinucci: *Vite di Pittori*, Bib. Naz. Florence, MSS. Palat. 565, vol. i, fol. 70 v; *Roma Antica e Moderna*, Rome, 1750, vol. ii, p. 24; V. Golzio in *Archivi d'Italia*, Ser. ii, Ann. I, 1933–1934, pp. 306–308; L. F. von Pastor: *The History of the Popes*, London, 1957, vol. xxx, p. 379.

4. S. Agnese in Piazza Navona. Two stucco angels over the high altar, 1729. Titi remarks that they were made 'modernamente con un particolar disegno sono di Gio. Battista Maini'. Documents reveal that the sculptor was paid 1,500 scudi for them in 1729.
Bibl.: F. Baldinucci, *op. cit. loc. cit.*; F. Titi: *Studio di Pittura di Roma*, Rome, 1763, p. 131; S. Sciubba and L. Sabatini: *Sant'Agnese in Agone*, Rome, 1962, p. 100.

5. Convent of S. Agostino (ex). Marble statue of Benedict XIV on cloister staircase. The contract for this work is dated 15 October, 1747, and refers to a price of 1,450 scudi; it was in place before 1750.
Bibl.: *Roma Antica e Moderna*, 1750, vol. i, p. 555; T. von Wahl: 'Archivalien zu L. Vanvitelli und G. B. Maini' in *Repert. f. Kunstwiss.*, XXXIV, pp. 14 ff.; W. Hager: *Der Ehrenstatuen der Päpste*, Leipzig, 1949, pl. 42.

6. S. Andrea delle Fratte. Transept altar with marble statue of St. Anne 1750–1752. *Roma Antica e Moderna* records that Luigi Vanvitelli was the architect of the chapel, Lodovico Mazzanti painted the altarpiece and 'le scolture saranno di Gio: Battista Maini'. However, Riccoboni suggested that if by Maini it must be an early work.
Bibl.: *Roma Antica e Moderna*, 1750, vol. ii, p. 223; A. Riccoboni: *Roma nell'Arte: Le Sculture*, Rome, 1942, p. 286.

7. S. Giovanni in Laterano. Relief of *St. John Preaching* in portico c. 1734. Mentioned by Gaddi as the work of one of the 'più celebri scultori de' nostri giorni' and ascribed to Maini by Titi.

Bibl.: G. B. Gaddi: *Roma Nobilitata . . .*, Rome, 1736, p. 31; Titi, *op. cit.*, p. 221.

8. S. Giovanni in Laterano. Bronze statue of Clement XII and marble statue of Cardinal Neri Corsini in the Corsini chapel, 1735. Cracas records, 22 October, 1735, that the statue of the Pope had been cast successfully by Francesco Giardoni at the Apostolic Foundry and, 4 August, 1736, that the bronze and other statues of marble were in place in the Corsini chapel. Gaddi describes both without mentioning Maini's name.
Bibl.: Cracas: *Diario Ordinario*, nos. 2843 and 2966; G. B. Gaddi, *op. cit.*

9. SS. Luca e Martina. Stucco reliefs with angels and the symbols of St. John and St. Luke in the squinches of the dome, c. 1731. The slightly complicated story of these reliefs is explained by a document dated 6 May, 1731, in the archive of the Accademia S. Luca (kindly communicated to us by Mr. Anthony M. Clark). Giovanni Odazzi originally proposed to paint the squinches but Camillo Rusconi wished them to be reliefs and modelled the St. Matthew in wax and all four in papiermâché, but died in 1728 before any could be executed in stucco. The St. Matthew was executed by Giuseppe Rusconi, the St. Mark by Filippo della Valle and the other two by Maini. The same document reveals that all four were modelled under the direction of the painter, Sebastiano Conca. Maini's reliefs are mentioned also by Gabburi who gave the other two to Filippo della Valle.
Bibl.: N. Gabburi: *Vite di Pittore*, Bib. Naz. Florence, MSS. Palat. 1377–1381, p. 1382.

10. S. Luigi dei Francesi. Stucco relief of a Doctor of the Church (St. Augustine?) in a squinch of the dome, 1750–1752. *Roma Antica e Moderna*, 1750, states that the 'cupola sarà ornata di statue'. Cracas records 3 April, 1754, that the whole work was finished and that the reliefs were by Maini, Filippo della Valle, Monsu Gilè (N.-F. Gillet) and Monsu Scial (Simon Challes)—though three reliefs must have been finished by 1752 when Gillet and Challes left Rome and Maini died. The similarity of the four reliefs suggests that they were executed from designs by a single artist, possibly the architect Antoine Deriset.
Bibl.: *Roma Antica e Moderna*, 1750, vol. i, p. 558; A. de Montaiglon and J. Guiffrey: *Correspondance des Directeurs de l'Académie de France à Rome*, Paris, 1887, vol. x, p. 244; V. Moschini in *L'Arte*, XXVIII (1925), p. 187.

11. S. Maria delle Fornaci. Stucco figures of two angels, a group of cherubs round a cross and a relief of a glory of cherubs, above the first altar on the right.

The angels are similar to those in S. Agnese (no. 3) and probably date from the 1730s.
Bibl.: *Roma Antica e Moderna*, 1750, vol. i, p. 115.

12. S. Maria Maggiore. Statue of Virginity on the left of the tympanum of the façade, 1741–1743.
Bibl.: *Roma Antica e Moderna*, 1750, vol. ii, p. 530.

13. S. Maria Maggiore. Relief of the Madonna of St. Luke, *c.* 1743, in the portico (near the Porta Santa). One of four reliefs, the others being by Pietro Bracci, Bernardo Ludovisi and Giuseppe Lironi.
Bibl.: *Roma Antica e Moderna*, 1750, vol. ii, p. 531.

14. S. Maria in Publicolis. Marble monument to Prince Scipione Santacroce, 1747. The earlier monument to Marchese Santacroce and his wife, facing this work, is by L. Ottoni (R. Wittkower in *Thieme-Becker*, vol. xxvi, p. 94), erroneously ascribed to Maini by Riccoboni.
Bibl.: *Roma Antica e Moderna*, 1750, vol. i, p. 584.

15. S. Maria della Scala. Two stucco angels above the altar in the chapel of St. Teresa, *c.* 1739–1745. The chapel appears to have been completed shortly before October, 1745 when the Pope visited it and Cracas printed a description of it.
Bibl.: Cracas: *Diario Ordinario*, 16 and 23 October, 1745; *Roma Antica e Moderna*, 1750, vol. i, p. 171.

16. SS. Nome di Maria. Stucco relief in the dome (the Presentation?). A document in the church archive reveals that Maini was paid 50 scudi for a 'medaglione' in 1746. The other seven reliefs are by M. L. Slodtz, Carlo Tantardini, Francesco Quierolo, Bernardo Ludovisi and Filippo della Valle.
Bibl.: A. Martini and M. L. Casanova: *SS. Nome di Maria*, Rome, 1962, pp. 61, 91.

17. S. Pietro. Marble statue of St. Francis of Paola (fourth pilaster of nave), 1732. Ratti reveals that Pietro Bianchi provided the design for this statue as for Filippo della Valle's nearby St. John of God.
Bibl.: F. Baldinucci *op. cit. loc. cit.*; *Roma Antica e Moderna*, 1750, vol. i, p. 65; C. G. Ratti: *Delle Vite de' Pittori . . . Genovesi*, Genoa, 1769, p. 304.

18. S. Pietro. Marble statue of St. Philip Neri (third pilaster of nave), *c.* 1735.
Bibl.: *Roma Antica e Moderna*, 1750, vol. i, p. 65.

19. S. Pudenziana. Stucco angels. *Roma Antica e Moderna* ascribes to Maini 'Angeli che reggono l'Organo, ed il Coretto incontro'. According to Riccoboni they were still there in 1942 but there is now no trace of them.

Bibl.: *Roma Antica e Moderna*, 1750, vol. ii, p. 595; Riccoboni, *op. cit.*, p. 287.

20. Oratorio di S. Francesco Saverio (del Caravita). Stucco decorations in the upper room. The lower floor of the oratory was redecorated in 1711 and it therefore seems likely that the stuccoes in the room above are early works by Maini, possibly dating from the period when he was still working under Rusconi.
Bibl.: *Roma Antica e Moderna*, 1750, vol. i, p. 515.

ROME—SECULAR BUILDINGS

21. Accademia di S. Luca. Terracotta relief of St. Francis of Paola. Probably presented to the Academy by Maini on his election in 1728.
Bibl.: V. Golzio: *Le Terrecotte della R. Accademia di S. Luca*, Rome, 1933, p. 33.

22. Palazzo della Consulta. Statues of Justice and Religion on the tympanum of the façade. Ascribed to Maini by Cracas who mentions their unveiling 31 October, 1739. Erroneously attributed to Filippo della Valle in *Roma Antica e Moderna* and many later publications.
Bibl.: Cracas, *op. cit.*, 31 October, 1739; *Roma Antica e Moderna*, 1750, vol. ii, p. 626; L. Bianchi: *Disegni di Ferdinando Fuga*, Rome, 1955, p. 34.

SIENA

23. Cathedral. Relief of the Death of the Virgin in Cappella Chigi, 1748, signed: I. B. MAINI.

WORKS IN OTHER COUNTRIES

ENGLAND

24. Wentworth Woodhouse, Yorkshire. Marble copy of the Callypigian Venus (Museo Nazionale, Naples), signed: G. B. MAINI. Commissioned in Rome, together with statues by Filippo della Valle and B. Cavaceppi, also after the antique, by Lord Malton for his father the Marquess of Rockingham, 1750.
Bibl.: H. Honour in *The Connoisseur*, May, 1958, p. 224.

PORTUGAL

25. Mafra, the Basilica. Statues of the Archangels Gabriel and Michael in the chapel of S. Pedro de Alcantara, both signed: GIO. BAT. MAINI, *c.* 1737. Ayres de Carvalho also ascribes unsigned statues of St. Elizabeth of Hungary and St. Clare, in the same church, to Maini.
Bibl.: Ayres de Carvalho: *A Escultura em Mafra*, Mafra, 1956, p. 17, pls. 3, 4, 125, 126.

ANTHONY M. CLARK

Agostino Masucci: A Conclusion and a Reformation of the Roman Baroque

In 1765 Mariette regretted that there was no life of Agostino Masucci, an artist whose great name Sir Joshua Reynolds found fallen, a generation later, 'into what is little short of oblivion'. Masucci died old and famous in October, 1768, and his son Lorenzo (died 1785) was a successful painter who amalgamated Agostino's style with that of Mengs but apparently was unable to honor his celebrated parent with even one of those short biographies customary in the Roman art publications of the 1770's and 1780's. Mariette knew possibly the only biography of Masucci, that of Niccolò Pio, written doubtlessly in cooperation with the artist and apparently in 1723, or while the Florentine Gabburri began his contacts with Roman artists for a similar purpose. Gabburri ignored the young painter who had just come into prominence but the more serious Pascoli did not, and in Pascoli's 1730 volume there is a shrewd and courteous citation.[1]

The Pio biographies of contemporary artists[2] I believe date from somewhat before 1715 down to the date the manuscript bears of 1724. An illustrative collection of drawings and prints was to accompany short biographies of the important dead and living masters. Portraits of all the artists were gathered by Pio in the form of drawings, self-portraits of the living artists and portraits by a group of the living masters of their predecessors. The majority of the portraits seem to have been in hand in 1715 (when they and most of the other drawings are said to have passed to Crozat) and may have been done in 1714 and 1715. Many of the biographies are of the early 1720's as is Masucci's, in which the biographer refers to the artist's thirty-second year. The self-portrait of Masucci (giving his birth date as 1692) passed from the Crozat sale to Count Carl Gustaf Tessin, and I have found it in the National-museum of Stockholm along with that of Andrea Procaccini, Masucci's teacher (Figs. 1 and 2).[3]

Pio says Masucci was born in Rome, studied first with Procaccini and then with Maratti who 'l'amava come

figlio' until his death (December, 1713). Thereafter Princess Pamphilj[4] supported him 'per molto tempo a disegnar le stanze di Raffaele in Vaticano' and Masucci also produced 'belle ritratti istoriati' in pen and watercolor with some success. One of Masucci's first oil paintings was exhibited at S. Salvatore in Lauro (possibly in 1715) and his first public work, now lost, were two laterals to Garzi's high altar[5] in S. Venanzio de' Camerinesi followed by the oval paintings in S. Maria in Via Lata (c. 1716–1717?). Pio then states that Masucci was currently preparing 'un quadro d'altare per una Cappella' in S. Maria Maggiore and had done numerous works for Monsignor del Giudice the papal Majordomo.[6] The altar in S. Maria Maggiore may be the painting presently there but this is signed and dated 1743.[7]

From Pio we discover Masucci at the beginning of the third decade of the century as a young painter just established. Until several years after Maratti's death the young man supported himself not as a monumental painter but as a supplier of drawings. One may note that in 1706 Masucci took second prize in the S. Luca painting contest and in 1707 the first prize. Aside from these works, which of course were prize

---

1. An actual biography of a slightly later date may occur in Pascoli's manuscripts at Perugia. The mention in Pascoli's *Vite* should be compared with the ill-judged note in Mariette's *Abecedario*.

2. *Vat. Cod.*, 257. Masucci appears at fol. 201 and fol. 202.

3. Masucci in Nationalmuseum 3063/1863; Procaccini 652/1863.

4. Presumably the widow of G.B. and the mother of Camillo Pamphilj Juniore.

5. This still exists, anonymously, in Galleria Nazionale, Rome (see photograph G.F.N. E 25122). The Masuccis are reported as having shown miracles of St. Venantius. A painting for a similar but unknown commission exists in the *Miracle of a Carmelite Saint* formerly at Castel Gandolfo and more recently in the Vatican storages (Arch. Fot. Gall. Mus. Vaticani, VII, 29, 2), as anonymous although surely by Masucci, and with the date 1726.

6. Masucci's patron was Niccolò del Giudice (1660–1743, cr. June, 1725), Prefect of the Sacred Palaces since the time of Clement XI and soon to be created a cardinal. His uncle was the notable cardinal Francesco del Giudice (cr. 1690, died October, 1725) who resembled Masucci's early portrait drawing of a cleric at Windsor (Blunt and Cooke, no. 534). In September, 1740, the younger del Giudice gave the new pope, Benedict XIV, an *Adoration of the Kings* by Masucci (*Cracas*, 3661, p. 6). See also note 19, below.

7. Although the painting is in want of cleaning, the signature and date are perfectly clear and, in 1743, the oval was paid for and in full, joining a series of matching ovals which were certainly new and upon new altars. A drawing of the composition in the National Gallery of Scotland (D. 1927) appears to me to date from the early 1740's.

drawings done by a student of painting, what seems to be the earliest known drawing is an academy in the style of Procaccini (similar to one by that artist from the Pio group)[8] and it is likely that the close relation to Maratti was somewhat overemphasized by Masucci for quite obvious reasons. Procaccini probably taught Masucci more than Maratti, although not the final orientation and ambition, and it may be recalled that this master was prominent in Rome from 1715, when he entered the Academy, until his departure for Spain in 1720.[9] In 1722, P. L. Ghezzi drew Masucci, noting that 'con il tempo' he would do well,[10] and in the same year he was proposed for S. Luca[11] and his portrait of the new pope (probably done for Monsignor del Giudice) was engraved.

This is the beginning. After Pio a biography would list considerable prominence achieved in the 1720's: election to the Academy; very fashionable portrait and other private commissions; pictures and altars for S. Francesco di Paolo and S. Marcello in Rome and for the cathedral of Prague.[12] In 1727 a youth from Lucca, Pompeo Batoni, sampled the two most obvious studios in Rome, Sebastiano Conca's and Masucci's. In the 1730's Masucci was the chief painter of the official tradition, becoming the prime continuator of Maratti on the death of Giuseppe Chiari (1727) and also the Regent of the Virtuosi al Pantheon (1735), as well as the Head (*Principe*) of the Accademia di S. Luca (1736–1738). For the courts of Savoy, Spain and Portugal, he produced a number of important pictures[13] and he had emerged as the leading portrait painter in Rome. As we shall see, the last two decades of Masucci's life present a somewhat unsatisfactory career, but at the beginning of 1740 only Conca, who succeeded him as Head of the Academy, was a serious rival and the general judgment was that given by Cochin in 1750 when he listed Masucci with Mancini, Giaquinto and Batoni as the best painters in Rome.[14]

The basic factors in Masucci's style are his position as the last of the *Maratteschi* and his contribution to and renovation of the official classicistic inheritance. The *Maratteschi* were the extensive group of Maratti's pupils prominent in Rome from about 1680, tremendously and consistently effective until well into the 1720's. While Maratti's pupils participated in the production of the master's works during his later years and while they were heavily employed in making the numerous, faithful copies of his pictures, yet the variety of the pupils' styles was rather great, great enough for one to find counted among the *Maratteschi* such alien innovators as Luti and Trevisani and even the old Baciccio. During Maratti's last decades the original production of the true *Maratteschi* had departed from the High Baroque position of the master for proto- or early Rococo positions. This was done carefully and quietly within an official mode of remarkable unanimity and consistency. The other elders of the Accademia di San Luca are distinguishable from Maratti just as his pupils are—although one must remember that this is generally considered one of the hardest moments in any European school to distinguish individuals and it is true that basic artistic agreement was exceptionally strict. The Academy was never more strong nor, in a sense, more 'academic' even if, until the 1720's, there was no large problem of exclusiveness. Just as Pio's lives are packed with Maratti's pupils, so the Academy; against Solimena's strictures in his letter to Onofrio Avellino[15] may be placed Luti's desire to be thought a pupil of Maratti, as well as the general artistic vigor in Rome throughout the reign of

8. The Masucci was at Sotheby's on May 5, 1964, in lot 63. It should be compared with a Masucci academy at Windsor of *c.* 1740 (Blunt and Cooke, no. 535). The Procaccini academy is Stockholm, Nationalmuseum 653/1863.

9. Procaccini is last recorded at the meetings of S. Luca on April 7, 1720, and wrote from Spain on June 18, 1721.

10. *Vat. Ottobon.*, 3113, fol. 155, dated May 14, 1722.

11. September 7, 1722. Consideration was postponed until May 14, 1724, and Masucci was elected on June 11. The reception piece may have been the *Martyrdom of St. Barbara* still in the Academy's collections.

12. The *Glory of St. John Nepomuck* in Prague is dated 1729. The S. Marcello altar was copied in 1729 and probably dates from 1728 which could also be a terminal date for Masucci's scenes in the sacristy of S. Francesco di Paolo. Among the portraits are those of Cardinal Banchieri (1728) formerly in the Rospigliosi collection, Princess Vittoria Altoviti Corsini (1735) in the Corsini collection, at Florence, and the anonymous woman (*c.* 1725?) formerly in the Chigi collection, Castelfusano. The cartoon for the large portrait mosaic of Clement XII and Cardinal Corsini still in palazzo Corsini, Rome, may be due to Masucci. The earliest engraved portrait is the Innocent XII of 1722 (I. Frey after 'Mastucci'). Incidentally, Masucci is rather often engraved after 1729 in which year he produced the drawing for the frontispiece to the *Vocabulario dell'Accademia della Crusca*.

13. For Savoy see below. An untypical *Annunciation* of the 1720's at La Granja is published by A. Griseri in *Boll. Piemontese della Società di Archeologia e Belle Arti*, XII–XIII,

1958–9, Fig. 145. Aside from the 1735 *Alexander and the Gordian Knot* (done for La Granja and now at the Escorial), the self-portrait of 1740 (formerly with the Marques de Santillano) and the portrait of Juvara of *c.* 1736 (Accademia di S. Fernando, published by Griseri, *op. cit.*, Fig. 144), there appears to be a number of commissions untraced in Spain. Before the major commissions of 1747 for S. Roque in Lisbon is the large *Assunta* of 1731 in Evora Cathedral and at least two equally large canvases in the palace at Mafra: a *Coronation of the Virgin* and what is said to have been John V's favorite painting, the *Holy Family with God the Father* (the date of which now reads 1721 but which is documented to 1730).

14. Cochin ignores a number of painters definitely but only slightly less important: Benefial, Conca, Costanzi, Mazzanti, Pozzi and Zoboli. In 1750 Subleyras, a very considerable rival of Masucci's from the 1730's, was dead.

15. See M. Loret, *Capitolum*, x, 1934, pp. 541 ff.

Clement XI. The problem of exclusiveness arose at the very end of the second decade of the century because stylistic innovations and solutions were suggested which could not be permitted by either of the two leading groups, the pacified late Baroque of such older masters as Garzi or the strict Marattism shrunken to febrile early Rococo of such younger masters as Giuseppe Chiari.

Maratti miniaturized and domesticated is the type and contribution of the true *Maratteschi*, and their *difference* from the master, which Pascoli clearly recognized in the case of Masucci, has been lost sight of in modern criticism. The key to the difference is the gradual Rococo adaptation of the High Baroque which moved by various steps in Rome to a culmination on its own terms in the 1720's and then a faltering and verging on obsolescence in the 1730's. The early Rococo is basically important to the generation just before Masucci and someone someday will point out that it is such *Maratteschi* as Procaccini and Chiari who represent more clearly than Trevisani and Luti the characteristic Roman approach to the Rococo. Both Trevisani and Luti are in a sense gathered, from slightly earlier and more radical but transitional positions, into the more effective style of the *Maratteschi* in the century's second decade. It is from this notable style that Conca, Rocca and Panini departed on their voyage to those greater Rococo feats which Masucci was strongly to oppose.[16]

To the *Maratteschi* of Chiari's generation the new classicism in the wind in Rome from just after 1710 (but more effectively from 1720) was not important and was not an immediate threat to the classicistic authority of Maratti and the continuance of much of his vocabulary in new Rococo terms. The proto-Neoclassicism (hideously so called) was consciously critical of the late Baroque and increasingly so of the Rococo, attempting to reform these by a return to the masters of the Renaissance and of the early Baroque and through an infusion of the new archeological enthusiasm. The new classicism and the Rococo influenced Masucci in that order and within a careful insistence upon tradition (i.e. Maratti).[17] I would now like to examine a series of Marattesque 'history pictures' to show the background and achievement of Masucci. Procaccini's *Tarquin and Lucretia* at Holkham (Fig. 3) is a fine Maratti school piece, less frothy and Rococo than the artist became by 1715 and, with little concession to the new century, almost reproducing the teacher. Chiari's *Perseus and Andromeda* in the same collection (Fig. 4) is Maratti remade for the early Rococo. Kittenish and slightly frenchified, eliminating the genuine heroic rhetoric and grandeur of the High Baroque, its minor eighteenth-century heroics would have been perfectly appropriate for Cardinal Ottoboni's theater. Chiari often handles paint more lavishly and delicately than here, but the general style was to be standard in Rome from Maratti's death to the early works of Masucci's most famous pupil, Gavin Hamilton—I am thinking of Hamilton's *Jupiter and Juno*, also at Holkham.

Luigi Garzi, an older and equally prominent Maratti pupil (died 1721), is also represented at Holkham with a bland but attractive *Cincinattus* (Fig. 5). Masucci was well aware of Garzi, whose traditional correctness, simplicity and sense of atmosphere and detail were highly regarded. Garzi's main concession to the new century was to sweeten and make more fond the late *seicento* painting while continuing its more classical positions. His classicism, as that of such related painters as D. M. Muratori and G. M. Morandi, was celebrated for its supposed dismissal of rhetoric old and new, its naturalism and even its realism.

Garzi's classicism is deeply indebted to France and

16. Panini's frescoes for palazzo Alberoni, palazzo De Carolis, etc., in the figural parts are closely dependent on Chiari and similar *Maratteschi* and not upon Luti or Conca as one would expect from Dottoressa Brunetti's careful review of Arisi (*Arte Antica e Moderna*, 26, 1964, pp. 167 ff.). Dottoressa Brunetti rightly stresses Luti's importance as a major artist, an importance which resides in his originality and quality and not in his notoriously restricted influence. Both Luti's main pupil, Pietro Bianchi (whose work finally denies his master's style), and his main spiritual heirs, Benefial, Batoni and Corvi, go very far afield from him and, as Conca and Panini—or even various late works of Luti himself—are heavily indebted to the *Maratteschi*. In Rome the more extreme Rococo painting was obviously considered especially appropriate to elegant *staffage*—both Panini and the constant shifting of position of Conca are testimony enough. Monumental painting, as Conca immediately found on his arrival in Rome, was to be based securely on classicistic principles or would be unacceptable. Chiari, whose major importance in Roman painting is not yet remembered, quite often decorated large compositions secure in their *bel disegno* with most gracious and nervous Rococo handling. The reverse approach of Conca or Rocca was fatal to the latter's career as a painter of large pictures and meant for the former a constant and complicated problem, sometimes avoided (in the very successful smaller pictures), sometimes solved by tempering the Neapolitan idiom with a strong dose of Chiari (as in the S. Cecilia ceiling), and sometimes surpassed (in such 'academic' works as that in Pisa Cathedral, or in such individual Rococo works as the Siena *Piscina Probatica*).

17. Mariette questioned Pio's insistence on Masucci's close relation with Maratti although recording that the paintings by Masucci he knew were only 'une imitation servile' (an opinion Pascoli opposes, as do the works themselves). Obviously Masucci strongly insisted, and more and more as both his position and his classicistic bias grew, upon his relation with his great drawing teacher and the possibility of duplicating in himself the pre-eminence of Maratti. In the 1720's Masucci became well known for his *Madonnas* with a good deal of publicity about ('Carlo delle Madonne') Maratti renewed. This was not an unimportant part of the campaign plus the favorable reports that Masucci was also especially good in Albani's realm of the infantile supporting cast.

Garzi's paintings are sometimes attributed to Charles Le Brun and his contemporaries. An *Alexander and the Family of Darius* (Fig. 6) last seen in auction as de Lairesse[18] and also a drawing for a *Coriolanus* in San Francisco (Fig. 7) may be said to carefully follow the great precedent of Le Brun's 1660 *La Tente de Darius*. It is notable that the classicism involved here is far more strict and less showy than that of Maratti in his 'history pictures'.

The sources do not connect Garzi and Masucci[19] but the visual connection will soon be apparent and I regard Garzi as one of the three main sources, with Procaccini and Chiari. Not a source but a friend was Francesco Fernandi called Imperiali,[20] of whom a pair of pictures exists in England, one completed and signed and the other apparently left unfinished at Imperiali's death in November, 1740, and finished by Masucci (Fig. 8). The co-authorship is noted in contemporary descriptions and is quite apparent: the pair of soldiers at left; at least the head of Coriolanus; all of the child in arms; and the activity at right are Masucci showing none of Imperiali's heavy and rather rustic manner.

Imperiali did not influence Masucci but the completion of his *Coriolanus* suggested a composition of Masucci's. A drawing reversing and amplifying the *Coriolanus* (as an *Alexander and the Family of Darius?*) exists (Fig. 9). This also reverses the traditional composition of Le Brun and, as might be expected, is more academic and grandiose than Imperiali's composition. Thus freed of Imperiali's suggestion, Masucci painted the composition in the original direction as can be seen in a version curiously attributed to Benjamin West and possibly a studio replica (although not by West: Fig. 10). In spirit, this is closer to Garzi's drawing of the subject than to the Imperiali Masucci finished. One notices the empty but 'correct' figurative style and coloring of Chiari and finds the novelty of the painting in the extremely rational and clear spatial structure, the plainness, and the cold bloodlessness of the execution.

The effect of the new Roman classicism is apparent in

Masucci's *Alexander* and it is worth examining a key work of this movement, Jacopo Zoboli's 1724 *Death of Caesar* (Fig. 11). Precedents for Zoboli's picture can be found in France and even among the academic Venetians before Tiepolo, but now the attempt at archeological correctness is increased as is the limitation of the use of stock Baroque poses and the emphasis upon plain, bold narrative. There is proud use of the most recent archeological source-books for convincing details and a flurry of Republican togas and stern grimaces which are both sensitive to Roman sculpture (as distinct from academic vocabulary) and prophetic of the 1780's. Sebastiano Conca, regularly the most frivolously Rococo of the important painters in Rome, also painted similar subjects and, in composition, also *à la Poussin*, but Conca is hardly so stern. In 1724 portraits conceived in the ancient style had been current, in medals and busts, for some few years. But, only the growing demand for careful drawings of the best antiquities and for more knowledgeable presentation and more faithful details had begun to bring the new classicism home to the painters, plus the pressure for a more serious, a more noble and classical art, as was to be publicized so strongly in France over a decade later. The Zoboli was painted three years before Raguzzini built Piazza S. Ignazio, the year Luti died, the year Masucci was elected to the Academy, the year before Conca's S. Cecilia ceiling.

Masucci's 1738 *Judgment of Solomon* (Fig. 12) is an excellent example of his mature work. The lighting, the style, the gestures, the surface handling are subordinated to the extraordinary logical clarity of narrative, composition, space and individual forms. The spectators on the far balcony seem to comment that the world of Panini can be as impeccable as Poussin (and, not incidentally, as ancient Rome) and as authoritative as Raphael. In the claustrophobia of conventional correctness, with the deliberately studied elements, there is a foretaste of the hieratic preciousness and odd ornamentalism of the true Neoclassical and of the Empire style. The next and final step before the Neoclassical might be represented by Mengs' 1760 *Augustus and Cleopatra*, in which Rococo graciousness is exhausted and the lingering Baroque pictorial devices, quietly present in the Masucci, may be said to disappear.

At Mentmore, attributed to Ghezzi and Maratti, are two paintings (Figs. 13 and 14) engraved in Rome before 1750 as by Masucci. The *Baptism of Charles Edward Stuart* employs engraved portraits all of which date before 1722, a date a year or two after the occasion. The other scene, the 1719 *Marriage of James III*, copies its likeness of Clementina Sobieska from a marriage portrait by Trevisani but shows the Pretender

18. Christie's, May 31, 1926. The attribution is supported by the preparatory drawing, Louvre 3116. Another large drawing was, in 1965, in the New York art market.

19. It is interesting that the Princes of Cellamare, the parents of the cardinals del Giudice, were important patrons of Garzi. The Achenbach drawing is part of a collection largely formed in Naples at the beginning of the nineteenth century.

20. See the author's article in *The Burlington Magazine*, CVI, 743, May, 1964, pp. 226 ff. The two artists were first proposed for the Academy within two months of each other and, with Conca, Costanzi and Trevisani, were selected by Juvara as the Roman artists appropriate for the throne room of La Granja. (On completing this commission Masucci became Head of the Academy and his first act was to honor the architect, apparently by the presentation of his posthumous portrait of Juvara.)

as he appeared in the mid-1730's. The *Marriage* is a gracious genre scene in which the same classicistic structure and correctness occur as in the Turin *Solomon*, enhanced by elegant reportage. Rococo frippery is eliminated, the majesty of the Baroque is stilled. From the *Baptism* and its crude composition and dubious perspective one could argue that Masucci's style was due to a genuine inability to take advantage of the old or new forms of the late Baroque and that careful draughtsmanship was no cure for feeble invention or native stiffness. Such indeed was the criticism of Benefial who was temporarily suspended from the Academy in 1755, particularly for his attack on Masucci.[21] In this case there is some defense: the author of the *Baptism* is by no means certainly Masucci. There is considerable visual evidence of Masucci's participation but I would suggest that not only is the artist traditionally its author responsible for the composition, but also that Ghezzi is himself shown in the background (behind the last group of women to the right) with Masucci close beside him. I believe the *Baptism* dates anywhere between 1722 to 1735 and the *Marriage* is slightly after 1735.

Masucci's investment in the Rococo was only skin deep, with the grace and pretty surface handling put upon compositions clearer and colder than those of any of his teachers. The early *Adoration of the Kings* in S. Maria in Via Lata (Fig. 15) is a brilliant essay in latter-day Marattism, exceptionally careful, delicate, gracious and rich. The opulence is not pictorial but technical, not grandiose and Baroque (or even purely Rococo) but academic and draughtsmanly, with some appeal to the pre-Baroque. A late Baroque painting in the gentle early Rococo mode, this work is an attempt at pure academic authority, and the authority supersedes the given style.

At S. Maria in Via Lata another oval is an *Annunciation*, a no less cool, small crystalization of the Marattesque idiom. By 1748, Masucci produced the pictorial decoration for the famous chapel in S. Roque at Lisbon. The Minneapolis *modello* of the *Annunciation* (Fig. 16)[22] may be compared with this and with a painting dated 1748 by Conca (Fig. 17) who lost the commission. The three paintings derive from the *Annunciation* in Rome by Guido and Lanfranco by way of a famous Maratti. Conca is all exquisite bravura and infantile grace; Luca Giordano for the *settecento* boudoir. Masucci in 1748 is Maratti prettified, rationalized and neated up. Indications of the grandly simple furniture in the Maratti *Annunciation* became the prow-like Juvarian *prie-dieu* in Conca, but in Masucci are clearly seen and recorded household furniture. Our artist's angel kneels on no traditional cloud mattress but walks, a nervous bird, on stone floor, in a clear volume of space. And yet, the 1748 *Annunciation* is Masucci at his most grand with a clear indebtedness to the Rococo. More so than in the S. Maria in Via Lata picture which is more plain and far less realized, with the best of the Rococo yet to come, yet to be assimilated or refused.

Masucci had fluctuated until 1740 between the various degrees of the Rococo adaptation of the High Baroque and the degrees of the new classicism. Works from the 1720's and 1730's are more open and florid, or more pretty and more delightfully handled than the S. Maria in Via Lata *Annunciation*, less somber and intense than the Lisbon *Annunciation*. It should be remembered that after the various rivalries and consolidations of the Rococo and new classical tendencies there came about in Rome at the end of the 1730's a new and surprising solution which stepped above and beyond the conflicting tendencies. The style characteristic of the reign of Benedict XIV eliminated from fashion the trivial strain in the Rococo, resurrected something of the grandeur of the High Baroque, continued the authority of classicism while mitigating its austerity in the richness of a strong mid-century style.[23] Almost fifty in 1740, Masucci had concluded his flirtation with the Rococo and had developed the strongly academic and classicistic reform obvious in the Turin *Solomon*. He never departed from the small, intimate forms of the Rococo and can only be found grandiose in his attempt at an austere conventional authority.

Cultivating no grand manner or effect, and more stiff

---

21. The story of the difficulty is given by Ponfredi, naming no names. From the Academy records one finds that Benefial taught the nude classes (where the criticism occurred) in June and July, 1755, that the *crise* came on July 22 and that Benefial was expelled on July 27. He was reinstalled in the Academy on November 16. That Masucci was the main victim is known from the Marchionni caricature of Benefial (Museo di Roma, 1, 2).

22. The actual painting copied in mosaic for the chapel is apparently not the signed and dated (1748) work now in Copenhagen. A model of the chapel with the three Masuccis in place and these possibly executed by the artist himself is in Portugal, as are several replicas. See M. da Camara Fialho, in *Boletim de Arte Antiga*, Lisbon, vol. 11, no. 2, 1951, pp. 22 ff. Models for the paintings, including the *Annunciation*, were sent at the end

of 1742. Masucci was seriously ill from late 1743 into 1745 and the paintings were shown in 1747.

23. The change into this style can be watched as the early work of Batoni (1732–8) passes into that of the early 1740's, a change from a pronouncedly proto-Neoclassical approach to a grander manner employing elements from the late Baroque, from Luti, from Subleyras, from Giaquinto. Subleyras' own manner became grander and more free at the same time. Giaquinto's painting, the importance and success of which at this moment overshadow and eliminate from prime consideration the work of his teacher, Conca, is another sample of the style of Benedict XIV. A cultural and artistic solution of importance is plainly involved although the actual sources of the confidence, grandeur and brilliance are somewhat obscure.

than genial and fresh, Masucci was found wanting by Benedict XIV, who became pope in 1740 and died the year Masucci died. Under Benedict XIV, Masucci was hardly neglected but it is very important to notice that he received no commission for St. Peter's. This final prize was then very rarely lacking to a painter of such note: an altar was a natural expectation of Masucci and it could have been no consolation that Conca and Giaquinto were not even given ceiling commissions as were such artists as Benefial and Zoboli. Masucci's ceiling to the Quirinal *Coffee-House* appeared tame, hard and empty beside Batoni's matching ceiling, and Batoni was immediately given an altar in St. Peter's.[24] The new pope was grateful to receive small devotional pictures by Masucci as gifts, but while his position was carefully preserved, further patronage came from the more conservative sources.[25] For the younger painters, however, Masucci had now become one of the most advanced and obvious painters of the classical position, if something of an old fogy.

A genuine disaster did befall Masucci as a portrait painter. Prominent, as has been seen, from 1722 and all but the official portraitist of Rome since the 1730 likeness of Clement XII (Fig. 18), Masucci began to encounter serious rivalry from a new luminary in the mid-1730's. Pierre Subleyras was certainly no more advanced a portraitist than the Masucci of the *Clement XII*—no one was. The balance of severity, directness and graciousness in this portrait is so adroit one need not notice that it is more severe in presentation, structure and finish than any portrait painted in Rome since Domenichino's and Sassoferrato's time, or that no other portraitist in the Europe of 1730 had so thoroughly extricated himself from the flimsy delights of the portraiture of Largillière. Until the 1780's, no Roman painter is as severe and in that sense as advanced, as appropriate for the next and Neoclassical step. Nevertheless, Benedict XIV unfortunately asked Subleyras and Masucci to compete in producing his official likeness. Masucci chose the traditional pose for

the active pope and presented him as a chilled hippopotamus (Fig. 19). Subleyras was a born and brilliant painter, fresh and poetic, and (perhaps luckily) academically more shallow than Masucci. Subleyras' portrait (Fig. 20) was preferred.

Masucci emerged in the second decade of the eighteenth century as Maratti's last and youngest pupil. This was potentially a most considerable advantage, and Masucci was able to seek and, on the death of Chiari, to achieve the prime succession from Maratti, and thus the leadership of the most effective tradition in Rome, supposedly with the pure inheritance of the authority of Raphael and Annibale. From the first it might have been argued that Masucci was an artist only of the fine but secondary virtues of a Calandrucci or a Pietro de' Pietris, but the weight of the Marattesque counted heavily, Masucci was more 'correct' than any obvious rival, a fine traditional draughtsman, and a more serious artist than his predecessor, Chiari. The principal paintings of the 1720's and 1730's were (as could be seen in a more extensive treatment) beautiful, if not, aside from their authority, powerful or very exciting or original. 'Ce peintre est froid' wrote Mariette, but Masucci did not become unusually 'cold' until the mid-1730's, nor did he, until that decade, offer anything especially new, newer at least than far older *Maratteschi* had offered. The coldness and extreme logical clarity of form and space of such later paintings as the *Solomon* were new and really defeat and terminate the Baroque style. Codified, quieted, even frozen, the Baroque presentation dies in Masucci's leaned, novel and rather provincial final manner. This manner excited younger artists and is close to a final step into the Neoclassical. However, there is no final step, no resolution, and only a limited reformation. The old achieved its last, straightened and crystalized terms in Masucci's work, and it is more that he finally closed a door than that he set forth something which made it obvious, necessary and easy to step forward.[26]

---

24. Lanzi says Benedict XIV liked Masucci's ceiling. But then Lanzi also calls it a fresco.

25. His late work in the advanced church of SS. Nome di Maria is considerably after the replacement of Derizet, and Masucci had been earlier employed there with Mauro Fontana as part of the repudiation of the French architect. Masucci's presence, however, apparently represented authority rather than reaction, as a decade earlier in his mediation between Salvi and Maini for the Fontana di Trevi.

26. I am grateful to the owners of the works illustrated for their kind patience and generosity. I would also like to thank for most generous help Keith K. Andrews, Giuliano Briganti, Per Bjustrom, Ayres de Carvalho, Frederick den Broeder, Antonio De Matta, Hans van Erffa, Italo Faldi, Andreina Griseri, Carroll T. Hartwell, Peter Murray, Mary Opsahl, Erich Schleier, Gunther Troche, Ellis Waterhouse, and the Staff of the Witt Library. A shorter version of this study was presented, through Professor Wittkower's tolerance and kindness, at the 1965 College Art Association Congress.

CHARLES MITCHELL

Benjamin West's *Death of Nelson*

In May 1815 the Liverpool packet brought George Ticknor from Boston to England to begin four years of study and travel which acquainted him with half the learned celebrities of Europe and prepared him for a distinguished professorship—in which Longfellow succeeded him—at Harvard College. In Liverpool he met Roscoe; on the 25th of the month he arrived in London, where he was soon calling on Sir Humphry Davy and Lord Byron; and on June 23, as he recorded in his Journal, he paid a visit to his compatriot Benjamin West, P.R.A., at his house in Newman Street.

> We spent half the forenoon in Mr. West's gallery, where he has arranged all the pictures that he still owns. . . . He told us a singular anecdote of Nelson. . . . Just before he went to sea for the last time, West sat next to him at a large entertainment given to him here, and in the course of the dinner Nelson expressed to Sir William Hamilton his regret, that in his youth he had not acquired some taste for art and some power of discrimination. 'But', said he, turning to West, 'there is one picture whose power I do feel. I never pass a print-shop with your "Death of Wolfe" in the window, without being stopped by it.' West, of course, made his acknowledgments, and Nelson went on to ask why he had painted no more like it. 'Because, my lord, there are no more subjects.' 'D—n it,' said the sailor, 'I didn't think of that,' and asked him to take a glass of champagne. 'But, my lord, I fear your intrepidity will yet furnish me such another scene; and if it should, I shall certainly avail myself of it.' 'Will you?' said Nelson, pouring out bumpers, and touching his glass violently against West's,—'will you, Mr. West? then I hope that I shall die in the next battle.' He sailed a few days later, and the result was on the canvas before us.[1]

It was a set-piece in West's best later manner: Nelson modestly deferring to the connoisseurship of his old friend Sir William Hamilton, the courtly President of the Royal Academy so responsive to high heroism and so gravely convinced of his call to paint it for posterity, the gay gallant rejoinder of the Admiral sitting between them, a frail battered figure with shaded eye and empty sleeve.

It is true that in dating the conversation so poignantly to the very eve of Trafalgar—he was an old man of seventy-six when he told the story—West allowed his memory to play him false. Hamilton was then more than two years dead. The meeting probably occurred during Nelson's previous spell ashore, before his long sea-watch in Mediterranean command and his baffled chase of Villeneuve across the Atlantic, that is to say sometime between 1801 and 1803, when he was much fêted and about in public with Sir William.[2] Nevertheless, despite the pathetic license of the date, we cannot doubt the substantial truth of West's recollection. Nelson, we know, was an eager frequenter of the print-shops;[3] he had premonitions that one day he would pay for victory with his own life; and the example of Wolfe's death at Quebec had long stuck in his memory. In 1794, when timid military colleagues hesitated to attack Bastia in Corsica in force, he wrote indignantly to Hamilton, then British Minister at Naples: 'What would the immortal Wolfe have done? as he did, beat the Enemy, if he perished in the attempt.'[4] And after Trafalgar Dr. Beatty, the surgeon of the *Victory* who tended Nelson in the cockpit, recalled that he 'often talked with Captain Hardy on the subject of his being killed in battle', and had asserted that it was 'the most ambitious wish of his soul to die in the fight, and in the very hour of a great and signal victory'.[5] Thus when Nelson and West toasted each other over their brimming glasses each in his way meant what he said; and West, in the sequel, kept his promise. How he contrived to do so is our topic now.

* * *

The news of Trafalgar—the overwhelming defeat of the combined fleets of France and Spain, the surrender of nineteen enemy sail of the line, and Nelson's death in the middle of the action—reached the Admiralty on

1. *Life, Letters and Journals of George Ticknor*, ed. George S. Hillard, 1, Boston, 1876, p. 63.

2. Oliver Warner, *A Portrait of Lord Nelson*, Harmondsworth, 1963, p. 291.
3. A. M. Broadley and J. Holland Rose, *Napoleon and Caricature, 1795–1821*, 1, London, 1911, p. 60.
4. Sir Nicholas Harris Nicolas, *Dispatches and Letters of Lord Viscount Nelson*, 1, London, 1845, p. 378.
5. William Beatty, *Authentic Narrative of the Death of Lord Nelson*, London, 1825 (3rd ed.; 1st ed. 1807), p. 73.

November 6, 1805, sixteen days after the battle; and after the first shock of dismay and relief (for this was the end of all Napoleon's designs and England's fears of invasion) the whole nation began to busy itself, as never before, to devise memorials to its saviour.[6] The popular mementoes and tokens of grief came first— the politer ones significantly as quickly as the vulgar. Then amid the preparations for Nelson's lying-in-state at Greenwich and his state funeral in St. Paul's there were prompt official proposals for permanent monuments in London and the provinces. In November the City of London appointed a committee under the chairmanship of Alderman Josiah Boydell, the fashionable Pall Mall picture-dealer, to organize a competition (eventually won by the sculptor James Smith) for a Nelson monument in the Guildhall,[7] and similar civic schemes were speedily launched in Liverpool, Dublin and elsewhere. Next the King intervened with the first suggestion for a national memorial. On December 11, only a week after the *Victory* arrived home at Spithead with Nelson's body on board, the Home Secretary, Lord Hawkesbury, wrote to the Royal Academy inviting its members to submit designs for the King's choice for a public monument in St. Paul's—a letter which aroused much debate among the Academicians as to whether designs for paintings as well as sculptures were admissible and whether the Academy should press for a say on the siting of the monument in the cathedral by way of countering the influence of the 'Committee of Taste' set up by the Treasury in 1802 to advise on national monuments generally.[8] This royal initiative, however, was soon superseded. Early in the New Year Parliament voted to erect the National Monument to Nelson in St. Paul's at public expense,[9] an act which deprived the Academy, to its chagrin, of the exclusive privilege of tendering designs and put the Treasury and the Committee of Taste in control of the competition.[10] In March 1807 they awarded the commission to Flaxman.[11]

Meanwhile, along with these official projects, the picture-dealers and print-publishers were quick to come forward with commercial schemes for historical paintings of Nelson's death to be exhibited in their shops and engraved by subscription. One print-seller, for example, with an eye perhaps to another 'Death of Chatham' or another 'Peirson', commissioned a big 'Death of Nelson' from Copley—a picture that Copley began but does not seem to have finished.[12] On the whole, however, the level of these efforts, aimed at a public who could afford a guinea or two for a stirring patriotic print, was much lower. To catch a competitive market, the trade was generally content to repeat the sort of thing that had become increasingly popular during the French Revolutionary and early Napoleonic Wars with the victories of Howe at the 'Glorious First of June', Jervis at St. Vincent, Duncan at Camperdown, and Nelson at Copenhagen—a quickly produced mixture of grandiosity, topical (if not always accurate) journalism, and sensational popular appeal. Edward Orme's 'Death of Nelson', engraved by Cooper after the hack painter William Craig and published on June 1, 1806,[13] is a typical example (Fig. 4).

There were two men in the business, however, who rose to the occasion with an apter sense at once of art and history: Josiah Boydell and the engraver James Heath. The news of Nelson's death in the moment of victory at Trafalgar immediately called to the minds of many people the death of Wolfe at Quebec; it was the only recent parallel in national history with anything like the same pathos and finality.[14] What the occasion demanded, therefore, was not just another Craig, another Mather Brown or a Daniel Orme, or even another Copley, but nothing less than a painting and a print to match Benjamin West's classic 'Death of Wolfe' (Fig. 3) and Woollett's famous engraving of it (1776)—a print with which Alderman John Boydell, Josiah's uncle, had made a fortune.[15] Accordingly Josiah Boydell, who had recently succeeded the elder Boydell as head of the family firm, put a notice in the newspapers, dated November 22, advertising a competition for the best painting by a British artist of the Battle of Trafalgar and the Death of Nelson for a prize of five hundred guineas, which Boydell and Co. would have engraved 'the size and in the manner of the Death of General Wolfe, at present their Property'.

6. An excellent conspectus of Nelson memorials has recently been made in an unpublished M.A. thesis of Columbia University, which I have gratefully consulted: Arthur S. Marks, *The Impact of Nelson's Death on English Art, 1805–1825* (1965). See also Nicolas, *Dispatches*, VII, London, 1846, pp. 352 ff.
7. Joseph Farington, *The Farington Diary*, ed. James Greig, London, 1922–8, III, p. 128.
8. Royal Academy of Arts, London, General Assembly Minutes, II, p. 314; Farington, III, p. 133. I am indebted to Mr. Sidney Hutchison, Librarian of the Royal Academy, for his courtesy and kindness in permitting me conveniently to consult the Minute Books.
9. Nicolas, VII, p. 327.
10. Royal Academy, Council Minutes, III, pp. 380, 383, 387–90, 392–3; General Assembly Minutes, II, pp. 329–31.
11. Farington, IV, p. 100.

12. Farington, III, p. 137; Martha Babcock Amory, *The Domestic and Artistic Life of John Singleton Copley*, Boston, 1882, p. 281.
13. The subscription ticket was published on January 9, 1806, the day of Nelson's funeral.
14. Marks, pp. 30–31.
15. C. Mitchell, 'Benjamin West's "Death of General Wolfe" and the Popular History Piece', *Journal of the Warburg and Courtauld Institutes*, VII, 1944, pp. 20 ff.

The Directors and Visitors of the British Institution were to be invited to judge the entries; the winning painting would be presented to the Admiralty or some other suitable public body; and subscribers were assured that they would get their prints 'with every kind of dispatch, consistent with excellence'.[16]

Heath, meanwhile, had done one better by going straight to the fountain-head. On November 29 West told his friend Joseph Farington, R.A., that Heath had approached him 'sometime since' with the proposition that they should together do a 'Death of Nelson' as an explicit companion-piece to his 'Wolfe', and he added that he had already come to terms with Heath and had begun his design.[17] According to this agreement, a draft copy of which survives, West was to keep the painting and pay Heath twelve hundred guineas for engraving it, and they were to publish the print jointly on their own, sharing expenses and profits equally.[18] In earlier days West might well have been less receptive to such a plainly commercial venture, but now he had pressing personal reasons to welcome it. In the first place, after more than thirty years as the King's favourite and familiar painter, he had recently lost his post and his income as History-Painter to the King, and was in need of commissions. Secondly, he was hurt and angered by personal enmities within the Academy, of which he had been the respected President since the death of Reynolds, and was on the point of resigning. He later told Farington that 'a great motive' in undertaking the 'Death of Nelson' was to 'shew the Academy what they had done in causing the author of it to withdraw himself [as President] and an architect [Wyatt] to be placed in his room'.[19]

Now let us see the outcome of the two projects.

*   *   *

West, with his usual prodigious industry, produced his painting in just under six months (Fig. 1). On May 11, 1806, Farington visited his studio and found him seated in front of the finished work with copies of his 'La Hogue' and the 'Death of Wolfe' alongside for comparison.[20] It is now in the Walker Art Gallery in Liverpool.[21] The picture shows Nelson dying in full uniform on the deck of the *Victory* in the arms of

Dr. Scott the chaplain of the ship, Mr. Burke the purser, and Dr. Beatty, while Captain Hardy kneels alongside reading from a paper in his hand the number of the nineteen enemy ships that had struck—a total not in fact known until after Nelson's death. Surrounding the central group is an enormous concourse of figures extending to the edges of the canvas either side, each face meticulously delineated like the faces in a school photograph; and in the background we see a vast panorama of billowing smoke, wind-blown flags and toppling rigging, with a distant prospect of the battle behind.

How did West set about composing this extraordinary scene? In the first place he went to great pains to ascertain—in the phrase he later himself used with reference to his 'Wolfe'—the true 'facts of the transaction'.[22] He assembled and studied all the authentic records and reports of the battle and of Nelson's death that he could lay hands on; many people from the *Victory* came to his house to tell their tale and to have their portraits taken;[23] and for three months Thomas Goble, who became Secretary of the Fleet when Mr. Secretary Scott was killed early in the action and saw it all from the *Victory*, was by his side to give technical advice.[24] At the same time, while West took every care to see that nothing in his picture was casually fictitious or fanciful, the last thing he aimed at was a piece of mere factual realism. His subject was 'The Death of Lord Viscount Nelson, or the Naval Victory off Trafalgar'; and this, as he conceived it, was a theme of such high heroism and national importance that it demanded an 'Epic Composition'—a composition in which everything should conspire to 'show the importance of the Hero'. This epic purpose he emphasized in the note he printed in the Royal Academy catalogue of 1811, when the painting was exhibited along with Heath's engraving which, after many difficulties and delays, had at last appeared.[25] Accordingly, West did not represent Nelson dying, as he did, in the cockpit of the *Victory* but on the open deck. And around the Hero, in a single synoptic and synchronistic vision, he displayed all the contributory moments and characters of the victorious day. Some groups he showed 'sympathizing with each other in the sufferings of

16. Farington, III, p. 128. I owe many thanks to Mr. Edward Croft-Murray, Keeper of Prints and Drawings in the British Museum, for sending me a photostat of this press notice, and for other information.
17. Farington, III, p. 127.
18. Marks, p. 29.
19. Farington, III, p. 226.
20. *Ibid.*
21. Oil on canvas, 70 × 96 inches. Signed and dated 1806. In possession of 'Mr. Stroud of Wardour Street' in 1846 (Nicolas, VII, p. 252 n.); presented by Bristow H. Hughes to the Walker Art Gallery in 1866.

22. Cf. West's apology for his procedure in the 'Death of Wolfe' to Reynolds given by John Galt, *The Life, Studies and Works of Benjamin West* (1820), quoted by Mitchell, *art. cit.*, pp. 20–21.
23. Marks, p. 29.
24. I am indebted for this information to Mr. Michael Robinson of the National Maritime Museum, Greenwich.
25. The note is printed in Algernon Graves, *The Royal Academy of Arts*, VIII, London, 1906, p. 220. For the protracted history of Heath's engraving see Farington, III, pp. 127, 269, 272, and IV, 150, 236. Heath's plate is approximately the same size as that of Woollett's 'Wolfe'.

their wounded Friend and expiring Commander';
others he 'introduced as episodes to commemorate
those with honour who fell on board the Hero's ship';
and in the background he gave a view of the 'flags and
signals of the other triumphant British Admirals, as
well as those of the vanquished enemy, which are
marked with all the wrack of battle, and that defeat
which took place on October 21, 1805'. It was a
picture, as he explained when he showed it to Farington, 'of what might have been, not of the circumstances
as they happened'.[26] Nor, though he elaborated and
varied on his earlier formula, did West fail to make his
composition tally with that of the 'Death of Wolfe',
its designated pendant. Nelson like Wolfe is supported
by three faithful companions; a swirl of flags, like the
single standard in the earlier picture, is silhouetted
against a darkened smoke-racked sky; again to the left
there is a solid group of figures waving hats to proclaim
the victory like the running messenger in the 'Wolfe';
the line of figures on the quarterdeck corresponds with
the crowded skyline beyond the Heights of Abraham;
to the right a tall sailor stands with clasped hands like
the tall grenadier in the 'Wolfe'; and beside him a
kneeling seaman—the seaman Saunders who liked to
visit West's studio and entertain his company with
stories of Trafalgar[27]—contemplates mortality like the
Cherokee Indian who gazes into the face of the dying
Wolfe.

The moment the painting was completed, West
hastened, in studied disdain of the concurrent Royal
Academy show, to exhibit it in his own house. It was a
triumph exceeding even that of his 'Death of Wolfe'
thirty-five years earlier. In a little over a month thirty
thousand people went to see it, and by royal command
West took it to show the King and the royal family.[28]
From a conversation West had with Farington the
following year we learn, moreover, something both of
the effect the picture had on the crowds who flocked
to Newman Street and of West's own estimate of his
achievement.[29] He had been spending the morning at
Christie's looking at Rembrandt's 'Woman taken in
Adultery', which he declared to be 'in its way the
finest piece of Art in the world'. And he went on to
remark how the people in the auction-room were un-
covering their heads in reverence as they came near it
—a thing, he added, which he had observed only once
previously: when his own 'Death of Nelson' was on
exhibition at his house. 'By an instinctive motion', as
he quaintly phrased it, 'the hand accompanied the

mind, and when the picture was approached, the Hat
was taken off.'

*   *   *

The history of Josiah Boydell's competition is obscure.
He was still apparently having to canvas it after
January 13, 1806, the closing-date (according to other
advertisements) for the submission of trial sketches, for
at an Academy meeting in March Hoppner was furious
at the way Boydell had sent copies of his press notices
to Academicians and hoped that none of them would
invite him to the Academy dinner.[30] There is no
evidence, however, that the competition ever got
properly under way. No competitors' names are
recorded, and the minutes of the British Institution do
not show that it was ever called upon to provide a
jury.[31] Nevertheless, whether by competition or otherwise, Boydell did in the end secure his picture—a
painting whose progress he watched from the start,[32]
later purchased,[33] and eventually published in a fine
print by William Bromley the same size as Woollett's
'Wolfe'. This was Arthur William Devis's celebrated
'Death of Nelson', now at Greenwich (Fig. 2).

Devis was probably induced to undertake the picture,
a huge canvas over eight feet by ten in size, in response
to Boydell's tempting prize-offer. At the time of
Trafalgar he was in very low water and, not for the
first time, in prison for debt.[34] Now let us compare his
procedure with West's. Like West he was anxious to
inform himself exactly of what occurred, and he
decided to get his information first-hand. He therefore
obtained permission from the King's Bench—his way
perhaps smoothed by his patron Alexander Davison,
Nelson's prize-agent—to go down to Portsmouth to
meet the *Victory*. He found the ship just arrived—the
date was probably December 5—lying off-shore await-
ing orders. So he had himself taken aboard, pushed his
way on deck among the men refitting the rigging after
the long and stormy passage home from Gibraltar,

26. Farington, III, p. 272.
27. *Ibid.*
28. Farington, III, pp. 269–70.
29. Farington, IV, p. 150.

30. Farington, III, p. 159.
31. Marks, p. 19. The Minute Books of the British Institution
are in the Library of the Victoria and Albert Museum.
32. On December 4, 1805, he told Farington (III, p. 128) that
Devis was planning to paint a 'Death of Nelson'.
33. When Boydell tried to sell it in 1809 (see note 39 below) he
was probably acting on Devis's behalf, since the British Institution required exhibited pictures to be the property of the artists;
in the printed description of Bromley's print of 1812 (see
below) Boydell stated that he had purchased the original. The
painting is in oils on canvas, 100 × 125 inches. There is a small
version in oils, probably not a preliminary sketch, in H.M.S.
Victory, Portsmouth.
34. On Devis see Sydney H. Pavière, *The Devis Family of
Painters*, Leigh-on-Sea, 1950. On Devis's imprisonment and his
visit to the *Victory* I follow the credible circumstantial account,
related to the author by Captain Edward Williams, in Joseph
Allen, *Life of Nelson*, London, n.d. (1853), p. 295.

introduced himself to Edward Williams, the first lieutenant, and explained his purpose. Williams was too busy to attend to him and sent him below to the wardroom, where he made himself very agreeable to the officers. As a result he was allowed to stay three weeks on board talking to the ship's company about their experiences, drawing their portraits, sketching the cockpit (Fig. 6) of which a small model was made for him on board, and even persuading those who were near Nelson when he died to pose for him in their original positions.[35] Devis owed his chance to stay so long on the ship, incidentally, to Dr. Beatty. On December 11 the *Victory* left Spithead for the Nore where Nelson's body was to be taken off for transport to Greenwich, and in the normal way (like Turner who also went on board the *Victory* at Portsmouth to gather materials for a painting) Devis would probably have been put ashore. But the day the ship weighed anchor Dr. Beatty had Nelson's body removed from the leaguer of spirits in which it had been brought home in order to conduct an autopsy, and he wanted Devis by him to help him record it.[36] It was Devis, accordingly, who made the drawing of the fatal ball, extracted from Nelson's spine, which Beatty reproduced in his *Authentic Narrative of the Death of Lord Nelson* (1807), the source from which so many of our best known and most pathetic anecdotes of Nelson's last hours derive ('Kiss me, Hardy', and the rest); and Devis was privileged to be the last artist to see Nelson in the flesh.[37]

Devis took more than a year longer than West in executing his painting; it was not finished until the summer of 1807.[38] Nor did it bring him anything like the same glory. It was exhibited at the British Institution in 1809 with a quotation in the catalogue from Beatty's *Narrative* without apparently creating any special stir, and Boydell's hopes at that time of selling it to Greenwich Hospital for a thousand pounds were disappointed.[39] How did Devis conceive of his task? First of all, as Boydell required, he designed his composition to match that of the 'Death of Wolfe'. Though he worked on a much larger scale and in a style whose slow rhythms and soft smouldering chiaroscuro have little in common with West's hard lighting and flinty drawing, his whole *mise-en-scène* shows how closely

and sympathetically he had studied his given model. The central group—Scott chafing Nelson's breast, Burke supporting his pillow, Beatty, anxiously watched by Chevalier, Nelson's steward, feeling his pulse—is a reversed variant of West's earlier one, while Hardy leans over behind like West's men with the flag. Once more there is a dense mass of figures on the left (Lieutenant Yule with his extended arm being the counterpart of West's pointing officer), and a sparser towering group to the right. Again, a prominent pair of expressive and anonymous figures in the foreground establish a kind of proscenium for the pathetic spectacle beyond. The mourning marine on the right, hiding his face from the sight of Nelson's sufferings like Agamemnon at the sacrifice of Iphigenia, is analogous to West's standing grenadier, while the kneeling sailor in the striped shirt opposite (whose pose seems also to owe something to the kneeling sailor in West's 'Nelson') performs a function similar to that of West's Indian brave. And both paintings have a deliberately sacred air. West's 'Wolfe', as Devis must surely have recognized, borrowed the traditional *Pathosformel* of a 'Lamentation'.[40] Devis's picture, with its great crossbeams above, the man shouldering a bundle of drapery on the left, and the seaman kneeling with his lantern like an adoring shepherd before the radiant Nelson, has the hushed Rembrandtesque atmosphere at once of a 'Deposition' and a 'Nativity'.

Secondly, Devis clearly sought to emulate, and indeed to surpass, what impressed him and the general public as the realistic character of his exemplar. He wanted to give the spectators of his picture that same feeling of intimate participation in the actual event which the contemporary dress, individual portraiture, and modern surroundings of the 'Death of Wolfe' had aroused in countless breasts ever since it was painted. It is true that, in accord with his model and in the interests of harmonious and dignified composition, he rearranged and multiplied his characters (Hardy, for example, was not present when Nelson died) and heightened the cockpit (where Hardy, in reality, would have had to stoop almost double). But within this prescribed framework he adhered as closely as he could to the 'facts of the transaction', with a minimum of telescoping and artistic license. He was economical in invention, scrupulous over the details of costume and portraiture, and he set his scene in exactly the spot where Nelson died (Fig. 6). When the painting was done he told Farington of the 'care he had taken in painting the death of the Hero to represent everything faithfully'.[41]

35. Allen, *loc. cit.*, and Boydell's printed description of Devis's painting issued with Bromley's print in 1812. There is a copy of the latter, and of the key to Heath's print of 1811, in the Print Room of the National Maritime Museum, Greenwich.
36. Beatty, pp. 67 ff.
37. This would not have helped him with his portraits. In a private memorandum Dr. Beatty reported that Nelson's features could then no longer 'be easily traced' (N.M.M., Greenwich, MS. 51/040/2 and B.M. Add. 34,992, f. 48).
38. Farington, IV, p. 150.
39. Farington, V, p. 156.

40. Mitchell, *art. cit.*, p. 31.
41. Typescript of Farington's Diary, June 5, 1807, pp. 3732–3 (Print Room, British Museum).

It was this 'fidelity to History' that Boydell especially emphasized in the printed description which he issued with Bromley's print in 1812.[42] 'Mr. Devis has adopted the plan of making TRUTH *alone* the object of his delineation; and has consequently depicted this awful scene exactly as it occurred.' And if he exaggerated, and said not a word about what Devis owed to West's example, who can blame him? For West was now his competitor and rival. Not only had West completed his 'Nelson' before Devis completed his, but Heath and West, only the previous year, had come out first with their print—a print accompanied by a key and description which, in terms very similar to those of the 1811 Academy catalogue, extolled Epic principles quite contrary to Devis's realistic ones. It was in competition with this that Boydell had to market Bromley's engraving.

*   *   *

So much for the commercial aspect of the case; but there is more to say on the theoretical side. When West himself saw Devis's picture in 1807—they were then neighbours in Newman Street—he perceived that Devis had neither risen to the essential dignity of his theme nor grasped the essential character of the 'Death of Wolfe', his model. He communicated his views to Farington on June 10.[43] The painting, he granted, 'had much merit, but it had more convinced him that there was no other way of representing the death of a Hero but by an *Epic* representation of it. It must exhibit the event in a way to excite awe and veneration; and that which may be required to give superior interest to the representation must be introduced—all that can show the importance of the Hero. Wolfe must not die like a common soldier under a bush; neither should Nelson be represented dying in the gloomy hold of a ship, like a sick man in a prison hole. To move the mind there should be a spectacle presented to raise and warm the mind, and all should be proportioned to the highest idea conceived of the Hero. No boy, said West, would be animated by a representation of Nelson dying like an ordinary man. His feelings must be roused and his mind inflamed by a scene great and extraordinary. A mere matter of fact will never produce this effect.'

This is a revealing document, both historically and psychologically. It not only expounds—more simply and directly than the note in the Academy catalogue and the description of Heath's print—the theory on which West contrived his 'Death of Nelson'. It also asserts, by clear implication, that thirty-five years

earlier he had contrived his 'Death of Wolfe' on precisely the same epic principles. But was this true? Admittedly, neither the 'Wolfe' nor the 'Nelson' represent the historical events as they actually happened. Nelson died in the cockpit of the *Victory*, and Wolfe died with only two attendants. But still there is a fundamental difference between the two pictures. The 'Death of Wolfe' achieved such a delicate balance of *vraisemblance* between the ideal and the actual that it appeared to contemporary spectators, as it has appeared to generations since, to be historically true. The 'Death of Nelson', on the other hand, was so patently and explicitly idealized and made up that nobody could possibly suppose that Nelson died in that way and in such circumstances. However impressive it was as an epic construction, *vraisemblance* was not one of its qualities: nobody, surely, could regard it as a picture of Nelson's death 'as it might have been'. How then—since West's candour can never be in doubt—are we to account for his curiously partial and undiscriminating view of his two achievements? Had some film of over-rationalized and over-moralizing doctrine, we wonder, interposed itself between his aged eyes and his own youthful creation? Did he look at the 'Death of Wolfe' in 1807—sincerely enough—through distorting spectacles which he was pretty certainly not wearing when he painted it in 1770? When we look into the matter, this indeed is what appears in fact to have happened.

The man through whose writings and conversation West imbibed the schematic doctrine of epic history-painting which he applied in his 'Death of Nelson' and projected back, apparently, into his 'Wolfe' was his friend the Rev. Robert Anthony Bromley, B.D., Rector of St. Mildred's in the Poultry and brother of the writer on portraits. It was the common belief of West's fellow-Academicians that Bromley helped him to get up his presidential Academy discourses.[44] In 1793 Bromley published the first volume of a *Philosophical and Critical History of the Fine Arts*, dedicated to George III, in which he extolled 'the display of moral subjects' as 'the purest office of painting as a means of instruction',[45] and explained and defined what he claimed to be a quite new and original classification of painting into two distinct kinds—the 'historic' and the 'poetic'.[46] The purpose of history, he declared, whether written or painted, was to instruct; and if instructive 'historic' painting was not to fly off into absurd poetical fancies it had to obey three rules. First, it had to be 'perspicuous', that is to

42. Boydell engaged Bromley late in 1806 to make the print in two years (Farington, IV, p. 55).
43. Farington, IV, p. 151.

44. John Knowles, *The Life and Writings of Henry Fuseli*, I, London, 1831, p. 185.
45. Bromley, I, pp. 24–32.
46. *Ibid.*, pp. 45–86.

say, it had 'to keep near to the history' represented. Secondly, it had to observe the rule of 'costume'—to clothe its characters strictly in the dress of the age and country in which they lived. Thirdly, it had to avoid any anachronisms as regards place or persons. Within these rules, however, the 'historic' painter enjoyed certain freedoms. He was allowed to use allegory, so long as it appeared 'natural and artless, and partici- pating ... in the event represented', and eschewed any 'mere creature of the brain, or of fabulous system'. Furthermore, if his work was to attain proper elegance and power to instruct the mind and move the feelings, he was not only permitted but emphatically required to change the order, time and place of events by fresh inventions and combinations, provided all the time that the three basic rules of perspicuity, costume and chronology were not infringed. Such 'excursions with- in the compass of the facts' were as admirable and legitimate as Livy's invented speeches. The purpose of 'poetic' painting on the other hand was not to instruct but to please. The 'poetic' painter, no less than the 'historic' painter, was still required to obey the three rules of perspicuity, costume and (as Bromley termed it in this case) consistency; but subject to these he was at liberty to take in 'the whole range of Nature, and the whole scope of imagination, to dress his scenes and give them force and attraction'.

And Bromley gave examples of each kind of painting. In 'poetic' painting, among the Old Masters, Michel- angelo and Rubens, and at times Raphael and Poussin, were exemplary; and the most excellent demonstration of its principles in recent times was to be found in James Barry's great cycle of pictures on the 'Progress of Science and the Cultivation of Society' in the Society of Arts' rooms in the Adelphi. As for 'historic' painting, Raphael among the Old Masters occasion- ally observed the rules and the finest, if not impeccable, exponent of them was Poussin. But for a really 'just and close exemplification of the boundaries of "his- toric"' painting Bromley deemed it 'necessary to select a composition recording an event which is minutely known to us, and which therefore has happened within our memories'. And for this perfect example he went to West's 'Death of Wolfe', which he judged to be 'one of the most genuine models of historic painting in the world'. He devoted seven pages to its exegesis,[47] explaining and praising its perspicuous setting of the scene, its appropriate use of modern rather than antique dress, its apt introduction of contemporary portraits, its felicitous use of allegory in the figures of the Indian warrior and the standing grenadier, and above all its 'most legitimate, judicious, and masterly,

though abundant, freedom of variation from the real circumstances of the case'.

So far, in enunciating his system, Bromley did not employ the term 'epic'. This emerged in the course of a pretty rumpus which his first volume aroused in the Academy and the press. West, without apparently informing the Council, got the Academy to subscribe for Bromley's flattering publication; and all was quiet for some months. But on December 10, 1793, Copley proposed[48] at an Academy meeting that the book be removed from the library and the subscription for the second volume cancelled, on the ground that Bromley had insulted Fuseli and the late President by calling the 'Shepherd's Dream', the 'Nightmare' and 'Little Red Riding Hood' 'frivolous, whimsical, and unmean- ing subjects', degrading to moral instruction.[49] It must have been an electric occasion. West sat in the chair saying nothing, but everybody in the room knew that Bromley was his friend and admirer and Copley his enemy. He was thus under two fires: from Copley on one side who was notoriously jealous of him, and from Fuseli on the other who was fuming under the direct insult of West's confidant. After a long debate it was decided to defer the motion until more members, including (if Bromley is to be credited) Copley himself, had read the book. At a meeting on February 10, 1794, Copley therefore again moved that the book be re- moved from the library, but his motion was defeated.[50] Finally, on February 20, 1794, at a heated and con- fused meeting in which Fuseli, Chambers, Tyler, Smirke and Bacon took a prominent part, and in which Fuseli's personal quarrels with Bromley seem to have been the main topic, it was voted to keep volume I in the library, but not to subscribe for volume II.[51]

Meanwhile, before Copley raised the matter of Brom- ley's first volume in the Academy, Fuseli had witheringly reviewed it in the press, impugning Bromley's learning and his knowledge of Greek, and ridiculing him for being 'unacquainted with the com- prehensive system which allots to painting the epic, the dramatic, and the historic departments', and for cutting them down to 'what he calls poetic and historic paint- ing'.[52] Bromley rejoined in letters of March 20 and April 8, 1794, which appeared in the *Morning Herald*, and in a series of letters culminating in a long one of September 10 he attacked Copley for his Academy

47. *Ibid.*, pp. 56–63.

48. Royal Academy, General Assembly Minutes, I, pp. 309–10.
49. Bromley, I, pp. 36–37.
50. Royal Academy, General Assembly Minutes, I, p. 322.
51. *Ibid.*, pp. 327–8.
52. *Analytical Review*, XVI, May–August, 1793, p. 242. Another review of Bromley's first volume by a partisan of Fuseli's appeared in the *Critical Review*, VII, 1793, pp. 377–88.

motions.[52a] Then at last in 1795 he produced his second volume. The bulk of it was concerned with modern art, but the Preface was virulently polemical and reprinted the two letters to Fuseli and the final letter to Copley. And it was in the letter to Copley[53] that Bromley designated the higher inventive type of 'historic' painting, so faultlessly exemplified by West's 'Wolfe', as 'epic', contrasting it pointedly with Copley's own performances. He jeered at Copley's 'Boy with a Squirrel', accused Copley of wishing that he had cited his 'Gibraltar' (which he classed as the 'bathos' of history-painting, barely distinguishable from mere portraiture) as his prime example of epic principle, and had three pages of heavy sarcasm on Copley's 'Watson and the Shark'—a ridiculous instance of how epic should *not* be managed. Genuine epic, on the other hand, he explained—again with reference to the 'Death of Wolfe'—thus: an 'historic painting, in that superior character which becomes epic, does not depend for the legitimacy or the sublimity of its composition on matters of fact . . . if the incidents which constitute the scene are so naturally connected with the real action that they may as probably have happened as any others, it may be as pure as an historic display, but may be raised to a greater climax, with the freest choice of those incidents, although not one of them, in fact, made a part of the event which is represented'.[54]

This, point by point, was unquestionably the doctrine—hammered out perhaps to some extent between West and Bromley in conversation, but formulated by the latter—which West relied upon when he devised his 'Death of Nelson', which he read back into his 'Wolfe', and used as a touchstone whereby to stigmatize Devis's 'mere matter of fact'.[55]

*　　*　　*

The rest of the story is quickly told. West's epic canvas was not his only tribute to Nelson's memory. Just as years earlier he had added his 'Death of Epaminondas' and the 'Death of Bayard' to his 'Death of Wolfe' as examples respectively of antique, medieval and modern valour,[56] so in the same systematic way he found occasion to eternize Nelson in other modes. Only a few weeks after West had made his contract with Heath, the King, as we have seen, commanded the Academicians to make designs for the Nelson monument in

St. Paul's. Here was a chance for West to return to the King's good graces, and he immediately began to design, simultaneously with the painting, a great tripartite allegorical memorial, embodying (as he put it) the 'three branches of the Academy'—painting, sculpture and architecture. Such was his Olympian comment, as he withdrew, on the Academy's cautious speculations as to whether anything except sculpture was eligible. This scheme he abandoned, however, when the vote of Parliament took the matter out of the King's hands. But later on, after the big painting was achieved and when the St. Paul's commission had gone finally to Flaxman, he went back to his triune allegorical design and made a painting of it which he exhibited, with a long description, in the Academy in 1807.[57] It is now in Mr. Paul Mellon's collection. Meanwhile, he had been approached to make two paintings for reproduction as plates in Clark and McArthur's monumental *Life of Nelson* (1809). For the frontispiece of this work he painted another version of the central painted feature of his St. Paul's design—an allegory of 'Victory presenting the dead body of the hero to Britannia, after the battle of Trafalgar, from the arms of Neptune'. Farington saw West at work upon it in March, 1807,[58] and it was exhibited that year in the Academy along with the painting of the triple monument.[59] His second painting for Clark and McArthur's work was a 'matter of fact' picture of Nelson's death in the cockpit of the *Victory*—a side view of the actual scene which perhaps in its lighting and in some details owes something to Devis himself (Fig. 5).[60] This was exhibited at the Academy in 1808, and a doctrinally non-committal description of it, no doubt furnished by West himself, was printed by Clark and McArthur. Both these pictures now hang at Greenwich. Finally in 1812 West persuaded the Governors of Greenwich Hospital to set up another allegorical memorial: the huge bas-relief in Coade stone of the 'Apotheosis of Nelson' that occupies one of the pediments of the King William Block—a work which taxed West almost beyond his strength.[61]

This was the last of what West called 'his works on the subject of Lord Nelson's victories'; and when he looked back on the whole series of them he could indeed congratulate himself on having faithfully and conscientiously discharged the promise he made to Nelson at the dinner-table. Time, however, has not

52a. On this correspondence see now J. D. Prown, *John Singleton Copley*, Cambridge, Mass., 1966, II, p. 338, n. 6.
53. Bromley, II, Preface, pp. xxvii–xlii.
54. *Ibid.*, p. xxxiv.
55. Bromley's doctrine also gives us a consistent frame of reference within which to interpret West's late version of his famous exchange with Reynolds on his 'Wolfe' (see note 22 above).
56. Mitchell, *art. cit.*, pp. 31–32.

57. Graves, VIII, pp. 218–19. Reproduced in Grose Evans, *Benjamin West and the Taste of his Times*, Carbondale, 1959, pl. 67.
58. Farington, IV, p. 100.
59. Graves, VIII, p. 219; reproduced by Grose Evans, pl. 66.
60. Graves, VIII, p. 219; reproduced by Grose Evans, pl. 65.
61. Farington, VI, p. 198.

ratified all his counsels. In 1815, when Ticknor visited him, the 'Death of Nelson' was still on his hands unsold, and even before his death in 1820 the taste for his more grandiose works was waning. In 1825 Thomas Uwins wrote regretfully of him to Keats's friend Joseph Severn: 'Poor man! he felt that his pictures were not legitimate art, and to cover his childish folly, he called them not historic, but epic! It pains me to think on what a mass of impertinent matter he crowded into his picture of "Christ Rejected", though he had the simple majesty of Scripture before his eyes.'[62]

Devis's 'mere matter of fact' has fared better. Though Boydell failed in hopes of selling it to Greenwich, it found its way there in 1825, the year Uwins wrote, when Edward Hawke Locker, the founder of the Naval Gallery in the Painted Hall, bought it from one Dyson at Christie's, presumably on behalf of Lord Bexley who then presented it to the Hospital.[63] And there, soon displayed alongside the authentic relics of Nelson's death, the uniform coat and white breeches so faithfully depicted in it, it gradually took its place in the hearts of Victorian visitors as the popular naval counterpart, in effect, of West's 'Death of Wolfe', as the artist had always intended it to be. Troops of schoolboys in the National Maritime Museum still crowd around it. West's epic, meanwhile, has hung in Liverpool since 1866, an almost forgotten curiosity— and a warning to artists never to put too much faith in the nostrums of art-historians.

62. S. Uwins, *A Memoir of T. Uwins, R.A.*, London, 1858, II, p. 202. I am indebted for this reference to Mr. Arthur Marks.

63. Pavière, p. 132, no. 119.

I owe many thanks for various help and information in the preparation of this paper to Mr. Edward Croft-Murray, Mr. Sidney Hutchison, Mr. Arthur Marks, Mr. George Naish, Mr. Michael Robinson, Mr. Timothy Stevens, and Mr. Oliver Warner.
Figs. 2, 4, 5 and 6 are reproduced by kind permission of the Trustees of the National Maritime Museum, Greenwich; and Figs. 1 and 3 by courtesy of the Walker Art Gallery, Liverpool, and the National Gallery of Canada respectively.

THEODORE REFF

Puget's Fortunes in France

It has been observed that 'during the last hundred and fifty years Bernini's star has lost much of its brilliance. What Winckelmann, the classicist doctrinaire, had begun, Ruskin, the medieval revivalist, completed.'[1] Even more than in Germany or England, it was in France that the Roman Baroque style identified with Bernini conflicted with the national ideals of order, harmony, and restraint which were firmly established in the age of Louis XIV. The incompatibility of Bernini's style with this dominant classical taste was already evident at the time in the rejection of his plans for completing the Louvre and the transformation of his equestrian monument of the King.[2] Later it prevented the acceptance of his art even in periods of an essentially neo-baroque character, such as Romanticism in painting and sculpture and Art Nouveau in architecture and the minor arts. Thus Delacroix, who admired certain aspects of the Baroque in Rubens and Rembrandt, observed in 1857 of Bernini and Pietro da Cortona, the other *bête noire* of nineteenth-century French critics: 'Leur manière particulière, ce qu'ils croient ajouter ou ajoutent à leur insu à la nature, éloigne toute idée d'imitation et nuit à la verité et à la naïveté de l'expression.'[3] As recently as 1911 the author of the first French monograph on Bernini regretted that 'aujourd'hui encore bien des gens en France, sur la foi des guides de voyage, croient qu'il est de bon ton de dire du mal du Bernin.'[4]

Yet Puget, the one French sculptor of the Baroque whose work can seriously be compared with Bernini's in boldness of conception and virtuosity of technique, and who was in fact influenced by the latter, has been highly regarded in France since the eighteenth century. Not only does the Salle de Puget in the Louvre contain all his major secular figures, including the *Milon de Crotone* and *Persée Délivrant Andromède* once at Versailles,[5] but a colossal bust of him stands beside one of Poussin at the entrance to the Ecole des Beaux-Arts, thus proclaiming him the patron of the national school in sculpture, as his contemporary is in painting.[6] Perhaps the two busts were inspired, as a biographer of Puget assumed in the mid-1860's at the height of his revival, 'par un sentiment de justice nationale. . . . C'est qu'en effet dans ces deux hommes se résume le suprême effort du génie artiste de notre nation. La France ne comprend pas la peinture sans la pensée, la sculpture sans la passion.'[7] Nevertheless, to historians outside France the presence of Puget, a pupil of Cortona and follower of Bernini, at the very entrance of this conservative institution is a paradox. It is in order to explain this paradox, and in so doing to clarify the status of the High Baroque in France, that we shall follow the history of Puget's fortunes in the nineteenth century.

*　　　*　　　*

That Mercier's monumental busts of Poussin and Puget were probably installed by 1838, when the new courtyard of the Ecole des Beaux-Arts was completed,[8] seems the more remarkable in that the most extreme neo-classical criticism of Puget had appeared less than twenty years earlier. Almost inevitably, it was written by a foreigner: in his authoritative *Storia della Scultura* Leopold Cicognara, a friend and biographer of Canova, stated flatly that Puget's statues are not truly sculptural since they must be viewed from one position, that they lack compositional unity, good proportions, and correctness of detail, and that they display a vulgar realism far removed from the nobility of ancient sculpture.[9] Of the *Persée Délivrant Andromède*, for example, Cicognara wrote, 'Non parliamo dei dettagli molto scorretti che sarebbe inutile andare sminuz-

1. R. Wittkower, *Gian-Lorenzo Bernini, the Sculptor of the Roman Baroque*, London, 1966, p. 1. Cf. *The Works of John Ruskin*, London, 1903-12, XIII, pp. 520-1, and XXII, pp. 423-4.
2. See L. Mirot, 'Le Bernin en France', *Mémoires de la Société de l'Histoire de Paris et de l'Ile de France*, XXXI, 1904, pp. 161-288.
3. E. Delacroix, *Journal*, ed. A. Joubin, Paris, 1932, III, p. 59, entry of January 25, 1857; cf. also III, p. 430, undated entry, on the superiority of Le Brun to Cortona.
4. M. Reymond, *Le Bernin*, Paris, n.d. [1911], p. 8. The allusion is probably to the famous essay on 'Bernini et son école' in J. Burckhardt, *Le Cicerone*, French trans., Paris, n.d. [1894], II, pp. 472-89.

5. See Musée National du Louvre, *Catalogue des sculptures*, Paris, 1922, II, nos. 1465-9.
6. See E. Müntz, *Guide de l'Ecole Nationale des Beaux-Arts*, Paris, n.d. [1889], p. 29; and E. H. Denby, 'The Ecole des Beaux-Arts Revisited', *Légion d'Honneur*, III, no. 3, January 1933, p. 5, for a photograph of the entrance.
7. L. Lagrange, *Pierre Puget*, Paris, 1868, p. v. First published in the *Gazette des Beaux-Arts*, 1er sér., XVIII, 1865, p. 193.
8. See Müntz, *op. cit.*, p. 19. No date for the busts is given in S. Lami, *Dictionnaire des sculpteurs de l'école française au 19e siècle*, Paris, 1919, III, pp. 438-9.
9. L. Cicognara, *Storia della scultura*, Venice, 1813-18, III, pp. 141-2.

zando', and of the *Milon de Crotone*, 'Non diremo della scelta delle forme, . . . nè della ignobilità che regna in tutte l'estremità specialmente.'[10] If the severe tone of these judgements was never matched by French critics, who recognized Puget's importance in the national school, the most doctrinaire neo-classicists clearly agreed with them in substance. Thus Quatremère de Quincy, the distinguished archaeologist and chief spokesman of this group, observed in reviewing Cicognara's book in 1819: 'Il n'est pas étonnant qu'un œil habitué à la perfection des beaux et éternels modèles de l'art se trouve violemment blessé du manque de noblesse, de la fausseté de composition et des écarts de dessin qui sont non-seulement les défauts accidentels des ouvrages du Puget, mais qui font l'essence même de sa manière.'[11] Indeed, Quatremère differed from his Italian colleague only in acknowledging Puget's extraordinary surface realism—a theme that would recur often in French criticism.

Although Quatremère de Quincy continued to attack 'cette manière hardie, facile et incorrecte qu'il porta dans la sculpture' as late as 1832,[12] when the tide had begun to turn in Puget's favor, his most severe critics outside France had objected in the previous decade to what a Scottish biographer of Canova called 'the national vanity of the French . . . in speaking of their art and artists', a vanity which prevented them from recognizing that 'in every intellectual beauty of art Puget's works are imperfect, presenting little of elevation, nobleness or grace'.[13] There were in fact several indications, when this Scottish critic wrote in 1825, that Puget was already 'the favourite artist of native writers'. In the previous year the Salle de Puget in the Louvre had opened and his most famous group, the *Milon de Crotone* (Fig. 1), had first been exhibited in Paris.[14] It was praised, at the expense of Canova's no less famous *Amour et Psyché*, even by such conservative writers as E.-J. Delécluze, the art critic for the *Journal des Débats*, who remarked after visiting the new gallery: 'Canova ne brille pas. Ses deux groupes

sont mignards d'expression et faibles d'exécution. Le Puget est naturel, fort, mais brutal.'[15] In the same year the Comte de Clarac, curator of sculpture at the Louvre, described the *Milon* as 'l'un des chefs d'œuvre de la sculpture moderne, et qui, si l'on y retrouvait la noblesse de formes et de proportions des anciens, pourrait rivaliser avec leurs plus beaux ouvrages, par l'énergie de son expression et la vie dont il est animé'.[16] On this issue there was almost universal agreement in France, Quatremère de Quincy himself admitting that Puget, 'doué du même sentiment en sculpture que Rubens en peinture', had succeeded in carrying illusionism to such a point that 'ses marbres doivent se compter dans le petit nombre de ceux qui semblent cesser d'être de la matière inanimée'.[17]

The comparison with Rubens, although a repetition of the familiar formula that Puget was 'le Rubens de la sculpture', may help to explain why his statues were regarded highly while Bernini's were not. For Rubens, despite the neo-classical cult of Poussin and the Carracci, was admired in France throughout the Revolution and the Empire, as is evident from the number of Louvre acquisitions and ambitious publications of his works and from his influence on Gros and Géricault among David's pupils.[18] But this revived taste for the colorism and dramatic realism of Northern Baroque art, nourished by greater contact with examples of it in the recently established museums, could not also accept what were considered the exaggerations and affectations of the less well-known Roman Baroque. To the French critics Bernini was 'le premier qui, sous le prétexte de la grâce, introduisit les licences de l'incorrection la plus outrée. Ses chairs, traitées avec trop de mollesse, s'éloignent du beau et outrepassent le vrai; son expression n'est souvent qu'une grimace et toujours une affectation.'[19] Also significant, no doubt, at least in the Revolutionary period, was the fact that the most familiar works of Puget, those in the vicinity of Paris, were mythological subjects, whereas Bernini was identified with sacred art and the papacy.

It is not surprising, then, that from the eighteenth century on, and even in the neo-classical era, Puget's monumental groups were admired in France for their realism and energetic movement, despite their supposedly imperfect proportions and lack of nobility. In

---

10. *Ibid.*, p. 142. Cf. the critique of Cicognara's book by T. B. Eméric-David, *Histoire de la sculpture française*, Paris, 1853, pp. 211–86.

11. A. C. Quatremère de Quincy, 'Tome troisième de l'Histoire de la sculpture en Italie, par M. Cicognara', *Journal des Savants*, 2ᵉ sér., IV, 1819, pp. 408–9. On his doctrine see T. M. Mustoxidi, *Histoire de l'esthétique française, 1700–1900*, Paris, 1920, pp. 95–102.

12. A. C. Quatremère de Quincy, *Dictionnaire historique d'architecture*, Paris, 1832, II, p. 325.

13. J. S. Memes, *Memoirs of Antonio Canova*, Edinburgh, 1825, pp. 111–13; for this writer's position cf. pp. 565–6 on Canova, who is described as 'hardly to be ranked inferior to the greatest names in the annals of ancient greatness'.

14. See Comte de Clarac, *Description des ouvrages de la sculpture française . . . de la Galerie d'Angoulême*, Paris, 1824, pp. 56–61.

15. E.-J. Delécluze, *Journal (1824–1828)*, ed. R. Baschet, Paris, 1948, p. 232, entry of June 5, 1825. Cf. his article on the Galerie d'Angoulême in the *Journal des Débats*, June 23, 1825.

16. Clarac, *op. cit.*, p. 57.

17. Quatremère de Quincy, *op. cit.*, 1819, p. 409.

18. See F. Benoit, *L'Art français sous la révolution et l'empire*, Paris, 1897, pp. 115–19 and 129–30.

19. A. C. Quatremère de Quincy, 'Architecture', in *Encyclopédie méthodique*, Paris, 1788–1825; quoted in Reymond, *op. cit.*, pp. 5–6.

1811 Alexandre Lenoir, the founder and conservator of the Musée des Monuments Français, affirmed that Puget, 'malgré les grandes négligences que l'on remarque dans son style, ... émeut l'âme par des attitudes vraies qu'il a rendu pour ainsi dire mobiles, et par des expressions énergiques'.[20] And as early as 1805, at the height of David's dominion over French art, the neo-classical painter and critic Charles Landon wrote of the *Milon de Crotone*, which he reproduced in pure outline in a typically severe engraving (Fig. 5): 'L'expression de ce groupe est parfaite: la tête de Milon exprime la rage et le désespoir; le lion est d'une vigueur effrayante.'[21] Indeed, David himself admired a Puget drawing so highly that he inscribed on it, 'Je vous engage à garder ce dessin, il est aussi beau qu'un Michel-Ange', whereas his attitude toward the Roman Baroque is expressed in his well-known slogan, 'écraser la queue du Bernin'.[22]

In this sharp distinction between Bernini and Puget nationalism undoubtedly also played a part, as the Scottish critic had recognized. When a distinguished group of sculptors, including Houdon, Pajou, Masson, and Foucou, that is, representatives of both the Rococo and Revolutionary generations, petitioned the Government in 1801 to purchase a group then attributed to Puget for the Musée des Monuments Français, they emphasized that his name was one 'que la France peut citer avec orgeuil et à qui les plus célèbres artistes ses contemporains rendirent les hommages dus à sa supériorité'.[23] This sentiment also led Lenoir to incorporate the group, a few years after its acquisition by the Musée, into a pseudo-mausoleum that he had erected in Puget's honor; its inspiration was probably the monument of Frédéric-Maurice de Bouillon in Cluny, which Lenoir had tried persistently to acquire around 1800 in the erroneous belief that the principal figures were carved by Puget.[24] With the same motives —historical and patriotic rather than aesthetic— Lenoir had attempted in 1797 to have the famous *Hercule Gaulois* transferred from the gardens at Sceaux to the Musée des Monuments Français,

explaining that 'elle remplira dans le dix-septième siècle une lacune que la réputation de Puget ne peut souffrir'.[25] Equally unsuccessful in this project, he had to content himself with casts of the *Milon de Crotone* and *Persée Délivrant Andromède*, of which the originals remained at Versailles.

An illustrious national artist associated with the grandeur of Versailles, Puget was also the most important figure in the history of Provençal art and as such the object of a regional fame. Eighteenth-century writers from Pitton de Tournefort on had established this tradition of local esteem, to which Bougerel's long biographical memoir of 1752 contributed a great deal. Widely read for its vivid anecdotal detail, it portrayed Puget both as an authentic type of the Midi, 'extrêmement vif, impatient, brusque, colère', and as a universal genius, 'qu'on appelloit à juste titre le Michel-Ange de la France'.[26] This favorable comparison was developed further in such publications as the *Dictionnaire de la Provence* of 1787, where Puget, '[qui] fut tout à la fois et presque au sortir de l'enfance grand Architecte, excellent Peintre et Sculpteur sublime', was hailed as Michelangelo's equal in every respect.[27] It was obviously the same local patriotism, rather than an innovation in taste, which led the academy of Marseilles to propose an 'Eloge historique de Puget' as the title of its prize competition in 1801. Several writers submitted essays, among them Alphonse Rabbe of Aix-en-Provence, an art critic for *Le Courrier Français*, and Zénon Pons, an antiquarian and professor of rhetoric in Toulon, both of whom were conscious of the sculptor's local importance.[28] Thus Pons went beyond even the *Dictionnaire de la Provence* in comparing him with Michelangelo: 'Dans la représentation des dieux et des héros, par-tout où le génie déploie sa fierté, sa force et sa majesté, Puget se place à côté de Michel-Ange. Mais combien ce dernier est loin de notre compatriote dans les ouvrages que le sentiment et la grâce doivent embellir!'[29] Among the other essayists in the competition, however, were Duchesne l'Aisné, conservator of the Cabinet des Estampes in Paris, and T. B. Eméric-David who, although a Provençal figure and partly drawn to the

20. A. Lenoir, *Histoire des arts en France, prouvée par les monumens*, Paris, 1811, p. 78.
21. C. P. Landon, *Annales du Musée et de l'école moderne des beaux-arts*, Paris, 1805, IX, pp. 139–40; cf. also XI, pp. 85–86, on the *Persée Délivrant Andromède*.
22. On the drawing, now at Chantilly, see Lagrange, *op. cit.*, p. 396, no. 156; for the slogan, P. E. Giudici, in *Gazette des Beaux-Arts*, 1er sér., I, 1859, p. 116.
23. See L. Courajod, *Alexandre Lenoir, son journal, et le Musée des Monuments Français*, Paris, 1886, II, pp. 192–3.
24. On the monument to Puget see *ibid.*, p. 192; on the mausoleum at Cluny, the *Inventaire général des richesses d'art de la France: Archives du Musée des Monuments Français*, Paris, 1883–97, I, pp. 146–9 and 180–2, where Lenoir refers to it as 'le monument du Puget'.

25. *Ibid.*, I, pp. 83–85; cf. also I, pp. 222–5, on his acquisition of a statue of Neptune which was then attributed to Puget.
26. J. Bougerel, *Mémoires pour servir à l'histoire de plusieurs hommes illustres de Provence*, Paris, 1752, pp. 61 and 63. Cf. J. Pitton de Tournefort, *Relation d'un voyage du Levant*, Paris, 1717, I, pp. 8–13.
27. *Dictionnaire de la Provence et du Comte-Venaissin*, ed. C. F. Achard, Marseilles, 1787, IV, pp. 129–30.
28. A. Rabbe, *Eloge de Pierre Puget*, Aix-en-Provence, 1807; Z. Pons, *Essai sur la vie et les ouvrages de Pierre Puget*, Paris, 1812.
29. Pons, *op. cit.*, pp. 40–41. Cf. also his earlier publication, *Notice sur les cariatides du Puget*, Toulon, 1810.

subject for that reason, was well known nationally as an archaeologist and historian of sculpture.[30] His conception of Puget thus had more than a regional significance, and in fact anticipated the Romantic criticism of the following generation.

Rejecting the strictures of incorrect proportion and faulty details, already current in eighteenth-century discussions of Puget before the neo-classicists took them up, Eméric-David insisted that 'ses incorrections n'atteignent jamais les lignes centrales de ses figures. L'ensemble est toujours juste; les mouvements en sont toujours précis.'[31] Correctness was indeed no longer the essential issue, since Puget was not an intellectual artist like Michelangelo, but an intuitive one: 'Tout, ou presque tout, en lui, est le produit du sentiment. Ses émotions le dirigent, plutôt que la théorie de l'art.'[32] And these emotions, raised from the level of Provençal temperament to that of Romantic genius, reveal a personality 'dominé par une âme sensible mais ardente, par un caractère brusque et impétueux. . . . Son âme élève son ciseau, parce qu'elle est elle-même forte et élevée.'[33] Although published in 1823, this prophetic passage was undoubtedly derived from Eméric-David's prize-winning 'Eloge', as was the almost identical passage in his *Recherches sur l'art statuaire* of 1805, where the image of the 'fougueux Puget', the self-willed artist who refused to submit to the official classicism of Versailles, was already visible.[34]

The cult of Puget as an illustrious Provençal, especially in Marseilles and Toulon where he had worked, also produced a number of less important tributes to him in the nineteenth century. In 1815 the neo-classical sculptor Foucou, who had been a student at the academy in Marseilles, carved a bust of Puget, now in the museum there, which anticipated Mercier's bust at the entrance to the Ecole des Beaux-Arts by twenty years; Foucou had already exhibited a statue of Puget in 1801 and a smaller version of it still earlier.[35] In the late 1820's the *Cariatides* of the Hôtel-de-Ville in Toulon were restored at the municipal government's expense by Louis Hubac, a native of that city, who also proposed at this time to place statues of Puget, Massillon, and other famous Provençal figures in the Salle des Séances of the local academy.[36] During the restoration of the *Cariatides*, casts were commissioned by the State, and copies of them were installed in the Salle de Puget of the Louvre, thus making accessible to a larger audience these famous figures around which many legends had already accumulated; they were in fact so popular by the 1850's that a poet of Toulon wrote rapturously in praise of them.[37] Marseilles, too, chose to honor Puget in this decade, but the monument erected there by the local sculptor Ramus was so mediocre in quality that it was later removed, and the creation of a Salle de Puget in the municipal museum, although widely discussed around 1859, was realized only forty years later.[38] On the popular level, however, he had long been regarded as an almost legendary figure in Marseilles, where the profile of one of the mountains overlooking the city was commonly called 'la tête de Puget'.[39]

*   *   *

Despite the many signs of a growing admiration for Puget in the first third of the nineteenth century, his works themselves literally suffered from neglect. When the Salle de Puget in the Louvre opened in 1824, it contained nothing of his but the *Milon de Crotone*, which had been brought from the gardens of Versailles, where it was slowly deteriorating, only a few years earlier.[40] The *Deux Anges Enfants*, a small group purchased as an original in 1817, was not exhibited, the attribution perhaps already being in question; and the *Hercule Gaulois*, which Lenoir had tried to obtain in 1797, was moved from one ignoble location to another in the Palais du Luxembourg, where it remained almost inaccessible until its transfer to the

30. J. Duchesne l'Aisné, *Eloge historique de Pierre Puget*, Paris, 1807; T. B. Eméric-David, *Vie de Pierre Puget, peintre, statuaire et constructeur de vaisseaux*, Marseilles, 1840 (based on the unpublished 'Eloge' of 1801–7).

31. T. B. Eméric-David, 'Pierre Puget', in *Biographie universelle, ancienne et moderne*, ed. L.-G. Michaud, Paris, 1823, XXXVI, p. 302. For the eighteenth-century position, a mixture of high praise and harsh criticism, see C.-N. Cochin, *Voyage d'Italie*, Paris, 1758, III, pp. 284–5; and A. N. Dézallier d'Argenville, *Vies des fameux sculpteurs*, Paris, 1787, pp. 181–202.

32. Eméric-David, *op. cit.*, 1823, p. 301.

33. *Ibid.*, pp. 289–90 and 301. On his position see Mustoxidi, *op. cit.*, pp. 82–83.

34. T. B. Eméric-David, *Recherches sur l'art statuaire considéré chez les anciens et chez les modernes*, Paris, 1863 [1st ed. 1805], pp. 297–8.

35. See S. Lami, *Dictionnaire des sculpteurs de l'école française au dix-huitième siècle*, Paris, 1910, I, pp. 349–53.

36. See E. Saglio, 'Le Sculpteur Hubac', *Gazette des Beaux-Arts*, 1er sér., I, 1859, pp. 344–51; and Lagrange, *op. cit.*, 1868, pp. 370–1.

37. C. Poncey, 'Les Cariatides de Puget, à Toulon', *Bulletin Semestriel de la Société des Sciences, Belles-Lettres et Arts du Département du Var*, XX, 2, 1853, pp. 203–6. These casts remained in the Louvre until 1886, when they were transferred to the Musée de Sculpture Comparée; see G. Berthold, *Cézanne und die alten Meister*, Stuttgart, 1958, p. 52.

38. On the monument, exhibited in the Salon of 1855, see P. Auquier, 'Pierre Puget', *L'Art et les Artistes*, IV, 1907, pp. 291–5; on the projected Salle de Puget, L. Lagrange, in *Gazette des Beaux-Arts*, 1er sér., II, 1859, pp. 255–6.

39. See P. Mariéton, *La Terre provençale*, Paris, 1894, p. 279; and Lagrange, *op. cit.*, 1868, p. 328, n. 1.

40. See Eméric-David, *op. cit.*, 1823, p. 303. As early as 1752 La Font de Saint-Yenne had argued that the *Milon* and the *Andromède* 'mériteroient l'honneur d'être dans les appartemens à l'abri de la gelée et des outrages de l'air' (*L'Ombre du grand Colbert, le Louvre, et la Ville de Paris*, Paris, 1752, pp. 234–6).

Louvre in 1849.[41] More serious was the continued exposure to moisture of the *Persée Délivrant Andromède* at Versailles. In 1831 Gustave Planche, one of the most influential critics of the Romantic period, remarked that 'malgré les dégâts nombreux qu'elle a déjà subis, on continue de la laisser se détruire de jour en jour',[42] and in 1844 Delacroix, lamenting the 'déstruction totale [d']un des ouvrages les plus capitaux du plus grand sculpteur français', conducted a vigorous campaign for its preservation.[43] But it did not enter the Louvre until the galleries of Renaissance sculpture were reorganized in 1849. And when the relief *Le Rencontre d'Alexandre et de Diogène* was finally transferred from the Louvre basement around 1836, it was so badly installed that Delacroix complained it could hardly be seen.[44]

It is also true, however, that Romantic writers like Delacroix and Planche exaggerated the extent of this neglect, and that the number of Puget's works exhibited in the Louvre had increased eightfold by the time the new installations were completed in 1850. Besides those already mentioned, they included a model of the equestrian *Alexandre Vainqueur*, purchased in the previous year, and a self-portrait in oil, acquired at great expense in 1842.[45] Thus, all the sculptures shown in the Salle de Puget today, and a few casts no longer there, had entered the Louvre in the preceding thirty years. During this period his reputation had grown to such an extent that Théophile Gautier, surveying the new galleries of Renaissance sculpture in the newspaper *La Presse*, could declare: 'Pierre Puget est devenu le plus grand statuaire de son époque, et peut-être l'artiste le plus franchement français dont nous puissions nous glorifier.'[46] If Gautier, like the majority of his readers, admired little more in Puget than the brilliance of his illusionism—'sous son marbre palpitant

courent le sang et la vie; quand on y porte la main, on est surpris de la trouver rigide et froid'—the historian Michelet, equally popular but more original, saw in Puget the very embodiment of his age and its only authentic witness. Of the widespread suffering and persecution in the reign of Louis XIV, he wrote in his *Histoire de France*, 'Le seul historien ici, c'est Puget, le grand solitaire de Toulon.'[47] His *Cariatides*, supposedly modelled on galley slaves in Toulon, would represent the victims of the Revocation of the Edict of Nantes; his *Persée Délivrant Andromède*, the abduction of women and children by government soldiers; and his equestrian *Alexandre Vainqueur*, an 'étrange et violente satire', Louis XIV himself crushing the people beneath his tyranny.[48] This curious interpretation, although obviously unfounded, indicates that by 1860 Puget's work was so universally appreciated in France that he could be considered not only the greatest sculptor of the age of Louis XIV, but an historical figure as important for understanding that age as the King himself. He had become, as Michelet wrote elsewhere, the 'grand artiste en qui fut l'âme souffrant d'un siècle malade'.[49]

Although this notion of the ethical and historical value of the work of art is typical of Michelet and in general reflects the importance attached to the visual arts in the Romantic period,[50] his choice of Puget as a protagonist remains significant. It is the climax of a revaluation observable on all levels of culture, from the popular to the most scholarly, and in all segments of opinion, from the liberal to the most conservative, during the previous thirty years. Contemporary with Gautier's enthusiastic appraisal of Puget in *La Presse* were the first publications in the *Archives de l'Art Français* of documents concerning his activities in Marseilles and Toulon and the first critical examination of the anecdotes reported by his early biographers.[51] The symbolic value of Puget's bust opposite

41. On the *Deux Anges Enfants*, now attributed to Veyrrier, Puget's pupil, see Courajod, *op. cit.*, II, pp. 198–202; on the *Hercule Gaulois*, the *Inventaire général des richesses d'art*, I, p. 85, n. 1.

42. G. Planche, 'Pierre Puget', *L'Artiste*, II, 1831, p. 105.

43. E. Delacroix, 'Sur le groupe d'Andromède de Puget', *Les Beaux-Arts*, III, 1844, pp. 121–5. Cf. also his *Correspondance générale*, ed. A. Joubin, Paris, 1936, II, pp. 170–3, letters of May 1844. According to Joubin, Delacroix had written the *Beaux-Arts* article in 1831, but his letter to Soulié implies that he was writing it in 1844.

44. Delacroix, *op. cit.*, 1844, p. 124, n. 1. The installation date of the relief, not found in the Louvre catalogue cited above, note 5, is given by T. Thoré, 'Etudes sur la sculpture française depuis la Renaissance—II', *Revue de Paris*, nouv. sér., XXVI, 1836, p. 40.

45. On the portrait, now attributed to François Puget, see F. Villot, *Notice des tableaux du Musée National du Louvre*, Paris, 1886, III, p. 299, no. 462.

46. T. Gautier, 'Etudes sur les musées—IV: le Musée français de la renaissance', *La Presse*, August 24, 1850; reprinted in his *Tableaux à la plume*, Paris, 1880, pp. 89–90.

47. J. Michelet, *Louis XIV et le duc de Bourgogne*, his *Histoire de France*, XIV, Paris, 1862, p. 116.

48. *Ibid.*, pp. 116–18; and J. Michelet, *Louis XIV et le Revocation de l'Edit de Nantes*, his *Histoire de France*, XIII, Paris, 1860, pp. 331–2. On the fallaciousness of this argument see Lagrange, *op. cit.*, 1868, pp. 289–91.

49. J. Michelet, *L'Amour*, Paris, 1920 [1st ed. 1858], pp. 36–37; here Michelet also interprets the *Persée Délivrant Andromède* in ethical terms as a model of the relations between the sexes.

50. See L. Rosenthal, *Du Romantisme au réalisme*, Paris, 1914, pp. 56–59; and J. Pommier, *Michelet interprète de la figure humaine*, London, 1961.

51. For the documents see J. Boilly and M. Chambry, in *Archives de l'Art Français*, III, 1852–3, pp. 236–41; P. Margry, in *ibid.*, VII, 1855–6, pp. 225–310; and L. Lagrange, in *ibid.*, XI, 1858–60, pp. 88–93. On the early biographers see D. M. J. Henry, 'Sur la vie et les ouvrages de Pierre Puget', *Bulletin Semestriel de la Société des Sciences, Belles-Lettres et Arts du Département du Var*, XX, 2, 1853, pp. 109–99.

Poussin's at the entrance to the Ecole des Beaux-Arts has already been discussed. Its counterpart in a more sacred precinct was the statue of him, his arm resting on a small replica of the *Milon de Crotone*, which was installed beside statues of Poussin, Corneille, Racine, and other immortals in the Salle de l'Académie des Sciences of the Institut, also around 1837.[52] A few years earlier Rude had introduced a copy of the *Milon* as an emblem of sculpture into his relief *Prométhée Animant des Arts* (Fig. 3) over one of the entrances to the Chambre des Députés, while his famous *Marseillaise* on the Arc de Triomphe, carved in the same period, was obviously inspired by Puget's dramatic types and vigorous execution.[53] The latter's influence on Romantic sculpture can in fact be observed in a number of works, including Barye's group *La Guerre* on the façade of the Louvre, whose principal figure was based on the *Hercule Gaulois*, and David d'Angers's statue of *Philopœmen*, whose anatomical realism is no less clearly dependent on the *Milon de Crotone*, as he himself recognized.[54] Imbued with admiration for the Baroque artist's intensity of expression—'on vole sur ses ailes vers la passion traduite par ses marbres ou sa toile', he once wrote—David d'Angers also tried in 1845 and again in 1851 to obtain the commission for the Puget monument in Marseilles.[55] It is surprising, however, that Géricault and Daumier, two of the most original sculptors of this era, whose passionate temperament and deep affinities with Michelangelo would have made Puget, long known as 'le Michel-Ange de la France', seem particularly congenial, neither wrote of him nor apparently felt his influence.[56]

If the Puget monument finally erected in Marseilles was mediocre in quality, the conception of such a tribute had been realized in Paris in a more impressive form as early as 1828, when Eugène Devéria, then at the height of his fame, was commissioned to paint a mural of *Puget Présentant le Groupe de Milon de Crotone à Louis XIV dans les Jardins de Versailles* (Fig. 2) on the ceiling of one of the recently created galleries of ancient ceramics in the Louvre.[57] The titles of Puget's other major statues were inscribed on medallions in the corners of the room, and in the voussoirs were smaller pictures representing similar episodes from the cultural history of the reign of Louis XIV. In one of them appeared Le Brun, the former dictator of the arts, now reduced to a marginal position while Puget was proclaimed the leading artist of his time and the real successor to Poussin, who was shown with Louis XIII in the ceiling of an adjacent gallery.[58] The choice of subject for Devéria's mural was the more significant in that it required a distortion of the facts; as Planche remarked in 1831, even before it was unveiled, Puget himself had not been present at Versailles and in general had received little recognition from the King throughout his career.[59] Instead of welcoming the tribute implied in this revision of history, however, the Romantic critic chose to interpret it in bitterly ironic terms: 'On a voulu remercier Louis XIV d'avoir donné à la France Pierre Puget. Maladroite mensonge, gauche remerciement!' This, too, involved a certain amount of distortion, since Puget was in fact shrewder and more successful than Planche admitted.[60]

Underlying the critic's bitterness was a typically Romantic conception of the alienated and ill-treated artist which, although contradicted by the acclaim that Puget actually received during this period, dominated the discussion of him for the next thirty years. Its most poignant statement was in Baudelaire's poem 'Les Phares', published in 1857, where Puget was pictured not only as the brutal realist whose statues were inspired by plebeian figures—a familiar idea at the time—but as the traditional type of the melancholic:

> Colères de boxeur, impudences de faune,
> Toi qui sus ramasser la beauté des goujats,
> Grand cœur gonflé d'orgueil, homme débile et jaune,
> Puget, mélancolique empereur des forçats.[61]

52. See the *Inventaire général des richesses d'art de la France: Paris, monuments civils*, Paris, 1879, I, p. 19; the statue, exhibited in the Salon of 1836, was by Desprez.
53. On the *Prométhée* relief see L. de Fourcaud, *François Rude sculpteur, ses œuvres et son temps*, Paris, 1904, pp. 215-16 and 467-8; on *La Marseillaise, ibid.*, pp. 216-17.
54. On *La Guerre*, carved in 1854, a few years after the *Hercule Gaulois* entered the Louvre, see R. Ballu, *L'Œuvre de Barye*, Paris, 1890, pp. 109-13. On the *Philopœmen*, exhibited in the Salon of 1837, see H. Jouin, *David d'Angers, sa vie, son œuvre, ses écrits et ses contemporains*, Paris, 1878, I, pp. 317-21, and II, pp. 483-4; cf. also II, p. 494, on his medal of Puget, exhibited in the Salon of 1841.
55. For his essay on Puget of *c.* 1853 see *ibid.*, II, pp. 211-13; on the Puget monument, *ibid.*, I, pp. 412-13, and II, pp. 443-4.
56. However, Daumier and Puget did share certain specifically Provençal traits, according to G. Bazin, 'Le Baroque Provençal', in Musée de l'Orangerie, *Monticelli et le Baroque Provençal*, Paris, 1953, pp. v-xxiii.

57. See M. Gauthier, *Achille et Eugène Devéria*, Paris, 1925, pp. 49-55. The oil sketch, also in the Louvre, is reproduced in our Fig. 4.
58. On the Louis XIV gallery see Musée National du Louvre, *Catalogue des peintures*, ed. G. Brière, Paris, 1924, I, pp. 298-9, Salle C; on the Louis XIII gallery, *ibid.*, p. 298, Salle A.
59. Planche, *op. cit.*, p. 104. Cf. also his remarks on this mural in the *Revue des Deux Mondes*, 2e sér., II, 1833, p. 192.
60. See, for example, the inventory of his possessions and estimate of his fortune in Lagrange, *op. cit.*, 1868, pp. 315-20.
61. C. Baudelaire, *Les Fleurs du Mal*, ed. J. Crépet, Paris, 1930 [1st ed. 1857], pp. 20-21; the only other sculptor included is Michelangelo. Diderot had already remarked a century earlier,

In the first monograph on Puget, written ten years later, Lagrange suggested in pseudo-art-historical terms that this morose spirit, which he did not find in the artist's paintings, was somehow conditioned by the nature of sculpture: 'Il semble que la résistance du marbre, en le provoquant à une lutte pénible, le tienne sous le joug de la douleur.'[62] But most writers emphasized the passionate, tragic character of the sculptor himself and, like Planche, Delacroix, and David d'Angers, all of whom made this observation independently, saw in the inscriptions carved into the ornament of Puget's house in Marseilles—'Nul bien sans peine' and 'Salvator mundi, miserere nobis'—appropriate mottoes of his life.[63] For Delacroix, however, Puget's inadequate recognition at the court of Louis XIV, whose official style was the academic classicism of Le Brun, and the frustration of Puget's great decorative projects at Versailles, had a more personal significance. As in his essays on Poussin and Baron Gros, where he dwelled at length on the abuse of talented artists in France, Delacroix evidently had his own unfortunate experiences in mind, particularly the severe criticism of his *Mort de Sardanapale* in 1827 and his lack of public commissions for many years thereafter.[64] Hence his pessimistic remarks on the deterioration or poor installation of Puget's works and his pathetic picture of the sculptor himself, 'harcelé de son vivant par les envieuses passions des artistes, ses rivaux, méconnu et délaissé par les grands et les ministres'.[65] In this respect, too, Puget was obviously a more congenial figure to the Romantics than the worldly and successful Bernini, who had been treated ceremoniously by 'les grands et les ministres' during his trip to Paris.

An image of the ill-used and melancholy creator, Puget also appealed to the Romantic critics in more positive terms as a model of independence and originality. In a second, much longer article on him published in 1852 Planche wrote: 'Passionné pour l'indépendance, Puget n'a jamais tenu compte, dans ses actions comme dans ses ouvrages, que de ses idées personelles, et le récit de sa vie est un des plus nobles exemples qui se puissent proposer.'[66] His volatile temper and uncompromising

attitude were of course familiar from the anecdotes reported by his eighteenth-century biographers, and as early as 1805 Eméric-David recognized that these personal traits were somehow linked with his unique style, which was 'grand, énergique, sublime, mais irrégulier'.[67] But the recurring words 'irrégulier' and 'incorrect' indicate that Eméric-David, despite his emphasis on the expressive aspects of Puget's art, still tended to judge it by conventional standards, whereas for Planche—at least at the time of his first essay in 1831—its originality lay precisely in its rejection of the classical: 'Il faut le dire hautement, la sculpture de Puget est une formelle insurrection contre l'art grec et romaine. C'est un art nouveau, étrange aux deux autres, mais aussi haut que les deux autres, plus profond et plus difficile peut-être. C'est la lutte corps à corps du marbre et de la nature.'[68] Thus, the legends of Puget's intransigence in dealing with political authority were linked with his independence of the accepted classical tradition and his achievement of an absolute or naïve realism. Modern scholarship has, of course, destroyed this direct connection by showing the extent of Puget's dependence on ancient models, especially of the so-called Pergamene Baroque;[69] but in the 1830's it seemed well established. Stendhal, too, for example, considered Puget 'admirable parce qu'il est naturel . . . ses formes n'ont rien de mesquin; elles ne portent jamais à l'esprit pour première impression *l'idée de l'imitation de l'antique*'.[70] In scrutinizing Puget's self-portrait bust in Marseilles with a novelist's eyes, Stendhal found the same qualities there: 'Il est plein de naturel comme ses ouvrages. Tête carrée, bouche serrée d'un homme qui *s'efforce* habituellement, yeux inégaux, le droit beaucoup plus bas que le gauche; en général beaucoup de *vérités* rendues avec scrupule.'[71]

Despite their insistence on Puget's independence of classical sources, the position of Planche and Stendhal did not differ radically from that of the neo-classical critics, who had also recognized that '[il] émeut l'âme, par des attitudes vraies qu'il a rendu pour ainsi dire

in speaking of the sculptor Slotz: 'Mais quel est sur l'homme l'effet de son talent ravalé? Le chagrin, la mélancolie, la bile épanchée dans le sang. . . . Son sort rappelle celui du Puget' (*Salons*, ed. J. Seznec and J. Adhémar, II, Oxford, 1960, p. 224; from the 'Salon de 1765').

62. Lagrange, *op. cit.*, 1868, pp. 331–3.

63. Planche, *op. cit.*, 1831, p. 103. David d'Angers, in Jouin, *op. cit.*, II, pp. 211–13. E. Delacroix, 'Puget', *Le Plutarque Français*, 1845; reprinted in his *Œuvres littéraires*, ed. E. Faure, Paris, 1923, II, pp. 122–3.

64. See E. Faure, 'Delacroix et son temps', in *ibid.*, II, pp. 225–8.

65. Delacroix, *op. cit.*, 1844, p. 125.

66. G. Planche, 'Peintres et sculpteurs modernes de la France:

Pierre Puget', *Revue des Deux Mondes*, nouv. pér., XV, 1852, p. 782. Zénon Pons had already praised this aspect of Puget in 1812; *op. cit.*, p. 2.

67. Eméric-David, *op. cit.*, 1805, pp. 297–8. Cf. Thoré, *op. cit.*, p. 38: 'On rapport une foule d'anecdotes qui prouvent l'indépendance du Puget et la fierté de son caractère.'

68. Planche, *op. cit.*, 1831, p. 106.

69. See C. Vermeule, *European Art and the Classical Past*, Cambridge, Mass., 1964, pp. 115–17; and A. Blunt, *Art and Architecture in France, 1500 to 1700*, Baltimore, 1953, p. 285, n. 47.

70. Stendhal [H. Beyle], *Mémoires d'un touriste*, ed. L. Royer, Paris, 1932, II, pp. 433–4, entry of 1837; italics in the original.

71. *Ibid.*, III, pp. 219–21, entry of 1838; italics in the original. Cf. also his remarks on Puget's statues in Genoa, in *ibid.*, II, pp. 442–3, entry of 1838.

mobiles, et par des expressions énergiques'.[72] The specifically Romantic conception of his realism was formulated only later, in the 1850's and 1860's, by writers who no longer considered the overwhelming actuality of his figures a product of sincerity or mere skill, but rather an expression, through the deliberate choice of plebeian types as models, of an unidealized, even brutal naturalism that was congenial to their own taste. Baudelaire's image of the sculptor, 'qui sus ramasser la beauté des goujats', and Michelet's image of the *Cariatides*, 'où l'on croit reconnaître les saints forçats de la Révocation', have already been mentioned.[73] The same sentiment led a poet of Toulon to link the *Cariatides* with the humble origin and democratic spirit of Puget himself:

> C'est que, né dans le peuple et lui restant fidèle,
> L'artiste qui signa ce groupe colossal
> S'inspira des tanqueurs et fit, sur leur modèle,
> De la réalité jaillir son idéal.[74]

On the stylistic level, too, an athletic figure like the *Hercule Gaulois* was for Lagrange and others a triumph of purely naturalistic representation, despite its mythological title: 'Pugent l'a pris tout vivant dans la nature réelle, sans se préoccuper de distinction ni de style; il a choisi l'homme qui lui représentait le mieux un homme fort, il l'a copié avec amour, et le seul idéal qu'il ait mêlé à cette reproduction fidèle, c'est l'esprit de la vie.'[75] Yet these attitudes, typical of the egalitarian and realistic tendencies of the Romantic period, were not shared by Théophile Thoré, the one writer on Puget who believed that art should express the intimate sentiments of common people rather than abstract ideals. For Thoré his sculpture was impressive in its intensity and powerful naturalism, but outmoded in its mythological content: 'Sous ce rapport, nous oserons dire que l'art du Puget est un art incomplêt et arriéré, puisqu'il ne satisfait pas les exigences spiritualistes de notre temps.'[76]

Thoré's was not the only negative comment on Puget, even in this period of his greatest renown. On the contrary, some of the most astute critics, including those who had praised him highly in the 1830's, became sharply critical of certain aspects of his work in the 1850's as their own positions changed; and nothing demonstrates more clearly the problematic status of the High Baroque style in France than these unexpected reversals.[77] This is particularly true of Planche, who became more conservative and dogmatic during these years and, while still appreciative of Puget's independent spirit, far more dissatisfied with his faults of composition and excessively pictorial effects. Whereas in 1831 he had only touched on the poor proportions of the *Persée Délivrant Andromède*, in 1852 he dwelled at length on such features of the *Milon de Crotone* as 'la draperie que rien ne motive et qui ressemble à un chiffon oublié sur une haie' and 'le corps même de l'athlète, qui ne présente qu'un seul côté satisfaisant', concluding that in this respect Puget 'eût agi plus sagement en suivant les conseils de l'antiquité'.[78] This familiar neo-classical stricture, to which Stendhal had wittily replied, apropos the relief in Marseilles of *La Peste de Milan*, 'Ce bas-relief est un tableau, comme nos tableaux modernes sont des bas-reliefs',[79] was also revived, perhaps more surprisingly, by Delacroix. Discussing the inherent limitations of painting and sculpture, itself a traditional theme, in an article published in 1857, he maintained that 'toutes les fois que la sculpture a essayé de présenter avec un certain mouvement ces images interdites, à cause de leur expression trop véhémente, elle a produit des ouvrages monstrueux, plus voisins du ridicule que du sublime', and he cited Puget's relief *Le Rencontre d'Alexandre et de Diogène* as 'un exemple signalé de ce ridicule et de cette impuissance'.[80] In the following year Delacroix took up in his journal the equally familiar issues of Puget's poor composition and lack of nobility: 'Des parties merveilleuses, ... mais point d'ensemble: des défaillances à chaque pas, des parties défectueuses assemblées à grand'peine, l'ignoble, le commun à chaque pas.'[81] It was perhaps only in

---

72. Lenoir, *op. cit.*, p. 78. On Stendhal's aesthetic in relation to that of the Revolution see P. Martino, *Stendhal*, Paris, 1934, pp. 72–86.

73. See above, notes 61 and 48, respectively. As early as 1848 Philippe de Chennevières, one of the future editors of the *Archives de l'Art Français*, wrote an historical tale describing Puget's use of a Norman peasant girl as a model for his statue of *Cybèle* at Le Vaudreuil: 'Suzanne, ou la terre normande; épisode d'un séjour de Pierre-Paul Puget au Château du Vaudreuil, en 1660', *Revue de Rouen et de Normandie*, XVI, 1848, pp. 5–21.

74. See above, note 37. Legends of Puget's youthful poverty and genius were current since the eighteenth century; see Bougerel, *op. cit.*, pp. 1–8, among others.

75. Lagrange, *op. cit.*, 1868, pp. 62–63; elsewhere, however, he criticizes the banality which accompanies this naturalism.

76. Thoré, *op. cit.*, p. 40. On his social conception of art see P. Grate, *Deux critiques d'art de l'époque romantique: Gustave Planche et Théophile Thoré*, Stockholm, 1959, pp. 151–60.

77. This is the more remarkable in that they occurred in a period of essentially neo-baroque character; see K. Scheffler, *Verwandlungen des Barocks in der Kunst des Neunzehnten Jahrhunderts*, Vienna, 1947, pp. 96–132.

78. Planche, *op. cit.*, 1852, pp. 796–7; cf. Planche, *op. cit.*, 1831, p. 106. On the development of his thought see Grate, *op. cit.*, pp. 130–5.

79. Stendhal, *op. cit.*, III, pp. 236–7, entry of 1838.

80. E. Delacroix, 'Des variations du beau', *Revue des Deux Mondes*, July 15, 1857; reprinted in his *Œuvres littéraires*, I, p. 49.

81. Delacroix, *Journal*, III, p. 173, entry of February 23, 1858; cf. the similar remarks in II, p. 283, and III, p. 303, entries of October 4, 1854 and August 6, 1860, respectively.

France, where classicism remained the national ideal in taste, that the leading figure in Romanticism could agree so well with a doctrinaire neo-classicist like Quatremère de Quincy in this judgement of Puget's sculpture.

*   *   *

That the extraordinary increase in interest in Puget's art and life in the second third of the nineteenth century was a product of specifically Romantic attitudes, rather than of the general expansion of art history, is suggested by the almost equally radical decrease in interest after about 1870. He was, of course, respected as a major artist of the national school, and was well represented in both the Louvre and the collections of casts in the Palais du Trocadéro and the Ecole des Beaux-Arts,[82] where students copied the torso of the *Milon de Crotone* as they would the Belvedere Torso. Typical of these copies in its anatomical realism and careful articulation of planes is a charcoal drawing of the *Milon* cast made by the young Seurat around 1878 (Fig. 4), when he was a student at the Ecole des Beaux-Arts.[83] Nevertheless, Puget was no longer the important influence on contemporary sculpture that he had been earlier: characteristically, Dalou turned to the Rococo tradition, and Carpeaux, whose cult of Michelangelo might have led him to Puget, also preferred in French sculpture the lighter, more graceful style of the eighteenth century. Even Rodin, who later spoke in typically Romantic terms of Puget's 'indescribable abnegation, . . . a consolation, as well as a sorrow to every true artist', and admired his 'fine perfection of form', was actually inspired by the Baroque sculptor only in his early decorative figures for a building in Brussels, which were based on the Toulon *Cariatides*.[84] His subsequent work sometimes suggested similarities, as Rodin himself once recognized, but these were coincidental.[85] Nor did Renoir and Degas, the most interesting sculptors in the

Impressionist movement, reveal an admiration for Puget in their work or writings, although both of them were deeply absorbed by the study of older art.[85a] More significant than Rodin's few remarks, but also more exceptional in the period of Impressionism, was Cézanne's sustained interest in drawing after Puget's statues in the Louvre and the Palais du Trocadéro. Together with an *Amour* then attributed to Puget, of which he owned a cast, they were models for one-quarter of all his copies after sculpture, not only in his early Baroque phase where they would be expected, but throughout his classical one in the 1880's and 1890's.[86] Indeed, as late as 1899, while painting his almost archaically frontal and symmetrical portrait of Vollard, Cézanne drew often after the *Milon de Crotone*, the *Hercule Gaulois*, and casts of the *Cariatides*. Although his interest was undoubtedly in the exercise of drawing as such—'Il prétend être ainsi tout disposé à bien *voir* le lendemain', Maurice Denis reported in his journal at the time[87]—it is remarkable that Cézanne should have chosen these works, perhaps the most extreme examples of High Baroque sculpture available in Paris, as his models. That his response to them was not simply formal, as is usually maintained, is evident from his copies themselves (e.g. Fig. 6), where the graphic style is bold and emphatic and the viewpoint chosen is one that seizes the most pathetic aspect of the figures.[88] Ultimately, then, the dramatic content of Puget's figures and the vigorous style in which they were carved were as inseparable for Cézanne as they had been for the Romantic writers, and nourished a taste similar to theirs. His profound admiration for Delacroix and Baudelaire, both of whom had stressed these elements in Puget's art, is well known. The poem 'Les Phares', from which the stanza on Puget has already been quoted, was in fact one of Cézanne's favorites in *Les Fleurs du Mal*.[89] However, the specifically Provençal aspect of Puget, to which he returned more than once in conversations reported by Joachim Gasquet, probably also appealed to the painter who, despite his frequent contacts with Parisian culture,

82. See Musée de Sculpture Comparée, *Catalogue des moulages de sculptures*, Paris, 1890, pp. 85–87; and Ecole Nationale et Spéciale des Beaux-Arts, *Catalogue des moulages*, Paris, 1881, p. 175.

83. See R. Herbert, *Seurat's Drawings*, New York, 1962, pp. 45–46. The torso of the *Milon* had in fact been one of the accepted models in the academy from the early nineteenth century on; see the *Archives du Musée des Monuments Français* cited above, note 24, III, p. 206.

84. For Rodin's statements see T. H. Bartlett, 'Auguste Rodin—IX', *The American Architect and Building News*, xxv, 1889, p. 262; on his early caryatids, A. Elsen, *Rodin*, New York, 1963, pp. 15–16 and 206.

85. On the resemblance between his *Adam* and Puget's *Faune* in the Marseilles museum, acknowledged by Rodin in a letter of 1878, see J. Cladel, *Rodin*, English trans., New York, 1937, pp. 69–70. According to Elsen, *op. cit.*, pp. 49–50, a more direct source was Michelangelo's *Pietà* in the Cathedral of Florence.

85a. Degas did, however, admire the bravado in Puget's famous boast to Louvois, to which he alluded in a letter of *c.* 1885 to the sculptor Bartholomé: 'Certainement le marbre tremblera devant nous . . . ' (unpublished; coll. David Daniels, New York).

86. See G. Berthold, *Cézanne und die alten Meister*, Stuttgart, 1958, catalogue, nos. 96–142; and L. Venturi, *Cézanne, son art —son œuvre*, Paris, 1936, nos. 1081–4 and 1608–9.

87. M. Denis, *Journal*, Paris, 1957, I, p. 157, entry of October 21, 1899. Cf. the similar account by Ambroise Vollard, who was then posing for his portrait: *Paul Cézanne*, Paris, 1914, p. 94.

88. See Berthold, *op. cit.*, nos. 100, 102–5, and 107 for copies of the *Milon de Crotone* probably done at this time, and nos. 127–30 and 108–13 for those of the *Cariatides* and *Hercule Gaulois*.

89. See L. Larguier, *Le Dimanche avec Paul Cézanne*, Paris, 1925, p. 147; also P. Cézanne, *Correspondance*, ed. J. Rewald, Paris, 1937, pp. 260 and 290.

remained deeply attached to that of his native Provence.[90]

Yet Cézanne's friend Zola, who was also raised in Aix-en-Provence, evidently did not share his interest in Puget, for there is no mention of the latter in his art criticism, his correspondence, or his novel of artistic life, *L'Œuvre*. This is the more remarkable in that Zola's novels of the 1860's, like Cézanne's early pictures, reveal a fascination with the passionate and the tragic, expressed in a starkly realistic manner, that is close to Puget's own.[91] Nor did any of Zola's colleagues in the circle of Naturalism—Flaubert, the Goncourt brothers, and Huysmans, all of whom were concerned with the visual arts—show any interest in Puget, unlike their counterparts in the Romantic period.[92] On the contrary, in 1903 Gustave Geffroy, the most active art critic in the group, severely criticized Puget's works in the Louvre in terms reminiscent of neo-classicism. He found the *Hercule Gaulois* vulgar, the *Milon de Crotone* exaggerated and artificial, the *Persée Délivrant Andromède* poorly proportioned and unintelligible, and in general believed that Puget 'n'a pas le même goût, la même mesure, la même force contenue que Coysevox. Il a subi les décadents italiens plus que l'antique'.[93] It is ironic to recall that for Stendhal, who was a much less conscious naturalist than Geffroy, Puget was 'admirable parce qu'il est naturel'.

Geffroy's conception of Puget as a product of the decadent Italian Baroque, whereas his contemporary Coysevox was an embodiment of the best national tradition, 'un grand artiste [en qui] le sentiment de la Renaissance est resté, ... très noble, très fin',[94] is characteristic of what had become the dominant position in later nineteenth-century criticism. Twenty years earlier Henry Jouin, a distinguished historian and member of the Académie des Beaux-Arts, had made precisely the same comparison: 'Tandis que Puget s'est instruit en Italie, à une époque de décadence, et que sa fougue l'a conduit à outrer les

défauts de ses initiateurs, Coysevox, sans violence, s'est arrêté devant la nature.'[95] Inevitably, this negative judgement was supported by the familiar arguments: 'De la méthode, Puget n'en a pas. La nature dans l'harmonie de ses lignes ne l'a pas frappé ... le Milon nous émeut, mais Puget s'y montre incorrect et indiscipliné, non moins peintre que sculpteur.'[96] Implicit in Jouin's celebration of Coysevox as the supreme national sculptor, at the expense of Puget, was a decisive shift in taste since the 1850's, when Gautier had declared the latter 'l'artiste le plus franchement français dont nous puissions nous glorifier'. It led ultimately to a rejection of the official position of the Romantic period, when Puget's bust had been placed beside Poussin's at the entrance to the Ecole des Beaux-Arts. In his famous 'Leçons' given at the Ecole du Louvre, Louis Courajod, curator of sculpture there, admonished his audience in 1893: 'Ne croyez pas ce que semblent vous dire les deux bustes à l'antique, à la fois rébarbatifs et débonnaires, qui se dressent rue Bonaparte.... Si grands que soient les noms de Poussin et de Puget, ces artistes sont de faux parrains, de faux patrons de l'école française, j'entends de l'école vraiment nationale.'[97] In this view, which was typical of the neo-classical reaction of the 1890's in its emphasis on the pure French tradition, Puget represented a completely Italianate style, 'plus Berninesque que le Bernin lui-même', although of course 'meilleur que tout ce qu'a pu produire l'Italie coalisée et repliée sur elle-même'.[98]

In the decades preceding this reaction, however, several writers no less influential than Courajod and Jouin had praised Puget highly. Thus Eugène Guillaume, a professor at the Collège de France and former director of the Ecole des Beaux-Arts, ranked him historically with the very greatest sculptors, Phidias and Michelangelo: 'Tous trois sont supérieurs par la science, par la grandeur et par l'expression de la vie. Tous trois sont la manifestation la plus haute de leur art à des époques qui marquent parmi les plus grandes de l'histoire.'[99] And Paul Lenoir, a widely read aesthetician of the 1880's, considered him the major figure in the

90. See J. Gasquet, *Cézanne*, Paris, 1926, pp. 191–2. The language is obviously Gasquet's, but the sentiment may well be Cézanne's.

91. This was also observed by A. E. Brinckmann, 'Ein unbekannten Bozetto von Pierre Puget', *Zeitschrift für Bildenden Kunst*, LIX, 1925–6, p. 319.

92. The same is true of the Symbolist art critics of the following generation—Fénéon, Kahn, and de Wyzewa—although Kahn later admired 'the vehement contortions of Puget and the powerful modelling of his colossal figures'; see G. Kahn, *Auguste Rodin*, English trans., London, n.d. [1909], p. 24.

93. G. Geffroy, *La Sculpture au Louvre*, Paris, n.d. [1903], pp. 129–30. Cf. also his somewhat more favorable remarks in 'La Salle Puget', *La Vie artistique*, 6ᵉ sér., Paris, 1900, pp. 29–35.

94. Geffroy, *op. cit.*, 1903, pp. 128–9. On his art criticism see R. T. Denommé, *The Naturalism of Gustave Geffroy*, Geneva, 1963, pp. 169–202.

95. H. Jouin, *Antoine Coysevox, sa vie, son œuvre, et ses contemporains*, Paris, 1883, pp. 84–85.

96. *Ibid.*, pp. 172–4. Cf. also the comparison of Puget and Coysevox in L. Gonse, *La Sculpture française depuis le XIVᵉ siècle*, Paris, 1895, p. 189.

97. L. Courajod, *Leçons professées à l'Ecole du Louvre*, ed. H. Lemonnier and A. Michel, Paris, 1903, III, p. 42, lecture of 1893.

98. *Ibid.*, p. 43. On the reactionary classicism of the 1890's see T. Reff, 'Cézanne and Poussin', *Journal of the Warburg and Courtauld Institutes*, XXIII, 1960, pp. 164–7.

99. E. Guillaume, 'Michel-Ange, sculpteur', in *L'Œuvre et la vie de Michel-Ange*, Paris, 1876, p. 112; reprinted in his *Etudes d'art antique et moderne*, Paris, 1888, pp. 104–5.

development of realism in French sculpture: 'La force et le mouvement, le feu, la vérité, l'expression réaliste enfin sont les qualités maîtresses de Puget. Nous lui devons ainsi leur apparition dans la sculpture française.'[100] It was even possible to appreciate the classical aspects of his art, at least in his drawings, which were now studied with increased interest. 'Le fougueux tailleur de marbres était un dessinateur des plus corrects et des plus soigneux', wrote Clément de Ris in 1880. 'Ses dessins sont tracés avec une délicatesse, une préciosité, une correction surprenantes.'[101] Yet these isolated statements, although indicative of an enduring admiration for Puget, are hardly equivalent to the fascination he had held, both as an artist and as a man, for the Romantic imagination.

The scholarly investigation of Puget's work, begun in the 1850's, also continued throughout the later nineteenth century, but not unaffected by the general decline in his reputation; for it was undertaken almost exclusively by Provençal historians inspired by local patriotism. The numerous archival and biographical studies of his activities in Toulon, published by Octave Teissier in the 1870's and by Charles Ginoux in the following decades,[102] are characteristic of this return to a regional attitude reminiscent of the 'Eloges' submitted to the Marseilles academy at the beginning of the century. The one exception by a famous critic, Ernest Chesneau's small monograph, was written for a popular audience and contributed nothing new.[103] In the late 1890's, too, the revival of interest in Provençal culture, well known in the history of French literature, resulted in the establishment of a Salle de Puget in the Marseilles museum, which was soon filled with casts of his statues in Paris and Genoa and a few original pieces.[104] 'Après deux siècles d'oubli', wrote the conservator of this museum in 1908, and eighty years after a similar gallery was inaugurated in the Louvre, 'Marseille rend enfin au plus glorieux de ses fils l'hommage qui lui était dû.'[105] At the same time a new monument in Puget's honor, replacing the unsuccessful one that had been erected in the 1850's and later removed, was placed in the center of the city.[106] But for many years thereafter his sculpture itself remained, like his statue in Marseilles, more an object of local pride than of authentic interest.

100. P. Lenoir, *Histoire du réalisme et du naturalisme dans la poésie et dans l'art*, Paris, 1889, pp. 663–4.
101. L. Clément de Ris, 'Exposition des dessins d'ornement au Musée des Arts Décoratifs', *Gazette des Beaux-Arts*, 2e sér., XXII, 1880, pp. 15–16. Cf. also P. de Chennevières, 'Les Dessins des maîtres anciens exposés à l'Ecole des Beaux-Arts', *ibid.*, xx, 1879, p. 133.
102. O. Teissier: *Documents inédits sur Pierre Puget*, 1871; *Histoire des agrandissements et des fortifications de Toulon*, 1873; etc. C. Ginoux: *Les Arts du dessin de l'école de Puget à Toulon*, 1881; *Notice historique sur les portiques et les cariatides de Pierre Puget*, 1886; etc.

103. E. Chesneau, *Pierre Puget* (Bibliothèque des Ecoles et des Familles), Paris, 1882; he relies heavily on Lagrange's monograph and stresses the idea, also typical of the 1860's, of 'les grandes qualités de puissance, de force, d'émotion, la vie énergique que l'artiste a su imprimer à son œuvre tout entière' (*ibid.*, p. 12). More important, but inspired by a purely local, antiquarian interest, was the article by G. Le Breton, 'L'Hercule de Puget au Musée de Rouen', *Gazette des Beaux-Arts*, 2e sér., XXXVII, 1888, pp. 224–41.
104. On the Salle de Puget see P. Auquier, *Pierre Puget, son œuvre à Marseille*, Marseilles, 1908, pp. 7–18; on the Provençal revival, M. Reymond, *De Baudelaire au Surréalisme*, Paris, 1952, pp. 89–97.
105. Auquier, *op. cit.*, 1908, p. 7.
106. See above, note 38. I owe the photograph reproduced in Fig. 3 to my colleague, Albert Boime.

ILLUSTRATIONS

1. 'Carrey' Drawing of the Right Half of the West Pediment

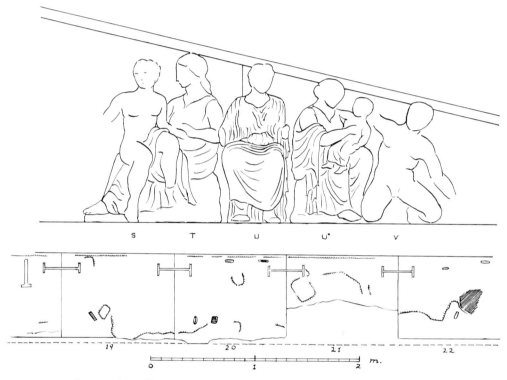

2. Restoration of West Pediment Figures S–V. Floor Marks after Carpenter

3. Statuettes from Eleusis, Casts

4. Acropolis 1363, Right Side   5. Acropolis 1363, Left Side

6. Acropolis 1363, Front   7. Fragment in British Museum, Smith 12

8. Statuette from Eleusis in Athens, N. M. 201

9. Statuette from Eleusis, N. M. 202

10–11. Statuette from Eleusis, N. M. 202

12–13. Fragment in Eleusis with Cast of N.M. 201

14–15. Fragment in Eleusis with Cast of N.M. 201

16. Acropolis 888, Right Side

17. Acropolis 888, Front

18. Statuette in the Athenian Agora, S 289

19. Statuette in the Athenian Agora, S 1429

1. Engraving of fresco: *Birth of Venus*. Formerly Celian Hill, Rome

2. Mosaic: *Birth of Venus*. Sétif

3. Mosaic: *Birth of Venus*. Ostia

4. Mosaic: *Birth of Venus*. Bulla Regia

5. Mosaic: *Birth of Venus*, from Carthage.
Tunis, Musée Alaoui

6. Fresco: *Birth of Venus*. Pompeii

7. Mosaic Fountain: *Birth of Venus*. Pompeii

8. Sarcophagus. Rome, Galleria Borghese

9. Sarcophagus. Paris, Louvre

10. Sarcophagus. Rome, Lateran Collection

11. The Projecta casket. London, British Museum

12. Silver patera. Paris,
Palais des Beaux-Arts

13. Mosaic from El-Djem. Susa, Museum

14. Mosaic from Hemsworth.
London, British Museum

15. Silver handle from Bourdonneau. Paris, Louvre

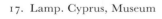

16. Gem.
Berlin, Museum

17. Lamp. Cyprus, Museum

19. Coptic relief, from Ahnâs. Cairo,
Coptic Museum

20. Ivory diptych. Sens,
Cathedral Treasury

18. Coptic relief, from Ahnâs. Cairo, Coptic Museum

21. Gold and lapis pendant.
Washington, D.C., Dumbarton Oaks Collection

1. Hrabanus Maurus, *De universo*, XV, 6 (*De diis gentium*):
Vulcan, Pluto, Bacchus, Mercury. Montecassino, Cod. 132, p. 386

2. Hrabanus Maurus, *De universo*, XV, 6 (*De diis gentium*):
Vulcan, Pluto, Bacchus, Mercury. Vatican Library, Cod. Pal. lat. 291,
fol. 190, right-hand column

4. Hrabanus Maurus, *De universo*, XX, 36 (*De theatro*): *Decapitation Scene*.
Montecassino, Cod. 132, p. 489

3. Hrabanus Maurus, *De universo*, XX, 36 (*De theatro*):
Decapitation Scene. Destroyed miniature originally belonging to
Berlin, Staatsbibliothek, Cod. fol. lat. 930

5. Hrabanus Maurus, *De universo*, XX, 36 (*De theatro*):
Decapitation Scene. Vatican Library, Cod. Pal. lat. 291
(here XX, 35), fol. 248 v.

6. Hrabanus Maurus, *De universo*,
VII, 2 (*De portentis*): *Fifteen Species
of Monsters*. Montecassino,
Cod. 132, p. 166

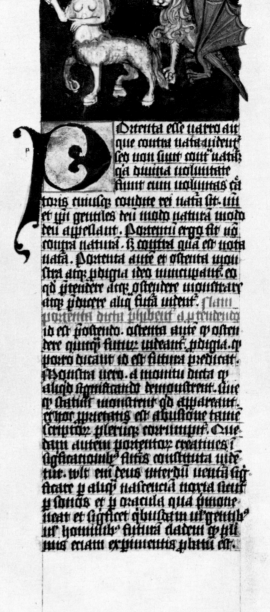

7. Hrabanus Maurus, *De universo*, VII, 2 (*De portentis*): *Fourteen Species of Monsters.*
Vatican Library, Cod. Pal. lat. 291, fol. 75 v.

8. Hrabanus Maurus, *De universo*, XV, 6 (*De diis gentium*): *Hercules, Mars, Apollo.*
Montecassino, Cod. 132, p. 387

9. Hrabanus Maurus, *De universo*, XV, 6 (*De diis gentium*):
Hercules, Mars, Apollo Medicus, Apollo Sagittarius.
Vatican Library, Cod. Pal. lat. 291, fol. 190 v.

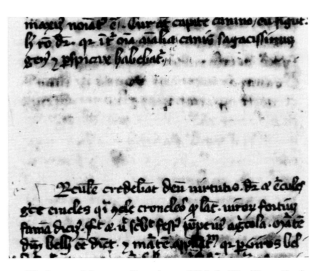

10. Hrabanus Maurus, *De universo*, XV, 6 (*De diis gentium*):
Space intended for a miniature showing Hercules,
Mars and Apollo; below, the text referring to Hercules.
Vatican Library, Cod. Reg. lat. 391, fol. 111

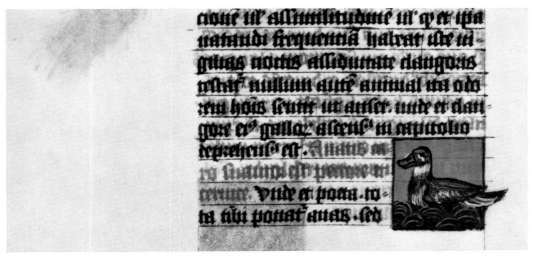

11. Hrabanus Maurus, *De universo*, VIII, 6 (*De avibus*): *Duck.* Vatican Library, Cod. Pal. lat. 291,
fol. 102 v., left-hand column

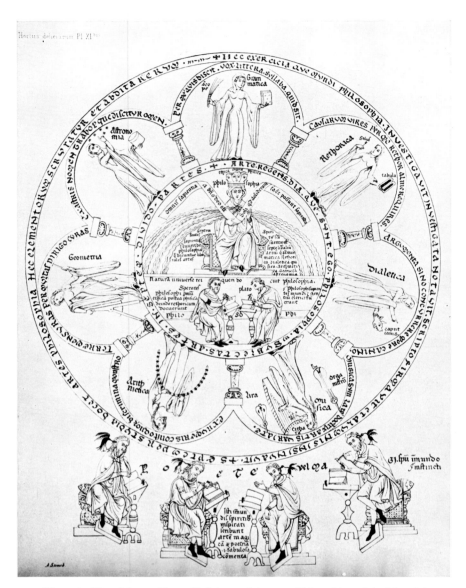

1. Herrad of Landsberg, *Hortus Deliciarum*, fol. 32 r.: *Philosophia and the Liberal Arts*

2. Herrad of Landsberg, *Hortus Deliciarum*, fol. 31 r.:
The Nine Muses

3. Roman sarcophagus: *The Nine Muses*. Paris, Louvre

4. Roman sarcophagus: *Socrates and Sophia*. Paris, Louvre

5. Roman sarcophagus: *Homer and Poiesis*. Paris, Louvre

6. Roman sarcophagus: *Couple with six Sages and eight Muses*. Rome, Villa Torlonia

7. Roman sarcophagus: *Philosopher with Sophia*. Rome, Lateran Museum

8. German tapestry: *The Wedding of Mercury and Philologia*. Quedlinburg

9. German woodcut: *Theologia, Petrus Lombardus and the Liberal Arts*

10. Roman mosaic: *The Nine Muses*. Trier, Landesmuseum   11. Monnus Mosaic. Trier, Landesmuseum

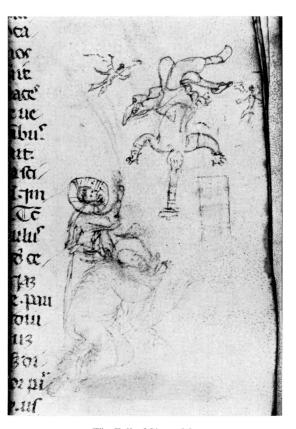

1. *SS. Peter and Paul before Nero*.
Turin, Biblioteca Nazionale, I. II. 17, fol. 156v

2. *The Fall of Simon Magus*.
Turin, Biblioteca Nazionale, I. II. 17, fol. 159

3. *SS. Peter and Paul before Nero, and the Fall of Simon Magus*. Monreale, Cathedral

4. *SS. Peter and Paul before Nero*. Palermo, Cappella Palatina

5. *The Fall of Simon Magus.*
Palermo, Cappella Palatina (Courtesy of the
Dumbarton Oaks Center for Byzantine Studies)

6. *St. Benedict and Exhilaratus.*
Biblioteca Vaticana, Vat. lat. 1202, fol. 52v. (detail)

7. *St. Benedict and Exhilaratus.* Turin, Biblioteca Nazionale, I. II. 17, fol. 104v.

8. *St. Benedict and St. Scholastica.* Biblioteca
Vaticana, Vat. lat. 1202, fol. 72v. (detail)

9. *St. Benedict and St. Scholastica.*
Turin, Biblioteca Nazionale, I. II. 17, fol. 108

11. *The Fire in the monastery kitchen.*
Turin, Biblioteca Nazionale, I. II. 17,
fol. 103

10. *St. Benedict and King Totila.* Biblioteca Vaticana, Vat. lat. 1202, fol. 44

1. *Image of Pity*, with silver frame. Rome, Sta. Croce in Gerusalemme

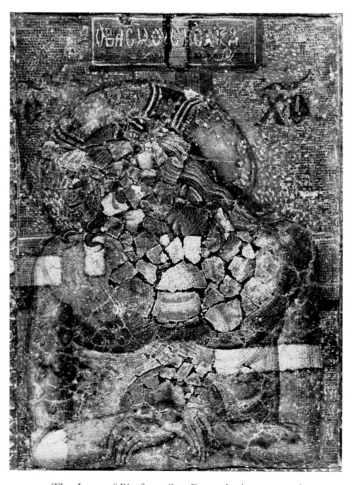

2. *Image of Pity*. Byzantine, early fourteenth century.
Rome, Sta. Croce in Gerusalemme

3. The *Image of Pity* from Sta. Croce during restoration
(courtesy Istituto Centrale del Restauro)

4. Reliquary attributed to St. Gregory the Great, open. Rome, Sta. Croce in Gerusalemme

5. Reliquary attributed to St. Gregory the Great, closed.
Rome, Sta. Croce in Gerusalemme

6. The shutters of the reliquary of Sta. Croce,
with their leather cover unfastened

7. *Image of Pity* (*Basileus tes Doxes*), Byzantine, fourteenth century. Tatarna, Evrytania, Monastery of the Genethlion tes Theotokou (courtesy the Byzantine Museum, Athens)

8. *Image of Pity*. London, British Museum (from Campbell Dodgson)

9. *St. Catherine*. Adriatic school, fourteenth century, painted on the back of the mosaic icon in Sta. Croce

10. Icon of St. Theodore. Sinai

11. Coat-of-arms
of Raimondello Orsini del Balzo,
from his tomb. Galatina

12. Mosaic icon, Byzantine, late thirteenth century. Galatina

13. Pediment on the main portal of the church of St. Catherine in Galatina,
late fourteenth century

14. *The Virgin*. English, fifteenth century, from Add. MS. 37049, fol. 1 v. London, British Museum

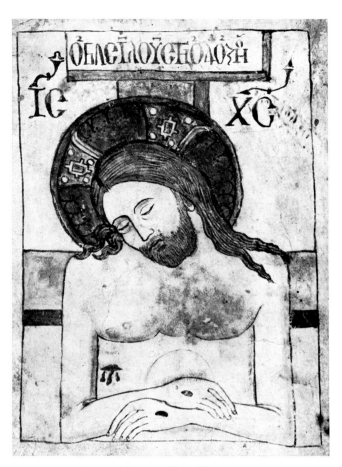

15. *Image of Pity*, English, fifteenth century, from Add. MS 37049, fol. 2 r. London, British Museum

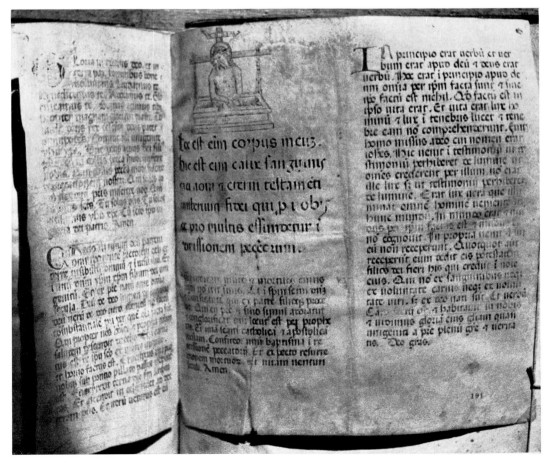

16. Sheet inserted in MS Cas. 1394, fifteenth century. Rome, Biblioteca Casanatense

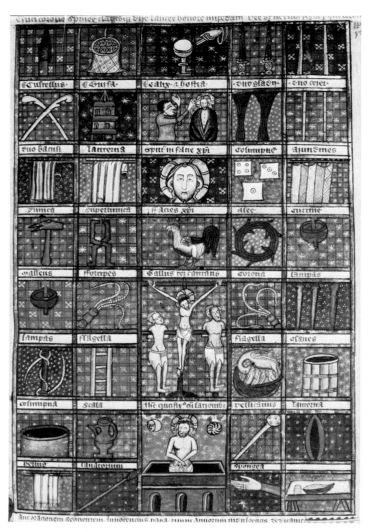

17. *Arma Christi*, English, fourteenth century. Royal MS 6. E. VI, f. 15r.
London, British Museum

18. *The Visions of St. Benedict and of St. Paul*. English,
fourteenth century, Royal MS 6. E. VI, f. 16r.
London, British Museum

19–20. *Benedict XII and the Beatific Vision*. English, fourteenth century. Royal MS 6. E. VI, fol. 16v. London, British Museum

21. E. Charonton: The vision of Moses and the vision of St. Gregory,
detail from the *Crowning of the Virgin*. Villeneuve-les-Avignons
(after G. Ring)

22. *Nota delle Indulgenze*. Parchment, eighteenth century.
Rome, Sta. Croce in Gerusalemme

23. *Nota delle Reliquie*. Parchment, eighteenth century.
Rome, Sta. Croce in Gerusalemme

1. Florentine, c. 1400: *Filippo Balducci and His Son*. Paris, Bibliothèque nationale, ital. 482, fol. 79v.

2. Cité des Dames Workshop: *God as Beginner and as Master Painter*. Vatican Library,
Pal. lat. 1989, fol. 189v.

3. Florentine, 1427: *Andrevuola and Gabriotto*. Paris, Bibliothèque nationale, ital. 63, fol. 150

4. Cité des Dames Workshop: *Androlla and Gabriel*. Vatican Library, Pal. lat. 1989, fol. 136

5. Flemish Master, c. 1440: *Androlla and Gabriel*. Paris, Bibliothèque de l'Arsenal,
MS 5070, fol. 164 v.

6. Cité des Dames Master: *Sire Frosin and Iosse (Giotto)*. Vatican Library, Pal. lat. 1989, fol. 188 v.

7. Cité des Dames Workshop: *Richard and Catelle*. Vatican Library, Pal. lat. 1989, fol. 97

8. Egerton Workshop: *Birth of the Virgin*. London, British Museum, Harley 2897, fol. 385

9. Cité des Dames Master, 1401: *Assumption*. Barcelona, Biblioteca Central, MS 1850, fol. 2

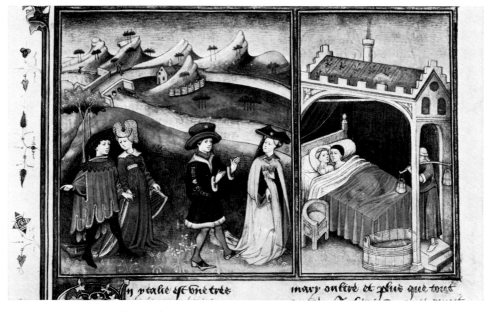

10. Master of Guillebert de Mets: *Richard and Catelle*. Paris, Bibliothèque de l'Arsenal, MS 5070, fol. 116

11. Cité des Dames Workshop, c. 1410: *Cremation of the Wife and Children of Hasdrubal.* Paris, Bibliothèque de l'Arsenal, MS 5193, fol. 218

12. Cité des Dames Workshop: *Régnier and Hélène on Christmas Night.* Vatican Library, Pal. lat. 1989, fol. 242 v.

13. Cité des Dames Workshop: *Battle* in *Chroniques de Normandie.* Vienna, National-Bibliothek, MS 2569, fol. 1

14. Cité des Dames Workshop: *Henry III Watching a Couple in the Snow.* The Hague, Royal Library, MS 72 A 24, fol. 10

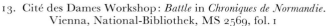

1. *Kneeling Persian*. Aix-en-Provence, Musée des Beaux-Arts

2. *Kneeling Persian*. Rome, Vatican

3. *Adam and Eve*. Chantilly, Musée Condé, 'Très Riches Heures du
Duc de Berry', f. 25 r.

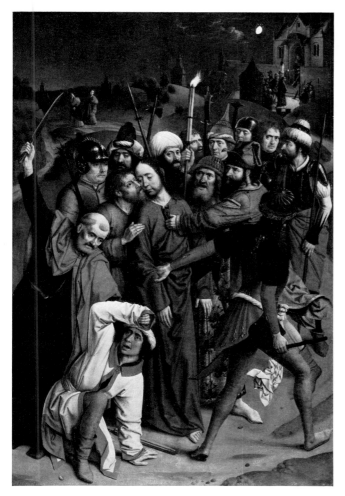

4. Follower of Dierick Bouts: *The Betrayal of Christ.*
Munich, Alte Pinakothek

5. Follower of Dierick Bouts: *The Resurrection of Christ.*
Munich, Alte Pinakothek

6. Etruscan terracotta urn, second century B.C. Perugia, Museo Civico

7. Follower of Fra Angelico: *Detail from the Martyrdom of Saints Cosmas and Damianus.*
Florence, Accademia

8. Etruscan alabaster urn, second century B.C. Florence, Museo Archeologico

9. Antonio Pollaiuolo: *Battle of Nude Men.* Drawing. Windsor Castle, Royal Collection

10. A. Dürer: '*Orpheus*'. Drawing. Hamburg, Kunsthalle

11. A. Dürer: *Christ succumbing under the Cross*. Woodcut from the 'Large Passion', 1498–1499

12. P. Picasso: *Fight in the Arena*. Etching, dated 1937

13. Byzantine mosaic: *Abel assailed by Cain.*
Monreale, Cathedral

14. 'Neville Hours': *The Betrayal of Christ*, c. 1407

15. Tombstone of Dexileos. Detail. Greek, about 394 B.C.
Athens, National Museum

16. Icon: *The Transfiguration of Christ*. Detail. Italo-Byzantine, c. 1600.
Recklinghausen, Ikonen-Museum

17. Giotto: *St. Francis receiving the Stigmata*. Florence, Sta. Croce

18. Pol de Limbourg: *St. John on the island of Patmos*. Chantilly, Musée Condé

1. Coluccio Salutati's script, from a Seneca MS, British Museum, Add. 11987, fol. 12. (XIV Century)

2. Poggio Bracciolini's script, Salutati's *De Verecundia*, Florence, Bibl. Laur. Strozz. 96 fol. 22 v. (1402–03)

3. North Italian, first half of twelfth century, from a MS of St. Gregory's *Dialogues*, Oxford, Bodleian Library, Canonici, Pat. lat. 105, fol. 3 v.

4. Florentine, 1458, from a Lactantius Firminanus MS. Oxford, Bodleian Library, Canonici, Pat. lat. 138, fol. 2 r.

5. The Baptistery, Florence (exterior)

6. The Baptistery, Florence (interior)

7. Window, Palazzo Medici-Riccardi, Florence,
middle of the fifteenth century

8. Window, Palazzo del Podestà (Bargello), Florence,
first half of the fourteenth century

9. *The city of Florence*, from a fresco in the Bigallo, 1352.

10. *The Florentines feeding the Siennese*, from the Biadaiolo MS.
Florence, Bibl. Laur. Cod. Laurenziano Tempiano No. 3 fol. 58 c. 1340

11. *View of the Baptistery*, from a Florentine cassone painting, c. 1430. Florence, Museo Nazionale

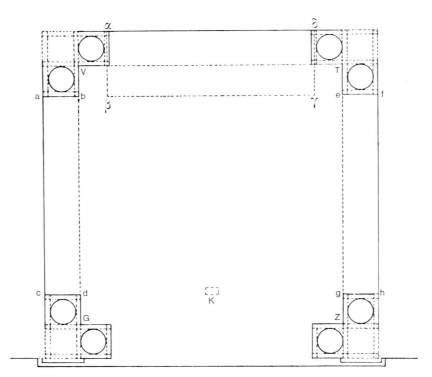

1. Ground Plan of Masaccio's Chapel, from Kern

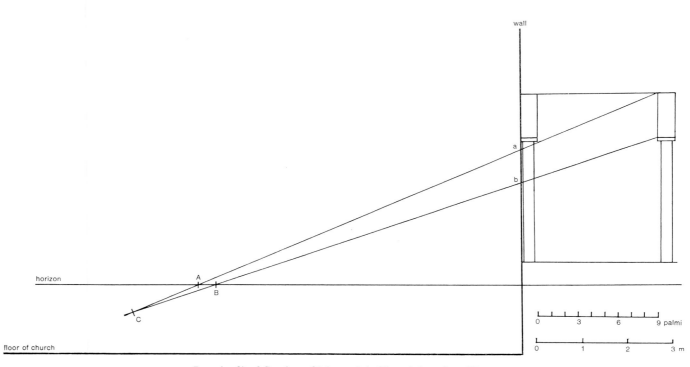

2. Longitudinal Section of Masaccio's Chapel, based on Figure 3

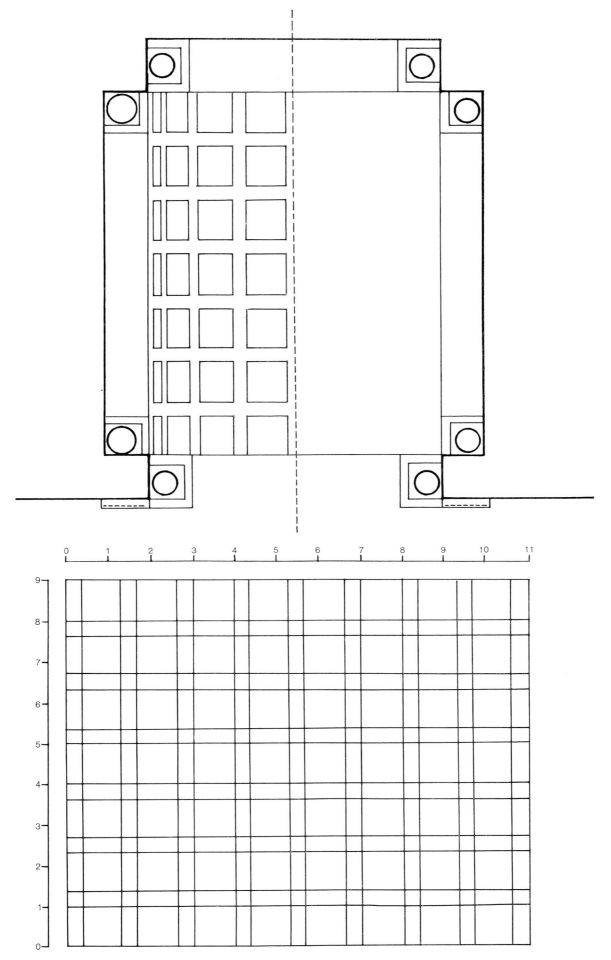

3. Ground Plan of Masaccio's Chapel as here proposed: the scales are calibrated in palmi (29.18 cm.)

4. Grid calibrated in palmi superimposed on Figure 5

5. Masaccio: *The Holy Trinity with Mary, John, two Donors, and a Skeleton*

8. Detail of Figure 5

7. Upper Portion of Figure 5 before restoration, with the lost areas outlined by Leonetto Tintori

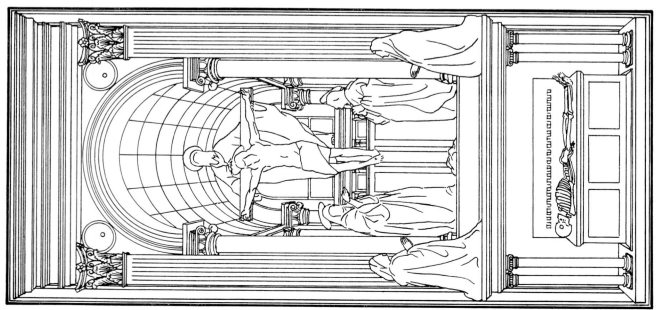

6. Reconstruction of the Original Appearance of Figure 5, from Schlegel

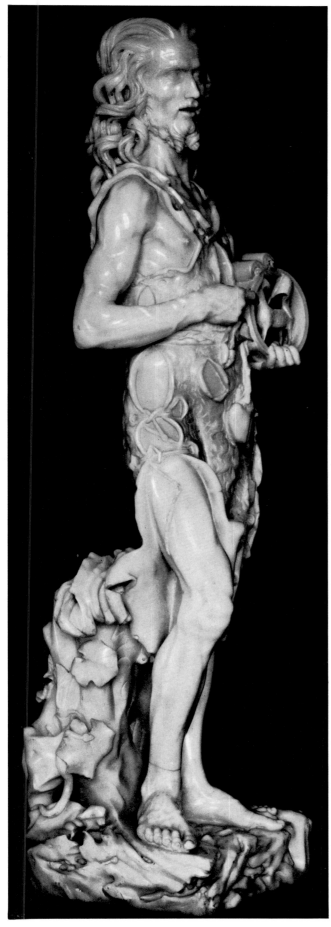

1–2. Niccolò dell'Arca: *St. John the Baptist*. Escorial

3. Niccolò dell'Arca: *St. John the Baptist* (detail). Escorial

1. Giorgio Vasari: Detail from fresco representing the triumphal entry of Leo X into the Piazza della Signoria, Florence, in 1515, showing Bandinelli's colossal Hercules in the Loggia de' Lanzi. Florence, Palazzo Vecchio, Sala del Papa Leone Decimo, 1561

2. Baccio Bandinelli: Pair of Stucco Colossi, before restoration. Rome, Villa Madama. About 1520

1. Niccolò Tribolo: *Sibyl* (here so identified). San Petronio, Bologna. (Photo: Fotofast)

2. Giovanni Pisano: Detail of Pulpit. Sant'Andrea, Pistoia. (Photo: from A. Venturi, *Giovanni Pisano, sein Leben und sein Werk*, 11, Munich, 1907, Plate 77)

3. San Petronio, Bologna. Detail of the Central Portal. (Photo: Beck)

4. Drawing of the Muses Sarcophagus, Villa Medici, Rome. Detail (from Reinach,
Repertoire de Reliefs Grecs et Romains, LL 1, p. 311, 3)

5. Niccolò Tribolo: *Lot Fleeing from Sodom*. Left portal, right pilaster, San Petronio,
Bologna. (Photo: Villani)

6. Jacopo della Quercia: *The Nativity*, detail.
Central Portal of San Petronio, Bologna, (Photo:
Courtesy of Professor Charles Seymour, Jr.)

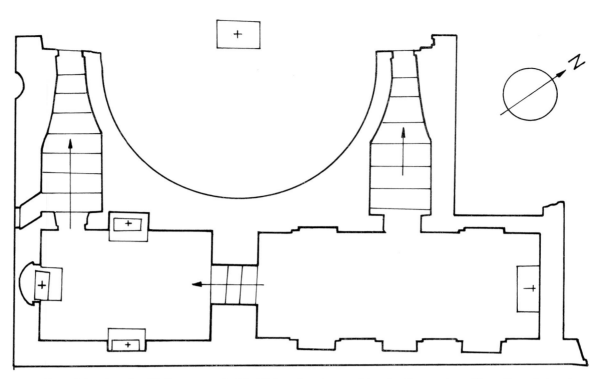

1. Plan of the chapels of S. Gregory and of St. Helen, showing corridors leading to them (from Krautheimer)

2. View of the South corridor

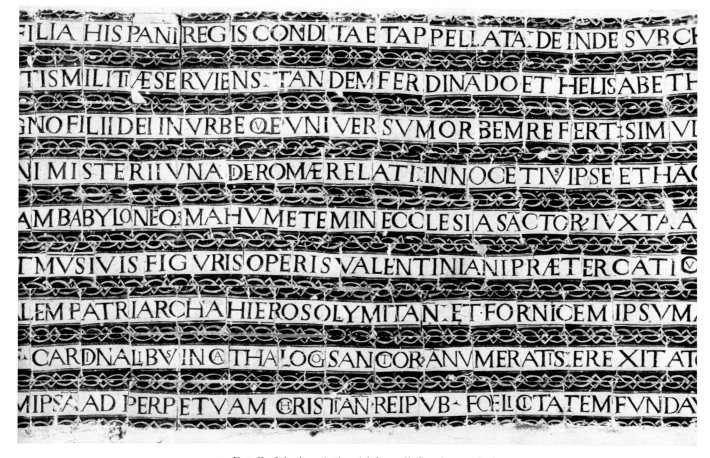

3. Detail of the inscription (right wall, South corridor)

4. The inscription on the entrance to the chapel of St. Helen

1. Michelangelo: *S. Matteo*. Firenze, Accademia

HÆC VISVNTVR ROMÆ, IN HORTO CARD. A VALLE, EIVS BENEFICIO, EX ANTIQVITATIS, RELIQVIIS IBIDEM CONSERVATA

2. Loggia del Palazzo della Valle. Disegno del Cock

3–4. *Busto di Polifemo*. Copia romana da originale ellenistico

5. Gruppo mutilo di *Atamante e Learco*. Copia romana da originale
di Scuola rodia. Disegno del Poelenburg

6. Sebastiano del Piombo (attr.): *Studio di figura*. Parigi, Louvre 716

7. Michelangelo: *Studio di figura*. Firenze, Casa Buonarroti, 69 F recto

Nymphae cuiusdam dormientis simulacrum e marmore mira arte factum, in uiridario
Vaticano Romae quidam, propter adiectum serpentem Cleopatrae imaginem putant.

6

1. G.B. Cavalleri: Engraving after the Fountain (destroyed).
Stanza della Cleopatra (Atrio del Torso), Vatican Palace

2. Daniele da Volterra (?): Lunette landscape. Stanza della Cleopatra (Atrio del Torso), Vatican Palace

3. Decorated pilaster (altered). Stanza della Cleopatra (Atrio del Torso), Vatican Palace

4. View of the ceiling decoration. Stanza della Cleopatra (Atrio del Torso), Vatican Palace

5. Daniele da Volterra: *The Finding of Moses*. Stanza della Cleopatra (Atrio del Torso), Vatican Palace

6. Daniele da Volterra: *The Israelites Crossing the Red Sea*. Stanza della Cleopatra (Atrio del Torso), Vatican Palace

7. Daniele da Volterra: *The Baptism of Christ*. Stanza della Cleopatra (Atrio del Torso), Vatican Palace

8. Daniele da Volterra: *Christ and the Woman of Samaria*. Stanza della Cleopatra (Atrio del Torso), Vatican Palace

9. Daniele da Volterra: *Navicella*. Stanza della Cleopatra (Atrio del Torso), Vatican Palace

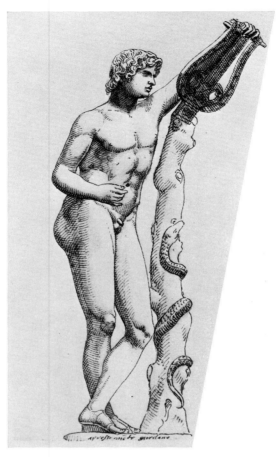

1. *'Apollo' Lisca*. Album of Pierre Jacques, folio 16 (Paris, Bibliothèque nationale)

2. *Satyr statue*. Brussels, Musées royaux du Cinquantenaire (Photo: Courtesy of the Museum)

3. Cavalieri, III–IV, plate 86: *Bacchus* in the Garimberti Collection

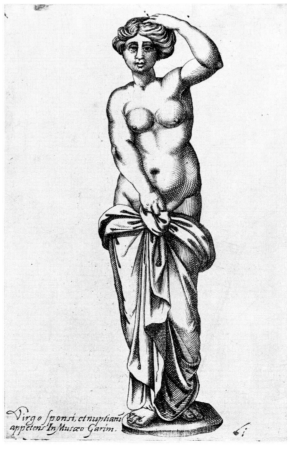

4. Cavalieri, III–IV, plate 73: *Venus* in the Garimberti Collection

5. *Venus statue*. Florence, Uffizi

6. Cavalieri III–IV, plate 54:
Pomona in the Garimberti Collection

7. Cavalieri III–IV, plate 72:
Bacchante in the Garimberti Collection

8. Cavalieri III–IV, plate 62:
'*Hymenaeus*' in the Garimberti Collection

9. Cavalieri III–IV, plate 55:
Cybele in the Garimberti Collection

10. Cavalieri III–IV, plate 21:
Diana

1. Paolo Veronese: *Susannah and the Elders*. Vienna, Kunsthistorisches Museum

2. Paolo Veronese: *The Annunciation*. Florence, Uffizi

3. Paolo Veronese: *The Annunciation*. Venice, SS. Giovanni e Paolo

4. Mantegna: *Virgin and Child with Saints and Angels*. Milan, Castello Sforzesco

5. Paolo Veronese: *The Martyrdom of St. George*. Verona, S. Giorgio in Braida

1. Hans Holbein the Younger: *Erasmus of Rotterdam with the Renaissance Pilaster*. Oil and tempera. Dated 1523 (Courtesy the Earl of Radnor, Longford Castle, near Salisbury). 30 × 20¼ inches (76.2 × 51 cm.). Our photographs, kindly supplied by the National Gallery, were obviously taken prior to the cleaning at an unspecified date.

1 a. Detail of Fig. 1 : the bookshelf

1 b. Detail of Fig. 1 : book and hands

2. Holbein: *William Warham, Archbishop of Canterbury, Aged 70*. Oil and tempera. Dated 1528. Paris, Musée du Louvre. The composition of the figure closely agrees with that of the Longford Castle *Erasmus*

3. *Emperor Marcus Aurelius* (*ca.* A.D. 180). Third-century marble (Courtesy the Ny Carlsberg Glyptotek, Copenhagen, Inv. no. 700). The incarnation of the Stoical ideal of Tranquillity

4. Quentin Matsys: *Erasmus of Rotterdam*. Oil and tempera. Dated 1517. Rome, Palazzo Corsini. The painter interrupted the sittings so that the model could recapture his serene expression. For its counterpart, see Fig. 5

5. Quentin Matsys: *Aegidius*, i.e. *Peter Giles of Antwerp*. Oil and tempera, 1517. Antwerp, Musée des Beaux-Arts. A close variant of the original at Longford Castle, which formed a diptych with the panel in our Fig. 4

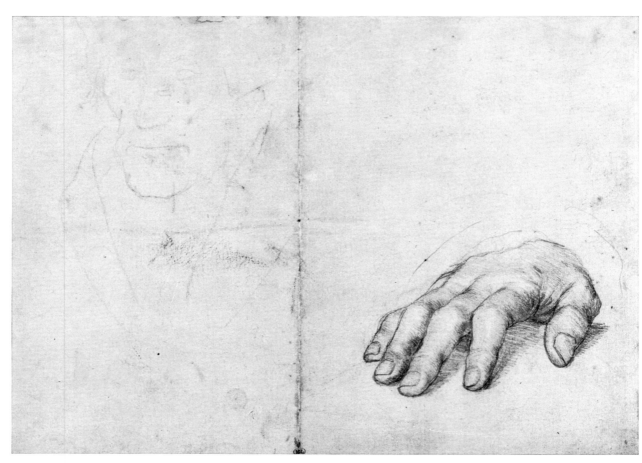

6. Holbein: *Leaf with Two Sketches*. About 1523. (a) Erasmus's right hand of the Longford Castle portrait, done in metal-point with touches of sanguine; (b) the head, in pencil, possibly a compositional design made after the model
(Courtesy Musée du Louvre, Cabinet des Dessins, Inv. no. 18.698)

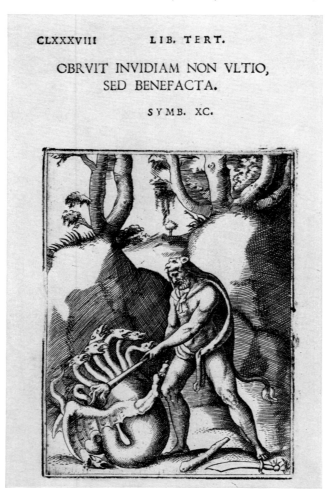

CLXXXVIII   LIB. TERT.

OBRVIT INVIDIAM NON VLTIO,
SED BENEFACTA.

SYMB. XC.

LIB. TERT.   CLXXXIX

VOTVM HERCVLI FERRARIAE DVCI INCLYTO.

SYMB. XC.

Qua fera Lernæi potuit ui colla draconis
   Confeciſſe heros Amphitrioniades?
Dic rogo diua: tui nullo sic tempore fama
   Inclyta diuini nominis intereat.
M. *Tot capitum ille olim haud dubiè exitiabile monſtrum*
   Non ferro, at graio contudit igne magis.
Ignis enim graius medijs quoq; flagrat in undis:
   Igne hoc infelix uritur Inuidia.
Si qua lace ſſierit te iniuria fortè malorum,
   Si ſapis ignem adhibe hunc fortis, & aſſiduus.
Iam nec cede malis, nec te malè ſana cupido
   Vindictæ quicq; diſtrahat. illa Dei eſt.
Nec desiſte tamen benè de quocunq; mereri.
   Perpetuo Inuidia extinguitur officio.

7. Acchille Bocci: 'OBRVIT INVIDIAM NON VLTIO, SED BENEFACTA', *Symbolarum quaestionum*, Bologna, 1555, Bk. III, Symbolum XC, pp. CLXXXVIIIf. One of the comparatively rare instances where, in Renaissance art, the Lernean Hydria is associated with Envy. The two pages are shown in order to illustrate the three elements of a typical Renaissance emblem (here called Symbolum): Motto, Icon, and Epigram. The engraving is by Giulio Bonasone.

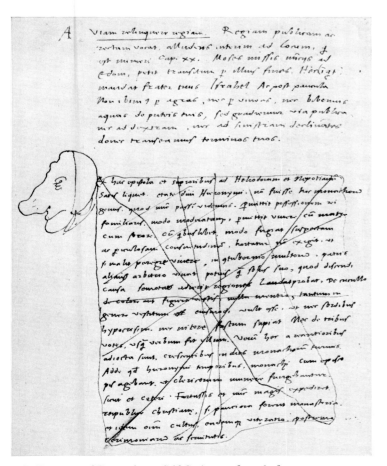

8. Erasmus of Rotterdam: *Self-Caricature*, from before 1524; manuscript draft in a convolute of miscellaneous Erasmus MSS. (Courtesy Basel, Universitätsbibliothek), MS. C. VI. a. 68, p. 146. Considering the fact that the first Self-Caricatures date from about 1600, this and the related sketches are quite remarkable

9. Cesare Cesariano: *Capital of a 'Columna Thuscanica'*, from: Vitruvius, *De architectura*, IV, vii, ed. Como, 1521, fol. LXIII. The woodcut was Holbein's direct source of inspiration for the 'Mermaid-Siren Capital' in the Longford Castle picture

10. Philippus Picinelli: *Mundus symbolicus*, Augsburg, 1687, XII, ii, 20, p. 679. The gold ring with diamond, worn by Erasmus, had powerful apotropaeic virtues. It was a gift of Cardinal Campeggio

11. Holbein: Marginal pen and ink drawing no. 66, inscribed 'Holbein', from: Erasmus, *Stultitiae laus*, ed. Basel, 1515 (Courtesy Kupferstichkabinett, Basel, Inv. no. 1662.166). Almost everyone of Holbein's marginal drawings is a commentary on a specific text or scholium passage of the *Praise of Folly*. Although the inscription is not in the artist's hand, the 'Epicurean pig' may well have been intended as a satirical self-portrait

12. Albrecht Dürer: *St. Jerome in his Study*, engraving dated 1514.
The sixteenth-century *beau idéal* of the scholar in his nest

13. Diagram to demonstrate the significance of the 'Portrait Bust with Parapet'; the Bust, the *effigies* of the Living, serves to preserve the model's appearance; in contrast, the stone parapet may traditionally stand for Death, Decay, Oblivion

14. Pietro Torregiano (?), *Tomb Memorial of Dr. John Colet*. London, St. Paul's Cathedral (destroyed 1666), engraved by Daniel King, 1641. Colet's 'imago ad viuam effigiem' presides as it were over his own cadaver

1. *Portrait of Sir John Luttrell*. Collection of Colonel Walter Luttrell, Dunster Castle

2. *Portrait of Sir John Luttrell* (before restoration). Courtauld Institute Galleries, London

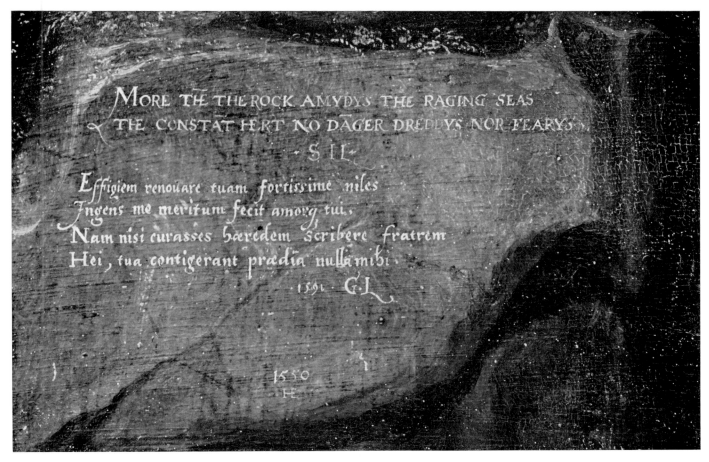

3 (a). The Rock in the Dunster Version

3 (b). The Rock in the Courtauld Version

4. *The Peace Allegory*. Courtauld Version (before restoration)

5 (a). '*Peace*'. School of Fontainebleau. Museum of Aix-en-Provence

5 (b–c). The Canning Jewel. Victoria and Albert Museum, London

6a. Miniature in Peace Treaty between France and England, 1527. Public Record Office, E. 30/1110

6b. Miniature in Peace Treaty between France and England, 1527. Public Record Office, E. 30/1111

7a. Detail of the Ship, Courtauld Version (before restoration)

7b. Detail of the Ship, Courtauld Version (before restoration)

8. *Portrait of Captain Thomas Wyndham.* Collection of the Earl of Radnor, Longford Castle

1. Giovanni Cariani (nach Giorgione?): *Doppelbildnis*. Paris, Louvre

2. Maso di San Friano: *Zwei Architekten*. Rom, Palazzo Venezia

3. *Heinrich Rubenow mit sechs anderen Professoren*. Greifswald, St. Nikolai

4. Adam de Coster (?): *Doppelbildnis*

5. George Desmarées: *Kurfürst Max III. Joseph von Bayern und sein Intendant Graf Seeau.* München, Residenzmuseum

6. Philippe de Champaigne und Nicolas de Platte Montagne: *Selbstbildnisse.* Rotterdam, Museum Boymans-van Beuningen

1. Cavallino: *Esther and Ahasuerus*. Florence, Uffizi

2. Furini: *Antiochus and Stratonice*. Auckland, City Art Gallery

3. Bassano: *Dives and Lazarus*. Detail. Cleveland, Museum of Art

4. Annibale Carracci: *Jupiter and Juno*. Rome, Borghese Gallery

5. Scarsellino: *Diana and Endymion*. Rome, Borghese Gallery

6. Vouet: *The Lovers*. Rome, Galleria Pallavicini

1. Rubens: *Het Pelsken*. Vienna, Kunsthistorisches Museum

2. Rubens School: *Bathseba*. Private collection (?)

3. J. Collaert after Marten de Vos: *Susanna*. Engraving

4. Rubens School: *Venus*. Potsdam

5. Rubens School: *Venus*. Conde de Adanero

6. Rubens: *Venus with a mirror*. Lugano, Thyssen Collection

2. A. Andreani: *Virtue Defeated*. Chiaroscuro woodcut after Ligozzi, 1585.
Munich, Staatliche Graphische Sammlung

1. L. Büsinck: *Virtue Defeated*. Chiaroscuro woodcut after Ligozzi, 1646.
Kassel, Staatliche Kunstsammlungen

4. Federigo Zuccari: *Porta Virtutis*. Drawing, 1580–81. Coll. J. Scholz, New York

3. M. K. Prestel: *Virtue Defeated*. Chiaroscuro aquatint after Ligozzi, 1777. Frankfurt, Städelsches Kunstinstitut

3. P. F. Mola: *Studio per una pala d'altare*

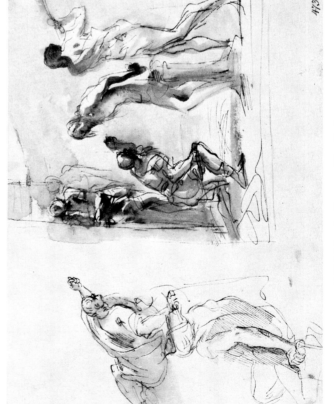

1. P. F. Mola: *Agar e Ismaele*

2. P. F. Mola: *Studi per una Flagellazione*

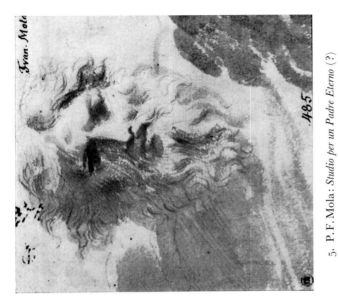

5. P. F. Mola: *Studio per un Padre Eterno* (?)

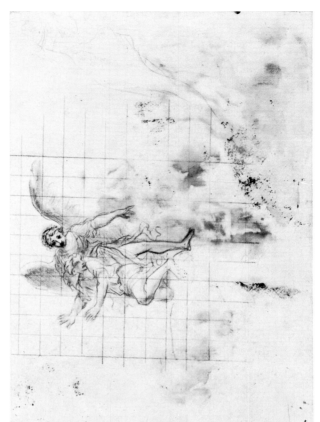

7. P. F. Mola: *Studio per un Tobiolo*

4. P. F. Mola: *Caricature*

6. P. F. Mola: *Scena mitologica*

10. P. F. Mola: *Studio per un Battista*

8. P. F. Mola: *Studio per un 'Battesimo di Cristo'*

9. P. F. Mola: *Studi per ritratti*

14. P.F. Mola: *Studio per la Pala di S. Carlo Corso*

12. P.F. Mola: *Studio di un albero*

11. P.F. Mola: *Studio di alberi*

13. P.F. Mola: *Studio per il 'Giuseppe riconosciuto dai Fratelli'*

1. Poussin: *Self-Portrait*. Detail. Paris, Louvre (photo: Réunion des Musées Nationaux)

2. Rubens and assistants: *Providence*. Lille,
Musée Wicar (photo: A.C.L., Brussels)

3. Errard: Illustration for Leonardo da Vinci, *Trattato della pittura*, 1651.
(Photo: Courtesy Stevens Institute of Technology)

1. *Mercury with scroll*

2. *Onore*

The photographs for Figs. 1–14 have been taken by André Ostier.

3. *Ignoranza*

4. *Donkey's head*. Detail of *Ignoranza*, fig. 3

5. *Scienza*

6. *Pile of books*. Detail of *Scienza*

7. *Distinzione del bene dal male*

8. '*Magnificenza nella libreria*': *Furore and Spia*

9. *Cannon and flask of vinegar*. Detail of *Furore*, see fig. 8

10. *Scandalo*

11. *Cicero in defence of sculpture*

12. *Giacomo Robusti*

13. *Symbolic figure between windows*

14. *Pianta's signature.* Detail from fig. 12

1. Bernini: *Ecstasy of St. Teresa*. Cappella Cornaro, S. Maria della Vittoria

2. Bernini: *Study of Head of St. Teresa.* Leipzig
(from Brauer-Wittkower, Tafel 24 a)

3. Bernini: *Drapery study for St. Teresa.* Leipzig
(from Brauer-Wittkower, Tafel 24 b)

4. Montage of Figs. 2 and 3

6. Bernini, *St. Sebastian*. Lugano, Thyssen Collection

5. *Ecstasy of S. Francesco*. Cappella Raimondi, S. Pietro in Montorio

2. Bernini: *Design for the tomb of a Doge.* London, Sir Anthony Blunt

1. Bernini: *Sketch for the Tomb of Countess Matilda.* Brussels, Musée des Beaux-Arts

1. E. Tesauro, C. Morello, B. Botto: *Intagli;* dipinti di Dufour, B. Caravoglia e A. Prelasca.
Torino, Palazzo Reale, Sala dell'Alcova

2. E. Tesauro, G. L. Boffi: *Fregio con simboli di Fedeltà*. Torino, Palazza Reale, Sala di Udienza

1. Magnasco: *Eruption of a volcano*. Collection W. T. Hassett, jr.

2. Magnasco: *Monk seated in a landscape*. Collection Janos Scholz

3. Magnasco (?): *Landscape*. Collection Janos Scholz

1. P. Legros: *Due statue mediane;* C. A. Tantardini: *Due statue centrali.* Torino, S. Cristina, facciata (gli originali del Legros sono ora in Duomo). (Archivio Museo Civico, Torino)

2. P. Legros, circa 1715: *S. Cristina.* Torino, Duomo (da S. Cristina). (Archivio Museo Civico, Torino)

3. C. A. Tantardini, 1718: *Angelo adorante.* Marmo. Torino, S. Teresa (altare della Sacra Famiglia). (Archivio Museo Civico, Torino)

4. Giuseppe Muttoni, circa 1720: *Stucchi decorativi* (su disegno di F. Juvarra?). Torino, Palazzo Madama, Scalone.
(Archivio Museo Civico, Torino)

5. C. G. Plura, circa 1730: *Angelo annunziante*. Torino, Chiesa della Misericordia. (Archivio Museo Civico, Torino)

6. Simone Martinez, 1731: *Putti in marmo*, Altare di S. Giuseppe. Torino, S. Teresa. (Archivio Museo Civico, Torino)

7. Simone Martinez, circa 1740–50: *Fontana della Nereide*. Torino, Giardino del Palazzo Reale. (Archivio Museo Civico, Torino)

8. Simone Martinez: *L'Estate*. Torino, Palazzo Reale, Giardino. (Archivio Museo Civico, Torino)

9. F. Ladatte, 1732: *Placchette e rilievi bronzei al mobile del Piffetti*. Torino, Palazzo Reale, Gabinetto di toeletta della regina. (Archivio Museo Civico, Torino)

10. F. Ladatte, 1732: *Arpie in bronzo*, applicate al mobile del Piffetti, Torino, Palazzo Reale,
Gabinetto di toeletta della regina. (Archivio Museo Civico, Torino)

11. F. Ladatte, circa 1732 (?): *Cervo in bronzo*. Stupinigi, cupolino della Palazzina di Caccia. (Archivio Museo Civico, Torino)

12. F. Ladatte, 1741: *Giuditta*. Marmo. Parigi, Museo del Louvre.
Archives Photographiques du Louvre, Paris

13. F. Ladatte (derivazione da): *Giuditta*. Terracotta
dorata. Torino, Museo Civico d'arte antica.
(Archivio Museo Civico, Torino)

14. F. Ladatte – P. A. e M. A. Slodz, 1746: *Martirio di S. Filippo*. Bronzo (da bozzetto di F. Ladatte, 1738).
Versailles, Cappella del Castello. Cliché des Musées Nationaux, Château de Versailles

15. F. Ladatte, 1744: *Trionfo delle arti liberali*. Terracotta. Parigi, Musée des Arts décoratifs. Cliché du Musée des Arts décoratifs

16. F. Ladatte, circa 1744: *Coppia allegorica di putti*. Terracotta. Torino, Museo Civico d'arte antica. (Archivio Museo Civio, Torino)

17. F. Ladatte (?), circa 1748: *Ratto di Proserpina*. Terracotta. Torino, Museo Civico d'arte antica. (Archivio Museo Civico, Torino)

18. F. Ladatte e A. Boucheron, 1750: *Tabernacolo del Sacro Pilone*. Bronzo e argento dorato. Vicoforte, Santuario. (Archivio Museo Civico, Torino)

19. F. Ladatte e A. Boucheron, 1750: *Tabernacolo del Sacro Pilone*. Bronzo
e argento dorato. Vicoforte, Santuario. (Archivio Museo Civico, Torino)

20. Lorenzo Lavy e Stefano Tamiatti (?): *Paiola in vermeil*. Vienna, Österreichisches Museum für angewandte Kunst.
(Archivio Museo Civico, Torino)

21. P. A. Paroletto, argentiere, 1741 (su disegno di F. Ladatte?): *Parte di paramento d'altare*, in argento. Torino, Chiesa metropolitana di S. Giovanni Battista. (Archivio Museo Civico, Torino)

22. P. A. Paroletto (su disegno di F. Ladatte?): *Zuppiera in argento*. Torino, collezione privata. (Archivio Museo Civico, Torino)

23. F. Ladatte, 1763: *Putto portacero*. Bronzo. Torino, Chiesa del Carmine. (Archivio Museo Civico, Torino)

24. F. Ladatte, circa 1770: *Candelieri con scene di caccia*. Bronzo (particolare). Torino, Palazzo Reale, Galleria del Daniel. (Archivio Museo Civico, Torino)

25. F. Ladatte, circa 1750: *Ventole in bronzo*. Torino, Palazzo Reale, Galleria del Daniel. (Archivio Museo Civico, Torino)

26. F. Ladatte (?), circa 1760: *Ventole in bronzo*. Torino, Museo Civico d'arte antica. (Archivio Museo Civico, Torino)

27. F. Ladatte, 1773: *Vittorio Amedeo III di Savoia*. Bronzo dorato. Torino, Museo Civico d'arte antica. (Archivio Museo Civico, Torino)

28. F. Ladatte, circa 1770–75: *Calamaio col Tempo*. Biella, Collezione Fila.
(Archivio Museo Civico, Torino)

29. F. Ladatte, 1775 (firmato): *Pendolo col Tempo*. Torino, Palazzo Reale.
(Archivio Museo Civico, Torino)

30. C. G. Plura (o cerchia): *Risurrezione* (su disegno di F. Ladatte?). Torino, Basilica Mauriziana. (Archivio Museo Civico, Torino)

1. *Monument to Pope Innocent X* by G.B. Maini, probably executed to a design by Camillo Rusconi. S. Agnese in Piazza Navona, Rome

2. *Monument to Pope Clement XII* with bronze statue of the Pope modelled by G.B. Maini and cast by Francesco Girdoni: the marble statues of Magnificence and Abundance are by Carlo Monaldi. Corsini Chapel, S. Giovanni in Laterano, Rome

3. *Monument to Cardinal Neri Corsini* by G.B. Maini. Corsini Chapel, S. Giovanni in Laterano, Rome

4. *The Madonna of St. Luke*, relief by G. B. Maini. S. Maria Maggiore, Rome

5. *Monument to Prince Scipione Santacroce* by G. B. Maini. S. Maria in Publicolis, Rome. (Photograph courtesy of the Bibliotheca Hertziana, Rome)

6. *Statue of Pope Benedict XIV* by G. B. Maini. Ex-convent of S. Agostino, Rome. (Photograph: Vasari, Rome)

7. *Venus*, statue after the antique by G. B. Maini. Wentworth Woodhouse, Yorkshire

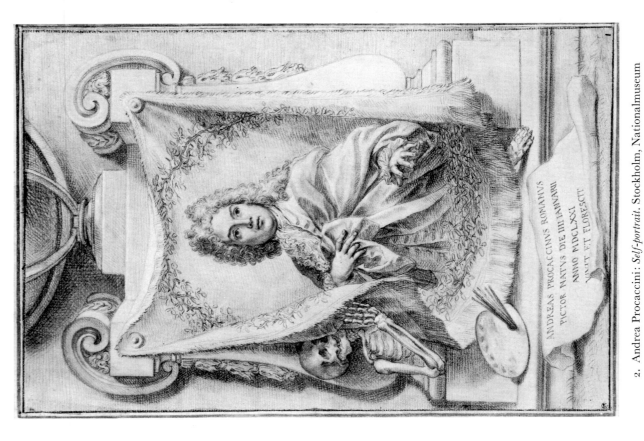

2. Andrea Procaccini: *Self-portrait*. Stockholm, Nationalmuseum

1. Agostino Masucci: *Self-portrait*. Stockholm, Nationalmuseum

4. Giuseppe Chiari: *Perseus and Andromeda.* Holkham Hall

3. Andrea Procaccini: *Tarquin and Lucretia.* Holkham Hall

5. Luigi Garzi: *Cincinnatus at the Plough*. Holkham Hall

6. Luigi Garzi: *Alexander and the Family of Darius*. Present whereabouts unknown

7. Luigi Garzi: *Coriolanus and his Family*. San Francisco, Achenbach Foundation for Graphic Arts

8. Francesco Imperiali and Agostino Masucci: *Coriolanus and his Family*. England, Private Collection

9. Agostino Masucci: *Alexander and the Family of Darius (?)*. Private collection

10. Agostino Masucci: *Coriolanus and his Family*. Amherst College, Mass.

11. Jacopo Zoboli: *The Death of Caesar*. Rome, Galleria Gasparrini

12. Agostino Masucci: *The Judgement of Solomon*. Turin, Palazzo Madama. Photograph: G.F.N.

13. P. L. Ghezzi and Agostino Masucci: *The Baptism of Charles Edward Stuart*. Mentmore

14. Agostino Masucci: *The Marriage of James III*. Mentmore

15. Agostino Masucci: *The Adoration of the Magi*. Rome, S. Maria in Via Lata.
Photograph: G. F. N.

16. Agostino Masucci: *The Annunciation*. Minneapolis
Institute of Arts

17. Sebastiano Conca: *The Annunciation*. New York,
Mr. Victor Spark

18. Agostino Masucci: *Clement XII*. Cantelupo, Palazzo Camuccini.
Photograph: G. F. N.

19. Agostino Masucci: *Benedict XIV*. Rome, Accademia
di S. Luca. Photograph: G. F. N.

20. Pierre Subleyras: *Benedict XIV*. Versailles.
Photograph: Musées Nationaux

1. Benjamin West: *The Death of Nelson*. Liverpool, Walker Art Gallery

2. Arthur William Devis: *The Death of Nelson*. Greenwich, National Maritime Museum

3. Benjamin West: *The Death of General Wolfe*. Ottawa, National Gallery of Canada

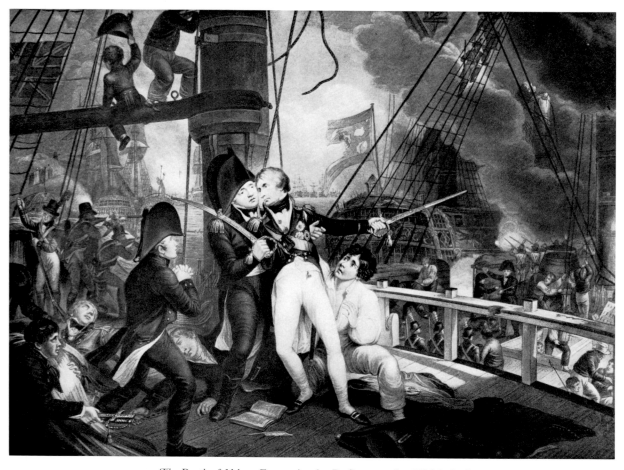

4. *The Death of Nelson*. Engraving by R. Cooper after W. M. Craig.

5. Benjamin West: *The Death of Nelson*. Greenwich, National Maritime Museum

6. Arthur William Devis: '*The Cockpit of the Victory, sketched on board, at Portsmouth*'.
Drawing in the National Maritime Museum, Greenwich

1. Pierre Puget: *Milon de Crotone*. Paris, Louvre

2. Eugène Dévéria: *Puget présentant le Groupe de Milon de Crotone à Louis XIV*. Paris, Louvre

3. François Rude: *Prométhée Animant les Arts*. Paris, Chambre des Députés

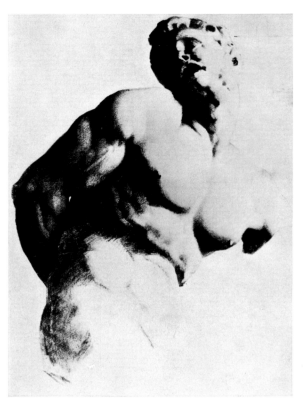

4. Georges Seurat: Copy of Puget's *Milon de Crotone*.
Paris, Private Collection

5. Engraving of Puget's *Milon de Crotone* from Landon's,
Annales du Musée, 1805

6. Paul Cézanne: Copy of Puget's *Milon de Crotone*.
Basel, Öffentliche Kunstsammlungen

THE WRITINGS OF RUDOLF WITTKOWER

The Writings of Rudolf Wittkower

Note: The following is a complete list of Professor Wittkower's major publications up to June 22, 1966, omitting detailed notice of such work as the entries in Thieme-Becker (1925–1934), revisions of the 16th edition of Baedeker's *Rome and Central Italy* (Leipzig, 1930), entries in *Chambers's Encyclopedia* (1950) and the *Encyclopedia Britannica* (1953, 1956), and obituaries (e.g., those of Fritz Saxl and Ludwig Schudt). The periodical literature has been grouped according to content although there are, of course, some conflicts of classification. Within each group the listing is chronological.

BOOKS

Michelangelo-Bibliographie, 1510–1926 (Römische Forschungen der Bibliotheca Hertziana, vol. I). In collaboration with Ernst Steinmann. Leipzig, 1927.

Die Zeichnungen des Gianlorenzo Bernini (Römische Forschungen der Bibliotheca Hertziana, vols. IX–X). In collaboration with Heinrich Brauer. 2 vols. Berlin, 1931.

Catalogue of the Collection of Drawings by the Old Masters, Formed by Sir Robert Mond. In collaboration with Tancred Borenius. London, 1937.

The Drawings of Nicolas Poussin. Edited by Walter Friedlaender in collaboration with Rudolf Wittkower and Anthony Blunt. Vol. I, London, 1938. Vol. II, London, 1949.

British Art and the Mediterranean. In collaboration with Fritz Saxl. London, 1948.

Architectural Principles in the Age of Humanism. London, 1949. 2nd ed., London, 1952. 3rd ed., London, 1962. Spanish ed., Buenos Aires, 1958. Italian ed., Milan, 1964. American ed. (Columbia Studies in Art History and Archaeology, vol. I), New York, 1965.

The Drawings of the Carracci in the Collection of Her Majesty the Queen at Windsor Castle. London, 1952. American ed., Garden City, L.I., 1953.

Gian Lorenzo Bernini, the Sculptor of the Roman Baroque. London, 1955. 2nd ed., London, 1966.

Art and Architecture in Italy, 1600–1750 (The Pelican History of Art). Harmondsworth and Baltimore, 1958. 2nd ed., Harmondsworth and Baltimore, 1965.

Born under Saturn: The Character and Conduct of Artists; A Documented History from Antiquity to the French Revolution. In collaboration with Margot Wittkower. London, 1963. German ed. under the title *Künstler—Aussenseiter der Gesellschaft*, Stuttgart, 1965.

Dupérac, Disegni de le ruine di Roma e come anticamente erono. Facsimile ed. with Introduction by Rudolf Wittkower. Milan, 1963.

The Divine Michelangelo: The Florentine Academy's Homage on his Death in 1564. Introduced, translated, and annotated in collaboration with Margot Wittkower. London, 1964.

La cupola di San Pietro di Michelangelo. Florence, 1964.

PAMPHLETS

Exhibition of Architectural and Decorative Drawings at London University, the Courtauld Institute of Art. In collaboration with Anthony Blunt. London, 1941.

The Earl of Burlington and William Kent. York Georgian Society Occasional Papers, no. 5, 1948.

Bernini's Bust of Louis XIV. London, 1951.

The Artist and the Liberal Arts. An inaugural lecture delivered at University College, London, January 30, 1950. London, 1952.

The History of the York Assembly Rooms. Compiled for and on behalf of the York Corporation, York, 1952.

ARTICLES

I. MIGRATION AND INTERPRETATION OF SYMBOLS

'Miraculous Birds. 1. "Physiologus" in Beatus Manuscripts. 2. "Roc": an Eastern Prodigy in a Dutch Engraving', *Journal of the Warburg and Courtauld Institutes*, I (1937–8), pp. 253–7.

'Eagle and Serpent: a Study in the Migration of Symbols', *Journal of the Warburg and Courtauld Institutes*, II (1938–9), pp. 293–325.

'Interpretation of Visual Symbols in the Arts', in *Studies in Communication* (London University, Communications Research Centre), London, 1955, pp. 109–24.

'Introduction', *East-West in Art, Patterns of Cultural and Aesthetic Relationships* (ed. Theodore Bowie), Bloomington and London, 1966, pp. 13–19.

II. STUDIES IN PROPORTION AND PERSPECTIVE

'Some Observations on Medieval and Renaissance Proportion', *Festschrift in Honor of Johannes Wilde* (unpublished typescript), 1951.

'International Congress on Proportion in the Arts', *Burlington Magazine*, XCIV (1952), pp. 52–5.

'Systems of Proportion', in *Architect's Yearbook*, V (1953), pp. 9–18.

'Brunelleschi and "Proportion in Perspective"', *Journal of the Warburg and Courtauld Institutes*, XVI (1953), pp. 275–91.

'The Perspective of Piero della Francesca's "Flagellation"', *Journal of the Warburg and Courtauld Institutes*, XVI (1953), pp. 292–302 (with B. A. R. Carter).

'The Changing Concept of Proportion', *Daedalus* (Winter, 1960), pp. 199–215.

III. ICONOGRAPHY

'Patience and Chance: The Story of a Political Emblem', *Journal of the Warburg and Courtauld Institutes*, I (1937–8), pp. 171–7.

'A Symbol of Platonic Love in a Portrait Bust of Donatello', *Journal of the Warburg and Courtauld Institutes*, I (1937–8), pp. 260–1.

'Chance, Time and Virtue', *Journal of the Warburg and Courtauld Institutes*, I (1937–8), pp. 313–21.

'"Grammatica": From Martianus Capella to Hogarth', *Journal of the Warburg and Courtauld Institutes*, II (1938–9), pp. 82–4.

'Transformations of Minerva in Renaissance Imagery', *Journal of the Warburg and Courtauld Institutes*, II (1938–9), pp. 194–205.

'Titian's Allegory of "Religion succoured by Spain"', *Journal of the Warburg and Courtauld Institutes*, III (1939–40), pp. 138–40.

'Death and Resurrection in a Picture by Marten de Vos', in *Miscellanea Leo van Puyvelde*, Brussels (1949), pp. 117–23.

IV. MEDIEVAL ART

'Marvels of the East: a Study in the History of Monsters', *Journal of the Warburg and Courtauld Institutes*, V (1942), pp. 159–97.

'Marco Polo and the Pictorial Tradition of the Marvels of the East', in *Oriente Poliano* (Istituto Italiano per il medio ed estremo oriente), Rome, 1957, pp. 155–72.

V. RENAISSANCE AND MANNERIST ART AND ARCHITECTURE

'Studien zur Geschichte der Malerei in Verona. I and II: Domenico Morone. III: Die Schüler des Domenico Morone', *Jahrbuch für Kunstwissenschaft* (1924–5), pp. 269–89; (1927), pp. 185–222.

'Ein Selbstporträt Michelangelos im Jüngsten Gericht', *Kunstchronik*, LIX, n.f. XXXV (1925–6), pp. 366–7.

'Das Problem der Bewegung innerhalb der manieristischen Architektur', *Festschrift für Walter Friedländer zum 60. Geburtstag am 10.3.1933* (unpublished typescript), pp. 192 ff.

'Zur Peterskuppel Michelangelos', *Zeitschrift für Kunstgeschichte*, II (1933), pp. 348–70.

'Michelangelo's Biblioteca Laurenziana', *Art Bulletin*, XVI (1934), pp. 123–218.

'Sculpture in the Mellon Collection', *Apollo*, XXVI (1937), pp. 79–84.

'Physiognomical Experiments by Michelangelo and his Pupils', *Journal of the Warburg and Courtauld Institutes*, I (1937–8), pp. 183–4.

'A Note on Michelangelo's Pietà in St. Peter's', *Journal of the Warburg and Courtauld Institutes*, II (1938–9), p. 80.

'Alberti's Approach to Antiquity in Architecture', *Journal of the Warburg and Courtauld Institutes*, IV (1940–1), pp. 1–18.

'A Newly Discovered Drawing by Michelangelo', *Burlington Magazine*, LXXVIII (1941), pp. 159–60.

'Federico Zuccari and John Wood of Bath', *Journal of the Warburg and Courtauld Institutes*, VI (1943), pp. 220–2.

'Holbein und England', *Die Auslese*, I (1945), pp. 55 ff.

'El Greco's Language of Gestures', *Art News*, LVI (1957), pp. 44–49 and 53–54.

'The Arts in Western Europe: Italy', in *The New Cambridge Modern History*, vol. I: 1493–1520, Cambridge, 1957, pp. 127–53.

'L'architettura del Rinascimento e la tradizione classica', *Casabella*, no. 234 (1959), pp. 43–9.

'Montagnes sacrées', *L'Œil*, no. 59 (1959), pp. 54–61 and p. 92.

'Individualism in Art and Artists: A Renaissance Problem', *Journal of the History of Ideas*, XXII (1961), pp. 291–302.

'La cupola di San Pietro di Michelangelo', *Arte antica e moderna* (no. 20) (1962), pp. 390–437 (revised and enlarged translation of 'Zur Peterskuppel Michelangelos', 1933).

'L'arcadia e il Giorgionismo', in *Umanesimo europeo e umanesimo veneziano*, Florence, 1963, pp. 473–84.

'The Young Raphael', *Allen Memorial Art Museum Bulletin*, xx (1963), pp. 150–68.

VI. PALLADIO, PALLADIANISM AND ENGLISH ARCHITECTURE

'Pseudo-Palladian Elements in English Neo-classical Architecture', *Journal of the Warburg and Courtauld Institutes*, vi (1943), pp. 154–64. (This paper appeared in a revised and improved form in a volume published by the Oxford Press.)

'Principles of Palladio's Architecture', *Journal of the Warburg and Courtauld Institutes*, vii (1944), pt. i, pp. 102–22; viii (1945), pt. 2, pp. 68–106.

'Lord Burlington and William Kent', *The Archaeological Journal*, cii (1945), pp. 151–64.

'Inigo Jones—Puritanissimo Fiero', *Burlington Magazine*, xc (1948), pp. 50–1.

'Palladianism in England', *The Listener*, xliii (May 18, 1950), pp. 866–8 and p. 879.

'Lord Burlington and the York Assembly Rooms', *York Georgian Society, Reports*, 1950–1, pp. 42–54.

'That Great Luminary of Architecture', *The Listener*, l (December 24, 1953), pp. 1080–1.

'Inigo Jones, Architect and Man of Letters', *Royal Institute of British Architects Journal*, lx (1953), pp. 83–90.

'The Influence of Palladio's Villas', *Country Life*, cxv (February 25, 1954), pp. 516–7.

'Burlington and his Work in York', *Studies in Architectural History*, ed. W. A. Singleton, London and York, 1954, i, pp. 47–66.

'Giacomo Leoni's Edition of Palladio's *Quattro Libri dell'Architettura*', *Arte Veneta*, viii (1954), pp. 310–6.

i: 'Sviluppo stilistico dell'architettura palladiana'; and ii: 'Diffusione dei modi palladiani in Inghilterra', *Bollettino del Centro Internazionale di Studi di Architettura Andrea Palladio*, i (1959), pp. 61–9.

i: 'Il "Pre-Neopalladianesimo" in Inghilterra'; ii: 'I principii informativi del nuovo movimento'; and iii: 'L'architettura di Lord Burlington e il suo ambiente', *Bollettino del Centro Internazionale di Studi di Architettura Andrea Palladio*, ii (1960), pp. 77–87.

'L'influenza del Palladio sullo sviluppo dell'architettura religiosa veneziana nel sei e settecento', *Bollettino del Centro Internazionale di Studi di Architettura Andrea Palladio*, v (1963), pp. 61–72.

'Le chiese di Andrea Palladio e l'architettura barocca veneta', in *Barocco europeo e barocco veneziano* (ed. V. Branca). Florence, 1963, pp. 77–87.

'Palladio nel mondo anglosassone', *Rotary Club Vicenza*, December 1965, pp. 7–8.

VII. BAROQUE ART AND ARCHITECTURE

'Die vier Apostelstatuen des Camillo Rusconi im Mittelschiff von S. Giovanni in Laterano in Rom, Stilkritische Beiträge zur römischen Plastik des Spätbarock', *Zeitschrift für bildende Kunst*, lx (1926–7), pp. 9–20 and 43–9.

'Die Rolle des Modells in der römischen Barockplastik', *Sitzungsberichte der kunstgeschichtlichen Gesellschaft Berlin*, Oktober–Mai 1928, pp. 5–7.

'Un bronzo dell'Algardi a Urbino', *Rassegna Marchigiana*, vii (1928), pp. 41–4.

'Ein Werk des Stefano Maderno in Dresden', *Zeitschrift für bildende Kunst*, lxii (1928–9), pp. 26–8.

'Eine Bronzegruppe des Melchiorre Cafà', *Zeitschrift für bildende Kunst*, lxii (1928–9), pp. 227–31.

'Ein Bozzetto des Bildhauers Lorenzo Ottoni im Museo Petriano zu Rom', *Repertorium für Kunstwissenschaft*, l (1929), pp. 6–15.

'Die Taufe Christi von Francesco Mochi', *Zeitschrift für bildende Kunst*, lxiv (1930–1), pp. 158–60.

'Zu Hans Sedlmayrs Besprechung von E. Coudenhove-Erthal: *Carlo Fontana*', *Kritische Berichte zur Kunstgeschichtlichen Literatur*, iv (1931–2), pp. 142–5.

'Le Bernin e le Baroque romain', *Gazette des Beaux-Arts*, s. 6, xi (1934), pp. 327–41.

'Pietro da Cortonas Ergänzungsprojekt des Tempels in Palestrina', *Festschrift für Adolph Goldschmidt zu seinem siebenzigsten Geburtstag am 15. Januar 1933*, Berlin, 1935, pp. 137–43.

'Carlo Rainaldi and the Roman Architecture of the Full Baroque', *Art Bulletin*, xix (1937), pp. 242–313.

'Piranesi's "Parere su l'Architettura"', *Journal of the Warburg and Courtauld Institutes*, ii (1938–9), pp. 147–58.

'Domenico Guidi and French Classicism', *Journal of the Warburg and Courtauld Institutes*, ii (1938–9), pp. 188–90.

'A Counter-Project to Bernini's "Piazza di S. Pietro"', *Journal of the Warburg and Courtauld Institutes*, iii (1939–40), pp. 88–106.

'Domenichino's Madonna della Rosa', *Burlington Magazine*, xc (1948), pp. 220–2.

'Un libro di schizzi di Filippo Juvarra a Chatsworth', *Bollettino Società Piemontese d'archeologia e di belle arti*, iii (1949), pp. 94–118.

'Documenti sui modelli per la Sacrestia di S. Pietro a Roma', *Bollettino Società Piemontese d'archeologia e di belle arti*, iii (1949), pp. 158–61.

'Il Terzo Braccio del Bernini in Piazza S. Pietro', *Bollettino d'Arte*, xxxiv (1949), pp. 129–34.

'Bernini's Famous Marble Group "Neptune and

Glaucus'", *Illustrated London News*, II (1950), p. 129.

'Works by Bernini at the Royal Academy', *Burlington Magazine*, XCIII (1951), pp. 51–6.

'Bernini Studies I. The Group of Neptune and Triton', *Burlington Magazine*, XCIV (1952), pp. 68–76.

'Bernini Studies II. The Bust of Mr. Baker', *Burlington Magazine*, XCV (1953), pp. 19–22.

'Bernin', in *Les sculpteurs célèbres* (ed. Lucien Mazenod), Paris, 1954, pp. 246–9.

'S. Maria della Salute: Scenographic Architecture and the Venetian Baroque', *Journal of the Society of Architectural Historians*, XVI (1957), pp. 3–10.

'Melchiorre Cafà's Bust of Alexander VII', *The Metropolitan Museum of Art Bulletin*, n.s. XVII (1959), pp. 197–204.

'Impressioni di Varallo', *Atti e memorie del terzo congresso piemontese di antichità ed arte, Congresso di Varallo Sesia* (Sept. 1960), Turin, 1962, pp. xxx–xxxiii.

'Algardi's Relief of Pope Liberius Baptizing Neophytes', *The Minneapolis Institute of Arts Bulletin*, XLIX (1960), pp. 28–42.

'Cornacchinis Reiterstatue Karls des Grossen in St. Peter', *Miscellanea Bibliothecae Hertzianae zu Ehren von Leo Bruhns* (Römische Forschungen der Bibliotheca Hertziana, XV). Munich, 1961, pp. 464–73.

'The Vicissitudes of a Dynastic Monument: Bernini's Equestrian Statue of Louis XIV', in: *De Artibus Opuscula XL, Essays in Honor of Erwin Panofsky*, New York, 1961, pp. 497–531.

'Art and Architecture', in *The New Cambridge Modern History*, V: The Ascendancy of France 1648–88. Cambridge, 1961, pp. 149–75.

'Piranesi as Architect', in *Piranesi* (Exhibition at Smith College Museum of Art, Northampton, Mass.), 1961, pp. 99–109.

'Il barocco in Italia', in *Manierismo, Barocco, Rococò: Concetti e Termini* (Convegno Internazionale, Rome, April 21–24, 1960, Problemi attuali di scienza e di cultura, Accademia Nazionale dei Lincei), Anno CCCLIX, ser. 8, XVII, no. 52 (1962), pp. 319–27.

'S. Maria della Salute', *Saggi e memorie di storia dell'arte*, III (1963), pp. 33–54.

'The Role of Classical Models in Bernini's and Poussin's Preparatory Work', in *Studies in Western Art* (20th International Congress of the History of Art), 1963, III, pp. 41–50.

'Imitation, Eclecticism and Genius', in *Aspects of the Eighteenth Century* (ed. Earl Wasserman). Baltimore, 1965, pp. 143–61.

'Introduction', *Art in Italy, 1600–1700* (ed. Frederick Cummings), The Detroit Institute of Arts, 1965, pp. 11–21.

'La teoria classica e la nuova sensibilità', *Lettere italiane*, XVIII (1966), pp. 194–206.

VIII. CONTEMPORARY PROBLEMS AND MODERN ARCHITECTURE

'Die Eröffnung des Museo di San Pietro in Rom', *Kunstchronik*, LIX, n.f. XXXV (1925–6), pp. 83–5.

'Die dritte Römische Biennale', *Kunstchronik*, LIX, n.f. XXXV (1925–6), pp. 138–9.

'Jahresausstellung der "Accademia di Francia" in Rom', *Kunstchronik*, LIX, n.f. XXXV (1925–6), p. 180.

'Die städtebauliche Zukunft Roms im 20. Jahrhundert', *Kunstchronik*, LIX, n.f. XXXV (1925–6), pp. 673–7.

'Ankauf der Villa Aldobrandini durch den Staat', *Kunstchronik*, LIX, n.f. XXXV (1925–6), pp. 690 f.

'Museumspolitik in Russland', *Die Weltkunst*, Dezember 1931, p. 1.

'Camillo Sitte's *Art of Building Cities* in an American Translation', *Town Planning Review*, XIX (1947), pp. 164–9.

'An Exhibition of American Art at Chicago', *Burlington Magazine*, XCI (1949), p. 254.

'Restoration of Italian Monuments', *Burlington Magazine*, XCI (1949), pp. 141–2.

'Art History as a Discipline', *Winterthur Seminar on Museum Operation and Connoisseurship*, 1959. Winterthur, Delaware, 1961, pp. 55–69.

'Le Corbusier's Modulor', in *Four Great Makers of Modern Architecture* (Symposium from March to May, 1961, School of Architecture, Columbia University). New York, 1963, pp. 196–204.

IX. BOOK REVIEWS

From among the host of reviews—published over the course of the years in such publications as the *Burlington Magazine, Bibliography on the Survival of the Classics* (Warburg Institute, 1931), *Kunstchronik, Zeitschrift für Kunstgeschichte, Kunstgeschichtliche Anzeigen, Architectural Review, The Listener, Review of English Studies, Erasmus*, etc.—the following have been selected for their length, importance, or interest.

'Ernst Heimeran: *Michelangelo und das Porträt*', *Repertorium für Kunstwissenschaft*, XLV (1925), p. 44.

'Leopold Zahn: *Caravaggio*', *Zeitschrift für bildende Kunst*, LXII (1929), p. 96.

'*Notizen und Nachrichten*', *Zeitschrift für Kunstgeschichte*, I (1932), pp. 177–82.

'Josef Weingartner: *Römische Barockkirchen*', *Deutsche Literaturzeitung*, LIII (September 25, 1932), pp. 1854–8.

'A. E. Richardson: *An Introduction to Georgian Architecture*', *Burlington Magazine*, XCII (1950), pp. 331–2.

'C. H. C. and M. Baker: *The Life and Circumstances of James Brydges, First Duke of Chandos, Patron of the Liberal Arts*', *Review of English Studies*, n.s. II (1951), pp. 184–6.

'M. Borissavliévitsch: *Les théories de l'architecture*', *Architectural Review*, CXI (1952), p. 265.

'F. Barbieri: *Vincenzo Scamozzi*', *Burlington Magazine*, XCV (1953), p. 171.

'A proposito dei *Disegni inediti di G. L. Bernini e di L. Vanvitelli* di A. Schiavo', *Palladio*, n.s. IV (1954), p. 89.

'E. Wüsten: *Die Architektur des Manierismus in England*', *Erasmus*, VII (1954), pp. 614–7.